EDEXCEL A LEVEL

BUSINESS

YEAR 2

IAN MARCOUSÉ

ANDY HAMMOND

NIGEL WATSON

In order to ensure that this resource offers high-quality support for the associated Pearson qualification, it has been through a review process by the awarding body. This process confirms that this resource fully covers the teaching and learning content of the specification or part of a specification at which it is aimed. It also confirms that it demonstrates an appropriate balance between the development of subject skills, knowledge and understanding, in addition to preparation for assessment.

Endorsement does not cover any guidance on assessment activities or processes (e.g. practice questions or advice on how to answer assessment questions), included in the resource nor does it prescribe any particular approach to the teaching or delivery of a related course.

While the publishers have made every attempt to ensure that advice on the qualification and its assessment is accurate, the official specification and associated assessment guidance materials are the only authoritative source of information and should always be referred to for definitive guidance.

Pearson examiners have not contributed to any sections in this resource relevant to examination papers for which they have responsibility.

Examiners will not use endorsed resources as a source of material for any assessment set by Pearson.

Endorsement of a resource does not mean that the resource is required to achieve this Pearson qualification, nor does it mean that it is the only suitable material available to support the qualification, and any resource lists produced by the awarding body shall include this and other appropriate resources.

The Publishers would like to thank the following for permission to reproduce copyright material.

Every effort has been made to trace all copyright holders, but if any have been inadvertently overlooked, the Publishers will be pleased to make the necessary arrangements at the first opportunity.

Orders: please contact Bookpoint Ltd, 130 Milton Park, Abingdon, Oxon OX14 4SE. Telephone: +44 (0)1235 827720. Fax: +44 (0)1235 400454. Email education@bookpoint.co.uk Lines are open from 9 a.m. to 5 p.m., Monday to Saturday, with a 24-hour message answering service. You can also order through our website: www.hoddereducation.co.uk

ISBN: 978 1 4718 4781 3

First published in 2016 by
Hodder Education,
An Hachette UK Company
Carmelite House
50 Victoria Embankment
London EC4Y 0DZ

www.hoddereducation.co.uk

Impression number 10 9 8 7 6 5 4 3 2 1

Year 2020 2019 2018 2017 2016

Cover photo © Sergey Nivens - Fotolia

Illustrations by Integra

Typeset in Bembo Std, 11/13 pts by Aptara Inc.

Printed in Italy

A catalogue record for this title is available from the British Library.

Contents

Theme 3
Business decisions and strategy

1 Corporate objectives

Definition

Aims are a generalised statement of where a business is heading, from which objectives can be set. A mission is a more fervent, passionate way of expressing an aim. Corporate objectives turn the aims into SMART targets, i.e. Specific, Measurable, Ambitious, Realistic and Timebound.

Linked to: Corporate strategy, Ch 2; SWOT analysis, Ch 4; Growth, Ch 7; Reasons for staying small, Ch 10; Corporate influences, Ch 15

1.1 Introduction

Some children, as young as ten or eleven years old, are clear about what they want from life. They are determined to become a doctor or a vet. The clarity of their **aim** makes them work hard at school, choose science subjects and overcome any setbacks (a weak maths teacher, perhaps). So whereas most GCSE and A level students drift from one day to the next, these individuals are focused: they have their eyes on their prize. This is the potentially huge benefit that can stem from clear aims.

Indeed, you could say that some of these focused students are driven by a sense of **mission**. Their aim is not just to get the label of 'doctor' but also to help make the world a better place. The drive shown by these students will be the most impressive of all.

For new small businesses there can also be a powerful sense of mission. A chef may open his or her own restaurant, driven largely by the desire to win a Michelin star (the *Michelin Guide* to restaurants is the world's most prestigious). In Gordon Ramsay style, the approach to achieving this may prove to be ruthless or even fanatical. Such a person is far more likely to achieve this aim than one who opens a restaurant thinking 'It would be nice to get a star; let's see if it happens'.

Figure 1.1 Gordon Ramsay

'A small body of determined spirits fired by an unquenchable faith in their mission can alter the course of history.'

Mahatma Ghandi, founder of modern India

'A lot of economists feel you do incentives and nothing else. I disagree. You have to motivate people around a central mission, a set of values, and then the incentives become the frosting on the cake; they become the payoff.'

Bill George, professor, Harvard Business School

1.2 Corporate aims

Aims are the generalised statement of where a business is heading. Possible examples of aims include:

- 'To become a profitable business with a long-term future' (Zayka Indian restaurant, started in January 2011)
- 'To become a Premier League club' (Nottingham Forest FC, at the time of writing in football's second tier)
- 'To diversify away from dependence on Britain' (the implicit aim of Tesco between 2003 and 2013).

One of the stated aims of the McDonald's fast food chain is to provide 'friendly service in a relaxed, safe and consistent restaurant environment'. The success of the organisation depends upon turning this aim into practice. In order for this to be achieved, employees must understand and share the aim. When a customer enters a McDonald's restaurant anywhere in the world they know what to expect. The organisation has the ability to reproduce the same 'relaxed, safe and consistent' atmosphere with different staff, in different locations. This has built the company's reputation. This corporate aim is effective because it recognises what lies at the heart of the organisation's success.

The Tesco example above shows that aims can be mistaken. In Tesco's case the aim of diversification led to specific disasters such as the £2 billion wasted on trying and failing in America. It also meant that successive Tesco bosses took their eye off changing customer requirements in Britain. The British shopper's image of Tesco lurched from believing 'Every Little Helps' to 'Every Little Helps Tesco' – and they switched to Aldi, Lidl or Waitrose.

Whether right or wrong, corporate aims act as the basis for setting the organisation's objectives. The success or failure of each individual decision within the firm can be judged by the extent to which it meets the business objectives. This allows authority to be delegated within the organisation, while at the same time maintaining coordination.

1.3 Mission statements

A **mission statement** is an attempt to put corporate aims into words that inspire. The mission statement of Wal-Mart, the world's biggest retailer, is 'to give ordinary folk the chance to buy the same thing as rich people'. Shop floor staff are more likely to be motivated by a mission statement of this kind than by the desire to maximise profit.

Businesses hope that by summarising clearly the long-term direction of the organisation, a focus is provided that helps to inspire employees to greater effort and ensure the departments work together. Without this common purpose each area of a firm may have different aims and choose to move in conflicting directions.

Real business

Examples of mission statements

- Google: 'organise the world's information and make it universally available'
- Coca-Cola: 'To refresh the world – in mind, body and spirit'
- Prêt à Manger (sandwich chain): 'Pret creates handmade natural food avoiding the obscure chemical additives and preservatives common to so much of the prepared and "fast" food on the market today'
- Nike: 'To bring inspiration and innovation to every athlete* in the world' (*If you have a body you are an athlete).

It is also important to note that not every company has a written mission statement. Some companies are clear that they and their staff 'live the mission' and therefore do not need to write it down. Marks & Spencer plc has stopped publicising a mission statement, perhaps because it has learned that one statement cannot sum up the driving forces behind a whole, complex business.

1.4 Influences on business mission

The model shown in Figure 1.2 shows the main influences on mission. It is necessary to link each of the four elements of the model so that they reinforce one another.

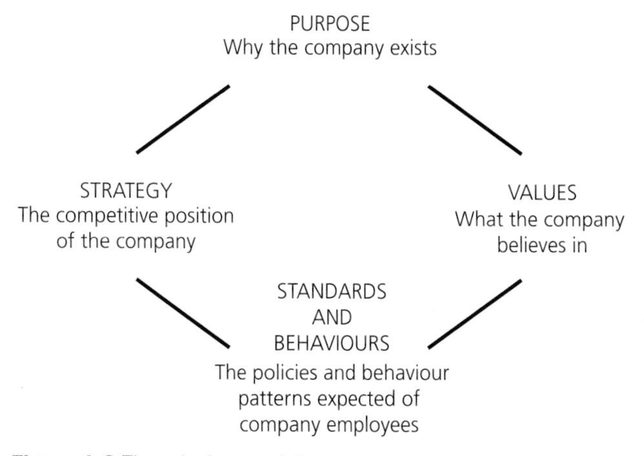

Figure 1.2 The mission model

In turn, each element suggests the following.

Purpose (reason why the company exists)

This is clearly shown by the Nike mission, which emphasises the desire to provide innovative products for athletes. In fact a sceptic could point out that Nike builds much of its branding around advertising, imagery and visual design rather than product innovation. Nike's brilliance has been to keep customers and staff confident that the company wants to support athletes rather than exploit them.

Values (what the company believes in)

In the case of Prêt à Manger, it is not just that it believes in natural, fresh food, but also that the business has always:

- used packaging that is made from recycled materials and can be recycled in future
- taken care to source its products from suppliers that treat staff fairly
- wanted to push customers to try new things, especially from sustainable sources.

The values of the business are a key part of its culture, and should also include the way staff are treated and other ethical considerations.

Standards and behaviours

This refers to the standards set by managers and the behaviour expected from staff. Cambridge graduate Polly Courtney has told the *Observer* newspaper about her experiences as a highly paid banker in the City of London. The work culture meant that people would send emails at 2.00 in the morning to show how late they worked, and Polly found sexism rooted in a 'lads'' culture in which nights out ended at the strip club. As the only woman in an office of 21, she was treated like a secretary and bypassed for the more important jobs. Polly wrote a book about her experiences, whereas others have successfully sued merchant banks on grounds of sex discrimination. Clearly the managements are wholly at fault in allowing such a situation to develop.

1.5 Critical appraisal of mission statements

As an example of the possible downsides of mission statements, it is interesting to look back at what companies used to say. At one time, Coca-Cola's mission statement said: 'Our mission is to get more people to drink Coke than water.' Today that seems quite a shocking idea. Clearly it would mean a dramatic worsening of the obesity problem that affects most of the developed world. The fact that Coca-Cola has dropped this statement in favour of the socially more acceptable 'to refresh the world' raises the question of whether mission statements are little more than public relations exercises.

Even more serious is the possibility that mission statements are a substitute for the real thing. They may be a bureaucratic management's attempt to provide a sense of purpose in a business that has none. If so, this would be the wrong way to approach the problem. If staff lack inspiration, the starting point is to find a real sense of purpose, probably through the staff themselves. For example, British doctors and nurses used to be hugely proud to work for the NHS; now they are more likely to moan about its shortcomings. Writing a mission statement would be treated with derision by the staff. Far more important is to find out from staff what they dislike about the current structure and discuss how to restore staff pride in the service.

A mission statement might be a genuine expression of an organisation's desire to succeed by doing good. Or it might be a cynical attempt to pretend that apathy has a sense of purpose.

> 'Facebook was not originally created to be a company. It was built to accomplish a social mission – to make the world more open and connected.'
>
> *Mark Zuckerberg, founder of Facebook*
>
> 'It takes a person with a mission to succeed.'
>
> *Clarence Thomas, US Supreme Court judge*

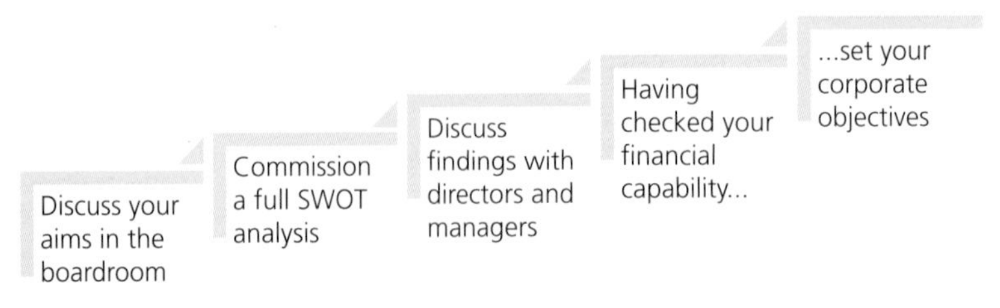

Figure 1.3 Logic chain: how to set objectives

Five whys and a how

Questions	Answers
Why may a clear sense of mission help a business to succeed?	A believable but inspiring mission can unite staff and customers behind the business.
Why may mission be especially important in a new business?	It's invaluable to have customers who 'buy in' to the business; they'll not only be loyal but will also spread the word.
Why may companies with aims outperform those with missions?	The weakness of mission is that it can blind the company to its weaknesses; aims are less powerful, so they can be appraised more coolly.
Why might the mission be lost from a company's strategy?	Because there's a stage in between: the objectives; if the objectives don't quite fit the mission, there may be a mismatch between mission and strategy.
Why might a new, clear mission help a giant but struggling company such as Marks & Spencer?	M&S needs something inspirational that will help customers and staff believe in the company again.
How might a company set about devising a new mission?	Aims and mission come from the top, so the directors need to spend time discussing and agreeing a suitable new mission.

1.6 Corporate objectives – evaluation

Good evaluation is based upon a questioning approach to the subject matter. This should apply to the case material being looked at and to the underlying theory. This section of the course provides huge scope for careful questioning; this should *not* be in the form of blanket cynicism ('all mission statements are rubbish'), but by carefully considering the evidence. Is a new boss genuinely trying to improve the motivation and behaviour of staff for the benefit of customers and the business as a whole? If so, perhaps a mission statement is a valuable centrepiece to a whole process of culture change.

At other times, though, the case material may present a new mission statement as no more than a sticking plaster over a diseased wound. Genuine problems need genuine solutions, not slogans. You need to make judgements about which situation is which, then justify your views with evidence from the case and drawn from the theory set out in this unit.

Key terms

Aims: a generalised statement of where a business is heading.

Mission: an aim expressed in a particularly inspiring way.

Mission statement: a short passage of text that sums up an organisation's mission. This may get displayed on walls throughout the business and placed prominently on its website.

1.7 Workbook

Revision questions

(25 marks; 25 minutes)

1. Explain why clear aims help people and businesses to achieve their goals. (4)
2. Explain the difference between mission and a mission statement? (4)
3. Outline one weakness of Nike's mission statement (in 1.3). (3)
4. Explain briefly what is shown by the 'mission model'. (4)
5. Explain why poor recruitment could lead to an ineffective business culture. (4)
6. Explain briefly who is responsible for setting a firm's objectives. (3)
7. Is it possible to have a SMART mission? Outline your answer. (3)

Revision activities

Data response

Figure 1.4 Fresh & Easy: Tesco's billion-pound blunder

In early 2007, Tesco confirmed rumours that it was to launch into the US grocery market: the world's biggest and most competitive. This would bring it face-to-face with Wal-Mart in a market worth $500 billion. Huge though Tesco had become, with 500,000 employees worldwide, it remained a shrimp compared with Wal-Mart. Despite scepticism by some analysts, most assumed that the magic touch of Tesco's long-time boss Terry Leahy would ensure success. Leahy had switched his best executives from China to America and allowed them to carry out a year's research and investigation into the US grocery market. Leahy never quite said it, but analysts were starting to wonder whether his real mission was to make Tesco the world's number 1 retailer.

In its 2007 annual report, Tesco confirmed its plan to invest £250 million a year for five years to develop a new grocery concept called Fresh & Easy. Its stores would be one-third of the size of a typical US supermarket, but double the size of the average convenience store. Tesco believed it had found a market gap. By Spring 2008, Tesco had 60 Fresh & Easy stores in operation, and was trumpeting that sales were 'ahead of budget'. It said 150 more would be opened in the 2008/2009 financial year. Break-even would be achieved, it said, within two years.

By 2009 it was clear that the original launch plan had been a flop. Not enough cash was coming through the tills to generate a profit. Tesco claimed that all it needed was 'scale', i.e. enough stores to deliver sufficient economies of scale to push the business beyond its break-even point. It announced a series of changes that would be made to store design and layout, and to the range of goods on offer. Effectively it was admitting 'we got it wrong' – but without acknowledging that if the concept was wrong it was time to cut the losses and withdraw.

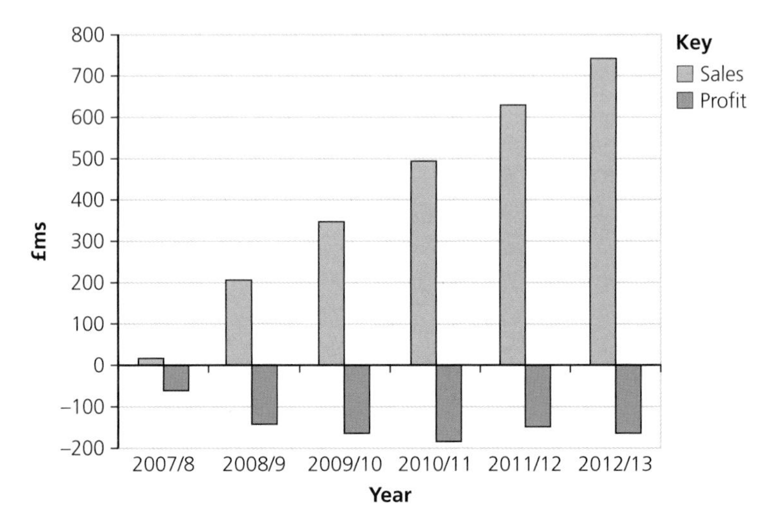

Figure 1.5 Tesco Fresh & Easy: annual sales and profits

Only after the retirement of Terry Leahy in 2011 did serious questions start to be asked within Tesco about the future of its US lossmaker. In February 2013, the new CEO Phillip Clarke made it clear that Fresh & Easy had to go. Embarrassingly, Tesco couldn't even give the stores away – it had to pay an American company to take some of the stores – and the rest of the business was liquidated. In 2013, Tesco said it would have to write-down its balance sheet by more than £1 billion to account for the failure of Fresh & Easy, but as nearly £900 million of operating losses had been made (see the Table 1.1), the total loss for Tesco was probably around £2 billion.

Important though £2 billion is, the long-term consequences of the Fresh & Easy fiasco may be much greater. In 2007/2008, Tesco was making a serious commitment to Asia, especially China. This commitment seemed to slip away as the American disaster required ever more management time. In 2013, Tesco effectively sold out of its long-term operational commitment to China. Worse still, perhaps, has been the impact on Tesco's UK performance, with sales, market share, profits and credibility being eroded away in 2013 and 2014. Not long ago Tesco was Britain's most admired company; no longer.

	Tesco USA (£ms)		Tesco Asia (£ms)	
	Sales	Profit	Sales	Profit
2007/8	16	–62	5,988	304
2008/9	208	–142	7,578	355
2009/10	349	–165	8,465	440
2010/11	495	–186	10,278	570
2011/12	630	–153	10,828	737
2012/13	740	–165	11,479	661

Table 1.1 Tesco's sales and profit in the USA and Asia

Questions (40 marks; 50 minutes)

1 Assess the mission and objectives Terry Leahy seemed to be pursuing through his Fresh & Easy strategy. (12)

2 Tesco decided to prioritise a developed economy over developing ones. Assess why it might have decided to do that. (12)

3 Such was Terry Leahy's status within Tesco that he was able to push ahead with quite a personal ambition to succeed in the US market. Evaluate how important the leader's views should be in setting the objectives and strategies of a business. (16)

Extended writing

1 In José Mourinho's first period as Chelsea manager the club won many trophies but failed to meet owner Abramovic's desire for exciting, beautiful football. Evaluate whether there is an inevitable trade-off between a mission for beautiful football and winning trophies. (20)

2 'In a small firm the mission can be absorbed by the staff. In a big business it's hard for it to get through to all staff, so it's written down as a mission statement.' Evaluate whether this big-business approach is likely to prove effective. (20)

2 Corporate strategy

Definition

Corporate strategy provides a medium- to long-term plan for meeting company-wide objectives.

Linked to: Corporate objectives, Ch 1; SWOT analysis, Ch 4; Growth, Ch 7; Reasons for staying small, Ch 10; Corporate influences, Ch 15

2.1 Introduction

To develop a successful corporate strategy means understanding how to turn an objective into a successful result. The starting point is to see the implication of different corporate objectives. The goals of fast-growing, low-cost AirAsia differ from those of long-established airlines such as Cathay Pacific or British Airways. As AirAsia targets growth, its corporate strategy has to find a way of achieving that without overstretching the company finances and its management hierarchy.

In addition to corporate strategies that are plans for meeting objectives, businesses often use the word 'strategic' to mean something bigger and broader. A 'strategic' initiative is one that cannot easily be reversed, for example Richard Branson's 2015 decision to sell 80 per cent of Virgin Active to a South African businessman (netting Branson £230 million of cash). Before then a boss of Waterstones decided that online retailing would never reach as much as a 10 per cent share of UK book sales. So he handed the Waterstones e-commerce site to Amazon! Today Amazon has nearly an 80 per cent share of UK online book sales; and they account for 30 per cent of total sales – and rising. Waterstones made a huge strategic mistake.

Real business

A classic quote from investment sage Warren Buffet is that 'It's only when the tide goes out that you see who's been swimming naked'. In the period 2008–2013 Morrisons seemed to be doing fine. Market share held up quite well and profit margins outstripped Sainsbury's. Yet when the pressure exerted by Aldi and Lidl forced Tesco to respond, Morrisons was the one that seemed stuck in the crossfire. As shown in Figure 2.1, Morrisons' profits evaporated in 2014 and 2015.

This example establishes the truism that companies need to think about their competitiveness even when things are going well. For a business such as Morrisons there is a balance to strike between customer benefits and price. It could offer free coffee to all customers, but would have to slip that cost onto prices somewhere along the line. In 2014, in the face of severe pressure, Morrisons decided to focus solely on price. It brought out a loyalty card that, it claimed, would reduce prices to the level found at discounters Aldi and Lidl. It was a major step away from the traditional Morrisons positioning of good food for all. It had no alternative: it had to find a way to compete. A year later it sold off more than a hundred convenience stores and closed eleven supermarkets.

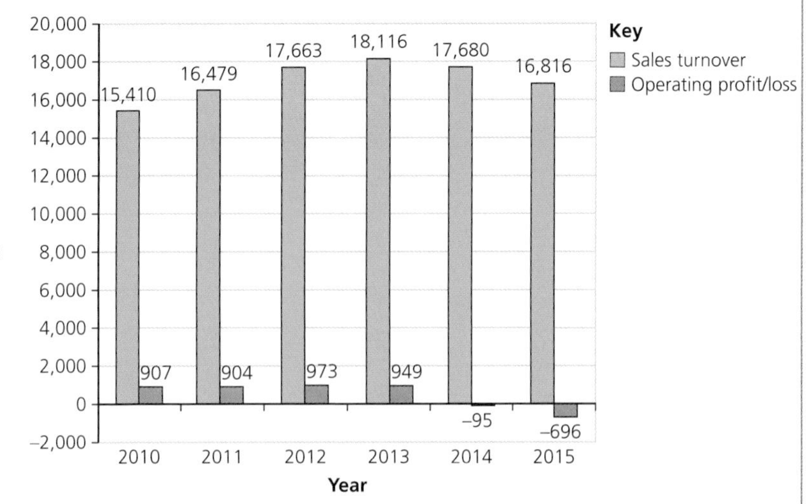

Figure 2.1 Morrisons' annual sales and profits 2010–2015 (source: Morrisons annual accounts)

2.2 Corporate strategy

The managers of a business should develop a medium- to long-term plan about how to achieve the objectives they have established. This is the organisation's corporate strategy (see Figure 2.2). It sets out the actions that will be taken in order to achieve the goals, and the implications for the firm's human, financial and production resources. The key to success when forming a strategy of this kind is relating the firm's strengths to the opportunities that exist in the marketplace.

Figure 2.2 Corporate strategy

Relating strengths to opportunities can take place at each level of the business, allowing a series of strategies to be formed in order to achieve the goals already established. A hierarchy of strategies can be produced for the whole organisation in a similar manner to the approach adopted when setting objectives.

- Corporate strategy deals with the major issues such as in what industry, or industries, the business should compete in order to achieve corporate objectives. Managers must identify industries where the long-term profit prospects are likely to be favourable.
- A business unit/division such as Costa Coffee, China must address the issue of how the organisation will compete in the industry selected by corporate strategy. This will involve selecting a position in the marketplace to distinguish the firm from its competitors; in the case of Costa Coffee, China, the question is how to differentiate the business from Starbucks.
- Functional (or department) strategy is developed in order to identify how best to achieve the objectives or targets set by the senior managers.

If a strategy is to achieve the objectives set, it must match the firm's strengths to its competitive environment (see Figure 2.3). Whitbread plc decided that the market for health clubs in the UK was saturated, so it would be better to sell off its David Lloyd health clubs and put its money behind the rapidly growing Costa chain. It proved one of the cleverest strategic moves of the past 25 years.

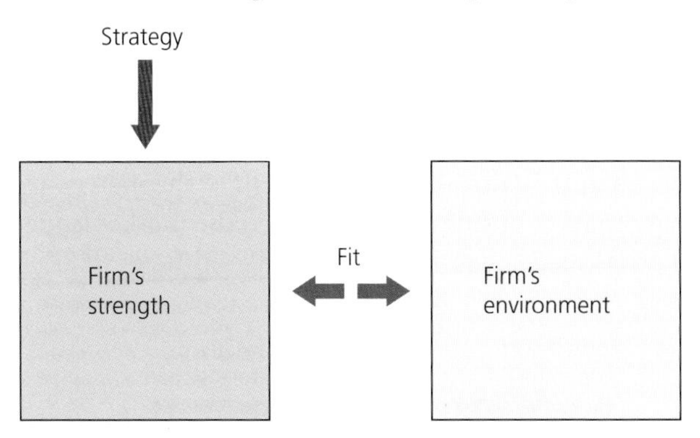

Figure 2.3 If a strategy is to achieve the objectives set, it must match the firm's strengths to its competitive environment

'The essence of strategy is deciding what not to do.'

Michael Porter, strategy guru

'Standing in the middle of the road is very dangerous; you get knocked down by the traffic from both sides.'

Margaret Thatcher, former Prime Minister

'Strategy is about making choices, trade-offs; it's about deliberately choosing to be different.'

Michael Porter, strategy guru

2.3 Porter's (Generic) Strategic Matrix

If Morrisons had been able to afford Michael Porter as a consultant (his charges start at $100,000 a day) the message would have been clear – years ago. Porter consistently warns against taking up a position in the middle of a market. He believes that long-term success is best built on either a super-low price position or else a positioning based purely on **product differentiation**. So he would applaud Aldi, Lidl, Asda and (at the other end of the scale) Waitrose – but criticise Sainsbury's, Morrisons and Tesco. At the time of writing (early 2015) customer purchasing patterns are right with Porter.

Porter's Generic Strategic Matrix suggests that all markets operate in the same way (hence the term 'generic'). They can be segmented in two ways: mass versus niche markets; and lowest cost versus highest differentiation strategies. In Figure 2.4 the example given is from the UK grocery sector. The bottom two quarters of the matrix represent niche markets (and low market shares). On the left are the two lowest-cost operators, Aldi and Lidl; their low costs enable them to charge low, everyday prices. According to *The Grocer* magazine, an Aldi shopping basket is usually 15 per cent cheaper than at Asda, and 25–30 per cent cheaper than at Waitrose. In the top half of the matrix are the mass-market businesses, with Tesco the market leader – and positioned squarely in the middle of the market.

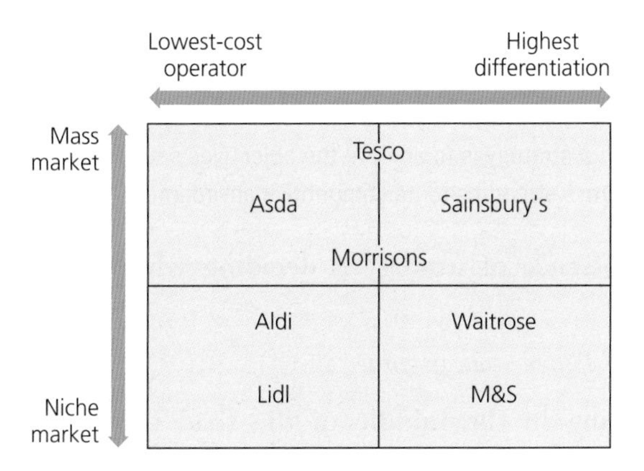

Figure 2.4 Porter's Generic Strategic Matrix

Porter's low-cost strategy

To Porter, there is no better position for long-term stability than to be the lowest-cost operator, as long as you have an advantage that others cannot copy. Producing in China can be copied by anyone. But Aldi and Lidl both have very strong positions that are difficult to copy. Since starting in 1973, Lidl has grown to have 10,000 shops across Europe, with sales (in 2013) of more than €63 billion – that's more than Sainsbury's and Morrisons combined. And Lidl operates with far fewer **stock units** than the main UK supermarkets. So vast buying power is focused on relatively few items in stock, giving enormous bulk-buying leverage. This provides a major cost advantage. Aldi operates in the same way. So not even Tesco has the same relative buying power as the German discounters.

As Porter makes clear, the joy of the lowest-cost position is that you can choose to either charge the lowest prices or to charge relatively high prices but enjoy high profit margins. In another market, Ryanair is the unrivalled lowest-cost operator in western Europe. But if you try to fly Ryanair at the last minute the price will be much the same as easyJet or British Airways.

Porter's differentiation strategy

Porter is clear that differentiation works when it adds greater value than the cost embedded in the differentiation. Customers will be prepared to pay a price premium for a differentiated item, as long as the difference is something they value. In the market for cars, brands such as BMW (status; driver excitement) and Volvo (safety) all have their specific differentiating factors. In essence, if customers buy the brand rather than the price tag, not only value added but also customer loyalty has been achieved.

In his book *Competitive Advantage*, Michael Porter emphasises that there are many ways to achieve differentiation beyond marketing. He believes that it could be derived from anywhere along the supply chain. Some businesses may be brilliant at purchasing, for instance a jeweller that keeps managing to obtain fantastic diamonds that can be turned into beautiful rings. Others may be brilliant at manufacture, producing the most reliable, durable cars on the market. As long as the consumer values the differentiating factor, the mission is accomplished.

One other factor is central to Porter's theme. Sustained advantage is only possible if the source of the differentiation can be protected. That's the wonderful thing about brand names. Coca-Cola has been able to sustain a price premium and some very loyal customers for more than a century based on its brand name and image. At the time of writing Coca-Cola is outselling Tesco Cola in Tesco stores even though Coke is priced at £1.83 for 1.75 litres while Tesco is 89p for 2 litres, i.e. Coke is more than twice the price.

Focused low cost

In the mass market the lowest-cost producer will enjoy **economies of scale** that come from size; this may not be the case in a niche market. To be the lowest-cost operator in the market for games apps targeted at the under-nines will require a well-considered approach to management – perhaps with a very flat management structure based on almost total delegation of development and marketing decision-making. If your business can succeed at that, there will still be a risk that success creates its own threats to your way of working. Sustaining a focused low-cost position will be hugely challenging; but when successful, Porter says it's a strong place to be.

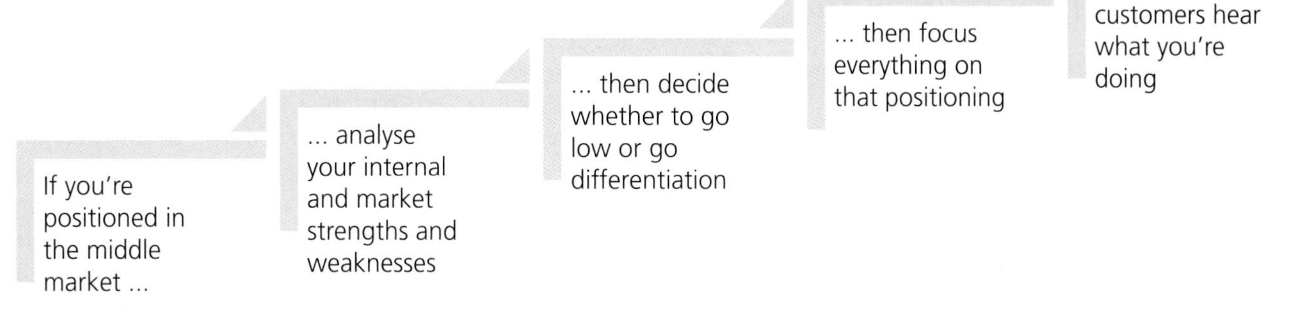

Figure 2.5 Logic chain: focus your strategic positioning

Focused differentiation

Perhaps the most sustainable competitive position is focused differentiation, i.e. within a niche market. Within the market for luxury goods, no brand is in a stronger position than Hermes of Paris. While companies such as Chanel sell bags for £3,000, Hermes is at £5,000 and upwards. It benefits from an exclusive image and can charge accordingly. In a different market the mobile phone brand Vertu charges upwards of £9,600 for a phone. 'Handcrafted in England from the finest rare materials', the Vertu phone doesn't want to compete with Apple's mass market dominance. It wants its own market positioning: focused differentiation.

2.4 Aim of portfolio analysis

Although portfolio analysis was conceived as a marketing tool, it can be adapted to the company-wide, corporate level. In boardrooms up and down the land, directors are making decisions about resource allocation; that is: what are our priorities? And how much cash and staffing do we put behind those priorities? Very few businesses are in Apple's position, with so much cash that they can do what they want. For most, resources are limited, with every decision having clear opportunity costs. The aim of portfolio analysis is to help that decision-making process.

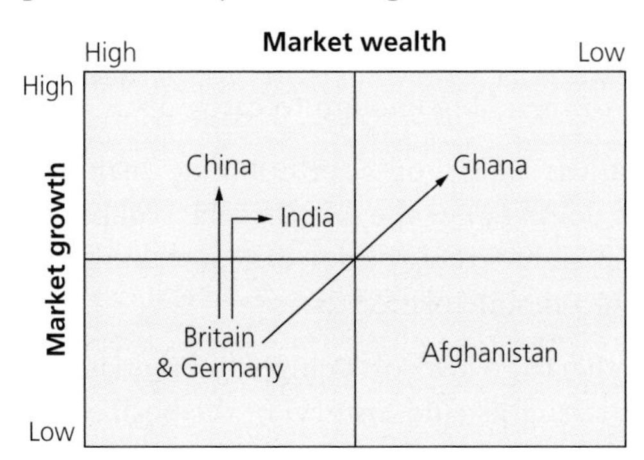

Figure 2.6 Portfolio analysis for corporate strategy

In the example shown in Figure 2.6, a UK business with successful operations in Britain and Germany is choosing whether to use cash generated in the west to put behind rising stars in China and India, or a potential rising star (but, for now, a problem child) in Ghana.

2.5 Achieving competitive advantage through distinctive capabilities

Every business should be clear on its main strengths and weaknesses. Ideally it wants to turn its strengths into **distinctive capabilities** that others cannot easily copy. When easyJet and Ryanair were growing rapidly, British Airways decided to launch its own low-cost airline called Go (in 1998). Within two years it was struggling and in 2002 was sold to easyJet! It proved to be that British Airways lacked the capability to run an efficient low-cost airline. It had neither the management skills nor the history. British Airways, then, has little choice but to pursue competitive advantage by being a differentiated operator. In addition to the background and traditions of the business, there are other possible influences on a company's distinctive capabilities:

- The operational skills within the business. If there is a highly talented research and development department it may be that differentiation is a viable future. If the skills lie in automation and cost reduction, then a low-cost strategy might be best.
- The company's ability to learn from both mistakes and successes, so that the business is constantly moving forward. This can be the result of a 'no-blame' culture in the business, encouraging staff to make bold decisions and therefore mistakes – as long as the company itself learns how to do things better in future.

2.6 Effect of strategic and tactical decisions on human, physical and financial resources

As explained above, strategic decisions are of an importance that makes them hard to reverse. By contrast tactical decisions are short-term responses to opportunities or threats. In January 2015, despite its general strategy of high differentiation/high prices, Waitrose chose to run an 'own brands at half price' promotion. This is a good example of a tactical decision: taken to boost customer numbers at a quiet time of year, temporary and easily reversible.

Whether a decision is long-term and strategic or short-term and tactical, there will be consequences for the company's human, physical and financial resources. In April 2015 Morrisons announced 700 redundancies among head office management in order to provide the finance for extra staff to provide better service on the shop floor. The managers were offered the opportunity to apply for shop floor jobs, but for many this seemed a backward career move. So they were out. Strategic decisions such as this are often accompanied by painful career decisions – and/or redundancies. By contrast a tactical decision may create a great deal of work and disruption in the short term – but is unlikely to threaten careers.

Similarly, strategic decisions may have an impact on physical resources. As part of a strategic rethink, Tesco announced 43 store closures on January 2015, together with the cancellation of many other store developments. In other cases, physical resources may be changed as a business wants to revamp its image. Tactical decisions are unlikely to require more than, perhaps, a temporary change to physical resources, such as hiring in extra equipment to cope with a planned sales promotion.

The impact of strategic and tactical decisions on financial resources should be regarded as an issue of cause and effect. However powerful, no boss can simply decide on a new strategic direction without having its financial implications 'signed off' by the board of directors, with the clear agreement of the chief financial officer. So if the new plan is unaffordable, it won't go ahead. But having agreed that it can go ahead, problems and unexpected extra costs might arise, with great implications for financial resources. Again, short-term tactical decisions are unlikely to have a significant impact on the finances of the business.

Five whys and a how

Questions	Answers
Why is corporate strategy so important?	Because finding the right strategy can put a business on course for success for decades to come, e.g. Apple in 2001, launching the iPod – its first consumer electronics product.
Why is Michael Porter associated most strongly with strategic decisions?	His focus is on the long-term competitiveness of businesses, so he has little interest in short-term, tactical issues.
Why might a business choose to take a central ('piggy in the middle') positioning?	Because that's where the bulk of the market is, i.e. it's tempting to try to become the Tesco of your own marketplace.
Why might focused differentiation be a more secure position than differentiation in the mass market?	Because it's easier to keep hold of a differentiated position when there's less competition (in a niche market, rivals often can't afford to spend big enough to catch up).
Why do differentiated businesses such as Nintendo ever struggle to be profitable?	Porter is sure of the value of a positioning such as Nintendo's, but it doesn't alter the fact that the company needs to make the right strategy choices, e.g. taking its software brands into mobile platforms.
How should a business react when it realises it's stuck in the over-competitive middle of the market?	It should choose either to go low cost or high differentiation depending on the strengths (and history) of the business.

'Firms are often different but not differentiated, as they pursue forms of uniqueness that buyers do not value.'

Michael Porter, author of Competitive Advantage

'Differentiation will lead to superior performance if the value perceived by the buyer exceeds the cost of differentiation.'

Michael Porter, author of Competitive Advantage

2.7 Corporate strategy – evaluation

Michael Porter is in no doubt that successful strategic positioning relies upon clarity. Be Lidl or be Waitrose; don't be a bit of each. This means that he appears to exclude some classically successful strategies. Who wouldn't want to be Wrigley, with more than a 90 per cent share of the UK market for chewing gum? Wrigley's approach is simple dominance of the chewing gum 'space'. But although one can find exceptions such as this, it is fair to view Porter's Generic Strategic Matrix as a genuine insight into the business world. Low cost versus differentiation works perfectly as a way to analyse the grocery sector, the airline sector and the car market; but it means far less in the chocolate market where differentiation is far more important than low cost. Possibly Porter's strategy isn't quite as generic as he wishes it to be, but it's certainly of huge value in many industries.

The strength of Porter's writings is the focus on relatively few messages. The key ones here are: find your point of differentiation ... hammer it home to the consumer and retailer ... and then you'll have a basis for sustained competitive advantage. Critics of Porter accept his ideas, but worry that his views are too static in a fast-moving competitive world. Today's competitive advantage (e.g. Nokia 2010) may be tomorrow's slide into mediocrity. So they want more uncertainty built into the theory.

Key terms

Distinctive capabilities: ways a firm operates that cannot easily be copied by rivals, e.g. Ryanair's obsession with cost minimisation.

Economies of scale: factors that cause average costs to fall as the scale of output increases.

Generic strategy: a strategic position that will prove effective in every market (i.e. generically). Porter said lowest cost and highest differentiation were the perfect positions of strength.

Product differentiation: the extent to which consumers perceive one product as being distinct from its rivals.

Stock units: the number of different brands and pack sizes stocked by a company; each has its own barcode; a Tesco hypermarket might have 75,000 separate products; an Aldi has 1,200.

2.8 Workbook

Revision questions

(30 marks; 30 minutes)

1 Explain what is meant by 'a sustained competitive advantage'. (4)

2 State whether each of the following is a strategic or a tactical issue:

a) Tottenham Hotspur building a new 56,000-seater stadium. (1)

b) West Ham offering 'Kids for a Quid' tickets for a match against Stoke City. (1)

c) Topshop running a 'mid-season sale' in November. (1)

d) Ryanair opening its first transatlantic route: Stansted to New York. (1)

3 Explain why 'focused differentiation' should be a stronger market position than 'differentiation'. (4)

4 Explain how effective focused differentiation might prove as a market positioning for one of the following

a) Porsche cars

b) New Look retail

c) Fat Face retail (5)

5 How does a distinctive capability differ from skills? (3)

6 Assess the possible effect of a decision by Fat Face to become a 100 per cent online retailer on the company's human, physical and financial resources. (10)

Revision activities

Data response

Tesco signs deal to enter India's supermarket sector

In the summer of 2013, Tesco shocked analysts by paying $500 million to a Chinese grocery chain to take Tesco China off its hands. Nine years after buying into an established Chinese hypermarket chain, Tesco was giving up on the world's fastest-growing grocery market.

Figure 2.7 An Indian kirana store

It was a slight surprise, then, that 20 March 2014 saw an announcement that Tesco had signed a deal to become the first foreign supermarket to enter India's $150 billion grocery market. If China was a complex, fragmented market, it was nothing compared with India, with its 8 million small, independent 'kirana' stores (see Figure 2.7). Tesco was committing itself to invest £85 million into a joint venture with the Indian Tata group. Tesco would be the first western retailer to venture into the Indian grocery market, implying considerable risks but perhaps the long-term benefit of first-mover advantage.

Until 2012, foreign retailers had been banned from investing in the country's retail sector. Now, following Indian government approval, Tesco would be investing about £85 million in the 50–50 deal to incorporate twelve supermarkets that already existed under the branding 'Star Bazaar'. Tesco has challenges but also amazing opportunities ahead. The 8 million small grocers divide the market up into minute fragments, with an average annual revenue of $18,750, i.e. about £12,000. In Britain a Tesco store might take £1 million in a week! It will be crucial to change people's shopping habits. Although 40 per cent of Indians' grocery spending is on 'wet' goods such as meat, fruit and vegetables, sales at groceries are heavily weighted towards 'dry', packaged goods. Only 3 per cent of grocery sales are of wet goods, so Indians are buying their wet goods at markets or in specialist butchers/fishmongers/greengrocers. Another interesting feature of the grocery market in India is that only 14 per cent of the population had internet access in 2014, so online grocery selling was not yet developed.

International firms are now able to buy up to a 51 per cent stake in multi-brand retailers, but the decision has led to much opposition in the country. The move to relax the rules in September 2012 came after a similar decision, in November 2011, was scrapped following widespread protests. Rules stipulating that foreign supermarkets had to source 30 per cent of their products from local firms were eased in August 2013 amid fears that the rule was blocking investment. The requirement remains, but foreign firms now have five years to hit the 30 per cent target, allowing them to import goods from overseas initially.

(Sources: various)

Questions (40 marks; 45 minutes)

1 From the evidence available and your wider knowledge of China and India, evaluate whether Tesco is making the right strategic choices. (20)

2 In entering the Indian grocery market, Tesco can choose what market positioning to adopt. Michael Porter might recommend following a 'lowest-cost, mass-market' strategy. Evaluate whether this is the best strategic positioning for the long-term future of Tesco in India. (20)

Extended writing

1 Evaluate whether Michael Porter is right to suggest that his approach to strategy is true in every industry, i.e. generically. (20)

2 Evaluate whether a high-differentiation strategic position would work for a business of your choice in an industry of your choice. (20)

3 Ansoff's Matrix

Definition

Igor Ansoff believed that businesses need greater awareness of the risks involved in developing new products or new markets, and especially in the combination of the two: diversification.

Linked to: Corporate objectives, Ch 1; Corporate strategy, Ch 2; SWOT analysis, Ch 4; Growth, Ch 7; Reasons for staying small, Ch 10; Corporate influences, Ch 15; Conditions that prompt trade, Ch. 32; Assessment of a country as a market, Ch 33

3.1 What are the keys to finding the right strategic direction?

The term 'strategic' implies looking to the long-term future and usually applies at the corporate, company-wide level. It should be based on a company's strengths, but not simply derived from what is working well now. Apple Inc set a good example in 2015. Just at the time it was launching its Apple Watch it was reportedly paying $250,000 starting bonuses to poach engineers from Tesla Motors (a producer of high-end electric cars). Apple was clearly thinking ahead to a possible iCar of the future. Doubtless this would be a self-drive car with fantastic entertainment features for its passengers.

Figure 3.1 Apple Watch

Strategy must be achievable

Strategy is concerned with what is possible, not just desirable. It must take into account market potential and company resources. The company needs to recognise its own limitations and potential. It also needs to consider economic and social circumstances. If the world economy is weakening, firms will be much more cautious about entering new export markets. If the home market is stagnating, businesses may well concentrate on lower-priced 'value' products.

Strategy must be company specific

Each company will have a different strategic direction. The strategy selected will reflect the individual circumstances of the business. Different companies within the same industry may be pursuing different goals. The directions they choose will reflect those different goals. Within the same industry, one company may be aiming to increase market share while another looks for cost reductions in order to compete on price. The tyre industry is a good example of this. The market leaders were faced with increasing price competition from developing countries. They chose different strategic directions: Goodyear reduced costs; Michelin put its effort into innovation and widened its product range; Pirelli decided to concentrate on the market for luxury and speed.

3.2 Strategic direction and Ansoff's Matrix

A useful way to look at the implications of changing strategic direction is to follow the approach taken by Igor Ansoff, who developed 'Ansoff's Matrix'. Ansoff's academic background was in mathematics, so he believed all decisions should be based on extensive research, i.e. gathering data.

In his 1965 book *Corporate Strategy*, Ansoff described strategy as a decision of medium- to long-term significance that is made in 'conditions of partial ignorance'. This 'ignorance' stems partly from the timescale involved If you look three years ahead there are huge risks that marketplace changes will make your plans and forecasts look foolish. Such decisions are usually discussed and decided at board level.

'I begged, borrowed and stole concepts and theoretical insights from psychology, sociology and political science. And I attempted to integrate them into a holistic explanation of strategic behaviour.'

Igor Ansoff, the 'father of strategic management'

Ansoff's Matrix (Figure 3.2) is constructed to illustrate the risks involved in strategic decisions. These risks relate to a firm's level of knowledge and certainty about the market, the competition and customer behaviour – both now and in the future. The key issue is that risk becomes ever greater the further a firm strays from its core of existing products/existing customers (i.e. the top left-hand corner of the matrix).

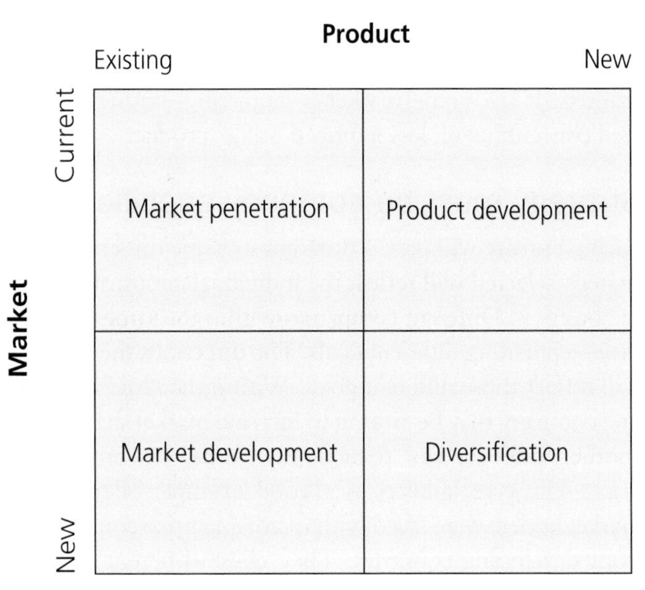

Figure 3.2 Ansoff's Matrix

Ansoff identified four types of strategy within his matrix; these are described below.

Market penetration

This is about increasing market share by concentrating on existing products within the existing market. It is the most common and safest strategy because it does not stray from what the company knows best. If Tesco has opened 400 stores in towns all over Britain, and all are profitable, it is a simple matter of market penetration to open store 401 in a good-sized town that has not yet got its first Tesco.

Market penetration opportunities arise by:

- finding new customers, perhaps by widening the product's appeal to attract additional buyers
- taking customers from competitors; this may be achieved by aggressive pricing or by offering additional incentives to the customer
- persuading existing customers to increase usage; many food companies give recipes with their products to suggest additional ways of using the product; shampoo manufacturers introduced a frequent-wash shampoo to boost product usage.

Market development

This is about finding new markets for existing products. It is more risky because the company must step into the unknown. For Cadbury to start selling chocolate in China requires a huge effort to learn to understand the Chinese consumer. Yet that is exactly what Cadbury is doing. Market development can be carried out by the following means.

- **Repositioning** the product: this will target a different market segment. This could be done by broadening the product's appeal to a new customer base. Land Rover's traditional market was farming and military use; it has now repositioned the product to appeal to town dwellers.
- Moving into new markets: many British retailers have opened up outlets abroad. Some, such as Tesco and Burberry, have opened up their own outlets. Others have entered into joint ventures or have taken over similar operations in other countries.

Moving Tesco into America was a major market development decision taken in 2006. Although backed by more than £1 billion of investment, Tesco 'Fresh & Easy' proved a disaster. In 2013, Tesco paid an American company to take the business off its hands. Even the mighty Coca-Cola has struggled to achieve success in India.

Why the difficulty? Surely market research can reveal whether customers in America want the same things as those in London? The answer to that is 'up to a point, perhaps'. But the skill with market research is to know what questions to ask and how to interpret the answers. This requires a degree of market knowledge that cannot always cross county boundaries, let alone national ones. This was why, over 80 years ago, the Ford Motor Company chose to set up a factory and offices in Britain, instead of relying on exporting from America. The rush of US firms that followed (for example, Heinz, Gillette and Mars) was followed much later by Japanese companies such as Sony and Honda. All took huge risks at the start, but believed they would only succeed in the long term by getting a deep understanding of local habits and needs. Famously, Sony budgeted for a 15-year payback period when it started up in Britain.

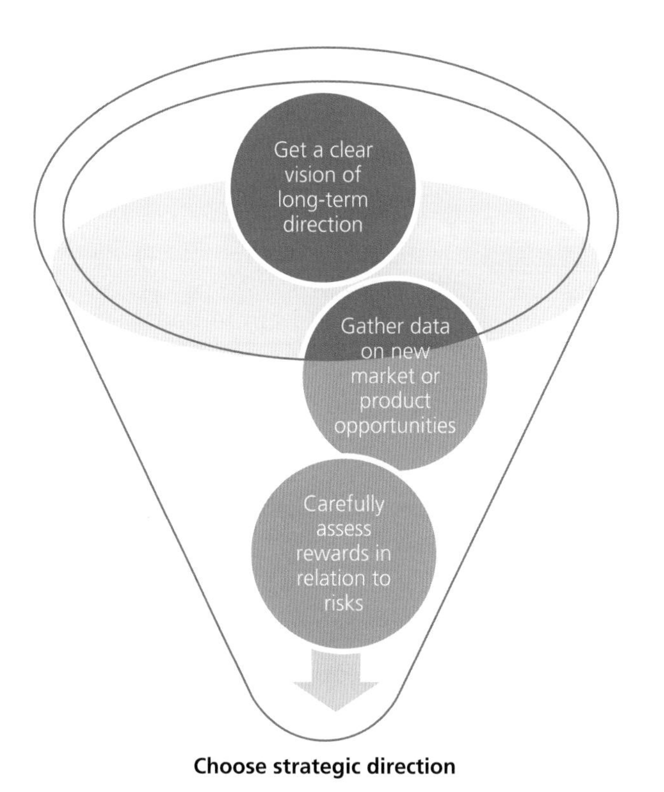

Figure 3.3 Logic funnel: implementing Ansoff's Matrix

Product development

Product development means launching new products into your existing market (for example, L'Oréal launching a new haircare product). Hard though market development can be, it could be argued that product development is even harder. It is generally accepted that only one in seven new products succeeds; and that is a figure derived from the large businesses that launch new products through advertising agencies. In other words, despite their huge resources and expertise, heavy spending on product development and market research, plus huge launch advertising budgets, companies such as Mars, Walls and L'Oréal suffer six flops for every success.

In highly competitive markets, companies use product development to keep one step ahead of the competition. Strategies may include those listed below.

Changing an existing product

This may be to keep the products attractive. Washing powders and shampoos are good examples of this. The manufacturers are continually repackaging or offering some 'essential' new ingredient.

Developing new products

The iPhone is a fantastic example of a new and successful product development, taking Apple from the computer business into the massive market for 'smartphones'.

Diversification

If it is accepted that market development and product development are both risky, how much more difficult is the ultimate challenge: a new product in a new market, or **diversification** in Ansoff's terminology. This is the ultimate business risk, as it forces a business to operate completely outside its range of knowledge and experience. Virgin flopped totally with cosmetics and clothing, WHSmith had a dreadful experience in the DIY market with Do It All, and Heinz had a failed attempt to market a vinegar-based household cleaning product.

Yet diversification is not only the most risky strategy; it can also lead to the most extraordinary business successes. Nintendo produced packs of playing cards until its new, young chief executive decided in the early 1970s to invest in the unknown idea of electronic games. From being a printer of paper cards, Nintendo became a giant of arcade games, then games consoles such as the Wii.

Ansoff emphasised the risks of diversification, but never intended to suggest that firms should fight shy of those risks. Risks are well worth taking as long as the potential rewards are high enough.

3.3 Ansoff's Matrix in international markets

Entering into international markets carries the extra risk identified by Ansoff as market development. Naturally, the extent of the risk will depend on just how different the new market is from the firm's home country. For Green & Black's to start selling chocolate in France may not be too much of a stretch. French tastes are different and the distribution systems are very different from those in Britain, but there are many similarities in climate and affluence. But what about selling organic chocolate to Saudi Arabia? Or China? Or Sierra Leone? Figure 3.4 shows the way Ansoff would indicate the increasing level of risk involved.

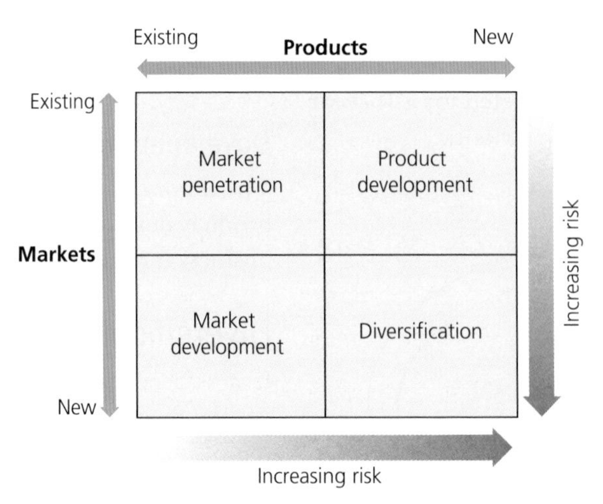

Figure 3.4 Ansoff's Matrix and risk

It is also possible that the product will need to be modified in order to be successful in the new market. International markets are littered with products and businesses that tried to shift their existing products and business models into overseas markets but failed. So even a business that plans to launch existing products into new overseas markets may find it has to adapt. In which case it will end up with a new product for the new market: diversification. More than 20 years ago Sony devised the corporate slogan: 'Think global. Act local.' It remains a valuable way to think.

	Risks	Rewards
Market penetration	• Few risks should arise, other than decline in the product life cycle • But lack of ambition may make your best staff look for more challenge elsewhere	• You know the customers and the competitors, so should make error-free decisions • Returns on extra investment will be predictable
Market development	• Subtle cultural differences add hugely to risk, e.g. many UK retailers who've flopped in the US • Practical differences matter too, such as distribution channels, consumer legislation and differences in managing staff	• There are huge potential economies of scale if your product succeeds elsewhere, e.g. Fever-Tree • If you take the time to understand the cultural differences, you may be able to localise your product range effectively, as McDonald's does
Product development	• Most new products fail (at a rate of about 6/7 in the UK) so the risk level is very high • Because new product success is tough, companies put their best people on it; this can mean too little brainpower devoted to ordinary brands (or, in Tesco's case, its UK supermarket heartland)	• As shown by Apple, nothing adds value and creates differentiation more than innovative product development • Continuous, successful product development should mean the organisation lives forever
Diversification	• Not knowing the market and having a brand new product means the risk level is multiplied by two • Therefore it's vital to plan for the operational risk of diversifying by making sure your financial position is especially secure	• When diversification works, it can transform the size of and opportunities for the business, e.g. Apple in the era since the iPod breakthrough • Radical diversification (Google making cars) can be hugely exciting for the workforce, helping you recruit the best

Table 3.1 Risks and rewards in different strategies

'The thing is, continuity of strategic direction and continuous improvement in how you do things are absolutely consistent with each other. In fact, they're mutually reinforcing.'

Michael Porter, theorist of competitive advantage

'There's danger of paralysis by analysis.'

Igor Ansoff

Five whys and a how

Questions	Answers
Why is it critical for a business to choose the right strategic direction?	Because a new direction is likely to tie up financial and human resources for several years – making the opportunity cost very high.
Why is it hard for businesses to move away from their customer heartland?	Because customer understanding is at the core of every business success; move away and you've lost your competitive advantage
Why might a UK retailer struggle to transfer its business model to another country?	Why not? Why should the Americans, or French or Brazilians want exactly what the British want?
Why is diversification a word that must be used with great caution?	Because although Ansoff showed that it's the riskiest strategic direction, successful diversification reduces the risk of over-dependence on one product or market.
Why might Ansoff's theory be of value to government as well as businesses?	Because governments often stray into territory they don't really understand, e.g. British foreign policy in Iraq and Libya.
How should a business such as ASOS use Ansoff's Matrix to help it evaluate its future strategic direction?	Ansoff would insist on the need for deep market knowledge before, for example, ASOS chose to move into the market for furniture – or to open a division in Africa.

3.4 Ansoff's Matrix – evaluation

Of all the business theories, none has been quite as illuminating as Ansoff's Matrix. The huge financial crash of 2007–2009 can be attributed to high street banks developing products and entering markets that they didn't really understand. And past corporate failings at Tesco (USA and China) and at Greggs (trying to open Starbucks-style coffee shops) may not have happened if the managements were sufficiently alert to the problems of straying from the core of the business.

Yet one should not focus purely on risk when considering strategic direction. Ansoff could see the huge benefits that might accrue from successful diversification. Among the great diversifications remains Nintendo's path from a producer of playing cards to one of the world's most successful designers of games consoles and the accompanying software. Another famous diversification – Nokia going from producing car tyres to become the world's biggest mobile phone maker – has had a less happy ending.

Key terms

Diversification: when a company expands its activities outside its normal range. This may be done to reduce risk or to expand possible markets.

Repositioning: changing a product or its promotion to appeal to a different market segment.

Further reading

Ansoff, I. (1965) *Corporate Strategy*. New York: McGraw-Hill.

3.5 Workbook

Revision questions

(30 marks; 30 minutes)

1. In the way business uses the terms, distinguish between 'strategy' and 'strategic'. (4)
2. How does strategic direction relate to the objectives of a business? (4)
3. Explain why strategic direction has to be company specific. (4)
4. Why is it important for a firm to examine its internal resources before deciding on a change of strategic direction? (3)
5. Explain the difference between market development and product development. (4)
6. Why is market research an important part of Ansoff's thinking? (4)
7. Why is market development more risky than market penetration? (4)
8. What might Ansoff mean by 'paralysis by analysis'? (3)

Revision activities

Data response

Morrisons' strategic direction

In the twelve weeks to 30 March 2014, sales at UK grocery discounter Aldi rose by 35.3 per cent while at rival Morrisons they fell by 3.8 per cent. This compounded a wretched two-year period for Morrisons – the worst since Dalton Philips took over as chief executive in January 2010 (see Figure 3.5). On 8 May 2014, the *Daily Telegraph* reported that:

'The supermarket chain slashed the price of 1,200 lines by 17 per cent last week to counter the rise of the discounters and to reignite its two-year attempt to report like-for-like sales growth. "I'm very confident we are doing the right things," Mr Philips said. "My job is to make big, bold decisions. The proof will be when there are more items in more baskets; how could it not be the right strategy to tackle this on price?"

Sainsbury's outgoing chief executive, Justin King, accused Morrisons of "playing catch-up" in lowering prices and said customers were enticed by ethically sourced products rather than simply price.'

Later, Phillips said that shareholders would 'hold our feet in the fire' if the price-cutting strategy proved unsuccessful, but he was convinced that this was the right long-term positioning for Morrisons.

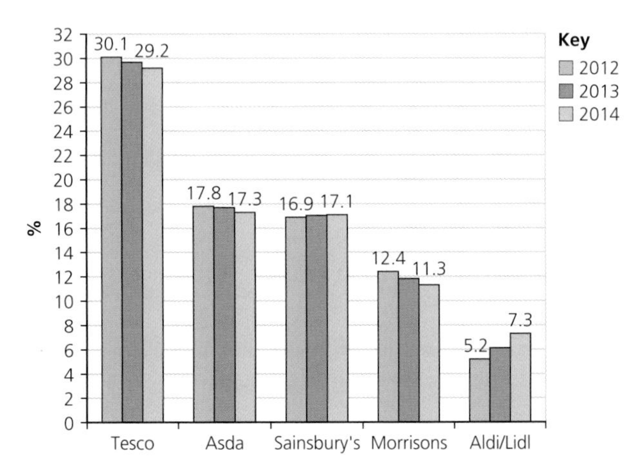

Figure 3.5 UK grocery market share 2012–2014, December–February data (source: Kantar Worldpanel)

Questions (30 marks; 35 minutes)

1. Explain why price cutting in this case can be called a strategy rather than a tactic. (4)
2. Explain two factors that may determine whether Morrisons' 2014 strategy proves successful. (8)
3. Assess one possible weakness in the strategy as outlined in the data provided. (8)
4. In Morrisons' circumstances, assess whether Ansoff would consider its new strategy to be 'market penetration' or 'market development'. (10)

Extended writing

1. Evaluate the extent to which the use of Ansoff's Matrix would eliminate the risk involved in Cadbury launching a new range of crisps in the UK. (20)
2. Scoop is an ice cream business with a production unit, four shops and 24 ice cream flavours. Its owners are ambitious for the company's future. Evaluate whether it would find the Boston Matrix or Ansoff's Matrix the more useful for its future development. (20)

4 SWOT analysis

Definition

SWOT analysis investigates a company's current Strengths and Weaknesses and uses them to help foresee future Opportunities and Threats (hence SWOT analysis).

Linked to: Corporate objectives, Ch 1; Ansoff's Matrix, Ch 3; Impact of external influences, Ch 5; The competitive environment, Ch 6; Corporate influences, Ch 15; Causes and effects of change, Ch 22

4.1 The purpose of SWOT analysis

When the appointment of new Tesco boss Dave Lewis was announced in July 2014, it was said that Lewis would conduct a 'root and branch', objective review of the whole Tesco operation. In effect Lewis was conducting a SWOT analysis – to try to gain insight as quickly as possible into the business he was now in charge of.

Dave Lewis's three predecessors had been Tesco career men, with decades of experience from the shop floor to the boardroom. Lewis had been appointed from outside – and with no retail experience. But he had to make sure that he knew enough about the business to not only make the right strategic decisions, but also to have full credibility when discussing Tesco issues with other staff who had decades of experience with the business.

By January 2015, Lewis was ready to announce his new corporate strategy for Tesco. This would emerge logically from the SWOT process. After all, once you've uncovered the firm's strengths and weaknesses, you can start to think about what should come next for a business. And that's the purpose of SWOT analysis: to provide sufficient insight into the current and potential position of the business to enable senior executives to make sound decisions based on good evidence.

4.2 How to conduct a SWOT analysis

There are two main ways to undertake a SWOT. The first is a top-down process, controlled by the boss and probably carried out by management consultants, answerable only to the boss. This has the advantage of being dispassionate, that is unaffected by emotion or tradition or 'the way we do things round here' – the culture. In a business such as Tesco, with half a million staff, it may be possible for an outsider to see opportunities for cutting 100,000 jobs. Unfortunately, long-established staff will know the threat posed by the outside consultants, and therefore try to hide weaknesses that might lead to job losses. So there is a risk that a top-down process will lack the insight required for a really helpful SWOT analysis.

The ideal SWOT would be conducted in a consultative manner, with the boss spending time in every key department, chatting to staff in an informal manner. There might also be elements of democratic delegation, in which middle managers are invited to conduct their own SWOTs – and then discuss the findings with the boss. This scenario highlights the benefit of appointing an outsider to the top job. No staff member need feel worried about what they say, when the blame for any blatant weaknesses can be pinned on the previous leadership team. A SWOT conducted by a long-established leader would be a very different beast.

TV programmes such as *Undercover Boss* (Channel 4) make a big thing of a boss being disguised to get an authentic flavour of working lives at the bottom of an organisation. A new outsider leader needs no disguise; staff will love to say what's been wrong in the past and how to improve things.

4.3 The theory behind SWOT analysis

SWOT must be broken down into two parts. Strengths and weaknesses represent the current situation for the business. In effect it is 'What are we good at? What are we bad at?' Opportunities and threats are external to the business and therefore largely outside management's control.

Naturally the current business situation has to be considered in relation to competitors, so it is useful to analyse strengths and weaknesses with the help of a **benchmarking** exercise. This shows how the business performs on key variables compared with the best in the industry. Nissan UK may be pleased that its labour turnover has fallen from 12 per cent to 10 per cent, but if it sees that Jaguar Land Rover's achievement is 2 per cent, it will perceive there's more to be done.

Among the external factors that can give rise to opportunities or threats are the following:

- Economic changes such as the sharp fall in the price of oil at the beginning of 2015; this would threaten the future of alternative energy provision such as wind power – but provide an opportunity to a specialist producer of acrylic clothes, as acrylic is made from oil, and will now be much cheaper than cotton or wool.
- Technological change such as the development of graphene, a form of carbon that's one atom thick, yet – gram for gram – is one hundred times stronger than steel. In markets where weight matters hugely, such as aerospace, companies that fail to master the potential for graphene may find their futures under threat.

4.4 Internal considerations: strengths and weaknesses

A key starting point in analysing strengths and weaknesses is to distinguish between those that *are* and those that *matter*. Inditex (owner of Zara) publishes a huge amount of environmental and human resource data that is presented as a strength, but perhaps doesn't matter much in relation to overall business performance. Eighty per cent of staff are permanent and only 20 per cent temporary (out of nearly 120,000 staff). In an era of outsourcing and contract labour, this is admirable. But does it actually matter?

To address this issue companies use the concepts of KPIs: key performance indicators. These are the numbers that a business acknowledges to be proper measures of strength or weakness. Typically these might include sales per employee, absenteeism, image ranking within the market sector and so on. These are measures that matter. Figure 4.1 shows how Tesco has prioritised returning the company's reputation to one that has empathy for customers as well as impressive size. This can be measured by regular quantitative research studies among Tesco users and non-users.

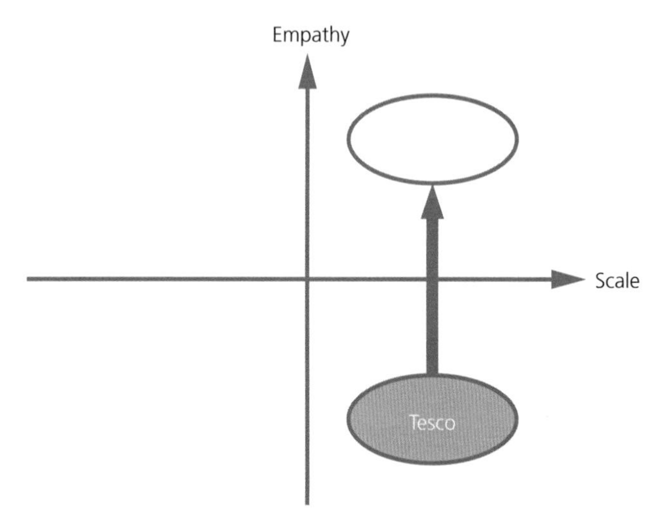

Figure 4.1 Logic chart (source: Tesco presentation by Dave Lewis, 23 October 2014)

When Googling 'KPIs', one site offered '75 KPIs for business success'. Actually that sounds like a recipe for disaster. What businesses need is relatively few KPIs that will – between them – add up to the achievement of the overall business goals. Among the most common KPIs are the following:

- Like-for-like sales, which show sales revenues this year compared with last, but eliminating any differences in shop floor space; so if a business has opened ten new stores in the past year, their sales will be excluded from the like-for-like comparison. On 6 January 2015 House of Fraser announced an 8 per cent improvement in Christmas 2014 like-for-like sales; the previous day John Lewis had boasted of its 4.8 per cent increase in like-for-like sales. In this case House of Fraser was the one showing strength.
- Market share: this is a number that every business cares hugely about. It is, after all, the ultimate comparison of you against your competitors. Even if your sales are rising rapidly you should worry if market share is falling; after all, when the market matures, continuing falls in market share would then mean falling sales. Rising market share is a strength; falling market share is a weakness.

- Capacity utilisation: even a business that's enjoying rising sales may have a fall in utilisation if it has expanded its capacity too greatly. Ryanair suffered exactly this problem in 2012 and early 2013. Sales were rising, but not fast enough to fill all the planes they had bought. An aircraft order can take as long as five years to fulfil, so it's very hard to keep supply and demand in balance. The falling capacity utilisation forced Ryanair to mothball some of its planes, and then forced boss Michael O'Leary into an unexpected backtrack – switching the sales strategy to be far more positive about customer care – to attract more customers.

So how should a business use its KPIs to address its strengths and weaknesses? The answer is simply to break them down as much as possible into their component parts. Capacity utilisation can first be broken down into size of capacity and the level of customer demand. In Ryanair's case there was a recognition that – for the first time – stories about bad customer experiences were denting demand. So the cause of the weakness was identified and tackled. On 5 January 2015 Ryanair reported a 20 per cent rise in passenger numbers for December, with their load factor (capacity utilisation) up from 81 to 88 per cent. In effect they had managed to turn a weakness into a strength, in less than 18 months.

4.5 External considerations: opportunities and threats

These relate to the external context of the business. They are therefore outside the direct control of managers – though in some cases (governmental and political, for example) companies will do everything they can to influence the decisions made by others.

Demography

An important factor to bear in mind is **demography**, i.e. population change. In the UK the population is rising by just over 0.5 per cent a year, but more important changes are occurring in the age distribution of that population. Not long ago, economists despaired at how a shrinking working population would cope with the huge rise in the elderly. Now immigration has solved that problem – though it hasn't altered the business opportunities in the sharp rise in the number of elderly consumers. See Figure 4.2.

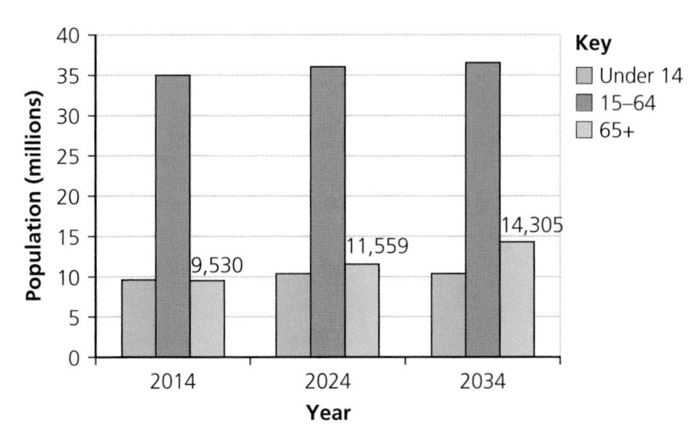

Figure 4.2 Changing age distribution 2014 to 2034 (source: Office of National Statistics 2014)

New laws and regulations

Changes in the law can have a dramatic effect on a business. A good example came from the regulation changes made to child car seats, which came into effect in September 2006. They forced all motorists to provide 'seat restraints' for children sitting in the back of a car. Children under the age of twelve must sit on a 'booster seat' and babies must have their own special car seat.

Overnight, this regulation created a huge boost for businesses like Britax, the car seat manufacturer, and Halfords, the biggest motoring retailer. Because the government gave 18 months' notice of the change, the companies had plenty of time to build production capacity and stock levels.

Technological factors

Technological change can also create opportunities and threats for firms. Before the advent of digital technology, ITV had only two competitors: the BBC and Channel 4. Today the situation is dizzying. Technological advances mean that ITV has to compete against the hundreds of channels provided by Sky and cable TV, plus subscription providers such as Netflix. In addition, the opening up of social media has provided indirect competition with conventional TV. These technological advances threaten ITV's ability to generate revenue from selling advertising slots. On the other hand, these same technological advances have created opportunities for the entrepreneurs behind Twitter, Facetime, Instagram and so many more.

Commodity prices

Commodities are internationally traded goods that include oil, copper, wheat and cocoa. Commodities are normally

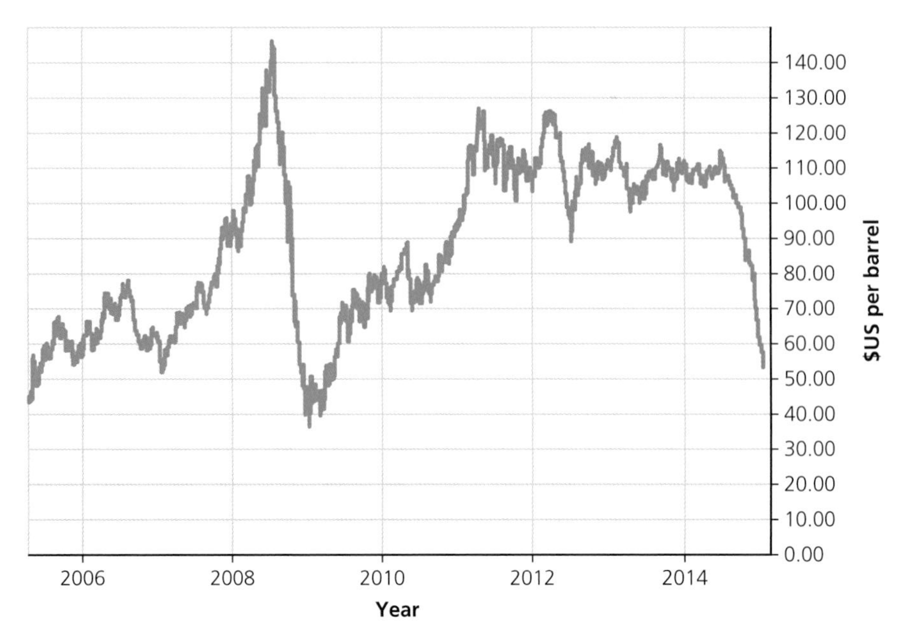

Figure 4.3 Oil prices 2006–January 2015

bought by firms as raw materials. As Figure 4.3 shows, the price of oil has fluctuated dramatically between 2006 and 2015. The price of oil is an important external influence for most firms. It not only affects transport costs directly, but also affects the costs of road building, as oil forms a key part of road construction materials.

Oil is also a very important raw material. Even companies such as Apple will be affected by rising oil prices because it will cost Apple more to buy in the plastic pellets needed to produce the casings for its laptop computers, iPads and iPhones. The price of oil is determined by the relative strength of the world supply and the world demand for oil. The world oil price is beyond the control of any single firm, making it an excellent example of an external influence.

Economic factors

Individual firms have no influence over economy-wide factors such as the rate of economic growth, the level of unemployment and the rate of inflation. However, these factors will definitely affect firms. Firms will also be affected by government fiscal and monetary policy responses. For more details see Chapter 45 of the AS book (*Business Year 1* for Edexcel).

Real business

If the SWOT technique were applied to the hotel industry, Table 4.1 might be a reasonable summary of the findings.

Strengths	**Opportunities**
• Inward tourism has been rising steadily: a major strength in London and Edinburgh • The industry has quite a high, positive income elasticity, so as people get more affluent they use hotels more	• British hotels such as the Ritz, the Savoy and Claridges are world-famous; this gives huge potential for growth overseas • After five years of dither, the British government committed itself in 2015 to cutting the crazily high price of a visa for Chinese citizens; this should help boost tourist numbers
Weaknesses	**Threats**
• Inherently a seasonal business, especially away from city centres such as London; this makes cash flow and capacity utilisation problematic • Lack of commitment by young English people means the industry is heavily reliant on immigrant – and therefore possibly transient – labour	• Airbnb threatens to offer unmatchable price competition from individuals renting out their own rooms – an online/clicks threat to hotel bricks • Economic downturns hit the hotel industry hard. When the next economic recession begins, hotels will be among the hardest hit

Table 4.1 Strengths, weaknesses, opportunities and threats for the UK hotel industry

'Build your weaknesses until they become your strengths.'

Knute Rockne, US football player and coach

'Strength does not come from winning. Your struggles develop your strengths.'

Arnold Schwarzenegger, film star and politician

4.6 What can firms do to influence opportunities and threats?

Organisations seem to spend an increasing amount of time and senior manpower on attempting to influence – even control – their environment. In some ways this is logical. Why would you wait for a train to hit you if you could a) stop it setting off or b) find out when it was coming and then get out of the way? So businesses began – many years ago – to 'lobby' their MPs. **Lobbying** usually meant local businesses going to London to put their case to their MPs, who would then ask questions in parliament. Today lobbying is an industry which allows unelected, professional lobbyists access to ministers or even the prime minister. Tony Blair made significant policy changes after personal lobbying by Formula 1 boss Bernie Ecclestone. David Cameron met media baron Rupert Murdoch on seven occasions between 2010 and 2012. There must come a point when the term lobbying should no longer be used for such direct involvements.

The point remains a simple one, though. Companies want to encourage favourable legislation and discourage unfavourable legislation (from the perspective of the companies) and switch the balance of taxation away from companies and towards households. In many ways this is perfectly sensible. The only problem comes when legitimate influence goes too far. Young mothers, skilled workers and those with disabilities are groups with as much right to lobby the government as business. They just don't have as much money or as much access to those with power.

'Strengths are not activities you're good at, they're activities that strengthen you.'

Marcus Buckingham, business consultant

'So it is said that if you do not know others and do not know yourself, you will be imperiled in every single battle; if you do not know others but do know yourself, you win one and lose one; if you know others and know yourself, you will not be imperiled in a hundred battles.'

Sun Tzu: The Art of War *(written about 500 BC)*

Five whys and a how

Questions	Answers
Why may it be hard for some senior managements to get to know their company's strengths and weaknesses?	Because they aren't asking the right questions of the right people; they're operating in their own boardroom bubble, like Tesco in the period 2007–2013/2014.
Why don't all strengths matter?	Because some have little bearing on the company's success or failure; consistent use of the colour orange may be one of easyJet's strengths, but does it make a difference to sales?
Why do some companies focus on their strengths while others tackle their weaknesses?	Most strategists would say build on your strengths, but Ryanair showed in 2014/2015 the value of tackling their (service) weakness; so there's no single 'right' way.
Why do some firms seem blind to their opportunities?	Up until early 2015 neither Primark nor Topshop had opened a single store in China; this lack of ambition is hard to fathom; a risk-averse board perhaps?
Why do threats so often seem to hit companies by surprise?	If they'd been anticipated they may never have emerged as a real threat; it's unexpected events such as the severity of the 2009 financial crash that threaten a firm's stability.
How often should a business conduct a SWOT analysis?	Many keep an ongoing one, updated each year. There's a case for starting from scratch every year, so that the material is really up to date.

4.7 SWOT analysis – evaluation

Regarding strengths and weaknesses the most important factor is to distinguish fact from hearsay or even delusion. One of the key characteristics of bosses who turn out to be failures is that they insulate themselves from real news. They effectively lock themselves away, listening only to 'yes-men' (usually men) and visiting the real world only as the Queen does – with plenty of warning and lots of security. Fred Goodwin, boss of RBS bank (which had to be bailed out by £46 billion from UK taxpayers in 2009) knew little about the real strengths and nothing of the weaknesses of his own business. If the person at the top is blind, it's very hard for others to see.

An important aspect of any evaluation of external factors is to distinguish between external change that is predictable and change that is not. For example, tourist businesses had five years to plan for the opportunities opened up by the 2012 London Olympics. By contrast no one would have expected that the Brazilians would have staged huge protests against their government immediately before the 2014 World Cup. Managers that fail to deal with predictable events are exceptionally weak. Those that succeed in unexpected situations are especially impressive.

Key terms

Benchmarking: comparing your own performance with that of rivals, to try to identify and learn from best practice.

Demography: factors relating to the population, such as changes in the number of older people or in the level of immigration.

Lobbying: the term originated in the 'lobby' between the House of Commons and House of Lords; it was where electors came to talk to their local MP.

4.8 Workbook

Revision questions

(30 marks; 30 minutes)

1 a) State two possible strengths and two weaknesses of McDonald's. (4)

b) Explain how McDonald's might tackle one of those weaknesses. (4)

2 Explain how a company such as Cadbury might be affected by a decision by Britain to withdraw from the European Union. (4)

3 Explain two possible reasons why a company might reject an opportunity. (6)

4 Explain how the quote from Sun Tzu (see page 25) relates to SWOT analysis. (4)

5 Several parts of Britain have suffered from floods in recent years. Explain how a retail business might prepare for that. (4)

6 Outline one UK business opportunity and one business threat that may emerge from global warming. (4)

Revision activities

Data response

Rolls-Royce to shed 2,600 jobs

John Rishton, chief executive of Rolls-Royce, sought to show he had a firm grip on the struggling FTSE 100 engineer as he unveiled the company's biggest job reduction programme in six years. Analysts welcomed initiatives that would reduce the group's 55,000 workforce by 2,600 and bring down annual costs by £80 million when fully implemented. However some raised concerns about the ability of the UK's flagship industrial company to innovate in future if the cuts hit its engineering capability.

Figure 4.4 Rolls-Royce engine on a Boeing 787 Dreamliner

'This implies they are firing engineers. That is surprising to me,' said Christian Laughlin of Bernstein Research. Mr Rishton insisted the reduction would not hit the group's ability to compete against its bigger rivals, such as General Electric. 'The measures announced today will ... contribute towards Rolls-Royce becoming a stronger and more profitable company,' he said. 'We will work ... to achieve the necessary reductions on a voluntary basis where possible, while making sure we retain the skills needed for the future.'

A large engineering team had been required for the development phase of the Trent 1000 and Trent XWB engines, the group said, but with the development phase complete, the need for engineers was reduced. These two engines are the main engines for the hugely successful Boeing Dreamliner and Airbus A350 wide-bodied jets. Orders for the Trent 1000 and Trent XWB run into tens of £billions.

The news of the job cuts sent shares in Rolls-Royce 1.4 per cent higher to close at 846p. The market took heart from signals that another cost-cutting programme was being planned for the power systems and marine business. The current job cuts would come over the next 18 months and largely be made across its aerospace division. The majority of the job cuts would be achieved in 2015. Two-thirds of the 2,600 job cuts will come in the UK. The company employs 24,800 people in Britain out of 55,200 worldwide. The job cuts will include engineers as well as managerial, operational and administrative positions.

Rolls-Royce is the world's second largest aero-engine maker, with a market share of 34 per cent.

(Source: *Financial Times*, 4 November 2014)

Questions (20 marks; 25 minutes)

1 Based on the information provided, carry out a SWOT analysis on Rolls-Royce Aero Engines. (20)

Extended writing

1 Tesco is a complex organisation employing half a million staff in more than 20 countries. Evaluate whether the boss of Tesco can be expected to know fully the company's strengths, weaknesses, opportunities and threats. (20)

2 Consider an online or social media business that you use regularly and know well. Briefly research its company history and financial background. Then conduct a full analysis of its strengths, weaknesses, opportunities and threats. (20)

5 Impact of external influences

Definition

An external influence is a factor beyond a firm's control that can affect its performance. Examples include: changes in consumer tastes, laws and regulations and economic factors such as the level of spending in the economy as a whole.

Linked to: Corporate objectives, Ch 1; Corporate strategy, Ch 2; The competitive environment, Ch 6; Growth, Ch 7; Corporate influences, Ch 15; Causes and effects of change, Ch 22

5.1 The impact of external influences on firms

Some external influences have a favourable effect on firms. The holiday company Saga specialises in providing trips targeted at the elderly. So an ageing population will enlarge Saga's target market, giving the company a good opportunity to increase its revenue and profit.

Other external influences can have adverse effects on firms. In 2015, it emerged that rising temperatures in the North Sea were causing problems for stocks of haddock. This staple of fish and chip shops in the north of England will probably see a sharp rise in price. Bad news for chippies, but perhaps good news for competitors such as Chinese and Indian takeaways.

It can be helpful to analyse external factors under the overall heading PESTLE, which stands for:

Political

Economic

Social

Technological

Legal

Environmental

5.2 Political factors

Despite the fuss made by businesspeople in the lead-up to elections, politics is rarely a huge influence on business success or failure. In 2010–2015, the coalition government cut corporation tax from 28 to 20 per cent, to the applause of the business community. The result was negligible: research and development spending fell; spending on training fell, though there was a small rise in investment spending. More significant was a hike in dividend payments to shareholders which pushed share prices up. In other words the actions of politicians did little to improve the real economy: jobs, innovation and economic growth.

The same could not be said of a political move to withdraw Britain from the European Union. That would be very serious. At the time of writing, Jaguar Land Rover has been complaining about the lack of UK-based 'Tier 1' suppliers of car components. With UK car production having been buoyant lately, it is possible to see German and Japanese, perhaps even Chinese, component suppliers building factories in Britain, perhaps close to Nissan's huge factory in the North-East. But not if there's a threat that the UK might withdraw from the European Union. That would create too much uncertainty for an overseas company – even a Chinese one. (Figure 5.1 shows the promising trend in UK car production for export in the period 2004 to 2014.)

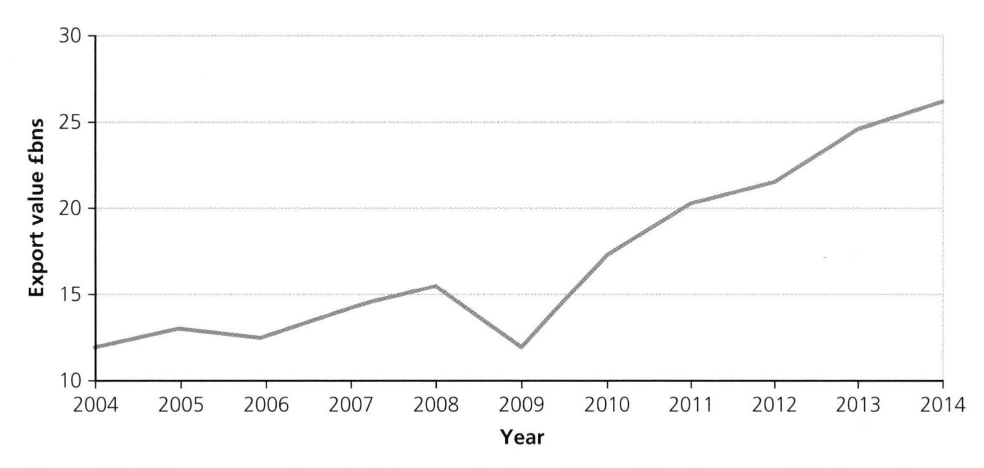

Figure 5.1 UK car exports (by value) (source: Society of Motor Manufacturers & Traders using figures from ONS)

5.3 Economic factors

Of all the economic factors that can affect a business, none is more important than the path of economic activity, as measured by the GDP: the Gross Domestic Product. Shown below in Figure 5.2, it is clear that the 2008/2009 recession was a dramatic event in the economy – and therefore business too. Particularly in the early part of the recession, there were dramatic falls in sales of luxury cars, posh holidays and champagne. Even the UK housing market took a huge hit, with prices falling 16.5 per cent nationally in the year from January–March 2008 to 2009. (This was nothing compared with Dubai, where property prices fell by 40 per cent in a year.)

Sales of most items are linked in some way to GDP and therefore people's real incomes. For Aldi and Lidl, the grinding economic woes between 2008 and 2014 meant a glorious boom in demand. Families had to take more care of their pennies – and they did.

Among other economic factors of importance, it is important to consider:

- the exchange rate, and its effect on the international competitiveness of our businesses, especially manufacturers
- the inflation rate, with its possible impact on the value of people's money savings and on their real wages (if incomes rise by 3 per cent but inflation rises by 4 per cent people are 1 per cent worse off in real terms – and therefore buy fewer items)
- the rate of unemployment, within which the figure for youth unemployment (under-25s) is perhaps the most concerning. Table 5.1 shows the sometimes extraordinarily high rates in certain countries.

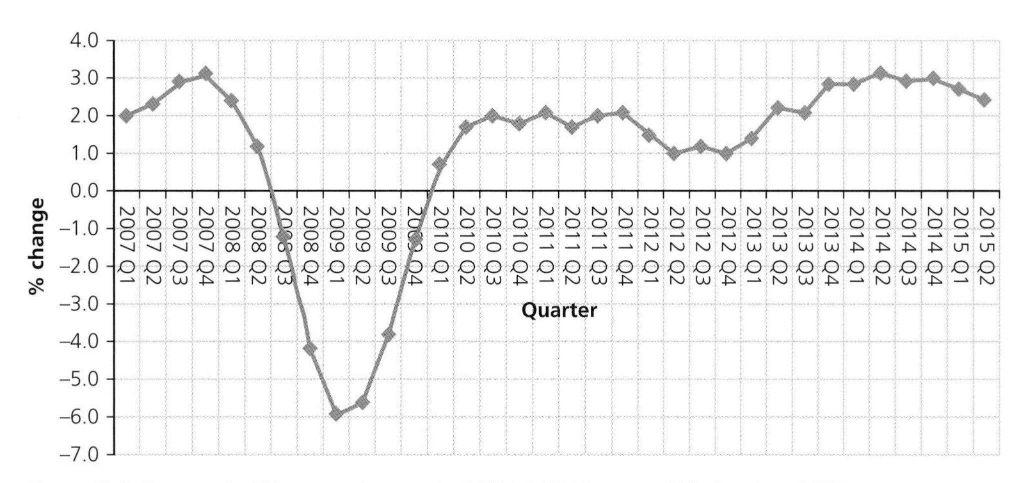

Figure 5.2 Changes in UK economic growth, 2007–2015 (source: ONS October 2015)

Level	Adult unemployment %	Youth unemployment %	Ratio of youth to adult unemployment
United Kingdom	6.1	16.1	2.64 times
France	10.3	24.6	2.39 times
Germany	5.0	7.4	1.48 times
Greece	26.5	51.1	1.93 times

Table 5.1 Unemployment data for selected countries, 4th quarter 2014 (source: Calculation based on Eurostat data)

5.4 Social factors

Among the key social factors are changes in social attitudes and behaviour. Sales of manufactured cigarettes in the UK began in 1871 and peaked in 1973. Since then they have fallen by more than two-thirds. Although legal and economic (tax/price) factors have played an important part in that decline, another factor has been a real social change from a 1960/1970s' you're-a-bit-of-an-outsider-if-you-don't-smoke type of attitude to the modern view that smoking is an outsider activity. That social change has been a consequence of numerous health reports about the dangers of active and passive smoking.

Although the changes in smoking seem to have been rational, some other social forces seem less so. Dramatic switches in diet from low-cal to low-fat to low-carb are little to do with the conflicting medical evidence. Producers simply have to weather different storms. Then there can be extraordinary crazes such as Loom Bands (2013) and *Frozen* (2014) in which a fad becomes a storm – until it blows out suddenly.

5.5 Technological factors

Although it feels like we are in the grips of the greatest ever technological revolution, it's important to keep some perspective. An online and super-connected life is very different from 20 years ago, but nothing like as different as before and after transport links (railways, then the car) or before and after electricity. IT was supposed to have brought about a productivity revolution, but there's no evidence of it in the growth rates of America, Japan, Germany or the UK.

So 'technological revolution' doesn't just refer to IT. It refers to any new, **disruptive** force that changes the way an industry or a sector works. The success of the Land Rover Evoque owes a great deal to its innovative use of aluminium instead of steel. The vehicle that looks like it should be towing tractors actually is nippy and fun to drive because it's nothing like as heavy as most 4 × 4s. And its lightness gives it far greater fuel and emissions efficiency. This has been great for the company and for skilled workers in the Midlands and North-West where Land Rover manufactures them.

Despite this, it would be daft to ignore the importance of IT as a major category within technological factors. In the department store sector, John Lewis has shone and Marks & Spencer wilted in a world of online shopping. And in the grocery sector Morrisons has been the big loser. And that's without even considering the huge new business opportunities for apps, games and social media.

> 'I'm a technological optimist in that I do believe that technology will provide solutions that will allow the world in 2050 to support 9 billion people at an acceptable standard of living.'
>
> *Martin Rees, astronomer*

5.6 Legal factors

Changes in the law can have a dramatic effect on a business. On 1 September 2014 a new European Union rule came in banning the sale of vacuum cleaners with more than 1,600 watts of power. Prior to this, media scare stories about low-power vacuums prompted a buying stampede with online sales rising by 400 per cent. The changes were especially helpful to James Dyson, whose design-led products had long offered plenty of cleaning power with relatively low-energy motors. So legal changes can affect total market sales and companies' market share statistics as well.

Because of the importance of legal factors, companies in Britain and (especially) the United States spend time and a great deal of money on lobbying parliament and government. Broadly, businesses want the minimum in the way of employment, health and safety, consumer protection and environmental legislation. Pressure groups such as the Confederation of British Industry (CBI) can put enormous pressure on governments that plan to intervene in the free market desired by firms. The introduction of the National Minimum Wage in 1998 was hugely controversial, with industry groups lobbying hard to prevent or postpone the legislation. In the event it proved a minor inconvenience.

Parliament has been intervening in business activity at least since 1833, when the Factory Act banned firms from employing children under the age of nine. Every intervention has been accompanied by warnings about competitiveness and 'freedom'. The fact that the European Union initiates quite a few laws to achieve common rules throughout Europe is seen by some as an important reason to leave the community.

5.7 Environmental factors

This category of external factors must be looked at from a short- and long-term point of view (and perhaps internationally as well, in a UK versus elsewhere comparison). Of all the topics in business, this is the one fraught with the greatest difficulty in establishing fact from opinion. In mid-nineteenth century Britain, average life expectancy was slightly below 40; today it's over 80. The amazing improvement is due to many things, but one is certainly the massive reduction in air and water pollution. Nineteenth-century public spending on water and sewage systems corrected much of the water problem, and the worst of the air pollution ended with the Clean Air Act of 1956. Yes, diesel exhaust emissions are a bad thing, but there's no excuse for making it sound as if environmental factors are a huge short-term problem in Britain.

Perhaps the most important short-term issue is particulate matter (specks in the air that can get into your lungs). Known as PM2.5, in 2014, the World Health Organization stated that in London it was five times the recommended level. New Delhi, in India, proved to be the world's most polluted city with a PM2.5 reading more than 30 times the recommended level (Beijing's is half that). Even New Delhi's though would be low compared with nineteenth-century Britain.

Then there is the long-term issue – global warming. This is the reason why European governments wrongly encouraged diesel over petrol engines – because diesel gives out less CO_2 per mile. Unfortunately it compensates by emitting far more nitric oxide and particulate matter. Theories relating to global warming have pushed governments to undertake other specific policy measures, such as the huge 35-year subsidy to be paid to the French/Chinese consortium that will build a new nuclear power plant at Hinckley Point. If the efforts prove inadequate and global warming continues, businesses will have to prepare for warmer winters and dust-bowl summers. Ice cream and soft drink producers are going to love it.

> **'Progressive companies regard global warming as an opportunity not a threat.'**
>
> *Tom Delay, Chief Executive, the Carbon Trust*

5.8 What can firms do about external influences?

Make the most of favourable external influences while they last

Luck can play an important role in determining whether a business flourishes or not, especially in the short run. However, over time good and bad luck has a habit of evening out. The key to success then is to make the most of any favourable external influence while it lasts. For example, the debt-fuelled consumer spending boom between 1997 and 2007 greatly assisted companies supplying luxury goods and services.

However, these firms should not have relied on this frothy boom for their success, because it was a factor over which they had no control. They should have made the best of the situation while it lasted, but also asked themselves a series of **'what if' questions**. In this case, 'What if interest rates were suddenly increased?' or 'How would we respond to a sudden drop in demand for our product if the commercial banks withdrew cheap and easy credit?'

Minimise the impact of unfavourable external influences

When faced with adverse external influences, successful firms make compensating internal changes to their business to offset the external constraint. Ryanair can do nothing about rising oil prices; however, it can attempt to cut other costs within the business to compensate for the rising oil price. If Ryanair can improve its internal efficiency the impact of the adverse external influence can be minimised. Successful businesses try as far as it is possible to internalise external constraints.

'The nine most terrifying words in the English language are "I'm from the government and I'm here to help".'

Ronald Reagan, former President, USA

Five whys and a how

Questions	Answers
Why might a change of government matter to UK companies?	It might mean a significant change in policies such as employment law, corporation tax rates and whether to stay in the European Union.
Why might a depreciation of the pound be welcomed by UK manufacturers?	Because their export sales would become more price competitive, while importers to the UK would find it harder to compete.
Why might a company such as Coca-Cola spend to finance academic research on a subject such as soft drinks and obesity?	The company would argue that it's part of its CSR practices; critics say that such research is directed at obscuring the evidence linking sugar and overweight.
Why, if new digital technologies are so powerful and efficient, has productivity growth slowed in the past ten years?	It's a bit of a mystery; some say the big productivity gains (and perhaps job losses) are still to come; others point out that IT and the internet are nothing like as fundamental as discovering engines or electricity.
Why do national leaders obsess about long-term global warming, yet do so little for short-term air quality (which is a killer)?	Another mystery; perhaps because it means *doing* something *now*, instead of setting ambitious long-term targets for governments in the future.
How might a company set about changing a proposed law that might damage its interests?	Lobbying is the start, which today means paying a 'consultancy' to get access to key government ministers or MPs; there will also be payments to public relations firms to get media coverage that favours your cause.

5.9 Impact of external influences – evaluation

The idea of PESTLE is that it provides a framework for analysing the context of a business – above all, to answer the question 'Is the business really in charge of its destiny?' City analysts hate it when a company blames poor performance on the weather or, still worse, on a factor that is external but predictable, such as a well-trailed piece of new legislation. If management knew a change was about to happen, why weren't they fully prepared?

In truth, though, there are external factors that appear to be manageable, but are not. A political swing to Jeremy Corbyn's Labour Party would create some panic among the directors and shareholders of railway franchises. As was shown in Figure 5.2, a sudden economic downturn can happen – and inevitably causes havoc with company plans and budgets.

In the long run, a management will succeed if it shows that it's very largely in control of its destiny, and clever at coping with the remaining external factors that threaten to push it off course.

Key terms

Disruptive: technology would shift a whole sector towards a new way of doing things. This is very painful for those left behind.

'What if' questions: these are hypothetical (that is, they are used to test out different possibilities or theories).

5.10 Workbook

Revision questions

(30 marks; 30 minutes)

1 What is an external influence? (2)

2 Look again at the recession period shown in Figure 5.2. Briefly explain the probable effect of a sharp recession on:

a) an airline that focuses on long-haul flights such as Virgin Atlantic. (4)

b) a clothes retailer that focuses on value-for-money fashion clothes such as Primark. (4)

3 Based on your knowledge of economic trends over the past three months, explain how one economic factor may be having a positive impact upon UK firms. (4)

4 In 2015, the steelworks at Redcar was closed down, with 1,700 jobs lost. Outline three examples of the types of firms in and around Redcar that would be adversely affected by this decision. (6)

5 Record companies find it increasingly difficult to generate revenue because of file sharing sites that enable music lovers to illegally download music. What actions should record companies take to minimise this external constraint? (4)

6 Table 5.1 shows that youth unemployment is relatively high in the UK. Explain how that might affect two different businesses of your choice. (6)

Revision activities

Data response

Black day for retail?

So what was that all about? People fighting in store, queues of up to an hour online – yes, that's the new American novelty of 'Black Friday'. Probably a number of retail chains had severe doubts about joining in – but what can you do? Amazon.com sold 4 million items in the UK on Black Friday 2013 – a record number. And in 2014, the figure was 5.5 million, an amazing 37.5 per cent increase. Other growth figures were even more impressive, though perhaps from a lower base. John Lewis boasted a 307 per cent increase in online sales compared with last year – and Currys bettered that by saying their online sales rose fivefold.

Black Friday stems from the US tradition of 'Thanksgiving' on the last Thursday of November. After that, Christmas can start to take its commercial grip – hence the sales as a spur to shoppers to get going on Christmas presents. But in 2014, US shops reported a slight dip in Black Friday sales. It's a long-established event in America, whereas in Britain it's still a real novelty.

But will it help the retailers? Some argue that it's better to sell at 20 per cent off before Christmas than 50 per cent off in the January sales. That would be true if shops were so good at forecasting that they knew exactly what stock would be left unsold at Christmas. Furthermore, some experts are worried that: 'All Black Friday is likely to do is bring forward business from December, reduce gross margins and undermine consumers' willingness to pay full price again before Christmas,' said retail analyst Nick Bubb.

Figure 5.3 Shoppers wrestle over goods on Black Friday

Questions (35 marks; 40 minutes)

1 The Black Friday phenomenon could be analysed using the acronym PESTLE. Explain which aspect of PESTLE was the most important factor. (5)

2 Assess the possible impact on stock management of having a day when online sales may be 307 per cent higher than you expect. (10)

3 Evaluate Nick Bubb's criticism of Black Friday from a business point of view. (20)

Extended writing

1 Evaluate whether the components of PESTLE are the main factors in holding Tesco back from rebuilding its profits back to their pre-2013 level of £4 billion a year. (20)

2 Evaluate which of the six PESTLE factors is likely to be the most influential in the long run for a producer of luxury, branded handbags. (20)

6 The competitive environment

Definition

Competitiveness measures a firm's ability to shine in comparison with its rivals.

Linked to: Corporate strategy, Ch 2; Impact of external influences, Ch 5; Causes and effects of change, Ch 22; Scenario planning, Ch 24; Factors contributing to increased globalisation, Ch 29

6.1 The changing competitive environment

The competitive environment was introduced in Chapter 47 of the AS book (*Business Year 1* for Edexcel). This A level chapter moves the topic on in the direction of competitive change and the global environment. Up until 2010, Nokia was the global leader of smartphone sales. Figure 6.1 shows how the brand was demolished by 2014. Innovative competition from Apple, then Samsung, then the Chinese newcomers Huawei and Xiaomi wiped out the company that had founded the mobile phone market. A changing competitive environment indeed.

The graph is also notable for what it shows about Apple. The arrival of Samsung's Galaxy S3 model (2012) plus the growth of low-priced Chinese competition pushed Apple's global market share down from 18.8 per cent to 11.6 per cent between 2011 and 2014. Apple's saviour was the hugely well received S6 model which boosted sales, profits and market share in 2015 – especially in China. So the company's answer to a tougher competitive environment was to invest more heavily in creative innovation (definitely not in price competition).

So is it inevitable that the competitive environment is changing? In some cases, no. At over 100 years old, Heinz Baked Beans is hardly in the growth phase of its life cycle, but in 2014, its UK sales of £217 million were slightly up on the previous year. By contrast sales of its nearest challenger, Branston, fell by 37 per cent. Heinz Baked Beans enjoyed a 68 per cent market share. Actually, canned foods as a market sector is in decline, so Heinz has to work hard to tackle that aspect of its competitive environment. Overall, though, it's in a comfortable position.

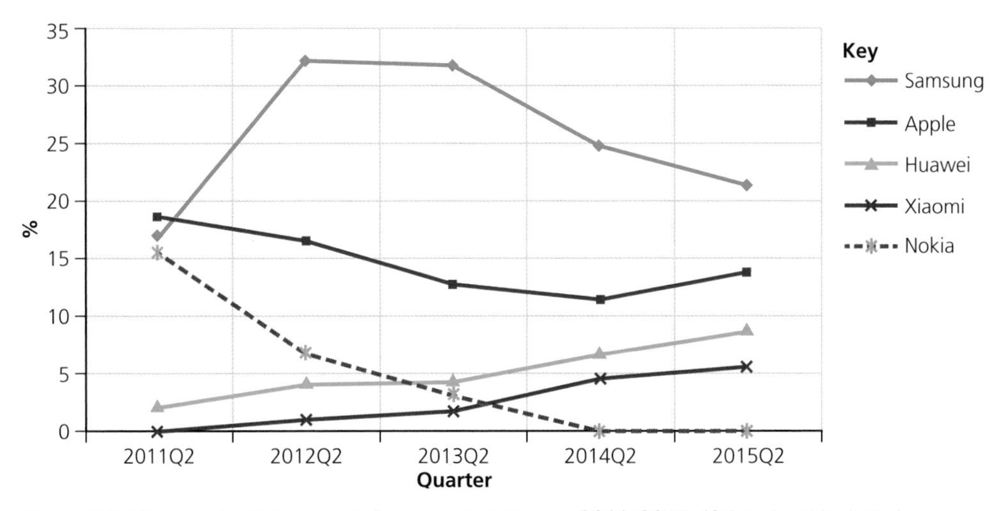

Figure 6.1 Changes in global smartphone market shares: 2011–2015. 'Others' not included so figures do not add up to 100 per cent (source: IDC)

By contrast, the UK bread market is in a whirlwind of change. In the year to December 2015 Kingsmill bakery's sales fell by £77 million. That was a decline of 23 per cent. Big brands in staple foods such as bread would never expect such a slide in sales. It lost out because the whole market for wrapped bread fell, but Kingsmill's position was worsened when Tesco decided to stop distributing its bread products. When the retailer with more than a quarter of the market stops stocking you, the impact on sales cannot be doubted.

Most commentators would feel that the big factors leading to a changing competitive environment include:

- shortening product life cycles; in turn driven by rapid developments in technology
- more rapid changes in consumer taste, such as the switches to 'free from' foods
- globalisation, meaning that more UK markets can be disrupted by competition from overseas (membership of the European Union has the same effect); in the UK chocolate market, the two big gainers in 2015 were Lindt (with Lindor) and Ferrero (with Kinder eggs); in sugar confectionery, the German Haribo was the big winner
- ever-tougher profit pressures on companies, both from the stock market and from 'private equity' financiers who buy up companies (such as Boots the Chemist) and demand that their profit levels should improve sharply.

In an attempt to devise a theory that would include all these pressures, Michael Porter came up with a form of analysis known as 'Porter's Five Forces'.

6.2 Porter's Five Forces

In 1980, with the publication of *Competitive Strategy*, Michael Porter became an instant business guru with his theory known as the Five Forces. Porter's target was to help businesses figure out how to achieve and sustain a **competitive advantage**. By this he meant establish a strength that rivals would struggle to copy. Coca-Cola has managed to stay the number one soft drink for more than 125 years. It, of course, has branding on its side – and the benefits of scale. Porter's theory showed the main pressures on businesses that would determine their ability to compete and succeed.

Crucial to Porter's success was the simple and accessible diagram that shows the Five Forces he identified. See Figure 6.2.

Figure 6.2 Rivalry among existing competitors (source: Michael E. Porter, 'The Five Competitive Forces That Shape Strategy', *Harvard Business Review*, January 2008)

6.3 Force 1: Rivalry among existing competitors

No one would doubt that competition is tough among Britain's eight supermarket chains. Even though Tesco once had a 32 per cent share of UK grocery sales, competition from Lidl/Aldi on price and Waitrose on quality squeezed its share down to 28 per cent by late 2015. At the other end of the scale is WHSmith, which overwhelmingly trades from local monopoly positions: at airports, at railway stations and so on. As a result WHSmith has the power to price its stationery stiffly, such as charging £3.39 for a 400-page refill writing pad: yours for £1 at Poundworld.

Where intensity of rivalry is low	Where intensity of rivalry is high
• A few companies dominate the market • Branding is very important to consumers • Booming market gives opportunities for all • Little spare capacity • High barriers to entry, e.g. a new Chinese aeroplane facing consumer credibility issues • No direct competition from abroad, e.g. 'bricks' retailing such as retail petrol	• Many competitors of roughly equal size • Products are relatively undifferentiated • Market growth is slow • Capacity utilisation is low • Low barriers to entry, so it's cheap and easy to enter the market • Directly faces overseas competition, e.g. manufactured goods and some services

Table 6.1 Characteristics of markets where rivalry is low and high

As shown in Figure 6.2, Michael Porter sees rivalry among existing competitors as the central factor in the Five Forces that shape the strategies that business must adopt. In a highly competitive market, cost control becomes a critical factor in long-term survival. The least efficient supplier will always be vulnerable to financial crisis. For businesses in less competitive markets, marketing, branding and product innovation become the focus of business strategy.

On a global scale the issues are the same, but the priorities might change slightly. To be as successful as Toyota requires an appreciation that competitive forces are different in every one of the 120+ countries in which it operates. It can be fairly sure that it will face its two most direct challengers for the global number one spot, Volkswagen and General Motors, but there might be local strengths for companies such as Ford (USA and UK), Peugeot (France), Nissan (Japan, USA and UK) or Suzuki (India). Whatever the local situation, Toyota arms itself with lean production systems that keep costs down. This plus the differentiation involved in its development of hybrid vehicles and its Lexus brand enables it to be markedly more profitable than its rivals. Toyota makes more than five times the profit of General Motors, allowing it to invest far more in product development and capacity expansion. Table 6.2 emphasises Toyota's competitive strength.

	General Motors (USA)	Volkswagen (Germany)	Toyota (Japan)
Annual sales revenue	£99.53bn	£162.1bn	£147.7bn
Annual operating profit	£2.71bn	£10.16bn	£14.91bn
Operating profit margin	2.72%	6.27%	10.1%

Table 6.2 Size and profitability of the world's top 3 car makers 2014 (source: annual reports for 2014: currencies converted to £s at Bank of England exchange rate data for December 2014)

6.4 Force 2: Threat of new entrants

One of the world's biggest and most profitable air routes is London–New York. The partnership between British Airways and American Airlines controls 60 per cent of the traffic. So why are there no significant new competitors? In practice the problem is the lack of 'landing slots' at Heathrow airport (no airline really wants to fly to Gatwick or Stansted because Heathrow commands higher ticket prices). But this could be overturned if, say, a wealthy airline such as South-West Airlines (of America) bought up a European airline with plenty of Heathrow landing slots, i.e. competition on the New York route could happen quite suddenly.

The threat of new entrants might constrain British Airways and American Airlines from being too greedy in their pricing. In other words even if their 60 per cent market share gives them strong pricing power, they may choose to keep prices down for fear that new entrants will be attracted like bees to a honey pot.

The degree of threat from new entrants depends on the barriers to entry. Starting a new discount airline is relatively easy, as you can open one route at a time – and choose routes that no one else yet offers. In the long term you will need to build a brand name, but the little-known Wizz Air enjoyed its twelfth birthday in 2015, operating with record profitability. Contrast the low barriers to entry in airlines with the huge barriers in the manufacture of aircraft. The global market for large passenger planes is controlled 50/50 by America's Boeing and Europe's Airbus. Among the barriers to entry to this market are:

- huge development costs; the new Airbus A350 cost at least £10 billion to develop
- huge extra costs to build up the global engineering network to ensure that the planes are serviced properly
- potential customer resistance based on lack of track record regarding quality and therefore safety (China's Comac aircraft maker wants to break into the market, but will face massive resistance from sceptical airline executives – and perhaps also from the travelling public).

Accordingly, the threat of new entrants may be an everyday one for some firms (pizza delivery firms, for example) but a distant one for others.

> 'The ability to learn faster than your competitors may be the only sustainable competitive advantage.'
>
> *Arie de Geus, author and former Head of Planning, Shell*

6.5 Force 3: Changes in the buying power of customers

If you produce ready meals that you sell to Morrisons, you are selling to a business that has an 11 per cent share of the UK grocery market. Morrisons is a big and powerful company. But if the buyers at Morrisons become too demanding of discounts and longer credit terms, you can negotiate with Sainsbury's or Asda (each with a 16.5 per cent market share). If the negotiations go well, you can tell Morrisons you no longer wish to supply it. So you, the producer, have some power in this relationship.

But what if Asda made a successful takeover bid for Morrisons. The combined business would have a 27.5 per cent market share (close to Tesco's 29 per cent) and your options would be restricted greatly. OK, Sainsbury's might still be your saviour, but it's easy to see that Morrisons' buying power is much greater when combined with Asda than when it's on its own. So changes in the buying power of customers can make a huge difference to a supplier's profitability, stability and long-term health.

6.6 Force 4: Changes in the selling power of suppliers

A manufacturer of ready meals will have a wide number of suppliers, delivering food ingredients plus packaging materials. Most will be commodities such as chicken, which can be bought from a wide range of suppliers. But what if there's a range of premium ready meals that comes in special 'flavour-seal' packs? This has been available from two packaging companies – but one has just gone into liquidation. So now you have to buy from the sole, monopoly supplier of the flavour-seal packs. Clearly the increase in the selling power of the supplier is going to mean higher prices and therefore higher costs for you. Your profit margin will be squeezed until you can find a solution – a completely different type of packaging perhaps.

6.7 Force 5: Threat of substitutes

Whereas 6.4 looked at the threat of new entrants to a market, the threat of **substitutes** means new competition from outside the traditional industry. Twenty years ago BP competed with Shell and Esso. Arguably, today they compete also with wind power, solar power and liquefied petroleum gas. Technological development and innovation have brought new rivals to the market, giving customers some alternatives to traditional oil. This represents a new threat to the profitability of the oil companies, but is entirely in the best interests of consumers.

Real business

In 2005, HMV was a highly profitable retailer. In the UK it made a profit of £93 million on sales of £986 million. Its success was built on its 25 per cent market share in sales of music and film CDs and DVDs. Virgin Megastores was the main retail rival, and there was a growing threat from online retailers such as Amazon. At the time, though, online retail had a 10 per cent share of sales of CDs and DVDs and although it was rising, it may not have seemed a huge threat.

Then came the digital deluge. New substitutes arrived in the form of iTunes, Spotify and many forms of illegal downloading. Within a few years analysts were questioning whether HMV could survive. Indeed in January 2013 the business went into receivership. Shareholders lost everything, though some of the shops were bought up and still trade today. For HMV, though, the threat of substitutes proved a very real one.

Figure 6.3 HMV shop

'Constant change by everyone requires a dramatic increase in the capacity to accept disruption.'

Tom Peters, business author of Thriving on Chaos

'Now here, you see, it takes all the running you can do to keep in the same place. If you want to get somewhere else you must run at least twice as fast as that.'

Lewis Carroll, author of Alice's Adventures in Wonderland

6.8 How the Five Forces might shape competitive strategy

Competitive strategy is the company's medium- to long-term plan for how to keep ahead of the competition. The Five Forces can be used as an analytic tool – in effect intertwined with SWOT analysis. Careful investigation of each of the forces might reveal one serious weakness on the part of the business. In recent years Marks & Spencer has allowed itself to fall behind the online sales success of its rival John Lewis. Early investigation of this weakness would have helped management to realise that the threat of substitutes made it vital to invest more – and earlier – in a state-of-the-art website and online sales system.

It's important to tackle weaknesses, but perhaps even more important to build on strengths. Associated British Foods (owners of Primark) have done a remarkable job in identifying the potential for what was once a tiny part of a huge food business. By the end of 2014 Primark had over 300 shops, made £662 million in profit and was generating a 33.2 per cent return on capital employed. The directors spotted that despite the apparently low barriers to entry in fashion retailing, rivals were struggling to achieve the Primark balance between design and price.

6.9 Critique of the Five Forces

Many academics have criticised the Five Forces theory, or suggested a sixth or seventh force. The single biggest weakness is that it is oddly static. It ignores completely the vast strategic importance of trends in market size. Implicitly Michael Porter would have missed the profitable opportunities that Costa Coffee, Burberry and Jaguar Land Rover found in China. The theory is also criticised for underestimating the forces of change. From the original 100 Top UK companies that started in the FTSE 100 stock market index in 1930, only two remained in the index in 2015: BP and GKN. The risk with the Five Forces is that a company uses it once – and trusts its findings. In reality it should be updated each year, just like a budget or a cash flow forecast.

Five whys and a how

Questions	Answers
Why may it be hard for a business to sustain a competitive advantage?	Everyone copies successful products or processes, so it's hard to stay ahead, even if you've been the innovator.
Why may the power of suppliers be a barrier to new businesses trying to enter a market?	If suppliers demand to be paid cash on delivery, it will add to the cash flow strains faced by a new, start-up business.
Why may barriers to entry sometimes be psychological rather than real?	Time after time, new businesses have found ways to break into apparently rock-solid markets, such as Fever-Tree breaking the Schweppes hold on tonic water, and the successful competition of Lindt's Lindor with Cadbury Creme Eggs.
Why may the threat of a new competitor keep prices down?	A business might choose to keep prices down to make it hard for a new business to enter the market.
Why may some people critique the Five Forces?	Because they ignore a key market condition: whether the market size is expanding or declining.
How effective might the Five Forces theory have been in spotting the deteriorating position of Tesco in 2013 and 2014?	Not well at all. It would have overestimated the importance of Tesco's power over suppliers and the strength of its market share. But then, no theory is perfect.

6.10 The competitive environment – evaluation

As has always been the case, the best way a business can ensure its survival in a competitive world is to find something it is good at, and stick with it. Cadbury is great when it concentrates on making chocolate; Heinz is brilliant at making and marketing baked beans. Even if the massive Hershey Corporation brings its chocolate from America, Cadbury need not fear. Similarly the launch of Branston's Baked Beans made little impact on Heinz.

Sometimes, though, big judgements have to be considered, such as to risk launching a new product in a new country. When Tesco did this in 2007, launching Fresh & Easy stores in America, the questions to ask were whether it really needed to, and whether it was looking in the right direction. (Wouldn't China or India have made more sense?) In 2010, it finally admitted its mistake by increasing massively its investment into China. All too often, business leaders take actions that seem more to do with ego than logic. Models such as Porter's Five Forces are based on an assumption that business is about reacting to pressures, whereas a great deal of business decision-making is about choices and judgements.

Key terms

Competitive advantage: the factors that enable a business to sustain a profitable position in a competitive market.

Substitutes: rival products such as Galaxy and Cadbury's Dairy Milk; many customers are happy to substitute one for the other.

6.11 Workbook

Revision questions

(35 marks; 35 minutes)

1. Chinese phone maker Xiaomi is known for producing Apple-like phones at much lower prices. Explain how Apple might respond to the threat from Xiaomi's growth. (4)
2. Figure 6.1 shows Apple to be the global smartphone number two 'by volume'. What might be the impact on the figures if the data had been provided 'by value'? (3)
3. In Section 6.1 it was explained that Heinz has a stable, long-lived brand in Heinz Baked Beans. Explain briefly whether you think the following products are in dynamic/new or static/older markets.
   a) Cadbury's Creme Egg. (4)
   b) Netflix. (4)
4. Use Porter's Five Forces (Figure 6.2) to assess the competitive position of **one** of the following:
   a) Sainsbury's
   b) Primark
   c) Greggs. (10)
5. Explain how a business might be affected by an increase in the buying power of its customers. (4)
6. Outline two reasons why a supermarket might be concerned if the world's top two breweries plan to merge into one business. (6)

Revision activities

Data response

Cadbury and Porter's Five Forces

In February 2015, Mondelez International (MI) reported a 44 per cent dip in 2014 net earnings, blaming 'developed market consumers responding negatively to chocolate price hikes'. MI (the owner of Cadbury) stated that it would withdraw from certain retail customers in Europe that have refused to pay the price increases. In 2014, MI implemented price hikes in response to rising commodity costs, particularly cocoa. The main centre of resistance to the price rises was in France. Although Nestlé increased prices as well, Mars only increased prices in America and Lindt said it could weather cocoa cost increases without needing to increase prices. In Europe, sales fell 1 per cent due to retailer resistance and in America growth was held to 1 per cent due to 'intense competition in biscuits and crackers'.

Only a few days earlier, both MI and Mars were accused of 'exploiting small businesses' by extending payment terms to some UK suppliers from 60 to 120 days. The small business pressure group FPB declared that: 'At a time when the economic outlook remains uncertain it is fundamentally unfair that small businesses are being used as a line of credit for larger organisations and propping up big business.'

Perhaps part of the pressure to act in the above ways can be blamed on competition. Although in the UK, Cadbury is giving big rivals Nestlé and Mars a hard time, the real stars in the UK market currently are Italian Ferrero and Swiss Lindt. In the twelve months to July 2014, sales by value for Ferrero rose by 22.1 per cent compared with 0.7 per cent for the market as a whole. Ferrero has only a 3.3 per cent market share in the UK, but it hopes that it will rise to 5.5 per cent by 2019. Meanwhile Lindt's Lindor brand enjoyed sales of £80 million in 2014, up 13.6 per cent on 2013.

(Source: various, including The Grocer, *20 December 2014 and articles from www.confectionerynews.com)*

Questions (30 marks; 35 minutes)

1. Use Porter's Five Forces to assess the external pressures faced by Cadbury (MI) at this time. (10)
2. Evaluate whether MI's strategy for dealing with external pressures is the right one for the long-term health of the business. (20)

Extended writing

1. Evaluate the extent to which the use of Porter's Five Forces might help Marks & Spencer to overcome its continuing difficulties in clothes retailing. (20)
2. Evaluate whether Porter's Five Forces might benefit from including a sixth 'Force' – *change*. (20)

7 Growth

Definition

Growth means expansion, either due to rising sales or by increasing the scale of an enterprise by means of a takeover.

Linked to: Corporate objectives, Ch 1; Corporate strategy, Ch 2; The competitive environment, Ch 6; Reasons for staying small, Ch 10; International trade and business growth, Ch 28

7.1 Reasons why firms grow

Some firms can end up growing by accident. This is called unplanned growth. A good example is Baggit, which is now one of India's leading suppliers of luxury handbags. Nina Lekhi set up the business when she dropped out of university. Initially, Lekhi did not take her own business seriously; it was just a hobby. Fortunately, her brightly coloured bags proved to be very popular with Indian women who loved her bold designs. More and more retailers wanted to stock Baggit, which meant that Lekhi had to take on more staff and expand.

On the other hand, many firms grow in order to achieve an objective. This is called planned growth. The reasons for planned growth include:

- to increase profits
- to achieve economies of scale
- increased market power
- increased market share
- increased profitability.

To increase profitability

Many firms choose to pursue growth because they hope that it will cause their profits to rise. In August 2014, Netflix, an American company that sells streamed films and TV series, announced its intention to grow by launching its service in France and Germany. In 2013, Netflix made a total profit of £80 million from 30 million subscribers. This implies that it made a profit of £2.67 per customer. Assuming that Netflix proves as popular in France and Germany as it has in America and Britain, an additional 10 million French and German subscribers would add £26.7 million to Netflix's bottom line.

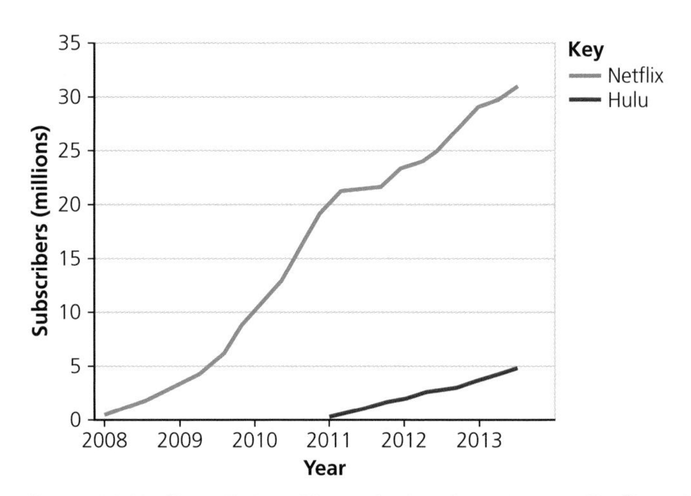

Figure 7.1 Netflix vs Hulu: millions of subscribers (source: Netflix and Hulu company data where available; author estimates otherwise)

To achieve economies of scale

Growth in the long run can cause cost per unit to fall due to **economies of scale**. This boosts competitiveness. This was the reasoning behind the merger of Carphone Warehouse and Dixons. Business leaders are attracted to growth by economies of scale, but often forget the drag caused by diseconomies (see below).

What businesses crave, more than anything else, is control. Growth itself is hard to control, but if it enables the business to become the market leader, with huge economies of scale, it may become virtually impossible for any competitor to hit back. Wrigley, with over 90 per cent share of the UK market for chewing gum, can't really be hurt by rivals; when Cadbury tried with its Trident gum brand, it spent many millions on an eventual failure. This is why businesses such as Amazon and Google worked so hard at growth (often profit-free) in their early years.

Economies of scale can be broken down into two types:

- Internal economies of scale: these are the economies that can arise within the business as its scale of operation expands, such as managerial, purchasing and technical economies.
- External economies: these may arise outside the business as it – or, more commonly, the whole industry – grows. For example, the West Midlands has long been an important area for car manufacturing in the UK. This attracted major car component supplier GKN to set up factories nearby. So Jaguar Land Rover's Solihull factory benefits from the external economy of scale of cheaper components from suppliers set up nearby. Another external economy of scale occurs when local education authorities respond to the growth of an industry by setting up colleges that specialise in teaching relevant vocational skills. This makes it cheaper for the companies to employ the staff they need.

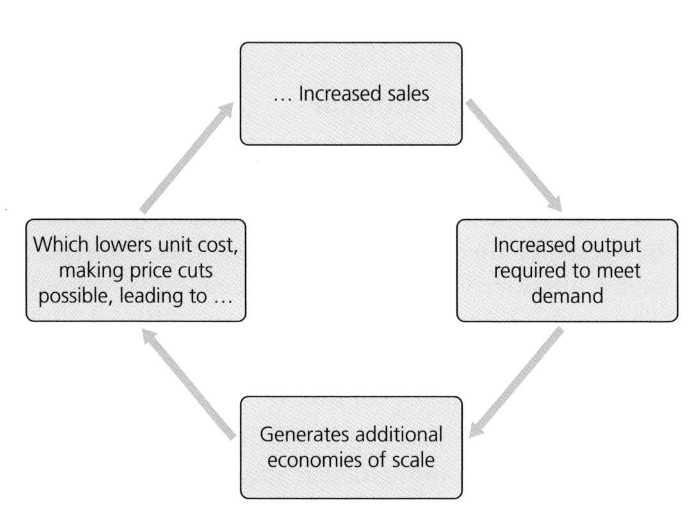

Figure 7.2 Logic circle: economies of scale

Increased market power over customers and suppliers

Power over customers

Colgate-Palmolive is an example of a company that has achieved a position of **market dominance** via growth. The company leads the global toothpaste market with a share of over 40 per cent. Colgate has a broad product portfolio ensuring that all market segments are covered, from 'gleaming white' to 'sensitive teeth'. Colgate's huge market share gives it substantial negotiating power with supermarkets and other distributors. This enables it to charge higher prices, whilst simultaneously benefitting from economies of scale. In 2015 Tesco's new strategy for boosting profits was to cut down on the number of suppliers, thereby ordering in bigger bulk from only one or two manufacturers. Many other companies would have been worried; not Colgate, as its market power is too great for Tesco to drop it.

Power over suppliers

In addition to its market power when dealing with customers, Colgate has a great deal of leverage in relation to its suppliers. In 2014 the company announced that it was building a factory for making its own toothbrushes. This puts pressure on current toothbrush-makers (suppliers) – forcing them to compete fiercely in order to win further Colgate contracts.

Some companies have been accused of abusing their market power. In August 2015 Topshop owner Arcadia upset clothes manufacturers by suddenly imposing a 2 per cent added discount, i.e. knocking 2 per cent off the pre-agreed prices being charged by suppliers. Tough negotiations over price and delivery dates are normal; but imposing an extra cut ('we're knocking 2 per cent off the bill') strays towards an abuse of market power.

Increased market share and brand recognition

There can be conflicts of interest between a company's internal stakeholders, but all love an increase in market share and brand recognition. Implicitly jobs are made safer, promotion prospects are better and profits can bloom. Furthermore increased market share can only be achieved by taking sales from your rivals, eating into their profitability and thereby undermining their ability to finance growth. To increase market share there are two main strategies:

- Work harder on innovation, perhaps by increasing the research and development budget; this should improve the long-term quality of the new product development pipeline; the goal is to be Apple rather than Nokia.
- Invest more heavily in branding and marketing, to try to differentiate your products more clearly.

Brand recognition can be both cause and effect of increased market share. If clever advertising boosts the image and recognition of your brand, that should help build market share. In the same way, rising market share leads to better distribution and therefore wider brand recognition. That, in turn, makes it easier to persuade retailers to stock new products launched under the same brand 'umbrella', e.g. the 2015 launch of Cadbury Dairy Milk 'Puddles'.

Increased profitability

If growth achieves greater economies of scale than diseconomies, **average costs** will fall in real terms. That would help to improve operating profit margins, allowing the twin benefit of rising revenues and rising margins. This can be the route to dramatic increases in profit. In Table 7.1 we can see how the fantastic growth of Costa Coffee has led to steady rises in operating profit margins (a good measure of profitability). This is only possible when total costs are falling in relation to revenue. Between 2009 and 2015 Costa sales rose 245 per cent, but profits by 483 per cent – nearly twice as much.

	Revenue (£ms)	Profit (£ms)	Operating profit margin (%)	Number of stores
2009	276.3	22.7	8.22	1,300
2010	340.9	36.2	10.62	1,600
2011	425.0	50.5	11.88	1,871
2012	541.9	69.7	12.86	2,203
2013	669.9	90.1	13.45	2,527
2014	807.7	109.4	13.54	2,861
2015	951.9	132.4	13.91	3,080

Table 7.1 Rising profitability at Costa Coffee, 2009–2015 (source: notes to Whitbread accounts)

Figure 7.3 Costa Coffee shop

7.2 Problems arising from growth

Diseconomies of scale

When firms grow, total costs rise. But why should costs per unit rise? This is because growth can also create **diseconomies of scale**. The most important of these is worsening internal communication.

Poor internal communication

Communication can be a significant problem when a firm grows. Effective communication is dependent on high levels of motivation. Communication is only effective if the person being communicated with is willing to listen. If growth has left the workforce with a feeling of alienation, communication can deteriorate alongside productivity. A second reason for poor communication in large organisations is that the methods chosen to communicate may be less effective. As a firm grows, it may become necessary to use written forms of communication more frequently. Unlike verbal communication, written communication is less personal and therefore less motivating. Written messages are easier to ignore and provide less feedback. Relying too much on written forms of communication could result in an increase in the number of expensive mistakes being made. It is also inevitable that growth leads to new managerial layers being added. With more layers of hierarchy, vertical communication becomes slower and more ineffective. This reduction in efficiency leads to increasing unit costs as the organisation grows.

Poor employee motivation

When firms grow, one consequence of poor internal communication is reduced personal contact between staff and management. In large organisations there may be a sense of alienation. If staff believe their efforts are going unnoticed a sense of indifference may spread. This is what happened at Tesco between 2010 and 2014.

Poor managerial coordination

Poor internal communication also affects coordination. In a small firm coordination is easy. The boss decides what the goals are, and who is doing what. As firms grow, it becomes harder for the person at the top to control and coordinate effectively. The leader who refuses to **delegate** 'drowns' under the weight of work. The leader who delegates finds (later) that manager A is heading in a slightly different direction from manager B. Regular meetings are arranged to try to keep everyone focused on the same goals through the same strategy. But not only are such meetings expensive, they are also often poorly attended and lead to grumbles rather than insight. Coordination works well and cheaply in a small firm, but is expensive and often ineffective in large corporations.

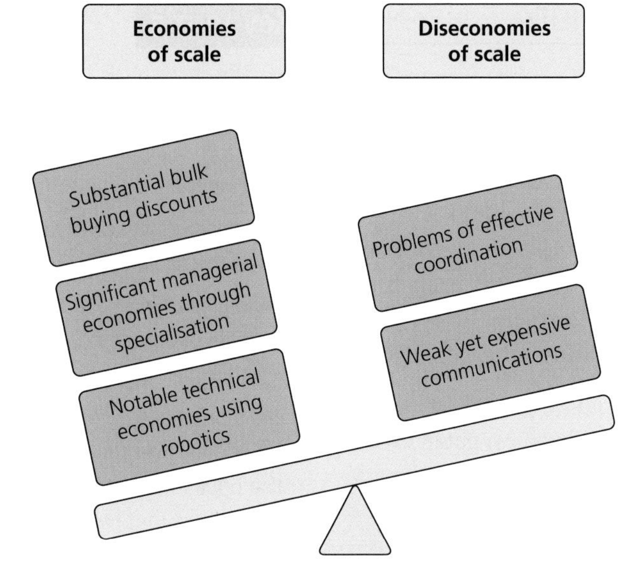

Figure 7.4 Logic balance: when economies outweigh diseconomies

Overtrading

A dangerous problem created by **organic growth** is overtrading. This occurs when a business suffers from cash-flow problems because it has tried to expand too rapidly with insufficient cash in the bank. When firms grow, cash flow can quickly become negative. This is because expansion creates additional cash outflows that occur before the extra cash inflows arrive. To prevent overtrading firms must forecast the cash-flow implications of growth and raise the additional working capital required well before the expansion programme begins. Banks and investors are willing to invest in a promising business that has sound financial management. If a business suffering from overtrading tries to borrow, a bank manager will probably refuse.

Real business

In 2011 Express Cafés Ltd was bought by a private company from the large Compass Group plc. From its Shropshire base it was soon able to claim to be the country's biggest supplier of small-unit temporary catering to sporting and music events and festivals. The business grew rapidly, picking up contracts for the 2014 Ryder Cup and Aintree Racecourse. Then in 2014 it made another leap forward, signing a deal with Levi Roots for 'Jammin' Jerk Burger' vans to go to the Reading Festival and the Formula 1 British Grand Prix. But in late October 2014 it went into voluntary liquidation, i.e. the directors closed the business down. Its growth had outstripped its ability to find the cash to pay the bills.

Five whys and a how

Questions	Answers
Why do newly established firms need to grow quickly?	To hit their break-even sales level. Most start-ups are short of cash; therefore, they cannot survive for very long if they are losing money.
Why might Costa Coffee's profit margin (see Table 7.1) start to fall in future?	Perhaps because the diseconomies it faces as it grows even bigger may start to outweigh the economies of scale.
Why might growth cause a firm to become more efficient?	Increasing output within existing facilities allows fixed costs to be diluted over more units of output. Growth can also allow a firm to benefit from economies of scale.
Why might diseconomies of scale outweigh economies of scale?	In a service business especially, there may be relatively few economies of scale, so problems such as weak and costly internal communication can hit overall efficiency.
Why might the founder of a small business need to delegate in order to let the business grow?	As the business grows, the boss may suffer from information overload without delegating. As a result, growth opportunities may be handled badly.
How might overtrading affect a business?	It creates the risk that bankers and other creditors may lose confidence in the management, making them reluctant to allow further credit. That would hasten a liquidity crisis.

7.3 Growth – evaluation

Many people in business believe that if you're not growing, you're dying. This is understandable, given the constant pressure of competition, but tends to underestimate the problems caused by growth. It's unlikely to be a coincidence that just as Toyota, then General Motors, then Volkswagen were about to be crowned number one global car maker (in the period 2009–2015) each hit a crisis caused by internal failings. Management eyed the prize a bit too greedily – to devastating effect.

If growth is unexpected and rapid, overtrading is the obvious risk. Less obvious is that as a business gets steadily bigger it becomes steadily slower at 'knowing what it knows'. People within the organisation know where the wheels are squeaking and about customer dissatisfactions – but this knowledge may fail to get to the boardroom – or reach it too late. Good decisions require full knowledge of what's going on. Bosses always struggle to get that, especially when growth means that more people are getting in between the top and bottom of the organisation.

Key terms

Average cost: this is the cost of producing one unit of output. It is calculated by dividing total cost by the current output level.

Delegate: passing authority down the hierarchy.

Diseconomies of scale: factors that cause average costs to rise as the scale of output rises.

Economies of scale: factors that cause average costs to fall as the scale of output increases.

Market dominance: describes a situation where a firm sells a product that achieves a very high market share. This ascendancy over the competition enables the dominant firm to raise prices without losing too many customers. According to the EU, firms that have a market share of more than 40–45 per cent are considered dominant.

Organic growth: comes from within the business, as compared with inorganic growth achieved by takeovers or mergers.

7.4 Workbook

Revision questions

(35 marks, 35 minutes)

1 In your own words, explain the value to a business of its growth being planned. (3)

2 a) Using examples distinguish between external and organic growth. (3)

b) Identify and explain one problem a firm might encounter as a result of rapid growth. (4)

3 The iPad has been a very successful product for Apple. Table 7.2 shows the number of iPads sold and the revenues generated worldwide since launch.

a) Calculate the percentage growth in the number of iPads sold between 2010 and 2011. (3)

b) Describe what happened to sales growth in terms of the number of iPads sold in the years after that. (4)

c) Using the information provided, calculate the average price of an iPad in each year shown. What conclusions can you draw? (6)

d) In July 2014 Apple announced that in the last three months only 13.2 million iPads were sold, compared with 16.3 million the quarter before. Should Apple be worried? (6)

4 Explain three difficulties that a sports retailer such as Sports Direct might face when attempting to grow organically. (6)

Year	2010	2011	2012	2013	2014
Units	7.46 million	32.4 million	58.31 million	71.03 million	67.98 million
Revenue	$4.96 billion	$20.36 billion	$30.95 billion	$31.98 billion	30.28 billion

Table 7.2 Number of iPads sold and revenues generated since launch in 2010

Revision activities

Data response

Stagecoach

Stagecoach is one of the biggest suppliers of public transport in the world, operating in eight countries, running 13,000 trains and buses, employing over 35,000 people. In 2014 the company's turnover was close to £3 billion, netting shareholders an operating profit of £223 million.

The business was not always this big. When Stagecoach was set up in 1980 it started with just three buses. The company's employers were the three founders: Brian Souter, who went on to be chief executive, did the driving, whilst his wife, Ann Gloag, made snacks to sell to their passengers. Robin, her brother, was the maintenance man.

Throughout Stagecoach's history, growth has always been the dominant corporate objective. In the early 1980s Stagecoach grew by buying out its local rivals. It also bought buses from local councils when they were privatised. In the 1990s there was a change in strategy as the company switched to organic growth. Instead of spending money on expensive takeovers, Stagecoach would expand its market share by stealing its rivals' passengers. The main method used to grow market share was low fares, which were designed to under-cut the competition. On several occasions Stagecoach was found guilty of predatory pricing, which involves cutting prices below average cost with the deliberate intention of forcing a rival out of business.

In more recent times Stagecoach has grown by diversifying. For example in Sheffield it runs trams, local train services, as well as bus services. This allows Stagecoach to set timetables for different modes of transport in order to minimise waiting time for passengers who need to change from one mode of transport to another in order to complete their journey. The company would like to offer passengers the same type of 'integrated' transport service in other British towns and cities.

Questions (30 marks; 35 minutes)

1 Explain how growth might help a transport company like Stagecoach to increase its profits. (4)

2 Apart from a desire to generate higher profits, explain two other reasons why a company might choose growth as its corporate objective. (6)

3 Evaluate the possible effect on its stakeholder groups if Stagecoach is able to achieve its ambition of running all forms of public transport in certain towns and cities. (20)

Extended writing

1 Table 7.1 shows that Costa Coffee grew by 245 per cent in terms of revenue in the period 2009–2015. Evaluate the problems it might face as a result of this pace of growth. (20)

2 Recently Barclays Bank declared an annual profit of over £3.5billion. At the time the chief executive revealed that the bank had cut 11,500 jobs in the previous year, and its intention in the coming year was to double this number of job losses. Evaluate the advantages and disadvantages of these management decisions. (20)

Section 3.2 Business growth

8 Organic growth

Definition

Organic growth comes from within a business, either from rising customer demand, or from the company launching successful new products or new outlets.

Linked to: Impact of external influences, Ch 5; Growth, Ch 7; Mergers and takeovers, Ch 9; Reasons for staying small, Ch 10

8.1 Distinction between inorganic and organic growth

Inorganic growth comes from outside a business. The most obvious example is a **takeover** bid such as Facebook's £11.4 billion purchase of WhatsApp in 2014. Instead of developing its own rival product and competing with the established WhatsApp messaging service, Facebook took the easy (but expensive) approach of buying the business, its products and its 450 million existing customers. Facebook was buying growth rather than creating growth from its own resources. Usually inorganic growth is the path taken by firms that are weak at innovation and product development, though in this case, Facebook's Mark Zuckerberg claimed that WhatsApp was just a great **strategic fit**.

Organic growth is a safer, but slower, method of growth than takeover. Its safety comes from the avoidance of the culture clashes involved in many takeovers. Steady growth also avoids the need to add debt to a company's balance sheet, since finance is more likely to come from retained profits. However, a reliance on organic growth could lead firms to miss out on surges of growth in their industry if they fail to develop sufficient capacity to cope with the potential demand. For example, when Coca-Cola saw the increasing consumer interest in juices and smoothies, it chose to buy up Innocent Drinks instead of developing its own brands.

Real business

Rapid organic growth

In 2010, General Motors (GM) was number one in China, selling nearly 2 million cars. Despite the financial troubles in America that forced the US government to bail it out, GM chose to keep this growth going by building nine new factories in China. It announced that it expected its sales in China to rise to 3 million by 2015. In fact sales grew organically to 3.5 million by 2014, so it hugely outperformed. The rapid pace of growth in China should have been great news for the US taxpayer, but the government sold its GM shares a bit too early – in December 2013.

Innovation within a business

Chapter 23 of the AS book (*Business Year 1* for Edexcel). focuses on innovation within a business (sometimes called intrapreneurship). This relates perfectly to the second-year theme of organic growth. For firms to grow from within their financial and human resources, clever ideas are needed backed by the drive to succeed. Intrapreneurs show the skills and dynamism of small business entrepreneurs, but within a corporate setting. The success of design guru Jonathan Ive at Apple is a good example of intrapreneurship.

8.2 Methods of growing organically

In 2009, newspapers ran a series of dismissive headlines about German retailer Aldi's decision to offer £40,000 starting salaries to graduate trainees. With Marks & Spencer offering just £25,000, Aldi's move was taken as a sign of desperation rather than ambition.

Figure 8.1 Aldi offers graduates a £40,000 starting salary

Yet since then, between 2010 and 2015, discount grocer Aldi doubled its share of the UK market from 2.8 to 5.4 per cent. Marks & Spencer stood still. Perhaps there's a German term for 'the last laugh'.

Organic growth may be sparked by external forces (for Aldi, the 2009 recession was a gift) but for continuous market share growth good management must be a factor. Fundamentally, organic growth is a function of financial and human resources; of the two, most bosses would say people are the main priority. At Google, the desire to keep staff committed to the business has led to remarkable working conditions and benefits. In the terms of Professor Herzberg, Google provides hygiene factors that go above and beyond meeting every need – to avoid job dissatisfaction (the work itself should provide the upward satisfactions). What could be called Googleperks include:

- free breakfast, lunch, and dinner; the organic food is chef-prepared
- free health and dental care; on-site doctors; free haircuts; free dry cleaning
- subsidised massages; free gyms and swimming pools
- 'nap pods'; on-site video games, football, ping pong.

(Source: www.google.co.uk/about/careers)

Ultimately, organic growth is the attempt to achieve success from within the company's staff, its culture and its resources. When this works well, the results can be outstanding. UK examples of this approach include JCB and Ted Baker plc. In some ways Ted Baker's success has been the more remarkable because it is a public limited company (plc) and therefore subject to outside shareholder pressures. But since it went public in 1997, Ted Baker has grown in what the strategy statement on its website calls 'considered expansion, controlled distribution and carefully managed development (of overseas markets)'. Ted Baker has never taken over another business – and never taken any risks with debt. Its dependence on debt is often 0 per cent and never rises above 5 per cent. In other words, Ted Baker's approach to organic growth even includes wanting to grow from within its own financial resources. Some outside shareholders might have complained at times about this cautious approach – but if they had held onto their shares they wouldn't have minded growth from 140p in 1997 to 2,800p in 2015. And over all that period Ted Baker has rarely made a serious mistake. It has gone from a men's shirt-only shop in Glasgow to a business with over 250 shops globally, and with womenswear outselling menswear. Its website boasts that Ted Baker has never advertised, therefore having to rely on word of mouth and stylish, quirky window displays. It is a remarkable success story.

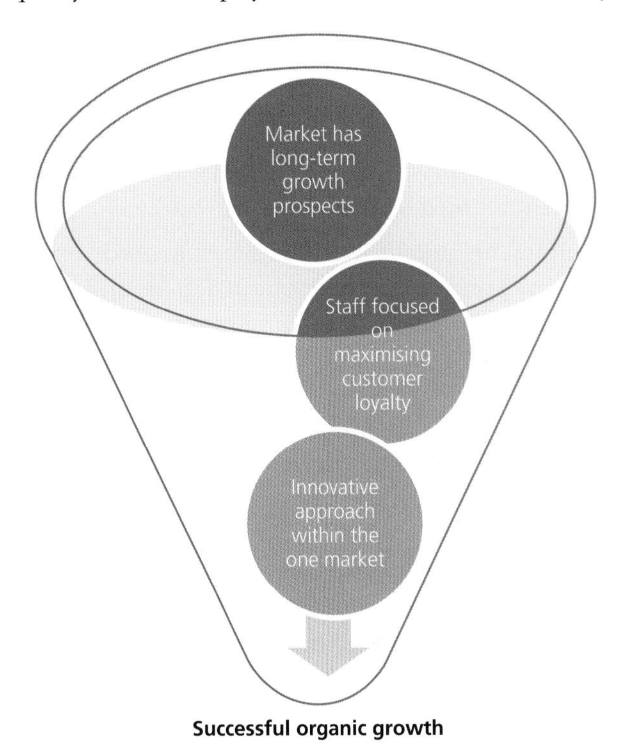

Figure 8.2 Logic funnel: successful organic growth

> 'Word of mouth marketing is a crucial component of organic growth for start-ups.'
>
> *David Rusenko, founder, Weebly Inc.*

8.3 Advantages of organic growth

Organic growth has many advantages, especially for a business that is growing satisfactorily. Among these advantages are the following.

Keeping it personal

Ted Baker is not a person; the person behind the brand is Ray Kelvin, who founded the business. For someone like him, it's a huge thrill to build up the company steadily. It enables him to influence the 2,800 staff – and to maintain the entrepreneurial culture. A takeover of another business would be far more likely to force Kelvin (or the directors) to look for a new, professional business manager to handle the consequences of the acquisition and take the company forward.

Minimising financial risk

It is fair to suggest that almost every takeover bid increases the debt level of the predator company. So inorganic growth is associated with debt. When Kraft bought Cadbury for nearly $20 billion in 2010, it needed to issue a huge amount more share capital to finance the deal. It also borrowed a lot more from American banks, making analysts worry about the huge interest payments it would be having to make (by 2013 Kraft's interest payments amounted to $500 million a year).

By contrast, organic growth can be controlled so that little or no extra borrowing is required. This minimises financial risk.

Providing a secure career path

Takeovers lead to a battle between staff for the single job of the future. For example, the marketing directors from each business battle for the one director position for the future. Many people are made redundant and many good members of staff leave. Organic growth means steady development of the business, with career opportunities opening up quite regularly. Well-run businesses give staff the opportunity to develop steadily from the shop floor to management and then leadership positions.

8.4 Disadvantages of organic growth

If the business has a single, simple focus, such as rolling out Costa Coffee bars around the world, it is fair to suspect that this might become rather predictable and dull. Consequently talented, ambitious and creative people might find work elsewhere. A single focus might backfire if a new competitor or changes in consumer taste make it necessary to rethink the strategy. This seemed to be a problem for Tesco in the period 2010–2014. Organic growth lacks the sudden opportunity (and threat) represented by a takeover bid or merger.

Other disadvantages of organic growth include:

- The difficulty of getting scale to match your competitors, especially if they are involved in takeover or merger activity; in other words, while you're growing gradually, they may be leaping ahead – giving them economies of scale that you cannot access (see Figure 8.3).

> **'Organic growth does not lend itself easily to moving into entirely new markets or developing completely new products.'**
>
> *Touch Financial website*

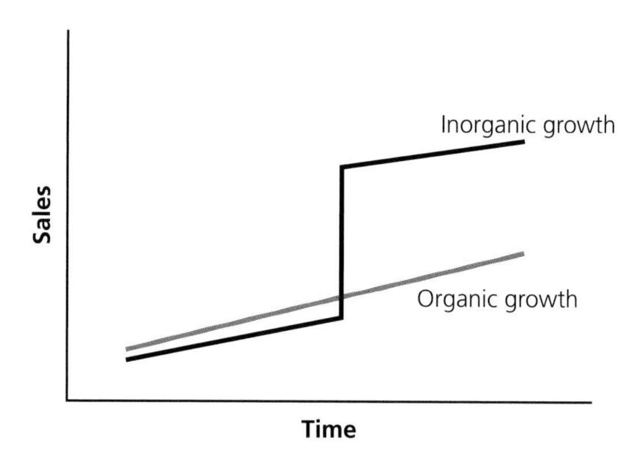

Figure 8.3 Organic vs inorganic growth

- Many products have relatively short life cycles. For those that have, it's vital to generate as much cash as soon as possible. Slow, organic growth may mean missing much of the economic opportunity from the growth and maturity phases of the life cycle. So it may be better to try to leap ahead while the going is good.

Five whys and a how

Questions	Answers
Why is internal growth called 'organic'?	Because it's like a plant growing steadily, day by day. No plant grows in sudden leaps forward.
Why might it be risky to grow slowly?	If a market is growing rapidly, slow growth by an individual business means losing market share – which might mean shops stop distributing your product.
Why might it be risky to grow in leaps and bounds, through takeover or merger?	Because long-term success hinges on the quality, motivation and culture of middle management – takeovers risk undermining a common sense of purpose (and carry higher financial risks).

Why might organic growth be risky, if it's financed from within?	Although (external) bank loans increase gearing, financing from within can mean too little capital – risking a liquidity crisis.
Why might an organic food producer decide to grow inorganically?	Why not? There's no link between organic food and organic growth. Of course an organic food producer such as Yeo Valley might choose to buy another such as Rachel's Organic.
How might organic growth be achieved rapidly?	If the demand is there (such as for Apple's iPhone 6), organic growth can be rapid as long as enough capital and manpower can be found to boost supply.

'For years I have made the point that progress is made not by high growth in any individual year, but by maintaining an expansion over a sustained period.'

Ian Macfarlane, Australian politician

8.5 Organic growth – evaluation

Fantastically successful businesses such as Apple, Costa, Ted Baker and Domino's have operated a largely or wholly organic strategy. Yes, Apple bought Beats Electronics in 2014, but headphones could only ever be a tiny part of Apple's long-term strategy.

Choosing organic versus inorganic growth is largely a statement of confidence in your business and the business model, in its culture and in the staff who work there. So even if organic growth sometimes seems strategically wrong, it may send out a signal to staff that emphasises loyalty and faith. That could result in a lot of potential benefits for the business.

Key terms

Inorganic growth: inorganic growth is via merger or takeover, not from within the business.

Strategic fit: buying another business that can provide a real boost to long-term growth and profitability, e.g. Mars buying Wrigley (massive cost-cutting potential but no overlap in terms of consumer sales).

Takeover: when one business buys majority ownership in another, thereby gaining full control.

8.6 Workbook

Revision questions

(25 marks; 25 minutes)

1 Explain two ways in which a business such as Jaguar Land Rover can achieve organic growth. (6)

2 In 2015, Costa Coffee set out a plan to expand in China from 350 outlets to 900 outlets by 2020. Explain how a clear target might make it easier to achieve organic growth. (5)

3 Why might financial resources prove a stumbling block to achieving organic growth? (4)

4 Working conditions such as those at Google are hugely expensive for the company. Are they relevant to the achievement of organic growth? Explain your answer. (4)

5 Explain the possible disadvantages of organic growth for a business such as SuperGroup plc, owners of the clothing brand Superdry. (6)

Revision activities

Data response

Domino's organic growth

Late in 1999, Domino's Pizza UK announced that it was accepting orders placed online. Nobody really noticed or cared. Ten years later, in 2009, online orders represented a quarter of all Domino's sales. By then it was acknowledged that the company's rapidly growing share of the pizza business owed a great deal to online sales. Five years later, in 2014, online ordering passed 50 per cent of total Domino's sales for the first time. The move to online was at the heart of revenue growth from £25.6 million in 2009 to £294.4 million in 2014 – providing a stunning annual growth rate of 17.7 per cent. Profits over that same 15-year period grew at an average of 25.2 per cent a year: organic growth on an amazing scale.

Part of the increase has been down to store openings, from 200 in 1999 to 900 by the start of 2015. This growth has overwhelmingly come from franchising; by 2014, the average franchisee owned eight Domino's outlets. One other factor has been important, though. In 2009, the business made a public confession that its pizzas had come joint bottom in a survey of customer attitudes to the taste of pizzas. This led to two new strategies:

- Spending six months experimenting to find better dough and better toppings – then a complete revamp of all their ingredients and flavours.
- Bringing back in-house the IT skills involved in programming the software that controlled the timing and efficiency of online ordering and delivery. Moving away from outsourcing proved a winner, as dedicated full-time staff made the delivery process faster than ever.

Despite 2010 being a year of recession, like-for-like sales at Domino's UK rose by 11.9 per cent – largely thanks to the new strategy. Overall, the Domino's story shows the potential of an organic growth strategy. Focus on making your products and processes better has worked at Domino's – just as it has at Costa Coffee and at Ted Baker.

Questions (40 marks; 45 minutes)

1. Assess two possible advantages to Domino's of pursuing an organic growth strategy. (8)
2. Assess the possible advantages to Domino's of pursuing a franchising development model for the business. (12)
3. To what extent does the Domino's case prove that the quality of the product itself is the single most important part of any long-term business strategy? (20)

Extended writing

1. Evaluate the extent to which organic growth could work for a brand new social networking site. (20)
2. After more than 20 years of organic growth, a new boss of Ted Baker plc decides to accelerate growth by buying a 100-shop chain of French fashion retail outlets. Evaluate the extent to which that might undermine the organic growth model. (20)

Section 3.2 Business growth

9 Mergers and takeovers

Definition

Mergers are where two firms of similar size agree to join forces permanently, creating a new company that is twice the size of each predecessor.

Takeovers occur when one firm buys a majority of the shares in another and therefore achieves full management control.

Linked to: Ansoff's Matrix, Ch 3; Impact of external influences, Ch 5; Growth, Ch 7; Organic growth, Ch 8; Reasons for staying small, Ch 10; Corporate culture, Ch 16.

9.1 Introduction

Every time a company's shares are bought or sold on the stock exchange, there is a change in the ownership of that company. However, the significant changes occur when a majority of shares is bought by an individual or company. Any individual or organisation that owns 51 per cent of a company's shares has effective control over that company. To successfully take over a company, a firm (or individual) must therefore buy 51 per cent of the shares. In America, this process is called mergers and acquisitions (M&A), acquisitions being another word for a takeover.

9.2 Reasons for mergers and takeovers

Some examples of takeovers and the reasons for them are given in Table 9.1.

Growth

The fastest way for any firm to achieve significant growth is to merge with, or take over, another company. The motives behind the objective of growth may be based on any of the reasons outlined below. However, as a basic motive behind mergers and takeovers, growth is often the overriding factor.

Figure 9.1 Mergers and takeovers are the fastest way to achieve growth

Cost synergies

Cost savings are often used as a primary argument for corporate integration. It is suggested that economies of scale will arise from operating on a larger scale. If two businesses merge, output will increase. As a result, they are more likely to benefit from economies of scale, such as cheaper bulk purchasing of supplies. Synergies are the benefits from two things coming together. In this context, it is that the two firms together will have lower costs (and higher profits) than the two firms separately. In effect, **synergy** means that 2 + 2 = 5.

> **'Promises of synergy are rarely fulfilled.'**
>
> *Tim Hindle,* The Economist

Diversification

This means entering different markets in order to reduce dependence upon current products and customers. Diversification is a way of reducing the risk faced by a company. Selling a range of different products to different groups of consumers will mean that, if any one product fails, sales of the other products should keep the business healthy. The simplest way to diversify is to merge with or take over another company. This saves time and money spent developing new products for markets in which the firm may have no expertise. This is why Mars bought Wrigley – in case there was a consumer shift away from high-calorie chocolate towards chewing gum.

Market power

When two competitors in the same market merge, the combined business will have an increased level of power in the market. It may be possible that this increased power can be used to reduce the degree of competition within the market. If prices can be increased a little as a result, margins will increase and the market will become more profitable.

Reasons for takeovers	Examples
Growth	• Facebook paid $19 billion for mobile messenger WhatsApp in 2014 • Kraft's takeover of Cadbury in 2010
Cost synergies	• In May 2014 Carphone Warehouse and Dixons agreed to merge, saying they would enjoy annual cost savings of £80 million within three years • Co-op taking over Somerfield (it bid £1.7 billion in 2008); the result has been a disaster
Diversification	• Tesco buying 49 per cent of Harris + Hoole coffee shops in 2013 • Kellogg's buying Pringles crisps for $2.7 billion in 2012
Market power	• Indian car producer Tata (producers of the world's cheapest car) bought Jaguar Land Rover for £1.3 billion in 2008 • Holcim's 2015 merger with fellow cement giant Lafarge gave the combined group a 50 per cent market share in Canada, and not far short in Britain

Table 9.1 Reasons for takeovers, and some examples

9.3 Distinction between mergers and takeovers

A merger occurs when two firms of approximately equal size choose to come together, perhaps by agreeing that shareholders will share ownership 50/50. This is therefore a friendly coming-together in which the directors are likely to have met often enough to know whether they can work together. It is therefore striking that research suggests that mergers have an even lower success rate than takeovers. Most researchers conclude that this is because there is no clear 'winner' and therefore leadership tends to be confused and weakened. There may even be an attempt at sharing leadership – which rarely works well. In a merger, both sets of staff expect their bosses to fight for them – to gain the plum jobs. So the infighting may be worse in a merger than in a takeover. It is striking that perhaps the two most expensive M&A flops in corporate history were both called mergers: Mercedes–Chrysler and AOL–Time Warner. Each has been estimated to have destroyed more than $100 billion of economic value.

A takeover may be 'friendly' (agreed between both sets of directors) or 'hostile' (the target company's directors reject the bid), but in either case the final decision is taken by the target company's shareholders. They either sell their shares to the bidder or they don't. If the bidder can acquire 50.1 per cent of the target company's shares, that's that. Then the bidder takes 100 per cent control of the target's management. It might be brutal from the start, making the target company's directors and senior managers redundant. Or it might wait to get to know both sets of managers better, giving both sides a chance. But for cost synergies to occur, at some point redundancies are inevitable. Research suggests that it's better to be quick and brutal, i.e. get the pain over quickly so that staff can feel more secure in their roles and get on with their jobs (instead of fighting political battles to try to avoid redundancy).

9.4 Types of integration

There are three main types of integration (see Figure 9.2), as discussed below.

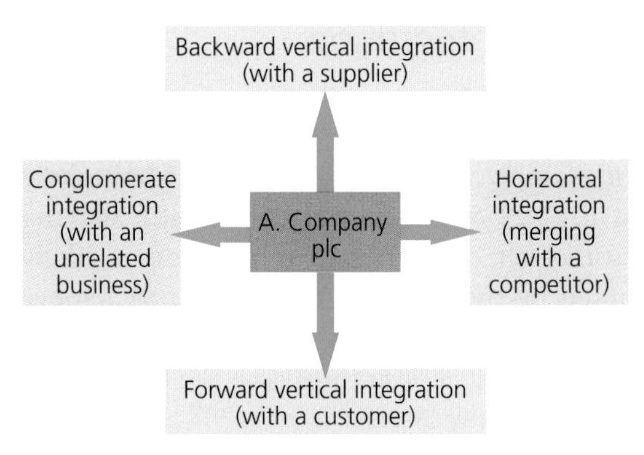

Figure 9.2 Vertical and horizontal integration

Vertical integration

Vertical integration occurs when one firm takes over or merges with another at a different stage in the production process, but within the same industry.

Backward vertical integration occurs when a firm buys out a supplier. In May 2014 advertising giant WPP bought Quirk London – which had been supplying WPP with advice on digital and social media strategy. A key benefit of a backward vertical takeover is security of supply.

Forward vertical integration means buying out a customer, such as the purchase by Burberry of the franchisee that ran its shops in China. At the time Burberry made it clear that it wanted to be closer to its Chinese consumers – to help develop the right product design and image for the rapidly developing Chinese market.

Table 9.2 explains the major advantages and disadvantages of backward and forward vertical integration for three important stakeholders: the company (and its shareholders), the workforce and the customers.

	Backward vertical integration	Forward vertical integration
Advantages to the company	• Closer links with suppliers aid new product development and give more control over the quality and timing of supplies • Absorbing the suppliers' profit margins may cut supply costs	• Control of competition in own retail outlets; prominent display of own brands • Firm put in direct contact with end users/consumers
Disadvantages to the company	• Having bought your supplier, its staff may become complacent if they know you will order from them • Costs might rise, therefore, and delivery and quality become slack	• Consumers may resent the dominance of one firm's products in retail outlets, causing sales to decline • Worries about image may restrict retail decision-making, e.g. Levi stores rarely discount Levi products
Advantages to the workforce	• Having a secure customer for the suppliers may increase job security • Larger scale of the combined organisation may lead to enhanced benefits such as pension or career opportunities	• Increased control over the market may increase job security • Designers can now influence not only how the products look, but also how they are displayed
Disadvantages to the workforce	• Becoming part of a large firm may affect the sense of team morale built up at the supplier • Job losses may result from attempts to cut out duplication of support roles such as in personnel and accounting	• Staff in retail outlets may find themselves deskilled. Owner may dictate exactly what products to stock and how to display them, which would be demotivating
Advantages to the consumer	• Better coordination between company and supplier may lead to more innovative new product ideas • Ownership of the whole supply process may make the business more conscious of product and service quality	• With luxury products, customers like to see perfect displays and be served by expert staff, e.g. at perfume counters in department stores • Prices may fall if a large retail margin is absorbed by the supplier
Disadvantages to the consumer	• The firm's control over a supplier may reduce the variety of goods available, e.g. Sony restricts Blu-Ray to its own products • Supplier complacency may lead to rising costs, passed on to customers as higher prices	• Increased power within the market could lead to price rises • If the outlet only supplies the parent company's products, consumer choice will be hit, as in brewery-owned clubs or pubs

Table 9.2 The advantages and disadvantages of backward vertical integration and forward vertical integration

Horizontal integration

Horizontal integration occurs when one firm buys out another in the same industry at the same stage of the supply chain. In 2014, the restaurant booking site Bookatable bought 2book – a direct competitor specialising in Sweden and Norway. This meant that Bookatable now represented more than 10,000 restaurants in 19 countries (and gave it a 90 per cent share of restaurants in Sweden and Norway). In the UK, if the market share of the combined companies is greater than 25 per cent, the Competition and Markets Authority (CMA) is likely to investigate before the integration will be allowed.

Horizontal integration (buying up a competitor) is the most common type of takeover and the most likely to be a commercial success. Typical examples include:

- Adidas buying Reebok
- Holcim cement company's 2015 merger with the Lafarge cement company
- British Airways merging with Iberia to form International Airlines Group.

For the purchaser, horizontal integration offers three major attractions:

1. huge scope for cost cutting by eliminating duplication of sales force, distribution and marketing overheads, and by improved capacity utilisation
2. opportunities for major economies of scale
3. a reduction in competition should enable prices to be pushed up.

Of course, no purchaser states publicly that the plan is to push prices up. But if you owned four consecutive motorway service stations covering over 190km of driving, would you not be tempted to charge a bit more?

As horizontal takeovers have particular implications for competition, they are likely to be looked at by the competition authorities. In the UK, the CMA looks at all takeovers and mergers where the firms have a turnover exceeding £70 million and a combined market share of 25 per cent or more. If there is believed to be a threat to competition, the CMA will launch an investigation. It has the power to refuse to allow the integration, or recommend changes before it can go through. For example, if Unilever (which produces Walls ice cream and much else) made a bid for confectioner Mars, the CMA might let the takeover through on the condition that Mars sells off its ice cream business.

Conglomerate integration

Conglomerate integration occurs when one firm buys out another with no clear connection to its own line of business. An example was the purchase by the household goods giant Procter & Gamble of the Gillette shaving products business. Conglomerate integration is likely to be prompted by the desire to diversify or to achieve rapid growth. It may also be done for purely financial motives such as asset stripping (breaking the business up and selling off all its key assets).

Although the achievement of successful diversification helps to spread risk, research shows that conglomerate mergers are the ones least likely to succeed. This is largely because the managers of the purchasing company have, by definition, little knowledge of the marketplace of the company that has been bought.

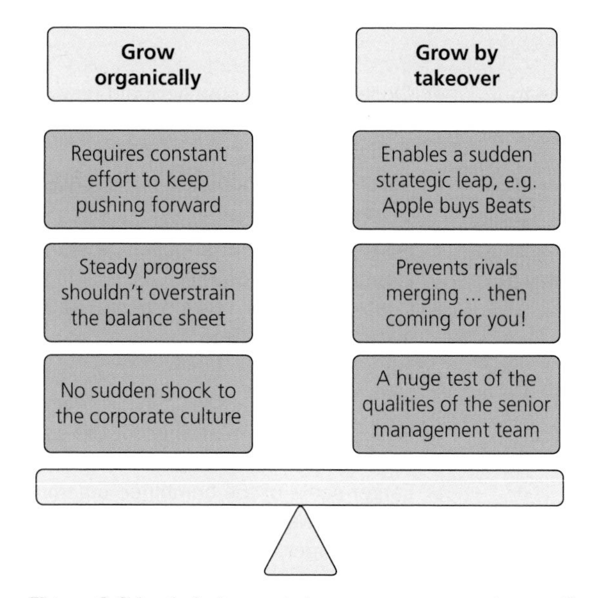

Figure 9.3 Logic balance: takeover versus organic growth

9.5 Takeover decisions and Ansoff's Matrix

A useful way to analyse the risks and rewards from a takeover is to apply Ansoff's Matrix (see Chapter 3). This considers the extent to which a business is keeping close to its core business (and knowledge/experience) or whether it is moving into new territory. For example, in February 2007 the US retail giant Wal-Mart paid $1 billion to buy a Chinese business with 101 hypermarkets in China. In 2014, it announced the closure of 29 of these huge stores and a refocus on smaller, local stores. In other words its big takeover was a mistake. On Ansoff's Matrix, this radical move into a new market would have been represented as a major, high-risk move. If Wal-Mart had bought a store chain in Canada (or Britain, where it owns Asda), it would have been much safer.

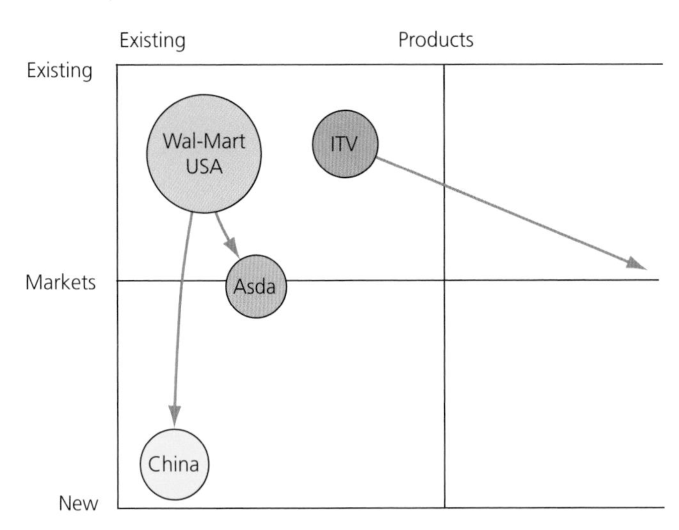

Figure 9.4 Ansoff's Matrix applied to takeovers

9.6 Financial risks and rewards

Although business leaders claim that takeovers are 'strategic', implying part of a long-term business plan, many are to do with financial engineering. That engineering is largely based on debt. Share prices rise during times of rising business optimism – and at those times City 'experts' urge companies to borrow more to boost their growth. This will magnify the profits – but only if the extra profit exceeds the cost of the capital, i.e. the interest charges. A classic way to achieve growth (and extra debt levels) instantly is via takeover bids. Time after time, stock market booms lead to takeover booms.

This might seem extraordinary given that higher debts mean higher risks. And while some takeovers will be successful, such as Kraft's purchase of Cadbury, many others prove disastrous, such as AOL's purchase of one-time Facebook rival Bebo (bought for $850 million in 2008 and sold back to its founder for $1 million in 2013).

Takeovers have always taken place between trading companies, for example BP buying the US oil giant Amoco. However, a major new force has emerged in takeovers. Half the money spent on takeovers in the UK comes from **private equity**, not from ordinary companies. In 2015, a private equity business snapped up discount retailer Poundworld for £150 million. Private equity firms own a series of apparently ordinary British businesses such as Boots UK, Center Parcs, Fat Face, Evans Cycles and Total Fitness, plus utilities such as Thames Water.

Private equity is a management group backed by sufficient bank finance to make a takeover, which is usually of a public limited company. The financing of these takeovers is usually reliant upon debt. If the business is doing well (perhaps because the economy is in an upturn), the high debt levels boost the profits made by the investors. Unfortunately, if there is an economic downturn, trading losses will quickly eat away the small shareholders' funds within the business, pushing it into liquidation. This is what happened to La Senza in 2014. The mechanism is very similar to what happens with UK households and the housing market. Some people borrow huge sums to buy big, risking losing their houses if interest rates rise to unaffordable levels; but if they are lucky they can magnify their wealth.

A serious criticism of a business such as Boots 'going private' is that it no longer has to provide the accounting information demanded from a public company. The people who felt like stakeholders in the old public company (staff, customers and, of course, shareholders) no longer have access to the accounts. Nor can they question the directors personally, as you can at a plc's **annual general meeting**. More serious still is that most private equity-owned businesses are deliberately structured to avoid paying UK corporation (profit) tax. For example, the extremely profitable UK leisure business Center Parcs was owned by the American private equity giant the Blackstone Group until 2015. In the four trading years 2011–2014, Center Parcs made £438.6 million of operating profit. In that time they paid zero corporation tax, despite paying huge dividends to the Blackstone Group (source: Center Parcs Annual Reviews, 2011–2014).

9.7 Problems of rapid growth

Whereas organic growth allows business culture and business processes to develop steadily as a business expands, a takeover bid represents a sudden, probably unwelcome, crashing together of two organisations. The scale of the operation jumps ahead, perhaps doubling in size overnight. No wonder there are problems.

Middle managers who are used to popping in to chat with the boss now find barriers – personal assistants whose key role is to keep staff at arms' length. The boss is (genuinely) too busy. So staff with good ideas feel frustrated and start to click through the job ads. When one or two of the brightest leave for better jobs elsewhere, there is a risk that all the good staff will go.

All this can have an impact on customers. They too had important business relationships with middle and senior managers, but now find the staff are focused inward on who-gets-which-job battles. The speed with which a takeover transforms a business organisation is just too great.

Management consultants earn huge fees giving advice to bosses about how to manage the rapid growth inherent to mergers and takeovers. Evidence shows, though, that sudden changes in culture are virtually impossible to achieve. When Anthony Jenkins took over as boss at Barclays bank in 2012, he warned that changing the bank's culture would take five to ten years. No one argued.

Five whys and a how

Questions	Answers
Why might a business be keen to make a horizontal takeover bid?	Quite apart from any economies of scale, there are bound to be profit gains from eliminating a competitor.
Why might organic growth prove more successful than takeovers in the long term?	Because it comes from within the business, giving time for the culture to develop gradually; it avoids a sudden shock as two workforces merge.
Why are so many takeovers unsuccessful?	Because bosses underestimate the significance of unquantifiable factors such as weakened motivation and clashes in culture.
Why might a business choose to grow through a conglomerate takeover?	Because it has an objective of reducing dependence on one product or market, or may be looking for an asset-stripping opportunity.
Why can't talented business leaders overcome problems when merging business cultures?	In some cases they can, but when the cultures are very different (e.g. one entrepreneurial and one bureaucratic), it might take ten years to break down the barriers.
How do takeovers actually work?	A cash bid means that one firm is buying up the shares in another for cash; a 'paper' bid means swapping shares in the bidder's company for those of the company being bought.

'It's far better to buy a wonderful company at a fair price than a fair company at a wonderful price.'

Warren Buffett, investment and takeover superstar

'Go for a business that any idiot can run, because sooner or later, they probably will.'

Peter Lynch, businessman

9.8 Mergers and takeovers – evaluation

When looking at takeover bids, a key judgement is to see through the public relations hype. Company leader A makes a bid for Company B, claiming that 'synergies will lead to better service and lower prices to our customers'. Really? Or will it mean factory closures, the elimination of small niche brands and – later – higher prices for all? Similarly, the leader may claim that the reason for a takeover is very businesslike, such as 'creating a world-leading company'. Yet the high failure rate of takeovers must imply that many claimed business benefits are a 'fig leaf'. The real reason for many takeovers is arrogance, and perhaps greed, on the part of the executives concerned.

An explanation for the problems firms may encounter after a merger or takeover is resistance to change. This will be especially true if the business cultures are widely different at the two companies. One may be go-getting and entrepreneurial; the other may be cautious and bureaucratic. Judgement is again required to consider whether a takeover is especially vulnerable to a clash of culture when the firms come together.

Key terms

Annual general meeting: a once-yearly meeting at which shareholders have the opportunity to question the chairperson and to vote new directors to the board.

Private equity: investment groups that buy up businesses in the expectation that they'll be able to sell them on for a profit – usually within three years.

Synergy: this occurs when the whole is greater than the sum of the parts (2 + 2 = 5). It is often the reason given for mergers or takeovers occurring.

9.9 Workbook

Revision questions

(30 marks; 30 minutes)

1 What is horizontal integration? (2)

2 For what reasons might a manufacturer take over one of its suppliers? (4)

3 For each of the following, outline two reasons why British Airways might like to make a takeover bid for:

a) easyJet (4)

b) high-street retailer Flight Centre. (4)

4 Explain why diversification might be a bad idea for a fast-growing firm. (4)

5 Explain the meaning of the word 'synergy'. (3)

6 Explain why businesses should consider Ansoff's Matrix before making a takeover bid. (4)

7 In March 2015, Philip Green's Arcadia retail business sold the BHS chain of 180 department stores for £1. Was the new buyer guaranteed to be able to make a profit on this deal? (5)

Revision activities

Data response 1

Apple buys Beats

2014 saw the purchase of Beats Electronics by Apple Inc, which paid $3 billion for the headphones and music-streaming business. It would mean combining the 300 staff at Beats with the 80,000 employees at Apple. Some analysts saw this as a horizontal acquisition, with Apple putting its iTunes business together with Beats' subscription music-streaming business to fight off Spotify (at the time of the takeover Beats had 110,000 subscribers; Spotify had 10 million). Others saw it as a vertical acquisition, with Beats headphones being put together with iPhone or iPad to create a compelling consumer proposition.

What was not in question was the valuation placed on Beats. In September 2013 Beats had raised extra capital at a price that valued the company at $1 billion. Six months later Apple paid three times that amount. Great for founders Jimmy Iovine, Dr Dre and will.i.Am, but a curious comment on the heady valuations often placed on companies when takeover bids are made.

Questions (40 marks; 45 minutes)

1 Assess two possible motives behind Apple's purchase of Beats Electronics. (8)

2 Assess the possible difficulties that Apple may encounter within Beats following the takeover. (12)

3 Apple could decide to incorporate all the Beats staff and products into its own operations, or keep it at arms' length, i.e. keep it as a separate operation. Evaluate which might be the better option. (20)

Data response 2

Dixons merges with Carphone Warehouse

Carphone Warehouse and Dixons have agreed a £3.8 billion 'merger of equals' to create an electricals retailer selling phones to fridges, and offering service and support alongside a multitude of gadgets. With 3,000 stores and sales of almost £11 billion, the new company, called Dixons Carphone, will bring the household names Currys, PC World and Carphone Warehouse under one umbrella. In bringing together fridges to computers (Dixons) and mobile phones (Carphone Warehouse), there is hope that the business will be ready for 'the internet of things' – a world in which mobile devices provide control over every aspect of the home: from robot vacuum cleaners to internet-enabled fridge-freezers.

The combined entity aims to branch into domestic heating, lighting and security services – all controlled by mobile phone. Carphone and Dixons said the merged company would benefit from greater buying power, extra growth options and annual synergies of at least £80 million within three years.

Dixons and Carphone shareholders will each own 50 per cent of the combined group under the deal, and Carphone concessions will be built into every Dixons outlet.

In a leadership compromise, Carphone's chairman and founder, Sir Charles Dunstone, will lead a 14-strong board that also includes two deputy chairmen, a chief executive, a deputy chief executive and a senior non-executive director. Dixons' boss, Sebastian James, will be chief executive, while Andrew Harrison of Carphone Warehouse becomes his deputy.

'This is a genuine merger of equals founded on core strategic principles rather than straight cost cuts,' said James, presenting the merger deal at London's Shard skyscraper on Thursday. 'We do things that are so adjacent that it makes sense to come together. Our markets are converging, and we are converging.'

One independent analyst, Louise Cooper, at CooperCity, was unimpressed with the deal: 'Two past-their-sell-by-date retailers merging does not an Amazon make.' She also criticised the top-heavy leadership structure, saying: 'The board is beginning to look as unwieldy as that of Co-op. Executives are not leading from the front. Mostly they are retaining their jobs. That is the wrong message to the workforce.' Investors appeared to agree, sending shares in both firms plummeting, with Dixons down nearly 10 per cent to 46p a share, and Carphone down more than 7 per cent to 303p.

(Source: adapted from the Guardian, 15 May 2014)

Questions (35 marks; 40 minutes)

1 Is this a conglomerate or horizontal merger? Explain your answer. (7)

2 Assess two possible cost synergies that might form part of the £80 million annual savings forecast by Dixons Carphone. (8)

3 Based on the evidence in the case and your wider knowledge of mergers, evaluate whether bringing together Dixons and Carphone is likely to be a business success. (20)

Extended writing

1 Evaluate whether it's inevitable that people management problems will occur within a firm that has just been taken over. (20)

2 'The high level of takeover activity in the UK leads to short-termism'. Evaluate whether this statement is justified. (20)

Section 3.2 Business growth

10 Reasons for staying small

Definition

According to the UK Companies Act, the definition of a small business is one that employs fewer than 50 employees and has a sales turnover of less than £6.5 million.

Linked to: Growth, Ch 7; Organic growth, Ch 8; Mergers and Takeovers, Ch 9

10.1 Introduction

While many businesses will seek to grow in size over time, some choose to remain small. Increased scale brings major advantages, not least through economies of scale. Scale also brings problems, however, such as overstretched communications and other diseconomies. Growth may also lead to the dilution of family ownership, leading to a family name such as Cadbury or Morrisons being controlled by people outside the family. Figure 10.1 shows just how significant small businesses are in the UK.

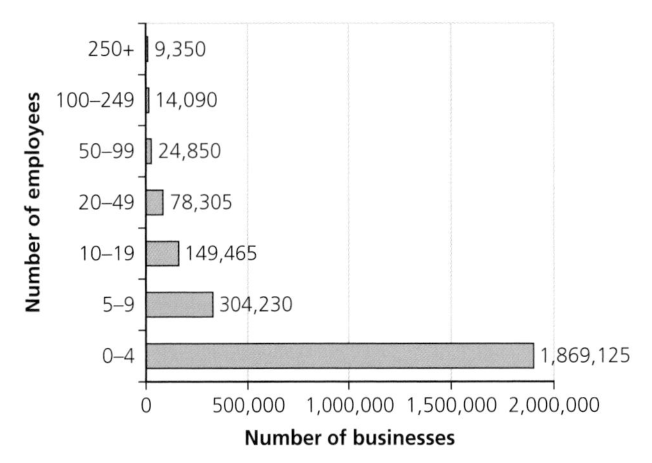

Figure 10.1: The importance of small firms in the UK (source: ONS October 2015)

The above bar chart shows that within the category 'small firm' it is sensible to look at a further category: the micro business, i.e. very small, in this case falling within the category 0–4 staff. These businesses are so small that the entrepreneur/owner will probably have complete power and will need to develop few managerial skills. So the following chart, which shows a variety of business objectives, will rarely apply to the majority of micro businesses. For most with fewer than five employees, success means surviving, and making enough to keep the family finances OK.

Objective	Importance of size
Survival	Smaller firms have lower fixed costs to cover, making it easier to break even, BUT, with smaller customer numbers and perhaps over-dependence on a single product, changes in the market can destroy a small firm quickly
Profit maximisation	Bigger firms are able to generate higher total profits due to their higher revenues, as well as economies of scale
Sales maximisation	Maximising sales is inextricably linked to growth as a business
Market share	Small firms may enjoy healthy shares of market niches, but to attain significant market share in a mass market requires growth
Cost efficiency	Although growth brings economies of scale, diseconomies of scale are likely to arise as a result of growth. Smaller firms may be able to more easily identify wastage and thus keep a tight rein on costs
Employee welfare	Although large firms may offer bigger bonuses and fringe benefits, working in a large firm can leave employees without the sense of belonging that comes from working in a small business
Customer satisfaction	With fewer customers, small businesses may be better placed to offer customer satisfaction, potentially building a personal relationship with all of their customers
Social objectives	Many social enterprises are set up to address local needs and thus want to stay small

Table 10.1 Business objectives and size

10.2 Small business survival in competitive markets

In 2007, when it was about to launch into America, Tesco had a 31 per cent share of the UK grocery market and a position that an analyst referred to as 'scale-proof against competition'. In other words Tesco was thought to be untouchable in the UK market because its market share gave it so many economic advantages over rivals: buying cheaper because of bigger bulk, able to secure the best locations and so on. As we know, it didn't work out that way. By 2015, market share was slipping back to 28 per cent.

What this proves is an important point: the benefits of scale are often overrated. Size matters, but it's often better to be small and nimble than big and slow. And it's important to remember that 'small' is an entirely relative term. The UK grocery market is worth about £180 billion a year. So a 1 per cent market share means sales revenue of £1,800 million a year. Iceland, with a 2 per cent market share, usually manages annual profits of £150–200 million a year.

Nevertheless, it's reasonable to suggest that small firms have to be alert, efficient and nimble to survive. A large business such as Mars can live on past glories (such as Maltesers, born 1937) but a small firm may have to reinvent itself regularly in order to keep up with changing tastes and sharp competition.

Figure 10.2 Gluten free is a niche market

10.3 Reasons to stay small

Product differentiation and USPs

Maintaining a level of product differentiation can be key to the success of small businesses. It enables them to avoid direct competition from mass market providers. However, differentiation may stifle growth because it limits the product to a small niche. A company that specialises in manufacturing gluten-free food should have limited sales because only 3 per cent of the population needs to avoid gluten. If the business uses 'free from gluten' as its point of differentiation or even uniqueness, its market will remain small, thus limiting growth. Expansion would rely on moving away from the very point of differentiation that created success – a decision that may be considered too dangerous by directors.

Flexibility in responding to customer needs

> 'Many leaders of small firms focus on making their business work efficiently and on delivering high-quality customer service. There is absolutely nothing wrong with these objectives. They are both essential aims. However, if they lead to rigidity and the exclusion of variation then they can undermine the key advantage that small businesses have over large businesses – agility.'
>
> *Paul Sloane, leadership speaker on innovation*

If firms are to maintain their popularity with consumers, it is vital that they adapt to changes in the marketplace. The easiest way to discover what consumers want is to monitor their behaviour in-store – shop-floor staff can provide invaluable feedback on changes in customer behaviour and tastes. The problem of growing too large is that organisational structures develop too many layers between shop-floor staff and senior decision-makers. These layers of middle management have an insulating effect, with middle managers often seeing their role as filtering the information their staff provide to prevent their bosses being overloaded. Of course, this filtering

Figure 10.3 Logic chain: successful flexible response

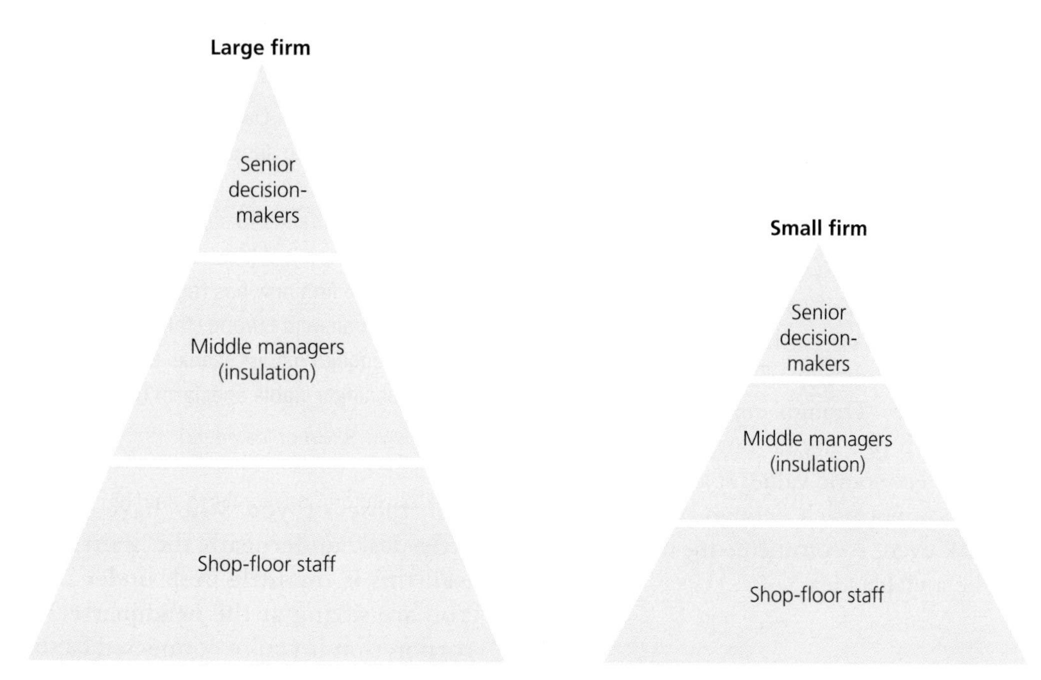

Figure 10.4 Small firms have fewer management layers between the top and bottom of the structure

can prevent vital insights reaching key decision-makers within the business. A firm that chooses to stay small may do so to ensure that there are fewer structural layers between shop-floor staff and senior managers.

Customer service

> 'Because I didn't have much money, I bought a small shop to fit my budget. The previous six owners had closed their business in three years. The store had no people traffic and, because of that, I was able to focus on figuring out how to provide a better service to each and every one of the customers that did come through.'
>
> *Do Won Chang, Founder of Forever 21*

Delivering excellent customer service needs staff who care about how they treat customers. This is easier to achieve when the contribution that each member of staff makes to the business is clear to them. Motivation theorists, notably Professor Herzberg, suggest that if the results of your work are easily identified, greater motivation and therefore better performance is likely to result. If a single employee can make a difference to the overall performance of a business they will work hard, rewarded by clear recognition of a job well done. Those who work for large companies may feel their own performance makes little difference to the business's success. For a business that is heavily reliant on great customer service, staying small can help to ensure that all staff deliver this.

Real business

Renowned for the level of product knowledge offered by owner and former cricketer Paul Cook, Cook and Matthews is a single sports shop, specialising in top-end cricket equipment. Started in 2009, the shop has built a strong reputation among keen amateur sportspeople as the place to go for impartial advice. The main problem that the business faces in expansion is that it has only one Paul Cook – i.e. the owner is the trusted source of advice for customers and he can only be in one place at a time. Despite initially planning to open more than one branch, at present Paul is more than happy to keep the business small and build its reputation.

e-commerce

Electronically generated commerce (e-commerce) occurs when commercial transactions take place online. This could be as simple as buying a book on Amazon or as complex as putting through a purchase for a complex, one-off production-line robot, ordered from Japan. In 2015, the average UK adult ordered more than £1,000 of goods online, creating an e-commerce market size in excess of £50 billion. Although more than 15 per cent of people's spending is now online, the scope for further growth seems huge. A lot of that growth will come from '**m-commerce**', that is, making purchase while on the move, using a smartphone or tablet device. Mobile ordering is already becoming dominant at Domino's Pizza and Just Eat.

In 2012, a 15-month-old company with 13 employees was bought for $1 billion by Facebook. The company was Instagram and there proved to be instant riches for the 13 staff, who shared $100 million between them. This story shows that in a digital world a 'small business' can be worth a fortune. Though small in terms of staffing, the global reach of a digital business gives rise to virtually unlimited economic value. If a small firm is so specialised that it cannot reach enough customers in its local area to break even, e-commerce means that the business may still be a viable idea.

Real business

888 Reptiles, based in Daventry, was set up in 2003 by a team of reptile fans to supply snakes, lizards, other reptiles and all the equipment needed to keep reptiles as pets. With such a specialist market to satisfy, the firm needed to service a wider market than just local customers. Using its website to take orders, the firm now has regular customers all over the UK as well as in mainland Europe. Though still small, the company has a large enough market thanks to the use of e-commerce to continue running a viable specialist business.

(Source: www.888reptiles.co.uk)

'For those of you who have as an office a little desk underneath the stairs, and you say, well this is my little desk under the stairs, no! You are sitting at the headquarters of a global corporation if you're connected to the Internet. What's happened is, we've changed the scale. Size and scale are no longer the same.'

Eddie Obeng, British organisational theorist, educator and author

Five whys and a how

Questions	Answers
Why do small firms react faster to change?	With fewer layers of structure for messages to pass through, messages get through more quickly, allowing senior managers to find out about market changes faster and implement their own changes faster.
Why are staff more likely to be motivated in small firms?	People who can easily see the impact on the business of their own contribution should see their working life as more 'meaningful', which Herzberg says is crucial to motivation.
Why can a USP limit growth?	If the unique feature of a firm's product appeals only to a tiny target market, then, assuming the firm continues to maintain its USP, growth will be limited by the size of that niche.
Why might some owners choose to avoid growth for personal rather than business reasons?	Growth is likely to bring an increased workload and less control over their work–life balance – something which may run contrary to their reasons for setting up the business.
Why may e-commerce raise a business's costs if customers pay for deliveries?	The cost of designing and then regularly updating and maintaining a website is significant, whilst more staff time is required to process orders and arrange for delivery.
How can small firms reach a global audience?	The use of e-commerce means that even a small, home-based business that sets up a website is able to show up on searches carried out anywhere in the world.

10.4 Reasons to stay small – evaluation

Some firms choose to stay small, whilst others, by their nature, will always find it very hard to grow beyond a certain size. The choice of staying small will often boil down to the personal objectives of the business's owner(s). For those that started their business to give themselves a better work/life balance than they could find in employment, the extra workload that comes from growth will be unattractive. Other businesses stay small because key aspects of the business simply cannot be expanded, perhaps due to a very unusual USP that appeals to only a tiny niche market, or because the business is totally reliant on the entrepreneur interacting directly with each customer.

The idea of staying small can often be frowned upon – there is a widely held belief that 'business success' depends, at least in part, on growing the business so it gets bigger and bigger. However, history is littered with examples of businesses that have failed due to their pursuit of growth, such as The Royal Bank of Scotland, or because their huge size made change hard to achieve in the face of a changing external environment – such as Nokia and Kodak. Sometimes, small can be great – bringing benefits of agility, flexibility and innovation. Indeed, the rise of concepts such as intrapreneurship suggest that even large firms understand there are benefits to be gained from harnessing the power of small-scale operations.

Key term

M-commerce: electronic transactions carried out while on the move, such as ordering an Asda delivery by smartphone.

10.5 Workbook

Revision questions

(30 marks; 30 minutes)

1 Explain two possible problems arising from growing as a business. (6)

2 Explain why customer service may be better in a small local garage than at a national chain such as Kwik Fit. (4)

3 As an organisation takes on more staff, explain briefly two possible impacts of this growth on the shape of its organisational structure. (6)

4 Explain two possible consequences for a small business of starting to sell via a website. (6)

5 Assess two possible impacts of opening three new outlets on a small cafe which is differentiated by the friendliness and customer service of its proprietor. (8)

Revision activities

Data response 1

Morris Ltd and VH Engineering plc are both manufacturers of components used in UK car factories. Although both were founded in the 1980s, Morris Ltd has remained small, in contrast with VH Engineering plc which has pursued a strategy of rapid growth over the past 20 years.

Shareholders at VH Engineering plc are concerned that the company has developed a reputation of being slow to respond to market change. Although sales remain high, analysts attribute this to the firm's willingness to cut prices on its products which tend to offer fewer features than those of market-leading businesses.

	Morris Ltd	VH Engineering plc
Employees	50	1,200
Total revenue (£m)	35	850
Marketing budget (£m)	0.5	15
Levels of hierarchy	3	8
Average manufacturing cost per unit (£s)	25	31.5
Product reject rate per 1,000	2	6
Operating profit	5	114

Table 10.2 Data for Morris Ltd and VH Engineering plc

Questions (40 marks; 45 minutes)

1 Calculate the operating profit margin for both firms. (4)

2 Assess two possible reasons why cost per unit may be lower at Morris Ltd. (8)

3 Assess two possible reasons why Morris Ltd is faster at responding flexibly to changing customer needs. (8)

4 Evaluate the possible consequences of VH Engineering plc responding slowly to market change. (20)

Data response 2

Hussein Hickmet's rise to fame was remarkable. Within just two years of graduating from one of London's top design schools, his fashionable menswear had featured three times on the front cover of men's style bible *GQ* magazine. With a small but elite group of customers, featuring many premier league footballers, other sports stars and Hollywood celebs, Hussein's business was hugely profitable. His advisors recommended that he reinvest the profits in order to allow the business to grow, developing a far wider range of designs that could be distributed through high-street fashion retailers. The pressure to grow was immense, with his wealthy customers also offering to invest extra capital into the business. Hussein, on the other hand, preferred to remain small. Industry analysts were left to speculate on the reasons for this decision as Hussein himself refused to talk to the press. He continues to produce designs that remain popular with his small, hardcore group of extremely loyal, and wealthy, customers.

Questions (35 marks; 40 minutes)

1 State three common objectives for business start-ups. (3)

2 Assess the possible problems Hussein may have faced if he had chosen to widen his product range and distribute through major high-street retailers. (12)

3 Evaluate the possible reasons why Hussein refused to grow his business. (20)

Extended writing

1 'Most established small businesses remain small because they cannot grow rather than actively deciding to avoid growth.' Evaluate this statement. (20)

2 'Sports car manufacturer McLaren sell such a highly differentiated product, it will always remain a small business in the context of the total global car market.' Evaluate this argument. (20)

11 Quantitative sales forecasting

Definition

Quantitative sales forecasting involves estimating possible future sales figures on the basis of available primary or secondary quantitative data.

Linked to: Sales forecasting, AS Ch 33, Impact of external influences, Ch 5; Investment appraisal, Ch 12; Decision trees, Ch 13; Scenario planning, Ch 24

11.1 Introduction

It is very important for managers to look ahead. They need to think about what is likely to happen in their industry and prepare accordingly in all areas of the business. One of the most important forecasts that needs to be made is the **sales forecast**. This forms the basis of most of the other plans within the organisation. For example:

- The human resource plan will need to be based on the expected level of sales; a growth in sales may require more staff.
- The cash flow forecast will depend on projected sales and the payment period.
- The profit and loss forecasts will depend on the level of revenue predicted.
- Production scheduling will depend on what level of sales is expected.

The sales forecast therefore drives many of the other plans within a business and is an essential element of effective management planning.

When a business starts up, it is extremely difficult to interpret its sales data. An ice cream parlour that starts up in April may find that sales double in May, again in June and again in July. Excited by the business success, the entrepreneurs may rush to open a second outlet. Yet a wet August may see sales knocked back, followed by a sales slump in the autumn. The business may be overstretched and in liquidation by February.

Figure 11.1 An ice cream parlour needs to take seasonal sales variations in to account

As long as a business can survive the first year or two, managers can start to interpret its sales data. Above all else, managers want to understand the **trend** in product sales and compare it to trends in the market as a whole.

There are three main methods used to provide a quantitative sales forecast:

- moving averages
- extrapolation
- correlation

Each is dealt with below.

> 'Good forecasting requires an understanding of your buyer's behaviour.'
>
> *Scott Edinger, Forbes magazine*

> 'If you have to forecast, forecast often.'
>
> *Edgar Fiedler, economist*

11.2 Moving averages

A useful way to show trends is by using a moving average. This is helpful in two main circumstances:

1 where there are strong seasonal influences on sales, such as in the ice cream parlour example

2 when sales are erratic for no obvious reason; wild ups and downs may make it hard to see the underlying situation.

The first column in Table 11.1 shows the 'raw data' for a small supermarket (that is, monthly sales figures). As you can see, they jump around, forming no obvious pattern.

	Raw data (monthly sales) (£)	Centred three-month total (£)	Centred three-month average (£)
January	48,000		
February	57,000		52,000
March	51,000	156,000	49,000
April	39,000	147,000	47,700
May	53,000	143,000	46,300
June	47,000	138,000	45,300
July	36,000	136,000	44,700
August	51,000	134,000	

Table 11.1 Example of a moving average

To find the moving average of the data:

- The first step is to calculate a moving total, in this case a three-month total – in other words, the January to March figures are totalled, then the February to April figures, and so on.
- The third column shows the centred average (that is, the January to March total of 156,000 is divided by 3 to make 52,000); this monthly average sales figure for January to March is centred to February, because that is the 'average' of January to March.

Note how well the three-month moving average clarifies the data, revealing the (very poor) underlying trend. The graph shown in Figure 11.2 simply plots column 1 and column 3 to show the value of the technique.

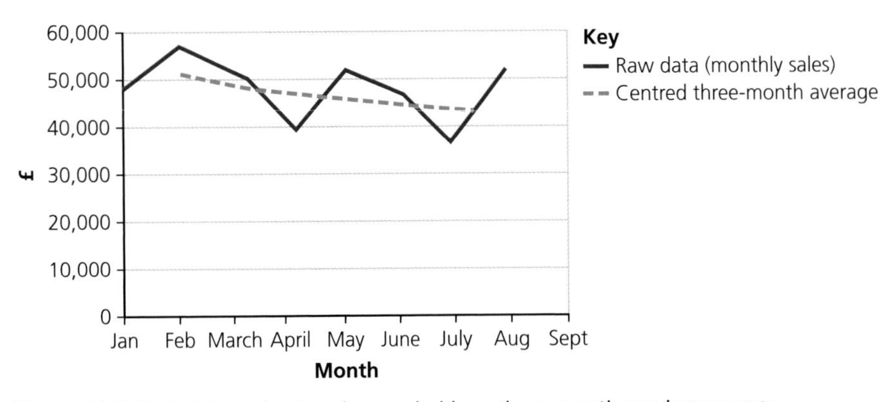

Figure 11.2 Underlying sales trends revealed by a three-month moving average

Seasonal factors and four-quarter moving averages

If the key factor affecting sales is seasonal, trends can only be identified by taking twelve-month or four-quarter moving averages. This eliminates **seasonal variations** due to Christmas because every moving average includes just one set of December figures (especially important for toys or perfumes). A good example is the Apple iPad, which has a strong seasonal sales peak at Christmas. As shown in Figure 11.3, the four-quarter moving average clarifies that demand for the iPad matured in early 2013 and was on a sharp downward trend by the first quarter of 2015.

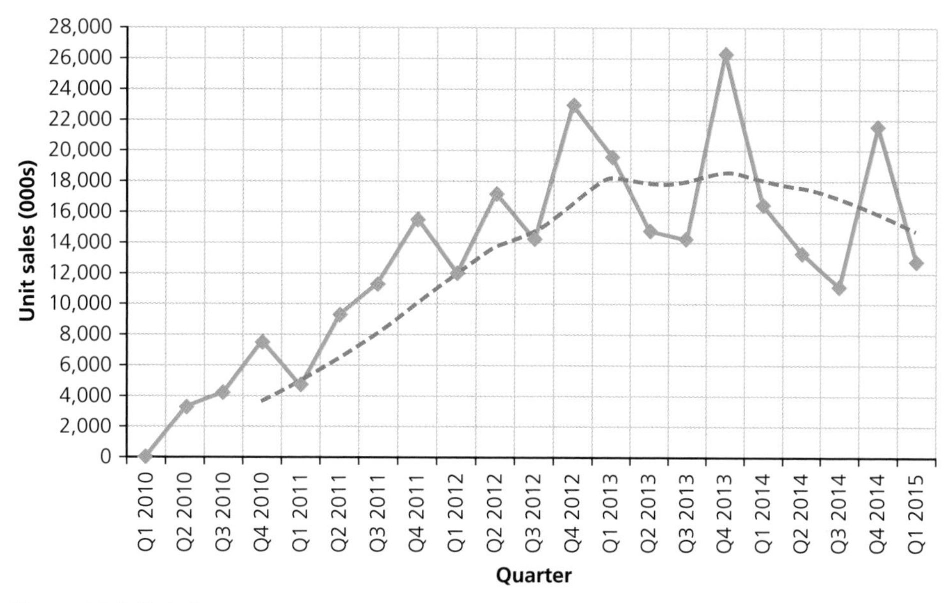

Figure 11.3 Global quarterly iPad sales since launch: raw data (solid line) and four-quarterly moving average (dashed line) (source: Apple Inc quarterly SEC filings)

11.3 Forecasting sales using extrapolation

The simplest way of predicting the future is to assume that it will be just like the past. For the immediate future this may be realistic. If demand for your product has been rising over the past few months, it is fair to assume it will continue in the foreseeable future. The process of predicting based on what has happened before is known as extrapolation. Extrapolation can often be done by drawing a line by eye to extend the trend on a graph (see Figure 11.4).

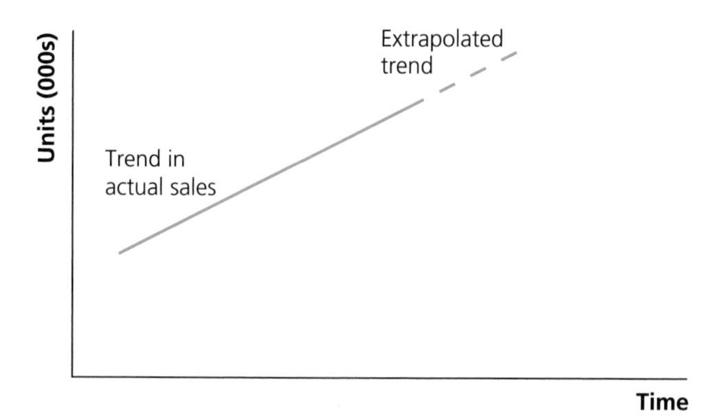

Figure 11.4 An extrapolated sales trend

Here a very steady upward trend over a long period may continue and be predicted to continue. However, such stability and predictability are rare. The values of data plotted over time, called time-series analysis, vary because of genuinely random factors. By definition these cannot be predicted. For example, a revaluation of the Chinese currency could lead to a huge wave of tourists coming to London. Despite the uncertainties, predicting sales based on extrapolated trends is the most widely used method.

As with every business technique, there is also a need for judgement. Look at Figure 11.5. Based upon the longer-term trend, you might believe that the recent downturn is temporary (perhaps due to bad weather). Or it may be that you believe that the recent figures have established the likely trend for the future. It is never wise to simply use a calculator, a computer or graph paper without thinking carefully about what makes the most sense.

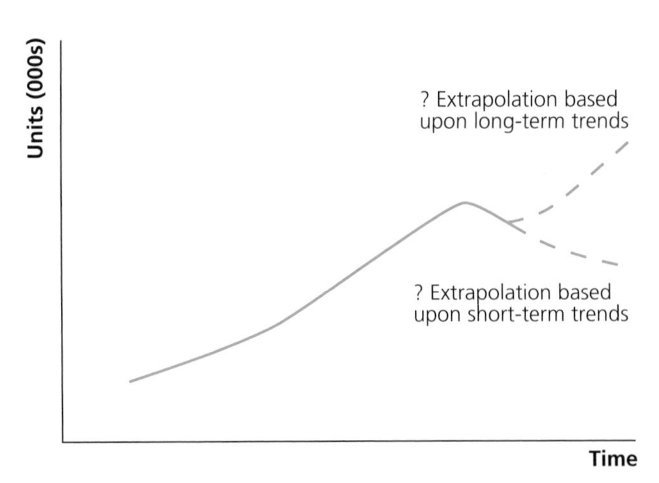

Figure 11.5 Requirement for judgement when extrapolating trends

Real business

Sales Forecasting Manager

Fast-moving consumer goods industry (fmcg)

Merseyside

Salary: £35,000–£40,000

We require a Sales Forecasting Manager for a large fmcg business. Reporting to the Supply Chain Manager, you will be responsible for producing sales forecasts, monitoring performance and detecting any deviations from plan to evaluate and take corrective action in order to drive and maintain high performance levels.

Who we're looking for

We require someone with an excellent forecasting background who has the proven ability to monitor actual targets against forecasts and to take action when needed. As Forecasting Manager, you will have a proven background and ability to improve accuracy to required standards. You must also possess excellent communication skills, excellent IT skills, be able to work as part of a team and also able to use your own initiative.

11.4 Scatter graphs (correlation)

Businesses are always keen to learn about the effect on sales of marketing strategies such as TV advertising, sales promotion or direct mailshots. Often researchers will compare sales volume and advertising expenditure. A good way to do this is on a graph. In Figure 11.6 there is clearly a strong relationship, or correlation, between the two. The correlation is positive: as one increases so does the other. It is important to realise that each point correlating the two variables represents one observation covering a period of time, e.g. spring 2016: advertising spending £30,000; sales 800 units.

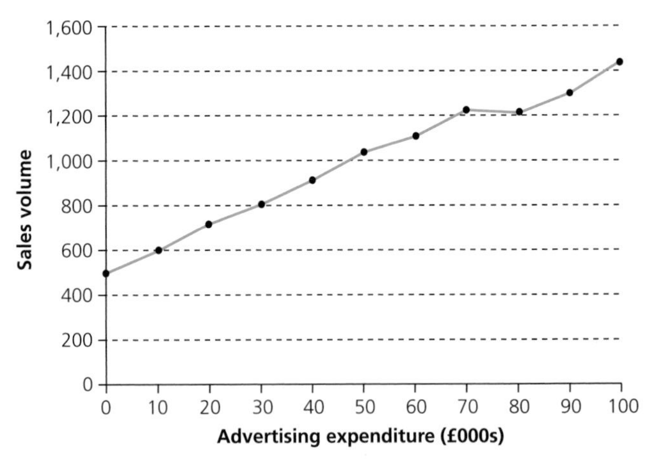

Figure 11.6 Strong positive correlation between advertising expenditure and sales

In Figure 11.7, however, there is not so much linkage, as the diagram is little more than a collection of randomly dispersed points. In this case there is low correlation between advertising and sales, suggesting that the firm should stop wasting its money until it has found a way to make its advertising work more effectively.

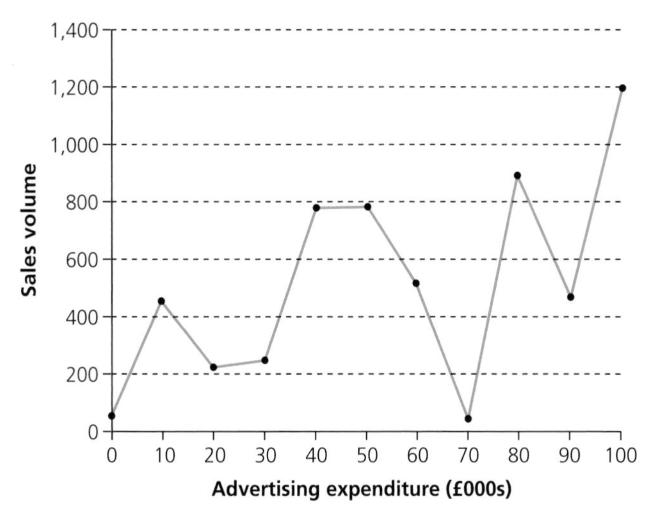

Figure 11.7 Loose correlation: are other variables important?

What the researcher is looking for is cause and effect, such as evidence that the advertising has caused the increase in sales. Correlation by itself does not indicate cause and effect. The sun rising in the morning may be strongly correlated with the delivery time of newspapers, but it does not cause them to be delivered. Strong correlation is evidence that cause and effect *may* be present. Further

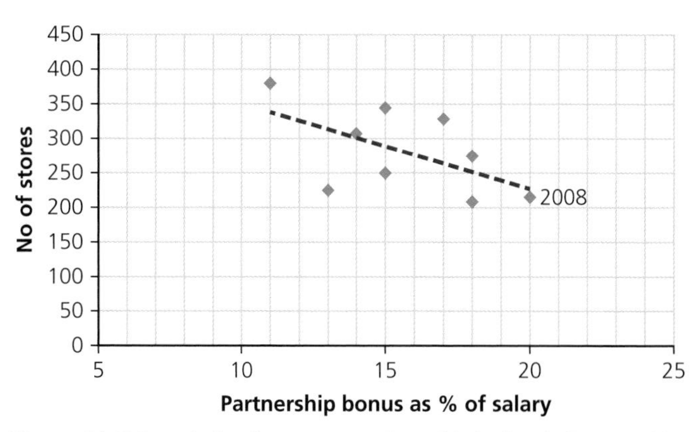

Figure 11.8 Correlation between number of John Lewis Partnership shops and staff bonus payments, 2007–2015 (source: John Lewis annual accounts)

evidence is needed to know how the variables are affecting each other.

A useful technique for interpreting scatter graphs is to look for the line of best fit. This shows whether the correlation is positive or negative. In addition, the degree of variation from the line of best fit gives a clear idea of the strength or the weakness of the correlation. In Figure 11.8 you can see that the more stores opened by the John Lewis Partnership (including Waitrose), the lower the bonus received by staff. Staff received their best bonus in 2008 when there were only 215 shops. The same negative correlation exists between the number of stores and the partnership's profits. (One might hope that John Lewis management might take a look at this!)

Real business

Correlation

In Britain, the Met Office offers businesses a weather-forecasting service, charging a fee for predicting the sales of products ranging from lemonade to cat food. It uses correlation analysis to predict how demand will vary according to the time of year and the prevailing weather. It has found that lemonade sales rise in the summer, but tail away if the weather is very hot (presumably consumers switch to non-fizzy drinks or to ice lollies). More surprisingly, cat food is weather-affected. Rainy days boost demand (the cats don't go out), while, if it's hot, cats eat less.

The website www.metoffice.gov.uk recently featured a producer of hot ready meals that used the Met Office's correlation software to find out that it lost £70,000 of sales for every 1 degree of temperature increase above 20°C. Needless to say, using a weather forecast could enable the business to forecast sales more accurately, and therefore reduce stock losses on its perishable goods.

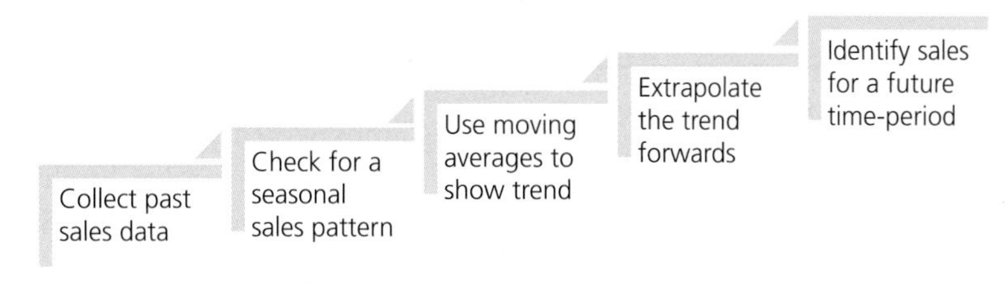

Figure 11.9 Logic chain: making a sales forecast

11.5 Limitations of quantitative sales forecasting techniques

Both extrapolation and correlation can only help to forecast if the future proves to be like the past. Certain future factors are certain, such as Christmas being in December. But many others are uncertain because of factors such as:

- new entrants into the market
- a sudden wave of viral, social media support for – or criticism of – your products or the celebrity who promotes your products
- population changes
- changes in weather conditions
- legal changes (for example, limiting particular forms of promotion or new taxes, perhaps on high-sugar drinks)
- internal factors such as changes in the sales force, changes in the amount of spending on promotion or the way that the money is being spent, or the launch of a new product.

In most cases the actual sales forecast will not be absolutely accurate. However, this does not make forecasting a waste of time; as long as it can provide an estimate that is approximately correct, it will have helped the firm to plan its staffing, funding and production. Better to plan and be approximately right than not plan at all and be unprepared. However, it is always important to review your sales forecasts and compare this with what actually happened; this can help the firm to improve its forecasting techniques and provide better estimates in the future.

'It is far better to foresee even without certainty than not to foresee at all.'

Henri Poincare, French scientist and philosopher

'The key to making a good forecast is not limiting yourself to quantitative information.'

Nate Silver, US election forecasting guru

Five whys and a how

Questions	Answers
Why is it harder to make an accurate sales forecast for a new product than an existing one?	With an existing product you can plot actual sales figures, then extrapolate forwards; with a new product all the data is based on market research, not reality.
Why do quantitative sales forecasts get progressively less accurate the further ahead you look?	Because external factors such as the economy can pull customer demand further and further away from expectations.
Why might qualitative judgements sometimes outweigh quantitative methods of forecasting?	With a radically innovative product it may be impossible to forecast sales accurately – so judgement/hunch might be better than data/science.
Why is correlation useful for sales forecasting?	Careful measurement of the past correlation between advertising and sales makes it easier to forecast the impact of next year's advertising budget.
Why is extrapolation both essential and simplistic?	Projecting forward on the basis of established trends makes huge sense – but of course the future is never exactly like the past.
How is correlation measured?	By plotting two variables on a scatter graph, then identifying the line of best fit.

11.6 Sales forecasting – evaluation

Sales forecasts can be very important to a business because so many other plans rely on them. They can determine how many people to employ, how much to produce and the likely dividends for investors. They may not always be accurate, but they can provide important guidelines for planning.

A badly run business will find itself in a crisis because its precisely forecast future turns out to be surprisingly different in reality. An intelligent manager tries hard to predict with precision, but thinks about the effect of sales being unexpectedly high or low. Nothing demoralises staff more than a sudden lurch by management (hiring one minute, firing the next). So the future needs to be planned with care.

Key terms

Sales forecast: a method of predicting future sales using statistical methods.

Seasonal variation: change in the value of a variable (for example, sales) that is related to the seasons.

Trend: the general path a series of values (for example, sales) follows over time, disregarding variations or random fluctuations.

11.7 Workbook

Revision questions

(30 marks; 30 minutes)

1 What is a sales forecast? (2)

2 Explain how you can show the trend in a series of data. (4)

3 Explain how **two** of the following Heinz managers could be helped by two weeks' warning that sales are forecast to rise by 15 per cent:

a) the operations manager

b) the marketing manager, Heinz Baked Beans

c) the personnel manager

d) the chief accountant. (8)

4 What do you understand by the term 'extrapolation'? Explain how it's used to make a sales forecast. (6)

5 Explain how Coca-Cola may be helped by checking for correlations between the following factors:

a) sales and the daily temperature

b) staff absence levels and the leadership style of individual supervisors. (6)

6 Explain why it is risky to assume cause and effect when looking at factors that are correlated. (4)

Revision activities

Data response

The US aircraft manufacturer Boeing has predicted an increase in demand from airlines for smaller aircraft, but large jumbo jet sales are expected to be lower than predicted over the next 20 years. Boeing raised its projected sales of commercial jets by all manufacturers by $200 billion to $2.8 trillion (£1.4 trillion) in the next two decades. Regional, single-aisle and twin-aisle jets for non-stop routes would prove more popular than expected, it said. However, it reduced its forecast for jumbos carrying more than 400 people. Boeing now expects that the market will buy 960 of the bigger craft, down from the 990 it set out in last year's forecast.

The 20-year industry forecast is as follows:

- 17,650 single-aisle aeroplanes seating 90–240 passengers
- 6,290 twin-aisle jets seating 200–400 passengers
- 3,700 regional jets with no more than 90 seats, up from 3,450 forecast last year
- 960 jumbo jets seating more than 400 passengers.

According to Boeing, passenger numbers would rise by about 5 per cent a year, while cargo traffic would increase by 6.1 per cent. Emerging markets are crucial for future sales, with about one-third of the demand coming from the Asia–Pacific region.

Boeing believes its success is secure thanks to its relatively small 787 plane. It believes this will take sales from its rival Airbus. Twin-engined but with a long range, it will be able to fly direct to far more of the world's airports. This means that passengers will not need to make a connecting flight first to travel a long distance.

Questions (30 marks; 35 minutes)

1 Assess the ways in which Boeing might have produced its industry sales forecasts. (10 marks)

2 Evaluate the possible consequences for Boeing of the findings of its research. (20 marks)

Extended writing

1 'Since we can never know the future, it is pointless trying to forecast it.' Evaluate this statement. (20)

2 Although it used quantitative sales forecasting techniques, Sony was taken by surprise about the launch sales success of the PS4. Evaluate why that might have been so. (20)

12 Investment appraisal

Definition

Investment appraisal involves using forecast cash flows to estimate the value of an investment decision based on quantitative criteria, then backing up the calculations with an assessment of non-financial factors.

Linked to: Corporate objectives, Ch 1; Quantitative sales forecasting, Ch 11; Decision trees, Ch 13

12.1 Introduction

Every day managers make decisions, such as how to deal with a furious customer or whether a cheeky worker needs a disciplinary chat. These can be regarded as **tactical decisions** because they are short-term responses to events. Investment appraisal applies to decisions that concern strategy rather than tactics (that is, the medium to long term). As they are significant in the longer term, they are worth taking a bit of time over; ideally, by calculating whether or not the potential profits are high enough to justify the initial outlay (the sum invested).

To carry out a full investment appraisal might take a manager several weeks, even months. This is because it takes time to gather the relevant data about costs and benefits. For example, if trying to choose whether to launch new product A or B, a sales forecast will be essential. Carrying out primary market research might take several weeks until the results are received and analysed. Only then can the investment appraisal begin.

Table 12.1 gives an idea of the data required to take effective decisions using investment appraisal.

Financial methods of assessing an investment

Having gathered all the necessary facts and figures, a firm can analyse the data to answer two main questions.

1 How long will it take until we get our money back? If we invest £400,000, can we expect to get that money back within the first year, or might it take four years?

2 How profitable will the investment be? How much profit will be generated per year by the investment?

To answer these two questions there are three methods that can be used:

1 payback period

2 average rate of return

3 net present value.

All three methods require the same starting point: a table showing the expected cash flows on the investment over time. An example would be an investment of £60,000 in a machine that will cost £10,000 per year to run and should generate £30,000 cash yearly. The machine is

Decisions requiring investment appraisal	Information needed to make the decision
Should we launch new product A or B?	Sales forecasts, pricing decisions, and data on fixed, variable and start-up costs
Should we make a takeover bid for L'Oréal?	Forecast of future cash flows into and out of L'Oréal; compare the results with the purchase price
Shall we expand capacity by running a night shift?	Forecast of the extra costs compared with extra revenues

Table 12.1 Information needed to take effective decisions using investment appraisal

expected to last for five years. The cash flow table would look like the one shown in Table 12.2.

	Cash in	Cash out	Net cash flow	Cumulative cash flow
NOW*		£60,000	(£60,000)	(£60,000)
Year 1	£30,000	£10,000	£20,000	(£40,000)
Year 2	£30,000	£10,000	£20,000	(£20,000)
Year 3	£30,000	£10,000	£20,000	
Year 4	£30,000	£10,000	£20,000	£20,000
Year 5	£30,000	£10,000	£20,000	£40,000

Table 12.2 Example cash flow table (*NOW = the moment the £60,000 is spent; can also be called the initial outlay or the sum invested)

Exam papers may present this information in the form of a graph. The graph in Figure 12.1 shows the **cumulative cash** total based on the above figures.

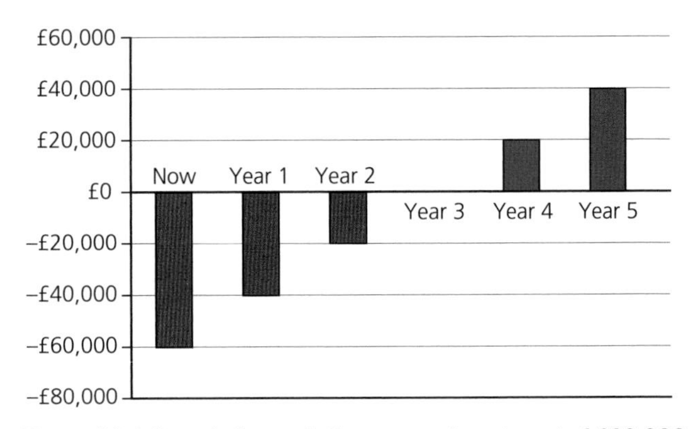

Figure 12.1 Cumulative cash flows on an investment of £60,000

These figures will be used to explain the workings of each of the three methods listed above, which we will now look at in more detail.

12.2 Payback period

Calculation

This method focuses on one issue alone: how long it takes to get your money back. In the above case, the £60,000 investment takes exactly three years to get back, as can be seen in the right-hand column: the cumulative cash total. All the £60,000 is recovered in three years because the business is generating £20,000 of cash per year.

If the annual net cash flows are constant over time, a formula can be used to calculate the payback period:

$$\text{payback} = \frac{\text{sum invested}}{\text{net cash per time period}}$$

$$\text{e.g. } \frac{£60{,}000}{\text{net cash per time period}} = 3 \text{ years}$$

What if the cash flows are not constant over time?

This can make it a little harder to work out a precise answer, though the principles are the same. For example, take the investment of £40,000 shown in Table 12.3.

	Cash in	Cash out	Net cash flow	Cumulative cash flow
NOW	–	£40,000	(£40,000)	(£40,000)
Year 1	£20,000	£5,000	£15,000	(£25,000)
Year 2	£30,000	£10,000	£20,000	(£5,000)
Year 3	£36,000	£24,000	£12,000	£7,000

Table 12.3 Finding the payback period

In this case, payback has not yet occurred by the end of year 2 (there's still £5,000 outstanding). Yet the end of year 3 is well beyond the payback period. So payback occurred in two years and x months. To find how many months, the following formula will work:

$$\frac{\text{outlay outstanding}}{\text{monthly cash in year of payback}}$$

In this case, the year of payback is year 3 and the monthly net cash flow is £12,000/12 months = £1,000 per month. Applying the formula therefore gives:

$$\frac{\text{outlay outstanding}}{\text{monthly cash in year of payback}} = \frac{£5{,}000}{£1{,}000} = 5 \text{ months}$$

In this case, then, the payback period was two years and five months.

Interpretation of payback period

The word investment suggests spending money now in the hope of making money later. Therefore every investment means putting money at risk while waiting to make a surplus. The payback period is the length of time the money is at risk. It follows that every business would like an investment to have as short a payback period as possible. Company directors may tell their managers to suggest an investment only if its payback is less than 18 months. This yardstick is known as a **criterion level**.

Although managers like a quick payback, it is important to be beware of **short-termism**. If directors demand too short a payback period, it may be impossible for managers to plan effectively for the long-term future of the business. Quick paybacks imply easy decisions, such as for Primark to expand its store chain by opening its fifteenth store in London. A much tougher, longer-term decision would be whether Primark should open up stores in New Delhi. This could prove to be a clever move in the longer term, but the high costs of getting to grips with Indian retailing may lead to a minimum of a three-year payback.

The advantages and disadvantages of payback are set out in Table 12.4.

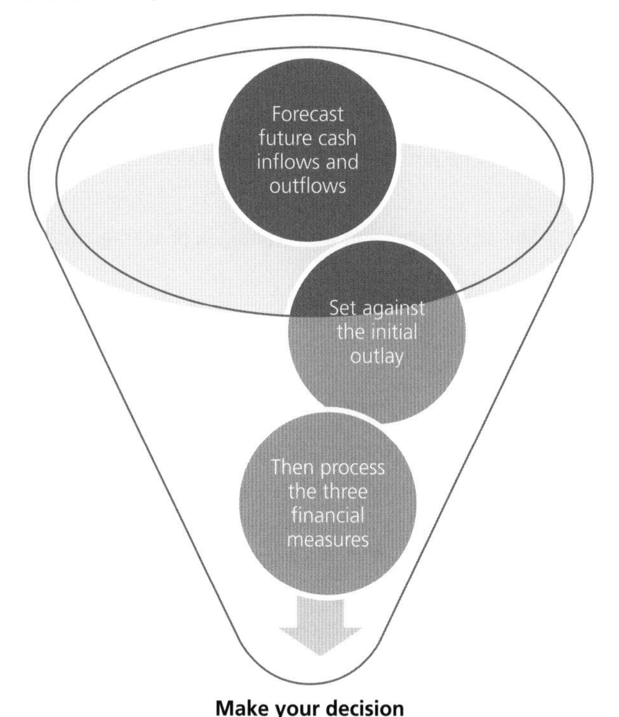

Figure 12.2 Logic funnel: making the investment decision

Advantages of payback	Disadvantages of payback
Easy to calculate and understand	Provides no insight into profitability
May be more accurate than other measures, because it ignores longer-term forecasts (the ones beyond the payback period)	Ignores what happens after the payback period
Takes into account the timing of cash flows	May encourage a short-termist attitude
Especially important for a business with weak cash flow; it may be willing to invest only in projects with a quick payback	Is not very useful on its own (because it ignores profit), therefore is used together with average rate of return or net present value (see below)

Table 12.4 The advantages and disadvantages of payback

12.3 Average rate of return (ARR)

This method compares the average annual profit generated by an investment with the amount of money invested in it. In this way, two or more potential projects can be compared to find out which has the 'best' return on the sum invested.

Calculation

Average rate of return is calculated by the formula:

$$\frac{\text{average annual return}}{\text{initial outlay}} \times 100$$

Real business

The opposite of short-termism

In 2012, JCB, manufacturer of construction equipment, opened a new, $100 million factory in Brazil. Supplied with parts from its UK plant, the Brazilian factory was planned to take advantage of an expected construction boom in Brazil on the back of the 2014 World Cup and 2016 Olympic Games. In March 2013, the company announced a £40 million order from the Brazilian government for 1,000 of its 'backhoe loaders'.

JCB hopes to repeat its amazing success in India, where it is market leader with a 50 per cent market share. It started in India in 1979, and kept going even though it took more than 15 years to make meaningful profits. Now it has four huge factories in India, with the latest opening in 2014. By looking beyond the payback period JCB has grown into one of the world's top three in the market for construction vehicles.

Figure 12.3 JCB: global manufacturing success

There are three steps in calculating ARR, as follows.

1 Calculate the total profit over the lifetime of the investment (total net cash flows minus the investment outlay).

2 Divide by the number of years of the investment project, to give the average annual profit.

3 Apply the formula: $\frac{\text{average annual profit}}{\text{initial outlay}} \times 100$.

For example, BJ Carpets is considering whether to invest £20,000 in a labour-saving wrapping machine. The company policy is to invest in projects only if they deliver a profit of at least 15 per cent a year (see Table 12.5).

Year	Net cash flow	Cumulative cash flow
0	(£20,000)	(£20,000)
1	+ £5,000	(£15,000)
2	+£11,000	(£4,000)
3	+£10,000	+£6,000
4	+£10,000	+£16,000

Table 12.5 Figures for BJ Carpets

Here, the £20,000 investment generates £36,000 of net cash flows in the four years. That represents a lifetime profit of £16,000 (see bottom right-hand corner of Table 12.5). To apply the three steps, then, proceed as indicated in Table 12.6.

Step 1	Identify lifetime profit	£16,000
Step 2	Divide by number of years (4)	£4,000
Step 3	Calculate annual profit as a percentage of initial outlay	$\frac{£4,000}{£20,000} \times 100 = 20\%$

Table 12.6 BJ Carpets: applying the three steps

BJ Carpets can therefore proceed with this investment, as the ARR of 20 per cent is comfortably above its requirement of a minimum ARR criterion level of 15 per cent.

Interpretation of ARR

The strength of ARR is that it is easy to interpret the result. Firms want as high a rate of profit as possible, so the higher the ARR the better. This makes it easy to choose between two investment options, as long as profit is the key decision-making factor. (It may not be, because some firms are pursuing objectives such as growth or diversification.)

Table 12.7 sets out the advantages and disadvantages of average rate of return.

Advantages of average rate of return	Disadvantages of average rate of return
Uses all the cash flows over the project's life ...	... but, because later years are included, the results will not prove as accurate as payback
Focuses upon profitability	Ignores the timing of the cash flows
Easy to compare percentage returns on different investments, to help make a decision	Ignores the time value (opportunity cost) of the money invested

Table 12.7 The advantages and disadvantages of average rate of return

Real business

Estimating average rate of return

In January 2016, Alan Travis bought a flat in north London for £360,000. His plan was to let it out to tenants for a rental of £1,800 a month (£21,600 a year). Although his mortgage payments would be slightly higher than this, he was sure that the property would enjoy a rise in value over the coming years. His forecasts suggested a 7 per cent average rate of return over a five-year period, and a possible 18 per cent ARR if he holds on to the property for ten years. Of course, these figures (as with all investment appraisal) depend entirely on the accuracy of his forecasts.

12.4 Net present value (NPV) of discounted cash flows

Useful though payback and ARR can be, they can work effectively only when used together. ARR provides information on average profitability, while payback tells you about the timing of the cash flows. It is better, surely, to have one method that incorporates profits and time. This is the third method of investment appraisal, which is based on 'discounted cash flows'.

Discounted cash flow (DCF) is rooted in opportunity cost (the cost of missing out on the next best alternative). If a firm invests £10,000 in computer software, it is important not only to ask 'What is the rate of return on my investment of £10,000?', but also 'What opportunities am I having to give up as a result of this investment?' At its simplest, £10,000 tied up in software prevents the firm from enjoying a 5 per cent return on its money in the bank (when interest rates are 5 per cent).

From the idea of opportunity cost, businesses want to know the implication of the timing of cash flows on different projects. If one investment generates +£40,000 in year 1, while another provides that inflow in year 4, the firm must consider what it is missing out on by waiting three years.

In short, it is better to have money now than the same cash sum in the future. This is because money held at the present time has a greater value than the same quantity of money received in the future. If interest rates are 10 per cent, £100 in the bank for a year would become £110. So £100 in a year's time is worth 10 per cent less than £100 today.

When considering potential capital investments on the basis of predicted future cash flows, it makes sense to ask, 'What will the money we receive in the future really be worth in today's terms?' These **present values** are calculated using a method called **discounting**.

To discount a future cash flow, it is necessary to know:

- how many years into the future we are looking, since the greater the length of time involved, the smaller the present or discounted value of money will be
- what the prevailing rate of interest is likely to be.

Once these have been determined, the relevant discount factor can be found. This can be done by calculation, or looked up in 'discount tables'. An extract from a discount table is given in Table 12.8.

Table of selected discount factors

Years ahead	4%	6%	8%	10%	12%	15%
0	1.00	1.00	1.00	1.00	1.00	1.00
1	0.96	0.94	0.93	0.91	0.89	0.87
2	0.92	0.89	0.86	0.83	0.80	0.76
3	0.89	0.84	0.79	0.75	0.71	0.66
4	0.85	0.79	0.74	0.68	0.64	0.57
5	0.82	0.75	0.68	0.62	0.57	0.50

Table 12.8 Extract from a discount table

The future cash flows are then multiplied by the appropriate discount factor to find the present value. For example, the present value of £100 received in five years' time, if the expected rate of interest is 10 per cent, would be:

$$£100 \times 0.62 = £62$$

The higher the rate of interest expected, and the longer the time to wait for the money to come in, the less that money is worth in today's terms.

So how does a firm decide which discount factor to choose? There are two main ways.

1. The discount factor can be based on the current rate of interest, or the rate expected over the coming years.
2. A firm may base the factor on its own criteria, such as that it wants every investment to make at least 15 per cent; therefore it expects future returns to be positive even with a 15 per cent discount rate.

The Edexcel A level uses just one technique of discounted cash flow: the net present value method.

Net present value (NPV)

Calculation

This method calculates the present values of all the money coming in from the project in the future, then sets these against the money being spent on the project today. The result is known as the net present value of the project. It can be compared with other projects to find which has the highest return in real terms, and should therefore be chosen.

The technique can also be used to see if *any* of the projects are worth undertaking. All the investments might have a negative NPV. In other words, the present value of the money being spent is greater than the present value of the money being received. If so, the firm would be better off putting the money in the bank and earning the current rate of interest. Projects are only worth carrying out if the NPV is positive.

For example, a firm is faced with two alternative proposals for investment: Project Z and Project Y (see Table 12.9). Both cost £250,000, but have different patterns of future cash flows over their projected lives. The rate of interest over the period is anticipated to average around 10 per cent. The calculation would be as shown in the table.

	Project Z			Project Y		
Year	Net cash flow	Discount factor	Present value (£s)	Net cash flow	Discount factor	Present value (£s)
0	(£250,000)	1.00	(£250,000)	(£250,000)	1.00	(£250,000)
1	+ £50,000	0.91	£45,500	+£200,000	0.91	+£182,000
2	+£100,000	0.83	£83,000	+£100,000	0.83	+£83,000
3	+£200,000	0.75	£150,000	+ £50,000	0.75	+£37,500
		NPV =	+£28,500		NPV =	+£52,500

Table 12.9 Project Z versus Project Y

Despite the fact that both projects have the same initial cost, and they bring in the same quantity of money over their lives, there is a large difference in their net present values. Project Y, with most of its income coming in the early years, gives a much greater present value than Project Z.

Interpretation

This method of investment appraisal has an in-built advantage over the previous techniques. It pays close attention to the timing of cash flows and their values in relation to the value of money today. It is also relatively simple to use the technique as a form of 'what if?' scenario planning. Different calculations can be made to see what returns will be obtained at different interest rates or with different cash flows to reflect different expectations.

Table 12.10 sets out the advantages and disadvantages of NPV.

Advantages of NPV	Disadvantages of NPV
Takes the opportunity cost of money into account	Complex to calculate and communicate
A single measure that takes the amount and timing of cash flows into account	The meaning of the result is often misunderstood
Can consider different scenarios	Only comparable between projects if the initial investment is the same

Table 12.10 The advantages and disadvantages of NPV

12.5 Limitations of these techniques

All three quantitative methods of investment appraisal use the same base data: forecast cash flows. Therefore inaccuracies in those forecasts damage the reliability of all three approaches. This makes it essential to focus on getting independent, unbiased and realistic data. Optimism is a wonderful quality in a manager, but not when putting together a cash flow forecast.

It should also be borne in mind that the results of ARR and NPV calculations depend on data that may be looking four or more years ahead. At the time of writing, the chief executives of Tesco plc and Sainsbury's plc would be thrilled if they knew what their sales figures would look like in a year's time, let alone four. The further ahead the cash flows are projected the greater the likelihood of inaccuracies. Just think of the things that could go wrong when forecasting cash flows three or four years ahead:

- Costs could rise unexpectedly, perhaps because of a fall in the value of the pound.
- A new competitor might push prices down, undermining forecast cash inflows.
- Consumer tastes might move away from your product.
- A cyclical downturn might turn into a full-blown recession.

In addition to these general problems, Tables 12.4, 12.7 and 12.10 set out the specific limitations of each of the three quantitative techniques.

> 'The value of any stock, bond or business today is determined by the *cash* inflows and outflows – discounted at an appropriate interest rate – that can be expected to occur during the remaining life of the asset.'
>
> *Warren Buffet, investment guru*

12.6 Other factors affecting investment decisions

Non-financial factors in investment appraisal

Once the numbers have been calculated, there are decisions to be made. On the face of it, the numbers point to the answer, but they are only part of the decision-making process. For example, perhaps a board of directors can afford no more than £2 million for investment and must choose between the two alternatives shown in Table 12.11.

	Investment A	Investment B
Type of investment	New R&D laboratory	Relaunching an existing product with flagging sales
Investment outlay	£2 million	£2 million
Payback period	4.5 years	1 year
Average rate of return (over next five years)	8.2%	14.2%
Net present value	£32,000	£280,000

Table 12.11 Investment A versus Investment B

Investment B is clearly superior on all three quantitative methods of appraisal. Yet there may be reasons why the board may reject it. Some of these are outlined below.

- **Corporate objectives:** if the business is pursuing an objective of long-term growth, the directors might feel that a relaunch of a declining brand is too short-termist; they may prefer an investment that could keep boosting the business long beyond the next five years.
- **Company finances:** if the £2 million investment capital is to be borrowed, the company's balance sheet is an important issue. If the business is highly geared, it may be reluctant to proceed with either of these investments, as neither generates an irresistible ARR.
- **Confidence in the data:** the directors will ask questions about how the forecasts were made, who made the forecasts and what was the evidence behind them. If the investment B data came from the manager in charge of the product with flagging sales, may they be biased? Ideally, data used in investment appraisal should come from an independent source and be based on large enough sample sizes to be statistically valid.
- **Social responsibilities:** investing in recycling or energy-saving schemes may generate very low ARRs, but the firm may still wish to proceed for public relations reasons, to boost morale among staff or because the directors think it is ethically right.

Investment criteria

As explained above, company directors may set out minimum financial targets for investment, so that no boardroom time is wasted on projects yielding inadequate returns. If the directors' criteria say at least 10 per cent ARR and no more than 18 months' payback, there is clarity for all concerned.

Risk and uncertainty

Every investment means putting money at risk in the hope of a satisfactory return. As the process includes estimates that will look years, or even decades, into the future, every cash flow figure is subject to uncertainty. And the level of uncertainty grows the further ahead the figures are projected. Successful businesses never invest in a new project unless they can afford it to go wrong. In other words the firm's underlying liquidity and gearing must be satisfactory enough to withstand losing the initial outlay on an investment.

Five whys and a how

Questions	Answers
Why are all investment appraisals based on forecast cash flows?	Because cash is being spent on the outlay, so cash should be the measure of success.
Why shouldn't payback be used on its own to appraise investments?	Because it says nothing about profitability and focuses too much on the short term.
Why is NPV great in theory, but difficult to use in practice?	Because you can't easily compare investments of different sums or covering different timescales (as you can with ARR).
Why might all three appraisal measures be wrong?	Because they're all based on the same cash flow forecast; if the forecast's wrong, all three will give wrong answers.
Why may it be necessary to set aside the findings from the financial methods of appraisal?	Sometimes principle is more important. In 2015, HSBC's Swiss bank was found to be at the centre of tax avoidance and the financing of drug deals; doubtless they had high ARRs.
How might a long-termist business set its criterion levels?	They should accept high payback periods as long as the long-term ARR and NPV figures look attractive.

'Most of our executives make very sound decisions. The trouble is many have turned out not to be right.'

Donald Bullock, US executive

'As far as the laws of mathematics refer to reality, they are not certain; and as far as they are certain, they do not refer to reality.'

Albert Einstein, Nobel prizewinner

12.7 Investment appraisal – evaluation

Investment appraisal methods will often give conflicting advice to managers, who must be willing to make decisions based on a trade-off between risks and profit. This must be taken alongside the objectives of the business, which could well dictate which of the criteria involved is of most importance to the firm.

The size of the firm will also have an impact. Small firms will often have neither the time nor the resources to undertake a scientific approach to investment appraisal. They will often rely on past experience or the owner's hunches in making decisions such as these. In larger firms, the issue of accountability will often lead managers to rely heavily on the projected figures. In this way, should anything go wrong, they can prove they were making the best decision possible at the time, given the information available (and might keep their job).

Key terms

Criterion level: a yardstick set by directors to enable managers to judge whether investment ideas are worth pursuing (for example, ARR must be 15+ per cent or payback must be a maximum of twelve months).

Cumulative cash: the build-up of cash over several time periods (for example, if cash flow is +£20,000 for three years in a row, cumulative cash in year 3 is +£60,000).

Discounting: applying a discount factor to a money sum to take into account the opportunity cost of money over time.

Present values: the discounting of future cash flows to make them comparable with today's cash. This takes into account the opportunity cost of waiting for the cash to arrive.

Short-termism: making decisions on the basis of the immediate future and therefore ignoring the long-term future of the business.

Tactical decisions: those that are day-to-day events and therefore do not require a lengthy decision-making process.

12.8 Workbook

Revision questions

(40 marks; 40 minutes)

1 Distinguish between quantitative and non-financial factors when carrying out an investment appraisal. (4)

2 Why should forecast cash flow figures be treated with caution? (4)

3 How useful is payback period as the sole method for making an investment decision? (3)

4 Briefly outline the circumstances in which:

a) payback period might be the most important appraisal method for a firm (4)

b) average rate of return might be more important than payback for a firm. (4)

5 How are criterion levels applied to investment appraisal? (3)

6 Explain the purpose of discounting cash flows. (4)

7 Using only qualitative analysis, would you prefer £100 now or £105 in one year's time, at an interest rate of 10 per cent? (3)

8 Outline two possible drawbacks to setting a payback criterion level of twelve months. (4)

9 What qualitative issues might a firm take into account when deciding whether to invest in a new fleet of lorries? (4)

10 Why is it important to ask for the source before accepting investment appraisal data? (3)

Revision activities

Data response 1

Questions (30 marks; 30 minutes)

1 Net annual cash flows on an investment are forecast to be as shown in Table 12.12.

	£000
NOW	(600)
End of year 1	100
End of year 2	400
End of year 3	400
End of year 4	180

Table 12.12 Forecast of net annual cash flows on an investment

a) Calculate the payback period based on the above data (4)

b) Calculate the average rate of return based on the above data. (4)

2 The board of Burford Ltd is meeting to decide whether to invest £500,000 in an automated packing machine or into a new customer service centre. The production manager has estimated the cash flows from the two investments to make the calculations given in Table 12.13.

	Packing machine	Service centre
Payback	1.75 years	3.5 years
NPV	+£28,500	+£25,600

Table 12.13 Estimated cash flows from two investments

a) On purely quantitative grounds, which would you choose and why? (6)

b) Outline three other factors the board should consider before making a final decision. (6)

3 The cash flows on two alternative projects are estimated to be as shown in Table 12.14.

Carry out a full investment appraisal to decide which (if either) of the projects should be undertaken. Interest rates are currently 8 per cent. (10)

	Project A		Project B	
	Cash in	Cash out	Cash in	Cash out
Year 0		£50,000		£50,000
Year 1	£60,000	£30,000	£10,000	£10,000
Year 2	£80,000	£40,000	£40,000	£20,000
Year 3	£40,000	£24,000	£60,000	£30,000
Year 4	£20,000	£20,000	£84,000	£40,000

Table 12.14 Estimated cash flows on two alternative projects

Data response 2

Dowton's new finance director has decided that capital investments will be approved only if they meet the criteria shown in Table 12.15.

Payback	30 months
Average rate of return	18%
Net present value	10% of the investment outlay

Table 12.15 Criteria required for approval of capital investments

The assembly department has proposed the purchase of a £600,000 machine that will be more productive and produce to a higher-quality finish. The department estimates that the output gains should yield the cash flow benefits shown in Table 12.16 during the expected four-year life of the machine.

Year	Net cash flow (£s)
0	– 600,000
1	+ 130,000
2	+ 260,000
3	+ 360,000
4	+ 230,000

Table 12.16 Yield of cash flow benefits during expected life of the machine

In addition:

- the machine should have a resale value of £100,000 at the end of its life
- the relevant discount factors are: end year 1, 0.91; year 2, 0.83; year 3, 0.75; year 4, 0.68.

Questions (30 marks; 35 minutes)

1 Conduct a full investment appraisal, then evaluate whether Dowton's should go ahead with the investment on the basis of the quantitative information provided. (12)

2 Assess two other pieces of information it may be useful to obtain before making a final decision. (8)

3 Assess which sources of finance might be appropriate for an investment such as this. (10)

Data response 3

3D Sports

Altrincham Sports (AS) had been the only independent sports shop in town for more than ten years, surrounded by Sports Direct and other multiples. AS had kept itself going by great customer service, but sliding revenues recently suggested that more was needed. Watching a news item on 3D printing made owner Jim Burn see a solution. Moulded trainers, made-to-measure and manufactured automatically in front of your eyes – surely that would be a real point of differentiation.

Jim found that the right grade of 3D printer would cost £12,000; with advertising, staff training and a few other fixed costs, the total investment outlay would be £20,000. The variable costs per pair would be about £10 and a selling price of £40 seemed realistic. Ongoing running (fixed) costs – including staffing – would be £1,000 a month.

But what was a realistic sales forecast? A Friday evening invite to the pub gave Jim the opinions of his staff. Most thought there'd be a great deal of interest at first, but that it would taper off. One said: 'But never mind, we need to get people out of Sports Direct and back to us. Even if you lose a bit on the printing, we might more than make up for it with customers buying other things.' Jim accepted the logic, but explained that he needed the printer to pay for itself. He would have to borrow the money from HSBC and they wouldn't lend it on a vague promise of selling 'other things'. As HSBC would be charging an interest of 8 per cent he really needed an average rate of return of at least 10 per cent to be credible.

After a lot of thought, Jim produced this sales forecast for the '3D shoe':

	Sales (pairs)
Year 1	1,000
Year 2	600
Year 3	400
Year 4	200

Table 12.17 Sales forecast for the 3D shoe

Now, before going to see HSBC, he needed an investment appraisal to work out whether the proposition was realistic.

Questions (40 marks; 45 minutes)

1 From the above information, assess two possible sources of inaccuracy in the underlying data being fed into the investment appraisal process. (8)

2 **a)** Turn the above data into a table showing cash inflow, outflow, net cash and cumulative cash. (4)

b) Calculate the payback period. (4)

c) Calculate the average rate of return. (4)

3 In the back of his mind, Jim has been wondering whether to drop the 3D idea altogether. Evaluate whether he should drop it. (20)

Extended writing

1 'Financial methods of assessing investment decisions are based on no more than educated guesses about future cash flows.' Evaluate whether that invalidates the use of these techniques. (20)

2 Evaluate whether making the wrong investment decision might threaten the survival of a medium-sized company. (20)

13 Decision trees

Definition

Decision trees are diagrams that set out all the options available when making a decision, plus an estimate of their likelihood of occurring.

Linked to: Corporate strategy, Ch 2; Corporate influences, Ch 15

13.1 Introduction

Decision trees provide a logical process for decision-making. The decision problem can be set out in the form of a diagram, like a tree on its side. It can take into account the occasions when a decision can be taken and the occasions when chance will determine the outcome. Chance can be estimated by assigning a **probability**, such as 0.2 (a 1 in 5 chance). While the estimate of the probability may sometimes be a guess, at other times there may be a logical basis. In the past, the chance of a new product launch surviving two years was 1 in 5, therefore it would be fair to give the probability of success for a new launch at 0.2.

The kinds of problems that are suited to decision-tree analysis are those where a sequence of events or options has to be followed in conditions of uncertainty. The decision whether or not to launch a new product, enter a new market, build a new factory, hire or buy machinery, for example, are all cases where decision-tree analysis is appropriate. It would also be possible to use investment appraisal. The advantage of a decision tree is that it allows for uncertainty or chance. This makes it a better model of the reality of an uncertain business world.

13.2 Step-by-step approach to decision-tree analysis

Step 1: the basics

1 The tree is a diagram setting out the key features of a decision-making problem.

2 The tree is shown lying on its side, roots on the left, branches on the right.

3 The decision problem is set out from left to right with events laid out in the sequence in which they occur.

4 The branches consist of:

a) a decision to be made, shown by a square (see Figure 13.1)

b) chance events or alternatives beyond the decision-maker's control, shown by a circle – a **node** (see Figure 13.2).

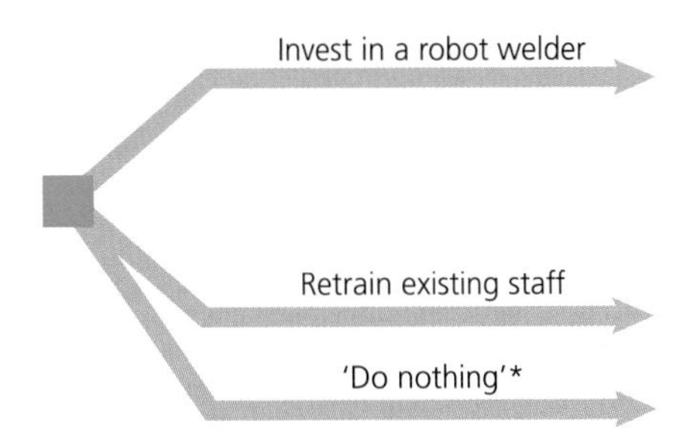

*Note that 'do nothing' is an option for every business decision

Figure 13.1

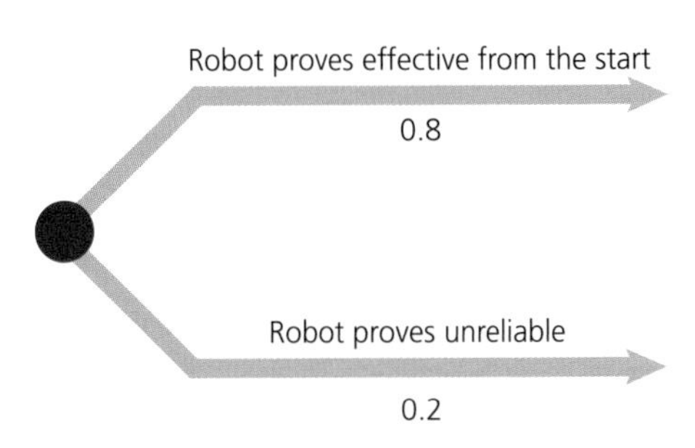

Figure 13.2

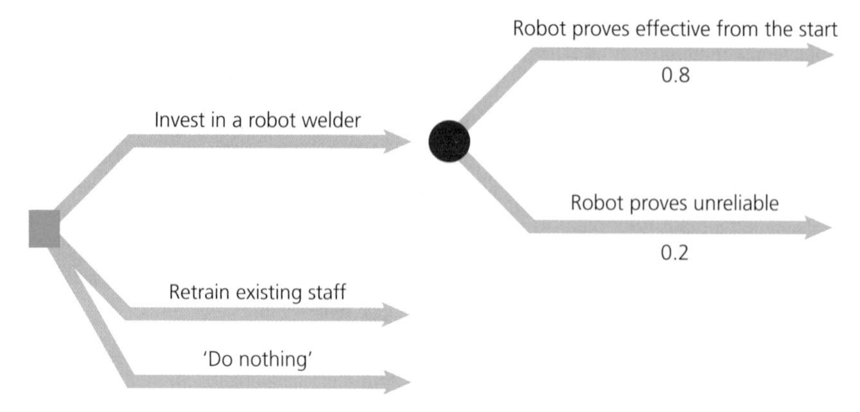

Figure 13.3

Note carefully that a square means a decision and a circle means a chance event, i.e. one of two or more events may follow. Therefore:

- there must be a probability attached to each of the chance events or alternatives
- these probabilities must add up to 1 as one of them must happen.

In Figure 13.2, the decision-maker has allowed for an 80 per cent (0.8) chance that the robot will work well and a 20 per cent (0.2) chance that it will prove unreliable. These figures could be arrived at from experience with robots in the past.

At any square, the decision-maker has the power to choose which branch to take, but at the circles chance takes over. You can choose whether or not to invest in a robot. But there is a chance that the robot may prove unreliable. The full tree so far is shown in Figure 13.3.

The decision-maker will choose which branch provides the better or best value.

If buying costs a net cash outflow of £1,000 per year while hiring costs £800, it is better to hire (see Figure 13.4).

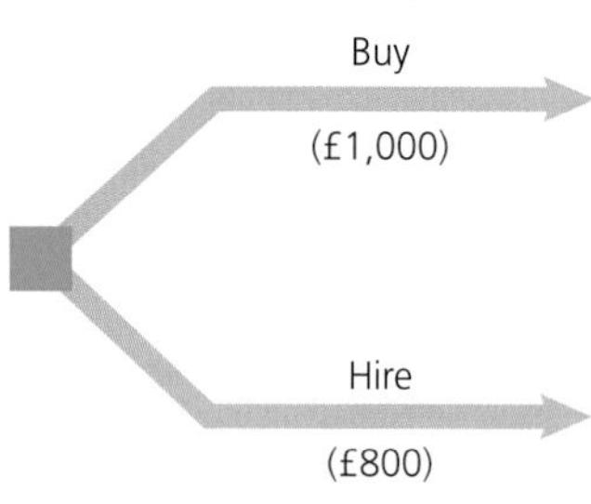

Figure 13.4

Note that the branch not taken is crossed out, as shown in Figure 13.5.

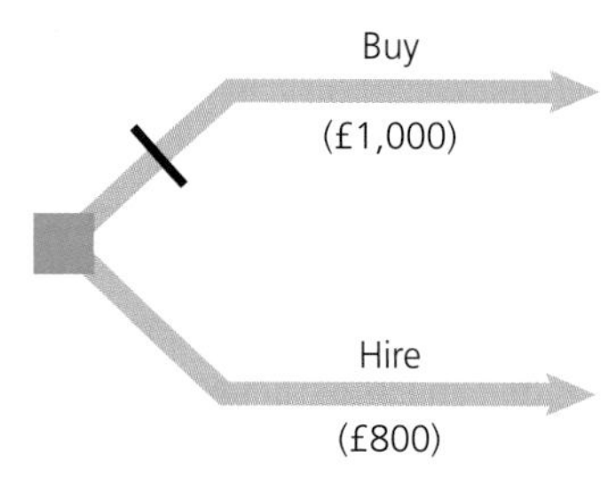

Figure 13.5

Step 2: drawing a decision tree

Bantox plc must decide whether to launch a new product (see Figure 13.6).

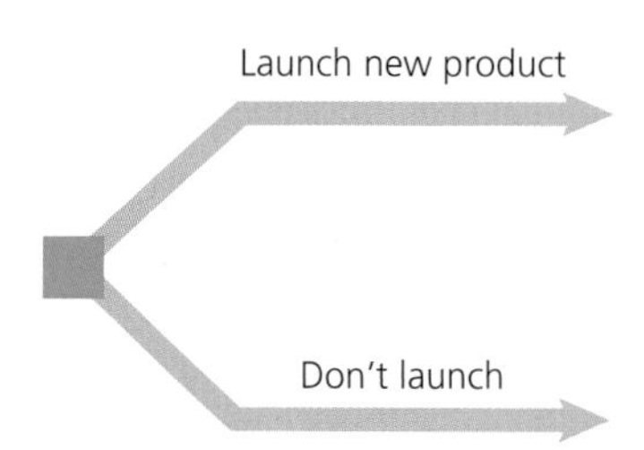

Figure 13.6

Research suggests there will be a 70 per cent chance of success in a new product launch. This would be shown as a probability of 0.7 (see Figure 13.7).

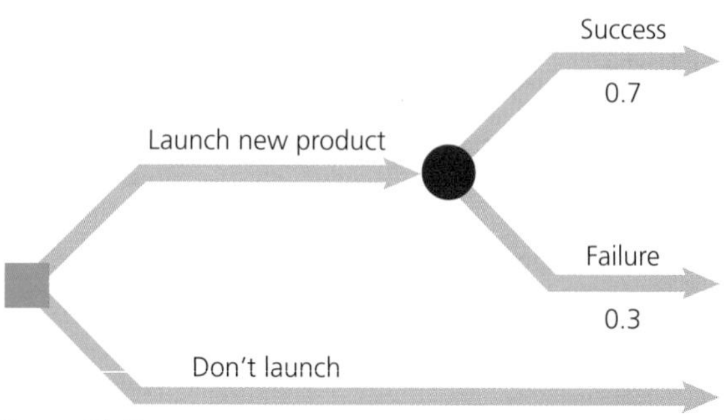

Figure 13.7

Note that, because probabilities must add up to 1, the implied chance of failure is 0.3.

To make a decision based on the above tree, estimates are needed of the financial costs and returns. In this case, let's assume:

- the new product launch will cost £10 million
- a new product success will generate £15 million of positive net cash flows
- a new product failure will generate only £3 million
- no launch means no movements in net cash.

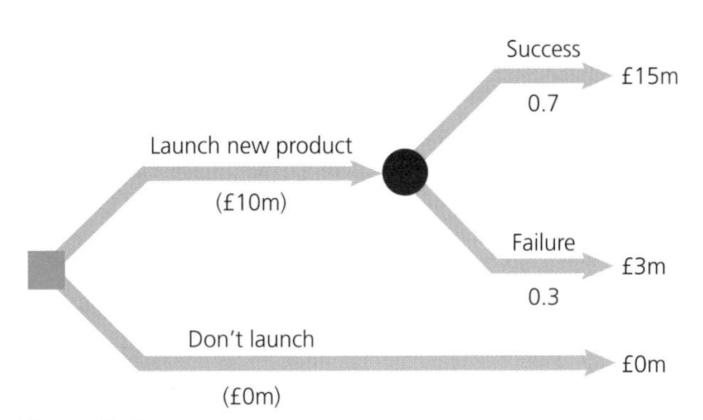

Figure 13.8

The full decision tree now looks like Figure 13.8.

Step 3: making calculations

At each probability circle, a calculation is required of the average outcome, given the probabilities involved. If a launch costing £10 million will generate either £15 million or £3 million, what will be the average result if the same circumstances happened several times over? Sometimes the firm would get £15 million and sometimes £3 million. Usually, to work out an average, you would add the numbers and divide by 2; that is:

$$\frac{£15m + £3m}{2} = £9m$$

That assumes, though, that there is an equal chance of £15 million and £3 million. In fact, the probabilities are not 50/50, they are 70/30. There is a 70 per cent chance of £15 million. So the correct (weighted) average **expected value** is:

£15m × 0.7	= £10.5m
£3m × 0.3	= £0.9m
Total	£11.4m

In decision trees, the expected values at probability circles are always calculated by weighted averages.

Calculations on decision trees are carried out from right to left, that is, working backwards through the tree, making calculations at each probability circle.

In the case of Bantox, only one calculation is needed. If there are several circles, it is helpful to number them, and show your weighted average calculations clearly (see Figure 13.9).

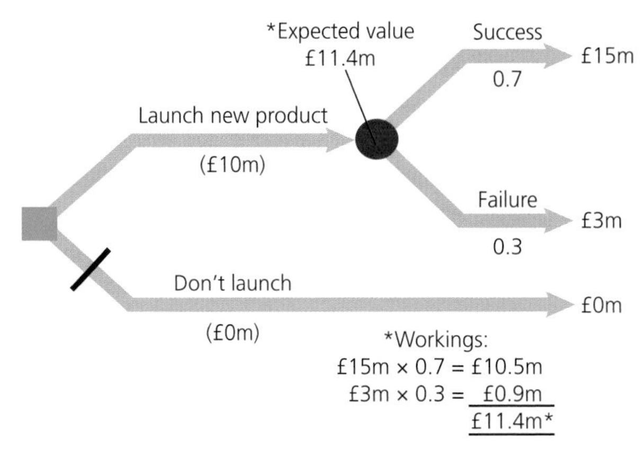

Figure 13.9

Step 4: showing your decisions

Having calculated the expected value (weighted average) at each probability circle, a rational decision can be made. As Figure 13.9 shows, launching the new product will, on average, turn £10 million into £11.4 million, i.e. generate a **net gain** of £1.4 million. Therefore it is preferable to launch. The decision to launch is indicated by crossing out the 'don't launch' option.

13.3 Summary of key points

A decision tree is a diagrammatic presentation of a problem involving decisions (squares) and chance events (circles).

1. The problem is laid out from left to right. Decisions are shown as squares, chance events as circles.
2. Each chance event has a probability estimated for it. The probabilities must add up to 1 since one of them must happen.
3. Two money values are shown:
   a) the cost of the decision (shown as a negative number, i.e. in brackets)
   b) the benefit or cost of a specific outcome occurring. These are shown at the end of each branch of the tree.

4 Working from right to left, the decision-maker calculates the expected value at each circle. These values are calculated by multiplying the money value by the probability, then adding the results.

5 Still working from right to left, the decision-maker decides at each square which branches to cross off, leaving only the better or best alternative open.

Real business

In 2014, the Head of Volkswagen America learned that the company's diesel cars were showing artificially low emissions data to the US regulators. He then faced a choice: go public, with the near-certain consequence of bad publicity and falling sales; or keep quiet, with a high chance that no one would ever know, but a huge scandal if the company were caught out. So the probability of being caught was perhaps as low as 0.2, but the cost might be huge if it became public knowledge. In September 2015 the diesel emissions scandal burst on the world; quite quickly analysts were talking of an eventual cost to the company of perhaps $50 billion. The US Head of Volkswagen was caught out. It might be said that he was unlucky. Or perhaps he should have ignored probabilities and chosen the morally correct option of stopping the manipulation of the data.

Figure 13.10

'Probability is the very guide of life.'

Thomas Hobbes, seventeenth-century philosopher

'We should never allow ourselves to be bullied by an either-or. There is often the possibility of something better than either of these two alternatives.'

Mary Parker Follett, business writer (1868–1933)

'Compromise is usually bad ... listen to both sides then pick one or the other.'

Robert Townsend, author of Up the Organisation

13.4 Advantages and limitations of decision trees

Advantages of using decision trees

1 The most important advantage of the technique is allowing for uncertainty. The most common technique for business decision-making is investment appraisal. This is based upon a single forecast of future cash flows, giving a bogus impression of certainty. In reality, every decision can result in a range of possible outcomes, not just one. The decision tree allows for this. By focusing firms on uncertainty, decision trees can help to ensure that managers' decisions are more carefully considered.

2 Decision trees also demand that managers consider all the possible alternative outcomes. Although it is important to be single-minded, too many managers adopt a strategy without fully considering the alternatives. They perhaps choose the approach that worked last time, or the one adopted by their competitors. Decision trees not only encourage careful consideration of the options, but also require an estimate of the actual outcome for each. This allows 'best case' and 'worst case' scenarios to be costed and considered.

Further advantages of decisions trees are set out below.

1 Decision trees set out problems clearly and encourage a logical approach. The discipline of setting out the problem in a decision tree requires logical thinking and can also generate new ideas and approaches.

2 Decision trees encourage a quantitative approach and force assessments of the chances and implications of success and failure.

3 Decision trees not only show the average expected values for each decision but also set the probability of a specific outcome occurring.

4 Decision trees are most useful when similar scenarios have occurred before so that good estimates for probabilities and predicted **actual values** exist.

5 Decision trees are most useful in tactical or routine decisions, rather than strategic decisions.

Limitations of using decision trees

All quantitative methods can be biased, consciously or unconsciously. Optimism is often a virtue in an executive, but it may lead to exaggerated sales figures or excessively high probabilities for success. This does not mean quantitative methods should be rejected, only that it is sensible to ask who provided the figures and assess whether they had any reason to want a particular outcome. Cynicism about decision trees is out of place; scepticism is wholly valid.

Further limitations of decision trees are set out below.

1 It may be difficult to get meaningful data, especially for estimated probabilities of success or failure.

2 Decision trees are less useful in the case of completely new problems or one-off strategic problems.

3 It can be relatively easy for a manager seeking to prove a case to manipulate the data. A biased approach to the estimated probabilities or values could 'prove' the pre-desired result rather than the logically determined outcome.

4 Decision trees may divert managers from the need to take account of qualitative as well as quantitative information when making a decision.

Five whys and a how

Questions	Answers
Why may decision tree analysis be more useful than investment appraisal?	Because it takes into account alternative possible outcomes and the probability of them occurring (investment appraisal is misleadingly 'certain').
Why are expected values calculated using a 'weighted' rather than a straight average?	Because it's the only way to gain accuracy when there are different probabilities of the possible outcomes occurring.
Why may the decision tree technique be useful even if you have no sound basis for estimating the probabilities?	The tree diagram will still indicate the best and worst possible outcomes – a vital part of decision-making (if the worst outcome would threaten the firm's survival, you'd say no).
Why may there be dangers in the apparent 'scientific' precision of the decision tree technique?	People may assume that the technique delivers more accuracy than is true given the degree of estimation involved.
Why may decision trees risk side-lining qualitative factors?	Because people are swayed by a 'definite', numerical 'answer' to a problem – so they subconsciously play down qualitative factors.
How are calculations done after the decision tree is drawn up?	Working back from right to left, calculating the weighted average at every chance node, then cutting off the less profitable decisions.

'One accurate measurement is worth a thousand expert opinions.'

Grace Hopper, computer scientist and US Navy Rear Admiral

'Exactitude is not truth.'

Henri Matisse, post-impressionist painter

'Human decisions affecting the future .... cannot depend on strict mathematical expectation.'

John Maynard Keynes, economist

13.5 Decision trees – evaluation

Small firms run by one person benefit from clear, speedy decision-making. The entrepreneur knows the customers, the competition and the staff. Therefore he or she can make effective decisions quickly, with no need to justify them to others. Some may prove faulty, but the quick responses of a small firm should ensure that damage is limited. The business will stand or fall on the hunches and judgements of the boss.

In large firms, the same rules do not apply. A successful career path at a company such as Mars or Unilever often depends upon avoiding mistakes. Therefore it is important to be able to justify why a decision was made. Even if it proves to be wrong, that should not matter as long as the method for making the decision was thorough and analytic. After all, if four out of five new products prove to be failures, what would be the reason for firing a manager who has just launched a flop?

It can be a matter for regret that methods such as decision trees are used to 'protect the back' of decision-makers. In other words, they may not be valued for themselves, only for their value as a protector. Often, though, the process of trying to protect themselves encourages managers to think hard about their decision-making methods. Those who use decision trees positively may find an improvement in their record of success, and help the big firms to compete with the faster-moving small firms.

Key terms

Actual values: although known as 'actual values' or 'payoffs', these are the forecasts of the net cash flow which result from following a sequence of decisions and chance events through a decision tree. They should always be shown at the ends of the branches of the tree.

Expected values: these are the forecast actual values adjusted by the probability of their occurrence. Although called 'expected', they are not the actual cash flows which result. Expected equals actual times probability.

Net gains (or losses): subtracting the initial outlay from the expected value to find out whether or not a decision is likely to produce a surplus.

Node: a point in a decision tree where chance takes over. It is denoted by a circle, and at that point it should be possible to calculate the expected value of this pathway.

Probability: the likelihood of something occurring. This can be expressed as a numerical value, which can be a percentage (for example 50 per cent chance), a fraction (for example $\frac{1}{2}$), or a decimal (for example 0.5). The probability of something certain is 100 per cent or 1. The probability of something impossible is zero. So probabilities range from 1 to zero.

13.6 Workbook

Revision questions

(30 marks; 30 minutes)

1 When drawing a decision tree, what symbol is used to show:

a) when a decision must be made

b) when chance takes over? (2)

2 If the probability of the successful launch of a new product is estimated to be 0.72, the probability of a failed launch must be 0.28. Explain why. (3)

3 State whether each of the following is a decision or a chance event:

a) choosing between three different new product options

b) a new product succeeding or failing in the marketplace

c) good weather on the day of the open air concert

d) whether to advertise or to cut the price. (4)

4 Explain the difference between an expected value and an actual value. (3)

5 State three advantages and three potential pitfalls of using decision trees. (6)

6 Explain the circumstances when decision trees are least useful. (4)

7 If the chance of achieving £200,000 is 0.2 and the chance of £20,000 is 0.8, what is the expected value of a decision? (4)

8 Explain how decision trees may help managers to assess the best decision by 'what if?' analysis. (4)

Revision activity

Look at the tree diagram below. Calculate the expected values at nodes 1–4 and state your decisions at decision points A–C. Indicate your decisions on the tree diagram.

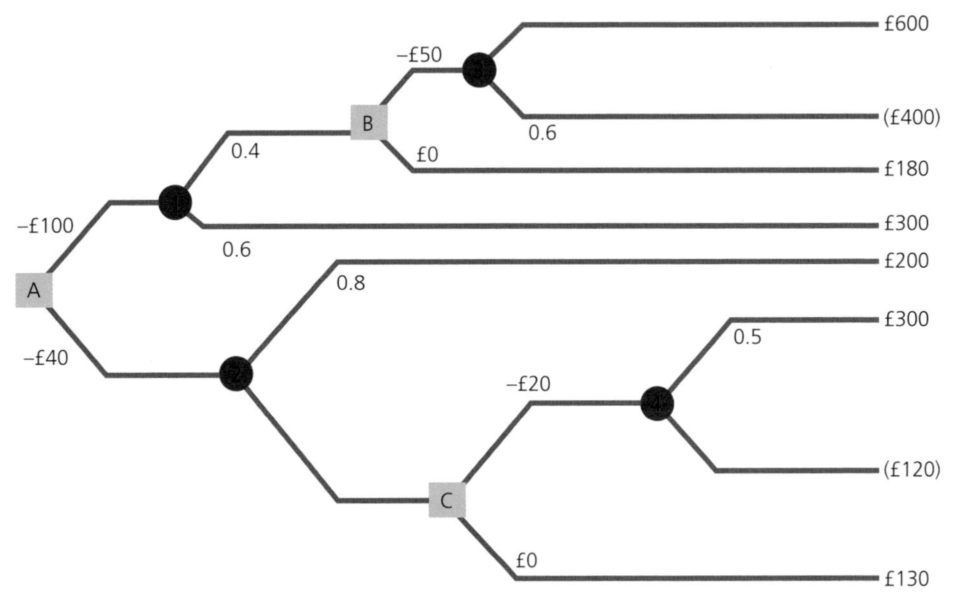

Figure 13.11

Revision activities

Data response 1

Denham Potteries has a capital spending budget of £100,000. The production manager has put in a bid for £100,000 for a new tunnel kiln. The marketing manager has countered with a proposal to spend £80,000 on launching a new product. This new product is in line with the firm's objective of diversifying, but may be rather risky given the firm's past record of only one success for every five new products.

Ken Coton, the marketing manager, has provided a handy table of figures to summarise the information. This is set out in Table 13.1.

Outcome	Probability (surplus over next 5 years)	Actual value (£)
New product		
Big success	0.1	900,000
Modest success	0.1	500,000
Failure	0.8	30,000
Tunnel kiln		
Success	0.8	200,000
Failure	0.2	60,000

Table 13.1 Denham Potteries

Questions (25 marks; 30 minutes)

1. Draw a fully labelled decision tree to set out the options. (10)
2. What decision should the firm make on purely numerical grounds? (3)
3. Outline the qualitative factors the board should take into account before making the decision. (12)

Data response 2

Mansfield Town FC is considering buying a South American centre forward player for its team. The club knows statistics show that only one in four overseas forwards succeeds in the lower divisions. But things are desperate. The player's contract will cost £500,000 and, if successful, could increase home attendances sufficiently to be worth £1.2 million over the three-year contract. Even if the player is unsuccessful, attendances should rise by £200,000.

Questions (20 marks; 15 minutes)

1 Draw a decision tree and label it carefully. (12)

2 On the basis of the tree, what decision should the club take? (4)

3 Outline two reasons why the club might decide to proceed. (4)

Data response 3

The research and development department in Gregson plc has just invented a new higher-quality version of the product sold by a rival business, Winder plc. The product is code-named 'Copycat'. At present Gregson lacks the technology to manufacture the product itself. After further research, it decides there are three immediate choices:

1 buy the technology to manufacture the product itself

2 sell all rights to Winder plc

3 sell all rights on a royalty basis to a third company.

The marketing department believes that Copycat, as it stands, has a 50 per cent chance of success, with no further development.

However, the research and development department in Gregson believes it could improve Copycat still further by some design enhancements. However, it only wants to do so if Copycat had already succeeded and if choice 2 above had not been taken. After design enhancement, the chance of a successful launch is estimated to be 60 per cent.

The forecast actual values are shown in Table 13.2.

Questions (25 marks; 30 minutes)

1 Prepare a decision tree to illustrate this situation, showing branches, probabilities, and actual values. (9)

2 Calculate the expected values. (4)

3 Explain the optimal decision strategy based on these calculations. (4)

4 Assess two other factors which Gregson may take into account before making the final decision. (8)

Decision outcome	Manufacture	Sell all rights to Winder	Sell on a royalty basis to a third company
Fails before design enhancement	–262.5	15	7.5
Succeeds after design enhancement	375	–	300
Succeeds but no design enhancement	150	15	82.5
Fails after design enhancement	–412.5	–	–142.5

Table 13.2 Forecast actual values for Gregson (all figures in £000s)

Extended writing

1 Whitbread plc made the brilliant decision in 2000 to move out of the beer market and concentrate on coffee (Costa) and hotels (Premier Inn). Evaluate the importance of decision trees when making long-term strategic decisions such as this. (20)

2 A restaurant business is considering opening its first outlet in America. Evaluate whether investment appraisal or decision trees are more likely to be useful on this occasion. (20)

Section 3.3 Decision-making techniques

14 Critical Path Analysis (CPA)

Definition

Critical Path Analysis is based on a network diagram that sets out which activities within a project can be done simultaneously and which must be done consecutively. A network diagram helps to identify the critical path – the activities that require the most careful management scrutiny.

Linked to: Corporate strategy, Ch 2; Human resources, Ch 21; Scenario planning, Ch 4

14.1 Introduction

Time has become an increasingly important competitive advantage, such as when two rivals are each trying to be first to market with a new product or business idea. To be first requires careful planning. The plan is turned into a critical path diagram to show supervisors and workers exactly what they should be doing: what, when and how. This provides the basis for monitoring and controlling actual progress to make sure the project is completed on time.

Network analysis is a way of showing how a complex project can be completed in the shortest possible time. It identifies the activities that must be finished on time to avoid delaying the whole project. These activities represent the **critical path**. Management effort can be concentrated on ensuring that these key activities are completed on time. This leaves greater flexibility in timing the non-critical items. The objectives are to ensure customer satisfaction through good timekeeping and to minimise the wastage of resources, thereby boosting the profitability of the project.

A **network** shows:

- the order in which each task must be undertaken
- how long each stage should take
- the earliest date at which the later stages can start.

If a house-building firm can predict with confidence that it will be ready to put roof beams in place 80 days after the start of a project, a crane can be hired and the beams delivered for exactly that time. This minimises costs, as the crane need only be hired for the day it is needed, and improves cash flow by delaying the arrival of materials (and invoices) until they are really required.

Figure 14.1 Network analysis can help building firms estimate when they will need materials and equipment

> 'In preparing for battle I have always found that plans are useless, but planning is indispensable.'
>
> *Dwight Eisenhower, former US General and US President*

14.2 Drawing Critical Path Analysis diagrams

A Critical Path Analysis (CPA) network consists of two components.

1. An 'activity' is part of a project that requires time and/or resources. Therefore waiting for delivery of parts is an 'activity', as is production. Activities are shown as arrows running from left to right. Their length has no significance.
2. A 'node' is the start or finish of an activity and is represented by a circle. All network diagrams start and end on a single node.

Rules for drawing CPA networks

1 The network must start and end on a single node.

2 No lines should cross each other.

3 When drawing an activity, do not add the end node straight away; wait until you have checked which activity follows.

4 There must be no lines that are not activities.

5 Due to the need to write figures in the nodes, it is helpful to draw networks with large circles and short lines.

14.3 Case example: the need for networks

A chocolate producer decides to run a '3p off' price promotion next February. Is there any need for network analysis? Surely not. What could be easier? Yet the risk of upsetting customers is massive with any promotion. What if a huge order from Tesco meant that Sainsbury's could not receive all the supplies it wanted?

To make this promotion work smoothly it would be necessary to:

- tell the sales force
- sell the stock into shops
- design the '3p off' packs
- estimate the sales volume for one month at 3p off
- get the special packs printed
- order extra raw materials (for example, a double order of cocoa)
- step up production
- arrange overtime for factory staff
- deliver promotional packs to shops ... ... and much, much more.

An efficient manager thinks about all the activities needed, and puts them in the correct time sequence. Then a network can be drawn up (see Figure 14.2).

Once the manager has found how long each activity is likely to take, she or he can work backwards to find out when the work must start. Here, the work must start 70 days before 1 February. This is because the longest path through to the end of the project is 70 (14 + 28 + 21 + 7).

Having drawn a network, the next stage is to identify more precisely the times when particular activities can or must begin and end. To do this, it is helpful to number the nodes that connect the activities. Figure 14.3 shows the 3p off example with the activities represented by letters and the nodes numbered.

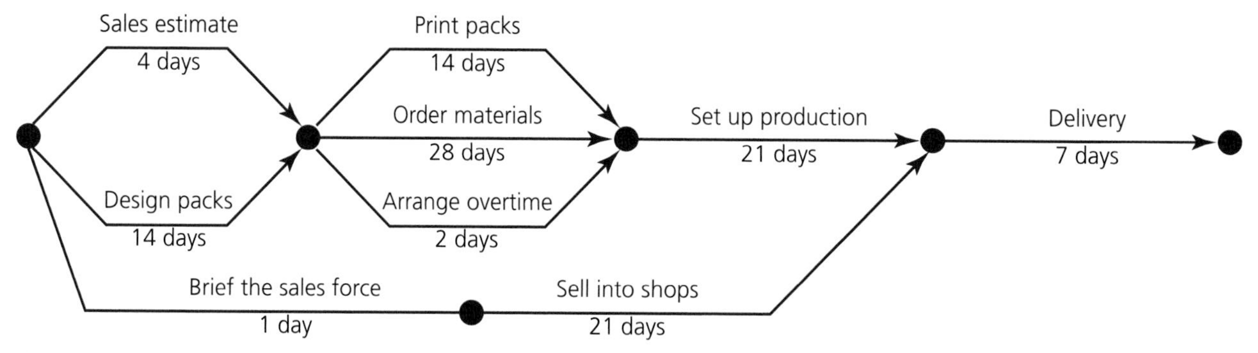

Figure 14.2 '3p off' network (1)

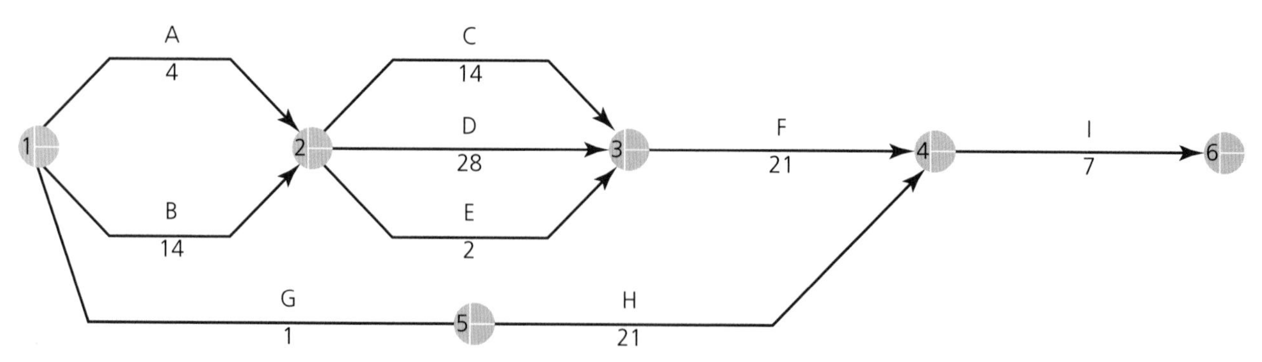

Figure 14.3 '3p off' network (2)

14.4 Earliest start times and latest finish times

Space has also been left in the nodes in Figure 14.3 for two more numbers: the earliest start time (EST) and the latest finish time (LFT). The EST shows the earliest time at which following activities can be started. On Figure 14.3, activities C, D and E can begin after 14 days, because that's when A and B are both finished.

Figure 14.3 shows the complete network, including all the ESTs. Note that the start of a project is always taken as 0 rather than 1. Therefore activities C, D and E can start on day 0 + 14 = 14. Activity F can start on 0 + 14 + 28 = 42. And the earliest the project can be completed is by day 0 + 14 + 28 + 21 + 7 = 70.

Calculating the ESTs provides two key pieces of information:

1 the earliest date that certain resources will be needed, such as skilled workers, raw materials or machinery; this avoids tying up working capital unnecessarily, for instance by buying inventory today that will not be used until next month

2 the earliest completion date for the whole project (this is the EST on the final node).

The EST on the final node shows the earliest date at which the project can be completed. So when is the latest completion date that a manager would find acceptable? As time is money, and customers want deliveries as fast as possible, if next Wednesday is possible, the manager will set it as the latest acceptable date. This is known as the latest finish time (LFT).

The LFT shows the time by which an activity must be completed. These times are recorded in the bottom right-hand section of the nodes. The LFT shows the latest finish time of preceding activities. The number 42 in the bottom right-hand section of node 5 (Figure 14.5) shows that activity G must be finished by day 42 in order to give activities H and I time to be completed by day 70.

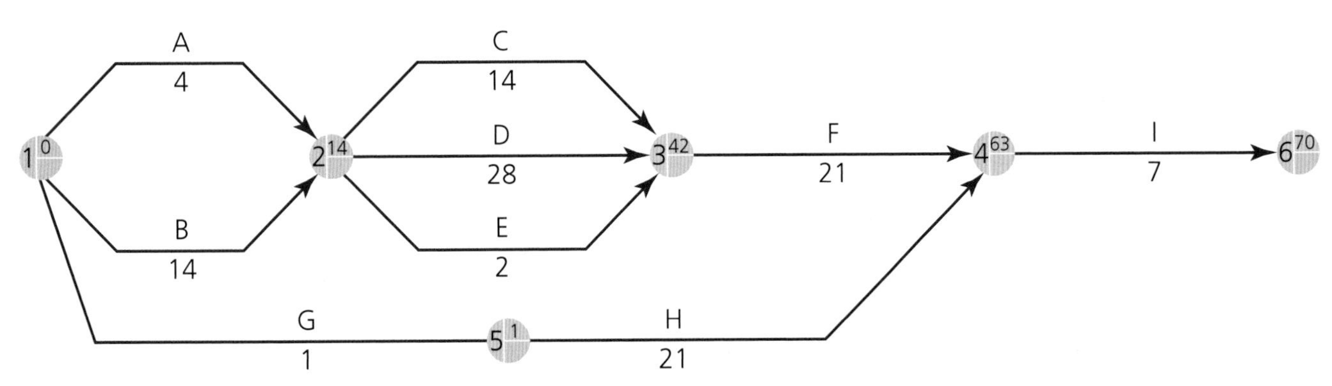

Figure 14.4 '3p off' network (3)

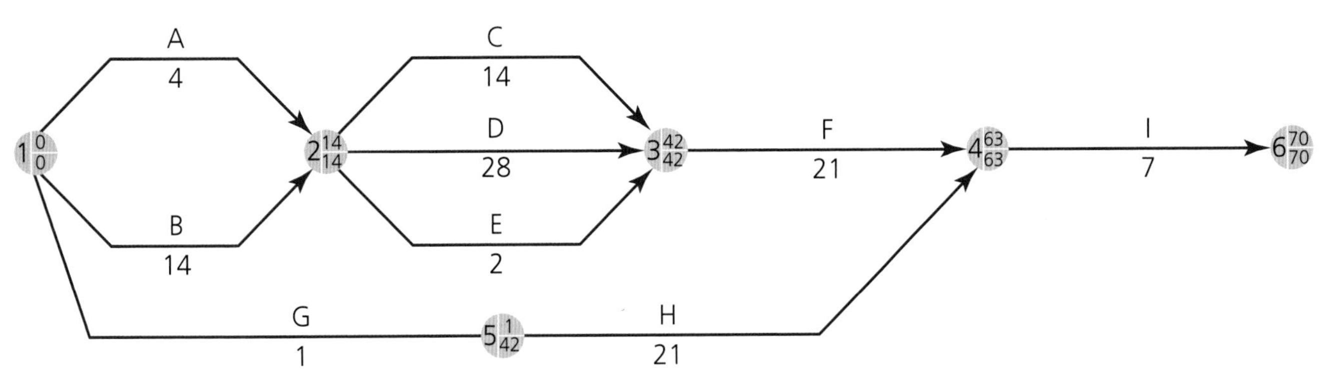

Figure 14.5 '3p off' network (4)

The LFTs on activities are calculated from right to left. In node 6 the LFT is 70, because that is the latest a manager would want the project to finish. Node 4 shows the LFT for activities F and H. Both must be finished by day 63, to leave seven days for activity I to be completed.

Calculating the LFTs provides three main pieces of information:

1. It provides the deadlines that *must* be met in order for the project to be completed on time.
2. It helps to identify the activities that have '**float time**' – in other words, some slack between the EST and the LFT; activity H can be started on day 1 and must be finished by day 63, but takes only 21 days to complete; so there is no rush to complete it.
3. It identifies the critical path.

14.5 The critical path

The critical path comprises the activities that take longest to complete. They determine the length of the whole project. In this case, it is activities B, D, F and I. These are the activities that must not be delayed by even one day. For then the whole project will be late. With C, a delay would not matter. There are 28 days to complete a task that takes only 14. But D is on the critical path, so this 28-day activity must be completed in no more than 28 days.

Identifying the critical path allows managers to apply **management by exception**; in other words, focusing on exceptionally important tasks, rather than spreading their efforts thinly. Of the nine activities within the 3p off network, only the four critical ones need to absorb management time. The others need far less supervision.

If a supervisor sees a possibility that an activity on the critical path might overrun, she or he can consider shifting labour or machinery across from a non-critical task. In this way the project completion date can be kept intact.

To identify the critical path, the two key points are:

1. It will be on activities where the nodes show the EST and LFT to be the same.
2. It is the longest path through those nodes.

When drawing a network, the critical path is identified by striking two short lines across the critical activities (see Figure 14.6).

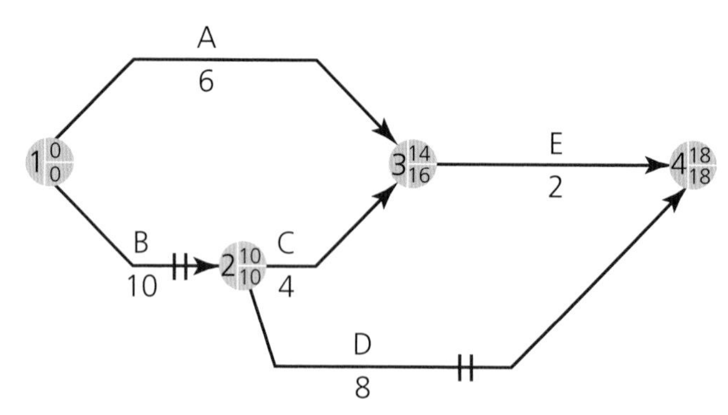

Figure 14.6 Indicating the critical path

14.6 Float time (non-critical activities)

Float is the spare time available for the completion of any activity. If an activity that takes three days must be completed within a week, there are four days of float time. These can be used to complete the task in a leisurely way, perhaps switching half the staff to another task. Alternatively, the task could be started on day four.

There are different ways of measuring float time, but this A level focuses solely on 'total float'. This measures the spare time available so that there is no delay to the overall project completion time. To work out the total float on any specific activity the following formula is required:

LFT (this activity) – duration – EST (this activity) = Total float

Applying this formula to Figure 14.5 gives the following calculations for total float times:

	LFT (this activity)	Minus duration	Minus LFT (this activity)	= Total float
Activity A	16	6	0	10
Activity B	10	10	0	0
Activity C	16	4	10	2
Activity D	18	8	10	0
Activity E	18	2	14	2

Table 14.1 Calculating total float

Note that the critical activities (B and D) have zero float time. This will always be the case. Once managers have calculated the total float on specific activities, they might get the job done straight away, then switch staff to other activities. Or the managers may allow staff the extra time to give more thought to the activity. For example, designing a new logo may need only two days, but it may well be that a better logo could be designed in five.

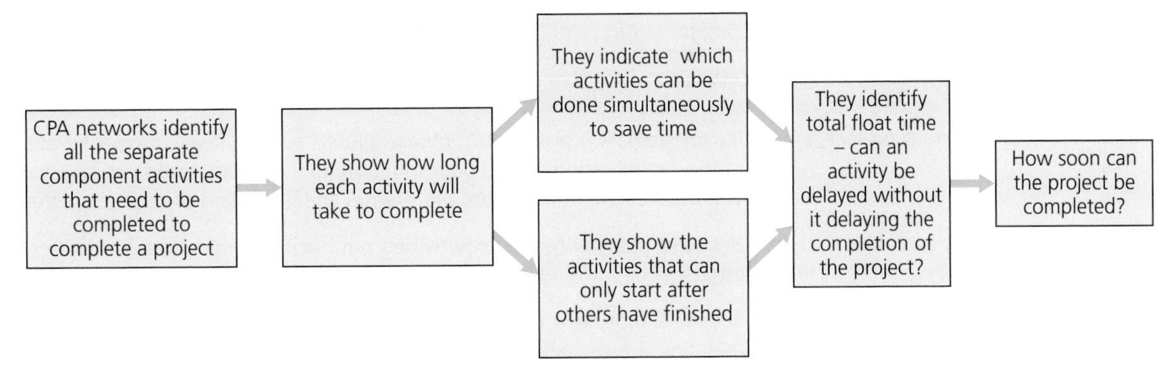

Figure 14.7 Logic chain: what do CPA network diagrams show?

14.7 Benefits and limitations of using network (critical path) analysis

Benefits

The benefits of using network (critical path) analysis are set out below.

- It requires careful planning of the order in which events need to occur, and the length of time each one should take. This should improve the smooth operation of an important project such as a new product launch.
- By identifying events that can be carried out simultaneously, it shortens the length of time taken to complete a project. This is an important element in the modern business focus upon time-based management. For example, if a law is passed that allows 14-year-olds to ride motorbikes with engines of less than 40cc, the first company to design and launch a suitable product would do extremely well.
- The resources needed for each activity can be ordered or hired no earlier than their scheduled EST. In this way cash outflows are postponed as long as possible, and the working capital tied up in the project is minimised.
- If the completion of an activity is delayed for some reason, the network diagram is a good starting point for working out the implications and deciding on appropriate courses of action.

Limitations

The limitations of critical path analysis are set out below.

- A complex project (such as the construction of the super-fast railway HS2) entails so many activities that a drawing becomes unmanageable. Fortunately, computers can zoom in and out of drawings, enabling small parts of the network to be magnified and examined.
- Drawing a diagram does not, in itself, ensure the effective management of a project. Network analysis provides a plan, but can only be as successful as the staff's commitment to it. This suggests that staff should be consulted about the schedule and the likely duration of the activities.
- The value of the network diagram is reduced slightly because the activity lines are not in proportion to the duration of the activities.

Real business

Delays can cost billions

In April 2015, American Airlines (AA) took delivery of its first Boeing 787 'Dreamliner'. It was three years late. AA placed the order for 42 787s in 2008, with a promised delivery date of 2012. That slipped back steadily into 2014, then 2015.

The problem arose because of difficulties with the new lightweight materials being used in the plane. The most serious was a redesign announced in 2009 to 'reinforce an area within the side-of-body section' of the plane! The direct cost to Boeing has been estimated at more than £4 billion. The indirect effects are no less severe. Before Boeing admitted that its project was behind schedule, its European rival Airbus was struggling to sell its competitor A350 plane. After Boeing's production delays became clear, Virgin Atlantic announced it was cancelling its Boeing order to buy Airbus planes. In 2010, Boeing received net orders for the Dreamliner of 36 planes, while Airbus enjoyed net orders for 78 A350s. Three years later the same issue continued to dog Boeing, with the Airbus 350 outselling the Dreamliner.

When the design problem became the critical one for Boeing, management failed to find a successful way of coping. In this case, poor critical path analysis cost Boeing £billions.

(Source: Airbus and Boeing websites: www.airbus.com and www.boeing.co.uk)

Five whys and a how

Questions	Answers
Why is it important to complete a project as soon as possible?	It's cheaper: if a project can be completed quickly, it will carry a smaller share of the organisation's fixed costs. In addition, customers do not like waiting. The quicker the completion, the greater the likelihood of repeat purchase.
Why is it important to identify activities that lie along a project's critical path?	Because delays on critical activities put back the final completion date for the project.
Why is it important to identify and calculate total float?	Activities that have float time are non-critical. They can be delayed without affecting the project's completion date. If a critical activity is delayed, resources can be transferred from other activities that have float time.
Why is it important to identify activities that can be completed simultaneously?	The goal should be to complete the project as soon as possible. If two activities can be carried out at the same time, they should be. It'll speed up the whole project.
Why is it important to calculate earliest start times and latest finish times?	This will help to ensure that specialist staff are only hired when needed. Don't hire bricklayers at the beginning of a project when they won't be needed for at least three weeks until the foundations are dug.
How do firms set about drawing network diagrams?	They identify all the component activities and estimate how long each will take to complete. Then they decide on the correct order for tackling the activities. Then they decide which activities can be carried out simultaneously. Now the critical path diagram can be drawn.

Key terms

Critical path: the activities that must be completed on time for the project to finish on time. In other words, they have no float time at all.

Float time: any spare time that arises between the completion of an activity and the starting time for the next.

Management by exception: the principle that because managers cannot supervise every activity within the organisation, they should focus their energies on the most important issues.

Network: a diagram showing all the activities needed to complete a project, the order in which they must be completed and the critical path.

Network analysis: breaking a project down into its component parts, to identify the sequence of activities involved.

'The P in PM is as much about People Management as it is about Project Management.'

Cornelius Fichtner, management consultant

'Time is the only commodity that's irreplaceable: invest it, share it, spend it ... never waste it.'

Tracy Sherwood, author

'Nothing is less productive than to make more efficient what should not be done at all.'

Peter Drucker, management guru

14.8 Critical Path Analysis – evaluation

The cliché 'time is money' has been around for years. Only recently, though, have systems such as just-in-time focused clearly on time-based management. Time is vital not only because it affects costs, but also because it can provide a crucial marketing edge. Primark's key advantage over Marks & Spencer is that it is much quicker at getting catwalk fashions into high-street shops. So time can add value. Careful production planning can also help to get a firm's new product to the market before the competition.

Critical Path Analysis is a valuable practical tool for taking time seriously. It involves careful planning and can be used as a way of monitoring progress. If critical activities are falling behind schedule, action can be taken quickly. This serves as a reminder that successful business management is not just about clever strategic thinking. Ultimately, success depends upon what happens at the workplace or at the construction site.

14.9 Workbook

Revision questions

(30 marks; 30 minutes)

1 Identify two objectives of Critical Path Analysis. (2)

2 Distinguish between an activity and a project. (2)

3 State three key rules for drawing networks. (3)

4 Explain how to calculate the earliest start time for an activity. (4)

5 Why is it important to calculate the latest finish time on an activity? (4)

6 What is meant by 'the critical path' and how do you identify it? (4)

7 Explain why it would be useful to know which activities have float times available. (3)

8 Explain the value of Critical Path Analysis for a small firm in financial difficulties. (4)

9 Explain how the use of Critical Path Analysis could help a firm's management of time. (4)

Revision activities

Data response 1

Activity	Preceded by	Duration (weeks)
A		6
B		4
C		10
D	A & B	5
E	A & B	7
F	D	3

Table 14.2 Data for constructing a network

Questions (40 marks; 40 minutes)

1 a) Construct a network from the information given in Table 14.2. (6)

b) Number the nodes and put in the earliest start times. (4)

2 a) Draw the following network:

Activity A and B start the project. C and D follow A. E follows all other jobs. (6)

b) Work out the earliest start times of the activities and put them in the nodes if, in the above question, A lasts 2 days, B = 9 days, C = 3, D = 4, E = 7. (4)

3 a) Use the information given in Table 14.3 to construct a fully labelled network showing ESTs, LFTs and the critical path. (12)

Activity	Preceded by	Duration
A	–	3
B	–	9
C	–	2
D	A	5
E	C	3
F	B, D, E	5
G	C	9

Table 14.3 Data for constructing a fully labelled network

b) If the firm were offered a £2,000 bonus for completing the project in twelve days, which activities should managers focus upon? Explain why. (8)

Data response 2

Every Friday needs managing

Last Friday had been a washout. Claire, Bren, Alliyah and Ruth had dithered over what to wear, where to go and how to get there, and ended up watching a rotten film in Bren's bedroom. This week was going to be different. Bren had just been taught critical path analysis and she was determined to use it to 'project manage' Friday night. As it was Bren's birthday on Friday, the others had to agree.

They sat down on Tuesday to agree all the activities needed for a great night out. They started by focusing on the activities:

Alliyah: We have the best nights when we start at Harry's Bar for a couple of hours, then on to the Orchid at about midnight.

Claire: I like Harry's but prefer RSVP; no argument, though, we should go to the Orchid.

After half an hour back and forth, the agreement was Harry's at 9.00 and the Orchid at 12.00.

Then they realised that there was a lot more to it than that. It would take half an hour to get to Harry's and they'd have to get ready beforehand: bath, hair, nails, make-up. And what about the preceding activities? Shopping for a new top ... and shoes ... and earrings ... and getting some highlights done.

They argued about which comes first, a top and then shoes and earrings to match? Or the other way round? It was time for Bren to set it all out. See Table 14.4.

Activity		Preceded by	Duration
A	Booking a hair and nails appointment	–	0.1 hours
B	Clothes shopping	–	4 hours
C	Shopping for shoes	–	3 hours
D	Shopping for earrings	B, C	1 hour
E	Hair and nails appointment	A	2 hours
F	Bath	D, E	1 hour
G	Make-up and get dressed	F	1 hour
H	Constant phone conversations	–	24/7

Table 14.4 Activities required for a night out

Questions (20 marks; 25 minutes)

1 Draw up Bren's critical path diagram, to help plan her birthday. (8)

2 Calculate the float time available on activities D and E. (4)

3 Assess two factors that might cause Bren's critical path network to prove inaccurate. (8)

Data response 3

Slightly Mad delays Project Cars

The video games industry has grown enormously over the last decade. Slightly Mad Studios is a London-based company that produces video games for PS4, Xbox and Nintendo Wii.

Gamers are notoriously fickle. As a result, the typical video game tends to have a very short life cycle. This means that in order to survive, companies like Slightly Mad Studios must constantly innovate and come up with new games that excite the imagination.

In early 2013, designers at Slightly Mad began to develop a new driving game called Project Cars. The goal was to create the most authentic driving experience for gamers. Developing new games is usually a very expensive business. To help raise the finance needed to develop Project Cars, Slightly Mad Studios asked gamers to crowdfund the project. In return for their money, gamers would receive a share of the profits generated from Project Cars. The crowdfunding project succeeded, and over £6 million was raised. The plan was for the new game to be available for Christmas 2014.

In October 2014, the news broke that the release date for Project Cars had been delayed until March 2015. According to Project director Andy Garton: 'This delay has come about because a couple of other big games are launching around the same time as our planned first date. ... This would have had a very significant impact on our initial sales.'

The boss of Slightly Mad Studios, Ian Bell, also tried to explain the delay by stating that: 'Our goal has always been to deliver a landmark title that encompasses the wishes and desires of racing fans from all around the world; something with features and content powered by the community that provide a truly unforgettable and pioneering experience.'

Questions (30 marks; 35 minutes)

1 Assess how video game companies, such as Slightly Mad Games, might benefit from using critical path analysis. (10)

2 Evaluate Andy Garton's view that delaying the launch of Project Cars until March 2015 will help the company to maximise its revenues. (20)

15 Corporate influences

Definition

Corporate influences are internal factors affecting business decisions including short- versus long-term horizons and scientific versus intuitive approaches to decision-making.

Linked to: Corporate objectives, Ch 1; SWOT analysis, Ch 4; Ratio analysis, Ch 20; Key factors in change, Ch 23

15.1 Introduction to corporate timescales

In October 2009, two years into the life of his brainchild Fresh & Easy (Tesco USA), boss Terry Leahy dismissed the one-year trading loss of $259 million by saying: 'we have been making good progress in developing the Fresh & Easy business'. Actually its 130 American stores were losing $2 million each per year. Oddly, Terry Leahy saw these facts as short-term problems that would seem unimportant in the long term. He hoped to create 1,000 Tesco stores in America and challenge Wal-Mart (the world's number one retailer). Now, with the benefit of hindsight, and the closure of the whole operation, it is clear that the £2 billion Tesco wasted on the whole venture was due to confusion between short- and long-term data analysis. Leahy thought the data was a short-term misreading of the long term. In fact it told exactly the right story: Tesco had nothing to offer the US grocery market.

15.2 Corporate timescales: causes and effects of short-termism

Short-termism is when the actions of managers show an obsession with immediate issues rather than long-term ones. Often such managers will use lots of long-term words such as mission, aims, strategy and legacy; but staff will soon learn when the real spur to action is this year or this month's budget. In a report on the topic, the Institute of Directors produced an interesting list of possible symptoms of short-termism:

- inadequate expenditure on research and development
- accounting adjustments that inflate current earnings
- a bias towards high dividend payouts and share buybacks, at the expense of investment
- adoption of executive pay schemes that reward achievement of short-term financial goals
- overly zealous cuts in employment levels, which destroy the company's stock of human capital
- a disregard for longer-term risks in the company's products, services or business strategy
- an excessive focus on acquisitions rather than organic growth.

The causes of short-termism

The most commonly cited explanation of short-termism by UK companies is the relationship with financial markets; many people believe that the plc structure encourages short-termism. Many years ago Richard Branson's Virgin Group was a publicly quoted plc; he eventually took the group private because he hated the pressures to prioritise immediate results over long-term strategy. The reason for these pressures is simple: City investors are more important today than private shareholders, and the City traders are measured on a quarterly basis. Pension funds controlling £billions judge their main advisors and investors every three months, to measure performance against a **stock market index** such as the FTSE 100. So if City investors are measured every three months, no wonder those investors care passionately about the short-term performance of the companies they've invested in.

Other important causes of short-termism:

- The widespread use in the City of short-term focused performance measures such as **Earnings Per Share** (EPS) as a way of judging the bonus level to be paid to the directors: EPS can be boosted by the ultimate

short-termism measure: buying shares back from shareholders; this boosts a company's debt level yet creates a higher share price and therefore bonus level.
- The threat of takeover: when share prices are high there is usually a fashion for making takeover bids. So companies like to make it harder (and more expensive) by boosting their short-term profit.
- The bosses of UK firms are unusually likely to have had a career based in finance: therefore they have no inherent understanding of the long-term thinking that is more instinctive among engineers, scientists and marketing executives. In Germany and Japan, engineers often become the chief executive.

The effects of short-termism

The most important effect of short-termism is underestimating or ignoring the opportunities that may exist in the long term. Primark's fashion/value retail positioning has long made it a natural for China. But Primark keeps opening safety-first stores in Britain and none in China. Quite probably it's now too late to enter this, the world's second biggest market for fashion clothes. By contrast Arsenal FC spent £400 million on the move from Highbury (35,000 capacity) to the Emirates Stadium (capacity 60,000). This showed the board's ability to think about the long-term interests of the club. Interestingly this 'long-termist' example is from a private company, not a plc.

Other effects of short-termism include:

- reluctance to invest in capacity, training, research and development and perhaps also in image-building advertising
- decisions that seem wise in the short term, but not down the line, such as when Waterstones sold its online book sales division – to Amazon!
- performance reward systems may over-focus on short-term gains, encouraging staff to achieve profit today even if it's at the expense of tomorrow; in the ten years to 2015 WHSmith constantly pushed their prices up; this was great for short-term profit but at the expense of long-term market share.

'Any jerk can have short-term earnings. You squeeze, squeeze, squeeze, and the company sinks five years later.'

Jack Welch, business super-leader

'Short-termism curtails ambition, inhibits long-term thinking and provides a disincentive to invest in research, new capabilities, products, training, recruitment and skills.'

Sir George Cox, businessman

15.3 Long-term thinking: the German Mittelstand

For many years big business in Britain has meant publicly listed companies, with shares bought and sold on the stock market. Generally the value of the British stock market is around 100–120 per cent of the value of annual GDP (the national income). Germany, by contrast, has a business sector dominated by world-class, medium-sized but family-owned and -run businesses – the **Mittelstand**. The value of the German stock market is only about 40 per cent of the value of annual German GDP. So whereas the business pages of British papers are dominated by the latest results from plcs, in Germany there is more likely to be reporting on business issues and market opportunities.

When Germans are asked about their Mittelstand, they mention two things: family-owned and humane management. Economists would add in two other features: long-term thinking and a focus on doing one thing well. The latter means that the typical Mittelstand firm is a world leader in a limited field, such as diesel car exhaust systems. A 2013 German government report showed that Germany had 20 times more 'world market leaders' than the UK – and strikingly more than America (see Figure 15.2). This is great for exports but also works well for employment, with the Mittelstand employing nearly 60 per cent of the German workforce, but 80 per cent of all trainees.

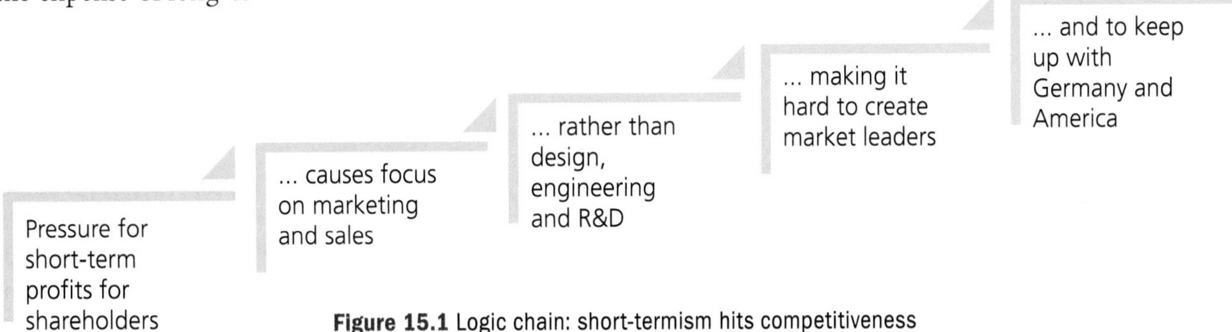

Figure 15.1 Logic chain: short-termism hits competitiveness

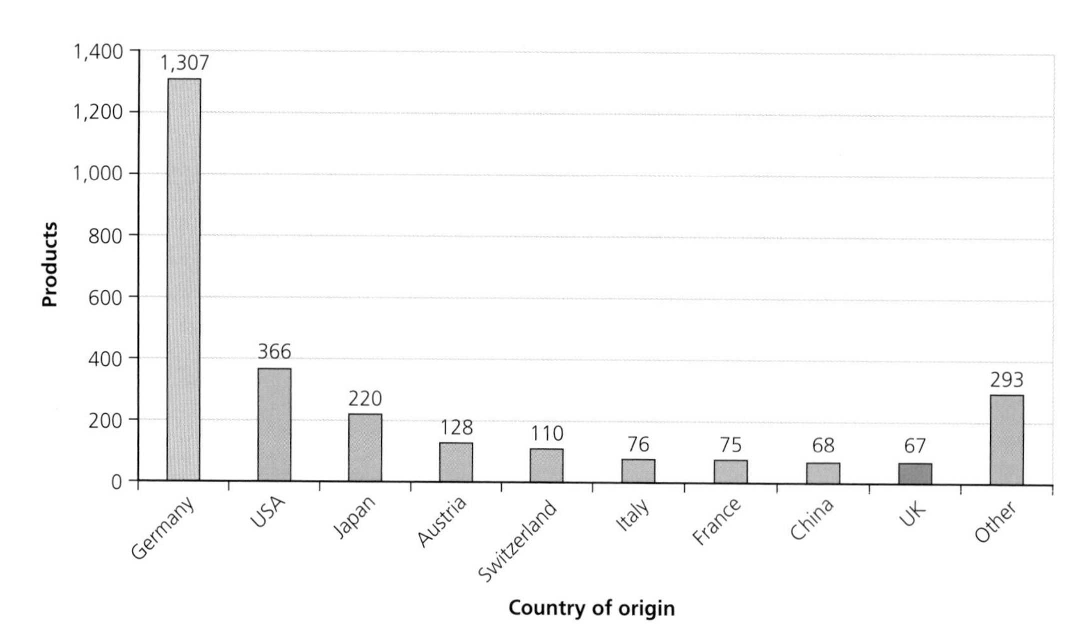

Figure 15.2 World market-leading products by country of origin (source: German Federal Ministry of Economics and Technology 2013)

The amazing success story of the German Mittelstand must be contrasted with the plc. First and foremost legal requirements force large plcs to report on profits and trading every six months. Then City analysts and the media will pore over the figures and declare the business a 'star' or a 'dog'. Tesco was unbeatable until it suddenly became untouchable. Every chief executive is in thrall to 'the market' and has to organise strategy and publicity accordingly.

The result is an excessive focus on the next set of results. This is rather more like the life of a Premier League manager than makes any sense. This helps to explain how a business such as Marks & Spencer can spend 20 years, under many different bosses – all failing to address the company's underlying problems. Long-term strategy can become empty words in the short-termist world of the plc.

	Plc	Mittelstand
Typical financial structure	Strong base of share capital with moderate gearing	Strong base of share capital with moderate gearing
Typical ownership structure	Owned by many, relatively small shareholders	Family-owned or majority family-owned with some shares listed on the stock market
Typical approach to spending on R&D and trainee staff	Varies, but many will look for a low-spend model with high levels of outsourcing (and low investment in staff)	Desire for very long-term success and a sense of moral duty creates a culture of investment in people and technology
Typical business objectives	Maximise short-term share price to keep the market happy, and to enjoy a big bonus due to the high share price	Maintain a world-leading position to hand over a continuingly successful business to the next generation

Table 15.1 The short-termist plc vs the long-termist Mittelstand

'The result of long term relationships (with suppliers) is better and better quality and lower and lower costs.'

W. Edwards Deming, quality guru

15.4 Evidence-based versus subjective decision-making

Evidence-based (or 'scientific') decision-making is becoming increasingly dominated by computers. For example, a McDonald's store manager is sent details of how many staff should be employed every hour for next Saturday. The computer makes the 'decision' based on a sales forecast using data from last year and recent weeks. In this way the decision-making can be 'scientific' – in the sense that it is based on objective, numerical data – as opposed to **intuition**, that is subjective decision-making.

When the decision is more strategic, by definition there will be more uncertainty. When Whitbread plc decided to back Costa Coffee, it couldn't know that it would be able to build the business from 50 outlets to 3,000 (including 350 in China). So computer programs can't punch out answers. Therefore there is a far greater need for opinion-based, subjective judgement. Whitbread made a brilliant call; Morrisons made a disastrous one when it bought online site Kiddicare for £70 million in 2011 and sold it for £2 million in 2014!

Evidence-based decision-making is the goal for most firms because it suggests a method that can be applied in a routine way to measure opportunities or problems. When considering whether to launch a proposed new product, large companies like to have a testing system that they can use for every proposal. Then, over time, enough data is gathered to start making accurate forecasts.

Real business

The *Grocer* magazine regularly features independent research into new product launches using a system called Cambridge Fast Foodfax. It uses various quantitative measures to test the likelihood of sales success. From the answers to those questions a rating score is devised. A look at the data below shows why Marks & Spencer felt optimistic about sales of its new lemonade.

From *The Grocer*: 2–9 August 2014	Asda Choc Chip Muffin Cheesecake £1.50	Cadbury Dairy Milk Banana Caramel Crisp £2.99	M&S Still Blackcurrant Lemonade £1.00
Pre-trial purchase	49%	46%	44%
Post-trial purchase	44%	39%	48%
Better than what's out there	30%	37%	54%
New and different	59%	93%	89%
Overall score	38/50	37/50	41/50

Table 15.2 Objective evidence about the potential of new product ideas

On these measures experience has shown that a score of 45+ shows a product of huge potential. Between 40 and 44 also shows promise. This approach enables big firms to scrap unpromising new products before taking them to market.

Evidence-based decision-making

The desire for a scientific approach to management dates back, at least, to F.W. Taylor and the late nineteenth century. Taylor wanted managers to find the 'one best way' to do things, and then instruct and incentivise workers to follow that one best method. Taylor believed in 'time and motion' studies that measured exactly how and when workers completed certain tasks. He also advocated high division of labour, forcing staff to do simple, repetitive tasks in the workplace. With simple tasks came ease of measurement; and from there it was only a short step to the business saying: 'measurement is management'. In other words, once you start measuring things in the workplace, staff pay more attention and start behaving differently.

Today managers still want to control business variables, from absenteeism to morale. They also want to control external variables as much as possible. So sales are forecast with great precision, and computer software is used to model every foreseeable situation, e.g. an August bank holiday with cloudy but not rainy weather. Evidence-based management tries to take the art out of business decision-making – replacing subjectivity with facts and quantitative forecasts.

Figure 15.3 Forecasting can help estimate sales given any potential condition, for example a cloudy bank holiday weekend in August

Good business decisions	Bad business decisions
Coca-Cola buys Innocent Drinks – giving it a real competitor to PepsiCo's Tropicana. The £200 million deal was completed in 2013	Waterstones bookshop decides to stop selling books online, because 'online will never be more than 10% of the market'
In June 2000, Nick Robertson and Quentin Griffiths launch 'As Seen on Screen'; first year sales are £3.6m. By 2014 ASOS has sales of £1,000 million.	Malcolm Walker, owner of Iceland Frozen Foods, takes the business upmarket – focusing on organic products: it didn't last
Unloved Mondelez (owner of Cadbury) launched Belvita Breakfast Biscuits in 2010. The grocery trade laughed at the idea, but by 2013 Belvita sales had grown to £58 million – that's more than Jaffa Cakes	Rupert Murdoch, media mogul, sells MySpace website for \$35m, having bought it for \$580m six years before
With recession biting, Waitrose launched its Essentials range of lower-priced groceries. By 2015 sales of Essentials exceeded £1 billion a year and Waitrose extended the range to 400 more items	Nestlé re-launches its Willy Wonka chocolate bar range in 2013 (sales were poor when it first launched in 2005); time is no healer and the whole range was discontinued in 2014

Table 15.3 Some good and some awful real business decisions

'The best class of scientific mind is the same as the best class of business mind. The great desideratum in either case is to know how much evidence is enough to warrant action.'

Samuel Butler, British novelist (1835–1902)

'Whenever decisions are made strictly on the basis of bottom-line arithmetic, human beings get crunched along with the numbers.'

Thomas Horton, US business leader

Five whys and a how

Questions	Answers
Why is business short-termism a problem for the British economy?	Because it limits our ability to innovate and makes it hard for engineering and manufacturing to grow and thrive – stifling economic growth.
Why doesn't a government change the rules, and allow financial reporting only once a year? Wouldn't that help?	It probably would help. Perhaps only allow an interim, six-month report in exceptional circumstances. It would take a degree of short-term pressure off the back of plc bosses.
Why doesn't the UK build a Mittelstand like Germany?	It's enormously difficult to change a national culture: in Britain, business is about making money; in Germany it's about building something great.
Why may middle managers be inclined to make decisions made on short-term criteria?	Because they are focused more on their next career step than on the long-term best interests of the whole business.
Why might 'short-termism curtail ambition' (quote from Sir George Cox, page 103)?	It's hard to have ambitions about the future when you're trying to cope with short-term pressures.
How can a firm make sure to take evidence-based decisions?	By gathering as much numerical data as possible and weighing it up using a standardised method such as decision trees (see Chapter 13).

15.5 Corporate influences – evaluation

A surprising feature of business is that whereas middle managers have to justify their decisions with evidence and data, those at the top are able to make subjective, quite personal decisions. Sometimes these come off, as with the launch of Apple's iPod and iPhone. On other occasions, they can be massive mistakes, as with the RBS purchase of ABN Amro Bank (loss: at least £50 billion), Tesco's launch into America (a mere £2 billion loss) and BP's careless attitude to safety in the Gulf of Mexico (which will end up costing more than \$50 billion, not to mention the appalling environmental impact).

Ultimately, though, the style of decision matters little compared with the issue of timescale. RBS was in too much of a hurry to win a battle against Barclays – and ended up with a dog. And BP's attitude to safety was probably influenced by a determination to meet short-term profit targets. Businesses that can take a long-term view will usually outstrip those that are focused on the next set of financial results.

Key terms

Earnings Per Share: company profits after tax divided by the number of shares issued; a rising EPS makes it easy to pay out rising dividends to shareholders.

Intuition: deducing something from circumstances without any direct evidence.

Mittelstand: the family-owned small and medium-sized businesses that are the backbone of the German economy.

Stock market index: a weighted average of the share prices of many companies are added together, adjusted to equal 100, then measured for percentage change over time.

15.6 Workbook

Revision questions

(30 marks; 30 minutes)

1 Explain one possible reason why Terry Leahy wanted to 'challenge Wal-Mart' (see Section 15.1). (4)

2 Explain why 'inadequate expenditure on research and development' might be a symptom of short-termism (see Section 15.2). (4)

3 Explain one possible benefit to a company if it appoints an engineer rather than an accountant to the role of chief executive. (4)

4 Explain why 'City analysts' play an important role in creating a business culture of short-termism. (4)

5 Explain why subjective thinking may be more important for a long-term, strategic decision than for a short-term one. (4)

6 Outline two factors that might undermine the accuracy of the data used in an evidence-based decision. (6)

7 Explain what Thomas Horton meant in the quote shown on page 106. (4)

Revision activities

Data response

Why strategy matters – Topshop, Zara and China

Back in 2002, when Philip Green bought Arcadia (Topshop), it and Inditex (Zara) were of a similar size. By 2013/2014 Inditex was making nearly 20 times more profit than Arcadia. Topshop was and is a retail jewel, with the potential to be huge internationally. It is a retail brand suited perfectly to the emerging young middle classes in China. But by early 2015, Zara owned over 150 stores in China and its owner Inditex had become the world's biggest clothes retailer. Topshop has no stores in China and is a minnow globally. What went wrong?

Green appears regularly in lists of Britain's most admired businesspeople. Yet a simple look at Arcadia's performance since 2002 makes it hard to see why. Britain needs business successes such as Zara, creating jobs and earnings from overseas. Why couldn't Topshop have achieved what Zara has? (In the graph of Zara vs Topshop, the actual figures are for Zara's owner Inditex vs Topshop's owner Arcadia Ltd.)

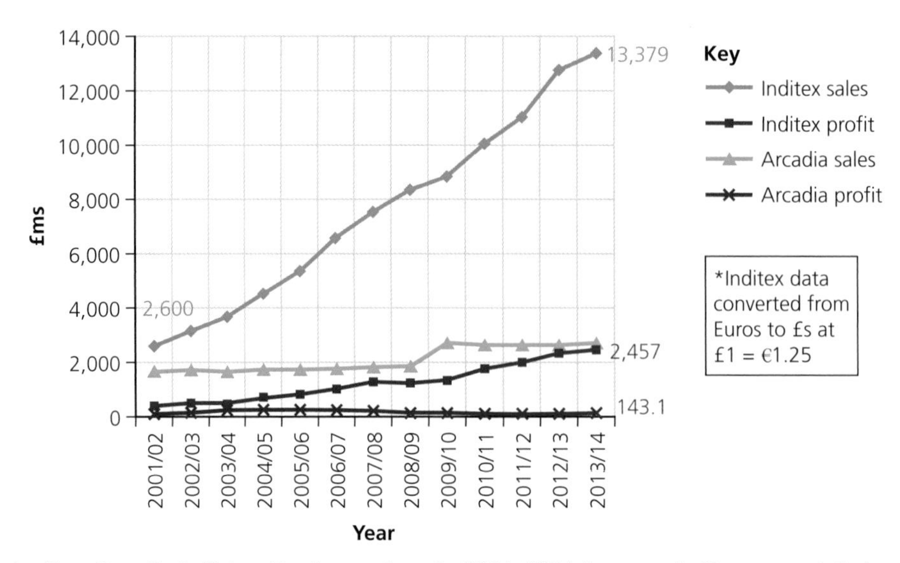

Figure 15.4 Booming Zara/Arcadia flatlining: Topshop vs Arcadia 2001–2014 (sources: Inditex accounts*; Arcadia press releases)

Zara began in 1975 and has grown thanks to the desire by owner Amancio Ortega to create something of lasting value. At a time when his rivals were getting all their clothes made in the Far East, Ortega was proud that more than half his supplies came from Spain and Portugal. His company Inditex has been famous for its long-term approach to the clothing industry, with care taken over suppliers, staff and the environment.

Cleverly, Zara turned its west European production into an advantage – being able to respond more quickly than others to changes in catwalk fashion. Today Zara delivers brand new designs twice a week to its stores worldwide, and can respond very quickly to any strong new trend. From early on, Zara adopted lean production as its way of working. Constant attacks on wastage suited Ortega's approach to business, as did minimising the amount of cash tied up in stock.

By contrast, Sir Philip Green's business has stood still for ten years, perhaps in part because of his famously short-term way of looking at investment. His rule of thumb has always been a twelve-month pay-back period – which is exceptionally rapid. Therefore only sure-fire, ultra-profitable investments work out. In Table 15.4 sales jumped in 2009 solely because Green decided to merge BHS in with the rest of Arcadia. Excluding that, there has been no significant growth.

	Arcadia sales (£millions)	Arcadia profits (£millions)
2006/07	£1,850	£293
2007/08	£1,840	£275
2008/09	£1,900	£214
2009/10	£2,800	£213
2010/11	£2,680	£133
2011/12	£2,679	£167
2012/13	£2,683	£148
2013/14	£2,707	£143

Table 15.4 Sales and profits of Arcadia (2006–2014)

It seems that owner Sir Phillip Green has been distracted by other priorities. In 2005, famously, Arcadia declared a £1,200 million dividend to be paid out to the sole shareholder of the business: his wife Mrs Green. As a resident of Monaco, no tax would be paid on this. To find this huge sum, Arcadia needed to borrow £1,000 million, which was not that hard to do in pre-crash 2005. Surely this sum would have been better invested taking Topshop to China. Ironically, it may have made Green more money in the longer term.

Is it too late for Topshop to make it in China? Perhaps not, though the middle-market positioning has been adopted in China by Zara, H&M, Gap and many others. Most striking, however, is the importance of focus on the long-term health of a business: Zara's Ortega had it, Arcadia's Green did not.

Questions (30 marks; 40 minutes)

1 Analyse two possible reasons why Zara (Inditex) was so successful between 2002 and 2014. (10)

2 Using this business example together with any other businesses you're aware of, evaluate whether short-termism is a particular problem for British businesses and businesspeople. (20)

Extended writing

1 Evaluate whether the government should try to tackle short-termism in British business. (20)

2 Former Apple boss John Sculley once said that 'No great marketing decisions have ever been made on quantitative data.' Evaluate whether this proves that subjective decisions are more effective than those based on evidence. (20)

16 Corporate culture

Definition

Corporate culture sums up the spirit, the attitudes, the behaviours and the ethos of an organisation. It is embodied in the people who work there via traditions that have built up over time.

Linked to: Mergers and takeovers, Ch 9; Reasons for staying small, Ch 10; Business ethics, Ch 18; Causes and effects of change, Ch 22; Key factors in change, Ch 23; Cultural and social factors in global marketing, Ch 39

16.1 Introduction

Culture is often described as 'the way we do things round here'. This will be built up over many years as a result of:

- the aims or mission of the business: if the aim is to be innovative, this will affect the business culture
- the behaviour of the company directors and other senior staff: if they pay themselves huge bonuses and jump at chances to fly business class to questionable conferences, staff will pick up the idea that 'me, me, me' is at the heart of the business culture
- the attitude of senior management to enterprise and risk: if an unsuccessful new product launch leads to the dismissal of the manager leading the project, this will send out a message to all staff to beware of taking on responsibility, which could be very damaging in the long term
- the recruitment and training procedures: dynamic companies have a mixture of different types of staff: some organised, some creative but chaotic; some argumentative, some 'yes-men' and so on. Many HR departments use **psychometric tests** to recruit 'our type of person'. The culture could become quite passive – safe but dull – if new recruits have similar backgrounds, personalities and behaviours.

Real business

Cultural differences in India

A recent report on takeovers in India cites cultural differences as a high-risk factor in corporate deals. There are twenty-nine different languages that are spoken by at least a million people in India, and customs and working styles differ significantly between regions. Companies in northern India tend to have more assertive, western cultures, while companies in the south are more traditionally Indian; that is, they have a more formal and subtle culture, emphasising protocol, seniority and indirect communication. Western predator companies often fail to understand these differences, seeing 'Indian' in a one-dimensional way. Indian companies have also come unstuck when trying to bring together two conflicting workplace cultures.

16.2 Strong and weak cultures

Quite recently banks turned their backs on tradition and turned themselves into casinos. For centuries, a culture of caution had been at the heart of banking. The successful banker was one who went through a career without making any awful mistakes. Suddenly this approach was considered old-fashioned. The focus was no longer on building a career; it was on building a bonus. As that bonus might be from £100,000 to £10,000,000 (a year!), who would look any further ahead than the coming months?

Nor was it difficult to make the profits required to get the bonuses. With plentiful cheap money (low interest rates) the clever thing was to borrow lots and lend it out as fast as possible. Why check on whether 'sub-prime' borrowers were likely to default in a year or two, if this year's bonus could be boosted to £500,000?

The collapse of this house of cards in 2008 and 2009 led to a predictable collapse into huge losses within the banking sector (estimated by the World Bank at

$1 trillion). The culture of recklessness and greed had been created by a crazy bonus system that gave people (non-returnable) rewards based on the short term. In the longer term, the shareholders, the bank customers, governments and taxpayers paid the bills.

This example shows that culture is at the heart (or *is* the heart) of every organisation. Even strong, generation-long cultures could be weakened and changed quite quickly, in certain circumstances. More often, businesses find that 'the way we do things round here' is very resistant to change. Strong cultures can be very hard to shift.

The strength of an organisation's culture is often very evident. One school will have a staffroom that is buzzing an hour before the start of the day; another's staff car park will still be empty. One clothes shop will have staff who take their time helping customers, while another's staff joke with each other. And one charity will be focused entirely on the people it is set up to help, while another will behave as if the charity itself is more important than its 'customers'.

Distinguishing between strong and weak cultures is not difficult. It can be summed up in the following:

- an attitude of 'can-do' rather than 'must we?'
- a conviction among staff that the organisation is a force for good (i.e. not just a money-making machine).

Signs of a strong culture	Signs of a weak culture
• Focusing on customers' real needs, allowing staff to make decisions, e.g. refunds	• Staff follow a script when dealing with customers (not trusted to know what's right)
• Staff show a real feeling for the organisation as 'us', as a long-term commitment	• 'Us' tends to be a department, not the business as a whole; and there may even be a feeling of them and us
• A united view among staff that the organisation is a force for good, e.g. staff at Greggs taking pride in the company's support for school breakfast clubs	• A cynical view among many staff, doubting the company's supposed principles and ethos; suspecting that there is too much PR spin; too little commitment
• Sticking together and working together at a time of crisis	• When things look bad, better qualified staff look to find another job

Table 16.1 Strong vs weak corporate culture

Real business

In June 2010 half the top medical staff at Great Ormond Street hospital signed a letter of no confidence in its chief executive, Jane Collins. Consultant Dr Kim Holt told the Daily Telegraph: 'Medical staff have growing concerns over patient care. They feel that Great Ormond Street is not really living up to its reputation.' Another consultant said: 'They (management) are completely unwilling to listen. Anyone who complains is treated as a troublemaker and bullied out.'

Dr Holt went on to report other consultants' view of a 'culture of fear and intimidation' within the hospital. In effect, there was a culture clash between the consultants' traditional view of patient care and the chief executive's desire for change. Even though Home Office government Minister Lynne Featherstone called on Jane Collins to resign in 2011, she only left Great Ormond Street in 2012.

16.3 Handy's classification of company cultures

In his book *Gods of Management,* Professor Charles Handy (Britain's only global business guru) developed four ways of classifying business culture. These are discussed below and can be used to analyse business culture in more depth.

Power cultures

Power cultures are found in organisations in which there is one or a small group of power holders. In effect the boss can become the spider in the middle of the web, with everything going through him or her. There are likely to be few rules or procedures and most communication will be by personal contact. This encourages flexibility among employees. Decision-making is not limited by any code of practice. This can result in questionable, perhaps unethical, actions being taken in an attempt to please the boss. The leadership style in such a situation is clearly autocratic, and has been displayed in recent times by leaders such as Sir Alex Ferguson of Manchester United and Sir Alan Sugar (boss of Amstrad and notorious as the central character in BBC TV's *The Apprentice*).

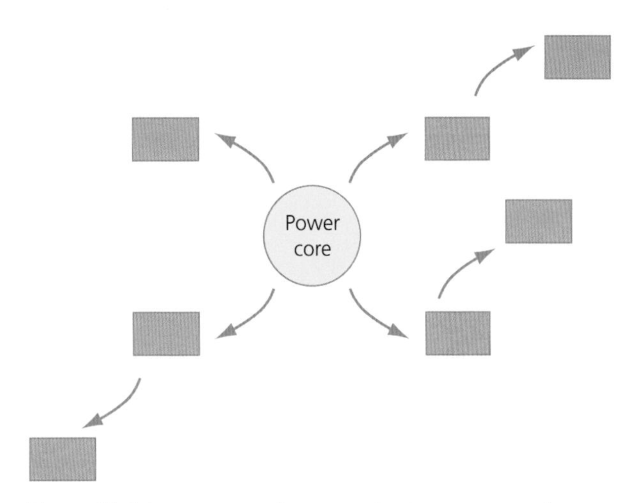

Figure 16.1 In a power culture, a web of power grows from the centre of the organisation

Role cultures

Role cultures are found in established organisations that have developed a lot of formal rules as they have grown. Power depends on the position an individual holds in the business, rather than the qualities of the person themselves. All employees are expected to conform to rules and procedures, and promotion follows a predictable pattern. This culture is **bureaucratic**, cautious and focused on the avoidance of mistakes. It may be appropriate when the competitive environment is stable, for example in industries with long product life cycles. However, if the pace of change becomes more rapid, staff will struggle to adapt to new market conditions. This is the approach taken in businesses such as Microsoft, where the key thing is to preserve its huge share of the software market. The leadership style could be autocratic or paternalistic.

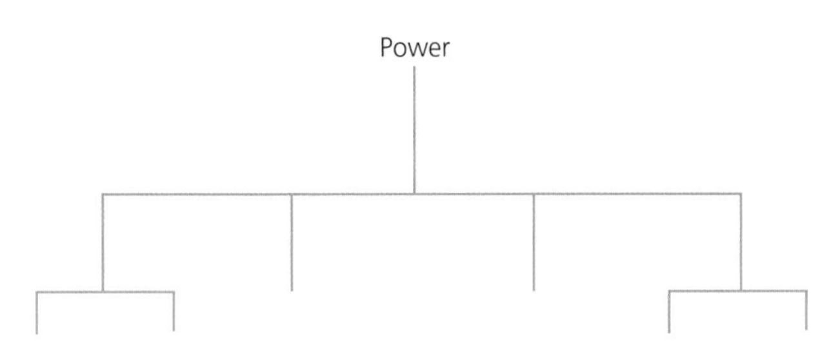

Figure 16.2 In a role culture, power flows down from the top of the organisation

Task cultures

Task cultures have no single power source. Senior managers allocate projects to teams of employees made up of representatives from different functional departments. Each group is formed for the purpose of a single undertaking and is then disbanded. Power within the team lies in the expertise of each individual and is not dependent upon status or role. This culture can be effective in dealing with rapidly changing competitive environments because it is flexible – for example, in markets with short product life cycles. However, project teams may develop their own objectives independently of the firm. The approach to leadership in such organisations is a mixture of paternalistic and democratic. This is just the approach taken by Indra Nooyi, boss of PepsiCo and probably the world's most important businesswoman.

Person cultures

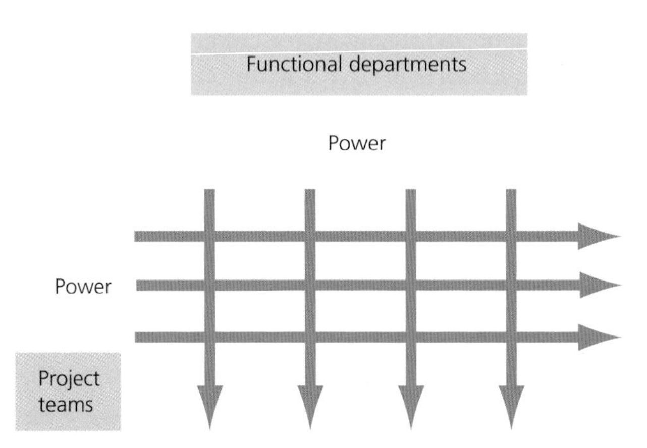

Figure 16.3 In a task culture, power flows down from the functional departments at the top of the matrix, but also lies horizontally within project teams

Person cultures are developed when individuals with similar training and backgrounds are encouraged to form groups to enhance their expertise and share knowledge. This type of culture is most often found within functional departments of large, complex organisations, or among professionals such as lawyers or accountants. It is largely associated with democratic leadership. The 'Real business' feature below shows how this culture can work in practice.

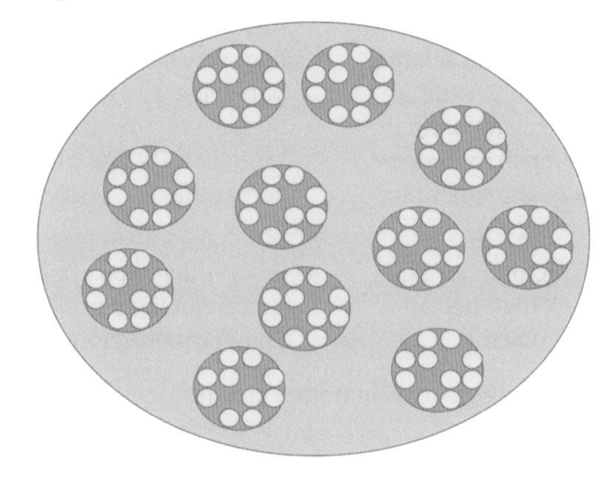

Figure 16.4 In a person culture, power lies within each group of individuals, flowing from their common knowledge and skills

Real business

At London's posh River Café restaurant, there's a friendly, chilled-out sense of teamwork among waiting and cooking staff. Perhaps uniquely, the waiters are incorporated fully into the business. They help prepare ('prep') the food before the lunch and dinner services and – like all the staff – enjoy at least one trip to Italy each year, to be taken to meet suppliers and to eat at some of the owner's favourite restaurants. All staff enjoy secure, permanent employment and wages that are far above the minimum-wage-norm in the catering trade. A waiter explains: 'We're paid well enough to not worry about tips: we can enjoy serving customers without needing to crawl to them.' The (privately owned) River Café is noted in London for great service, and is rated among the top ten restaurants in Britain.

Pros of Handy's approach	Cons of Handy's approach
Suggests four types: power, person, role and task	Overly focused on leaders and leadership
Useful for analysing existing situations	Takes a narrow view of culture, ignoring ethics and risk-taking
Used by managers in many parts of the world	Ignores the issue of cultural change

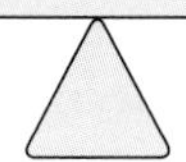

Figure 16.5 Logic balance: pros and cons of Handy's Cultures

'The thing I have learned at IBM is that culture is everything.'

Louis Gerstner, former Chief Executive, IBM

'Culture is one thing and varnish is another.'

Ralph Waldo Emerson, nineteenth-century American sage

16.4 How corporate culture is formed

Leadership style

An organisation may have been moulded to the personality of the founder, e.g. Branson, Jobs, Zuckerberg or Bezos; if so, the culture is derived from the founder/leader. And not just positive, entrepreneurial cultures; note the obsessive tax avoidance of Virgin, Apple, Facebook and Amazon, perhaps reflecting an insecurity summed up in the quote from Andy Grove of Intel: 'only the paranoid survive'.

Some non-founder leaders have the personality (and longevity) to transform culture, such as Terry Leahy, whose 14 years at the head of Tesco achieved profits but left a flawed legacy. Most leaders, however, are not in post long enough to make much difference to 'the way we do things round here'.

Real business

Google has an unusual culture. Its US headquarters (see Figure 16.6) looks more like an adult playground than a place for work. Google's success can partly be attributed to this culture. Google has people whose sole job is to keep employees happy and maintain productivity.

Hence the 'GooglePerks', which include (from a long list):

- free breakfast, lunch, and dinner; the organic food is chef-prepared
- video games, football, ping pong.

Figure 16.6 Google HQ

And does it all add up to a profitable business? Well, in 2014, Google's global revenues of $66 billion yielded a pre-tax profit of $17.25 billion. The only cloud hanging over the company is its approach to tax avoidance which, in Britain at least, is starting to raise serious questions about Google's famous motto: 'Don't be Evil'.

(Sources: various blogs plus the Google website)

Type of ownership

Public limited companies (plcs) have many external shareholders who seek 'shareholder value' (rising dividends and a rising share price) which derives from profit. In the UK plcs can have too short a profit horizon. Tight budgeting to meet profit forecasts can create its own narrow culture.

Some large, multinational corporations are family-owned and can take a longer-term view. Germany's BMW and Indian-owned Jaguar Land Rover are large companies that are family-controlled. Both have created a culture based on skilled engineering and entrepreneurial flair.

Real business

In late 2014 and early 2015, the big retail flops were Tesco, Marks & Spencer, Sainsbury's and Morrisons (all plcs) while the successes were Waitrose, Aldi and Lidl. Aldi and Lidl are privately owned companies while Waitrose is part of the John Lewis Partnership, effectively owned by its workforce. Aldi and Lidl boosted their combined grocery market share from 5 per cent in 2010 to 9.8 per cent by autumn 2015. The corporate culture at the plcs had drifted away from their customers towards growth and profit targets. By focusing on customers, Aldi, Lidl and Waitrose have enjoyed far better times.

Recruitment policies

In middle and senior management, some firms represent a monoculture: perhaps 'stale, pale and male' (old, white blokes). This may lead to a culture in which 'we' know best, even if 60 per cent of our customers are young women and 20 per cent non-white. Currently 7 per cent of FTSE 100 executive directors are women; non-white FTSE directors are in a tiny minority. Would the long-term weaknesses at Marks & Spencer, Game and HMV have persisted if the directors had been younger, more diverse, and more online savvy?

16.5 Difficulties in changing corporate culture

When a new chief executive joins a business, his or her first impressions will be of the culture. Is the customer embraced by the business, or kept at arms' length by voicemail and answerphone messages? Do staff enjoy Monday morning or only Friday afternoon?

If the new chief executive is unhappy about the culture, achieving change is unlikely to come easily. After all, some staff may have been working at the same place for 15 years, and will find it very difficult to change. Even more problematic is that staff collectively have a set of attitudes that may be tough to overcome. A manufacturing business may be dominated by middle-aged engineers who are sure they know best how to make cars or caramels. Switching to a more market-orientated business may be difficult.

The key to success in this process will be to ensure that all staff believe that the change is genuinely going to happen (and, preferably, that the change is the right one). There will be middle managers who are crucial to making things happen (for example, human resource managers or the finance staff who supervise the budget-setting process). If these people believe that the change is only skin-deep, they will hold back from supporting it. The engineers are likely to resist the change and perhaps they will prove right. Perhaps the new chief executive will be pushed aside by a board of directors who start to worry about whether a mistake is being made.

The key to cultural change, then, is to have a clear, consistent message. If everyone believes that the change is to be pushed through, they are far more likely to support it.

Not all cultural changes prove to be a success. Sometimes new leaders assume that a change in culture is essential, because they do not take the time to understand the strengths of the existing one. Past Conservative governments swept away the tradition of NHS hospital wards being run by an all-powerful 'matron'. A failure to clean the ward properly would have meant risking the wrath of matron; cleaners cleaned. The new approach was to award contracts to outside cleaning companies, then check that agreed targets had been met. The matrons were pushed aside in favour of professional, 'can-do' managers. The managers were supportive of the new cleaning businesses; unfortunately, the cleaners were not so committed to cleaning. The later wave of MRSA and *C. difficile* bacterial problems in hospitals can be put down to a management change based on inadequate understanding.

> 'Culture eats strategy for breakfast.'
>
> *Richard Plepler, Chief Executive, HBO*

> 'In most organisational change efforts, it is much easier to draw on the strengths of the culture than to overcome the constraints by changing the culture.'
>
> *Professor Edgar Schein, academic and author*

Five whys and a how

Questions	Answers
Why might 'culture eat strategy for breakfast'? See page 114.	Because you never know whether individual decisions or plans will turn out right, but with the right culture you'll keep being pleasantly surprised.
Why is role culture said to be bureaucratic?	Because individuals have to conform to their roles and everyone checks things out with the next role up in the organisation (their boss).
Why do Handy's theories make no mention of ethics?	Indeed a mystery. The culture of companies such as Barclays, Tesco and BP had ethical flaws at their heart. That will have soured every aspect of the culture.
Why might publicly quoted companies have a different culture from family-run ones?	Because focus on short-term profit creates a corporate culture based on fear of failure – failing to meet the next profit target.
Why might culture be dominated by short-term thinking?	If a company is focused on short-term profit, that will prevent any positive culture traits emerging.
How might a company measure the success (or otherwise) of a culture change programme?	By conducting regular research among customers – if positive change is happening among staff, customers will see or feel it.

16.6 Corporate culture – evaluation

Business leaders make many claims about the culture among their staff. They enjoy using words such as 'positive', 'can-do' and 'entrepreneurial'. Does the fact that the leader says these things mean that they are true? Clearly not. The leader cannot admit in public that the culture is 'lazy', 'negative' or 'bureaucratic'.

A well-judged answer to a question about culture will look beyond claims and public relations, and look for the evidence. Is there evidence that staff suggestions are welcomed and that they make an important contribution to the business? Is there evidence that mistakes are treated as learning experiences, rather than as reasons to be fired. And, perhaps most important of all, is there evidence that staff love their jobs and look forward to coming to work? All these things are tests of an organisation's corporate culture.

Key terms

Bureaucratic: an organisation in which initiative is stifled by paperwork and excessive checking and rechecking of decisions and actions.

Person culture: an organisation such as a legal practice, where common training practices mean everyone is trusted to get on with their jobs with minimal supervision.

Power culture: the boss as spider in the web, with every decision going through him or her. Power kept at the top.

Psychometric tests: designed to test the psychological make-up of a candidate - that is, the personality and character of an individual.

Role culture: where the job role is treated as of more importance than the individual; this will be a bureaucratic, risk-avoiding culture.

Task culture: making the task or project the focus, with staff brought in to form a temporary team empowered to get the task completed successfully.

16.7 Workbook

Revision questions

(35 marks; 35 minutes)

1 Explain why poor recruitment could lead to an ineffective business culture. (3)

2 Choose two of the following and briefly explain whether you think they would be likely to have an entrepreneurial or a bureaucratic business:

a) Marks & Spencer
b) Facebook
c) L'Oréal
d) Ryanair. (6)

3 Explain why it is unlikely that a task culture could exist in a business with an authoritarian leadership. (4)

4 Explain why a role culture would be inappropriate for a new software company seeking to be more innovative than Google. (4)

5 Sir Alex Ferguson was manager of Manchester United for 25 years. Examine two problems in changing the culture at an organisation dominated by one person, as at Manchester United. (6)

6 There was an entrepreneurial culture within the UK banking sector in the lead-up to the crash of 2008/2009. Does that prove that an entrepreneurial culture is a bad thing? Explain your answer. (6)

7 Recently a former quantity surveyor told the BBC that he had left the construction industry because he was so disillusioned by the problem of price fixing. Explain how a new leader of a construction firm might try to change the culture to one of honest dealing. (6)

Revision activities

Data response

Bakery culture

Gianni Falcone had built his Italian bakery up over a 40-year period in Britain. He came to escape a life dominated in the 1960s by the Sicilian Mafia, and started a bakery in south London. For the first ten years his life had been hard and very poor. Baking only white rolls and white bread, he had to keep his prices low to compete with local supermarkets. He would get up at 1.30 a.m. every day to prepare and then bake the bread, and his working day would end 12 hours later. With a young family of four, he could not get to bed until 8.30 in the evening. Five hours' later he would be back at work.

Eventually he started to see ways of adding value to his dough. A half kilogram loaf of bread with 30p of ingredients would sell for 80p, but roll it flat, smear tomato, cheese and herbs on it (cost: 25p) and it became a £3 pizza. A series of value-added initiatives followed, all adding both to the popularity of the shop and to its profitability. By 2000 the queues on a Saturday morning were legendary. Gianni was able to finance houses for all his family and he started to dream of owning a Ferrari.

By 2005 the business employed all the family members plus six extra staff. All worked the Gianni way. All knew the principles behind the business: ingredients should be as natural as possible and of as high a quality as possible. The customer is not always right (rowdy schoolchildren will be thrown out if necessary) but the customer must always be treated with respect. A slightly over-baked loaf will be sold at half price and day-old currant buns are given away to regular customers. Above all else, Gianni wanted to be honest with customers; they knew that all the baked goods were baked freshly on the premises.

Then, in 2012, Gianni was taken ill. The problem was with his lungs; quite simply, 40 years of flour in the bakery air had taken its toll. He had to retire. As none of his family wanted to take on the commitment to the awful working hours, he had to sell up. The only person with the inclination and the money to buy was an experienced baker from Malta, Trevi Malone. He bought the business for £250,000. Gianni was able to retire to the substantial home he had built in Sicily (now relatively Mafia-free).

From the start, Malone's approach was dramatically different. While Gianni had been ill, all the baking had been done by his bakery assistant Carol. She had worked miracles by herself, so that the shelves were full every morning. Now, from the first morning, Malone showed his distaste for her ways of working. Why did she use organic yeast when there were perfectly good, cheaper ones? Why did she 'knead' the dough in batches of 5kg when it would be better to do it by machine in 20kg quantities? And when she suggested that it would be good to start making hot cross buns, Malone snapped: 'This crazy place already makes too many different lines; just concentrate on what you're doing.' In the past, Carol's ideas had led to successful new products such as a top-selling apricot doughnut. Now she was silenced.

In the shop, Malone's approach was also quite different. Instead of casual clothes, everyone would wear uniforms; customers would be addressed as 'Sir' or 'Madam', and every order must be followed by an 'upselling' suggestion. The person who bought only a loaf of bread should be asked 'Would you like any doughnuts or cakes today?' The sales staff thought this was a daft idea, because – with so many regular customers – people would soon tire of being asked to spend more money. But they had quickly picked up the idea that Malone was not interested in discussion – he knew best.

Over the coming weeks things were changed steadily. The ham used on the meat pizza was changed from 'Italian baked ham' at £10 per kg to a much cheaper Danish one (with 20 per cent added water). As Malone said to Carol, 'Our customers don't see the ingredients label, so who's to know?' Malone noticed that doughnuts took longer to prepare than was justified by their 60p price tag, so he started to buy them in from a wholesale baker. Outsourcing was the sensible approach.

Within two months Carol began to look for a new job. She found it in another bakery, but soon left that as well, and went to college to retrain for a new career. Other staff steadily left, including all of Gianni's family. The newly recruited staff were accepting of Malone's rules, but none seemed particularly keen on the work. Perhaps that was fortunate, because sales started to slip after two months, and then fell at an increasingly rapid pace. Staff who left were not replaced, as they were no longer needed. Even more fortunate was that Gianni was not well enough to travel back to England. He never knew how quickly 40 years of work fell apart.

Questions (50 marks; 60 minutes)

1 Evaluate whether the example of Gianni's bakery proves that value added is at the heart of all business activity. (20)

2 Assess why outsourcing the doughnuts may not have been 'a sensible approach' for Malone. (10)

3 Malone paid £250,000 for a business that steadily went downhill. Evaluate whether this was primarily due to the change in culture within the workplace. (20)

Extended writing

1 When Anthony Jenkins took over as boss of Barclays in 2012, he said that it would 'take five to ten years' to change the bank's corporate culture. Evaluate whether this might be connected to the size of this multinational bank. (20)

2 Evaluate whether workplace culture might be the key factor in your own choice of job when you leave education. (20)

Section 3.4 Influences on business decisions

17 Shareholders versus stakeholders

Definition

A shareholder owns a proportion of a company's share capital and therefore has voting rights at the annual general meeting. A stakeholder is any individual or group affected by the activities of an organisation.

Linked to: Corporate objectives, Ch 1; Reasons for staying small, Ch 10; Corporate influences, Ch 15; Business ethics, Ch 18

17.1 Introduction

All firms come into contact on a daily basis with suppliers, customers, the local community and employees. Each of these groups has an impact on the firm's success and at the same time is likely to be affected by any change in its activities. If, for example, the managers decide to expand the business, this may lead to:

- overtime for employees
- more orders for suppliers
- a wider range of products for consumers
- more traffic for the local community.

Groups such as suppliers, employees and the community are known as the firm's **stakeholder** groups because of their links with the organisation. A stakeholder group both has an effect on and is affected by the decisions of the firm. Each stakeholder group will have its own objectives. The managers of a firm must decide on the extent to which they should change their behaviour to meet these objectives. Some, but not all, firms believe they can benefit from co-operating with stakeholder groups and incorporating their needs into the decision-making process. Examples include:

- improving the working life of employees through more challenging work, better pay and greater responsibilities, so that the business benefits from a more motivated and committed workforce
- giving something back to the community to ensure greater co-operation from local inhabitants whenever the business needs their help; for example, when seeking planning permission for expansion
- treating suppliers with respect and involving them in its plans so that the firm builds up a long-term relationship; this should lead to better-quality supplies and a better all-round service; if, for example, your supplier has limited availability of an item, it is more likely you would still get supplied because of the way you have treated the supplier in the past.

Despite the benefits that are evident in a stakeholder approach, many managers believe that an organisation's sole duty is to its investors (that decisions should be made in the best interests of **shareholders** alone). Generally, this means maximising **shareholder value** (increasing the share price and the dividends paid to shareholders). Even company directors who instinctively want to serve all the stakeholders often find that day-to-day pressures force them to pay primary concern to shareholders' interests – because shareholders are the only people with the power to get rid of the board of directors.

> 'If you look after your customers and you look after your staff then shareholders will do very well ... If you put shareholder interest – particularly short-term interest – first, you don't create a business.'
>
> *Ian Gregg, who built Greggs from one shop to 1,600*

Figure 17.1

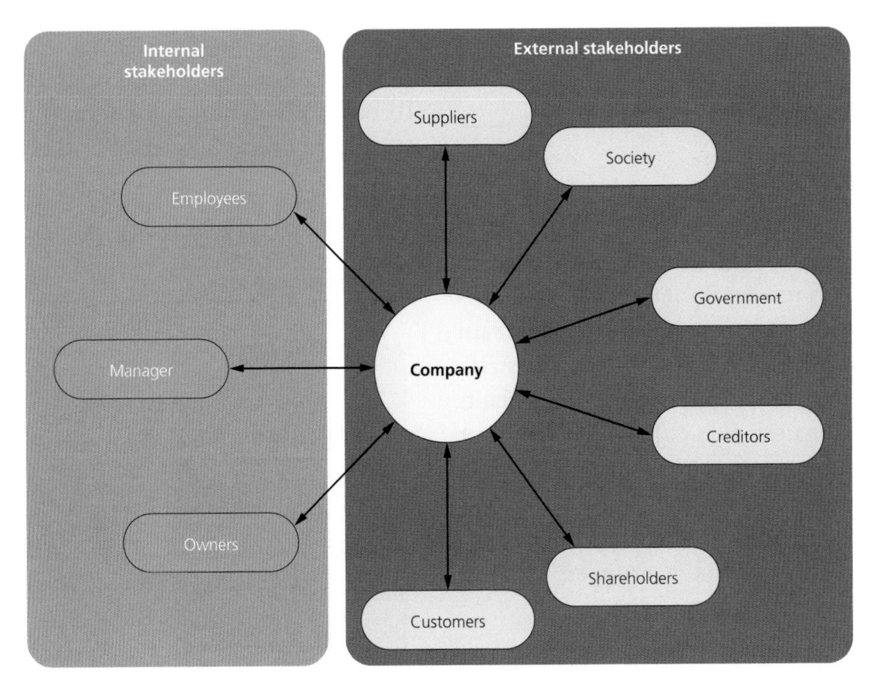

Figure 17.2 Internal and external stakeholders

17.2 Internal and external stakeholders

Although it is easy to come up with a long list of possible stakeholders, it makes sense to try to identify the more important groups. One way is to divide them into internal and external stakeholders. In Figure 17.2 it is important to take the dividing line between internal and external as no more than a guideline. After all, 'owners' are listed as internal while 'shareholders' are external – yet they are legally one and the same. The point is that whereas Ray Kelvin, founder of Ted Baker plc, owns a 35 per cent stake in the company (and is clearly an internal stakeholder), most small shareholders may only have £1,000 of shares and only a passing interest in the business. Therefore the latter are external stakeholders.

Well-run businesses think about the potential value of drawing relevant stakeholder groups away from the external towards the internal category. Franchise owners such as Subway want their franchisees to feel part of the 'family'. So although franchisees are really customers, they are treated as internal stakeholders. It would be a foolish franchisor who kept franchisees at arms' length, in a them-and-us stand-off.

17.3 Stakeholder objectives

Each stakeholder group is likely to have a primary objective that may or may not coincide with the objectives of the other groups. Staff are likely to prioritise stability and security. Shareholders, with an eye on the profit potential of robotics, may have other ideas. The objective that is most likely to create agreement is growth. But local residents may think of traffic congestion due to increasing deliveries. Table 17.1 shows the most likely objectives for the main stakeholder groups. Note that there is no reason to suppose that internal stakeholders have a common purpose – with or against external ones.

Stakeholder group	Main objectives
Staff	Growth (preferably organic); new technology by product, not process; rising profits (if they're shared in some way)
Managers/directors	Growth (organic or inorganic); new technology by process or product; rising profits (especially if bonuses are available)
Shareholders	Rising profits – short-term and long-term
Suppliers	Growth
Customers	Quality of product and service; innovative new products
Bankers	Stable profits
Local residents	Clean, green production with few deliveries or despatches

Table 17.1 Objectives of main stakeholder groups

17.4 Stakeholder and shareholder influences

Influence of stakeholders

There is no doubt that businesses today understand the public relations benefits that come from a positive corporate image based on respect for stakeholders. This is how Ben & Jerry's became America's favourite ice cream and how Innocent Drinks became Britain's favourite start-up. But ultimately both sold out to the corporate giants they claimed they were against: Ben & Jerry's to Unilever for $326 million and Innocent Drinks to Coca-Cola for a final valuation of £320 million. So was Innocent *really* concerned about providing something healthy for its customers? Surely, ultimately, the founders' actions showed that shareholders always came first.

Despite these reasons for scepticism, there are companies that make a consistent effort to consider all stakeholders when setting objectives and making decisions. In Britain, the John Lewis Partnership is held up as an exceptional example of how to deal with stakeholders fairly. Customers feel they are buying ethically sourced, high-quality products and suppliers feel better looked after than with Tesco, Boots and many other high-street retailers. Impressively, suppliers also speak warmly about their dealings with the 'hard discounters' Aldi and Lidl. And for customers, the low prices and high quality standards are pleasing. In its 2015 survey, *The Grocer* magazine's annual 'Own Label Product Awards' placed Lidl first and Aldi second. It is possible, then, to provide high quality, reasonable prices, yet keep suppliers onside.

Influence of shareholders

In the first quarter of its 2015 financial year, McDonald's suffered a sixth quarter of falling same-store sales in America and weakness in Europe as well. While McDonald's sales were declining, Domino's Pizza enjoyed a 14.5 per cent increase in sales in America. And how did financial analysts and stock market professionals respond to this crisis? By pressing its new chief executive about a series of issues that add up to nothing more than financial engineering, for example taking on more debt. That is an attempt to boost profits by financial means, not trading improvements. Surely shareholders should be taking the long view and asking whether McDonald's menu and its service standards are fit for the modern world?

If shareholders seem obsessed with quick fixes to boost profits and the share price, it's very hard for senior executives to buck this trend. In effect the directors inevitably end up doing what the shareholders want. To boost dividend payments and the share price, higher profits are needed. So they will be delivered.

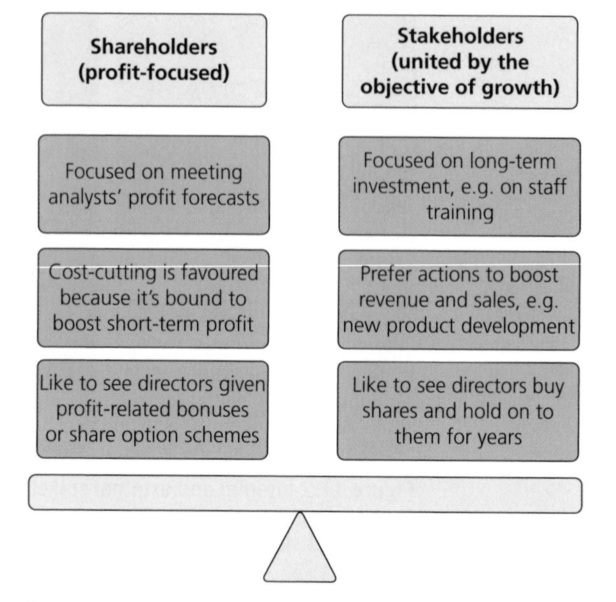

Figure 17.3 Logic balance: stakeholders vs shareholders

17.5 Potential for conflict between shareholder and stakeholder objectives

Certain business circumstances may be to the advantage of all primary stakeholders. If, like Primark, your business concept is working successfully overseas, there are benefits to staff (promotion prospects), the board (bonuses), suppliers, shareholders, financiers and distributors. Even among external shareholders there are potential benefits to Inland Revenue and the wider community. Perhaps the only negative comments might come from environmental **pressure groups**.

Sadly, this is not often the case. All too often different stakeholders seem unable to stop themselves taking advantage of any weakness in others. In July 2014 Lloyds Bank was fined £105 million by the UK's Financial Conduct Authority and ordered to pay the Bank of England £7.76 million. Lloyds had not only rigged markets but had also deliberately underpaid the British government for help given to keep Lloyds afloat during the tough days in 2009 and 2010. By attempting to benefit its shareholders at the cost of the government and the taxpayer, Lloyds' executives were showing clearly where their stakeholder priorities lie.

Situation	Shared interests/needs between stakeholders	Conflicting stakeholder interests/needs
Productivity advance – perhaps coming from a staff suggestion scheme	Shareholders, managers and customers	Managers and employees (threats of redundancy)
Fashion or weather turns in your favour	Shareholders, managers, suppliers and employees	Green campaigners may object to increased resource use
Consumer demand switches from shops to e- and m-commerce	Shareholders and customers	Managers and employees
High and rising inflation	Shareholders and managers	Employees, suppliers and customers

Table 17.2 Stakeholder needs in different business circumstances

'We intend to conduct our business in a way that not only meets but exceeds the expectations of our customers, business partners, shareholders, and creditors, as well as the communities in which we operate and society at large.'

Akira Mori, Japanese businessman

'Find the appropriate balance of competing claims by various groups of stakeholders. All claims deserve consideration but some claims are more important than others.'

Warren Bennis, business author

Five whys and a how

Question	Answer
Why may it be risky for a business to focus solely on shareholder value?	Because the interests of wider stakeholders may lead to bad publicity, for example Primark and its low-cost Asian suppliers.
Why might a company choose to act with social responsibility – but without publicising it?	It might see more advantage in focusing on the good than in publicising the good, e.g. knowing that staff like pursuing a goal other than shareholders' profits.
Why may staff feel that they should be treated as a higher priority than other stakeholders?	Because the staff are actually the heart of the enterprise. It's like football fans and football managers – the latter come and go but the former are there for the long term.
Why might it be sensible to give thought to who your internal stakeholders *should* be?	Because it's helpful to think about who the business really needs a strong relationship with, e.g. Jaguar Land Rover treating supplier GKN as a key part of JLR's success.
Why might a new small company treat customers as its only key stakeholder?	Because the business will stand or fall on repeat purchase and word of mouth from those customers.
How might a large clothing retailer establish effective consultation with its stakeholders?	It would be hard because there are potentially so many of them. Perhaps get two representatives from each stakeholder group – then meet regularly (every two months?)

17.6 Shareholders versus stakeholders – evaluation

In recent years, there has been much greater interest in the idea that firms should pay attention to their **social responsibilities**. Increasingly, firms are being asked to consider and justify their actions towards a wide range of groups rather than just their shareholders. Managers are expected to take into account the interests and opinions of numerous internal and external groups before they make a decision. This social responsibility often makes good business sense. If you ignore your stakeholder groups, you are vulnerable to pressure group action and may well lose customers and your brightest employees.

It may not be possible to meet the needs of all interest groups, however. Firms must decide on the extent to which they take stakeholders into account. Given their limited resources and other obligations, managers must decide on their priorities. In difficult times it may well be that the need for short-term profit overcomes the demands of various stakeholder groups. It would be naive to ignore the fact that TV consumer programmes such as the BBC's *Watchdog* keep exposing business malpractice. Even if progress is being made in general, there are still many firms that persist in seeing short-term profit as the sole business objective.

Key terms

Pressure group: a group of people with a common interest who try to further that interest (for example, Greenpeace).

Shareholder: an owner of (part of) a company.

Shareholder value: a term widely used by company chairmen and chairwomen, which means little more than the attempt to maximise the company's share price.

Social responsibilities: duties towards stakeholder groups, which the firm may or may not accept.

Stakeholder: an individual or group that affects and is affected by an organisation.

17.7 Workbook

Revision questions

(45 marks; 45 minutes)

1 What is meant by a 'stakeholder'? (2)

2 Distinguish between internal and external stakeholders. (3)

3 Some people believe that an increasing number of firms are now trying to meet their social responsibilities. Explain why this may be the case. (4)

4 Outline two responsibilities a firm may have to:

a) its employees (4)

b) its customers (4)

c) the local community. (4)

5 Explain how a firm could damage its profits in the pursuit of meeting its shareholder responsibilities. (4)

6 Explain why a firm's profit may fall by meeting its stakeholder responsibilities. (4)

7 Some managers reject the idea of stakeholding. They believe that a company's duty is purely to its shareholders. Outline two points in favour and two points against this opinion. (8)

8 What factors are likely to determine whether a firm accepts its responsibilities to a particular stakeholder group? (4)

9 Explain why a company in the public eye such as Next plc might find it difficult to pursue the shareholder concept. (4)

Revision activities

Data response

Marks & Spencer plc and Plan A

M&S has spent 20 years in a strategy vacuum. Bosses have come and gone, but nothing has altered the slide in the company's core business: women's clothing. It is curious, then, that the business has been consistent in one strategy for the past decade: 'Plan A': its Corporate Social Responsibility plan. From its inception it has been remarkably wide in its scope, covering staff diversity through to health and safety and on to a series of environmental commitments. In some ways, it's hard to see how Plan A has helped. Today John Lewis can do no wrong, while the reputation of Marks & Spencer is as low as it's ever been. But perhaps it has helped keep staff onside during such a turbulent period.

Plan A is supposed to keep M&S focused on a better tomorrow. Many of its targets are to be achieved by 2020. But it's surprising that some targets that are viewed as important one year disappear the next. The 2011/2012 report boasts of an 'employee engagement positivity score of 75 per cent' (previous year 76 per cent), but this measure had been dropped by the time of the 2014 report. Other measurements are covered with more consistency, such as (Figure 17.3) the dramatic reduction in customer use of single-use (plastic) carrier bags since a 5p charge was levied in 2006/2007.

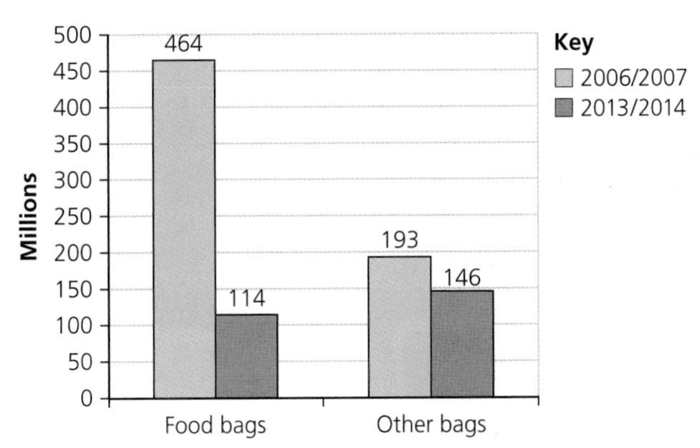

Figure 17.4 M&S Plan A: single-use carrier bags (source: M&S Plan A Report 2014)

	CO_2 emissions 2006/2007	CO_2 emissions 2011/2012	CO_2 emissions 2013/2014
Business travel	10,000 tonnes	14,000 tonnes	Not included
Total gross CO_2 emissions	730,000 tonnes	572,000 tonnes	566,000 tonnes
Carbon offsets purchased	0 tonnes	131,000 tonnes	566,000 tonnes
Net CO_2 emissions	730,000 tonnes	441,000 tonnes	0 tonnes

Table 17.3 M&S CO_2 emissions (source: M&S reports 2011/2012 and 2013/2014)

	2011	2012	2013	2014
Women employees	76%	74%	74%	73%
Women managers	65%	64%	64%	58%
Women in senior management	32%	35%	35%	39%
Ethnic minority employees	12%	13%	12%	11%
Ethnic minority managers	11%	12%	13%	14%

Table 17.4 Diversity data: UK figures as a % of the total UK workforce (source: M&S reports 2011/2012 and 2013/2014)

The same pattern of inconsistency occurs with the main environmental finding, showing an extraordinary change from 730,000 tonnes of CO_2 emissions in 2006/2007 to zero in 2013/2014, but dropping data for business travel.

Amidst many other pieces of data, the figures for workforce diversity are interesting. It is a pity there is no data provided to cover the percentage of senior management occupied by ethnic minority employees.

As mentioned above, it may be that Plan A has brought staff together, with a feeling of common purpose. From the outside, though, it is hard to see that it has achieved one of the goals M&S has set itself: 'To excite and inspire our customers at every turn'.

Questions (40 marks; 50 minutes)

1. Assess the data provided to examine two strengths and two weaknesses of Plan A so far. (10)
2. Assess whether Marks & Spencer is focusing most on its shareholders or its stakeholders. (10)
3. Evaluate whether Marks & Spencer should regard Plan A as a strategic success. Justify your answer. (20)

Extended writing

1. Evaluate whether the objectives of the different stakeholder groups necessarily conflict. Use real business examples to develop your answer. (20)
2. 'A manager's responsibility should be to the shareholders alone.' Evaluate this view. (20)

18 Business ethics

Definition

Ethics are the moral principles that should underpin decision-making. A decision made on ethical grounds might reject the most profitable solution in favour of one of greater benefit to society as well as the firm.

Linked to: Corporate objectives, Ch 1; Corporate influences, Ch 15; Corporate culture, Ch 16; Shareholders versus stakeholders, Ch 17; Ethics in global business, Ch 41

18.1 What are business ethics?

Business ethics can provide moral guidelines for the conduct of business affairs. These need to be based on common understanding of what's right and what's wrong. An ethical decision means doing what is morally right. It is not a matter of scientifically calculating costs, benefit and profit. Most actions and activities in the business world have an ethical dimension. This has been highlighted recently in relation to whole industries (such as soft drinks and fast food) and to businesses that use cheap labour in less developed countries.

Among the important ethical considerations in business are:

- dealing honestly and fairly with customers and with suppliers
- protecting the environment through actions such as the use of sustainable sources of raw materials
- dealing with bullying, harassment and discrimination within the organisation
- the provision of accurate financial and other numerical information
- anti-competitive practices
- testing products on animals
- **whistleblowing** on unethical practices within the business.

Two major influences shape the moral behaviour of businesses. First, an organisation is composed of individuals, who all have their own moral codes, values and principles. Naturally they bring these to bear on the decisions that they make as part of their working lives. Second, businesses have cultures that shape corporate ethical standards. The approach taken by the leaders of the business can have a big effect on both of these factors.

The extract below about ethics at GlaxoSmithKline illustrates a situation in which individuals and the **corporate culture** proved important.

Real business

Ethics at GlaxoSmithKline (GSK)

In March 2015 the UK pharmaceuticals giant GSK fired more than a hundred of its staff in China. This came after the company was fined £300 million for its guilt in bribing doctors in China (to get them to prescribe GSK medicines).

When the story first broke in 2013, GSK denied it. But later GSK chairman Sir Christopher Gent said: 'The illegal activities of GSK China were a clear breach of GSK's governance and compliance procedures and are wholly contrary to the values and standards expected.' The company was found to have funnelled billions of renminbi to hospitals, doctors and government officials in a programme of 'massive and systemic bribery'.

In 2010, the company had been forced by an American court to pay out a world record payout of $96 million to a 'whistleblower' who was sidelined and made redundant for warning of contamination problems at one of GSK's American factories.

Ethics is not about what companies say; it's about what they do.

(Sources: Guardian, *28 October 2010;* Financial Times, *6 March 2015)*

18.2 The ethics of strategic decisions

A strategic decision is one that is so major and so long term that is virtually irreversible. A good example is when Nokia sold its handset business to Microsoft in 2013. At the time commentators were 'shocked' at the low price (about £4 billion). When Microsoft later wrote off the whole sum and closed the business, people realised how wise Nokia had been.

Ethics enter strategic decisions in two main ways:

1. Whether the moral aspects of the decision have been fully thought through. In 2006, British Aerospace (BAe) sold its 20 per cent stake in Airbus for £1.9 billion (one of the worst business decisions of all time). The ethics of the situation seemed not to occur to the directors. It meant that BAe would now be 100 per cent reliant on sales of military aircraft and weapons systems. Quite apart from the ethics of selling arms, the fact is that arms sales are especially prone to bribery and other corrupt practices. BAe later paid £286 million in fines for corrupt dealings.
2. The level of risk – and are the risks borne fairly? In 2013, a private equity business bought the City Link parcel delivery service for £1. With more than 2,500 staff this big business could make the new owners a fortune if things went well. In fact the business was placed into administration on 24 December 2014, leaving delivery drivers horribly out of pocket (they had been encouraged to act as self-employed van owners). If the deal had gone well, the owners would have made millions. When it went badly, ordinary staff lost their jobs.

Figure 18.1 City Link was bought by a private equity firm for £1 in 2013

As strategic decisions are so important to a business's future, it is especially important that the directors consider the morality behind their decision as well as the potential profitability.

18.3 Trade-offs between profit and ethics

Businesses need profit. It is profit that provides the capital to withstand a bad trading period, or to keep up with new technology or to finance growth. But there can be a huge difference between profit needed and profit wanted. Profit needs to be enough to provide a satisfactory return for the risks involved in investing in a business. In 2013, at the time GlaxoSmithKline was embarrassed by its corrupt practices in China, bank interest rates of 0.5 per cent might suggest that a return of 5–10 per cent on capital would have been adequate. In fact the business had a 25.7 per cent return on capital in 2013, and the company's chief executive received £7.2 million in remuneration.

In a healthily run business, there *should* be a constant tension between ethics and profit. When a clever product developer comes up with an idea like Krave chocolate cereal, it's for a senior Kellogg's executive to question whether that's the right thing to do. In a public limited company, however, there will rarely be any such debate. Staff soon learn that questioning the ethics of sweets near the checkout (Marks & Spencer plc) or excess sugar in the cans of Cola (Coca-Cola and PepsiCo) is never a good career move. Only in a privately owned, preferably family-run, business or a co-operative is there a serious chance of a true ethical debate. And even then there are many instances of career ambition overtaking moral considerations.

When writing on the subject, it is vital to distinguish between ethics and business strategies such as 'ethical' marketing. Ethics is about morality; ethical marketing is the often-cynical pursuit of product differentiation through the manipulation of consumers. In August 2015 Innocent Drinks launched 'Light & Juicy' drinks, with each pack carrying the banner: 'Naturally 30 per cent lower in sugar'. Was this decision rooted in ethics? Or was it a response to a 10.8 per cent fall in sales of Innocent Drinks in 2014 (Kantar Worldpanel, quoted in the *Grocer* 1 August 2015)? Even though the 900ml carafes of the drink contain 14–15 teaspoons of sugar, it is wrong to jump to conclusions about the motives involved. If Innocent's executives genuinely saw this as a way of lowering consumers' sugar intake, it could be argued that the decision was ethical. Please excuse my scepticism.

The ultimate test of the ethics involved in a decision is whether the ethical course of action involves a loss of profit. When Lidl removed sweets and crisps from its checkouts in January 2014, it was clearly a good thing to do. It would have made a small dent in profit without making a significant difference to the brand's image. By contrast Aldi's decision to do the same in August 2014 can only really be seen as a reactive move. It is hard to see it as ethically driven. As mentioned earlier, the real test is whether the motive was ethical, and one can only be sure of that if one is part of the discussions and the decision. Outsiders can only hypothesise; they can rarely be sure.

18.4 Pay and rewards

In 2005, Arcadia (Topshop) boss Sir Philip Green paid himself a dividend worth £1,170 million, funded by bank borrowing. In other words the business took on the debt, and Philip Green took the cash. Well, strictly speaking it was paid to his wife who – living in Monaco – paid zero tax to the UK government. This huge exercise in tax avoidance may have come at a cost to the business. In 2005 Arcadia made £326 million in profit. By 2013/2014 (latest accounts at the time of writing), the figure had fallen to £143 million – and Arcadia announced 2,000 job losses.

Few would doubt that high-risk, high-pressure jobs deserve high rewards. Still fewer would doubt the value of a really talented business boss. Ray Kelvin, founder and boss of Ted Baker plc, has taken the business from one shop in Glasgow to an international brand with a stock market value of more than £1 billion. What pay and rewards does Ray Kelvin deserve? Well, for the year ended 31 January 2015 Mr Kelvin paid himself a salary of £374,000. He received further bonus payments taking his remuneration up to £757,000. In the same year, underachieving Marc Bolland, boss of Marks & Spencer plc, received remuneration totalling £2,076,000. Was he worth it? Hmm.

In the long run, the logic is simple. Business success is a team effort. The people at the top can only succeed through the efforts of those throughout the business. Therefore it must be a strategic mistake to separate the riches at the top from the scraps at the bottom. Long-term success will come from everyone feeling that there is fairness. Not equality, perhaps; but fairness. So, yes, the person at the top may receive 20 times the income of graduate trainees, but if those at the bottom are being restricted to a 2 per cent pay rise, it is grotesque to see those at the top receiving huge bonuses.

18.5 Corporate Social Responsibility

Corporate Social Responsibility (CSR) is – at its best – a form of self-regulation by which companies exceed legal minimum requirements in an attempt to be good social citizens. Such behaviour is claimed by businesses such as John Lewis, Unilever, Marks & Spencer and the Co-op. Critics, though, suspect that CSR is often no more than a branch of a company's public relations (PR) department – concerned with image, not substance. It may be that examples exist at both extremes, but the majority of businesses are somewhere in between.

What is undeniable is that these issues are complex. In 2005 Unilever plc came joint bottom of a ranking of corporate UK's ethical standards. Perhaps in response in 2010 the company launched its Sustainable Living Plan that it still claims to be the cornerstone of the business. This helped Unilever move up to 7th in the *Guardian*'s list of graduates' most-favoured employers. Yet in February 2015, an important health story broke showing evidence that 30 years of health advice was unfounded. Saturated fats were not a health problem and butter was no worse for your heart than margarine. Well, who had put out all this research into the evils of butter, years ago? Unilever, producer of Flora and many other margarines. Companies *may* adopt high standards, but it's wise to be sceptical of what they do and say. Their **vested interest** makes it harder than they realise for them to be objective.

18.6 Reasons for and against Corporate Social Responsibility (CSR)

Reasons for CSR

Companies receive many benefits from behaving, or being seen to behave, in a responsible manner. John Lewis and its supermarket business Waitrose both gain from consumer affection based on the assumption that these employee-owned businesses behave better towards their stakeholders. Reasons for CSR include the following.

Marketing advantages

Many modern consumers expect to purchase goods and services from organisations that operate in ways that they consider morally correct. Some consumers are unwilling to buy products from businesses that behave in any other way. Some companies have developed their apparent ethical behaviour into a unique selling point (USP). They base their marketing campaigns on these perceived differences. Examples include Lush cosmetics, Innocent Drinks and Toyota (which, in January 2015, had the two top-selling cars in America – all based on the company's green image due to its Prius hybrid car).

Positive effects on the workforce

Firms that adopt strong CSR practices may experience benefits in relation to their workforce. They may be able to recruit staff who are better qualified and motivated, because larger numbers of high-quality staff apply. Innocent Drinks has had an unusually low labour turnover rate since its start-up. This cuts the employment costs associated with recruitment, selection and training. Creating a culture of social responsibility can also improve employee motivation. In turn, that may boost the productivity and profitability of the business.

> 'There needs to be a balance between business and social responsibility ... The companies that are authentic about it will wind up as the companies that make the most money.'
>
> *Howard Schulz, boss of Starbucks*

Reasons for doubting CSR

Some shareholders criticise CSR as a distraction from the real business of making profits. For them the concerns are as follows.

Reduced profitability

Any business that really embraces CSR faces higher costs. Exploiting cheap labour or very low-cost supplies from less developed countries may be very profitable. If a business wants to act with responsibility, it must accept that principle may have to override profit. This is easier to do in a family-run business than in a public limited company, with its distant, profit-focused shareholders.

Reduced growth prospects

It may also be that the company has to turn down the opportunity to invest in projects offering potentially high returns. This would limit the long-term growth potential of the business – which might allow competitors to become stronger on the back of their high profits. Following the 2013 coup by the Egyptian army against a democratic leader, some travel agencies refused to carry on sending tourists to the country's Red Sea resorts. Others carried on, ignoring the moral issues. A true sense of CSR has to include refusing business profits that are tainted morally.

The bigger critique of CSR comes from those who doubt its authenticity. Their reasons against include the following.

Rejection of CSR as a tool of public relations (PR)

The actions of banks such as Barclays, Lloyds and HSBC have shown how hollow their CSR rhetoric can be. They pretended to be acting in the interests of the wider community as a cloak for some depressingly amoral, sometimes, immoral business behaviours.

Rejection of CSR as a distraction from a truly moral purpose

During the period 2010–2014, Aldi and Lidl received praise for their low prices, while Waitrose received praise for its socially responsible way of doing business. But surely not! During a time of heavily squeezed family budgets, Waitrose was charging higher prices than any other food retailer. Surely Aldi and Lidl were being socially responsible by helping people survive the squeeze.

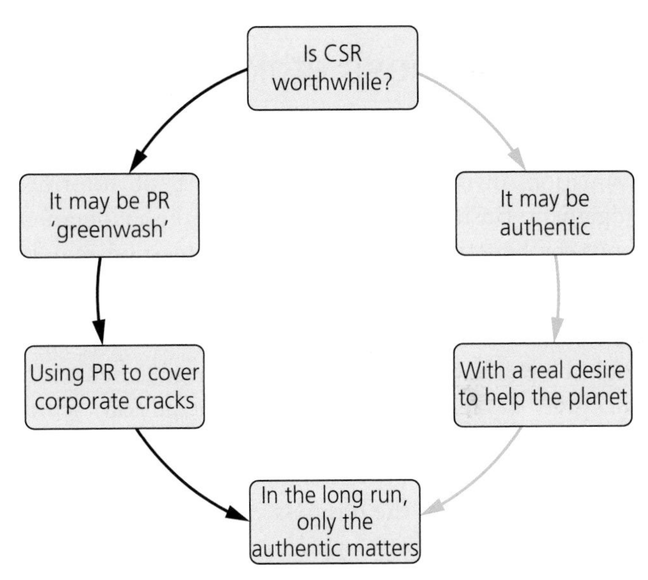

Figure 18.2 Logic circle: is CSR authentic or cosmetic?

> 'All company bosses want a policy on corporate social responsibility. The positive effect is hard to quantify, but the negative consequences of a disaster are enormous.'
>
> *Noreena Hertz, academic and athor*

> 'It takes 20 years to build a reputation and five minutes to ruin it.'
>
> *Warren Buffet, investor extraordinaire*

Five whys and a how

Questions	Answers
Why do some people believe that corporate social responsibility is a modern trend?	It's a mystery. Over a hundred years ago companies such as Cadbury and Unilever focused far more on social factors than anyone does today.
Why might ethics get in the way of profit?	By forcing a business to back down from a decision that makes money, but isn't right morally.
Why might a company choose to act with social responsibility – but without publicising it?	It might see more advantage in focusing on the good than in publicising the good, e.g. knowing that staff like pursuing a goal other than shareholders' profits.
Why are directors paid so much, even when they're underperforming?	Perhaps because the 'remuneration committees' that decide on pay are stuffed with people who are directors of other companies, i.e. it's a merry-go-round.
Why might CSR be handled by the PR department?	Because the company sees it as a tool for image-building, rather than a matter of substance.
How should a company set about being both profitable and ethical?	By identifying a product or service that has high enough value added that it is possible to pay suppliers and staff properly, while still making a reasonable profit margin.

18.7 Business ethics – evaluation

Evaluation involves making some sort of informed judgement. Businesses are required to make a judgement about the benefits of CSR. Their key question may be whether social responsibilities are profitable or not.

This chapter has put forward arguments as to why CSR might be profitable. For example, responsible behaviour can give a clear competitive advantage on which marketing activities can be based. Every John Lewis Christmas commercial is designed to make customers feel warmer towards the business.

Operating an authentic policy of social responsibility gives a USP if none of your competitors has taken the plunge. Being first may result in gaining market share before others catch up. In these circumstances a CSR policy may enhance profitability. It can also be an attractive option in a market where businesses and products are virtually indistinguishable.

Regarding ethics, however, the arguments have to be different. If the adoption of an ethical approach is down to calculation of self-interest, by definition it is not ethical. Ethics are about moral values and therefore must override calculation/profit. Many years ago, before cigarette advertising was banned, one London advertising agency took the decision to refuse to accept contracts from tobacco companies. This decision had no financial upside; it was simply based on the moral codes of the directors of the agency. That's ethics.

Key terms

Corporate culture: the culture of an organisation is the (perhaps unwritten) code that affects the attitudes, decision-making and management style of its staff.

Corporate Social Responsibility (CSR): a term intended to sum up the ethically driven activities of a business; but often it's an extension of the public relations (PR) department, making sounds that signify nothing.

Vested interest: when there's a personal, often hidden, reason for making a decision (often rooted in money).

Whistleblowing: when an employee decides they can't accept a moral dilemma (such as knowing of bribery), and exposes the unacceptable practice – perhaps first to senior management and then – if nothing is done – to the media.

18.8 Workbook

Revision questions

(25 marks; 25 minutes)

1 Define the term 'business ethics'. (2)

2 State two factors that may shape the moral behaviour of businesses. (2)

3 Outline one circumstance in which a company may face an ethical dilemma. (3)

4 Explain the difference between a business behaving legally and a business behaving ethically. (4)

5 Look at each of the following business actions and decide whether they were motivated by ethical considerations. Briefly explain your reasoning each time:

a) a private hospital refusing to accept an ill elderly person whose only income is the state pension (2)

b) a small baker refusing to accept supplies of genetically modified flour (2)

c) a small baker refusing to deliver to a restaurant known locally as a racist employer. (2)

6 Why could a policy of delegation make it more difficult for a business to behave ethically? (4)

7 Explain why a company's corporate social responsibility programme might do little to change irresponsible behaviour within the organisation. (4)

Revision activities

Data response

Virgin Galactic

With all Richard Branson's success as Britain's best-known business leader, his Virgin Group may yet achieve its greatest fame for space travel. The space-tourism project goes back to 1999 when Branson registered the name 'Virgin Galactic'. It started to take shape in 2004 when Branson adopted technology that engineers had used to win a $10 million space race prize. He was so confident at that stage that he announced that Virgin Galactic would fly within three years – and he started selling tickets at $250,000 a go.

Unfortunately three years later the programme hit the headlines only because of the detonation of a tank of nitrous oxide that killed three people and seriously injured another three. Ticketholders, including Brad Pitt and Angelina Jolie, would have to wait. In 2011 there were more glitches when a test flight malfunctioned. Far more serious, though, was the disaster on 31 October 2014, when a Virgin Galactic test flight exploded and then crashed shortly after launch at the Mojave desert. One of the pilots was killed instantly and the other (who ejected) was seriously injured. It emerged that the space ship was powered by a fuel mix that had not previously been used in flight. Branson's immediate response to the disaster was to say 'Space is hard – but worth it. We will persevere and move forward together'.

Just prior to the test flight and crash, Branson had been interviewed by the *Financial Times*. Here he set out the purpose behind his investment: 'The space company will be our flagship. Because we're the only private company in the world sending people to space, the next few months are obviously something that has a halo effect on every Virgin company.'

And after the crash, what's the future for Virgin Galactic? In April 2015 Virgin boasted that only 20 of 700 deposit-payers had asked for their money back. When an official safety report was published into the crash it blamed pilot error due to inadequate training. The safety problems may eventually force Branson to back down on his space dream. You wouldn't bet on it, though.

Questions (40 marks; 45 minutes)

1 As Branson states, the corporate objective for Virgin Galactic is to provide 'a halo effect' for every Virgin company. Assess whether this is a valid corporate objective. (10)

2 Given the safety problems the project has faced, assess whether it would be better, ethically, for Branson to close the project and return the deposits. (10)

3 Richard Branson is determined to proceed with Virgin Galactic. Evaluate whether he should first discuss this decision with Virgin Galactic's stakeholders. (20)

Extended writing

1 Evaluate the following statement: 'For a business such as Tesco, a strong commitment to social responsibilities is vital to the company's long-term success.' (20)

2 Evaluate the view that most businesses use CSR as a strategy for gaining a competitive advantage. (20)

Section 3.5 Assessing competitiveness

19 Interpretation of financial statements

Definition

There are two key financial statements: the balance sheet and the profit and loss account. The balance sheet shows an organisation's assets and liabilities at a precise point in time, usually the last day of the accounting year. A profit and loss account shows a firm's sales revenue over a trading period and all the relevant costs involved in generating that revenue.

Linked to: Ratio analysis, Ch 20; Key factors in change, Ch 23

19.1 Introduction

The function of accounting is to provide information to various stakeholder groups on how a particular business has performed during a given period. The groups include shareholders, managers, bankers and suppliers. The period in question is usually one year. There are two key financial documents from which this information can be drawn:

- The statement of comprehensive income is more widely known as the profit and loss account; generally, large plcs use the former phrase, while smaller companies use the latter.
- The statement of financial position is more widely known as the balance sheet; large plcs may use the former phrase, while smaller companies (and the media) use the latter.

By law, public limited companies must publish these accounting statements so that they can be investigated by journalists, competitors or staff. Late on 24 December 2014, City Link (a parcel delivery business) went into receivership. This was especially devastating for those of its drivers who had opted to be contractors, owning their own van and paying personally for it to be painted in City Link colours. They spent Christmas knowing not only that their income was at an end and that their investment in the van was wasted, but also wondering whether they would be paid any outstanding sums they were owed. If City Link had been a plc, its financial position would have been open for staff to consider. In fact, it was a private-equity-owned business so staff were completely in the dark right up until the Christmas Eve announcement.

For staff – or other interested parties – published accounts allow an analyst to find out:

- the amount of cash or near-cash the company holds in its bank accounts
- how that cash total compares with its short-term liabilities (the bills it needs to pay in the coming twelve months)
- how much of all the firm's long-term capital is in the form of debt – and therefore needs to be serviced with interest payments and eventually must be repaid
- how profitable the business is – both in absolute terms (the sum of money) and in relative terms, perhaps profit as a percentage of sales **revenue**. Between 2008 and 2015 operating profits at John Lewis rose from £394 million to £450 million. This seems less impressive when looked at as a percentage of sales: 6.5 per cent in 2008 down to 4.1 per cent in 2015. So in 2015 John Lewis made about 4p profit per £1 of sales.

Figure 19.1 John Lewis store

Real business

Between 2008 and 2015, John Lewis Partnership pursued growth objectives. Despite the difficult economic circumstances of the time, both divisions of the business (John Lewis and Waitrose) opened new stores throughout the UK. Financing this growth required huge extra borrowings, pushing long-term debts over £2.5 billion in 2015. The result of the extra debts was higher interest payments. Figure 19.2 shows the extraordinary growth in the net financing costs of John Lewis from £14 million in 2008 to £100 million in 2015. And all this at a time of record low interest rates.

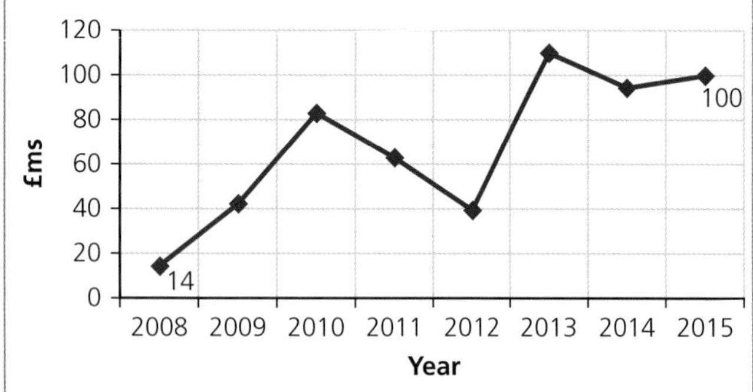

Figure 19.2 The increasing cost of coping with debt at John Lewis Partnership (source: JLP accounts)

'Debt is a prolific mother of folly and of crime.'

Benjamin Disraeli, nineteenth-century Prime Minister

19.2 Balance sheets (also known as 'statement of financial position')

This accounting document looks at the question: 'How rich are you?' To find out how rich someone is, you would need to find out what they own (big house?) and what they owe (fat mortgage?). The balance sheet does this for a business, adding up the totals on the last day of the financial year. Balance sheets show the wealth, or the indebtedness, of the business – vital information for shareholders, managers, financiers and other stakeholders.

The balance sheet shows where a business has obtained its finances – its liabilities. It also lists the assets purchased with these funds. Therefore, the balance sheet shows what the business owns and what it owes. For bankers, this is of vital importance when deciding whether or not to:

- invest in a business
- lend it some money
- buy the organisation outright.

The composition of the balance sheet

The balance sheet is a 'snapshot' showing the position of a company at a given point in time. It shows what the business owns and owes on one day; in other words, it shows an organisation's assets and liabilities.

The foundations of the balance sheet (at the bottom) consist of the firm's capital. This may have come from shareholders, bankers or from reinvested profit. If Spark plc has £400,000 of capital invested, it follows that it must have £400,000 of assets (see Table 19.1). The top section shows the type of assets bought.

Spark Ltd: Simplified balance sheet	£
Long-term (non-current) assets	300,000
Short-term (current) assets	100,000
Total assets	400,000
Balancing with: Total capital	400,000

Table 19.1 An example of a simplified balance sheet

Types of asset

Long-term (non-current) assets

Non-current assets are long-term assets such as:

- land and buildings: property owned by a business, either freehold or leasehold
- plant/machinery/equipment: anything from specialised machinery used in manufacturing to computers or even furniture
- vehicles: all types.
- patents/copyright: although patents are not physical assets such as a building, the exclusive rights to a technical advance can have huge long-term value.

Current assets

Current assets are short-term assets that change daily, perhaps hourly. There are three main types of current asset.

Inventories

This is the value of all the stock a firm holds, either on shop shelves or in warehouses; all these stocks are valued at cost in a balance sheet. This is because it's more **prudent** to value stock at the lower cost figure instead of at the higher figure for selling price (in case the stock doesn't sell and has to be sold off at a discount).

Receivables

Receivables are the sums owed by customers who have bought items on credit; for some firms this can be a large sum of money; for example, small suppliers to Boots the Chemist can be kept waiting for 105 days before

Boots pays up; if customers are big and powerful, small suppliers may have to invest a lot of their own cash in the balance sheet item 'receivables' (also known as debtors).

Cash

Cash means all forms of bank account that can easily be accessed, e.g. the balance on a current account; in business, the term **liquidity** is used to measure how able a business is to pay its bills and finance near-term spending; cash is the most liquid asset of all.

Spark plc: Fuller version of the firm's balance sheet	
	£
Property	180,000
Machinery and vehicles	120,000
Inventories	80,000
Receivables and cash	60,000
Current liabilities	(40,000)
Assets employed	400,000
Total capital	400,000

Table 19.2 An example of a fuller version of a balance sheet

Capital on the balance sheet

Companies have three main sources of long-term capital: shareholders (share capital), banks (loan capital) and retained profits (**reserves**). Loan capital carries interest charges that must be repaid, as must the loan itself. Share capital and reserves are both owed to the shareholders, but do not have to be repaid. Therefore they are treated separately. Added together, share capital and reserves are known as total equity.

Assuming Spark plc's capital came from £50,000 of share capital, £250,000 of loan capital and £100,000 of reserves, the final version of the balance sheet would look like the one shown in Table 19.3. Note that the two-column format allows sub-totals to be shown in the right-hand column.

Spark plc: Balance sheet for 31 December last year		
	£	£
Property	180,000	
Machinery and vehicles	120,000	300,000
Inventories	80,000	
Receivables and cash	60,000	
Current liabilities	**(40,000)**	
Total assets less current liabilities		**400,000**
Loan capital	(250,000)	
Net assets		150,000
Share capital	50,000	
Reserves	100,000	
Total equity		**150,000**

Table 19.3 An example of a final version of a balance sheet

19.3 Key information: assessing financial performance using a balance sheet

Financial performance really means the level of success (or failure) achieved by a business. Typically this is measured by profit – perhaps the percentage growth in profit compared with the previous year. That can be found in a firm's profit and loss account. The balance sheet gives a vital clue, though, to a company's real performance over time through the item known as reserves. This item shows the accumulated, retained profit ever since the business started trading. For a long-established business such as John Lewis, this should be a substantial figure. At the end of July 2014, the reserves figure for John Lewis was £1,861 million. If, in 2015, the business made an operating loss, that negative number would be added to the reserves total – bringing the accumulated figure down. If profits are made (and not all paid out to the owners in the form of **dividends** or bonuses), the reserves total will rise.

The value of this approach can be seen by a look at Tesco plc's performance over several years. As shown in the Figure 19.3 below, Tesco's reserves figure rose consistently in the period up until 2012. The decline in 2013 and 2014 shows the start of Tesco's financial problems. The collapse in reserves in 2015 is partly a reflection of Tesco's awful trading position, and partly due to one-off write-offs due to closure of overseas businesses and stores in the UK. The graph shows how profits accumulated in Tesco's balance sheets over many years collapsed from a value of £12 billion to £2 billion in just three years.

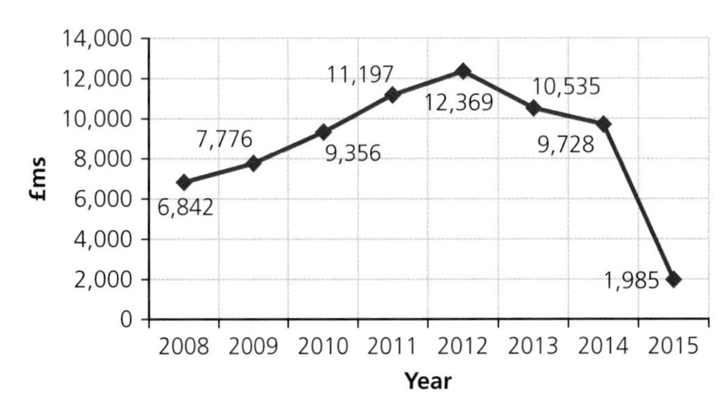

Figure 19.3 The collapse in value of Tesco's accumulated retained profits: its reserves (source: Tesco annual reports and accounts)

19.4 Stakeholder interest in balance sheets

Most companies believe that stakeholders, even shareholders, tend to steer clear of the balance sheet. The words and the numbers are assumed to be too confusing. This may be true and, if so, it's a great shame. A glance at the John Lewis Partnership accounts for 2015 suggests that stakeholders could use the data to ask some serious questions of management. These include:

- Bankers could ask: why have long-term borrowings risen nearly 50 per cent in 2015, from £629 million to £924 million? And what plans has the business for when the Bank of England starts pushing interest rates up?
- Suppliers could ask: why do you owe suppliers over £1,600m when you hold under £600 million of their stock? How long do you delay before paying your bills? (The answer is that they take 91 days to pay.)
- Staff (who are also – nominally – the owners of the business) could ask: why has the accumulated profit of the business (its reserves; its true store of wealth) declined year after year in recent times? The actual figures are as follows:

	John Lewis Partnership reserves
2012	£2,002 million
2013	£1,891 million
2014	£1,779 million
2015	£1,507 million

Table 19.4 John Lewis Partnership accounts 2012–2015

This means a quarter of the partnership's wealth has been wiped out in the period 2012–2015.

19.5 Profit and loss accounts (also known as statement of comprehensive income)

The profit and loss account (P&L) records all a business's revenues and costs within a trading period. This constitutes a vital piece of evidence for those with interests in a company. For many stakeholders, profit is the main criterion by which to judge the success of a business:

- Shareholders are an obvious example of those assessing profitability.
- Government agencies such as the tax authorities require data on profits or losses in order to be able to calculate the **liability** of a business to **corporation tax**.
- Suppliers to a business also need to know the financial position of the companies they trade with, in order to establish their reliability, stability and creditworthiness.
- Potential shareholders and bankers will also want to assess the financial position of the company before committing their funds to the business.
- Staff are also interested, especially if they receive a profit-related bonus; for partners in employee-owned John Lewis this is especially important. In 2008, a good year's profit allowed the business to pay a bonus worth 20 per cent of a year's salary to all permanent staff; poor management leading to faltering profitability explains why the bonus rate fell to 11 per cent in 2015.

Making a profit is one of the most significant objectives for business organisations. It is this profit motive that encourages many people to establish their own business or expand an existing one. Without the potential for making a profit, why should individuals and companies commit time and resources to what may be a risky venture? Even charities must seek to generate revenues to at least match their expenditure, otherwise they cannot survive. Therefore the P&L account is as important to a charity as it is to a company.

Figure 19.4 Logic chain: from daily data to the year's accounts

19.6 How a P&L account shows a company's profit or loss

Table 19.5 sets out the basic structure of a profit and loss account for a public limited company.

		£m
	Revenue	**26.0**
Less	Cost of sales	(17.0)
Gives	Gross profit	9.0
Less	Overheads	(4.0)
Gives	Operating profit	5.0
Less	Financing costs	1.5*
Gives	Profit before taxation	6.5
Less	Tax	(2.0)
Gives	Profit after taxation for the year	4.5

Table 19.5 The basic structure of a profit and loss account.
*In this case more interest was earned than paid out

The P&L comprises four main stages, as outlined below.

1. First, **gross profit** is calculated. This is the difference between the income (or 'turnover') and the cost of the goods that have been sold. The latter is normally expressed simply as 'cost of sales'.
2. Second, '**operating profit**' is calculated. This is done by deducting the main types of overhead, such as distribution costs and administration costs.
3. Next, profit before taxation is calculated, which is arrived at by the inclusion of interest received by the business and interest paid by it. These are normally shown together as a net figure labelled 'financing costs'.
4. The final stage of the P&L is to calculate profit after taxation (net profit). This is arrived at by deducting the amount of tax payable for the year and shows the net amount that has been earned for the shareholders.

Calculating gross profit

This top section of the profit and loss account shows how much revenue has been earned from sales less the **cost of sales**. In other words, it calculates gross profit.

revenue (turnover) – cost of sales = gross profit

When calculating revenue, sales taxes such as VAT are excluded as they are paid directly to the tax authorities.

Calculating operating profit

The next stage of the statement sets out the operating profit or loss made by the business. To calculate it, overhead expenses are deducted from gross profit.

Overhead expenses

Expenses are payments for something that is of immediate use to the business. These payments include cash expenditures on labour and fuel, as well as non-cash items such as depreciation.

Examples of overhead expenses include:

- wages and salaries
- rent and rates
- heating, lighting and insurance
- distribution costs.

Operating profit

Deducting overhead expenses from gross profit leads to operating profit. Most firms regard this as the key test of their trading performance for the year. At the very least a firm would want operating profit to be:

- up by at least the rate of inflation compared with the previous year
- at least as high a percentage of capital employed as that achieved by rival companies
- high enough to reinvest in the future of the business while still paying satisfactory dividends to shareholders.

Financing costs

Financing costs can add to or subtract from the operating profit of a business. Most companies have relatively high borrowings and therefore have to pay out a large proportion of their profit in interest charges. Japanese and German companies like to have substantial bank deposits earning interest, so this item can be a positive figure.

Profit before and after taxation

All businesses are required to pay corporation tax on their profits. In 2015, the rate of corporation tax paid by UK companies is 20 per cent. Once tax has been deducted, the final figure on the P&L is profit after taxation for the year. This figure is also known as net profit.

Using profits

Net profit can be used in two main ways: it can either be distributed or retained. Usually businesses retain some profits and distribute the remainder. The balance between these two uses is influenced by a number of factors.

- Distributed profit: the company directors will decide on the amount to be paid out to shareholders in the form of dividends; if the shareholders are unhappy with the sum paid out, they can vote against the dividend at the annual general meeting.
- Retained profit: any prudent owner or manager of a business will use some of the profit made by the business to reinvest in the business for the future.

> 'The substance of the eminent socialist gentleman's speech is that making a profit is a sin, but it is my belief that the real sin is taking a loss.'
>
> *Winston Churchill, UK politician and WW2 leader*

> 'The accounts are a snapshot of the business at a moment in time. Take a picture the following day and the scene may look very different. As with many of us, companies like to look their best when they are photographed and sometimes dress for the occasion.'
>
> *M.A. Pitcher, accounting author*

19.7 Key information: assessing financial performance using a profit and loss account

Public limited companies (plcs) are required by law to publish their accounts. This means that they are available for scrutiny not only by the owners (shareholders), potential investors and bankers, but also by competitors.

When a company draws up its profit and loss account for external publication, it will include as little information as possible. Public limited companies usually supply no more detail than is required by law. SuperGroup (owner of the Superdry brand) has no wish to give information to rivals such as Abercrombie & Fitch. But the following statement shows the level of detail provided by a public limited company.

	2015 (£m)	2014 (£m)
Revenue (sales excluding VAT)	486	431
Cost of sales	(190)	(174)
Gross profit	**296**	**257**
Administrative and other expenses	(236)	(212)
Operating profit	**60**	**45**
Net finance expense	(0.5)	-
Profit before tax	**59.5**	**45**
Taxation	(13.5)	(17.5)
Net profit for the year	**46**	**27.5**

Table 19.6 Summarised profit and loss account for SuperGroup plc (year ended 31 March 2015)

To assess SuperGroup's P&L, it makes sense to start at the top. In 2015, revenue rose from £431 million to £486 million, which is a rise of 12.8 per cent. This sparked a 15 per cent rise in gross profit. Administrative expenses rose, but not too much, allowing operating profit to rise by 33 per cent to £60 million. Helped by a lower tax bill in 2015, SuperGroup's net profit for the year was hugely up on the 2014 figure.

Real business

Profits and Candy Crush

In March 2014, King Inc, the company behind the Candy Crush phenomenon, launched onto the US stock market. It sold just 10 per cent of its share capital for $500 million, valuing the company at $5,000m. Many commentators were amazed that people were willing to buy shares in a business that relied on one game (Candy Crush) for 78 per cent of its revenue. But the startling growth figures shown in Table 19.7 give an idea of the attractions of the shares.

What happens when players get bored with Candy Crush, though? The share buyers hope that King will be able to come up with new products that work the same business miracle as Candy Crush.

King Digital Entertainment Inc		
	Revenue ($s)	Operating (net) profit
2011	64m	(1.3m)
2012	164m	7.8m
2013	1,880m	567.6m

Table 19.7 Starting growth figures of King Inc 2011–2013

Five whys and a how

Questions	Answers
Why do plcs have to publish their accounts?	So that any member of the public can check on the company's progress, from investor to employee.
Why is a balance sheet sometimes called a 'snapshot' of the finances of a business?	Because it's drawn up on a single day (usually the last day of the financial year). This restricts its usefulness.
Why do firms need to publish both a profit and loss account and a balance sheet?	Because the P&L shows the flow of revenue in and costs out, whereas the balance sheet shows the wealth at a point in time.
Why might it be useful to look at a company's balance sheet reserves?	Because they show how much profit has been made (and kept) in the past – and changes in reserves give insight into company performance.
Why might shares in King Digital (Candy Crush) be high risk?	Because the business is over-reliant on one game – and that game might be near or past its saturation point.
How difficult is it to get the figures right?	Tesco showed in 2014 that it's possible to get the figures wrong by £260 million; this would not surprise professors of accounting who acknowledge that it's hard to achieve the accuracy shareholders want.

19.8 Interpretation of financial statements – evaluation

Two evaluative themes can be considered in relation to published accounts. It is easy to make the assumption that a rising level of operating profit is evidence of a company that is performing well. There are a number of factors that need to be considered when making such a judgement. Has a new management pushed up prices, boosting profit for a year or so, but at the cost of damaged market share in the future? Is a company that pollutes the environment, uses materials from unsustainable sources, but makes a large profit, a successful business? Is profit necessarily the best measure of the performance of a business?

Even if we assume current profits are a good indication of how a company is performing, a number of other factors need to be taken into account. Is the market growing or declining? Are new competitors coming onto the scene? To what extent is the business achieving its corporate objectives? Is the profit earned likely to be sustained into the future? Information such as this is vital if a meaningful judgement is to be made about business success.

Key terms

Corporation tax: a tax levied as a percentage of a company's profits.

Cost of sales: all the costs arising from sales to customers, including raw materials, supplies and packaging.

Dividends: regular payments to shareholders as a reward for their investment.

Gross profit: revenue less cost of goods sold; profit made on trading activities.

Liability: a debt (that is, a bill that has not been paid or a loan that has not been repaid).

Liquidity: a measurement of a firm's ability to pay its short-term bills.

Operating profit: gross profit minus expenses.

Prudent: an accounting term meaning cautious ('being on the safe side').

Reserves: a company's accumulated, retained profit; it forms part of the company's total equity.

Revenue: sales revenue (that is, the value of sales made); also known as turnover.

19.9 Workbook

Revision questions

(40 marks; 40 minutes)

1 Outline two possible reasons why a bank would want to see a company's statement of comprehensive income. (4)

2 Look at Figure 19.2.

a) Calculate the per cent increase in the annual net financing costs for John Lewis between 2008 and 2015. (3)

b) Explain one possible effect of this increase on the business. (4)

3 Outline two ways in which employees may benefit from looking at their employer's balance sheet. (6)

4 Distinguish between gross and operating profit. (3)

5 Explain why even a charity such as Oxfam may want to make a profit. (4)

6 State two items that may be listed as current liabilities. (2)

7 Distinguish between non-current and current assets. (3)

8 Explain what may be included under the heading 'financing costs'. (4)

9 Look at the profit and loss account for SuperGroup plc shown in Table 19.6.

a) Revenue rose 12.8 per cent between 2014 and 2015, but what was the percentage change in the company's cost of sales? (3)

b) Explain one conclusion that can be drawn from those findings. (4)

Revision activities

Data response

Whitbread plc was once a brewery, but is now focused on three markets: coffee bars (Costa), budget hotels (Premier Inn) and restaurants (Beefeater Grill). Costa has been a great success both in the UK and China. Table 19.8 shows Whitbread plc's statement of comprehensive income summarised. Study the figures and answer the questions.

	Year to 28/02/15	Year to 27/02/2014
	£m	£m
Revenue (turnover)	2,608	2,294
Cost of sales	?	?
Gross profit	**1,660**	**1,472**
Operating expenses	(1,159)	(1,080)
Operating profit	**501**	**392**
Net finance income	(37)	(45)
Profit before taxation	**464**	**347**
Taxation	(98) s	(24)
Net profit for the year	**366**	**323**

Table 19.8 Adapted from Whitbread plc group report and accounts 2015

Questions (50 marks; 60 minutes)

1 a) Calculate Whitbread's cost of sales for both periods. (4)

b) Calculate each figure as a percentage of the company's revenue for the corresponding period. (4)

c) Comment on your findings. (6)

2 a) Calculate the percentage increase Whitbread achieved in 2015 compared with 2014 in:

i) revenue

ii) operating profit. (4)

b) Assess the data to suggest why the increase in operating profit was greater than the increase in sales revenue. (12)

3 Whitbread's two main operating divisions are Hotels and Restaurants (mainly Premier Inn) and Costa Coffee. UK hotel profits rose by 15.2 per cent in 2015 and at Costa UK rose by 20.7 per cent. Evaluate how Whitbread's management might respond to that information. (20)

Extended writing

1 People start businesses to make profits and from there to build a sellable asset. Evaluate how effectively the profit and loss account and balance sheet capture that information. (20)

2 'Profit is the most important thing and the way you get profit is through gross margins,' says Arthur Snyder, businessman. Evaluate whether this argument is robust. (20)

20 Ratio analysis

Definition

Ratio analysis is an examination of accounting data by relating one figure to another. This approach allows more meaningful interpretation of the data and the identification of trends.

Linked to: Interpretation of financial statements, Ch 19; Causes and effects of change, Ch 22

20.1 Introduction

The function of accounting is to provide information to stakeholders on how a business has performed over a given period. But how is performance to be judged? Is an annual profit of £1 million good or bad? Very good if the firm is a small family business; woeful if the business is KFC and annual sales exceed £10 billion. What is needed is to look at the £1 million profit in relation to another variable, such as sales revenue. This helps judge a firm's financial performance in relation to its size and its competitors. The technique used to do this is called ratio analysis.

Financial accounts, such as the profit and loss account and the balance sheet, are used for three main purposes:

1 financial control
2 planning
3 accountability.

Ratio analysis can assist in achieving these objectives. It can help the different users of financial information answer questions such as:

- Is this company/my job safe?
- Should I stop selling goods on credit to this firm?
- Should I invest in this business?

20.2 Interpreting final accounts: the investigation process

To analyse company accounts, a well-ordered and structured process needs to be followed. This should ensure that the analysis is relevant to the question being looked at. The seven-point approach shown in Figure 20.1 is helpful.

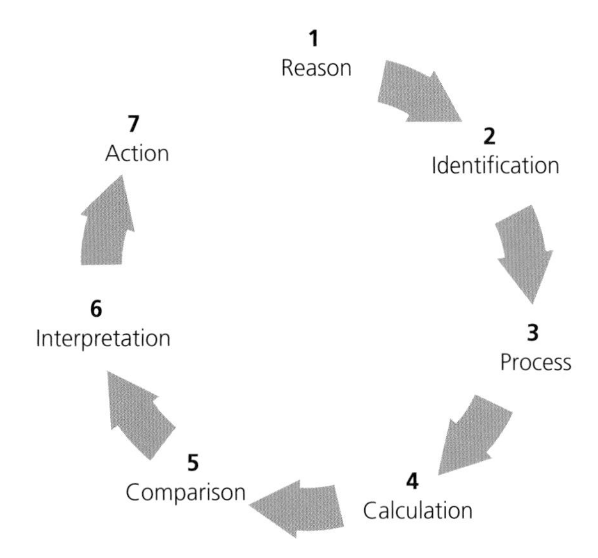

Figure 20.1 The seven-point approach to ratio analysis

20.3 Types of ratio

The main classifications of ratios are as follows.

- **Profitability ratios:** measure the relationship between gross/net profit and revenue, assets and capital employed. They are sometimes referred to as performance ratios.
- **Liquidity ratios:** these investigate the short-term financial stability of a firm by examining whether there are sufficient short-term assets to meet the short-term liabilities (debts).
- **Gearing:** examines the extent to which the business is dependent upon borrowed money; it is concerned with the long-term financial position of the company.

The following sections look at each classification of ratios in more detail. An explanation of the seven-point approach to ratio analysis is given in Table 20.1.

The investigation process		
Step 1	Reason	The starting point for interpreting financial accounts is establishing why you are doing so. If you are considering supplying a company with a large order of goods, you want to try to establish its financial stability and ability to pay.
Step 2	Identification	Identify the relevant figures from the financial accounts.
Step 3	Process	Decide which method(s) of analysis will provide you with the most useful and meaningful results.
Step 4	Calculation	Make a comparison between data by calculating one figure as a ratio of another. For example, profit as a percentage of sales revenue or borrowings as a proportion of total capital.
Step 5	Comparison	Compare the figures from this period with the results from the last period, those of your competitors or other companies under investigation.
Step 6	Interpretation	Look at the results obtained and interpret them in relation to values that would be considered poor, average or good.
Step 7	Action	If certain results are worrying, initiate further investigation (maybe into areas that are not covered in the financial accounts), or take corrective action.

Table 20.1 An explanation of the seven-point approach to ratio analysis

20.4 Liquidity ratios

These ratios focus on the short-term financial health of a business. If the ratios are too low, they may be indicating that the business will struggle to pay its bills when they come due.

Current ratio

This ratio looks at the relationship between current assets and current liabilities. It examines the **liquidity** position of the firm. It is given by the formula:

$$\text{Current ratio} = \frac{\text{current assets}}{\text{current liabilities}}$$

This is expressed as a ratio such as, for example, 2:1 or 3:1.

Example

Bannam Ltd has current assets of £30,000 and current liabilities of £10,000:

current ratio =	current assets	:	current liabilities
=	£30,000	:	£10,000
=	3	:	1

current ratio = 3

Interpretation

The above example shows that Bannam Ltd has three times as many current assets as current liabilities. This means that, for every £1 of short-term debts owed, it has £3 of assets to pay them. This is a comfortable position.

Accountants suggest the 'ideal' current ratio should be approximately 1.5:1 (that is, £1.50 of assets for every £1 of debt). Any higher than this and the organisation has too many resources tied up in unproductive assets; these could be invested more profitably (or the cash could be handed back to shareholders). A low current ratio means a business may not be able to pay its debts. It is possible that the result may well be something like 0.8:1. This shows the firm has only 80p of current assets to pay every £1 it owes.

The current ratios of a selection of public companies in 2015 are shown in Table 20.2. As this table shows, it would be wrong to panic about a liquidity ratio of less than 1. Huge firms such as Tesco have often had liquidity levels of below 1.

Company	Balance sheet date	Current assets £millions	Current liabilities £millions	Current ratio
French Connection plc	31/01/2015	£82,500,000	£37,700,000	2.19
Ted Baker plc	25/01/2015	£160,000,000	£91,100,000	1.76
Tesco plc	28/02/2015	£11,958,000,000	£19,805,000,000	0.60
Morrisons plc	01/02/2015	£1,228,000,000	£2,273,000,000	0.54
JD Wetherspoon	25/01/2015	£81,839,000	£262,784,000	0.31

Table 20.2 The current ratios of a selection of public companies in 2015

Altering the ratio

If the ratio is so low that it is becoming hard to pay the bills, the company will have to try to bring more cash into the balance sheet. This could be done by:

- selling under-used fixed assets
- raising more share capital
- increasing long-term borrowings
- postponing planned investments.

Acid test ratio

This ratio takes a sharper look at the relationship between current assets and current liabilities. It does this by excluding stock levels from the calculation. This is because when times are tough it can be very difficult to sell (to 'liquidate') stock.

Calculating the acid test ratio requires the following formula:

$$\text{Acid test ratio} = \frac{\text{current assets (excluding stock)}}{\text{current liabilities}}$$

This is expressed as a ratio such as 0.5:1.

Example

Bannam Ltd has current assets of £30,000 of which £18,000 is in the form of stock; its current liabilities are £10,000:

Acid test ratio = highly liquid assets : current liabilities

= £12,000 : £10,000

= 1.2 : 1

Interpretation

The above example shows that Bannam Ltd has 1.2 times as many highly liquid assets as current liabilities. This means that, for every £1 of short-term debts owed, it has £1.20 of assets to pay them. This is a comfortable position.

Accountants suggest the 'ideal' acid test ratio should be approximately 1:1 (that is, £1 of assets for every £1 of debt). A low acid test ratio means a business may not be able to pay its debts. It is possible that the result may well be something like 0.4:1. This shows the firm has only 40p of current assets to pay every £1 it owes.

The current ratios of a selection of public companies in 2015 are shown in Table 20.2. As this table shows, it would be wrong to panic about an acid test ratio of less than 1 (though the position of Morrisons and Wetherspoons looks worrying).

Company	Balance sheet date	Current assets excl. stock £millions	Current liabilities £millions	Acid test ratio
French Connection plc	31/01/2015	£47,000,000	£37,700,000	1.25
Ted Baker plc	25/01/2015	£48,500,000	£91,100,000	0.53
Tesco plc	28/02/2015	£9,001,000,000	£19,805,000,000	0.45
Morrisons plc	01/02/2015	£570,000,000	£2,273,000,000	0.25
JD Wetherspoon	25/01/2015	£57,757,000	£262,784,000	0.22

Table 20.3 The acid test ratios of a selection of public companies in 2015

20.5 Gearing

Gearing is one of the main measures of the financial health of a business. Quite simply, it measures the firm's level of debt. This shines a light onto the long-term financial stability of an organisation.

Gearing measures long-term liabilities as a proportion of a firm's capital employed. It shows how reliant the firm is upon borrowed money. In turn, that indicates how vulnerable the firm is to financial setbacks. The Americans call gearing 'leverage'. In boom times, banks and investors find leverage (debt) very attractive; but high gearing always means high risk.

Highly geared companies can suffer badly in recessions, because even when times are hard they still have to keep paying high interest payments to the bank.

The formula for gearing is:

$$\text{gearing} = \frac{\text{non-current liabilities}}{\text{capital employed}} \times 100$$

This is expressed as a percentage.

Interpretation

The gearing ratio shows the level of long-term risk in a company's balance sheet. If loans represent more than 50 per cent of capital employed, the company is said to be highly geared. Such a company has to pay substantial interest charges on its borrowings before it can pay dividends to shareholders or retain profits for reinvestment. The higher the gearing, the higher the degree of risk. Low-geared companies provide a lower-risk investment; therefore they can negotiate loans more easily and at lower cost than a highly geared company.

Real Business

Carlyle Capital Corporation

During the Credit Crunch, a US blogger with the fabulous name of Postman Patel warned that the Carlyle Capital Corporation (an American investment fund) was unable to pay its bills. Within a week it had collapsed, owing over $16 billion. It emerged that Carlyle Capital had a gearing level of 97 per cent. In other words, only 3 per cent of the money it invested was its own money; all the rest was borrowed. When times were good, its shares were worth $20 each. Now they were worth nothing. High gearing means high risk. Ridiculously high gearing means ridiculously high risk.

Altering the ratio

The gearing ratio can be altered in several ways, depending on whether the organisation wishes to raise or lower its gearing figure. Ways in which an organisation's gearing figure may be altered are shown in Table 20.5.

Raising gearing	Reducing gearing
Buy back ordinary shares	Issue more ordinary shares
Issue more preference shares	Retain more profits
Obtain more loans	Repay loans

Table 20.5 Altering an organisation's gearing ratio

20.6 Profitability ratios

For private businesses, a key objective is to make a profit. But how much profit? Consider the following example.

Company	Balance sheet date	Non-current liabilities (long-term loans)	Capital employed	Gearing (%)
Ted Baker plc	31/01/2015	£0	£140,574,000	0
Home Retail Group plc	28/02/2015	£311,300,000	£2,984,200,000	10.4
Morrisons plc	01/02/2015	£3,304,000,000	£6,898,000,000	47.9
Tesco plc	28/02/2015	£17,333,000,000	£24,404,000,000	71.0
JD Wetherspoon plc	25/01/2015	£781,187,000	£1,000,809,000	78.1

Table 20.4 The gearing ratios of a selection of companies in 2015

Example

Companies A and B operate in the same market. At the end of the year they report profits as follows:

	Company A	Company B
Profit	£100,000	£1 million

Table 20.6 Profits of Companies A and B

Which is the more successful company? Company B, surely. However, take into account the following additional information.

	Company A	Company B	As a %
Profit	£100,000	£1 million	10%
Sales revenue	£200,000	£10 million	2%

Table 20.7 Profits and sales revenue of Companies A and B

This shows that company A's profit is terrific in relation to its sales; better, in fact, than company B. Profitability ratios allow comparisons such as this to be made in detail. The figures can be compared in percentage terms. This makes comparison easier.

	Company A	Company B
Profit	£100,000	£1 million
Divided by	£200,000	£10 million
× 100 (to get a percentage)	50%	10%

Table 20.8 Profitabiliy ratios of Companies A and B

Company A's success can now be seen much more clearly.

Chapter 37 of the AS book (*Business Year 1* for Edexcel). looked into profit margins in detail. It is worth re-reading that section, but here is a summary of what you need to know to answer A level questions on profit margins:

	Gross profit margin	Operating profit margin	Net profit margin
Formula	Gross profit/ Sales revenue × 100	Operating profit/ Sales revenue × 100	Profit after tax/ Sales revenue × 100
What it shows	Gross profit per £ of sales	Operating profit per £ of sales	Net profit per £ of sales
How to improve it	Price up Unit variable costs down	Boost gross margin Cut overheads per £ of sales Increase sales	Boost operating profit margins Cut corporation tax bill (legally!)
Problem if it's too low	May not be enough gross profit to cover overhead expenses	May not be enough operating profit to reinvest into the business and so get growth	May be too low to provide shareholders with acceptable annual dividends

Table 20.9 Summary of profit margins and profitability

Return on capital employed (ROCE)

This is sometimes referred to as being the primary efficiency ratio and is perhaps the most important ratio of all. It measures the efficiency with which the firm generates profit from the funds invested in the business.

$$\text{ROCE} = \frac{\text{operating profit}}{\text{capital employed}} \times 100$$

Operating profit is profit after all operating costs and overheads have been deducted. Capital employed is all the long-term finance of the business (debt plus equity).

Interpretation

The higher the value of this ratio the better. A high and rising ROCE suggests that resources are being used efficiently. ROCE measures profitability and no shareholder will complain at huge returns. The figure needs to be compared with previous years and that of other companies to determine whether this year's result is satisfactory or not.

A firm's ROCE can also be compared with the percentage return offered by interest-bearing accounts at banks and building societies. If bank interest rates are 6 per cent, what is the point of a sole trader investing money in his or her business, working very hard all year and making a return on capital employed of 4 per cent? The sole trader would be better off keeping the money in the bank, taking little risk and staying at home.

So what is the *right* level of ROCE? There is no clear answer, but most companies would regard a 20 per cent ROCE as very satisfactory. The returns achieved by a selection of public companies in 2015 are shown in Table 20.12.

Real business

A difficulty with using the return on capital ratio is that modern balance sheets hide the figure for capital employed. The problem can be seen with these figures from John Lewis Partnership (see Table 20.11). To find the capital employed, it's necessary to understand a bit about the balance sheet. Capital employed is all the long-term finance within a business. It comes from three sources: share capital, reserves and long-term loans (known as non-current liabilities). In 2014, JLP had £1 million of share capital, £1,781 million of reserves and £2,037 million of long-term debt. Note that although the non-current liabilities are in brackets on the balance sheet, I don't treat the figure as a negative number. It's simply in brackets because it's a liability not an asset. So JLP's capital employed in 2014 was £3,819 million.

In 2014, the business had operating profits of £424 million, so its ROCE figure was £424/£3,819 million × 100 = 11.1 per cent.

In 2015, the figure was:

2015 share capital	£1m
2015 reserves	£1,518m
2015 non-current liabilities	£2,641m
Total 2015 capital employed:	£4,160m

Table 20.10

So 2015, ROCE was: £450.2m / £4,160m × 100 = 10.8 per cent.

All figures in £millions

	2015	2014	2013
Non-current assets	4,682	4,385	4,116
Inventories	581	554	514
Receivables	252	226	192
Cash	340	360	542
Current liabilities	(1,695)	(1,706)	(1,634)
Net current assets	(522)	(566)	(386)
Non-current liabilities	(2,641)	(2,037)	(1,828)
Net assets	1,519	1,782	1,902
Share capital	1	1	1
Reserves	1,518	1,781	1,901
Total equity	1,519	1,782	1.902

Table 20.11 John Lewis partnership balance sheet (last day of January)

Altering the ratio

The return on capital employed can be improved by:

- increasing the level of profit generated by the same level of capital invested, or
- maintaining the level of profits generated but decreasing the amount of capital it takes to do so.

Company (in Costa's case it is a division of a company)	Annual operating profit	Capital employed	ROCE
Costa UK (coffee bars)	£132,500,000	£286,100,000	46.3%
Ted Baker (retailing)	£49,759,000	£140,574,000	35.4%
Marks & Spencer (retailing)	£600,000,000	£6,085,000,000	9.9%
Mandarin Oriental (hotels)	£120,800,000	£1,537,000,000	7.9%

Table 20.12 The return on capital employed (ROCE) achieved by a selection of public limited companies in 2014/2015

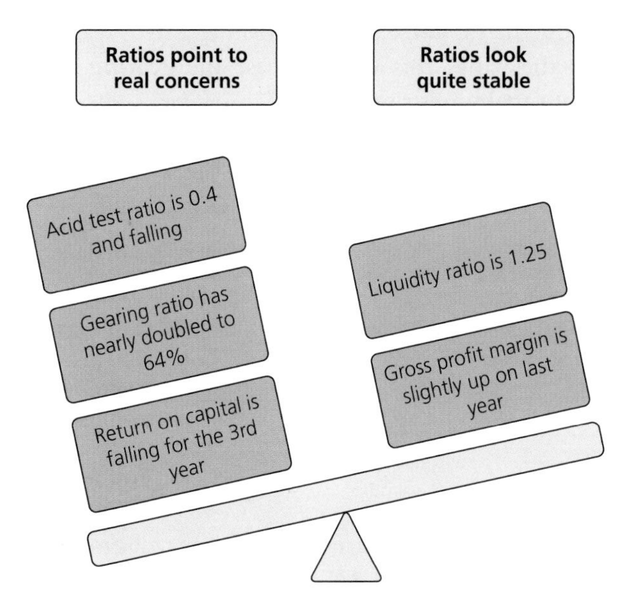

Figure 20.2 Logic balance: judging a company's finances using ratios

20.7 Interpret ratios to make business decisions

Money acts as the language of accounting, allowing business transactions to be measured, compared and added together. This means that accounts focus on items that can be given a financial value. Yet a successful business depends on a lot more than the price paid for property and equipment, or the size of its outstanding debt. For example, a firm's culture and its attitude to risk-taking will be at the heart of its performance. Similarly, a highly skilled, loyal and motivated workforce, a commitment to behaving in an ethical and environmentally friendly manner or a reputation for excellent customer service can increase a firm's ability to compete against rivals. These aspects of a business are likely to make it worth more, both to existing owners and potential buyers. However, such features are difficult to express in numerical terms and are therefore ignored by the main accounting statements.

To help make business decisions, the most important issue that ratios can help with is: can we afford it? The decision itself can be evaluated using investment appraisal or decision tree techniques. But can the business afford it? If not, it shouldn't proceed. There are three main ways of financing a decision:

- Use working capital, such as cash or the cash soon to come from customers; note, though, that taking cash from your working capital will worsen your liquidity ratios.

- Borrow the capital, e.g. in the form of a five-year loan from the bank; this will increase the gearing ratio, perhaps making it riskily high.
- Fund the expansion by asset sales; this will work well from a ratio viewpoint, but leave the business with too few assets to fall back on if times get tough.

Decision	Ratios	Evaluation
Can we afford to spend £50 million on launching in China?	Acid test 0.95 Gearing 24.5%	Finance can come from extra borrowing (to a 50% gearing maximum) plus some use of working capital (to an acid test minimum of 0.6)
Do we need to put our prices up?	Gross margin This year: 8.7% Last year: 10.2%	The problem should be addressed, but price elasticity of demand must also be considered before proceeding
Should we focus on Divisions A and B and sell off Division C?	ROCE figures for: Division A 22.6% Division B 31.4% Division C 5.7%	Unless Division C produces something of value to Division A or B, there's a strong case for selling it off and focusing on the strongest areas of the business

Table 20.13 Interpreting ratios to make decisions

20.8 Limitations of ratio analysis

Weaknesses

The main single weakness is to take the figures from ratio analysis as if they are facts; the reality is that they are more like averages – and averages can be deceiving. The average temperature for the year in London and in Calgary, Canada is similar at around 10 degrees centigrade. But in London a typical range is from +2 to +24 centigrade. In Calgary it's from –12 to +29. Consider the importance of this in relation to the following.

Receivables

Firms are usually content to sell goods on credit to customers in order to generate sales; any outstanding payments are recorded as a current asset on the balance sheet. However, this figure tells us very little about the nature of the receivables themselves. Does the overall figure consist of regular customers who can be relied upon to pay on time, or long overdue amounts that are unlikely to ever be received? A high proportion of receivables made up of **bad debts** will result in an overvaluation of a firm's current assets on the balance sheet. That would mean that the current and acid test ratio figures would overstate the true liquidity position of the business.

Stock

The value of stock at the end of a trading period affects both the value of the business due to its inclusion on the balance sheet (under current assets) and the value of profit (due to its effect on cost of goods sold in the trading account). But how reliable is the value attached to it? The value of stock can change rapidly, especially in industries subject to frequent changes in customer tastes. The traditional accounting practice is to value stock at cost or **net realisable value**, whichever is the lower. This means that the value of unsellable stock is potentially zero.

Profit quality

The ability to generate profit is generally accepted as a key indicator of success. However, it is also worth checking the source of this profit in order to assess the likelihood of such profits continuing into the future. Selling off a piece of machinery at a price above its book value will generate a surplus, but this can only happen once and is, therefore, described as being of low **profit quality**. It is important that a firm's accounts separate 'one-off' low-quality profit from the high-quality profit that results from its normal trading activities.

> 'How do you explain to an intelligent public that it is possible for two companies in the same industry to follow entirely different accounting principles and both get a true and fair audit report?'
>
> *M. Lafferty, banker and writer*

> 'Research evidence is consistent with the view that managers use latitude in existing financial reporting to benefit themselves.'
>
> *Lawrence Revsine, US academic*

20.9 Ratio analysis – evaluation

Ratio analysis is a powerful tool in the interpretation of financial accounts. It can allow for comparison between rival companies (**inter-firm comparison**), appraisal of financial performance and the identification of trends. It can therefore be of great help in financial planning and decision-making.

However, because of its usefulness and the range of possible applications, there is a tendency to attach too much importance to the results gained from this analysis. Other types of analysis exist such as market share trends, and there are sometimes more important issues at stake than just financial performance. A changing society has seen a greater interest in social and ethical aspects of business performance. Although ratio analysis is useful, it is limited in the area it investigates.

> 'When you combine ignorance and leverage (gearing), you get some pretty interesting results.'
>
> *Warren Buffet, investment guru*

> 'A pig bought on credit is forever grunting.'
>
> *Proverb*

Key terms

Bad debts: money owed to the business that will never be repaid; perhaps a customer has gone into liquidation.

Inter-firm comparisons: comparisons of financial performance between firms; to be valuable, these comparisons should be with a firm of similar size within the same market.

Liquidity: the ability of a firm to meet its short-term debts; liquidity can also be understood as being the availability of cash or assets that can easily be converted into cash.

Net realisable value: the price that can be obtained for second-hand stock after deducting the selling costs.

Profit quality: this assesses the likelihood of the source of the profit made by a business continuing in the future. High-quality profit is usually that which is generated by a firm's usual trading activities, whereas low-quality profit comes from a one-off source.

Figure 20.3 'Neither a borrower nor a lender be.' *W. Shakespeare, playwright:* Hamlet

Five whys and a how

Questions	Answers
Why are financial ratios needed at all?	Because they cut through the huge amount of data in company accounts, allowing the user to focus on a few key pieces of analysis.
Why is it sometimes said that ratios raise questions but don't answer them?	Because the ratio results don't tell you the thinking behind them, so a rise in gearing may be because the business is 'gearing up' for a major new product launch.
Why is ROCE usually regarded as the single most important ratio?	Because it shows the real profitability of the business – measured against all the capital invested, so it measures financial efficiency.
Why do some firms operate with acid test ratios as low as 0.3?	Because they have the market strength to be confident that suppliers will not press too hard to be paid on time.
Why do some businesspeople and City analysts find gearing exciting?	Because high gearing means high risks but also high rewards if things go well.
How many ratios do you really need to understand a company's performance?	The three most important ratios are ROCE (profitability), the acid test ratio (short-term financial health) and gearing (longer-term financial health).

20.10 Workbook

Revision questions

(30 marks; 30 minutes)

1 List four groups of people who may be interested in the results of ratio analysis. (4)

2 State the key stages in conducting an analysis of company accounts using ratios. (7)

3 Explain why the return on capital employed (ROCE) is regarded as one of the most important ratios. (3)

4 Explain why a financial analyst might criticise a company for having a current ratio that's 'too high'. (4)

5 Outline two problems that a company could experience if its gearing ratio rose significantly. (4)

6 Explain one reason why investors might treat the results of ratio analysis with caution. (4)

7 Explain how a business might set about improving its return on capital ratio. (4)

Practice exercises

(40 marks; 40 minutes)

1 A garden furniture producer wants to buy a garden centre. It has identified two possible businesses and conducted some ratio analyses to help it decide which one to focus on. Look at the ratios in Table 20.14, and decide which business you would recommend and why. (10)

	Blooms of Broadway	Cotswold Carnations
Gross profit margin	60%	45%
Return on capital	15.2%	14.6%
Gearing	52%	35%
Sales growth (last 3 years)	+3.5% per year	+4.8% per year

Table 20.14 Ratio analysis conducted for two garden centres

2 The balance sheet for GrowMax Co as at 31 December is shown in Table 20.15.

	£000
Non-current assets	860
Inventories	85
Receivables	180
Cash	15
Current liabilities	200
Non-current liabilities	360
Share capital	160
Reserves	420

Table 20.15 Balance sheet for GrowMax Co as at 31 December

a) Calculate the firm's net current assets and capital employed. (8)

b) Last year's revenue was £1,460,000 and operating profit margin was 10 per cent. Assess the firm's profitability this year. (10)

c) Assess the difficulties there may be in drawing firm conclusions from comparisons between the ratios of two rival companies. (12)

Revision activities

Data response

	Tesco 2015	Sainsbury's 2015	Morrisons 2015
Revenue	62,300	23,800	17,700
Cost of sales	(64,400)	(22,600)	(16,600)
Gross profit	(2,100)	1,200	1,100
Overheads and interest charges	(3,300)	(550)	(400)
Exceptional one-off profits/losses	(1,000)	(720)	(900)
Pre-tax (operating) profit	(6,400)	(70)	(200)
Tax	600	(90)	(50)
Profit after tax	(5,800)	(160)	(250)
Dividends	(900)	(330)	(280)
Retained profit	(6,700)	(490)	(530)

Table 20.16 Published accounts from three grocery retailers: Income statement (year to Feb/March 2015) (all figures in £millions)

	Tesco 2015	Sainsbury's 2015	Morrisons 2015
Fixed (non-current) assets	**32,200**	**12,000**	**7,950**
Stock (inventories)	3,000	1,000	660
Debtors (receivables)	6,300	2,200	330
Cash	2,700	1,300	240
Trade payables	(10,000)	(6,300)	(2,230)
Overdraft	(9,800)	(600)	(50)
Net current assets	**(7,800)**	**(2,400)**	**(1,050)**
Long-term (non-current) liabilities	(17,300)	(4,100)	(3,300)
NET ASSETS	**7,100**	**5,500**	**3,600**
Share capital	5,500	1,600	400
Reserves	1,600	3,900	3,200
TOTAL EQUITY	**7,100**	**5,500**	**3,600**

Table 20.17 Published accounts from three grocery retailers. Balance sheets as at Feb/March 2015 (all figures in £millions)

Questions (40 marks; 45 minutes)

1 a) Calculate the current ratio for each of the three retailers. (4)

b) Assess the liquidity of each on the basis of your findings. (10)

2 Assess the profitability of the three retailers using return on capital employed. (12)

3 a) Calculate the gearing levels for each of the three grocers. (4)

b) On the basis of this data, assess which is in the weakest position to raise extra loan capital. (10)

Extended writing

1 'The ability to assess the long- and short-term financial stability of an organisation is vital to every stakeholder.' Evaluate this statement. (20)

2 With the economy entering a recession, an investor wants to reassess her share portfolio. Evaluate whether she can rely solely on the return on capital ratio, given the economic circumstances. (20)

21 Human resources

Definition

Human resources is a common term for the personnel function of a business. HR professionals think of their role as central to the overall goals of the business, and set their HR objectives accordingly.

Linked to: Corporate strategy, Ch 2; Corporate culture, Ch 16; Causes and effects of change, Ch 22; Key factors in change, Ch 23; Scenario planning, Ch 24

21.1 Introduction

People are a resource of the business. Like any other resource, they have to be managed. Many organisations claim their people are their 'most important asset' and that HR management makes a significant difference to business success. All too often, though, staff are treated like a cost, not an asset.

21.2 The management of people

The management of people (otherwise known as human resource management) involves a wide range of activities. These begin with identifying the workforce requirements of an organisation in the future so that the appropriate plans can then be developed. For example, more staff may need to be recruited, existing staff may need training or redeployment, or redundancies may be needed.

In addition to managing the flow of people into and out of an organisation, human resource management involves activities such as those listed below.

- Designing the jobs that people do: this can have a big effect on their motivation and effectiveness; poor job design may be demotivating and lead to increased labour turnover.
- Developing appropriate reward systems: this will have a big impact on how employees behave. For example, a commission-based system is likely to push employees to make sales, but staff may be unwilling to do tasks that do not directly lead to a sale.
- Developing effective communication systems: these may include bulletins from managers, newsletters, systems of meetings or consultation with employee representatives. The communication systems will be designed to inform employees and at the same time achieve a desired level of consultation with staff.

The decisions taken by the human resource function will be linked to the overall business objectives and strategy. For example:

- If the business is growing, the HR function may need to recruit more staff; if it is expanding abroad, it will recruit staff with language skills.
- If the business is changing the nature of its operations, HR staff may need to invest more in training to ensure employees have the right skills; alternatively, it may mean some jobs are lost and others are created.
- If the business is trying to reduce its costs, then HR will be looking for ways of helping to bring this about; for example, combining jobs, boosting productivity or reducing the training budget.

> 'We treat our people like royalty. If you honour and serve the people who work for you, they will honour and serve you.'
>
> *Mary Kay Ash, American entrepreneur*

> 'We have always found that people are most productive in small teams with tight budgets, time lines and the freedom to solve their own problems.'
>
> *John Rollwagen, Chief Executive, Cray Research*

21.3 Monitoring the effectiveness of human resources

Staff costs are usually between 25 and 50 per cent of a firm's total costs. So firms try to measure the performance of their people objectively (that is, in an unbiased way). Accurate data can help point to areas of strength or weakness in the way staff are managed. Companies focus on calculating and interpreting the following personnel measures:

- labour productivity
- labour turnover and retention
- absenteeism.

21.4 Labour productivity

Labour productivity is often seen as the single most important measure of how well a firm's workers are doing. It compares the number of workers with the output they are generating. It is expressed through the formula:

$$\frac{\text{output per period}}{\text{number of employees per period}}$$

For example, if a window cleaning business employs ten people and in a day cleans the windows of 150 houses, then the productivity is:

$$\frac{150}{10} = 15 \text{ houses per worker per day}$$

Any increase in the productivity figure suggests an improvement in efficiency. The importance of productivity lies in its impact on labour costs per unit. For example, the productivity of AES Cleaning is 15 houses per worker per day; MS Cleaning achieves only 10. Assuming a daily rate of pay of £45, the labour cost per house is £3 for AES but £4.50 for MS Cleaning. Higher productivity leads to lower labour costs per unit. And therefore leads to greater competitiveness both here and against international rivals.

Figure 21.1 Higher productivity leads to more windows cleaned in a given time and therefore lower labour costs per unit

Real business

The UK's largest recruitment firm is 'on the front foot for the first time in years,' says its boss. Perhaps white-collar recruitment group Hays can teach Britain's economic policymakers a thing or two. While they fret about the country's low productivity, the UK's biggest recruitment firm has been investing heavily to ensure it becomes more productive.

That effort is now paying off, according to chief executive Alistair Cox, and helped Hays post a forecast-beating pre-tax profit up 10 per cent at £62.5 million as it delivered first-half results yesterday. 'We've had a diligent focus on productivity,' said Mr Cox. 'As a recruiter, we're the ultimate people business. We've brought in quality people, we've trained them, managed them, equipped them to do the job as best as is possible. We're the only recruiter to bother investing in technology.

Cynics might argue that he's taking the credit for an improving global economy that's actually driving the performance. However, credit where credit's due: net income rose by just 1 per cent to £363.4 million, so the 10 per cent profit increase was impressive. During the half-year in question, total operating costs fell by just over 1 per cent.

(Source: adapted from the Telegraph, *27 February 2014)*

21.5 Labour turnover

This is a measure of the rate of change of a firm's workforce. It is measured by the ratio:

$$\frac{\text{number of staff leaving the firm per year}}{\text{average number of staff}} \times 100$$

So a firm which has seen five people leave out of its staff of 50 has a labour turnover of:

$$\frac{5}{50} \times 100 = 10 \text{ per cent}$$

As with all business data, it is best to find a means of comparison: either with a rival business or with previous years' figures. Sometimes it will be hard to make a realistic comparison between labour productivity at two rival companies. After all, Nissan UK may produce more cars per employee than BMW Mini, but if Nissan uses more imported car parts, is its productivity really any higher?

There are other effective measures of productivity. In retail businesses a favoured measure is sales per square foot. This measures sales revenue in relation to the sales area of the business. Tesco might have found the decline in this figure quite depressing:

	2011	2012	2013	2014	2015
Tesco weekly sales per square foot	£24.95	£24.86	£24.15	£23.33	£22.41

Table 21.1 Tesco productivity measured by sales per square foot of shop-floor space

Fortunately it can easily find comparable data in the annual reports of Sainsbury's and Morrisons – both plcs. This makes better reading. Despite its decline between 2011 and 2015, Tesco still beats its rivals on this measure of productivity.

	2011	2012	2013	2014	2015
Sainsbury's weekly sales per square foot	£20.04	£19.47	£19.27	£18.93	£18.24
Morrisons weekly sales per square foot	£22.38	£22.52	£21.62	£20.58	£19.11

Table 21.2 Comparable data on productivity measured by sales per square foot of shop-floor space

Factors affecting labour turnover

If the rate of labour turnover is increasing, it may be a sign of dissatisfaction within the workforce. If so, the possible causes could be either internal to the firm or external.

Internal causes

Internal causes of an increasing rate of labour turnover could be:

- A poor recruitment and selection procedure, appointing the wrong person to the wrong post. When this happens, frustrated workers leave to find a job better suited to their particular interests or talents.
- Ineffective motivation or leadership, leading to workers lacking commitment to this particular firm.
- Wage levels that are lower than those being earned by similar workers in other local firms. If wage rates are not competitive, workers are likely to look elsewhere to find a better reward for doing a similar job.

External causes

External causes of an increasing rate of labour turnover could be:

- more local vacancies arising, perhaps due to the setting up or expansion of other firms in the area
- better transport links, making a wider geographical area accessible for workers. New public transport systems enable workers to take employment that was previously out of their reach.

Consequences of high labour turnover

Negative effects

A high rate of labour turnover can have both negative and positive effects on a firm. The negative aspects would be:

- the cost of recruiting replacements
- the cost of training replacements
- the time taken for new recruits to settle into the business and adopt the firm's culture
- the loss of productivity while the new workers learn the new ways of working (reach the peak on their learning curve).

Positive effects

On the positive side, labour turnover can benefit the business in several ways:

- New workers can bring new ideas and enthusiasm to the firm.
- Workers with specific skills can be employed rather than having to train up existing workers from scratch.
- New ways of solving problems can be seen by workers with a different perspective, whereas existing workers may rely on tried and trusted techniques that have worked in the past.

On balance, then, there is a need for firms to achieve the *right* level of labour turnover, rather than aiming for the lowest possible level.

Another way of measuring the loyalty and commitment of staff is to look at labour retention rates. This calculation is based on exactly the same raw data as labour turnover, but uses the information differently.

Formula for labour retention:

$$\frac{\text{staff not leaving in the past year}}{\text{average number of staff employed in the year}} \times 100$$

A high level of retention means a low level of labour turnover. The figures are based on the same raw data, but perhaps a focus on retention helps managers realise the importance of looking after existing staff. As Liverpool FC found out when Luis Suarez left the club, staff retention matters.

21.6 Absenteeism

Absenteeism is measured solely on the basis of staff days absent per year (or staff absences as a percentage of the available working days). The key point here is that the figures ignore the question of whether the absence was avoidable or unavoidable. It is simply time off – whether or not it is justifiable. According to the Chartered Institute of Personnel Management (CIPD), the correct formula is:

$$\frac{\text{Total absence (hours or days) in the period}}{\text{Possible total}} \times 100$$

According to the CIPD's own research, in 2014, the average workplace absenteeism level was 7.4 days which translates into 3.3 per cent of all working days. Out of their sample of 342 employers they found seven workplaces where absenteeism was higher than 10 per cent, i.e. three or more times higher than the average. For the average business, then, absenteeism is a relatively small issue; but there are some companies that put themselves at a serious competitive disadvantage because of high absenteeism.

21.7 Using employee performance data to help make business decisions

For young, dynamic companies such as Fever-Tree and Just Eat, each with annual growth rates of 50 per cent, the key to success is a working environment that fosters creativity, team working and intensity of effort. These qualities may not translate into measures such as productivity. After internal discussion, Just Eat's chief executive announced in August 2015 that 'Our competitors want to be in 50, 60 or 70 markets. That is not our strategy. We're about identifying the best 15 or 20 markets in the world and being the big winner in those markets.' This is a strategic decision that will determine whether Just Eat continues to be a success over the coming ten years or so.

For almost all companies, the heady days of youth are replaced by a more stable period of maturity. Think Coca-Cola, easyJet, Prêt à Manger and Next. In a more stable period, brilliant ideas may be largely irrelevant. Launching 'green' Coke Life, for example, made little difference to overall sales of Coke. In a company's maturity phase, efficiency becomes all-important. In 2015, the insurance company Direct Line declared first-half revenues that were unchanged on 2014; but because the business had

	Formula	Interpretation	Intervention
Labour productivity	$\frac{\text{output per period}}{\text{number of employees per period}}$	The higher the figure the higher the productivity (and therefore the lower the labour cost per unit).	Boosting productivity requires involved, motivated staff plus heavy investment in new technology, training and R&D.
Labour turnover	$\frac{\text{staff leaving per year}}{\text{Average number of staff}} \times 100$	The higher the figure the greater the threat to the culture, the efficiency and the consistency of the customer experience.	When recruiting it's vital to get staff who fit the culture and the ambitions of the workplace; otherwise they leave before they settle in.
Labour retention	$\frac{\text{staff } \textbf{not} \text{ leaving per year}}{\text{Average number of staff}} \times 100$	The higher the figure the better, though 'new blood' can inject new creativity – so 100% retention is unlikely to be successful for long.	To avoid established staff leaving, job enrichment and fair treatment are key (in effect, bosses should follow Herzberg's two-factor theory).
Absenteeism	$\frac{\text{Days absent per year}}{\text{Toatl number of working days}} \times 100$	Absenteeism implies something voluntary. A brilliant employee with elderly, sickly parents may have high absence levels, but still be invaluable.	It could be argued that this is an old-fashioned measure. The key is whether an employee does their job well; if someone works twelve-hour days for a week and then takes a day off, are they really 'absent'?

Table 21.3 Calculating and interpreting key measures of human resource effectiveness

cut its costs by almost 8 per cent, pre-tax profits jumped by 49 per cent to £315 million. In this world of mature companies, performance measures such as productivity and absenteeism may be crucial. After all, how is it possible for a big business such as Direct Line to cut costs by 8 per cent? Finding greater efficiencies will be the answer.

Two of the world's biggest car makers are Toyota (Japan) and General Motors (USA). Each produces about 10 million cars a year, generating revenues of $150–200 billion each. But in 2014/2015, Toyota made a pre-tax profit margin of 10.62 per cent while General Motors (GM) made 2.72 per cent. In other words, Toyota is four times more profitable than GM. This is unsustainable for GM in the long term. The American car maker needs to consider decisions such as the following:

- Addressing productivity levels head on; Toyota is the innovator behind much of lean production; perhaps GM needs to find new ways to boost productivity that fit in with lean production, such as minimising re-work by getting things right first time; high quality production means jobs are done once and once only – which helps boost productivity.
- Labour turnover and retention levels are affected by Toyota's support of the Japanese philosophy that a job is for life. Japanese firms like to have a big core of full-time, permanent staff who feel committed to the company; in America (as in Britain) there's a greater instinct by companies to treat workers as costs, not assets. This leads to short-term contract staff and therefore high labour turnover.
- Absenteeism is virtually unknown in Japan; this is partly cultural but also rooted in the teamwork approach prominent at companies like Toyota; to be absent would mean letting down your friends and those you respect (your bosses). In some western businesses it just means letting 'them' down – 'them' meaning management.

21.8 Human resource strategies to improve employee performance

In order to improve productivity, lower labour turnover and minimise absenteeism, businesses need to consider appropriate strategies. As mentioned above, the approach to personnel taken by Toyota may be an important element in the company's superior performance to General Motors. Among the possible strategies are:

- financial rewards
- employee share ownership
- consultation strategies
- empowerment strategies.

Financial rewards

Human resource managers are constantly on the lookout for a system of financial rewards that will raise productivity, boost participation and increase employee retention. Governments follow the same approach, believing that teachers or doctors can be motivated by a payments-by-results financial package. There is some excuse for this on the part of the HR professionals, because they need to justify their employment. For government there is no excuse, because research over many years has done little more than confirm Professor Herzberg's dictum from 1959: beware of meddling with hygiene factors (such as pay and working conditions that can cause job dissatisfaction).

Herzberg warned that manipulation of employee behaviour through financial means risks creating wrong incentives or even 'revenge psychology' on the part of staff. Ask Lloyds Bank. In July 2015, the bank upped its provisions for compensation payments on 'PPI' misselling to £13.4 billion. The bank's own financial reward system had encouraged its own staff to sell payment protection insurance (PPI) to people who didn't need it. Losing £13.4 billion may have persuaded Lloyds that financial reward systems distort behaviour. Better by far to employ good, honest people, train them well and pay them a decent salary.

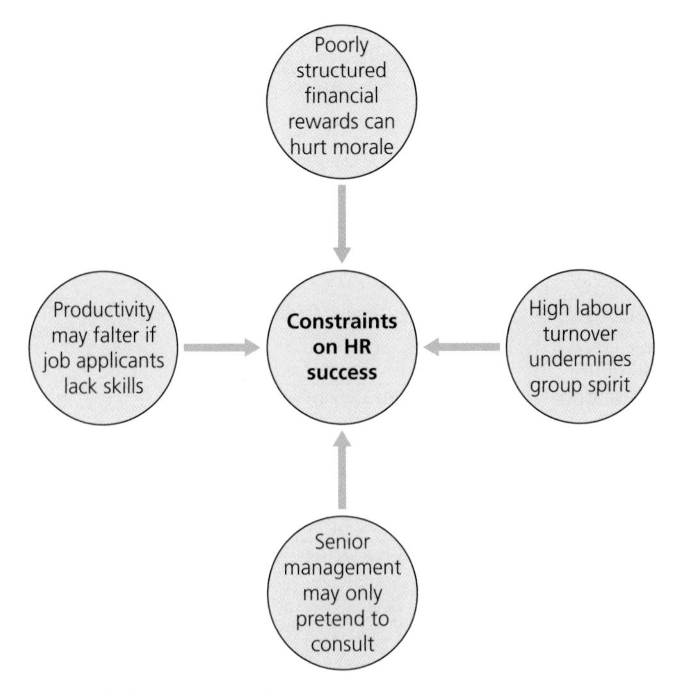

Figure 21.2 Logic circle: HR management isn't easy

Employee share ownership

The theory is clear: give staff a stake in the business and they'll feel part of the whole instead of seeing a them-and-us divide between management and staff. Therefore staff will be more motivated and more committed to long-term employment. *Financial Times* journalist Tim Harford says that 'A study by Alec Bryson and Richard Freeman of the Centre for Economic Performance at the London School of Economics found that employee ownership was positively correlated with productivity ... Mr Bryson and Mr Freeman also surveyed other studies and conclude that none found any negative impacts of employee share ownership and some found positive effects.'

It would be a mistake to overestimate the value of employee ownership, though. Every week the *Grocer* magazine does a 'mystery shopper' rating of a branch of the Big Five supermarkets. In the 25 July 2015 issue, the top rated store was Morrisons, Beverley, Yorkshire with 81/100; bottom was Waitrose, Beckenham, London with 47/100. The company's own data shows that labour turnover at Waitrose was 34.1 per cent in 2014/2015, which is far from impressive. So employee ownership (Waitrose is part of the John Lewis Partnership) proves little.

Consultation strategies

In its 2014/2015 annual report, John Lewis quotes a survey finding that 75 per cent of partners (full-time staff) agree with the statement 'we create real influence over our working lives'. For any business this would be an encouraging finding.

The John Lewis strategy for achieving this is to have a consultation forum called 'Partner Voice' that feeds through 'Divisional Forums' into the 'Partnership Council'. In effect, this is a fusion of democratic and consultative procedures. It certainly gives a theoretical input from the shop floor into the boardroom. However impressive the structures, though, the real issue is whether suggestions or complaints from the shop floor are acted upon by those at the top.

At a global giant such as Unilever, consultation becomes that much harder. With nearly 200,000 staff spread over more than 100 countries, the business chose in 2014 to use social media as a mechanism for a two-day management conference. Four hundred senior managers held a two-day online meeting with 16,000 **line managers**! Of the 16,000 employees invited to be part of the event, only 3,680 were active users of the company's internal chatsite before the event. During the conference this number rose to 7,520. Employees also reported feeling more included and motivated thanks to the initiative. When asked directly how useful participants found the experience, 86 per cent of respondents shared feedback like: 'It did provide real-time information on key programme results. It was like following an internal Twitter feed', 'I felt as though I were actually attending the event!', 'A big step in democratisation of information in Unilever'.

Empowerment strategies

Important though consultation can be, empowerment is at another level. Empowerment means delegating not only the power to decide how to tackle a task, but also to decide which task to tackle. In other words, it means allowing junior staff to set their own objectives and then the strategy for achieving them. A great example is at Google, where staff are allowed 20 per cent of their working hours to work on their own projects. They don't have to get approval for what those projects are (so designing a new bathroom might be someone's priority). In fact, important breakthroughs such as Gmail have come from this open approach to empowerment at the company.

The key to an effective empowerment strategy is to have such strong, clear organisational aims and culture that staff will know what's relevant and what's unacceptable. When Google staff started working on a self-drive car it probably seemed a wild gamble – but the staff knew that it was a way of leveraging various Google corporate strengths – notably a mastery of complex software algorithms.

Many other firms have followed (or preceded) Google's approach. In the 1990s, an inward-looking South Korean company called Samsung decided to send its best young staff to live for a year in different foreign countries. They returned with a good understanding of local habits – and this must surely have made it easier for Samsung to take on Apple in the global market for smartphones.

> **'There was a time when people were "factors of production" managed little differently from machines or capital. No more. The best people will not tolerate it.'**
>
> *Robert Waterman, business writer*

> **'Companies used to be able to function with autocratic bosses. We don't live in that world anymore.'**
>
> *Rosabeth Moss Kanter, business guru*

Five whys and a how

Question	Answer
Why might productivity fall during a period when sales are rising?	Management might get complacent, recruiting more staff than the revenue increase warrants.
Why does rising productivity tend to push labour costs per unit down?	Because employees' wages are being spread over more units of output.
Why might staff retention figures improve during a recession?	Staff are scared to risk unemployment, so they stay put even if they get little satisfaction from their jobs.
Why might a company's labour turnover figures have worsened steadily over the past four years?	There may be a new management approach that puts more pressure on staff, encouraging increasing numbers of them to look for work elsewhere.
Why might the Chancellor of the Exchequer be concerned if UK productivity figures failed to rise?	He or she would worry, because without productivity gains our economy has no prospects for sustained economic growth; rising efficiency makes it easier to export, and easier to fight off imported goods.
How might a head teacher view a big rise in labour turnover since his/her arrival?	He or she would probably ignore the possibility that staff are leaving due to disappointment with him/her; but that might be the real reason.

21.9 Human resources – evaluation

The term 'human resources' is a controversial one, smacking of treating people no differently from other resources such as land and capital. In fact, most successful companies see their staff as the beating heart of the organisation – to be paid well and treated well. If your people come up with sufficiently brilliant new products or new routes to market, competitive issues such as productivity and absenteeism will become minor matters.

The hard thing, though, is to move from a weak to a strong position. When David Potts took over at Morrisons in early 2015, he inherited a demoralised staff. To his credit, consulting with staff and acting quickly on staff grumbles allowed him to make a real impact. Interestingly, one of the new boss's first actions was to scrap 'scan rates' at checkouts as a measure of productivity. Staff objected to the conflict it created between speed and being friendly to customers. In the best organisations, measures of employee efficiency are used intelligently, not as a stick to beat managers.

Key term

Line managers: staff with responsibility for achieving specific business objectives, and with the resources to get things done.

21.10 Workbook

Revision questions

(25 marks; 25 minutes)

1. What may be the effects of managing human resources in the same way as all the other resources used by a business? (3)
2. Identify three important features of the job of a human resource manager. (3)
3. How could an increase in labour productivity help a firm to reduce its costs per unit? (3)
4. In what ways could a hotel business benefit if labour turnover rose from 2 to 15 per cent per year? (4)
5. Some fast food outlets have labour turnover as high as 100 per cent per year. What could be the effects of this on the firm? (4)
6. Explain two ways in which a human resources manager may be able to help increase productivity at a clothes shop. (8)

Revision activities

Data response

Employers face high staff turnover in 2014

A fifth of employees plan to quit their job this year, according to a survey from the Institute of Leadership and Management (ILM). The study, of 1,001 workers, found that of the staff who are preparing to change job, 16 per cent want to leave because they do not feel valued. Of this group, the vast majority would like a similar job (40 per cent) or a different post (39 per cent) at a new company, while one in ten would like to start their own business.

However, in addition to the fifth of workers planning to leave, a further 31 per cent are unsure about whether they will stay in their current roles, suggesting employers face a high staff turnover in the coming months.

Charles Elvin, ILM's chief executive, said: 'The New Year is always a popular time for workers to look ahead and think about how they can progress. Our findings show that UK employees are beginning to reassess the job market and look into a range of new opportunities, from starting a new job to developing a new business.

'The survey illustrates just how crucial it is that workers feel valued in the workplace. As many workers like to make a change at this time of year, it is important that organisations adapt to this phase by offering the chance to learn new skills and opportunities to progress wherever possible.'

The survey also asked employees about their workplace resolutions for the New Year. Most respondents (31 per cent) said improving their work–life balance was a top priority for 2014; this was closely followed by a desire to receive more training or attain a new qualification (28 per cent), to become a better manager (13 per cent), and be more productive at work (11 per cent). The ILM said that the findings revealed a desire to improve the standards of leadership in organisations, with 19 per cent hoping to improve their own leadership skills this year and 17 per cent hoping for more transparent leadership from their boss.

'The survey reinforces the importance of leadership to workers in the UK, and in particular the desire for greater transparency in the workplace,' Elvin added. 'This should be an important consideration for both current managers and those looking to improve their leadership skills.'

(*Source:* People Management Magazine *online, January 2014*)

Questions (40 marks; 45 minutes)

1. During the recent recession labour turnover fell. Assess two possible reasons why. (8)
2. Assess why labour turnover was expected to rise in Britain in 2014. (12)
3. Is high labour turnover always a course for concern? Evaluate the potential benefits and drawbacks of a high labour turnover for either Primark or Jaguar Land Rover. (20)

Extended writing

1. Evaluate the ways in which a firm may respond to an increasing rate of labour turnover. In your answer, refer to one retail business and one other organisation you have researched. (20)
2. In 2014, Tesco announced that it planned to open a supermarket chain in India, one of the world's fastest growing economies. Evaluate the extent to which Tesco's success or failure in India might depend upon a successful HR strategy. (20)

22 Causes and effects of change

Definition

Change is a constant feature of business activity. The key issues are whether it has been foreseen by the company – and therefore planned for – and whether it is within the company's control.

Linked to: Impact of external influences, Ch 5; Growth, Ch 7; Mergers and takeovers, Ch 9; Reasons for staying small, Ch 10; Key factors in change, Ch 23; Scenario planning, Ch 24

22.1 The value of change

No one should doubt that most businesses, like most people, hate change. Just try persuading football supporters that it's time for a new home ground, or children that it's time to try a new type of food. So most business leaders drool over:

- Coca-Cola, born 125 years' ago, but still with 2015 retail sales of £1,154 million in the UK alone
- Cadbury's Dairy Milk, more than 100 years' old and with 2015 sales of £486 million in the UK.

Businesspeople value lack of change, because it makes it easier to hang on to strong profits. For the consumer, though, change has potentially huge benefits. Although we may want Cadbury's Dairy Milk unchanged, we benefit hugely when online retailers force shops to push prices down, or when Netflix starts paying for its own, high-quality programming – to draw in more subscribers.

And when change comes, managements have to rethink their whole operation, to figure out how to be more efficient while simultaneously offering exciting new products or services to customers. It's at that point that change can be of value to many stakeholders: customers, shareholders, managers and perhaps the environment as well.

22.2 Internal and external causes of change

Change arises as a result of various internal and external causes. The internal ones (such as a change in objectives) should at least be planned for. External causes may be unexpected, which makes them far harder to manage. Table 22.1 sets out some possible internal and external causes of change.

Internal causes	External causes
• Changes in organisational size • Poor business performance • New ownership • Transformational leadership	• Changes in the market • Political • Economic • Social • Technological • Legal • Environmental

Table 22.1 Examples of internal and external causes of change

22.3 Internal causes of change

Changes in organisational size

Whether a business expands or contracts, there will be pressures for change to the organisational structure and to the balance between spending for growth (R&D, new technology, new capacity) and spending for survival (labour-saving capital spending, redundancy payments). In either case, the impact on the business is short-term disruption that, if mishandled, can damage long-term relationships within the business – especially those between management and staff.

Whenever management hierarchies are reorganised, there are winners and losers. At a time of growth, creating new horizontal management layers will be necessary to prevent spans of control getting too wide. But with every promotion opportunity there will be staff members who get passed over – and feel unfairly treated. Some will then harbour suspicions of discrimination or favouritism – and of course they may be right. If **downsizing** is needed, the implications are still worse, with people actually being selected for redundancy (an embittering process) and others left behind, wondering whether they may be next to go.

Handling this process well is a huge test of leadership skill. At the time of writing, new Morrisons boss David Potts seems to have been able to make redundancies to senior and middle management in ways that have impressed shop floor staff. Very clever.

Poor business performance

In most modern boardrooms, the chief executive is judged by whether agreed objectives have been achieved. In early 2014, the boss of Whitbread plc announced that his Costa Coffee division would be expanding its number of coffee bars in China from 300 to 700 by 2017. If, by late 2016, it becomes clear that this objective will not be achieved, the directors will ask serious questions. From this may come a demand for change. Either that change will be at the top, or the chief executive must be able to explain why the disappointment happened and what will be done to prevent a recurrence. Ultimately, the job of the directors is to make sure that poor performance is never tolerated.

New ownership

Business is unpredictable because different people make different decisions based on the same evidence. So if ownership changes, policies can change – even if things were going well before. This is especially likely when the reason behind a takeover was strategic. In July 2015, German rivals BMW, Mercedes and Audi (VW) together paid £2 billion for Nokia's digital mapping business (called 'Here'). They did it to seize control of car navigation software that had been included in 80 per cent of new cars sold in Europe. In effect, it was an attempt to prevent newcomers such as Apple and Google from easily being able to develop their new driverless cars. Needless to say, the new ownership is likely to cause significant change to the internal operations of the business. Here employs 6,000 staff – they will doubtless find a huge amount of change as their new owners refocus the business on the development needs of the German luxury car market

Transformational leadership

A transformational leader can achieve change in a situation that others might find too difficult. After its 2015 election defeat, the Labour Party collapsed into squabbling. It needed a new vision, new policies and a clear focus on a defined but large section of the population. It desperately needed a transformational leader. As of August 2015, there was no sign!

When Indian-born Rajeev Suri became chief executive (CEO) at Nokia in 2014, he was taking over a business that had been humiliated in the smartphone market by Apple and Samsung. It had just given up on a market for which it was once the global number one. Since then Suri has transformed the Finnish company, but without needing large redundancy programmes.

A new approach by a transformational leader might require flattening a hierarchy to create more empowerment and generate more creative thinking – or it might be focused on finding new efficiencies to cut costs and improve competitiveness. Either way, there will be significant human and structural change.

22.4 External causes of change

Changes in the market

Market change can come about from a combination of business, economic and social factors. In the UK grocery market, a remarkable market share boom pushed discounters Aldi and Lidl to the forefront, creating a panicky price-cutting reaction from the other grocers. In Figure 22.1, contrast Morrisons' position in 2012 compared with Aldi and Lidl, then do the same for 2015. The impact of Aldi and Lidl on Morrisons was dramatic. Asda/Wal-mart might also be needing an urgent change in management strategy.

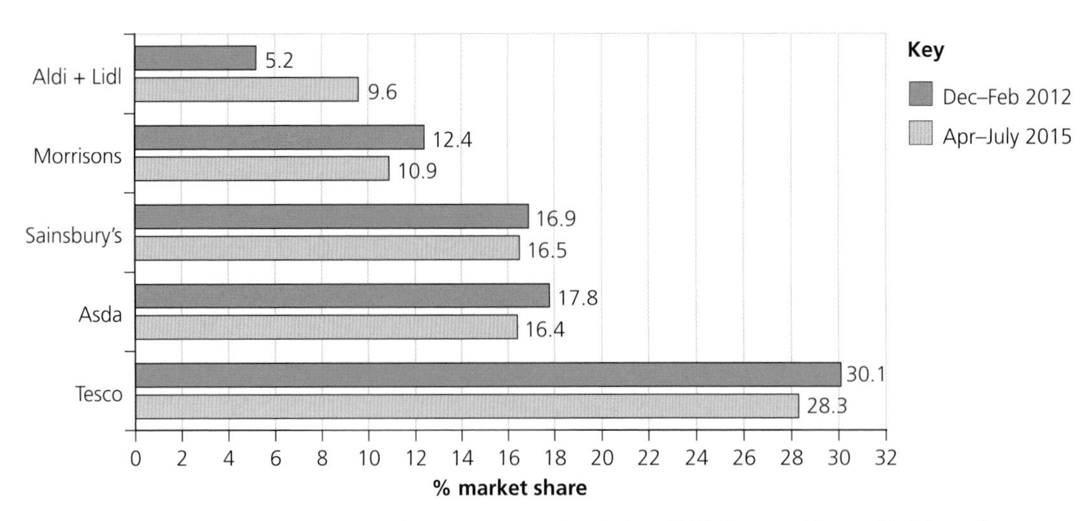

Figure 22.1 Grocery market transformation: booming Aldi and Lidl (source: Kantar Worldpanel)

'All great change in business has come from outside the firm, not from inside.'

Peter Drucker, business guru (1909–2005)

'Change is inevitable; except from vending machines'.

Anonymous

'When you play it too safe you're taking the biggest risk of your life.'

Barbara Sher, author

'It isn't the changes that do you in, it's the transition.'

Daniel Webster, US politician (1782–1852)

Political change

The Edexcel specification picks out the term **PESTLE** (covered more fully in Chapter 5) to indicate the value of seeing external influences from a broad perspective. Political change may impact mainly on business and market confidence. Although the Labour Party's election manifesto in 2015 was rather bland, businesspeople queued up to emphasise the threat they perceived from a potential Labour government. Some threatened to up and leave the country.

What is not in doubt is that business leaders care hugely about political outcomes. Businesses such as Virgin rely far more on the public sector than their publicity might suggest. Virgin Rail and Virgin Care are effectively outsourced government spending – and the Virgin Group's ability to use offshore tax minimisation techniques is a function of government policy towards business taxation.

Economic change

In 2015, with the economy growing at 2.5 per cent, companies and consumers felt quite confident about their future. Accordingly consumers spent 7.5 per cent more on their credit cards than in 2014. In the short term, businesses love to see consumers feeling flush; in the long run this has to be self-correcting. If people's spending outstrips their income (helped by debt), there has to be a cutback in future. This creates the familiar British cycle of confidence + debt = upturn, then faltering confidence + consumer spending cutbacks = downturn.

As economic growth varies through its cycle, businesspeople should be able to anticipate what might happen next, but the evidence is that they do not. When upturn becomes downturn there are always a number of companies caught out badly. Economic change is easily to rationalise with hindsight, but very difficult to anticipate.

Social change

Despite sustained media focus on diet and body shape, the biggest trend by far in consumer lifestyles is the desire for greater convenience. We want to spend less time cooking and less time eating. So breakfast cereals are in decline because we'd rather eat a snack bar, and retail bread sales are down because we'd rather buy a sandwich. That's good for Greggs and Prêt à Manger, but bad for Hovis and Kelloggs.

The key management skill, therefore, is to understand the consumers' reasoning and then refocus the business on the new social impetus. Apple understands the mobile phone user; Marks & Spencer understands food shoppers; underperforming businesses such as French

Connection, Tesco and Nestlé UK need to retune to modern social wavelengths.

Technological change

It is easy to think of the modern era as the most significant ever in terms of technological change and its impact on society and businesses. In fact, a strong case could be made for steam/the railways, oil/the car and the arrival of electricity. The key is to appreciate that technological change may come in waves, but it's always there, creating havoc for businesses that get complacent. In recent years a series of companies have been caught out by online selling, including Game, HMV, Marks & Spencer and Morrisons. Today, virtually every business talks about a multi-channel strategy – in other words making sure that they are as equipped for e-commerce and social media as they are for traditional distribution and traditional media.

Legal change

When parliament passes new laws, the impact on business can be immediate, such as the boom in crash helmet sales when motorbike riders were forced to wear one at all times. At other times, the warning period for a legal change is sufficient to allow extensive planning. Within the European Union, all car manufacturers had to ensure that their 'fleet average' yielded a maximum CO_2 level of 130 grams per kilometre by 2015. By 2021 the figure comes down to 95 grams. So producers have made CO_2 reduction a priority for their Research and Development teams.

Environmental change

As with technological change, historical perspective is crucial here. For the UK, the environmental change between the mid-nineteenth century and the mid-twentieth century far outweighs anything that hits headlines today. In 1851, male life expectancy was about 40; by 1951 it was 67. Life had largely moved on from constant pollution (in urban areas, anyway) to a much better-ordered life. Today there are real problems with diesel-based pollution in cities, but it's as nothing compared with years ago.

Companies often marvel at the irrational approach consumers take to environmental factors. Ultimately, though, companies can do no more than to reflect their customers' concerns. Sadly, these tend to be short-lived. One year 'food miles' is all-important; the next it's sustainability – then natural ingredients.

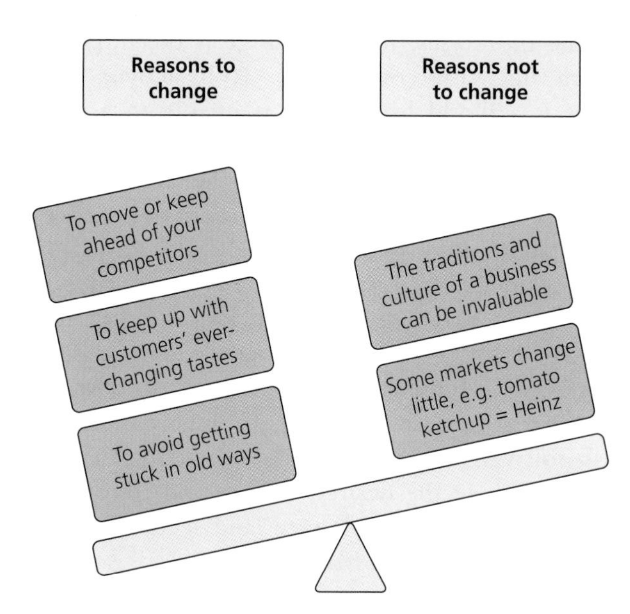

Figure 22.2 Reasons to change (or not to)

22.5 Possible effects of change

Effect of change on competitiveness

It would be very rare to have a business where competitiveness can survive unless changes are made. Let us take the example of Morgan Cars, where traditional British sports car motoring is the key source of differentiation and value added. Customers want a retro product, such as the Morgan Plus 4, which was introduced in 1950. Nevertheless modern customers don't complain if there's a heater in the car, or if the company has introduced new production techniques. Today Morgan produces 20 cars per week at its Worcestershire factory. Customers get a tailor-made car and are encouraged to come and see it being made. Even at Morgan, though, some change is needed.

Figure 22.3 Manufacturing at Morgan

For some businesses, radical change is the only way to catch up with competitors. Rolls-Royce Aero Engines is a world leader, but is unable to achieve the profitability of its key US competitor General Electric. Although the design of the Rolls-Royce engines is super high-tech, the production process remains labour-intensive – effectively job production. The company needs to change its working practices to become competitive with General Electric. Just such a change is slow coming, however. In Spring 2015, chief executive John Rishton was replaced, with the new boss recruited from ARM – a hugely successful British software business. Perhaps new boss Warren East will achieve the desired change and restore the competitiveness of Rolls-Royce (and secure the jobs of many staff in the East Midlands).

Competitiveness can be achieved in one of two ways:

- cost minimisation, i.e. changing the ways of working to squeeze all surplus costs out of the business and thereby become a Ryanair, a Primark or an Aldi
- high differentiation, i.e. mark yourself out as distinctly different from your rivals, in a way that adds value, such as BMW, Apple, Singapore Airlines and Galaxy chocolate.

Change must therefore be focused clearly on one (not both) of these positions in the market.

Effect of change on productivity

If you produce a middle-market car such as the Ford Focus with a labour productivity score of 24 cars per worker per year while your competitors achieve 36, you have a real problem. OK, if you produce those cars in Romania with wages of £60 a week, the low productivity matters less. But assuming that you produce them in Western Europe with wages of £400 a week, you need to make a change.

It may be that productivity can be improved by investing in automated systems, but it's important to remember that only 10 per cent of the British economy is based on manufacturing. So most firms are in the service sector. To boost productivity in services can be difficult, as indicated by Figure 22.4. It shows the extraordinarily flat productivity path for UK services between 2010 and 2015.

Realistically, boosting productivity in the service sector is likely to require a huge upheaval in workplace attitudes. Manufacturing companies learned from the Japanese that 'kaizen' (continuous improvement) requires the full commitment of staff to making things steadily more efficient. This change is required in service sector organisations in the public and private sectors if overall UK productivity is to rise significantly.

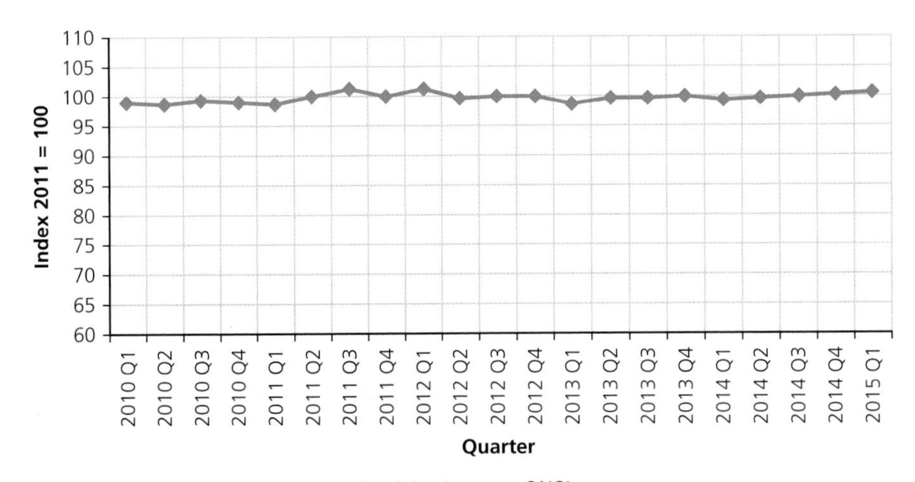

Figure 22.4 UK service sector productivity (source: ONS)

Effect of change on financial performance

Achieving major change can mean short-term pain for long-term gain. This is likely to be reflected in financial performance. In 2014 and 2015, Morrisons tried to reconfigure itself, with strategic moves into urban convenience stores and also online shopping, plus the removal of a layer of management in-store. In addition, when new boss David Potts arrived in 2015, the business hacked into its senior management ranks, cutting 700 head office jobs – and also initiated some serious price cuts. The full effects of the decisions made by David Potts won't be seen until the 2015/2016 figures, but already Table 22.2 is able to reflect the dramatic short-term pain felt by the supermarket chain. It has two problems: the decline in the underlying profitability of the business (that's what David Potts is really trying to tackle) and the short-term financial difficulty caused by huge one-off (exceptional) items. These are the effects of closing down under-performing stores, and cancelling contracts on new stores that are no longer going ahead.

As can be seen, change management can have a severe impact on short-term financial performance. But as long as the long-term problems are solved, no one will mind.

	2012/2013	2013/2014	2014/2015
Turnover	£18,116m	£17,680m	£16,816m
Gross profit	£1,206m	£1,074m	£761m
Underlying pre-tax profit	£880m	£719m	£345m
Exceptional items	***(£1m)***	***(£895m)***	***(£1137m)***
Effective pre-tax profit	£879m	***(£176m)***	***(£792m)***

Table 22.2 Morrisons revenues and profit at a time of change, 2013–2015 (source: Data from Morrisons accounts)

Effect of change on stakeholders

In the case of Morrisons, not only were the shareholders hit by the collapse into a lossmaking position in 2014 and 2015, employees also suffered as staff numbers fell by 9,000 between 2013 and 2015. Much of this reduction in staffing would have been achieved by non-replacement of staff (rather than actual redundancies) but there can still be negative impacts if staff find themselves over-stretched once a colleague has left.

Change can also have a devastating effect on suppliers. Tesco, as part of its turnaround strategy, chose to cut back on the number of suppliers. This is to ensure buying in greater bulk from fewer suppliers, thereby getting purchasing costs down (to compete more effectively with Aldi and Lidl). Horribly caught out by this in 2015 was the huge bakery Kingsmill, which was dumped by Tesco in favour of Hovis and Warburtons. Kingsmill stood to lose about £100 million of annual sales.

Another key stakeholder is the customer, and here change can also be significant. Spare a thought for elderly residents in care homes closed down as part of a structural reorganisation in a private care home business or as part of a local authority's response to cutbacks in central government funding.

'Change is hard because people overestimate the value of what they have – and underestimate the value of what they may gain by giving that up.'

James Belasco and Ralph Stayer, authors

'Change is the law of life and those who look only to the past or present are certain to miss the future.'

John F. Kennedy, former US President

'If past history was all there was to the game, the richest people would be librarians.'

Warren Buffett, investor extraordinaire

'The entrepreneur always searches for change, responds to it, and exploits it as an opportunity.'

Peter Drucker, management academic and author

Five whys and a how

Questions	Answers
Why do plc bosses tend to blame poor results on external causes, but good results on internal causes?	Because external factors are outside the firm's control, whereas internal causes are down to the management.
Why is social change happening faster now than ever before?	Much of the answer to this is technology – a cynic might say we waste more time online and therefore demand more convenience; others see social media and online shopping as ways to give consumers more power.
Why is social change hard to predict?	Although experts try to read early signs of changes in social behaviour or lifestyle, it is impossible to accurately forecast the future.
Why do some businesses seem to be in a permanent process of change?	They may keep failing to get a satisfactory answer to their underlying problems, and therefore keep trying; many companies seek quick-fix solutions (such as new financial incentive programmes) and then find that little has changed.
Why may change hit shareholders less than other stakeholders?	Shareholders own the business and therefore have huge sway over management; so when change happens, it tends to be more focused on the long-term needs of shareholders (i.e. profit) than on staff, customers or suppliers.
How might a small business effect major internal change among staff?	The key will be whether the business leaders have discussed its problems well enough to convince all important staff members to get involved.

22.6 Causes and effects of change – an evaluation

Seasonal, competitive, economic and other causes of fluctuation make change a regular part of business planning and management. Some change factors are so predictable (the lead-up to Christmas for a supermarket) that they can be handled by middle or junior management. Others are more fundamental and game-changing, and therefore need a higher-level strategic plan, such as whether or not to build a third runway at Heathrow airport. Many successful businesses do not have a formal strategic planning process. This does not mean that the issues raised here are not relevant to these organisations. The same problems must be dealt with when strategy emerges over time as when it is planned more systematically. The advantage of explicitly setting aside time for strategic planning is that managers' minds are concentrated on the key questions facing the firm in the future. Then the actions decided upon can be more closely integrated.

Key terms

Downsizing: rethinking staffing numbers and the organisational structure needed given that sales revenue has fallen; often used as a euphemism for redundancies.

PESTLE: key external factors that impact on business objectives and achievements: Political, Economic, Social, Technological, Legal and Environmental.

22.7 Workbook

Revision questions

(30 marks; 30 minutes)

1 Distinguish between internal and external causes of growth, using examples. (5)

2 Explain how social change has affected businesses operating in the following markets in the UK over the last 20 years:

a) grocery retailing

b) restaurants

c) consumer electronics retailing. (12)

3 Outline one example of how a social change might:

a) create a brand new market

b) destroy an entire market. (4)

4 Explain why it may be hard for young, inexperienced managers of a successful business start-up to cope effectively with an unexpected, dramatic change. (5)

5 Explain one reason why change may be of value to an established grocery business. (4)

Revision exercises

Data response

You've had your chips: award-winning chippy closes doors

In 2011, Ian Shaw ditched his day job and set up his own fish and chip shop. Using £15,000 of his own money, Shaw rented a bakery in Rochdale, converted it and, in early 2012, The Best Cod in Town opened its doors for the first time. The chippy proved to be a hit with customers. Shaw's business model was based on selling a top-quality product at low prices. This meant buying in the best fish and changing the oil used for frying more often than usual.

Like many other entrepreneurs just starting out, Ian worked very long hours, which helped to boost sales and keep staff costs down. Most of Shaw's customers who tried his fish and chips liked them, and came back for more, becoming regulars. Thanks to its popularity, the chippy generated good revenues. At the end of its first year, The Best Cod in Town was ranked in first place by Trip Advisor as Rochdale's best takeaway. Despite its substantial turnover, the business struggled to make a profit. This was because fixed costs were too high, which created a high break-even point. The biggest fixed cost that he had to pay was business rates. Every month The Best Cod in Town had to pay Rochdale council £1,872. This was even higher than the £1,200 he paid per month in rent to lease the premises. When the council increased his rates again, and said it would do so in the following years, Shaw decided that there was no other option; the writing was on the wall: 'We had a break clause in our lease after 18 months and I've decided it's best to get out sooner rather than later.' The Best Cod in Town closed its doors for the final time in September 2013. At the time Shaw said:

'The town centre is dying. Unless you want a payday loan, a television on hire purchase or to go to a charity shop, there just isn't a reason for people to come into Rochdale. With the changes that are coming in to the benefits system later this year, people will have even less money to spend. We're the fourth business that is closing at this end of the high street and I can't see things getting any better.'

MP Simon Danczuk, Rochdale's MP, was critical of the government, arguing:

'This government does not care about people like Ian, they are only interested in big business. Small businesses like Ian's are the lifeblood of the economy and if we're going to have a proper recovery, then they need to be given a fighting chance of survival. Big business seems to get all the support and subsidies from the government and are being allowed to exploit tax loop holes. At the same time, smaller firms are getting bigger and bigger business rate bills.'

The biggest employer in the town is Rochdale Council. Due to government spending cuts, unemployment has soared and spending is sharply down. In December 2014, nearly a quarter of Rochdale's shops were vacant. The council reacted by offering new businesses that were prepared to move into an empty shop an 80 per cent discount on their business rates in the first year, and a 50 per cent cut in the second year.

Questions (50 marks; 60 minutes)

1 Assess two factors that would have affected the break-even output level of The Best Cod in Town. (8)

2 Assess how private businesses like The Best Cod in Town might benefit from government spending. (10)

3 When The Best Cod in Town made losses, Ian Shaw responded by closing down the business. Were there any other options? Assess Ian Shaw's decision to shut down his business. (12)

4 The Best Cod in Town's competitive advantage was based around selling a high-quality product at a low price. Evaluate whether this business model can deliver long-run, sustainable success. (20)

Extended writing

1 The soft drinks' company Fever-Tree has grown at a rate of 50 per cent per year for nearly a decade. Evaluate whether it's inevitable that this pressure for change will cause setbacks for the business. (20)

2 Evaluate the extent to which UK net migration represents an opportunity for UK supermarkets. (20)

Section 3.6 Managing change

23 Key factors in change

Definition

Change is a constant feature of business activity. The key issues are whether it has been foreseen by the company – and therefore planned for – and whether it is within the company's control.

Linked to: Impact of external influences, Ch 5; Growth, Ch 7; Corporate culture, Ch 16; Causes and effects of change, Ch 22; Scenario planning, Ch 24

23.1 Successful change

There's a tendency on the part of senior managers to see change as a good thing. It can be their way of stamping their authority on the organisation. It's important to bear in mind, therefore, that as many as 70 per cent of change management initiatives prove to be a flop. Big management reorganisations, or quality initiatives, or customer service response programmes – all are more likely to fade away than to achieve anything. Therefore it's terribly important to make sure of the following:

- All staff understand the need for change.
- All staff understand what the new, changed world is going to look like.
- All staff understand the plan for getting from A to B.

Academics Carolyn Aiken and Scott Keller say that fundamental human issues get in the way of successful change:

- What motivates leaders doesn't motivate most of their employees.
- Leaders believe mistakenly that they already are the change.
- Money is the most expensive way to motivate people.
- The process and the outcome have got to be fair.

This highlights that successful change management is about people – not technology or software systems. Therefore a business is much more likely to beat the 70 per cent flop figure if it has an underlying position of trust between bosses and staff.

Among the key factors in successful change are:

- organisational culture
- the size of the organisation
- the timing/speed of change
- managing resistance to change.

23.2 Organisational culture

When David Moyes succeeded Sir Alex Ferguson as boss of Manchester United, he brought in new players such as the giant Belgian Marouane Fellaini. Brought up on the talents of Ryan Giggs and Paul Scholes, the home crowd struggled to take to the Belgian's muscular style. The expectations and conventions within the Manchester United crowd represented their culture – and the crowd would feel (just as company staff do) that they represent the 'real' Manchester United/company. Managers (and players) come and go; the fans are the constant. And the culture within the fans has been built up over years, perhaps generations. Newcastle fans expect excitement and goals; Chelsea fans expect home wins and trophies; Manchester United fans expect all of those things. Clever managers of companies and football clubs try to work with the grain of the organisational culture – not against it.

Figure 23.1 Football clubs have their own culture

Real business

In January 2013, Barclays Bank's new boss Anthony Jenkins told staff to 'sign up to ethics or leave'. After at least a decade in which success at Barclays meant creating more profit (and bonus) than the next guy, suddenly the bank was to become ethically pure. Fast-forward to July 2015 and it was Anthony Jenkins leaving. The chairman sacked him in favour of a man with a more ruthless, profit-focused streak. Anthony Jenkins was working against the culture of the business - and failed to make it change. (Don't weep for Mr Jenkins; he is expected to clear £28 million as a leaving present.)

To achieve successful change in a business with a strong organisational culture:

- Make sure you really understand that culture (it may seem jokey and carefree, with a focus on Friday nights, but underneath be seriously committed to the success of the business).
- Work with it not against it.
- Use consultation to make sure that key figures from every part of the organisation are with you because they understand and trust you.
- But don't waver; people want a very clear lead; as the saying goes: 'indecision is final'.

23.3 Size of the organisation

Logically it should be much harder to change a big organisation than a small one. Oddly there's no evidence for this. Businesses (or organisations such as schools) employing perhaps 50–100 staff also find it's hugely difficult to achieve change. Ultimately, though, change is achieved successfully when the boss changes the hearts and minds of staff; and organisational size must matter.

In a large organisation, it'll be necessary to do the following:

- Rely on upward information from middle managers, as the boss will never be able to get a real feel for the views of 200,000 staff (Unilever) or 500,000 staff (Tesco).
- Find a compromise between the different views and needs of different parts of the business; a change to temporary or outsourced staff may be right in one division, but not in another.
- Rely on cascading, with senior managers explaining the changes to middle managers who, in turn, brief the next layer down; this will be time-consuming and expensive, but more important is that it is likely to be ineffective. A passionate chief executive explains the new vision and changes to senior managers, whose explanations to their juniors are slightly less powerful and accurate – and so on.
- And with every aspect of the change programme, there's a chance that the different business functions will fail to work together effectively.

For small organisations, change may also be challenging because of the following:

- The business may lack the financial resources to both finance the change and to withstand any short-term problems caused by the change.
- Small businesses are usually dominated by one person (or family). There may be too few independent voices to persuade the boss to change.
- Large firms have staff with a wide range of skills, making it easier to cope with new ways of working. Small business may lack that flexibility.

'Plus ça change, plus c'est la même chose.'

Jean-Baptiste Karr, French journalist (1849)

'Give employees the information they need to understand the reasons for change.'

Carla O'Dell, businesswoman

'I always loved change, something new. Change is a challenge, an excitement.'

Dawn Sibley, Executive Vice President

23.4 Time and speed of change

Most businesses can cope reasonably well when the pace of change is relatively slow. A slow pace of change is referred to as **incremental change**. From as early as 2005, John Lewis appreciated that its world was changing. From a purely physical ('bricks') high-street retailer it saw that more and more people wanted to purchase online. Perhaps they might want to go to a store to choose which sofa or which TV to buy, but they would find it easier to make the transaction via a 'click' at home. To the operation's great credit, it worked hard to create an easy-to-use e-commerce site and encouraged sales staff to see it as a complement, not a competitor to the stores. By 2015, with Marks & Spencer floundering in its wake, John Lewis was getting close to 30 per cent of all sales arising online, but with a clear strategy to open new stores within Britain to act as a shop window for the website.

This incremental change (steady and quite predictable) towards online shopping was intelligently managed by John Lewis, but botched by Marks & Spencer (and

Morrisons). Quite simply, with years to look ahead and plan for this incremental change, there can be no excuses for the management failures of those who woke up to find they had missed the boat.

By contrast, **disruptive change** typically occurs within a timescale that makes planning almost impossible. In 2009, two years after the launch of the iPhone, Nokia held a 38.9 per cent share of the global market for smartphones. Two years later, its share was 8.2 per cent and dropping like a stone. Looking back, one could point to the mistakes Nokia made; but it simply didn't have enough time to rethink the new world created by Apple (and Samsung). In the same timescale as Nokia's collapse, Samsung's global market share went from 3 per cent to 30 per cent.

The unusual aspect of Nokia's collapse was that the disruptive change came from Apple's marketing and design brilliance. Usually the causes of disruptive change are either technology or legislation, i.e. external to the business. Banning smoking in public places meant that pubs had to adapt quickly – or die. Many died. And the onset of online retailing finished off HMV, Blockbuster and Game retail chains.

The problem for businesses faced with dramatic change is that managers don't yet know the timescale and therefore do not know how disruptive a given change will be. When General Motors launched its 'Volt' electric car in 2010, it forecast sales of 60,000 cars by 2012. In fact sales struggled to reach 24,000 units. The company had thought electric cars were the disruptive technology that would sweep petrol-based cars aside. Not yet. Now, as it plans its 2016 Volt, General Motors is trying hard to dampen down sales expectations.

23.5 Managing resistance to change

Academics Kotter and Schlesinger have identified a series of methods for dealing with resistance to change. Generally a mixture of methods should be used. They should be selected by carefully considering the methods that are most appropriate given the nature of the workforce and the nature and speed of the change. They are explained below:

Education and communication

A highly effective method for breaking down resistance to change is to successfully explain the need for change before it is implemented. This is especially effective where resistance is the result of misunderstanding or a different assessment of the firm's position before the change. However, this method relies on a level of trust between management and staff if the communication is to be believed by the staff whose resistance is to be overcome. Large-scale presentations, or even corporate films, can be used to try to provide the information and education needed for staff. Exactly these methods were used by British Airways in its difficult struggle to change working practices at the airline.

Participation and involvement

Involving unofficial staff leaders in designing the how and why of the change can be an excellent method of breaking down resistance before it becomes entrenched. The change managers must listen carefully to the views of staff and try where possible to take these views into account. Kotter and Schlesinger report that some managers believe participation of staff is vital, whilst others feel that it is highly dangerous. If staff feel that change is based on their ideas, they are far more likely to commit to the change. It is worth pointing out that this method is likely to take time due to the amount of consultation needed, and therefore be unsuitable as a way of overcoming resistance when change is needed fast.

Negotiation and agreement

This involves offering some kind of incentive to resistors if they accept the change. Often used where resistance is led by a trade union, staff may be offered a pay rise

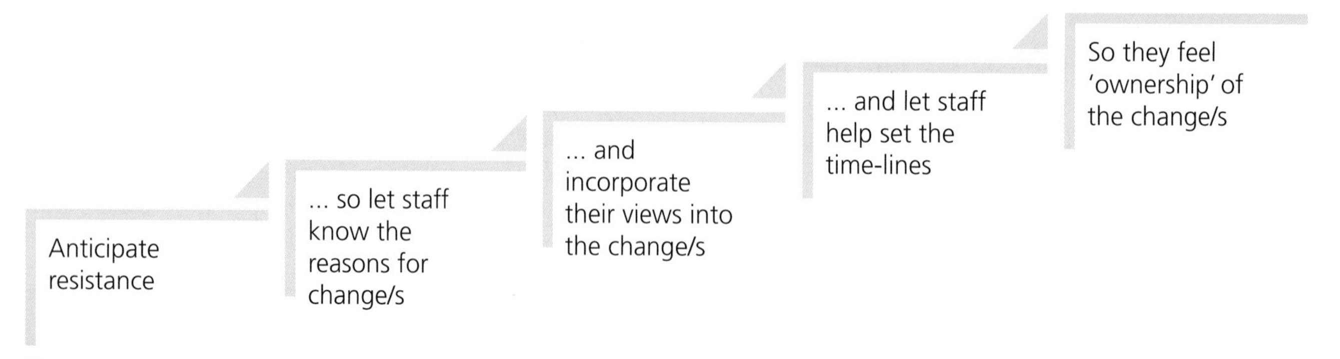

Figure 23.2 Logic chain: overcoming resistance to change

Five whys and a how

Questions	Answers
Why do people resist change?	Because change introduces uncertainty and therefore insecurity. They also frequently doubt that the goals of the people at the top fit the needs of the people further down the hierarchy.
Why do organisations need to change?	Changes in the markets in which firms operate force businesses to change in order to remain competitive.
Why is it important to manage change?	Changes must be planned and then managed to ensure that staff implement those changes in the way that was planned.
Why is change so hard when a business is growing rapidly?	All the inherent problems of change are multiplied by the pressure of rapid change; staff may fail to see the emerging problems because they can't keep up with the implications of rapid growth.
Why is commitment a key to successful change management?	Staff who feel that the changes are for the best will work harder to make new methods work – meaning the new methods are more likely to work as planned.
How should managers choose the best method to overcome resistance to change?	Managers must assess the changes planned, the extent to which they have all information needed to make the changes, the speed with which change must take place, the importance of managing costs during the change and the main causes of resistance to the particular changes planned.

for accepting changed working conditions, or perhaps offered the chance of early retirement. This method works particularly well when resistors are resisting due to parochial self-interest – since it is designed to reduce the extent to which the change will make them worse off. However, if this method is used, there is the danger that staff will feel that resisting future changes will always lead to compromise from managers. This would push up the costs of the next change programme (remembering that change is a constant in many firms).

> 'Everyone thinks of changing the world but no one thinks of changing himself.'
>
> *Leo Tolstoy, novelist*

23.6 Key factors in change – evaluation

Change is normal, not abnormal. Therefore firms need to be alert to causes of change and quick to devise a strategic plan for coping. It is also hugely important that those at the top should be self-critical about their motives and their chance of success. Staff hate to see what they believe to be a self-serving, 'I'm the new boss and I'm going to show everyone what I'm about' change-for-change's-sake approach. New football managers often sell and buy players with little net difference to the team – apparently just to prove themselves (and create '*my* team'). That can be contrasted with the situation of David Potts (Morrisons) and Dave Lewis (Tesco), both of whom were appointed in 2014/2015 at a time of serious crisis for the businesses. Few staff would have doubted the need for radical change.

In the long run, the business that will cope best with change is the one that has a good, trusting relationship between management and staff, strong enough finances to afford the 'right' change rather than the most affordable, and a leader with the skills to be able to paint a clear picture of how the future is to look.

Key terms

Disruptive change: this kind of change happens suddenly, unpredictably and with a substantial impact that shakes up the whole market.

Incremental change: this kind of change occurs in small, gentle steps, allowing a business to adapt gently.

23.7 Workbook

Revision questions

(30 marks; 30 minutes)

1 Examine the key factors that might make it difficult to change the age range of a school from 11–16 to 11–18. (5)

2 Identify three problems for a fast-growing firm caused by changes in the management structure. (3)

3 Explain one way in which your school/college could be affected by:

a) incremental change (4)

b) disruptive change. (4)

4 Explain why misunderstanding is more likely to cause resistance to change in branches of an international retailer. (3)

5 Explain two issues that a change management team should consider when deciding which approach to take to overcoming resistance to change. (6)

6 Explain why it may be hard for young, inexperienced managers of a successful business start-up to cope effectively with an unexpected, dramatic change. (5)

Revision activities

Data response

Hemmings and Bennett Ltd is a medium-sized engineering firm that specialises in manufacturing cutting-edge propulsion systems used in rockets. The firm has been established for over 25 years and has a loyal and exceptionally highly skilled workforce. Over recent years it has found it increasingly hard to generate the profit levels expected by shareholders as it has struggled to compete with emerging rivals from Europe and China. Chief executive Andy Bennett has been convinced by his finance director that the firm needs to reduce costs in order to maintain competitiveness. In order for this to happen, they have identified a number of steps that can be taken without damaging the quality of output produced:

- 30 per cent of the workforce to be made redundant.
- Staff holiday entitlement to be cut by 25 per cent.
- Several simple processes to be outsourced to a company in the Czech Republic.
- A 50 per cent cut in the training budget.

The shareholders agreed these proposals and gave Andy twelve months to make the changes. He and his directors held a series of planning meetings in order to decide how to proceed.

	Hemmings and Bennett Ltd before the changes	Industry average
Capacity utilisation	70%	85%
Average age of staff	46	32
Index of unit cost	124	100
Labour costs as a % of total costs	52%	38%
% of workforce who belong to a trade union	17%	12%
Net profit margin	8%	15%
ROCE	6%	16%

Table 23.1 Hemmings and Bennett Ltd – selected data before the change programme

Questions (40 marks; 45 minutes)

1 Using the information from the case study and Table 23.1, assess why change is needed at Hemmings and Bennett Ltd. (10)

2 Assess possible causes of resistance to the changes proposed at Hemmings and Bennett Ltd. (10)

3 Evaluate the best method(s) for Andy to use to overcome any resistance to change from staff. (20)

Extended writing

1 'Managing change is easier within a successful business than one that is struggling.' Evaluate this statement. (20)

2 Evaluate the difficulties a new boss would face in changing Marks & Spencer into a dynamic, young, fashion-conscious organisation. (20)

Section 3.6 Managing change

24 Scenario planning

Definition

Scenario planning means visualising possible futures for a business, then planning how to get the best out of the opportunities and how to deal with the threats.

Linked to: Corporate objectives, Ch 1; SWOT analysis, Ch 4; Growth, Ch 7, Causes and effects of change, Ch 22; Key factors in change, Ch 23

24.1 Introduction to scenario planning

Since its birth in 2005, soft drinks maker Fever-Tree has grown at a ferocious pace of around 50 per cent a year. By the first half of 2015, its sales had risen to an annualised £48 million. So what might the position of the business be in, say, five years' time? Three scenarios come to mind:

- It might carry on growing at 50 per cent a year; this compound growth would mean a £365 million revenue business by 2020 – a business the size of SuperGroup plc, and therefore needing strong, experienced financial management.
- Growth might slow to 20 per cent a year; that would mean a £120 million business by 2020 – probably not requiring any fundamental change from the current board of directors.
- Growth might tail away, leaving a business of £50 million by 2020, and probably facing tough competition from others catching Fever-Tree up; the current management set-up might need to be slimmed down to reflect the lack of growth.

The point is simple: look ahead and think about what might happen – and start planning for what you might do if a particular scenario happens. For big companies with big brands, years can go by with relatively little happening – then suddenly a decision is needed – and that decision must be right. In June 2015, a government department in India announced that Nestlé's Maggi noodles contained unacceptably high levels of lead. For several days Nestlé argued that the tests were wrong and that the products were fine. Ten days later the government banned further production or importing of the brand and Nestlé was forced to strip the product from Indian shop shelves. Maggi noodles had annual sales of more than £400 million in India; it remains to be seen whether they can recover to that level. Surely Nestlé should have withdrawn the product first – and argued second; that would have preserved the brand and company image. Such a misjudged response may point to poor scenario planning.

24.2 Identifying key risks through risk assessment

Risk assessment comes in three parts:

1. Identify the possible risks faced by the business.
2. Quantify their possible cost to the business.
3. Attempt to quantify the probability that each risk might occur.

If that sounds rather like drawing up a decision tree, that's good. It is.

In truth, you're unlikely to be able to quantify stages 2 and 3 with anything like accuracy. But that's not a problem. The key is to have gone through the thought process and therefore start a planning process – and perhaps even put one or two things into practice.

Among the key risks a business might consider are:

- natural disasters
- IT systems failure
- loss of key staff.

Natural disasters

Manufacturing businesses have some obvious vulnerabilities: to their sources of supply (earthquake in Turkey, where Ferrero gets its hazelnuts to make Nutella); to their own factory (local flooding makes roads impassable); and to the warehouses here or abroad where finished goods stocks are held. In the computing and consumer electronics business, a surprising number of companies and factories are based in earthquake zones: in California, in Japan and in China.

Real business

In March 2011, a massive undersea earthquake off the east coast of Japan sent massive waves that went deep inland, killing around 18,000 people. The flooding and the direct impact of the earthquake were compounded by a catastrophic failure at a flooded nuclear power plant. A senior manager of US Cisco Systems said that the scale was unprecedented:

'In the past we had incidents where five suppliers or a single contract manufacturer were shut down. But we had nothing like this before where we had we had 60 to 70 suppliers impacted in some form or fashion. In addition, the supplies affected included a wide range of production materials, including semiconductors, passives, wafers and chemicals.'

Car manufacturers were hit round the world, leading them to the view that in future they must make sure to get supplies from more than one region.

In the UK, serious natural disasters are rare, with the exception of localised flooding. It wouldn't be hard for a large business to plan for this eventuality, but there may be local service businesses that have no opportunity to diversify. For them, the key would be to try to build up cash reserves for that rainy day. There is always sense in **contingency planning**.

Figure 24.1 Outbreak of the Great East Japan earthquake and tsunami

> **'Individuals should think about the worst-case scenarios and plan for them. The world will be crazier than you think.'**
>
> *Nicolas Taleb, author of* The Black Swan

IT systems failure

On 8 August 2015, Carphone Warehouse warned that its website had been hacked three days before, risking the credit card security details of 90,000 of its customers. The company's security systems had failed, but the shock to customers was that the business had taken three days to own up to the problem. Proper scenario planning would have identified that the proper response was to inform customers immediately.

The Carphone Warehouse fiasco came just two months after a more widespread IT systems failure at RBS/NatWest Bank. RBS had tweeted: 'Some customer payments are missing this morning – we are investigating this issue as a matter of urgency'. In fact 600,000 customers were affected by a systems failure that meant deposits to their bank accounts failed to register. This would mean that thousands would be unable to withdraw cash as needed. Only seven months before, the bank had been fined £50 million for a previous systems meltdown that left 6.5 million customers locked out of their bank accounts for days. Both episodes had newspapers asking whether RBS is Britain's worst bank.

For any business today, scenario planning must include careful thought about the vulnerability of the firm's reputation to IT systems failure. Back-up systems may be expensive to install – but are surely an essential cost in doing business.

Loss of key staff

In most large companies, although the boss may be paid huge sums, the business is bigger than any individual. If the chief executive leaves, another can slot in without too much disruption. Businesses such as Mars, Next, Primark and Halfords would fall into that category. There are important exceptions, however. Ted Baker plc was started by Ray Kelvin, who still runs the business. Ray *is* Ted Baker; what would happen if Ray retired? And for many years shareholders in News International/Sky worried what would happen when Rupert Murdoch had to stand down (he's over 80).

No less important are key technical experts within a workforce. At Apple, Jonathan Ive is the design guru and

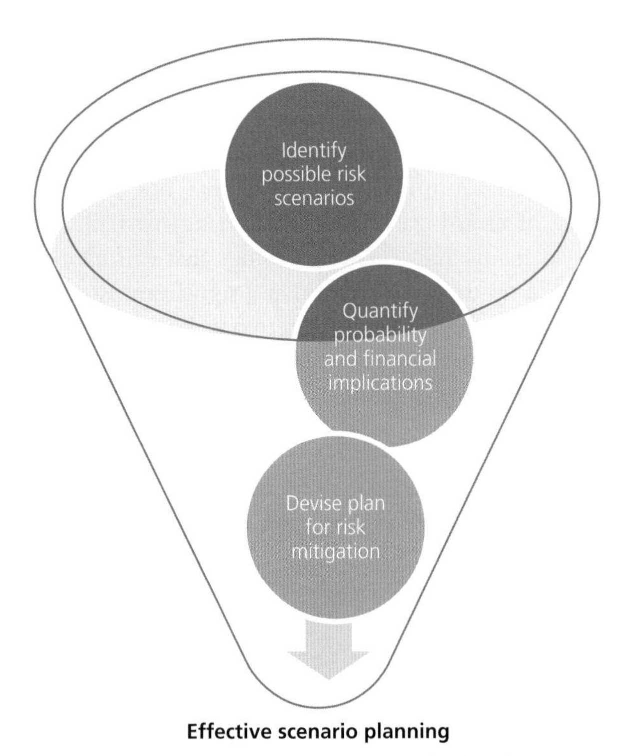

Figure 24.2 Logic chain: effective scenario planning

for Nintendo, Shigeru Miyamoto (designer of Donkey Kong, SuperMario and the Wii system) has long been the star. Quite clearly if either of these experts left the business, the implications would be significant. This scenario can be anticipated and planned for.

24.3 Planning for risk mitigation

Mitigating risk means taking actions that will reduce, even minimise it. No one can prevent natural disasters, but you can make sure that your supplies come from different companies in different regions, to minimise the possibility of disruption due to 'acts of god'. You can also make sure that your sales revenue isn't overly dependent on one product line. In the first half of 2015, Apple was 69 per cent dependent on the iPhone for its income. No wonder the company launched the Apple Watch and also started work on an Apple self-drive car.

Business continuity

Business continuity means planning how to restore things to normal after a setback or disaster has struck. This will have several aspects:

- There must be a strong enough financial position to be able to withstand short-term shock and finance any capital requirements to get the business straight again. For example, the cost to Nestlé of withdrawing all Maggi noodle products from shop shelves in India was about £50 million.
- The British government has a committee called COBRA that meets when security or other physical disasters occur. In a similar way, a company might set up a business continuity committee, including marketing and public relations staff as well as resource and personnel managers.
- There must be clear lines of authority showing who is responsible for making the key decisions at a time of crisis. This shouldn't be the chief executive, who should be more focused upon long-term strategy.

Succession planning

Succession planning means thinking hard and planning ahead for when a leader leaves and must be replaced. *Forbes* magazine has published research showing that 55 per cent of large companies recruit a new chief executive from outside the business. So only 45 per cent of appointees are the product of succession planning. Presumably the internal candidates were too weak to be worth appointing – which indicates poor planning. A successful succession plan would have identified the right person to be groomed for the role – and set up a suitable training plan.

The value of effective succession planning is that the new person understands fully the thinking behind current strategies and given insights into policies that have been trialled but failed. For middle managers, nothing is more frustrating than a new boss who seems determined to make the same mistakes as the previous one.

Eventually, every boss will go and so will every one of the business's most valuable specialist staff – so planning their replacement makes a huge amount of sense. Unfortunately what makes sense for the company doesn't necessarily suit the staff. Some may feel that 'succession planning' threatens their job security, as shown in the following case.

Real business

Dominic is a software expert working for a major oil company. He is employed on a consultancy contract which gives him a regular four days a week (at a huge daily rate). A new divisional boss employs two IT graduates and asks Dominic to train them up. Not unreasonably, Dominic suspects that he is being asked to plan his own succession, with his own job being scrapped as soon as the younger, cheaper staff can do the work. He doesn't hurry; nor does he explain things well enough for the younger staff to feel comfortable that they can take over.

Is there a solution to this problem? Probably not. Succession planning can only work effectively when the boss is a willing participant, perhaps because he or she wants to retire or to move on.

'Succession planning should be gradual and thoughtful, with lots of sharing of information and knowledge and perspective, so that it's almost a non-event when it happens.'

Anne Mulcahy, former CEO, Xerox Corp

'Good fortune is what happens when opportunity meets with planning.'

Thomas Edison, inventor

24.4 Scenario planning – evaluation

The logic behind scenario planning is not that you'll be able to predict what will happen. It's simply that if you've thought about what might happen, and how you might respond, you should be in a better position to cope. Nicolas Taleb, in his book *The Black Swan*, warns that totally unexpected things happen more often than we imagine, from planes falling out of the sky to companies suddenly collapsing into administration. He points out that the probability of each bizarre event occurring is small, but there are so many different weird things that can happen that they add up to a likelihood that a significant, strange event will happen quite often. Therefore, he says, always keep a strong enough balance sheet to cope with tough times. This is very sound advice.

Key term

Contingency planning: thinking through a Plan B in case Plan A goes wrong.

Five whys and a how

Questions	Answers
Why is scenario planning needed?	Because it's hard to cope with a sudden problem if you haven't thought it through beforehand.
Why do some companies focus on downside rather than upside risks?	Downside risks may threaten business survival; upside risks can just be seen as good news.
Why might scenario planning prove a mistake?	It might take up more time than makes sense, especially if there are so many different possibilities that none can be tackled in sufficient depth.
Why might scenario planning prove useful for a business such as British Airways?	It can plan for the downside implications of a price war or of even higher passenger taxes, and the upside risks of a major rival going into receivership or of new routes opening up to Africa.
Why might a company use risk mitigation methods?	To turn its scenario planning process into a way to smooth out potential future problems.
How might a small construction company use scenario planning?	It can think about what might go wrong, cost it out and then build those potential costs into its pricing method for quoting for jobs.

24.5 Workbook

Revision questions

(25 marks; 25 minutes)

1 Choose **one** of these companies and set out two positive and two negative scenarios that might impact on the business.

a) Heinz, in its management of its Tomato Ketchup brand

b) Sony, in its management of its PS4 console. (8)

2 Unusually high rainfall causes flooding throughout the Midlands, cutting off the Mini engine factory at Hams Hall. Explain two possible effects if the business had failed to carry out scenario planning. (8)

3 Explain why scenario planning might be of particular value to **one** of these businesses:

a) Primark

b) Jaguar Land Rover

c) Instagram. (4)

4 Explain why the leader of a business such as Marks & Spencer might be reluctant to carry through a full succession plan. (5)

Revision activities

Data Response

JCB: one of the UK's most successful manufacturers

In 2015, JCB hopes to break the £3 billion turnover mark for the first time in its history. One of the country's biggest and most important engineering companies, JCB's yellow and black construction vehicles are among the top three bestsellers globally. In its UK heartland of Staffordshire and Derbyshire, JCB employs over 5,000 people in highly skilled, secure jobs.

One of JCB's secrets has been its willingness to invest. Its 1979 decision to start up in India has led to the achievement of a 50 per cent market share in this huge, fast-developing country. India's new government is embarking on a huge programme of investment in roads and other infrastructure which should be great for JCB. Just in 2014, the company announced:

- a £25 million programme to double production in Germany
- a £45 million investment in a six-cylinder engine to slot into its fuel-efficient Dieselmax range
- a £150 million plan to expand production in the UK, with the expectation of creating 2,500 more jobs by 2018.

As Figure 24.3 shows, not long ago – in the 2009 recession – the company's plans were thrown into turmoil by a collapse in sales. That year the company was saved by sales growth in India and China. Even so, with an estimated total capacity of 72,000 units in 2009, the rate of utilisation was very poor.

To their credit, senior managers kept their heads and kept investing in the firm's future. From a struggle to break even in 2009, the company bounced back to make £365 million profit in 2012.

In 2014, JCB has been holding to its long-term plan for significant increases in its global capacity. Its factories in India and Brazil are getting greater investment and new factories are being built in Uttoxeter and Cheadle in Britain. JCB believes that developing countries will continue to plough funds into construction investment, and that JCB should be at the heart of this business. It shows no fear of its two huge global rivals: Caterpillar of America and Komatsu of Japan.

Another plan for the future is to improve the productivity of the JCB factories worldwide. In 2014, the 12,000-strong workforce produced 64,000 units. By 2018, the hope is to get annual productivity up to eight units per worker.

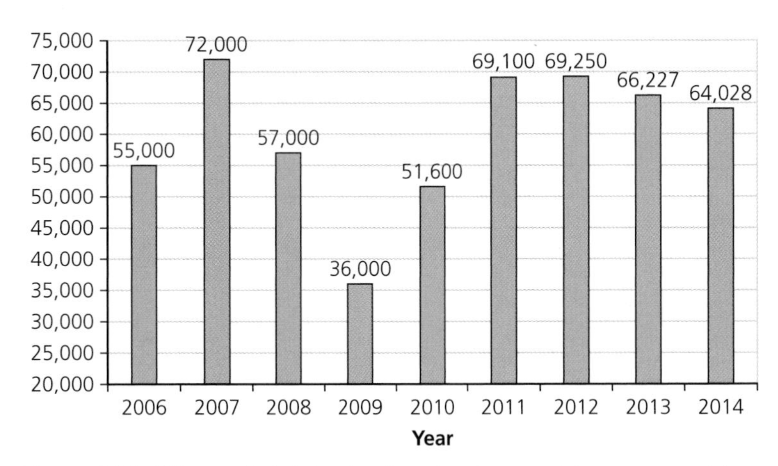

Figure 24.3 JCB annual global sales (in units) (source: JCB press reports)

Questions (40 marks; 45 minutes)

1 a) Calculate JCB's capacity utilisation in 2009. (3)

b) Explain how JCB might have set about rebuilding this figure. (4)

2 Assess the problems JCB might face in implementing a new strategy that matches output to demand. (10)

3 a) Calculate JCB's labour productivity in 2014. (3)

b) JCB's directors have asked managers to devise a new strategy to meet a productivity objective of eight units per worker by 2018. Evaluate how detailed scenario planning might help the business achieve this objective. (20)

Extended writing

1 Coca-Cola UK is having to face the possibility that its future will be much harder than its past. It believes there is a 40 per cent chance that a soft drinks' sugar tax will be brought in. Evaluate how scenario planning might help Coca-Cola UK face this prospect. (20)

2 Richard Branson has run the Virgin Group since he founded it in the 1960s. Evaluate whether it's inevitable that the Virgin Group will decline once Sir Richard retires. (20)

Theme 4

Global business

25 Growing economies

Definition

Over time, almost all economies grow thanks to rising productivity and population. This chapter focuses on economies that have growth prospects that are higher than average.

Linked to: China versus India, Ch 26; Business potential in Africa, Ch 27; International trade and growth, Ch 28; Reasons for global mergers or joint ventures, Ch 35'

25.1 Introduction

The most important thing is to realise that development happens. In 1981, 50 per cent of the world's population lived on less than $1.25 a day (about 80p). By 2015, World Bank estimates suggest that the figure was down to about 16 per cent. Let's be clear; that means 1,200 million people still living on extremely low incomes. That, in itself, is a disgrace in a world with so much wealth. But it is wrong to treat the issue of development with a shrug of the shoulders. There are hopeful signs. Table 25.1 shows the economic performance of a selection of less developed countries. Despite the figures in the right-hand column, the two central columns show that improvements are definitely occurring.

In the period since 1981, the big development wins have been achieved in China, in South East Asia more generally, and in South America. Without exception, these gains have come about as a result of economic development. In other words, poverty has not been reduced because rich Chinese have given more to poor Chinese; this has come about because the Chinese economy has been able to produce more wealth for all.

Does economic aid have much to do with this relative success? Not really, as governments and charities rarely do enough to make much impact throughout a country. In China, India and Bangladesh, for instance, the key factors have been:

- greater willingness to accept inward investment from multinational or other big, wealthy companies from the west or Japan
- greater enterprise on the part of the local business population
- more stable government than before, especially in India and Bangladesh
- easier access for exports to countries such as Britain, America and the rest of Europe, partly thanks to the World Trade Organization/**globalisation**.

	GDP at PPP 2014	Average annual growth in real GDP per head 1970–1990 (%)	Average annual growth in real GDP per head 1990–2013 (%)	Percentage of population below $1.25 a day 2009–2012
Bangladesh	$3,400	0.5	3.8	3.3
China	$12,900	6.5	9.4	11.8
India	$5,900	2.0	5.0	2.7
Bolivia	$6,200	–1.2	1.8	15.6
Nigeria	$6,000	–2.3	3.4	68

Table 25.1 Economic performance of selected countries. PPP means purchasing power parity, i.e. allowing for differences in the cost of living, which allows for more realistic comparisons
(sources: *CIA World Factbook* 2015 and Unicef Statistics, February 2015)

25.2 Growth rate of the UK economy compared with emerging economies

The term 'emerging' economy is a difficult one, because it is hard to pin down. Is China 'emerging'? Or has it emerged by now? After all, at purchasing power parity (PPP) it is the largest economy in the world. It will help to define an emerging economy as countries with low incomes per head, but high growth rates and good prospects.

The UK economy has grown at around 2.25 per cent a year for more than two hundred years. Consistency is everything in long-term development and wealth. At 2.25 per cent a year, incomes double every 30 years, i.e. every generation. But if other countries are growing faster, it is important to compete. In the long run, a business such as Jaguar Land Rover cannot succeed if it turns its back on fast-growing markets. In Figure 25.1 below, the amazing growth of Chinese car production (now world's number one) mirrors the growth in the Chinese market for cars. India also shows substantial percentage growth – but is dwarfed by China.

According to the United States Department of Agriculture, by 2030, America will still have the biggest economy, with China close behind. And India will have overtaken Japan to become the world's third largest economy. On these US forecasts, the UK remains one of the world's biggest economies, but increasingly falling behind China and India. Brazil, Indonesia, Mexico, Turkey and Nigeria are also important winners in this analysis (see Figure 25.2). British companies need to have plans for succeeding in these top markets.

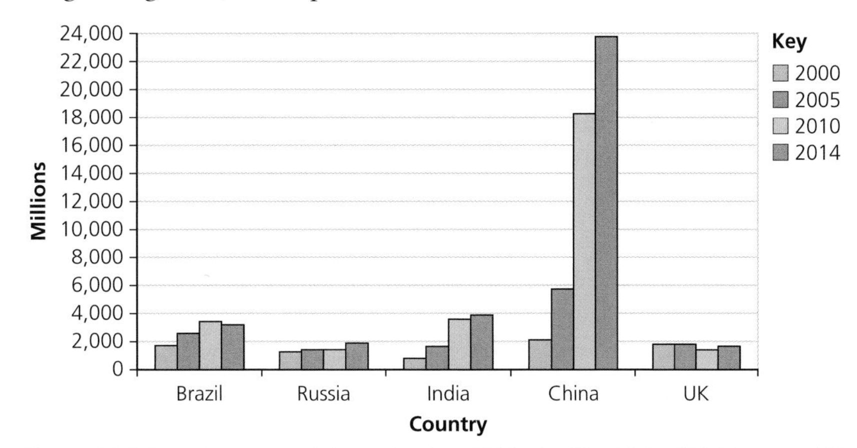

Figure 25.1 Annual motor vehicle production, BRIC plus UK, 2000–2014 (source: OICA 2015)

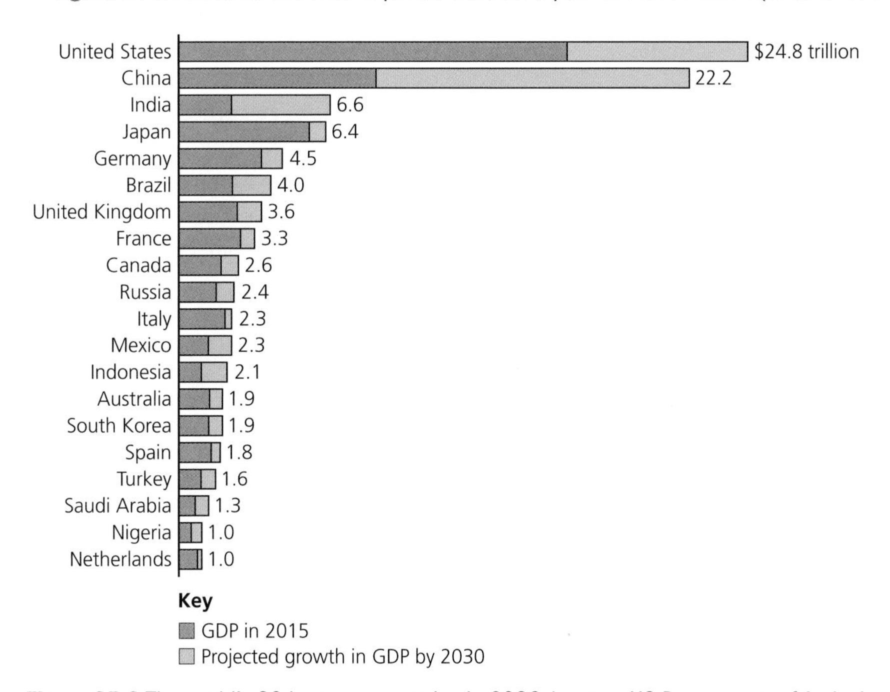

Figure 25.2 The world's 20 largest economies in 2030 (source: US Department of Agriculture)

Real business

2015 was a great year for Apple Inc, with its iPhone6 proving a huge hit against Samsung. In the early part of 2015, the stock market value of Apple was more than twice the figure than any other company in the world. Underpinning these figures was a simple fact – Apple was more profitable than ever. The main reason was that even though the Chinese economy was suffering a relative slow-down, its consumers were buying more Apple products than ever before. Between 2013 and 2015, Apple generated an *increase* in operating profit from consumer electronics of close to $20 billion. Of that increase, 59 per cent came from China. By 2015, China represented more sales and more profit to Apple than the whole of Europe. Developing economies matter.

25.3 Growing economic power of countries within Asia and Africa

Chapters 26 and 27 cover the main themes concerning China, India and Africa. There are a few more points to be made, though, about Asia:

- The growth of China in particular has become a regional hub that has sucked in supplies and therefore fostered greater growth among countries such as Vietnam, Indonesia and Cambodia; the first two are especially important because of their huge population sizes: Vietnam has a population of 95 million and Indonesia is the world's fourth most populous with 256 million.
- Many Asian countries follow the examples set by China and Japan and take education extremely seriously; this sets them up nicely for improved production of higher value-added products. It is a myth that countries such as China simply copy western products and designs.
- Historically, the west has been the focal point for global trade; the dramatic rise of China has changed much of this. This may have an ongoing impact not only on trade in goods but also services, including tourism as well as banking, insurance and so on. The opportunities for Britain get ever greater as these economies increase their need for the things we are best at: services.

> 'The developing world is full of entrepreneurs and visionaries, who with access to education, equity and credit would play a key role in developing the economic situations in their countries.'
>
> *Muhammad Yunus, Nobel-prizewinning pioneer of microfinance*

25.4 Implications of economic growth for businesses

Even though the United States is a vast and hugely valuable market, it is striking how American firms treat the globe as an extension of America. Businesses such as Gap, Forever 21, Google, Amazon, Microsoft, Apple and Facebook make a global approach look normal. In the UK, this is less common. Our retailers remember many examples of disastrous moves into America, China, Russia and even France. So strong propositions for developing countries such as Primark and Topshop keep thinking, but don't act.

To take advantage of economic growth elsewhere needs good strategic thinking backed by strong finances. It helps to have a clear idea about where UK firms have natural competitive advantages. For instance, British pop music is a success story virtually everywhere; and British education attracts a price premium throughout the world. Among other British economic strengths are:

- British design engineering and architecture
- British fashion design
- British culture, from books (Harry Potter, Sherlock Holmes) to films to the Premier League
- British tradition, not only schools but also cars, foods and especially alcoholic drink (we exported £12.5 billion of food and drink in 2015)
- financial and other business services.

In most markets, long-term success comes from adjusting your business towards your customers. In the period 2000–2014, the car market in China was growing so rapidly that western companies could get away with replicating their European-/American-designed cars for the Chinese consumer. Then a combination of factors led to a check to the ambitions of many. Volkswagen decided to respond to faltering sales in 2015 by announcing the design and development of a Chinese-focused range of economy cars. Their target prices of £6,000 to £9,000 would place them in a completely different market sector to VW's best-selling Audi and Porsche models. This strategic approach is sometimes known as 'glocalisation', that is, using a global brand strengths but designing products for the local market.

Figure 25.3 British beer

25.5 Implications of economic growth for individuals

For individuals, building a career or starting their own business, sustained economic growth in a country like Vietnam provides a whole range of opportunities. Developing markets don't just 'grow', they tend to change shape as they grow. New niches emerge, such as kids (yogurt, chocolate, films) or on-trend young adults (think Nike, Apple, Snapchat). With each emergence of a new niche there are chances to launch new products to challenge the existing ones. The creative, responsive executive or entrepreneur can scoop the prize.

With exciting prospects available globally, it's sensible for ambitious individuals to prepare themselves:

- Learn a foreign language at school (any one, because learning one makes it easier to learn others later on).
- Read broadly, perhaps using the *Economist* magazine to have a good understanding of global business and different economies.
- Learn to find a balance between business and morality, in which you can politely refuse an unethical proposal without being self-righteous; this is a skill that's useful throughout life, but there's no doubt that corruption is more widespread in developing countries than developed ones.

Implication of economic growth for employment patterns

In the early stages of economic development, the key cause of growth is the transfer of jobs from agriculture to factories or the service sector. Factory labour almost always generates higher value added than working the land. Therefore the very act of moving from farm to factory generates economic growth. When this process slows to a halt (as in Britain, with only 1 per cent of labour left on the land), economic growth becomes much harder to achieve.

So a key implication of growth is the transfer from physical labour on the land to machine-assisted labour in factories and then people-focused jobs in services. There is, though, an argument for saying the change in employment patterns is as much a cause of the growth as an effect/implication.

A further consequence of these broad shifts in employment is that factory and service operations have greater scope for growth – which leads to a greater need for management. So the rise of the middle classes tends to sit alongside the switch away from agriculture.

25.6 Indicators of growth

Gross Domestic Product (GDP) per head of population (per capita) at PPP

Gross Domestic Product (GDP) is the value of all the goods and services produced in a country in the course of a year. Economic growth is usually measured as the percentage change in this figure from one year to the next. The strength of GDP is that the methodology for calculating it has been developed internationally since its invention in the 1930s. So it provides meaningful comparable data between countries and within a country over time.

There is a strong argument for saying that GDP figures **per capita** should be used far more often than they are. Measuring GDP per head of population means that you have an effective measure of changes in living standards. Some African countries have annual population growth of 2.5 per cent. So if GDP growth is 1.5 per cent a year, people are effectively getting 1 per cent worse off per year. Percentage changes in GDP per capita are a much better measure of economic growth than looking at changes in total GDP.

PPP is another way to improve the validity and comparability of the data. PPP means adjusting the GDP figure in line with known differences in the cost of living. Usually, the cost of living in a poor country is far below that of a rich one. Typically, the basics are cheaper, such as bread, rice and buses to get to work. So to understand the true difference in living standards between an Indian and an American worker, the Indian's income is adjusted in line with the greater purchasing power of the money income. Table 25.2 shows this: an Indian worker's $1,640 of annual income actually buys more than three times that amount, i.e. buys $5,900 of goods and services.

	India	USA
GDP per capita (2014)	$1,640	$54,600
GDP per capita at PPP (2014)	$5,900	$54,600

Table 25.2 Incomes in India and America: raw data and adjusted to show PPP

Literacy

Important though income is, economic development must mean more than money. Illiteracy (being unable to read or write) in China in 1987 was 40.6 per cent among women. In Kenya, there was a similar figure (41.5 per cent). By 2015, the figure in Kenya had fallen to 25.1 per cent and in China to 5.5 per cent. Not only is this a flattering insight into Chinese economic growth (it's not just about cars and pollution), it also gives an insight into the sustainability of the growth. India also enjoys strong economic growth, but its high levels of illiteracy may act as a brake on the country's ability to expand. See Table 25.3 to see the stark difference between China and the other three developing countries.

	Male illiteracy %	Female illiteracy %	Adult illiteracy %
India 1987	45.2	74.3	59.2
India 2015	18.7	39.4	28.8
China 1987	16.9	40.6	28.6
China 2015	1.8	5.5	3.6
Nigeria 1990	37.7	60.5	49.3
Nigeria 2015	30.8	50.3	40.4
Kenya 1990	20.2	41.5	31.0
Kenya 2015	18.9	25.1	22.0

Table 25.3 Adults who can't read or write (sources: 1987/1990 figures from *United Nations Statistical Yearbook*, 28th edn; 2015 figures *CIA World Factbook*)

Health

As with literacy, so with health. In Britain in the 1850s, average life expectancy was 43 years. A similar figure was true of Bangladesh and Sierra Leone in the 1980s. As societies become more prosperous, malnutrition falls and life expectancy rises. An effective government can generate even better health outcomes if it invests in effective healthcare. In Table 25.4 you can see the impact of economic growth in South Korea, China and Mexico and a remarkable performance (for a poor country) by successive governments in Cuba. The data also shows the extraordinary differences in outcomes, especially in terms of infant deaths. A Nigerian baby is 20 times more likely to die before the age of one than one born in South Korea.

Although economic growth is an important element in improved health outcomes, the figures for Cuba confirm that even a struggling economy can provide good healthcare, as long as the government has the determination. And Nigeria, a wealthier country than Kenya, shows the shocking outcomes that poor governance leads to.

Human Development Index (HDI)

In an attempt to find a single measure of healthy economic growth, the Pakistani economist Mahbub ul Haq devised the HDI, which was launched by the United Nations in 1990. The idea was to get a more people-centred measure of economic development. The HDI was to be a single composite figure reflecting health,

	Rank (out of 180 countries)	HDI score (out of 1.00)
Norway	1	0.944
UK	14	0.892
Cuba	44	0.815
Mexico	71	0.756
China	91	0.719
India	135	0.586
Kenya	147	0.535
Nigeria	152	0.504

Table 25.5 HDI ranking and scores, selected countries 2014 (source: Courtesy of the United Nations and reproduced under the Creative Commons License, http://creativecommons.org/licenses/by/3.0/igo/legalcode)

	Infant mortality (under one yr) per 1000 births 1985	Infant mortality (under one yr) per 1000 births 2015	Life expectancy (from birth) 1985	Life expectancy (from birth) 2015
India	91	42	52	68
China	32	12	69	75
Nigeria	105	73	50.5	53
Kenya	72	39	58.5	64
Cuba	11	4	74	78
South Korea	25	4	71	80
Mexico	43	12	64	76
UK	8	4	75	80.5

Table 25.4 Health statistics (sources: 1985 figures from *United Nations Statistical Yearbook* 28th edn; 2015 figures *CIA World Factbook*)

education and economic progress. In its latest form, the measure combines three pieces of data:

- a decent standard of living, measured by Gross National Income per capita (at PPP)
- a long and healthy life: life expectancy at birth
- good educational standards: average years of schooling (the recent past) and expected years of schooling (the future).

Is the HDI the best way to judge economic growth? In fact, it would be reasonable to call the elements in the index relatively arbitrary. Mexico's relatively strong showing is a reminder that crime statistics are not included – and perhaps they should be. What is not in doubt is that it made sense to suggest that there was more to human development than the gross domestic product (GDP). The United Nations certainly believes in the approach, as it publishes an updated Human Development Index annually.

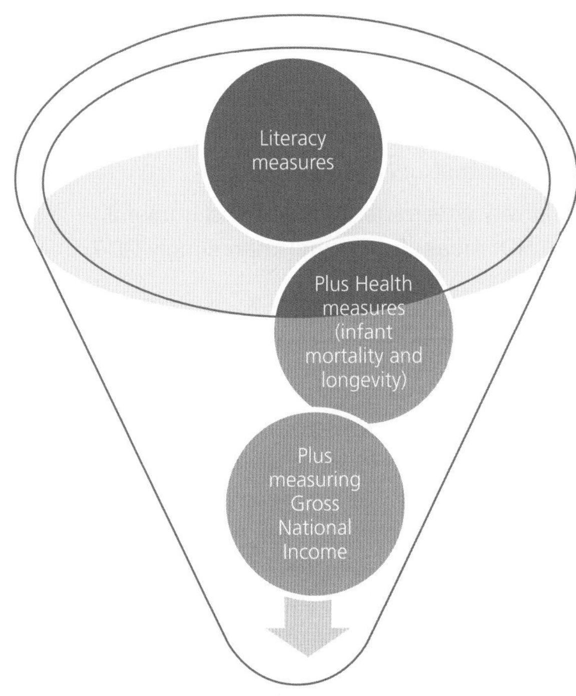

Figure 25.4 Logic chain: Human Development Index

'Development is about transforming the lives of people, not just transforming economies.'

Joseph Stiglitz, Nobel prizewinning economist

'People say that globalisation has negative aspects, but I don't believe globalisation is bad. It's criticised from a western perspective, but if you put yourself in the shoes of people in the developing world, it provides an unprecedented opportunity.'

Tadashi Yanai, super-rich Japanese founder of Uniqlo

Five whys and a how

Questions	Answers
Why do some poor countries grow faster than others?	Some say that growth comes to countries that trust more in the free market; others believe well-managed government intervention can help growth; everyone agrees that political stability is hugely important.
Why should British companies care about economic growth in the developing world?	Because it shows where the opportunities lie, and the potential value of those opportunities.
Why not measure economic progress simply by changes in GDP?	Humans want and need more than just to buy more stuff. They want health and happiness too.
Why not add more measurements to the HDI, to make it better-rounded?	Its simplicity may be an important part of its success; people understand the HDI and therefore trust it.
Why is literacy so important for its impact on economic growth?	Because if people can't read or write, they can't safely be employed in factories or in other roles.
How can small businesses succeed when launching into big developing countries?	As with any launch, the key is take time to understand the target market – then find the right financial backing to afford that launch.

25.7 Growing economies – evaluation

Britain's slow but stable growth provides a terrific platform for businesses in this country. But for those same businesses, it would be crazy to miss the opportunities provided by more rapid growth elsewhere. British companies such as JCB (India) and Burberry (China) have built their own businesses on the back of the opportunities they found in specific, rapidly growing economies. The British mystery is why there aren't more examples of this. Of the world's top ten car companies, three are American, three Japanese and three German (plus Hyundai, South Korea); no Brits there. Britain is the world's second-biggest aerospace producer, yet British Aerospace plc sold our stake in the hugely successful European Airbus project, leaving us with no direct stake in passenger aircraft. In relation to growing economies, there has been a lack of entrepreneurial and corporate enterprise going back over several generations. Somehow we focus on the risks more than the opportunities. It's time that changed.

Key terms

Globalisation: the growth of international trade that has made an increasing number of markets global rather than national.

Gross Domestic Product (GDP): is the value of all the goods and services produced within an economy over a specified time-period such as a year.

Per capita: this means looking at data per head of population, to make it easier to compare statistics from countries of different size.

25.8 Workbook

Revision questions

(30 marks; 30 minutes)

1 Explain two factors a British manufacturer might consider in deciding which developing country should be the base for its first overseas factory. (6)

2 In 1979, the African country of Benin had the world's highest rate of illiteracy (83.5 per cent of all adults). In 2015, Benin's annual GDP per capita of $835 was among the lowest in the world. Explain the possible connection between these figures. (5)

3 Explain why it may be useful to see GDP per capita figures shown 'at PPP'. (4)

4 Should wealthy countries increase the rates of tax on their own populations in order to finance greater help to people living on less than $1.25 a day? Explain your answer. (5)

5 Outline three possible reasons that may explain why China's growth rate is so much higher than that of Nigeria or India. (6)

6 Explain why governments might find it useful to see HDI measured, rather than simply GDP per capita. (4)

Revision activities

Data response

Global business strategy isn't easy

In 1980, it wasn't obvious whether India or Pakistan had the better economic prospects. Yes, India's population was hugely bigger (685 million compared with 85 million for Pakistan) but Pakistan had a higher GDP per capita. Whatever the reasons, Honda opted for Pakistan. By 2005, even though India was the growth story, Honda's 50 per cent share of Pakistan's car market was a big consolation. Honda Pakistan's position was very profitable, and its place was secured by owning Pakistan's only large car factory. For those growing up locally, the Honda Civic and Accord models epitomised luxury driving.

To keep its position strong, Honda embarked in 2005 on heavy investments in capacity expansion. The goal was to be able to produce 50,000 cars a year.

Then it all went wrong. From 2006, the market for passenger cars started to slide. Worse, competition from Toyota and Suzuki (in partnership with the Pakistan government) chipped away at Honda's market share. In 2007, Honda sales were just 18,709 cars – from a factory capable of producing 50,000. Worse was to come, as sales slid further in the face of world recession and a collapse in security and consumer confidence. Healthy operating profits turned into severe losses.

Naturally enough, Honda's strategy had been to focus on 'the market' – largely companies or government departments buying prestigious cars for managerial staff. Yet from about 2005, the market moved more towards individuals buying cars for themselves. A Honda Civic was priced at about £11,000; a Suzuki Swift cost half that. Honda's marketing strategy was facing the wrong way – looking backwards instead of forwards. In

2010, Honda's market share fell to 23 per cent and by 2014 it was 18 per cent. Toyota with 27 per cent and Suzuki with 55 per cent made up the rest of the market.

Meanwhile the difference in 2014 car production between Pakistan and India emphasised the poor choice Honda made back in 1980 (see Figure 25.5).

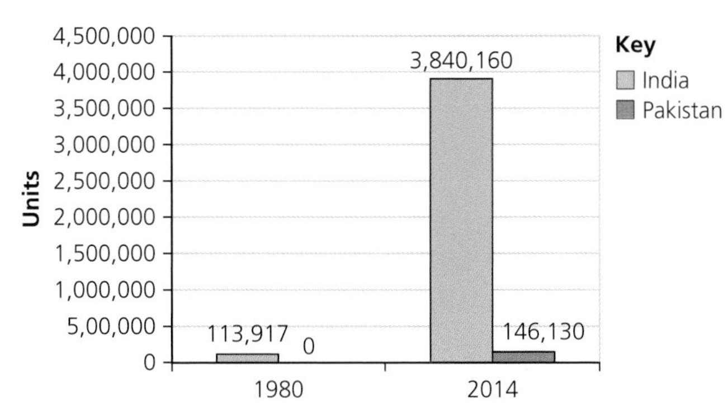

Figure 25.5 Total market car production, India vs Pakistan (source: OICA 2015)

Questions (40 marks: 45 minutes)

1 Assess why a business might make a mistake when choosing which country to focus on. (10)

2 Honda's international strategy has been hugely successful; but not in this case. Assess why a successful international company such as Honda might fail within one country. (10)

3 Evaluate two alternative strategies Honda might choose in the face of its current problems in Pakistan. Explain which you would recommend, and why. (20)

Extended writing

1 A British-educated entrepreneur chooses to start up a pizza delivery business in Mexico City, where the minimum wage rate is 45p per hour. Evaluate the problems the entrepreneur might face if she decides to run the business exactly as she would in Britain. (20)

2 Ella's Kitchen is a highly successful producer of baby food. Founded by entrepreneur Paul Lindley in 2006, it has already expanded successfully in Europe and America. Evaluate whether the brand should now be launched into faster-growing but less developed economies in Asia. (20)

26 China versus India

Definition

China and India are the two most populous countries on the planet. Both have populations of around 1.3 billion – more than four times the size of the next most populous country (America).

Linked to: Corporate strategy, Ch 2; SWOT analysis, Ch 4; Impact of external influences, Ch 5; Growing economies, Ch 25; International trade and business growth, Ch 28; Assessment of a country as a market, Ch 33

26.1 China?

In 2001, investment banks coined the term BRIC to sum up the huge growth potential of Brazil, Russia, India and China. In fact, the growth in China and India is far, far more significant than in the other two countries. In Brazil, a growth rate of 3 per cent is applauded; China sees a growth rate of 7 per cent as a disappointment.

In 1997, the streets of every Chinese city were dominated by bicycles. The private car was still quite rare. Fewer than four households in one thousand owned a car. Yet in 2009, China overtook America to become the world's biggest car market. Since 2009, Jaguar Land Rover has benefitted hugely, with sales in China rising from 15,000 in 2009 to over 100,000 in 2014 (at an average price of around £70,000 per car, that represents over £7 billion of sales in China). The boom in China has been incredible.

For more than 25 years, the Chinese economy grew at around 10 per cent a year. That is faster than any other major economy in history. During Britain's Industrial Revolution, the economy only grew at around 2 to 2.5 per cent a year. And, of course, China is not only remarkable for its rate of growth, but also its population size. This is a country with nearly one-quarter of the world's population. If 1.35 billion people have economic wealth, even the United States will have to step back. China is set to become the world's superpower. Or is it ...?

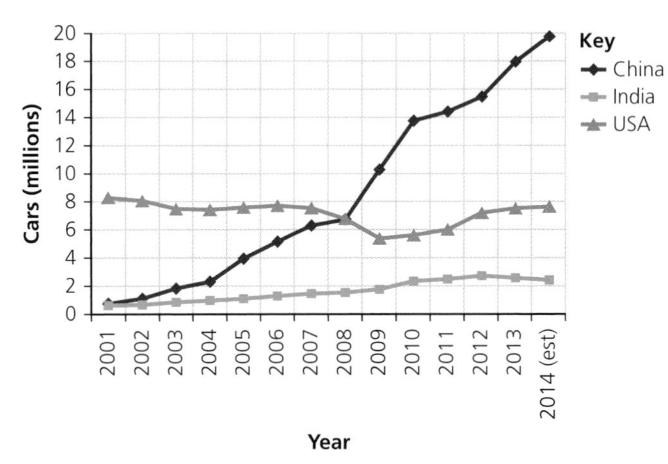

Figure 26.1 China becomes the world's largest car market (source: www.OICA.net)

Figure 26.2 Street Market in Hong Kong, China

26.2 Or India?

Some argue that India is in an even more powerful position. Although far behind China, its accelerating growth and population may make it the dark horse that eventually wins the prize. India has long been one of the world's poorest countries, yet one of the most populous. At 1.3 billion, its position as the world's second-most populated country puts it way ahead of America (in third place with 'only' 320 million).

India's population has two features that China cannot match: it is rising and it is very young. Over the next 20 years there will be far more keen 20-year-olds entering the Indian job market than in China. This is because China made huge efforts between 1979 and 2015 to curb population growth by pressing its people to have only one child per family. Due to this policy, only 22 per cent of the Chinese population is 18 or under. In India, the figure is 35 per cent. Details of the population figures for China and India are given in Table 26.1.

	China	India
Population growth per year (2015)	0.52%	1.26%
Population level 2015 (UN data)	1.376bn	1.311bn
Population level 2050 (UN est.)	1.348bn	1.705bn
Population under-20 (2015 data)	316m	501m

Table 26.1 China and India: population figures

26.3 Which has been growing faster?

Here the answer is clear. As shown in Figure 26.3, since 1991 the Chinese economy has completely outstripped that of India and managed to overtake first Britain, then Germany and then Japan. This has largely been due to massive increases in **fixed capital formation**. In the early 1990s, the Chinese government started investing heavily in the economy, and started to encourage western companies to invest as well.

Typically, western companies invested by building factories (taking advantage of extremely low-cost labour), while the government started building dams (for water and electricity), roads and other forms of infrastructure. Today that government investment is going into housing, railways, schools and hospitals. China is gearing up for continuing success. China spends more than 40 per cent of its annual output on investing in its future (fixed capital formation). For many years, India's investment spending was far behind this but since 2005 it has been much more impressive. It has been helped by the growth in foreign direct investment (FDI), though as Figure 26.3 makes clear, the world's investors still choose China ahead of India.

China's long-term success was largely built on export growth. Originally that was based on incredibly cheap labour (around 10p an hour in 1985–1990) and therefore outstanding cost competitiveness. In 2009, China's exports were seven times higher by value than India's. The recession that followed hit China's exports hard, as western markets dried up during 2009 and 2010, but China remains the world's largest exporter of manufactured goods. Furthermore, its exports contain a bigger proportion of high technology products than those of the UK, India or (amazingly) the United States (according to World Bank data).

As Table 26.2 shows, India is a relatively small-scale exporter of goods. At the heart of its commercial success are '**invisible exports**' such as software engineering and running English-speaking call centres. India has two important advantages over China: good English (the global language) and an education system that is

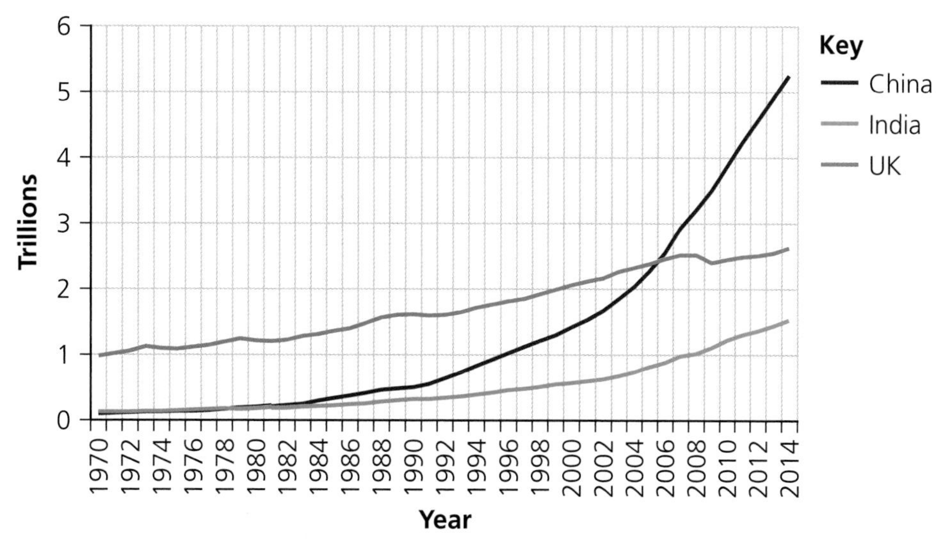

Figure 26.3 Total GDP for China, India and Britain (1970–2014) in constant 2005 US dollars (source: United Nations)

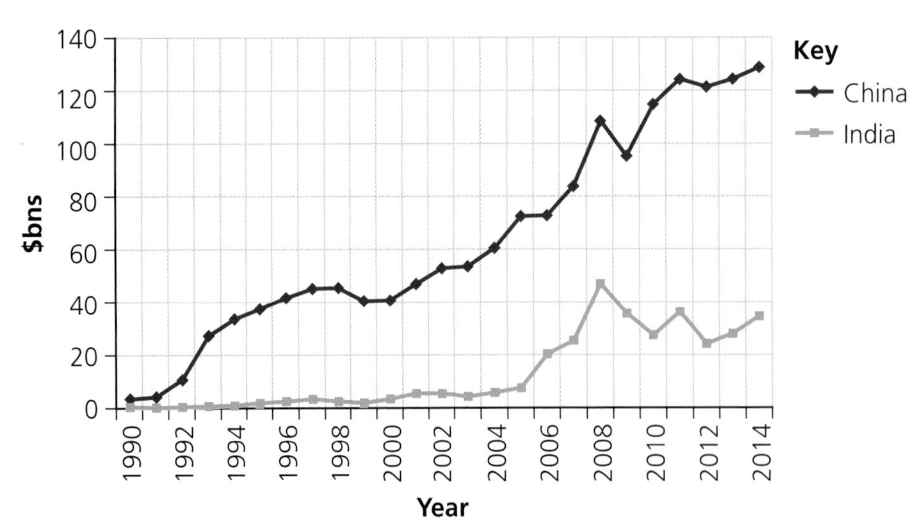

Figure 26.4 Foreign direct investment China vs India from 1990 to 2014 (source: UNCTAD database 2015)

excellent at the top end, so it produces many excellent managers and software experts.

Visible exports 2014	
	$bn
China	2,343
USA	1,610
Germany	1,547
UK	503
India	343

Table 26.2 Top three exporters of goods, plus UK and India (source: Courtesy of the Central Intelligence Agency, *CIA World Factbook* 2015)

The big question now is whether India can sustain its recent success.

26.4 Can India grow rapidly and consistently?

India has three key weaknesses in its attempts to keep up with China.

India's key weaknesses

India's key three weaknesses are set out below.

Its poor infrastructure

Under-investment means that the road system lags behind China's, especially in motorway construction. It is possible that the reason is political. In China, the government can dictate to the people that 40+ per cent of spending will be on investment. In India, there is a democratically elected government, and it may be that the public is unwilling to cut back too severely on today's spending, in order to invest in the country's future.

The narrow education system

Whereas the literacy level in China is 96.5 per cent, in India it is only 71 per cent (that is, 29 per cent of the population cannot read or write). Therefore, if the growth rate led to job opportunities for a wider range of people, many would be unable to take up the jobs due to illiteracy. At the top end the Indian education system is very strong, but for the mass of the population it is shockingly poor.

International trade: balance of payments deficit

Whereas in 2015 China had a current account surplus (more exports than imports) of $290 billion, India had a deficit of $25 billion. This implies that Indian consumers are overspending in relation to the goods foreigners want to buy from India. Running a large **balance of payments deficit** makes it hard for India to keep growing without an inflationary fall in the value of the rupee.

Inevitable overheating?

This is not an issue of global warming, but of economic performance. In the past, accelerations in India's industrial production have triggered rises in inflation. This has made the Bank of India respond by pushing up interest rates. As a result the growth spurt is choked off. India has consistently had higher levels of inflation than China. Therefore there must be reservations about India's ability to match China's remarkable growth rates.

Real business

CAT versus JCB

Thirty years ago, America's construction equipment giant Caterpillar (CAT) started investing heavily in China. Today its huge strength in China underpins its position as world number one. At much the same time, Britain's JCB chose to invest in India. Today its 50 per cent market share in India is crucial in securing JCB's 12 per cent share of the world market for construction equipment.

Now, both Cat and JCB are following similar strategies: build on strength, while dipping a toe in the weaker market. In 2014, Caterpillar announced that it had just opened its 26th factory in China, employing 15,000 staff. Caterpillar boss Doug Oberhelman said in March 2014 that 'in China we're in the lead position by a fairly nice margin'.

At the same time JCB announced that it would be opening a \$100 million factory complex in Jaipur – the company's fourth factory in India. JCB is also investing cautiously in new capacity in China, just as Cat is doing the same in India.

As things stand, it looks as if Caterpillar made the better bet, 30 years ago. Happily for JCB, even if it never breaks into China, its strength in India guarantees it a strong position in the world market for the foreseeable future.

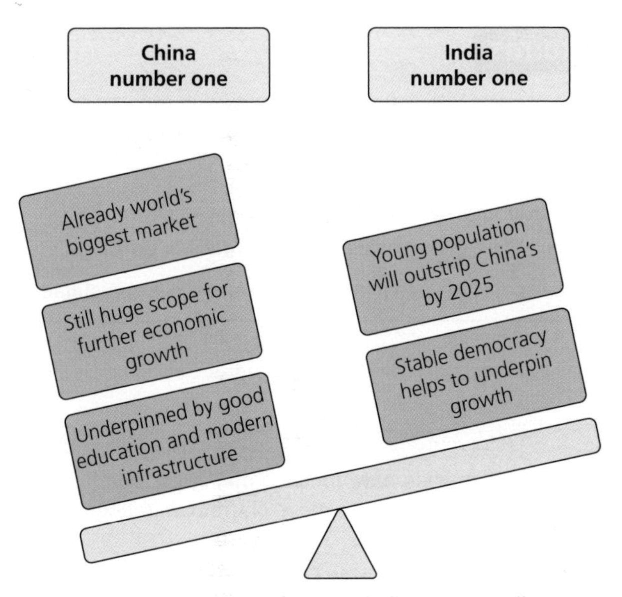

Figure 26.5 Logic balance: China vs India in the medium term

26.5 Can China outstrip America?

Some have expressed doubts about the sustainability of China's growth. They suggest that export growth must flatten out as Chinese wage rates increase. At present fast-food and factory workers in Beijing earn £1.15–1.30 per hour, so there is some way to go! In any case, this view assumes that China will remain a producer of low-cost items. In fact, in 2015, China was the world's biggest manufacturer of cars and produced 48.5 per cent of the world's steel (Japan came second with 6.5 per cent). Nevertheless, it is true to say that China will lose some low-cost production. For example, minimum wage rates in India are as low as 25p per hour. So India can already undercut China.

So can China's GDP overtake America's? Yes, it can – and arguably it already has. The US Central Intelligence Agency's figures show that China's total GDP (at PPP) for 2014 was slightly higher than America's at \$17.62 trillion compared with \$17.42 trillion. Of course, China's population is four times higher than America's, so this doesn't mean that the average Chinese is richer than the average American. But as recently as 2010, there were analysts arguing that America would never be overtaken by China.

What is not in doubt is that China's growth has serious environmental implications. There is no doubt that pollution is dreadful in industrial towns such as Linfen, and poor in cities such as Beijing and Shanghai. Nevertheless, China is investing heavily in cleaning up its rivers and air, and the country makes a relatively modest contribution to greenhouse gases (per capita). Table 26.3 shows the major contributors to global CO_2 emissions. Generally, the richer the country, the higher the total of CO_2 emissions.

	2014 tonnes of CO_2 per head p.a.	2014 total CO_2 tonnes (bns)	Est. 2019 total CO_2 tonnes (bns)
India	1.5	1.808	2.046
China	7.2	9.595	11.302
Japan	9.8	1.245	1.229
USA	16.5	5.261	5.441
Russia	11.5	1.633	1.732
World	4.7	33.186	35.998

Table 26.3 Global carbon dioxide emissions (source: U.S. Energy Information Administration 2014)

As China grows, its emissions will continue to rise. This is why emissions in developed countries will have to be cut if there is to be a chance of stopping the global figure from growing further.

26.6 What opportunities are there for British business?

Every director of every major public company knows the need for a China/India strategy. Tesco has its investment in Chinese superstores and in 2014 invested £85 million in a joint venture into the grocery market in India. UK-owned Costa Coffee had 300 stores in China at the start of 2015 and plans to have 900 open by 2020. Despite some British successes in China, the value of German exports to China is more than five times the value of Britain's; even France outsells Britain by 2:1. Of all China's imports, Britain supplies little more than 1 per cent.

What about India? Britain ran India (as a colony) for 150 years, so there must be trade links remaining. Indeed, in 2002, the British share of Indian imports was 4.96 per cent (about in line with Britain's share of world trade). By 2014, however, the British share had fallen to 1 per cent – one third of the level achieved by Germany. Despite this decline, Britain still has distinct advantages over France, Italy and Spain. The need is for British businesses to commit themselves to an effective long-term strategy for India.

> 'Asia's rise to global economic pre-eminence could see China and India leading the world by 2050.'
>
> *Pricewaterhouse Coopers: The World in 2050, published in March 2015*

> 'While Chinese companies succeeded because of the government, Indian companies succeeded despite the government!'
>
> *Girija Pande, Indian contributor to Forbes magazine*

> 'New car sales in China are forecast to contribute 35% of the world's car market growth until 2020. Still, car penetration (per household) will reach only about 15% by 2020.'
>
> *McKinsey & Company*

26.7 China versus India – evaluation

China has been growing at a rate of 7+ per cent for 30 years and looks capable of doing the same in the future. It may be short of younger people, but it has over 400 million people working on the land, many of whom would be pleased to earn higher wages in a factory. India also has good prospects, though it is less clear that it will be able to deliver high growth year in year out. It needs huge investments in education and infrastructure, but the Indian government is unwilling, or unable, to provide this. In this two-horse race, the one to back is China.

Nevertheless, for an individual business India may be the better bet. For a young British company lacking export experience, it would probably be easier to break into India than China, if only because there are fewer language and cultural barriers. Above all else, India lacks an effective manufacturing sector, so it may be a perfect place for British manufacturing exports or for setting up new factories. As always, each business case is different.

Key terms

Balance of payments deficit: imports outweigh exports; if it continues indefinitely, it means ever greater build-up of foreign currency debt.

Fixed capital formation: an economist's way of saying investment in long-term assets, such as roads or buildings.

Invisible export: the sale of a service to an overseas customer.

Five whys and a how

Questions	Answers
Why has China's growth not led to any world-leading brands?	Perhaps Chinese companies have focused mainly on their home market; or maybe it is struggling to move on from imitating western products and processes.
Why have UK firms been so slow to 'get' the China growth story – and therefore seize opportunities?	With impressive exceptions such as Costa, Land Rover and New Look, UK firms seemed determined to see more risks than rewards. Lack of long-term thinking?
Why has India struggled to keep up with China?	It's been far less welcoming to foreign direct investment, and has had a series of dysfunctional, bureaucratic governments.
Why doesn't China tackle its gross income inequalities?	For a supposedly communist government, it's odd – but perhaps the wealthy have as much power in China as elsewhere.
Why has President Xi set lower growth targets for China in the future (of 6.5–7.0 per cent)?	He says it's to allow greater priority for air quality and other environmental factors: the growth-at-all-costs phase is over.
How might India try to boost growth to exceed that of China?	By heavy investment in mass education and in infrastructure.

26.8 Workbook

Revision questions

(30 marks; 30 minutes)

1 Outline two reasons why China's growth prospects may be greater than India's. (4)

2 Outline two reasons why India's growth prospects may be greater than China's. (4)

3 Explain the implications of the quote by McKinsey & Company shown on page 190. (6)

4 Look again at Figure 26.3. Do you think businesses in the UK should be pleased or concerned about China and India's growth path? (5)

5 Outline two reasons why a British retail firm such as Next may choose to invest in China rather than India. (4)

6 Look at Table 26.3 and answer the following questions.

a) Why is Russia's environmental record sometimes criticised, given that its total carbon emissions are 'only' 1.633 billion tonnes? (2)

b) America regularly criticises China for its impact on global warming. Analyse this view based on the data provided. (5)

Revision activities

Data response 1

Grocery sales by outlet size			
	India	China	USA
Hyper/ supermarkets	1.66%	61.48%	65.10%
Small grocery	78.91%	13.35%	8.12%
Other grocery	3.76%	19.68%	19.27%
Specialist food/ drink	15.67%	5.49%	7.51%
Population	1.240 billion	1.350 billion	330 million

Table 26.4 Grocery outlets in India and China (source: Euromonitor Reports. © 2014 Euromonitor. Reprinted with permission from Euromonitor)

Questions (25 marks; 25 minutes)

1 Explain two key differences between grocery distribution in India and China. (5)

2 Assume you are the boss of Innocent Drinks, trying to decide whether to launch your fresh-fruit smoothie drinks into India or China. On the basis of the data given in Table 26.4, evaluate which country should be targeted first. (20)

Data response 2

The growth of the middle market in China

For many years the big business story in China was the growth of the luxury goods sector. Since late 2012, President Xi has made an impressive stand against corruption in China, which seems to have dampened down spending. This has allowed the biggest story of all to emerge: the rise of the middle market. Think shampoo, chocolate and toilet paper rather than Gucci bags and £50,000 watches. Table 26.5 tells the story: static demand for toilet paper in the west (with a little bit of inflation), but surging demand in China and India. In India, though, the 2008 starting point was 1.3 US cents per person per year, which makes it hard to make much of a 76.9 per cent growth rate.

Note that the populations of these four countries are: China 1.355 billion; India 1.24 billion; USA 320 million and the UK 64 million.

$ per capita spending on toilet paper, 2008–2013				
	China	India	USA	UK
2008	4.38	0.013	27.69	28.13
2009	4.81	0.015	28.69	28.9
2010	5.62	0.017	28.21	29.75
2011	6.81	0.02	29.24	30.12
2012	7.5	0.02	29.34	30.03
2013	8.33	0.023	29.74	29.85
2008–2013 %	+90.2%	+76.9%	+7.4%	+6.1%

Table 26.5 $ per capita spending on toilet paper, 2008–2013 (source: Euromonitor Reports. © 2014 Euromonitor. Reprinted with permission from Euromonitor)

Questions (40 marks; 45 minutes)

1 a) Calculate the market size for toilet paper in each country in 2008. (4)

b) Calculate the growth in the market between 2008 and 2013 for China, India and the UK. (4)

c) Assess the conclusions that might be drawn from that data by the chief executive of a UK-based producer of a major brand of toilet paper. (12)

2 Using extrapolation, evaluate the extent to which India might have better growth prospects than China in the future of the market for toilet paper. (20)

Data response 3

Costa: a middle-market British success story

Perhaps Britain's most successful middle-market brand in China is Costa Coffee. Owners Whitbread took the decision to follow Starbucks into the market for coffee bars in 2006. Although they were many years behind Starbucks (which started in China in 1999, without joint venture partners, and had 250 outlets by 2006) Costa's coffee bars proved profitable from early on. By the end of 2013, Costa had 253 outlets spread over 28 cities, accounting for 10 per cent of all Costa coffee bars worldwide. Starbucks, in the meantime, had raced ahead to 1,017 shops across 60 Chinese cities. This still leaves cities with more than a million inhabitants (bigger than Manchester) with no western-style coffee bars at all.

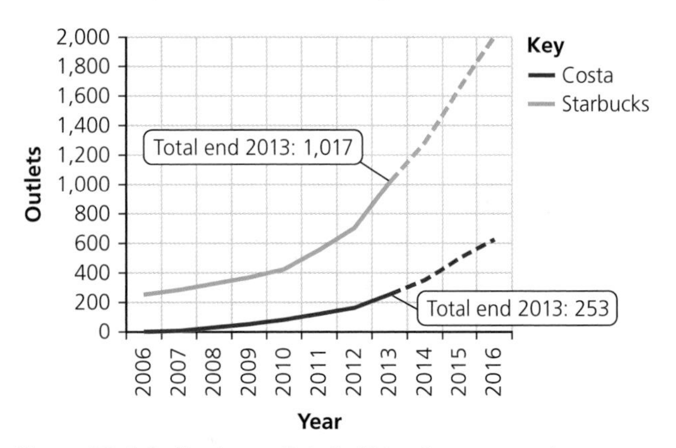

Figure 26.6 Coffee bar outlets in China (sources: various, including company accounts and media reports)

Whitbread plc seems careful to hide the turnover and profits of its Chinese outlets, perhaps in part at the behest of its joint venture partner the Yueda Group. The accounts of Starbucks, though, give an idea of the attractions of China as a market. Whereas the gross profit margin of running Starbucks outlets in America in 2013 ran at 21.5 per cent, in China Starbucks made a 35 per cent margin. This is, in part, because it is able to charge higher prices in China than America. As average incomes in China are about a fifth of those in America, this makes a visit to a western coffee bar a luxury.

Partly because of the high prices, the Chinese drink – on average – only three cups of coffee a year. This compares with 240 cups per person per year globally, and around 600 cups in America. According to Mintel the market for coffee in China has been growing at 30 per cent a year. Rapid growth plus huge upward potential make this a marvellous market to be in.

Questions (30 marks; 35 minutes)

1 Assess the advantages and disadvantages to Costa of operating in China. (10)

2 With reference to your own research and the text above, evaluate whether it is justifiable ethically for a British plc such as Whitbread to commit itself to major development in China. (20)

Extended writing

1 Sainsbury's is considering whether to open its first stores in China or India. Evaluate the extent to which a decision like that should be based on strategic vision or rigorous investment appraisal. (20)

2 Having opened 18 stores in China in 2014, low-cost fashion retailer New Look announced it would open 50 more in 2015. Evaluate whether long-term success for New Look in China is now inevitable. (20)

Section 4.1 Globalisation

27 Business potential in Africa

Definition

Africa is a continent with 20 per cent of the world's land and more than 50 countries. It can be split into North Africa, sub-Saharan Africa and South Africa. Its combined population of more than one billion is the world's youngest. More than 50 per cent of its people are under 20.

Linked to: Growing economies, Ch 25; China versus India, Ch 26; International trade and business growth, Ch 28

27.1 An introduction

In August 2015, the first ever scheduled airline route began between Japan and sub-Saharan Africa. An Ethiopian Airlines Boeing Dreamliner now links Tokyo to Addis Ababa three times a week. This highlights the remarkable growth in Japanese investment in Africa. During the five years to 2014, Japanese project finance commitments to Africa rose by 576 per cent to $3.54 billion, according to global law firm Linklaters. The head of Linklaters' Japanese office says: 'Japan has taken a much quieter and below the radar approach than China but has made serious inroads, particularly in countries such as Nigeria and Mozambique.' The message is clear: things are happening in Africa – and those things will generate business opportunities.

> 'Africa is the story. The big story is Africa. The Chinese and Japanese are fighting over Africa.'
>
> *Dr Ahmed Heikal, Chairman of Citadel Capital*

Since 2000, it has been noticeable that the economies of sub-Saharan Africa have been growing at a sustainedly impressive rate. Not quite at the level of China or India, but more rapidly than Latin America or the economies of Eastern Europe. Figure 27.1 gives a clear sense of how significant the change has been since 2000, with African growth rates of 5.5 per cent compared with 2.5 per cent in the west. There are three possible explanations for the recent African growth story:

- In the lead-up to 2000, Britain was prominent in pushing for debt write-offs in Africa. Many occurred at around 2000, perhaps helping the macro-economic balance within the main countries – and helping growth to be restored.
- The China-induced commodity price boom between 2004/2005 and 2014 boosted economies across Africa, boosting Nigeria (oil), Ghana (cocoa), Kenya

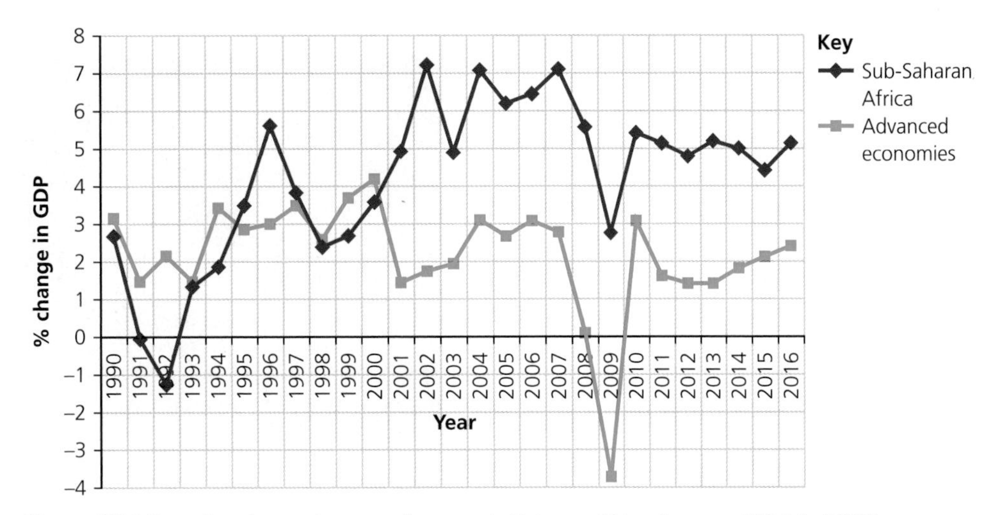

Figure 27.1 Growth: advanced economies vs sub-Saharan Africa (source: IMF July 2015)

(coffee) and many others. In fact, though, the African recovery story pre-dates the commodity story by about four years, making this an unlikely explanation of the change in economic performance.

- A broad improvement in governance, shown most notably in the sharp reduction in wars and civil wars. Other fantastically hopeful signs came from the acceptance of democratic handovers of power in Ghana in 2000 and 2009 and most important of all, in Nigeria in 2015. Issues of democracy and corruption remain hugely problematic, but there do seem to have been significant improvements in recent years.

These growth rates are compounded by very significant increases in population size, which the United Nations believes will continue for the rest of this century. This allows for projections of huge growth in consumer markets, especially in countries such as Nigeria. The globe is running out of new development stories: Africa may be the last great opportunity for business and economic growth. Figure 27.2 shows the extraordinary population growth in countries such as Kenya and Nigeria – and the expected rise to come.

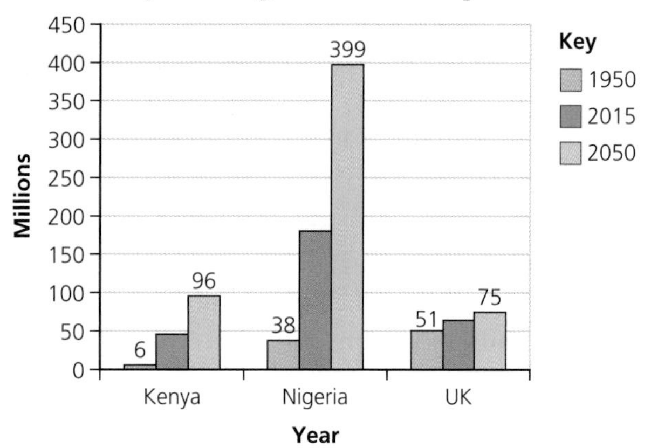

Figure 27.2 Population growth in Africa (source: United Nations 2015 projections)

27.2 What is Africa like?

To write sensibly about business opportunities or problems in Africa, it's necessary to get a feel for a 'typical' African country. Any resident of Kenya or Uganda would be clear on the differences between the countries, but from a British perspective it's reasonable to try to understand the broad differences between here and there. Table 27.1 risks providing too much data, but at least it provides enough to tell a story. Nigeria, Kenya and Cameroon have been chosen purely because secondary research agency Euromonitor provides some useful data on these three – alone among the countries of sub-Saharan Africa. India is set alongside the three African nations to provide a direct comparison and UK figures are there to help place the others into context.

Table 27.1 allows the following broad conclusions:

- Nigeria, Kenya and Cameroon are economies based on primary production, with high rates of poverty but quite high economic growth; income inequality is high, as is infant mortality.
- Nigeria and India have comparable growth rates and income levels, but Nigeria's more unequal society leads to wider poverty and shockingly high infant mortality.
- Nigeria's government has remarkably low income from taxation (that's because it gets income directly from the oil industry) and despite its reasonable level of income, government underspend probably explains the poor infant mortality and literacy figures.
- The UK has average incomes of around ten times higher than in the other countries, but lower growth; relatively high taxation has a payoff in low infant mortality and high literacy; whereas in India and the African countries half to three-quarters of people work in the fields, in the UK the figure is 1.3 per cent.

Real business

In Autumn 2014, Nigeria boasted the first car manufacturing business in West Africa. The Innoson Vehicle Manufacturing (IVM) Company showed off its first 500 cars, including a saloon car and a 4 × 4. The origins of the company came from a 2013 government initiative announcing a 70 per cent tariff on imported cars. This gave Innocent Chukwuma, a manufacturer of car parts and plastics, the incentive to start up his own car production business. Visitors to his factory have been surprised to see how labour-intensive it is - but Mr Chukwuma is happy to talk about job creation rather than efficiency. Commentators in Nigeria have noted that car production started in China thanks to big tariff walls (taxes on imports; it will surely not be long before one of the global car producers decides to try producing in Nigeria).

Figure 27.3 The Nigerian flag

	Nigeria	Kenya	Cameroon	India	UK
Population (million 2014)	182	46	24	1,252	64
GDP per capita at PPP*	$6,000	$3,100	$3,000	$5,900	$39,500
Economic growth % change 2014	6.3%	5.3%	5.1%	7.2%	2.6%
% of GDP from agriculture	20.6%	29.3%	19.9%	17.9%	0.6%
% of population working the land	70.0%	75.0%	70.0%	49.0%	1.3%
% of population below poverty line**	70.0%	43.4%	48.0%	30.0%	15.0%
Infant mortality (per 1000 births)	72.7	39.4	53.6	41.8	4.4
Household income % for richest 10%	38.2%	37.8%	35.4%	31.1%	31.1%
Household income % for poorest 10%	1.8%	1.8%	2.3%	3.6%	1.7%
Government taxes as a % of GDP	3.8%	18.8%	17.1%	9.1%	32.9%
Adult literacy (as a % of the population)	59.6%	78%	75%	71.2%	99.9%

Table 27.1 *PPP = **purchasing power parity**; **The poverty line is a moving target, set in relation to average incomes within that country; so UK poverty is at much higher income/spending than Kenyan poverty (source: Courtesy of the Central Intelligence Agency, *CIA World Factbook* August 2015)

Away from statistics, if you went to a major city in Nigeria, Kenya, Cameroon or India you'd be struck by wave after wave of activity and enterprise. UK media can leave one feeling that the default position for an African child is standing around, looking sad and holding out a bowl. In fact those children are trying to sell you something, or they're carrying large loads or they're working in fields, in factories or picking scraps in rubbish tips.

27.3 Getting trade right

For many years, the East African **trading bloc** has been successful. It has encouraged international trade and economic growth among a 'home market' of 140 million. In June 2015, a **free trade** agreement was signed between the East African Community and the Common Market for Eastern and Southern Africa, including South Africa. This potentially offers market access to 600 million consumers – more people than in the European Union. Already people are starting to talk about a complete African Economic Union, perhaps by 2017.

For a business such as Nigeria's Innoson, this opening up of free trade is vital. In the past African countries saw neighbours as bitter rivals. Opening up markets will encourage competition and therefore stimulate greater efficiency and productivity on the part of the key businesses. The World Economic Forum calculated in 2015 that whereas 65 per cent of trade by EU members is with other EU countries, only 10 per cent of African trade is with other African countries. The scope for improvement is colossal.

Perversely, at the moment, African companies find it easier to export to the west than to other African countries. This is because many have trade agreements with the European Union and/or America that keep import taxes down. So an African Economic Union might trigger a stronger, mutually reinforcing economic growth hub based on trading with each other.

'I have a dream that Africa should have one bloc – north to south – we could trade freely, people can move freely and that makes business sense.'

Chief Executive, Mohammed Enterprises, Tanzania

27.4 Opportunities for business in Africa

Africa is not just about possible opportunities in the future. Things are happening now. Nigeria's main city Lagos has become important for film production ('Nollywood' produces more films than Hollywood) and as a centre for games software. Top hotels and shops in London, and private schools throughout Britain, know that Nigeria is a significant source of wealth. Far more interesting, though, are figures such as those in Figure 27.4. The figures for soft drinks represent the middle market and show that growth rates in Africa can be as attractive as in China. Interestingly, the big growth sector in all cases is bottled water rather than fizzy drinks.

So which western businesses are making a move into Africa? Unilever has offices in 18 countries across Africa

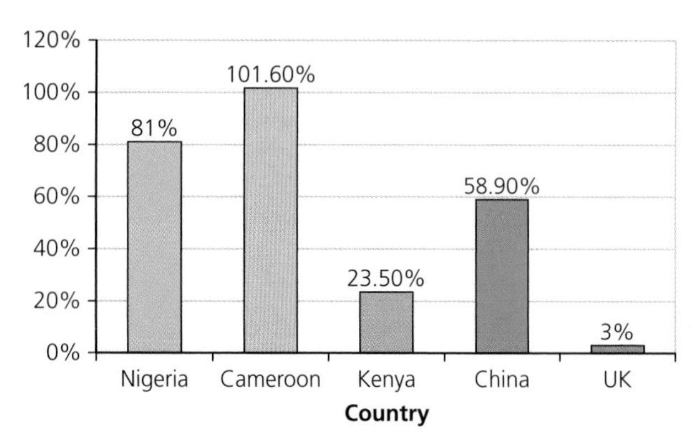

Figure 27.4 Percentage increase in soft drinks sales volume 2009–2014 (source: Euromonitor 2015)

and sells more than 50 brands, including Domestos (for hygiene and sanitation) and PureIt, a low-cost water purifier. In 2013, computer giant IBM chose Nairobi in Kenya as the base for its twelfth research and development laboratory globally. Chief scientist Dr Uyi Stewart heads the lab, following ten years working for IBM in New York. He told the BBC: 'Can you do African research from New York? Yes you can … but you will miss the mark … in order to capture value and deliver innovation that leads to commercially viable products that impact on people's lives, we have to be here, in the local ecosystem.' Other big movers have been Microsoft and the retail giant Wal-Mart, which bought African supermarket chain Massmart for $2.4 billion.

British investment groups are at the forefront of investing in developments such as shopping malls and upmarket housing developments in Africa. Regrettably this is not yet matched by British businesses. Despite the strong historical links between Britain and many countries in Africa, American companies are being much bolder than British ones.

27.5 Problems doing business in Africa

Among the key problems are corruption, poor infrastructure and the reluctance of outside investors to commit to countries they believe to be unstable.

Corruption

The World Economic Forum publishes an annual research report into the most problematic factors in doing business – in each country in the world. As shown in Table 27.2, corruption looms large in the three sub-Saharan countries this chapter is focusing on. The data from Mexico and China shows that corruption is a widespread problem in developing countries, while the addition of Ghana shows that not all African countries operate in the same way.

	Cameroon	China	Ghana	Kenya	Mexico	Nigeria
Corruption	18.6%	12.4%	6.2%	20.0%	18.6%	19.6%
Access to finance	17.9%	15.8%	20.2%	18.1%	9.8%	17.7%
Crime and theft	1.2%	1.8%	2.1%	10.3%	12.9%	2.6%
Poor infrastructure	12.5%	8.4%	3.0%	9.9%	6.1%	26.1%

Table 27.2 Most problematic factors in doing business (source: WEF Competitiveness Report 2014/2015)

Poor infrastructure

The figures for Nigeria point to another critical factor: infrastructure. Across Africa, but especially in Nigeria and South Africa, inadequate electricity supplies are a huge issue. In Nigeria, car manufacturer Innoson has no alternative but to have its own generators to provide electricity when the national grid is down. This adds significantly to the cost of doing business. The only upside is that it's such an obvious hole to plug that surely the Nigerian government will sort this problem out soon – and, if sorted, there may be a significant upswing in Nigerian economic growth.

Poor infrastructure means more than just electricity. Transport infrastructure, especially roads and rail, usually lack investment spending and are therefore slow and expensive to use. Lack of coordination means that a motorway may stop just short of a border, with

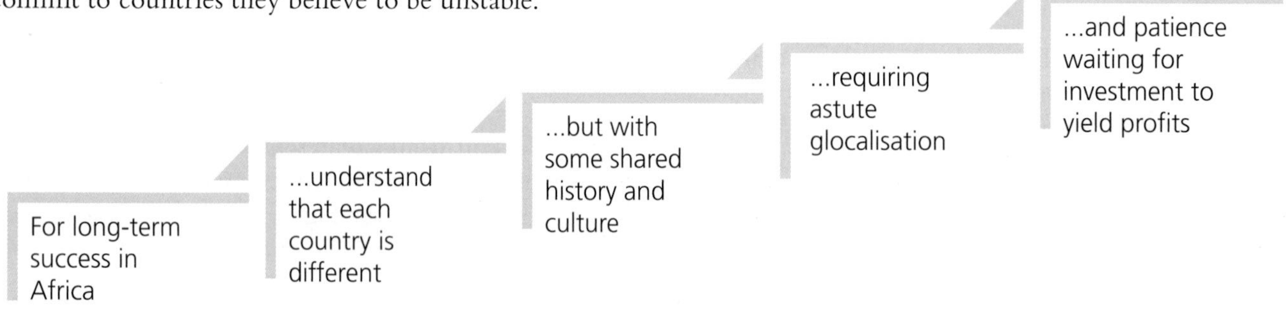

Figure 27.5 Logic chain: succeeding in Africa

little more than a dirt track on the other side. Good motorways linking capital cities across Africa would boost competition and boost trade. Exactly the same point can be made about high-quality broadband access. In the UK, there's often a view expressed that governments get in the way of business; in Africa good government is the starting point for a stronger economy.

Investor concern about stability

In 2012 and 2013, Sierra Leone was the world's fastest-growing economy, with an astounding 15 per cent (2012) followed by 20 per cent annual growth in GDP. Then in 2014, the country was laid low by the Ebola virus; growth collapsed to a still-not-bad 6 per cent. But the apocalyptic virus summed up what many investors see as the risk in dealing with Africa.

Of course, it's not just a matter of health. There are valid concerns about the stability of governments, whether democratic or military, and about the level of security within civil society. Nigeria's failure to deal with Boko Haram insurgents in the North East of the country must make investors think: well, if mighty Nigeria can't cope with threats to civil society, who can you trust? Figure 27.6 is based on accountants Ernst & Young's annual 'Africa Attractiveness Report'. It makes a telling point about the importance of stability – though the text emphasises that actual investors in Africa (i.e. there already) are far less concerned about many of these problems than outsiders looking in.

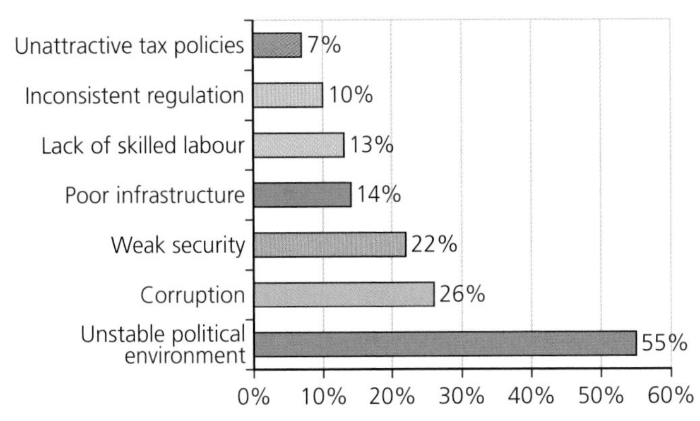

Figure 27.6 Perceived barriers to investment in Africa (source: Ernst & Young Africa Attractiveness Report 2015)

> 'We are enjoying in Africa what I call the democracy dividend. It has created an atmosphere for our young people to be creative, innovative.'
>
> *President Mahama, Ghana*

> 'Before you talk about economic growth, political stability is key.'
>
> *President Goodluck Jonathan, Nigeria*

Five whys and a how

Questions	Answers
Why would a British business target an African country over China?	For the long-term potential and because it may be easier to break into a relatively undeveloped country compared with quite sophisticated China.
Why might there be ethical concerns about doing business in Africa?	People will worry about child labour and about corruption, but that's a concern in virtually all low-income countries, so there's no reason for more concern than, say, in south-east Asia, e.g. Bangladesh.
Why might a British business such as Dixons/Currys regard sub-Saharan countries as too risky for now?	There are always huge risks in getting in early. Both B&Q and Tesco probably arrived in China too early. There may not yet be enough middle-class consumers for profitable business.
Why might the formation of an African economic union be a 'game-changer'?	In the long run, the key is that Africa needs to develop more successful businesses of its own; that will create the middle class that then become a worthwhile consumer market. Economic union would help that process enormously.
Why might British businesses have an advantage in Africa over others from, say, Japan or Spain?	Empire links mean that English is spoken widely among African middle classes – and there are cultural links that may assist our businesspeople.
How might a British firm decide which African country to choose as its base/headquarters?	Doubtless it would choose one of the many English-speaking countries such as Nigeria, then consider political stability, the level and conditions relating to profit tax and the skills and education of the local workforce.

27.6 Business potential in Africa – evaluation

In 2001, the roads of Beijing were full of bicycles and men pulling handcarts piled high with produce or building materials. The phrase 'the Chinese car market' meant nothing. BMW sold fewer than 5,000 cars in the whole of China in 2001. In most of western Europe businesspeople ignored China because of the poverty, the corruption, the lawless approach to patent rights and the believed inevitability of an uprising against the one-party state. In 2014, BMW sold 425,000 cars in China and the country contributed half the company's global profits. China is now the world's largest car market – by a mile.

So could it be that the same story will occur in Africa? Of course there are plenty of reasons *not* to invest in Africa, but with such vast potential it makes sense to get in at the start. Building shopping malls, setting up retail chains offering electrical appliances and household goods and setting up private schools – all these are sure-fire ways to participate in the rise of Africa. It would be nice if, for once, British companies were the modern pioneers.

Key terms

Free trade: when countries can export to each other without hurdles such as import taxes ('tariffs') or import quotas (limits to the volume of imports).

Purchasing power parity: adjusting income levels to allow for differences in the cost of living, e.g. a dollar might buy three times more groceries in India than in America.

Trading bloc: a regional grouping of countries agreeing to free trade and – sometimes – free movement of labour; the European Union is a trading bloc.

27.7 Workbook

Revision questions

(30 marks; 30 minutes)

1 a) From Figure 27.2, calculate the projected percentage rise in population between 1950 and 2050 for Kenya, Nigeria and the UK. (6)

b) Explain how a UK business such as Highland Spring (water) might use this information. (4)

2 Explain why high levels of corruption might discourage UK companies from investing in Africa. (4)

3 Assess why a sustained increase in economic growth might be more important than rising population levels to a UK fast-food business looking to expand into Africa. (8)

4 Explain what might be holding these British companies back from investing in Africa right now.

a) Primark (4)

b) Jaguar Land Rover. (4)

Revision activities

Data response 1

United Nations population forecasts, published in 2015, suggest dramatic changes in the distribution of the world's population by the end of this century. The two most significant changes will be the rise of Africa, to be the world's largest population centre and the sharp decline of population numbers in countries including Japan and China. In 2015, the population of all the countries in Africa was below that of China or India. By 2100, Africa's population will be greater than India, China and Europe combined. Look at this UN population data and answer the questions below.

	1980	2015	2050	2100
Nigeria	74	182	399	752
Africa (inc. Nigeria)	478	1,186	2,400	4,373
India	697	1,311	1,705	1,660
China	978	1,376	1,348	1,004
UK	56	65	75	82
Europe	694	738	785	780
World	4,450	7,349	9,725	11,213

Table 27.3 United Nations 2015 World Population Prospects (all figures in millions)

Questions (50 marks; 60 minutes)

1 a) Calculate Africa's share of global population in 2015, 2050 and 2100. (6)

b) Assess the importance of this information to a global business such as Coca-Cola. (12)

2 Assess the possible impact of an expanding African trading bloc on a UK-based low-cost airline with an existing enterprise in Africa. (12)

3 Forecasters expect that Africa will have above-average population growth and economic growth between 2015 and 2050. Evaluate the likely impact on the strategy of a UK-based international business such as Jaguar Land Rover. (20)

Data response 2

Look carefully at this data, then answer the questions below.

	Nigeria	Cameroon	Kenya	China	UK
Soft drinks volume growth 2009–2014	+81%	+101.6%	+23.5%	+58.9%	+3%
Forecast soft drinks volume growth 2014–2019	+68.9%	+201.2%	+28.9%	+40.4%	+4.1%
Total market value 2014	£6,640m	£440m	£570m	£52,600m	£13,500m
Population size	175.3m	21.4m	45.5m	1,360m	64.3m
Market value per capita (in £s)	£38 p.a.	£20.50 p.a.	£12.50 p.a.	£38.70 p.a.	£210 p.a.

Table 27.4 Soft drinks market – Nigeria, Cameroon, Kenya, China and the UK (source: Euromonitor Reports. © 2014 Euromonitor. Reprinted with permission from Euromonitor)

Questions (40 marks; 45 minutes)

1 a) Assuming no change in the price of soft drinks in each country over the coming years, calculate the growth in the value of soft drink sales in Nigeria, Cameroon, Kenya and the UK between 2014 and 2019. (8)

b) Assess the implication of these findings for a UK-based soft drinks producer such as Innocent Drinks. (12)

2 A British producer such as Fever-Tree can choose whether to get in early into the growth of the premium sector of the Nigerian soft drinks industry, or whether to wait until the sector is more fully developed. Evaluate which would be better for the company, giving clear recommendations. (20)

Extended writing

1 A London business consultancy has said that by 2050 there will be 40 million 'middle class' consumers in the UK and 150 million in Nigeria. Evaluate the extent to which starting a business focused on the Nigerian middle classes will inevitably be successful for a Business graduate born and educated locally. (20 marks)

2 A medium-sized UK food manufacturer is considering its first move into Africa. Evaluate the key factors in deciding *which* African country to start in. (20 marks)

28 International trade and business growth

Definition

International trade occurs when a firm either buys goods or services from an overseas business, or sells a product to an overseas buyer. Capital flows are an aspect of international trade of particular importance to Britain.

Linked to: Growing economies, Ch 25; China versus India, Ch 26; Business potential in Africa, Ch 27; Factors contributing to increased globalisation, Ch 29; Protectionism, Ch 30; Trading blocs, Ch 31; Conditions that prompt trade. Ch 32; Assessment of a country as a market, Ch 33; Global competitiveness, Ch 36

28.1 The logic behind foreign trade: international specialisation

Countries trade with each other because they want the benefits that can come from specialising in certain types of production, then trading with others that excel at producing other items. Years ago countries sought self-sufficiency – but that can generate a low standard of living because it can be wasteful and inefficient. For example, it might be technically possible to grow bananas in the UK. However, it would be bananas to try doing it on a commercial basis. The greenhouses needed to grow tropical fruit in Britain would be very expensive to run, requiring elaborate heating and lighting systems, and would be unsound environmentally. To make such an enterprise profitable, the bananas produced would have to be sold for very high prices, making them unaffordable for all but the very rich. Far better to buy the bananas from another country with a more suitable climate.

To pay for the bananas the UK needs to sell some of its own output abroad. The UK economy should specialise and focus on producing the sort of goods and services that we can produce efficiently. By doing so we will be able to pay for the products that we would like to consume, but cannot or no longer produce.

28.2 Distinguishing between imports and exports

Imports

Imports are products that are produced abroad that are consumed domestically. When we import, products come into the UK, but the cash needed to pay for these products flows out of the country. British imports include fast-moving consumer goods such as Becks Bier and Lindor chocolate. These products are popular with British households and are produced abroad in Germany and Switzerland. We enjoy these imported goods and value the increased consumer choice.

In some cases, we have to import because Britain no longer has mass-market producers of products like shoes, TV sets and refrigerators. To make these products available to buy in Britain, they must be imported. British retailers like Tesco therefore rely heavily on imports. Their success depends on the companies' ability to source the type of imported goods their customers want to buy.

Many manufacturing businesses also import. British manufacturers such as Jaguar Land Rover will import many of their materials, such as sheet steel, and components such as spark plugs. It may be that foreign suppliers are offering better quality products and/or sell their products for lower prices than UK suppliers. If British manufacturers were no longer able to access imports they would have no choice but to source what they need domestically. This could lead to higher costs and prices, and declining product quality. Like retailers, a manufacturer's competitiveness depends in part on its ability to source cheap but high-quality imported raw materials and components.

Some British businesses generate profit by selling imported services. A good example is tourism. TravelRepublic is a UK-based internet retailer of foreign holidays. To sell its products to British customers, TravelRepublic needs to buy services from foreign hotels and airlines.

Figure 28.1 shows the rise in UK import levels between 2000 and 2015.

Figure 28.1 UK import expenditure: 2000–2015 (source: www.tradingeconomics.com)

Exports

Exports are goods and services that are produced in Britain but consumed by people and businesses overseas. When the UK exports some of its output, products leave the UK's shores. When buyers abroad pay for the goods and services that they have bought, money flows into Britain.

According to the employers' pressure group the Confederation of British Industry (CBI), 20 per cent of UK firms export. The main reason why firms export is because they want to find new markets. Exporting can therefore help businesses to grow. A good example of a British business that has expanded by tapping into export markets is the Little Valley Brewery, located in the village of Hebden Bridge in West Yorkshire. The business was set up in 2005 by Wim van der Spek, a Dutch immigrant, who thought that a gap in a niche market existed for organic, bottle-conditioned beer. Initially the business was only able to grow slowly because UK supermarkets like Tesco were reluctant to stock its products. Little Valley's big breakthrough came when the company signed a distribution deal with two of Finland's biggest supermarket chains. By 2015, the business had increased its production to 2.5 million bottles a year, a fivefold increase on the brewery's initial capacity.

Britain's membership of the European Union has undoubtedly helped Little Valley to sell its beer to consumers in other European countries. This is especially important given that Little Valley's product is highly specialised and only likely to appeal to a relatively small market segment. Without its European export markets, Little Valley might have struggled to grow large enough to benefit from the economies of scale needed to survive.

Due to advances in technology, all economies tend to experience economic growth in the long run. Firms benefit from economic growth because the rising incomes created by growth make for bigger markets. Unfortunately, in the short and medium term, economic growth rates can vary greatly. During recessions, when incomes fall, domestic markets tend to shrink as households cut back on their expenditure. Exporting can help firms to even out their profits over the economic cycle of boom and bust. To offset falling sales at home during a recession, firms often try to compensate by seeking out new export markets.

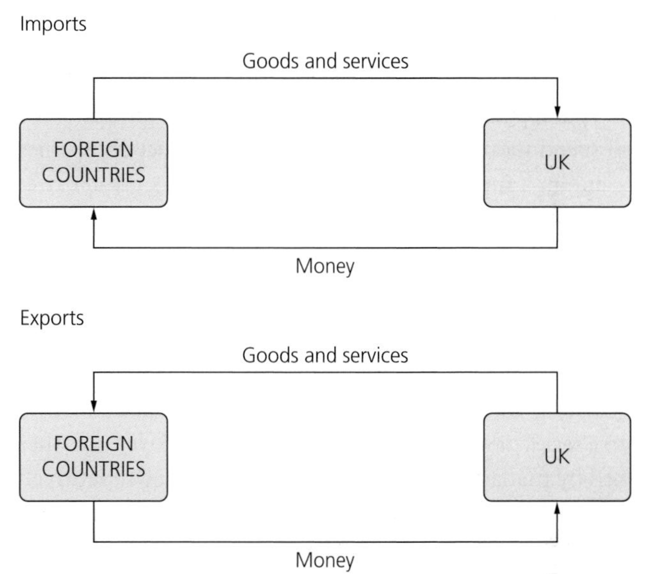

Figure 28.2 Logic chain: flow of goods and services in imports and exports

28.3 The link between business specialisation and competitive advantage

What is business specialisation?

Businesses specialise when they produce a limited range of products. At its most extreme, some businesses choose to only produce one product. These single-product firms can be very successful. A good example is Coca-Cola. For most of the twentieth century, the company produced only a single variety of Coke that was sold in the iconic glass bottle. Other firms produce a variety of products, but still specialise in the sense that they are only interested in supplying a particular market or market segment that they understand well. Morgan Cars, based in Worcestershire, produces several car models, but specialises in the sense that it sells only sports cars.

How can specialisation make a firm more efficient?

Firms become more efficient when they are able to produce more output from the same amount of raw materials, machinery, energy and labour. If firms can squeeze more output from the same inputs, average cost will fall. Specialisation can help firms to achieve this outcome. Firms that produce several products may need different machines to produce each of their products. If sales of some of a firm's products dip, capacity utilisation will dip with it, leading to higher average costs. Single-product companies that have chosen to specialise will in all probability require less machinery. Theoretically, lower capital costs should help a firm to reduce its unit costs. The same principle applies to training expenditure. Multi-product firms will spend more on training than single-product companies, because in a multi-product firm there will be a greater need for the workforce to be flexible, so that they are able to work on more than one production line.

The final argument used to justify the view that specialisation makes firms more efficient is advanced by those who believe in Taylorite **scientific management**. According to this view, all jobs should be broken down into a series of smaller component tasks. Employees are then asked by management to specialise, so that they repetitively perform just one of these component tasks all day long. The logic is that via practice each employee will become highly proficient at carrying out their task. Specialisation therefore speeds up production, allowing more to be produced from the same workforce every week. If total output rises without any addition to the firm's wage bill, the average cost of production will fall. On the other hand, critics of specialisation point out that repetitive work leads to employee boredom and alienation. This is a problem because product quality problems are often caused by a disillusioned and demotivated workforce.

How can efficiency gains created by specialisation create a competitive advantage?

Economists assume that specialisation makes firms more efficient, leading to lower average costs. If a firm can produce its product for a lower unit cost, the business should be able to benefit from a cost advantage over its rivals. In a highly competitive market, an efficient firm might use its cost advantage to lower its retail prices. If specialisation reduces average cost, managers could opt to cut prices for customers without any loss in the amount of profit made per unit supplied. A good example of a business that is trying to do this is the Co-operative supermarket. The UK market for supermarket groceries is very competitive. To survive, the Co-operative needs to get closer to the prices charged by Lidl, Aldi and Asda. To make these lower prices profitable, the Co-operative must lower its costs by becoming more efficient. To create this outcome the management is trying to specialise. The business used to run a nationwide chain of pharmacies and farms, but these have now been sold off. This allows the managers of the Manchester-based business to focus all its efforts on its core business – which is supermarket retailing.

For the Co-op the goal is to become more competitive by cutting prices. Other firms take a different approach and choose to benefit from the lower unit costs created by specialisation by keeping their retail prices constant. By doing this the firms will make more profit on every unit sold.

> 'Rising living standards – whether in a village, a region, a nation, or the world – depend first on specialisation: on letting people concentrate on what they do best and trade with others who specialise in other things.'
>
> *Virginia Postrel, writer*

28.4 Foreign direct investment (FDI) and business growth

What is foreign direct investment?

Foreign direct investment describes a situation where a company either sets up a new business abroad, or where a company takes over or merges with another business overseas. In recent times, the UK has received huge amounts of foreign direct investment from abroad. A good example of this type of **inward foreign direct investment** occurred in January 2015 when the British owners of Canary Wharf sold off a cluster of high-rise offices in London to investors from Qatar. This deal brought £2.6 billion into Britain. However, the rents paid every year by the likes of HSBC and Barclays to occupy these buildings will now flow out of the country to the new Qatari shareholders. **Outward foreign direct investment** occurs when a British firm builds or buys a facility abroad. A good example is Tesco, which has built supermarkets all across Eastern Europe during the last decade.

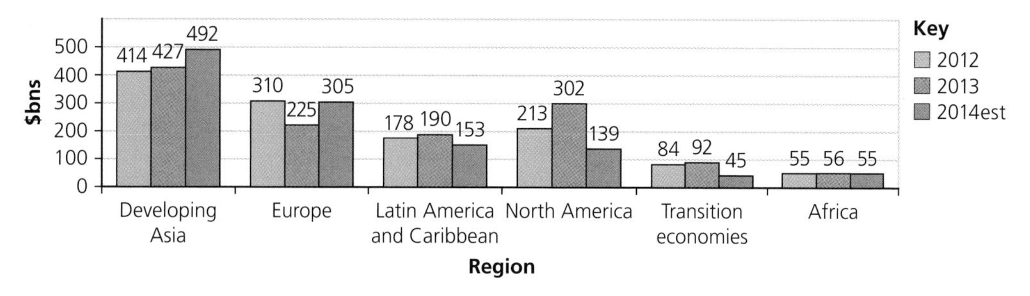

Figure 28.3 Foreign direct investment by region. Note: transition economies include South-east Europe, the Commonwealth of Independent States and Georgia (source: From United Nations Conference on Trade and Development. © United Nations. Reprinted with the permission of the United Nations)

It is interesting to look at where FDI flows towards. In Figure 28.3, you can see that ongoing western concern about economic slowdown in China hasn't stopped developing Asia continuing to be the region of the world of most interest to global businesses. The decline in Latin American FDI inflows mirrors the continent's weak economic performance in recent years.

How can foreign direct investment enable a firm to grow?

Most firms want to grow larger because higher sales levels help to boost total profit. Just as importantly, managers running big companies are keen to pursue growth because their own status and pay depend on it. Most entrepreneurs try to grow their businesses by finding additional customers close to home. However, the domestic market will eventually become **saturated**, making growth far harder to achieve. So managers look overseas to find new unsaturated markets abroad.

The most obvious way to supply an overseas market is by exporting. This approach can work very well, especially if domestic factories are running at low levels of capacity utilisation. This will make it relatively easy for a firm to produce the extra output needed to begin supplying customers abroad without the need for any expensive capital investment in new machinery.

Problems involved in export

There are however a number of problems of supplying an overseas market by exporting. Many of these problems can be avoided if a firm opts to use foreign direct investment in order to supply consumers locally.

Transport costs

It takes time and money to move products from one country to another. This can cut into profit margins, especially if the product to be exported is bulky and therefore expensive to transport. This is why Coca-Cola has been trying hard to open a new bottling plant in India.

Avoiding protectionist trade barriers

Some manufacturers use foreign direct investment to supply foreign markets, because it allows them to avoid tariffs and quotas. Governments that use tariffs hope to divert demand away from imports towards domestically produced substitutes. The European Union imposes both tariffs and quotas on imports from countries like Japan which are not members of the European Union. The European car market is huge – in 2015 over 13.5 million new cars were sold. Japanese companies like Toyota and Nissan want to export into this market without being subject to tariffs and quotas. To do this, both companies supply the European car market from factories they have built in the UK.

Access to natural resources

North American and European countries need natural resources such as oil, gas and minerals. Many of these commodities are scarce, which means that they can sell for high prices. This makes extracting them a highly profitable business. European and American multinationals use foreign direct investment to establish mines and oil wells in resource-rich countries. Glencore, an Anglo-Swiss mining multinational, makes profit by exporting copper and nickel from mines in African countries such as Zambia and the Democratic Republic of Congo. If the company wants to grow, it must build new mines in countries that possess the resources that it wants to sell. This type of foreign direct investment is controversial because of the environmental damage caused. In addition, most Africans do not benefit from the profits made from extracting their resources. This is because very few of Glencore's shareholders live in Africa. The profits made by Glencore's mines flow out of Africa, enhancing the living standards of shareholders living in North America and Europe.

Real business

In July 2015, the *Guardian* newspaper reported that the Church of England had just sold its shares in British oil company Soco International. The reason was the company's failure to unequivocally rule out drilling for oil in Africa's oldest national park.

The company had been criticised for two years by conservationists including the World Wild Fund for Nature and Sir David Attenborough. Their concern was Soco's plan to drill in Virunga in the Democratic Republic of Congo (central Africa), which is a World Heritage site and home to around half the world's mountain gorillas.

This was only the third time the Church had sold its shareholding in a company for ethical reasons.

(Source: Guardian, 1 July 2015)

Figure 28.4 A Mountain gorilla in the Virunga

Lower operating costs

Some firms choose to supply an overseas market directly via foreign direct investment because it is cheaper than exporting from a domestic base. This could be because wage rates abroad are lower than at home, or because environmental and labour laws are more relaxed, reducing the cost of regulatory compliance.

> 'Tobacco exports should be expanded aggressively because Americans are smoking less.'
>
> *Dan Quayle, US politician*

> 'In an age of specialisation people are proud to be able to do one thing well, but if that is all they know about, they are missing out on much else life has to offer.'
>
> *Dennis Flanagan, scientist*

Five whys and a how

Questions	Answers
Why are UK manufacturing firms keen to sell their products abroad?	Once domestic markets have become saturated, firms turn to overseas markets to maintain growth. Selling products in more than one market also reduces risk – while one country is in recession, another might be enjoying an economic boom.
Why might a UK-based retailer like Tesco prefer a strong pound to a weak pound?	Tesco like many other UK retailers imports a high proportion of its stock. If the exchange rate appreciates, the price paid in sterling for imported stock will fall.
Why is foreign direct investment surprisingly high in some of the poorest countries in the world?	Some of these countries might be poor economically but they are resource rich. Mining companies, such as Rio Tinto, invest heavily in poor countries because they have abundant supplies of scarce natural resources that are not available in other countries.
Why do some governments give tax breaks to multinationals in an attempt to boost foreign direct investment?	If a multinational builds a new factory in a country, employment levels in that country will rise, boosting income tax revenues for the government. In addition, the new factory will probably create new business opportunities for would-be suppliers.
Why have many Japanese car manufacturers chosen to supply the European car market by building new car factories in Europe, rather than exporting from Japan?	If Nissan and Mazda tried to supply Europe by exporting from Japan the companies' products would be subject to EU tariffs and quotas. Foreign direct investment within the EU allows Nissan and Mazda to avoid these protectionist trade barriers.
How can specialisation lead to lower average costs?	If firms produce only one product, they will need a single production line. If high capacity utilisation is achieved, this will reduce fixed costs per unit.

Key terms

Inward foreign direct investment: investment into a country such as the UK from companies abroad, perhaps in the form of buying up one of our businesses, or buying up property assets.

Outward foreign direct investment: investment from a country such as the UK, perhaps building a factory in Brazil (e.g. JCB) or buying property in Nairobi.

Saturated market: one where (nearly) everyone who wants an item already has it, so sales can stabilise or slip back, e.g. fridges in the UK.

Scientific management: F.W. Taylor suggested that managers should maximise worker productivity by calculating how best to divide up tasks into smaller fragments, then incentivise workers to produce exactly as set out by managers.

28.5 International trade and business growth – evaluation

There is no doubt that there's a correlation between economic growth and inward foreign direct investment (FDI). It's very clear in the long-term growth story of China between 1985 and 2015. But when considering correlation it's vital to also think about causation. It's the age-old question of which came first? The chicken or the egg? In this case it could be that inward FDI was an important causal factor in China's giddy growth. Or perhaps the western investors were attracted in after they saw the growth figures? On balance it's probably right to say it's a bit of both. Rising GDP and rising inward FDI represent a classic upward spiral. They feed off each other. In 2015, British media kept writing about slowdown in China. FDI figures held up well, implying that big business investors were rather more optimistic than the journalists.

28.6 Workbook

Revision questions

(40 marks; 40 minutes)

1. Using examples that are relevant to the UK, distinguish between imports and exports. (3)
2. Dyson vacuum cleaners used to manufacture its products from a factory located in Wiltshire in the UK. Today, the vacuum cleaners sold under the Dyson brand in Britain are all imported from a factory based in Malaysia. Assess the possible impacts of this decision on Dyson's various stakeholder groups. (10)
3. Use Figure 28.1 to estimate the value of UK imports in 2004 and 2013. Then calculate the percentage change. Show your workings. (4)
4. Assess two possible reasons why a small firm such as the Little Valley Brewery might choose to expand by exporting, rather than by foreign direct investment. (8)
5. Tesco tried to expand in America by setting up its own chain of Fresh & Easy grocery stores. Unfortunately for Tesco, its expansion into America failed because the new stores failed to attract sufficient numbers of customers to break even. Using the example of Tesco, assess the dangers of trying to grow via foreign direct investment. (10)
6. Comment on the quote by Dan Quayle (page 204). (5)

Revision activities

Data response 1

SABMiller targets the craft segment of the UK beer market

The market for beer in the USA is huge: £85 billion in 2014. One of the fastest growing segments of this market is craft beer. Craft brewers now produce one in every ten beers sold in America. This type of beer is typically made by smaller independent breweries using aromatic ingredients, such as coriander. The intention is to create a differentiated product that will appeal to sophisticated drinkers who are bored of the mass-produced corporate lager brands. To gain a foothold in this rapidly growing market segment, multinationals like SABMiller and Anheuser-Busch have tried taking over much smaller, specialist craft brewers.

One company that has used foreign direct investment to grow in this way is Duvel from Belgium. In October 2013,

Duvel bought the American Boulevard Brewing Company for $100 million. Boulevard was established in 1989 by John McDonald. Initially Boulevard operated on a very small scale, selling its product direct to customers from the back of a tiny Isuzu truck. Gradually the business grew and by the time of the takeover Boulevard was the twelfth largest producer of craft beer in America. The company's retro-style marketing, incorporating a distinctive green and red diamond logo, is well known.

Duvel could have tried to supply the American market by using its existing plant in Belgium. However, Duvel rejected exporting in favour of foreign direct investment because it valued the Boulevard Brewing Company brand and the company's knowledge of the tastes and preferences of the American drinker. The takeover was not met with universal approval. Many of Boulevard's consumers used social media to articulate their fears that the new owners might interfere with either the product or production process. Duvel reassured Boulevard's consumers that it would keep everything the same. The workforce was also told to expect new employment opportunities and investment, rather than rationalisation and redundancies.

Questions (40 marks; 45 minutes)

1. The craft beer segment of the American beer market is still relatively small. Given this fact, assess two possible reasons why companies like SABMiller and Anheuser-Busch want to enter this segment of the market. (8)
2. Duvel has chosen to supply the US market via foreign direct investment rather than by exporting. Assess the possible benefits of foreign direct investment over exporting in this case. (12)
3. Evaluate the importance of specialisation to smaller businesses such as the Boulevard Brewing Company. (20)

Data response 2

Westwood Rocks

Westwood Rocks specialises in selling hand-made gemstone jewellery. The business has seven shops located in affluent market towns in Surrey. All of the jewellery sold by Westwood Rocks is produced in-house from materials such as freshwater pearls and topaz that are imported direct from suppliers in Asia. The business was set up by its owner Lauren Westwood following a trip travelling around Asia. During her time abroad Westwood was enthralled by the distinctive and colourful Asian jewellery she had seen. She believed that these designs might also prove to be a hit with sophisticated British women. On her return to the UK in 2000, she used the last of her university student loan to set up her first retail outlet in the affluent market town of Godalming in Surrey. The business operates with a healthy profit margin. Her customer base is prepared to pay significant price premiums for something different. She also buys all of her gemstones direct from suppliers in Asia, which helps to keep her variable costs down.

Questions (35 marks; 40 minutes)

1. Explain why Westwood Rocks locates its shops in market towns such as Godalming, where average incomes are many times higher than the national average. (5)
2. Assess how a rise in the value of the pound against the Indian rupee might affect the profits made by Westwood Rocks. (10)
3. Westwood Rocks has chosen to specialise. It sells only hand-made gemstone jewellery that it has produced itself. Evaluate the importance of specialisation to businesses like Westwood Rocks that operate in highly competitive markets. (20)

Extended writing

1. In the first half of 2015, Britain had a worrying deficit between exports and imports. Evaluate whether the UK government should take action to try to boost the competitiveness of UK companies. (20)
2. Early in 2015, Jaguar Land Rover's first overseas factory opened in China – the result of £1 billion of investment by the UK-based company. Evaluate whether Jaguar Land Rover should continue to expand by investing overseas – or whether it would be better to expand UK production and rely on exporting. (20)

29 Factors contributing to increased globalisation

Definition

Globalisation is the trend towards closer economic, political and cultural ties between countries. This trend has made goods, services, people, capital, media, culture and even ideas more internationally mobile.

Linked to: Growing economies, Ch 25; China versus India, Ch 26; Business potential in Africa, Ch 27; International trade and business growth, Ch 28; Protectionism, Ch 30; Trading blocs, 31; Conditions that prompt trade, Ch 32; Assessment of a country as a market, Ch 33; Global competitiveness, Ch 36

29.1 Introduction

Globalisation is characterised by a growth in international trade. Much of this trade is undertaken by transnational companies that have bases in more than one country. Those that support globalisation argue that it has been a force for good, because it has helped millions of people living in formerly poor countries to trade themselves out of poverty. Critics of globalisation claim that it has undermined local businesses, tastes and cultures, creating an increasingly similar planet, where people the world over consume the same global brands, produced by the same global giant corporations.

As shown in Figure 29.1, international trade boomed between 1990 and the pre-recession year of 2008, but since then has struggled to recover to its previous trend level. Despite the World Trade Organization's (WTO) optimistic forecast for 2015, world trade fell back again in that year. This led some commentators to wonder whether the globalisation trend has ground to a halt.

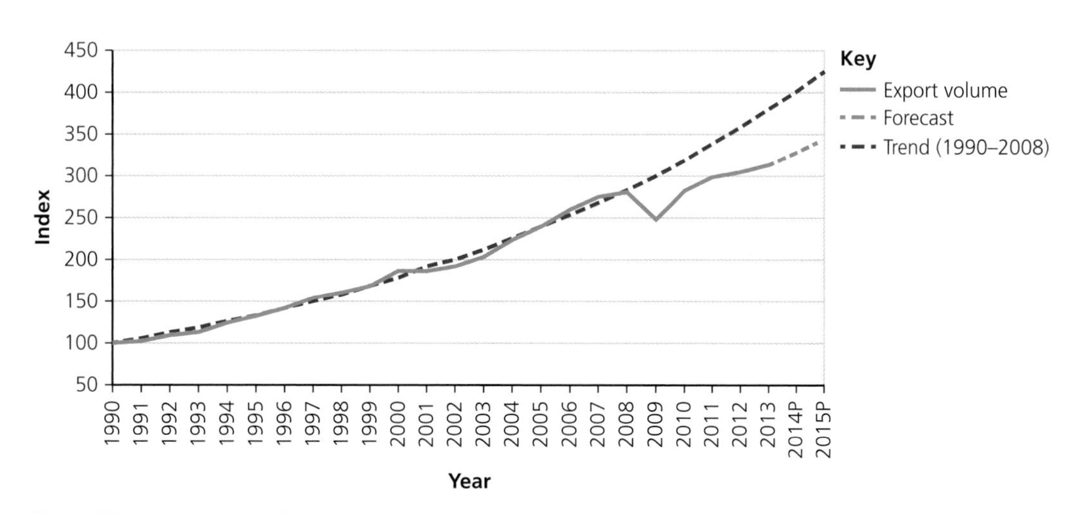

Figure 29.1 The volume of world merchandise exports, 1990–2015 (index 1990 = 100) (source: WTO)

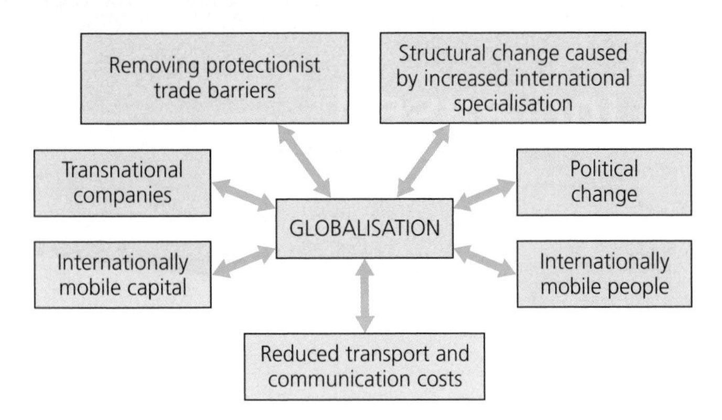

Figure 29.2 Logic chain: globalisation

> 'The word "overseas" has no place in Honda's vocabulary, because it sees itself as equidistant from all its key customers.'
>
> *Kenichi Ohmae, business author*

29.2 Trade liberalisation

Trade is liberalised when governments decide to remove international trade barriers such as tariffs, quotas and **regulations** that are designed to keep imports out of a country. Tariffs are taxes that are imposed on imports only. They work by making imports more expensive. The intention being that the higher price will divert domestic demand away from imports towards domestically produced substitutes. A quota is an annual restriction on the amount of a particular good that can be imported into a country. Once a quota has been filled, consumers will be forced into buying a domestic alternative. Trade **liberalisation** is usually a product of trade negotiations. Typically, politicians will only tend to drop the tariff and quota trade barriers that protect their domestic markets if their trading partners promise to do the same. The UK's trade with countries such as France and Germany is already liberalised. This is because Britain, France and Germany are all members of the free trade European Union (EU). One of the conditions of being a member of the EU is that countries are not allowed to impose either tariffs or quotas on each other's goods and services.

Opportunities created by trade liberalisation

Trade liberalisation can benefit domestic firms in two ways. If tariffs are removed, the price of imports will normally fall. This will help manufacturers who either buy raw materials or energy from abroad. If variable costs can be cut, the manufacturer could opt to pass these lower costs on to the consumer by lowering their retail prices. The resulting price cuts made possible by the abolition of tariffs could help the manufacturer to sell more of its product, creating a growth opportunity. For retailers such as Sainsbury's, which imports a high proportion of its stock, the same basic principle applies. However, rather than passing on the benefits of lower import costs to consumers, some supermarkets might be tempted to keep retail prices constant, thus allowing their profit margins to rise.

Trade liberalisation provides increased market access to businesses that are willing to sell their products abroad.

Real business

Ryanair: beneficiary of trade liberalisation

A good example of a business that has benefitted greatly from trade liberalisation is Ryanair, which was set up in Ireland in 1985. In the early years Ryanair grew slowly because it was only allowed to operate flights in and out of Ireland. This was due to protectionist regulations adopted by several European governments that stopped Ryanair from gaining the take-off and landing slots needed to operate new routes. In 1992, the European Union passed the Single European Act, which was designed to sweep-away hidden trade barriers between member states. As part of this act, the airline industry in Europe was de-regulated. The resulting 'Open Skies Agreement' forced European airports to offer take-off and landing slots to airlines from third countries. For the first time ever, Ryanair, an Irish airline, could set up bases in other European Union countries to supply and sell flights from say, Spain to Finland. Customers liked Ryanair's low prices. By 2005, Ryanair was carrying more passengers per year than British Airways. In March 2015, the airline announced that it had achieved a turnover in the last year of over €5.5 billion (see Table 29.1). Without doubt, Ryanair has benefitted greatly from trade liberalisation.

	2011	2012	2013	2014	2015
Turnover (€m)	3,630	4,390	4,884	5,036	5,654
Aircraft capacity utilisation % of seats filled	83	82	82	83	88
Number of employees	8,063	8,438	9,059	9,501	10,000 (est)
Profit after tax (€m)	375	560	570	523	867

Table 29.1 Ryanair's continued success story

Theoretically, if the UK ever voted to leave the European Union, goods or services produced in the UK could become subject to European tariffs and quotas. This would increase the price, and reduce the availability, of UK exports across Europe, potentially hitting the profits of British exporters.

Threats created by trade liberalisation

Trade liberalisation opens up domestic markets to foreign competition. Consumers nearly always benefit from the extra competition created by trade liberalisation because it forces firms into offering consumers the best possible products, at the lowest possible prices. Some firms lose out when trade is liberalised. These businesses tend to be less efficient than their overseas rivals. When tariffs and quotas protections are removed, inefficient businesses will probably struggle to attract enough customers to break even. In the airline industry the success achieved by the likes of Ryanair and easyJet has come at considerable cost to less efficient operators such as Alitalia and Air France. Both of these airlines have lost market share to Ryanair, and on several occasions have needed taxpayer-funded bailouts in order to survive.

29.3 Political change

Globalisation has been assisted by political change. The best example is probably China. During the period from 1948 to 1978, China was Communist. This meant that all the important economic decisions made in China were made by politicians. Chinese businesses were told by the government to focus on producing products for domestic consumption. There was very little foreign trade. In the late 1970s, significant political change took place in China following the death of Chairman Mao. For the first time businesses could now be privately owned. But perhaps the biggest change took place in 2001 when China joined the World Trade Organization (WTO). Membership of the WTO has given China access to the rich markets of the developed world. This political change allowed China to integrate with the rest of the global economy, which has been a significant driver of globalisation. The export-led economic growth made possible by globalisation has lifted living standards in China. This, coupled with China's huge population of 1.4 billion people, has created the largest car market in the world. Businesses such as Jaguar Land Rover have taken advantage of this new economic reality by opening up new factories in China. Foreign direct investment like this is also an important feature of globalisation.

Figure 29.3 shows the remarkable growth in China's international trade. In 2014, it was the world's biggest exporter and second largest importer. The value of its exports in 2014 was over $2,300 billion.

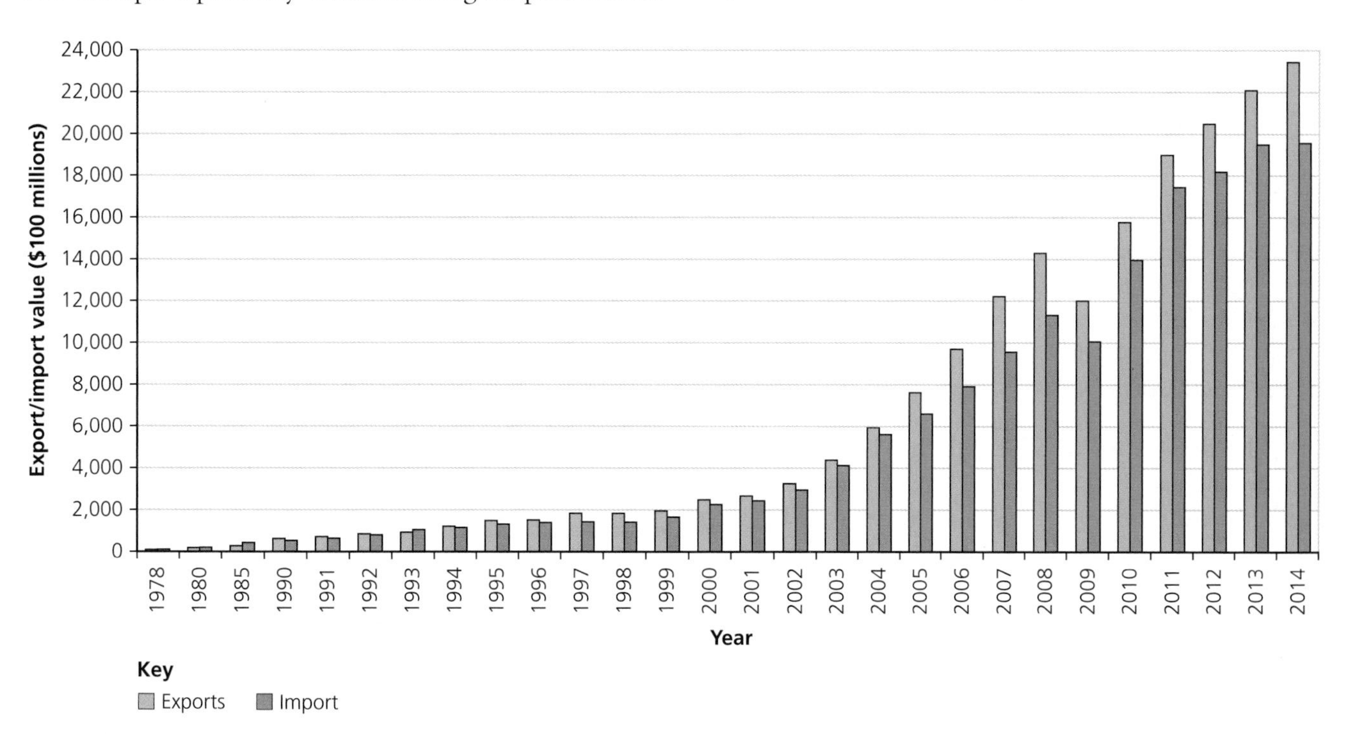

Figure 29.3 The breathtaking growth of Chinese exports 1978–2014 to become the world's number one exporter (source: National Bureau of Statistics of China)

29.4 Reduced cost of transport and communication

It costs money to move goods from one country to another. Transport costs therefore discourage international trade because they cut into an exporter's profit margin. Fortunately for the global economy, transport costs have fallen since the 1970s. These lower transport costs have undoubtedly contributed to the growth in world trade that we have seen over the same period. There are a number of reasons why transport costs have fallen in real terms. First, contrary to the gloomy predictions made in the 1970s, oil has not run out. In fact, the world's supply of oil continues to grow, which has helped to keep down the price of fuel. Technological advances have also held transport costs in check. The engines used to power today's planes, trucks and ships use far less fuel than their 1970s equivalents. In addition, the introduction of super-sized trucks, boats and aircraft are able to deliver lower costs per tonne kilometre. Figure 29.4 shows the 80 per cent reduction in aircraft fuel per passenger over time, due to improved technology and the increased size of aircraft.

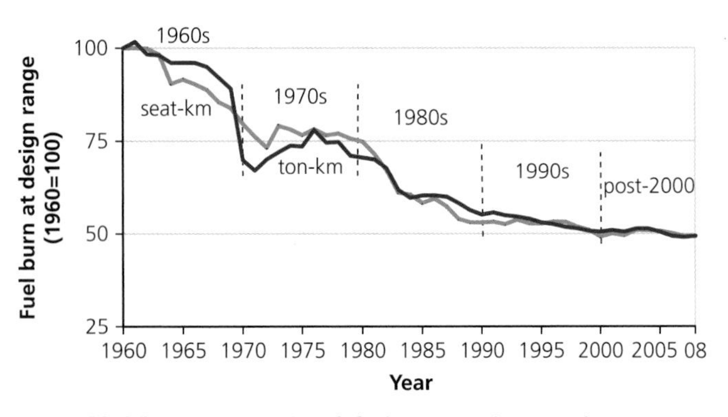

Figure 29.4 Reductions in aircraft fuel consumption over time (source: ICCT (2009) Abstract 1. Average fuel burn for new aircraft, 1960–2008. In 'Efficiency Trends for New Commercial Jet Aircraft, 1960 to 2008'. http://www.theicct.org/sites/default/files/publications/ICCT_Aircraft_Efficiency_final.pdf)

Since the mid-1990s, the internet has brought people in different parts of the world closer together. This digital revolution has also changed the way that many business services are bought and sold. The most well-known example of this type of globalisation is the offshoring of call centres. Companies such as Sky UK Ltd, British Telecomunications plc and E.ON have all tried to cut the costs of customer service by moving call centres to India to take advantage of lower wages. Other UK jobs have been lost in the same manner. A good example is engineering. Before the internet, most builders bought their planning drawings from local engineers. This was because architectural plans were done on paper, and in those days they were posted or delivered by hand. Today there is nothing to stop a builder using a cheaper foreign engineer. This is because complex documents can be sent rapidly and very cheaply down a fibre-optic cable. For documents, geographical distance no longer affects delivery time. Unlike 'snail mail', an email sent from an office in Poland takes the same time to arrive as an email sent from an office located around the corner. It is not just engineering that is being affected. Top London law companies, such as Slaughter and May, have outsourced low-level work, such as document review and due diligence, to Indian-based lawyers who are willing to accept much lower salaries.

In 2000 there were fewer than 1,800 jobs in legal process outsourcing in India. In 2005, the US-based research company, Forrester, forecast that the market would reach $4 billion with 79,000 jobs in India by 2015. This nearly came true, though the actual figure for jobs in 2015 was closer to 75,000. In the long term, salaries in India may catch up with those in the West, making this form of outsourcing obsolete. For now, though, a lawyer in India earns about a fifth of one in the UK: quite a cost-saving.

29.5 Increased significance of transnational corporations

Transnational corporations (TNCs) or multinationals are businesses that own factories, offices or shops in more than one country. They differ from multinational corporations simply because multinationals tend to localise their global offering (glocalise) whereas transnationals operate a one-size-fits-all approach, often from a single production base. This was traditionally true of Boeing, which only produced planes in Seattle, USA. These days it is building factories elsewhere, including Japan and China. Broadly, though, it is still a transnational because it offers the exact same product range globally.

A good example of a multinational company is Coca-Cola, which has over 900 bottling plants located in various parts of the world. Although North Korea is the only country in the world where Coca-Cola is not sold, the company does have plenty of brands that are largely local (such as Innocent Drinks in the UK). Other examples of multinationals include Nissan, Unilever and Zara. The sheer size of multinationals like Coca-Cola or Starbucks can make life tough for smaller businesses that are not able to benefit from the same economies of scale. In the 1990s, most of the UK's coffee shops were small independents, run by Italian immigrant families. Many of these shops no longer exist because they have not been able to compete against multinationals such as Starbucks and McDonald's. Some economists are concerned about what they see as the growing power and influence of the global giants because of the threats to both competition and consumer choice.

29.6 Increased investment flows

Globalised financial markets allow investors to move their money more easily around the globe to wherever returns are highest. According to research published by the McKinsey management consultancy in April 2014, more than one-third of all investment transactions are international. Some of these international investment flows are created when the likes of Coca-Cola and Jaguar Land Rover build new factories abroad. Cross-border takeovers and mergers also contribute to international investment flows. A good example occurred in January 2010 when British shareholders accepted a £11.5 billion bid for Cadbury from America's Kraft Foods. It is important to point out that the vast majority of international financial transactions are undertaken by the financial sector. For example, UK pension companies like Standard Life routinely buy shares in foreign companies that are not listed on London's stock exchange. Banks also borrow from abroad so that they can make more loans to households and firms. In 2008, a British bank called Northern Rock collapsed because it borrowed money from foreign banks that it subsequently struggled to re-pay. Some people argue that globalised financial markets have increased the risk of a financial crisis spreading from one country to another. It is widely acknowledged that the global financial crisis was triggered by a single event, which was the collapse of an America investment bank called Lehman Brothers in September 2008.

29.7 Migration (within and between economies)

Migration is an important aspect of globalisation, but is hardly a new phenomenon. Throughout human history people have moved from one town or country to another in search of a better life. Immigration is how America overtook Britain to become the world's paramount economy.

Figure 29.5 Migrants might bring valuable skills to a country

Immigration has two major benefits to an economy. First, migrants are a self-selected group of the most proactive and ambitious individuals, determined to make a better life for themselves and their families. Research makes it clear that they are unusually motivated, both to start their own businesses and to study to obtain higher qualifications. Second, they tend to be well educated and can use their IT or medical skills to fill jobs for which there are too few qualified candidates. Countries with high levels of immigration such as the US and Hong Kong tend to have strong economic growth rates.

It is important to realise that there are other motives that drive people to move from one country to another apart from economic factors. British and American foreign policy decisions have led to internal conflicts in countries such as Iraq and Libya. Unsurprisingly, this has caused a flow of refugees who are desperate to flee their own countries to avoid either death or persecution.

29.8 Growth of the global labour force

Globalisation has helped firms to reduce their operating costs. Wage rates vary greatly between countries. Some firms have sought to cut their labour costs by transferring production from Britain to other countries where wage rates are lower. This is called offshoring. In February 2010, Kraft Foods transferred chocolate production from a factory in Somerset to a new £100 million facility in Poland. As a result of this decision, 400 British workers lost their jobs. The move to Poland was great for Kraft's shareholders – labour costs were halved! This type of offshoring from high-wage to low-wage economies inevitably leads to an increase in international trade. In this case, most of the Cadbury's chocolate consumed in Britain used to be produced in Britain. The same chocolate is now imported into Britain from Poland.

A globalised workforce can also help firms to find the right type of labour needed to expand and grow. Manpower is one of Britain's biggest recruitment agencies. In 2015, it produced a report which stated that in the last year construction companies were turning away profitable contracts because they could not find enough workers with the right type of skills. These skill shortages are caused by a failure to train enough apprentices to replace those who retire each year. To fill the skills gap, employers are trying to hire the workers that they need from abroad. For example, in 2014, Manpower publicly claimed that foreign bricklayers were being paid £1,000 a week to work in Britain. None of this would be possible without globalisation.

29.9 Structural change

Economies go through structural change when they change what they produce. The structure of an economy matters enormously. Take South Korea; in the 1960s, the country was one of the poorest countries on the planet because most of the country's labour was used inefficiently to farm the land. Living standards started to increase when the South Korean economy began industrialising at the beginning of the 1980s. It could be argued that this structural change away from agriculture towards manufacturing would not have been possible without globalisation. Manufactured goods, such as cars and TV sets, sell for relatively high prices. When South Korea began industrialising, average household income was less than £2,500 per year. With incomes this low, the domestic market for manufactured goods was extremely limited. This meant that South Korea's fledgling manufacturers had to rely heavily on finding customers abroad in export markets.

The structure of the UK economy has also been affected by globalisation. In 1948, manufacturing made up over a third of Britain's output. By 2015, manufacturing output contributed only 10 per cent of the UK's total output. In contrast, over the same period, service sector output rose rapidly as the UK economy re-balanced. It is important to note that the demand for manufactured goods in Britain is as high as ever. However, thanks to globalisation, most of the manufactured goods that we now consume are produced somewhere else. Globalisation has encouraged countries to specialise more, which has created structural change.

> 'Globalisation is about homogenising differences in the world's markets, cultures, tastes and traditions. It's about giving big business access to a global market.'
>
> *Zac Goldsmith, politician*

> 'Globalisation means that for a high wage economy like Britain we need to focus our efforts on the highly skilled, added-value sectors, such as advanced manufacturing.'
>
> *Lucy Powell, politician*

Five whys and a how

Questions	Answers
Why have super-tankers led to significantly reduced transport costs?	Bigger ships burn less fuel per tonne kilometre because they have a lower surface area to volume ratio than smaller ships.
Why has the internet led to more international trade in services, such as accounting?	The internet has made communication almost instant, regardless of geographical distance. This has allowed firms to buy in services from other cheaper suppliers further afield
Why are transnational companies setting up new manufacturing bases in China, rather than supplying this market from existing factories locally?	By locating a new factory inside a new overseas market, protectionist trade barriers, such as tariffs and quotas, can be avoided. In addition, labour costs could also be lower.
Why do some countries decide to remove tariffs and quota protection?	Trade liberalisation happens because governments expect other countries to follow suit and open up their markets too.
Why are most big British retailers against any plans to limit immigration to the UK?	Supermarkets like Tesco benefit in two ways from immigration into Britain. First, if the UK's population increases, there will be a greater demand for supermarket groceries. This should help to boost Tesco's revenues. Second, immigration increases the supply of labour. This should help Tesco to find the staff it needs, without having to offer higher wages.
How has the increased globalisation of markets affected human resource management?	Thanks to globalisation, UK employers now have a bigger pool of skilled labour to recruit from. The growth of a globally mobile workforce enables firms to import whatever type of skilled labour is needed. Furthermore, in high-wage economies, employers can take advantage of migration from the developing world to solve domestic skill shortages, without having to raise wage rates.

29.10 Globalisation – evaluation

Steadily improving transport, from sail to steam and from boats to planes, has meant that globalisation has been growing for hundreds of years. Its economic dimension has had strengths and weaknesses, but many see only weakness in the cultural 'imperialism' implied by the Americanisation of many parts of the world. Despite all the growth that's occurred, it may be that much, much more is to come, especially culturally. It may be that online media such as YouTube and social media such as Facebook and Instagram are going to close dramatically the 'distance' between different countries. At the time of writing, one can see a political backlash against this in India and the Middle East. In the future, there might be a business backlash if different nationalities fight harder to preserve their distinctive national cultures.

Key terms

Liberalisation: minimising the rules and regulations faced by businesses; or, on a global scale, reducing the barriers to freely moving international trade.

Regulations: rules created as a result of laws passed by parliament.

29.11 Workbook

Revision questions

(40 marks; 40 minutes)

1 a) What is meant by the term globalisation? (2)

b) Give three examples of UK companies with a strong global presence. (3)

2 Study Figure 29.1 on page 207, which shows the volume of world merchandise exports by volume.

a) Calculate the percentage increase in export volumes between 1990 and 2013. (4)

b) Identify and explain two factors that could have contributed to this increase. (6)

c) Describe what happened to world exports during the period from 2008 to 2010. Can you explain what happened and why? (5)

3 a) Using Table 29.1, calculate Ryanair's revenue per employee in 2011 and 2015. (4)

b) Assess the extent to which the Ryanair success story can be attributed to the European Union's 1992 Open Skies Agreement. (10)

4 Explain two reasons why transnational corporations, such as Starbucks and McDonald's choose to operate in more than one country (6)

Revision activities

Data response 1

Political change: the Russian trade embargo

In 2014, a bitter war of words broke out between America and Russia. The disagreement stemmed from a difference in views regarding the revolution that had taken place in the Ukraine months earlier. The Americans were the first to act, imposing sanctions that froze the assets of Russian banks operating in the USA. The European Union quickly followed suit, imposing more sanctions on Russia. Unsurprisingly, the Russian government retaliated by imposing an embargo on food imports from the European Union. Under the embargo, farmers in Europe were prevented from exporting meat, fruit, vegetables, fish and dairy products to Russia.

The embargo hit some European farmers and food processing companies very hard, including Valio, one of the largest companies in Finland. In 2013, the company sold over €2 billion worth of milk, butter, yoghurt and cheese. Russia used to be a big export market for Valio – nearly 15 per cent of the company's turnover came from the Russian market. In April 2015, after the embargo hit, Valio announced plans to cut up to 320 jobs in Finland.

Questions (35 marks; 40 minutes)

1 Explain the difference between an embargo and a quota. (5)

2 Assess the possible reasons why Valio used to export 15 per cent of its output to Russia. (10)

3 Evaluate how Valio might respond to Russia's embargo on European dairy products. (20)

Data response 2

Brexit: would it really be a good idea?

In the lead-up to the general election held in May 2015, David Cameron promised a public vote on whether Britain should stay in the European Union. Following Cameron's election victory, a number of high-profile business leaders expressed their concerns about a possible Brexit (British exit from the EU) in the media. One of these people was the president of Airbus UK, Paul Kahn, who claimed that future investment and thousands of highly skilled jobs would be at risk if the UK left the European Union. According to Kahn, the European Union might be bureaucratic, but 'it's a hell of a lot more difficult, more bureaucratic and more costly to be outside the EU than within it'.

Airbus is a transnational company that manufactures passenger aircraft, such as the double-decker A380 used by airlines such as British Airways and Lufthansa and Singapore Airlines. The company is unusual in that the component parts of an aircraft are manufactured in different countries. For example, Airbus UK employs more than 16,000 people in the Britain to produce mostly plane wings. The Airbus factory in Hamburg, Germany, specialises in producing fuselage sections. When the components are ready, they are sent to Toulouse in France where the Airbus airliners are assembled.

Questions (40 marks; 45 minutes)

1 Assess two possible reasons why Airbus chooses to manufacture its aircraft in parts in more than one country. (8)

2 Assess the possible benefits of trade liberalisation for Airbus. (12)

3 Evaluate the possible consequences of a Brexit for the UK stakeholders of Airbus (20)

Extended writing

1 In 1960, car producers such as Toyota (Japan) and Volkswagen (Germany) largely operated in their own countries. Each country tended to have two or three dominant producers. Today, in almost every country, there are as many as twelve to 15 big global car companies competing. Evaluate the strengths and weaknesses of this new global reality. (20)

2 Companies such as Primark and New Look buy their clothes from Far Eastern producers that pay wages that are far below western levels. Evaluate whether that is a morally acceptable use of globalisation. (20)

30 Protectionism

Definition

Protectionism means giving preference to home producers by making it harder and more expensive for overseas companies to export to your country.

Linked to: Growing economies, Ch 25; China versus India, Ch 26; Business potential in Africa, Ch 27; International trade and business growth, Ch 28; Trading blocs, Ch 31; Conditions that prompt trade, Ch 32; Assessment of a country as a market, Ch 33; Global competitiveness, Ch 36

30.1 Introduction

Protectionism is an economic philosophy, or way of thinking. Advocates of protectionism believe that governments should intervene to change the pattern of international trade. The goal is to increase economic prosperity by either increasing a country's exports or by reducing the amount imported. Examples of protectionist trade policies include: tariffs, quotas, government regulations and subsidies. Protectionism is the opposite of free trade, where foreign trade is unrestricted and left to market forces.

In December 2014, the European Union imposed import taxes (tariffs) on solar panels made in China. These tariffs varied up to a maximum of 36 per cent of the factory price. It was said that this was due to Chinese manufacturers 'dumping' solar panels on Europe at below their cost of production. So the EU was protecting EU solar panel producers.

30.2 Tariffs

How do tariffs affect a firm's ability to export?

Mitsubishi charges Japanese consumers in its home market the equivalent of $25,000 for a brand new L200 pick-up truck. Unfortunately, Mitsubishi is unable to charge American consumers the same price. This is because the American government uses tariffs to protect its car and truck industry. In 2014, the American tariff rate on imported Japanese trucks was 25 per cent. This means that for every L200 sold in America, Mitsubishi pays $6,250 (25 per cent of $25,000) to the American government. To make the same amount of profit Mitsubishi will have to pass this tariff on to the American consumer by raising prices. Excluding the extra shipping costs, American buyers of the L200 will have to pay $31,250, rather than $25,000. The American tariff on imported Japanese trucks is a competitive disadvantage for Mitsubishi because it makes its vehicles artificially expensive. In 2014, Mitsubishi sold over 77,500 vehicles in America; this figure would undoubtedly have been higher without the tariff.

Why do countries impose tariffs?

Governments sometimes use tariffs to protect declining industries. Industries can end up declining because either a product has become technologically obsolete, or because the industry has become internationally uncompetitive. An example is the US car industry, which is centred on the city of Detroit. Unfortunately for Detroit, jobs and incomes in the city have been lost as Ford and General Motors have lost market share to foreign-owned rivals. Without tariffs on imported cars this decline would have been even more rapid. Tariffs in this circumstance can be used to prevent a sharp rise in **structural unemployment**.

Some economists and politicians believe that tariffs are also needed to protect 'infant' industries. Infant industries tend to be very small because they have not had time to grow. Small-scale producers can find it hard to survive because unlike their larger foreign rivals they will not be able to benefit from as many economies of scale. Advocates of protectionism argue that tariffs are needed to protect infant industries to enable them to survive and grow. When the infant industry has developed the economies of scale needed to survive, the tariff protection can be withdrawn.

Countries may impose tariffs on imports in retaliation to the protectionism of another country. This is called a **trade war**.

> 'As history has repeatedly proven, one trade tariff begets another, then another – until you've got a full-blown trade war. No one ever wins and consumers always get screwed.'
>
> *Mark McKinnon, US political advisor*

The pros and cons of tariffs

Tariffs help inefficient firms to survive. They therefore benefit the workers, managers and shareholders of these firms. The suppliers of these inefficient firms will also benefit too. In Detroit, bars and cafes have all been helped out by US tariffs on foreign vehicles. Without the tariffs more car workers would have lost their jobs, which would have further depressed demand in Motor City. The general public can also benefit from tariffs because the revenue raised from import taxes can be used to fund public services, such as health and education. On the other hand, tariffs disadvantage consumers because they make imported products more expensive than they should be. Higher prices reduce the amount that consumers are able to buy with their limited incomes. As such, it could be argued that tariffs cause the material standard of living to fall. Some economists also argue that tariffs cause long-run competitive damage to the very firms that they are designed to help. Tariffs can help inefficient firms to survive. If tariffs were removed, these firms would have a greater incentive to find internal ways of becoming more efficient.

Figure 30.1 Without the tariffs more car workers would have lost their jobs, which would have further depressed demand in Motor City.

The pace of economic change within a country can also be slowed by tariffs. It could be argued that long-term economic growth means that inefficient industries are allowed to decline. The labour and capital currently tied up in the inefficient industry can then be moved to other industries elsewhere in the economy that are more efficient.

Certain types of import are especially attractive for the tax authorities. The data on taxes on luxury cars tells a huge story in itself (see Figure 30.2).

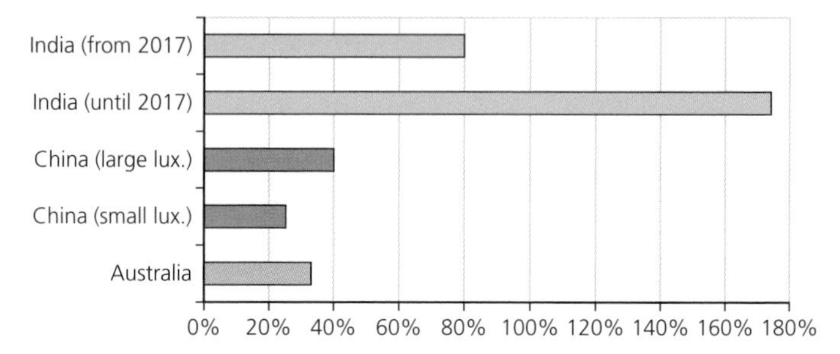

Figure 30.2 Luxury car import taxes, from Australia's 33 per cent to India's 174 per cent (sources: various)

30.3 Import quotas

An import quota is an annual limit on the quantity of a good that can be sold in an overseas market. Nigeria uses quotas to protect its own fishing industry. In the first six months of 2015, the government limited frozen fish imports to a maximum of 300,000 tonnes. Import quotas work by restricting consumer choice. When a quota limit has been reached, domestic consumers will have to buy a domestically produced substitute because there will no longer be imports left available to purchase.

How do import quotas affect a business's ability to sell overseas?

There are more cows (28 million) living in Australia than people (23 million). Due to Australia's relatively small human population, over 60 per cent of the beef produced in Australia is exported. Exports of Australian beef to Indonesia have been hit hard by an import quota. In 2009, the Indonesian government set an import quota of 750,000 tonnes on Australian beef. By 2014, this figure had been reduced to just 250,000 tonnes. This has limited the amount of beef that Australian farmers are allowed to export to Indonesia. The reduction in Indonesia's beef import quota has meant that Australian beef farmers have had to look for new export markets in other countries.

Why do some countries impose import quotas?

Countries impose import quotas to protect domestic producers. The Indonesian government has stated that it wants Indonesia to rely less on imported Australian beef. In the short run, the decision to reduce Indonesian import quotas decreased the supply of beef in Indonesia. This has led to higher beef prices. The Indonesian government no doubt hopes that higher beef prices will encourage local farmers to increase output. To raise beef production, farmers will probably have to take on extra workers. Therefore, it could be argued that quotas can help to reduce the rate of unemployment. Like tariffs, quotas can be used to protect uncompetitive infant industries and sunset industries. Indonesia's balance of payments will also improve if more of the country's beef is produced domestically, rather than being imported. In March 2015, the new president of Indonesia announced his intention to make the country self-sufficient in foods, such as beef.

The pros and cons of quotas

Quotas are not popular with consumers because they limit consumer choice. By decreasing supply, quotas also make products more expensive. The main beneficiaries of quotas are the workers, managers and shareholders of firms who will now face less foreign competition. Inside a protected domestic market, these firms are likely to generate higher revenues and profits. For the workers, the result is likely to be greater job security and an increased likelihood of inflation-busting pay rises. Shareholders who own companies that are protected by quotas stand to gain via bigger dividends and higher share prices. Unlike tariffs, quotas do not generate an additional source of income for the government. However, if quotas prevent job losses, the government could indirectly benefit because higher levels of employment will mean that there are more incomes available for the government to tax. In addition, the government will not have to spend as much on welfare benefits for the unemployed.

30.4 Government legislation

Most countries have consumer protection laws. Sometimes legislation is used to stop firms from selling dangerous products. For example, fat-free Pringles snacks are no longer sold in Britain because they contain an ingredient called Olestra, which has been banned in the UK. According to the British government, Olestra causes stomach cramps and diarrhoea. Other types of legislation are designed to protect the environment. For example, in 2014, the European Union acted to reduce electricity consumption by legislating that all vacuum cleaners must be fitted with motors less than 1,600 watts.

How does legislation affect a business's ability to sell overseas?

Sudden changes in legislation can be hard for exporters because their products must be redesigned to meet the new laws. This can take time. In some cases, exporters might be locked out of an overseas market for years. Between 1959 and 2014, no ordinary citizen in Cuba was allowed to import a car; therefore the Cubans did everything they could to keep pre-1959 (usually American) cars on the road.

Legislation does not always restrict a firm's ability to sell overseas. If product standards abroad are fairly similar to those at home, it should be possible to export without having to make too many expensive adjustments to raw materials, components, design, production methods and/or labelling. Since the development of the Single Market within the EU, it has been far easier for UK firms to export to other European Union countries. This is because from this point on, the European Union replaced various national product standards with single, pan-European standards.

Why do governments impose legislation to regulate business activities?

Most firms are run by entrepreneurs who are happy to live up to their social responsibilities. Despite this, legislation is needed. This is because there will always be a small minority running firms who are prepared to put their profits before their responsibilities to other stakeholder groups. These unethical firms can cause tremendous damage to society. Legislation is designed to protect consumers, employees and the environment. This was demonstrated in 2015, when Volkswagen was caught cheating on its diesel car emissions tests in America and Europe. VW's claims of 'clean diesel' encouraged people to buy; yet diesel emissions are killers through air pollution. So it could be argued that the company was willing to risk lives in order to sell more cars. It was only an alert US regulator that put an end to this.

Laws and regulations passed by politicians can also be used by some governments to reduce competition. For example, in Russia the government does not allow foreign airlines the legal right to run scheduled passenger services between Russian cities. This type of regulation works by limiting competition. If Ryanair were able to run a regular service between Moscow and St Petersburg, it would probably be very popular. As this service does not exist, Russians are forced into travelling with one of their domestic airlines.

The pros and cons of legislation

If legislation is passed to protect against imports, the main beneficiaries will be domestic firms. These firms will now face less competition. A reduction in competition should lead to higher profits for shareholders. For workers, a reduction in external competition should lead to greater job security.

The main drawback of using legislation for protectionist reasons is that it is likely to provoke retaliation. If a country unfairly bans another country's product, the victim is likely to fight back and introduce a ban of its own against the aggressor. The other key factor is that reducing importer competition means higher prices and less product choice for consumers.

> 'A good piece of legislation is like a good sentence or a good piece of music. Everybody can recognise it. They say, "Huh. It works. It makes sense".'
>
> *Barack Obama, US President*

30.5 Domestic subsidies

A subsidy is a sum of money given by the government to the producers of a particular product. Subsidies are normally paid on a per unit supplied basis. For example, in 2015, the European Union paid British farmers a subsidy of nearly 10p for every pint of milk produced. Governments hope that firms will respond to this incentive by producing more of the product receiving the subsidy.

Real business

In 2013, the UK Coalition government announced a subsidy deal with a French energy company. The French company (backed by Chinese money) would build a big new nuclear power station at Hinkley Point (Somerset) that could provide 7 per cent of all Britain's electricity needs. But the subsidy could amount to £1 billion a year for the 35 years the plant was expected to operate. That £35 billion would be subject to inflation – all of which would add still further to the subsidy. Later, in 2015, Chancellor George Osborne offered another £2 billion in the form of a government guarantee to underwrite the costs of building the power plant. This at the same time that the government was cutting back sharply on subsidies for renewable energy, especially wind power.

How do subsidies affect a business's ability to sell overseas?

Subsidies work by offsetting production costs. They increase the amount of profit made on every unit sold. This increase in profitability allows exporters to reduce their prices without any loss of profit margin. If firms decide to cut their export prices, their products will seem cheaper to consumers abroad compared with domestically produced alternatives. This should divert demand towards the export. Subsidies paid to exporters therefore enhance a business's ability to sell overseas.

Why do governments pay domestic firms subsidies?

Subsidies help inefficient firms by stimulating demand for their products. By keeping order books full, subsidies help to boost output and employment in an industry that might otherwise be in decline. Some governments defend their use of subsidies on the grounds that they are necessary because other countries are also paying subsidies to their firms. Subsidies have also been used for environmental reasons. By subsidising solar energy, the UK government hoped to reduce the UK's carbon footprint.

The pros and cons of subsidies

Subsidies can help the poor by lowering prices and by preserving jobs in internationally uncompetitive industries. They can also help to improve a country's balance of payments by reducing imports and increasing export sales. However, subsidies have to be financed. This is likely to lead to higher rates of taxation for households and for businesses operating in industries that do not receive government subsidies. Some economists argue that subsidies can encourage inefficiency, because firms receiving subsidies can become reliant on them. Subsidies are not always sufficient to save an uncompetitive industry. This is because consumers consider other factors apart from price when buying products.

'Protectionism will do little to create jobs, and if foreigners retaliate, we will surely lose jobs.'

Alan Greenspan, former President of the US Central Bank

'If the United States wants access to Chinese, Indian or Vietnamese markets, we must give access to their companies. US protectionism is very subtle but it is very much there.'

Azim Premji, Indian businessman

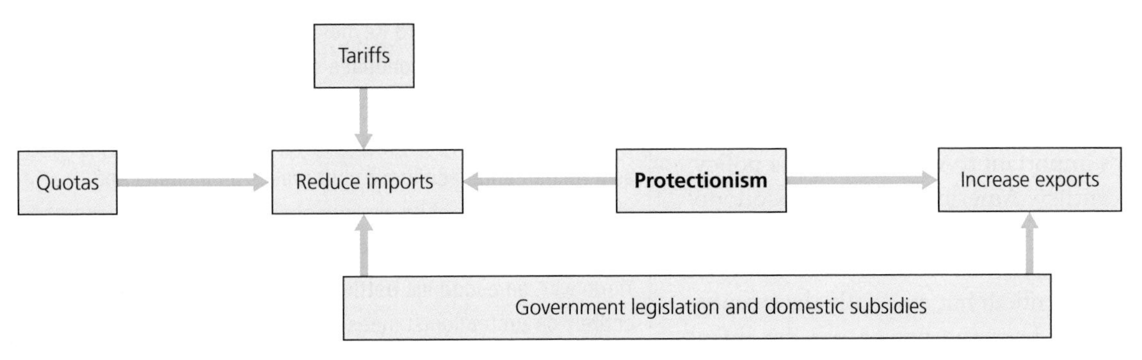

Figure 30.3 Logic chain: the key factors relating to protectionism

Five whys and a how

Questions	Answers
Why might a new American tariff on UK-produced cars cause British job losses?	The American tariff will increase the price of UK cars sold in America, making them less attractive to American car buyers. If UK car exports drop, British car manufacturers might cut production, leading to redundancies.
Why might the EU decide to impose an import quota on Chinese shoes?	Shoes are still made in some European countries like Italy. The wages paid to workers in Italy are higher than the wages paid to Chinese workers. As a result, Chinese shoe producers can under-cut their Italian rivals in terms of price. By limiting the amount of Chinese shoes allowed into Europe, the quota provides a domestic source of demand for Italian shoes.
Why do most big multinationals like Kraft Foods favour harmonising product standards across the whole of the European Union?	In the past, supplying Europe was a tricky business because each country had its own distinctive regulations. To comply with these regulations, firms had to produce different versions of their products. The result was higher costs, caused by shorter production runs. If a common standard can be agreed production can be continuous.
Why might a government agree to pay a subsidy to an uncompetitive industry that is in decline?	Because the government wants to protect the incomes and livelihoods of those working in this industry. The subsidy can be used as a temporary measure to buy time. Hopefully, a new industry can be enticed to set up in the same region, creating new jobs.
Why might a subsidised firm become less efficient?	Because necessity is the mother of invention. Subsidies enable inefficient firms to continue trading. This arguably reduces the incentive to make the internal changes needed to restore efficiency.
How might a Japanese car manufacturer get around American tariffs imposed on imported cars?	By supplying the American market from a new factory based inside America. The Japanese cars sold in America will no longer be classified as imports.

30.6 Protectionism – evaluation

After the 1929 'Wall Street Crash', the factor that turned a recession into a catastrophic depression (and the rise of Hitler) was global protectionism. Britain and France had empires, and could hide behind protectionist walls, and America was big enough to stand on its own two feet. But many other countries, including Germany, were hit dramatically by a collapse in export markets. The 2009 financial crash was the worst economic event since 1929, but the actions of governments proved much wiser. Protectionism didn't resurface and in late 2008 and 2009 governments such as America, Britain and China used **Keynesian counter-cyclical** economic policies to prevent a depression.

Although protectionism is far less widespread today than in years gone by, it's important to see its value as a policy. In the nineteenth century, America built up its economy behind tariff walls to protect it from British producers. In the twentieth century, Japan, then South Korea, did the same. And in the late twentieth but especially the twenty-first century, China has been the one to use the infant industries idea to build economic strength before taking on global allcomers.

Overused – or allowed to be used for too long – and protectionism is a recipe for complacent companies and under-served consumers. But it has an important role in helping baby industries start to walk.

Key terms

Counter-cyclical: expansionary government policies to counter a downturn in the economic cycle.

Keynesian: an economic policy based on the views of British economist John Maynard Keynes, who urged governments to take action to boost economies when hit by recession (so-called 'counter-cyclical policies').

Structural unemployment: potentially long-term unemployment as a fundamental economic shift makes an industry and therefore the skills of its workers obselete, e.g. the widespread closures of coal mines and clothing factories in 1980s Britain.

Trade war: an economic battle between two countries based entirely on protectionist measures such as import quotas; one starts, so the other retaliates and this can spiral out of control.

30.7 Workbook

Revision questions

(45 marks; 45 minutes)

1 Define the term 'protectionism'. (2)

2 **a)** What is the difference between VAT and a tariff? (3)

b) The American government imposes a 2.5 per cent tariff on Japanese cars. How much would a $60,000 Japanese car cost to buy in the USA after the tariff is imposed? (2)

3 In 2015, the European Union imposed a monthly quota on Moroccan tomatoes of 46,000 tonnes. Exports from Morocco to the EU had previously been 60,000–80,000 tonnes a month.

a) Explain how this quota has affected Moroccan farmers. (4)

b) Explain the benefits of the quota to European tomato growers. (4)

4 According to European Union legislation, cheese can only be sold as Mozzarella in Europe if the cheese is made in Italy from water buffalo milk.

a) Explain how this type of legislation has helped Italian producers of Mozzarella cheese. (6)

b) Apart from Mozzarella cheese producers, who else might benefit from this type of legislation, and why? (4)

5 **a)** What is a subsidy? (2)

b) Explain how subsidies can affect a business's ability to export. (6)

6 Evaluate whether it is fair for an underdeveloped African country such Sierra Leone to use tariffs to protect its first-ever steelworks. (12)

Revision activities

Data response 1

McDonald's hit by Russian legislation

McDonald's has been selling fast food in Russia since its first restaurant was opened in Moscow in 1990. Since then, economic growth has boosted Russian incomes and living standards. Unsurprisingly, the demand for fast food in Russia has grown. In 2013, Russians spent over £20 billion visiting burger joints. In the same year, McDonald's share of the Russian burger market was 40 per cent. According to a Russian market research firm, the largest Russian-owned chain held just 2.5 per cent of the market.

In October 2014, McDonald's was investigated by the Russian government for breaking consumer protection legislation. According to the Russian government, some of the items sold by McDonald's were illegal under Russian law because they contained too many calories. McDonald's was forced to close down branches and to pay fines to the Russian government for breaking Russian legislation. Most European and American analysts argued that the actions of the Russian government against McDonald's were motivated by anti-American politics. But the Russian government maintained it was protecting Russian consumers from the dangers of eating unhealthy food.

In 2015, the Russian government granted a Russian entrepreneur a £10 million loan to set up a nationwide chain of fast-food restaurants. The new chain has promised to use local ingredients. Its launch advertising slogan is: 'Let's eat at home'.

Questions (40 marks; 45 minutes)

1. Calculate the value of McDonald's Russian sales in 2013. Compare it with the sales of the largest Russian-owned chain. (4)
2. Explain how McDonald's was affected by Russian government legislation. (4)
3. Assess whether it is right for the Russian government to introduce legislation that restricts the calorie content of fast food. (12)
4. Evaluate whether the Russians' government actions were a form of protectionism or a way to improve public health. (20)

Data response 2

Subsidy wars: Airbus versus Boeing

The market for large passenger aeroplanes is dominated by two companies. Competition between Airbus, a European consortium, and its American rival, Boeing, is intense. Innovation in this market is very important because technological advances can make products obsolete. During the last 20 years, both companies have tried to steal each other's market share by launching new hi-tech modern aircraft. The new products – the Airbus double-decker A380 and the Boeing 777 – are both more efficient because they burn far less fuel per passenger kilometre than older aircraft such as the Boeing 747.

Airbus and Boeing regularly accuse each other of competing unfairly by being in receipt of government subsidies. For example, in 2014, the European Union accused the American government of offering Boeing tax breaks worth $8.7 billion. These tax breaks allegedly helped Boeing to pay for the costs of developing the new Boeing 777. In 2015, Boeing hit back at Airbus by claiming that the European Union was preparing to make a loan to Airbus to finance a new and improved version of the A380. In the past both companies have taken their cases to the World Trade Organization. The WTO investigates and rules on trade disputes between countries. Its goal is to discourage protectionism and to promote international trade.

Questions (40 marks; 45 minutes)

1. What is a tax break? Explain how a tax break can act as a subsidy. (4)
2. A Boeing 777 costs $300 million to buy. Calculate the number of aircraft covered by the US government subsidy. (4)
3. Assess the case for and against the European Union paying subsidies to private companies such as Airbus. (12)
4. Evaluate the role played by subsidies in creating competitive advantage within the market for civil aeroplanes. (20)

Extended writing

1 If Britain left the European Union, it would be free to set any import tariffs it wished, such as a 25 per cent tariff on all manufactured imports, to give a hand to our slightly struggling manufacturing business. Evaluate the probable effects of this. (20)

2 The single biggest area for European Union intervention and subsidy is agriculture. UK farmers produce 0.7 per cent of UK GDP but get £3 billion a year of subsidy payments. Evaluate the likely consequences if these subsidy payments were withdrawn completely. (20)

Section 4.1 Globalisation

31 Trading blocs

Definition

A trading bloc is an agreement between countries to have free trade within an external tariff wall. It is also possible, like the European Union, to have free movement of labour between the members.

Linked to: International trade and business growth, Ch 28; Conditions that prompt trade, Ch 32; Assessment of a country as a market, Ch 33; Assessment of a country as a production location, Ch 34; Global competitiveness, Ch 36

31.1 Introduction

Most economists would agree that trade between countries is a good thing. It encourages countries to specialise in what they're good at and buy in the products or services they're less good at. In this way people become better off and economic growth can be encouraged through trade.

For most of the period since 1945, countries have sought to move away from protectionism and encourage freer trade. This has been managed since 1995 by the World Trade Organization (WTO). Although global free trade is the goal of the WTO, regional trading blocs are also appealing. After centuries of war, the European countries began, from 1958, to bind themselves together politically by locking their economies together using a trading bloc. Few countries in the world are as interconnected economically as those of Europe. In 2014, 62 per cent of all exports from European Union (EU) countries were to other EU members.

31.2 Trading blocs: the attractions

If a British-based car producer wants to export cars to Turkey (outside the EU), it has to find out the local safety and pollution rules governing cars, and adjust production accordingly, perhaps with a special exhaust system. Years ago, every export to every country required the same expensive, time-consuming, jumping-through-hoops approach to trade. Today, the Nissan factory in Sunderland can produce 250,000 identical cars bound for 26 countries within the European Union. Naturally that cuts Nissan's cost per unit considerably, enabling the business to benefit from economies of scale. This, in effect, makes everyone in Europe better off, because cars can be sold at lower prices than would otherwise be the case.

Other attractions of trading blocs include:

- A degree of protection from a tough world. Churchill China plc (a Stoke pottery business) has been very happy with the protection provided by EU anti-dumping rules against china from China; an individual country of Britain's size would rarely stand up to the economic might of China or America. A trading bloc like the EU can.
- The beneficial pressures of competition. Companies within trading blocs have to compete directly with companies based in other countries within the bloc; the pressure forces them to be as efficient as possible, which helps keep prices down and choices up for consumers.

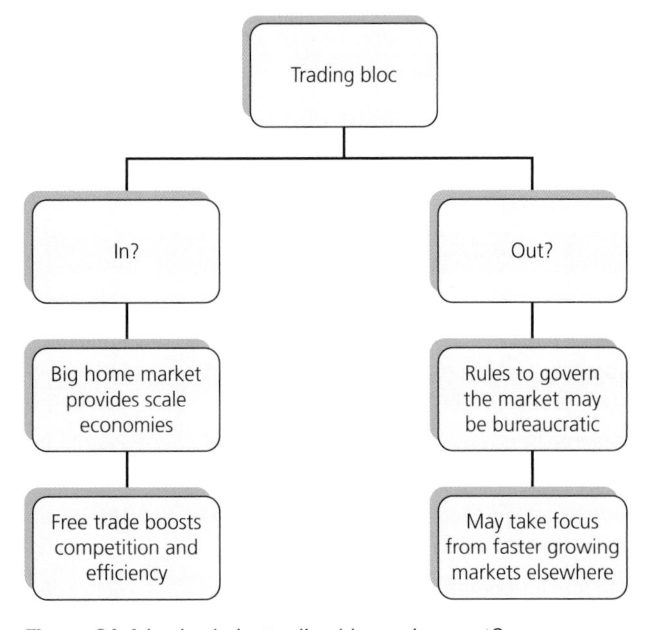

Figure 31.1 Logic chain: trading blocs – in or out?

31.3 Expansion of trading blocs

Since the original six members began the European Economic Community in 1958 (which became the EU in 1993) there have been two ways in which trading blocs have expanded:

1 More have started up.

2 Most have attracted more and more members.

New trading blocs

Following the successful formation of the European Community in 1958, a series of other trading blocs have opened up. Today there are at least 13 around the world, including the two most important: the EU and the North American Free Trade Association (NAFTA). Table 31.1 gives a summary of some important trading blocs, picking ones from all parts of the world. During 2014 and 2015, discussions took place between America and Europe with a view to forming the world's biggest bloc: the Transatlantic Trade and Investment Partnership (TTIP). This would bring together NAFTA and the EU, which together account for more than a third of the world's GDP. The negotiations stalled in mid-2015, but there is no denying the desire by many to develop trading blocs further.

Increase in membership

In addition to the increasing number of trading blocs, each bloc has tended to attract more members. The EU began with six members and now has 28. The Association of South-East Asian Nations (ASEAN) started with six and now has ten; and the plan for the East African Community (EAC) is that it will eventually expand to cover the whole continent of 50 countries.

Both the growth in numbers of trading blocs and the growth in members point to the continuing attractiveness of trading bloc membership. British politicians and citizens are unusual in finding a series of reasons to doubt our membership of the European Union. As at summer 2015 there were seven more countries wanting to join the EU, but only one voting whether to stay in.

31.4 The EU and the single market

Until it joined the European Union in 1973, Britain's economic growth rate had been disappointing. Since 1945, almost every leading economy (especially those in Europe) had grown faster than Britain. A key reason for this was assumed to be that Britain's **home market** was 60 million while America and EU countries each had home markets of around 250 million. Others had huge economies of scale that we lacked. So we were uncompetitive. Indeed, since joining, our economic growth rates have been much better in relation to competitors such as America, Germany, France and Japan.

Figure 31.2 shows the importance of size. China and the United States are the biggest global economies by far, but clubbing the 28 members of the European Union together makes Europe sit alongside them. This massive home market is why Nissan is so successful – exporting

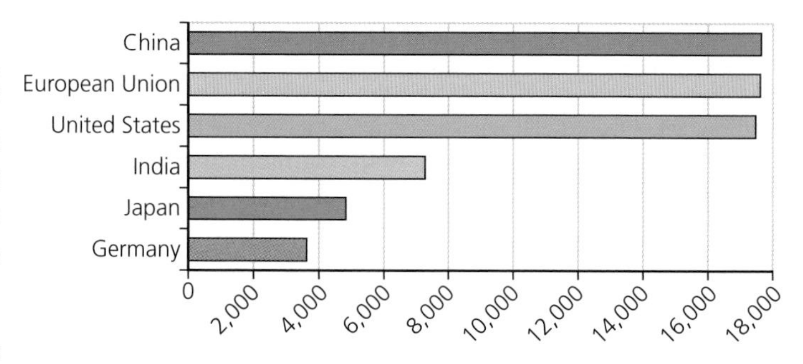

Figure 31.2 The world's biggest economies (total GDP at purchasing power parity in $bns) (source: *CIA World Factbook* 2015)

	Starting date	Main members	Total GDP 2014	Total population 2014
European Union (EU)	1958	Germany, France, UK (28 in total)	$16,000 billion	515 million
Association of South-East Asian Nations (ASEAN)	1967	Indonesia, Thailand, Vietnam (10 in total)	$2,600 billion	625 million
MERCOSUR (Spanish for South American Common Market)	1991	Brazil, Argentina, Uruguay (6 in total)	$3,600 billion	300 million
North American Free Trade Association (NAFTA)	1994	USA, Canada and Mexico (3 in total)	$21,000 billion	480 million
East African Community (EAC)	2000	Kenya, Tanzania (5 in total)	$110 billion	150 million

Table 31.1 Expansion of trading blocs

throughout Europe from its Sunderland base. Other UK-based manufacturers such as BMW Mini, GKN, Toyota, McVities and Fever-Tree all benefit from the scale provided by this European 'single market'.

The **single market** is at the heart of the European Union. By working hard to unify employment, health and safety and environmental rules and regulations, the European Union has provided the 'level playing field' employers demanded. With labour also allowed to move freely within the EU, companies are able to mass produce and also hire in skilled staff from elsewhere when necessary. When California's booming, no one minds if labour flies in from New York. Movement of labour helps businesses keep expanding during boom conditions. It's essential if Europe's single market is to achieve sustained economic growth.

31.5 The ASEAN trading bloc

Over the past 25 years, south-east Asia has been the globe's economic powerhouse – boosted by China and, to a lesser extent, India. The ASEAN bloc has been within China's magnetic field, sucking in raw materials but also benefiting from outsourcing of key tasks. The ASEAN free trade area began in 1992 with six members. Its success encouraged Vietnam, Cambodia, Laos and Myanmar (Burma) to join later. Today the ten members regularly invite representatives from China, Japan and South Korea to attend important meetings. The members of ASEAN have no illusions – they realise that their success depends on the bigger economies around them. Table 31.2 shows just how successful ASEAN has been. The data for the UK and Bolivia (South America) is there for comparative reasons – to help appreciate ASEAN's success – and to see the importance of China in that story.

	1990	2000	2014	% change in GDP 1990–2014
*Cambodia**	$700	$1,084	$3,242	+383%
Indonesia	$2,939	$4,659	$10,565	+259%
Thailand	$4,116	$7,085	$14,661	+256%
Vietnam	$970	$2,100	$5,629	+480%
India	$1,148	$2,020	$5,833	+408%
China	$980	$2,915	$13,217	+1,249%
Bolivia	$2,417	$3,432	$6,450	+167%
UK	$17,985	$27,340	$39,137	+118%

Table 31.2 Growth in GDP per capita at purchasing power parity to $US. *Italic = members of ASEAN (source: World Bank 2015)

31.6 NAFTA trading bloc

The combination of Mexico, Canada and the United States remains controversial in America. There's no doubt that the free trade area has helped bring jobs to Mexico, but many Americans blame NAFTA for the fact that median male incomes haven't improved in a generation. They say that low Mexican wages are doing Americans out of well-paid jobs – and forcing real wages down. Figure 31.3 appears to support that view until you remember that NAFTA started in 1994, whereas median real wages have been flat in America since 1973. There must be other factors in play. A decline in the trade union membership in the US is a plausible alternative explanation.

In the long term, trading blocs such as NAFTA may attract extra investment from outside companies because of the flexibility involved. For Japanese car companies such as Nissan and Toyota, it makes sense to supplement their US factories with lower-cost ones in Mexico. In

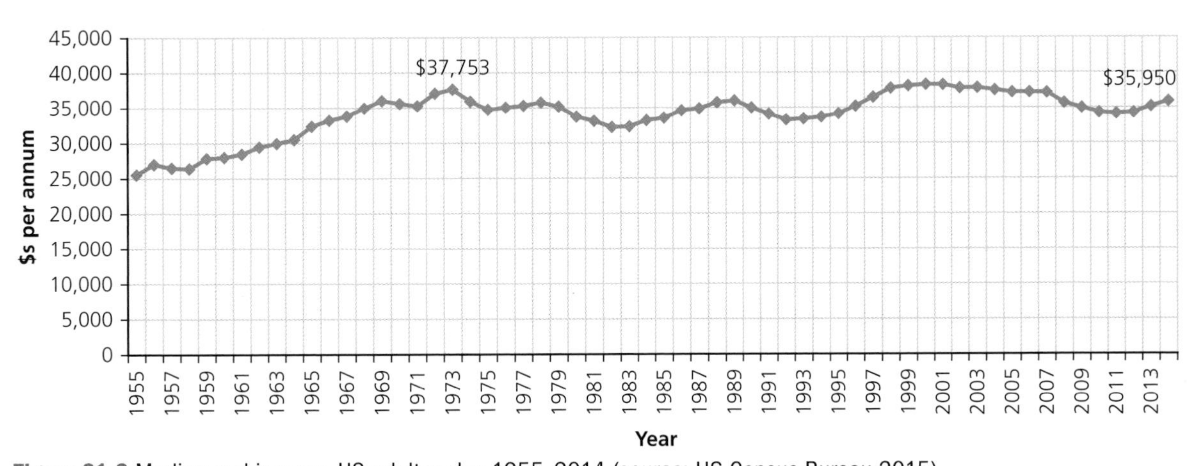

Figure 31.3 Median real income, US adult males 1955-2014 (source: US Census Bureau 2015)

America they can make the added-value, fancier cars; in Mexico they can make the more mass-market ones.

Real business

Auto industry's $23 billion investment in Mexico

Car makers from Nissan Motor Company to Mazda Motor Corporation are churning out record numbers of vehicles in Mexico destined for consumers abroad. But some executives are worried that the factory hum will slow in coming years as exports get bogged down by congestion at the nation's ports.

The Mexican government has targeted 70 billion pesos ($4.6 billion) for port infrastructure up to 2018, including building four new terminals in Veracruz. Some car makers are sceptical that the goal will be met or will be enough to handle the more than 5 million vehicles Mexico expects to produce annually by 2020 – a 56 per cent increase from the country's 2014 output.

In the past two-and-a-half years, car manufacturers, including Toyota Motor Corporation and Daimler AG, have invested or promised $22.6 billion for auto and parts plants, according to the government of Mexico. That success story, which made the sector the largest source of foreign cash in the country, may be imperilled if the government doesn't speed up plans for infrastructure improvements.

(Source: adapted from Bloomberg, http://www.bloomberg.com/news/articles/2015-05-26/carmakers-23-billion-mexico-venture-may-face-snarls-at-ports)

'The real end winner of NAFTA is going to be Mexico because we have the human capital. We have that resource that is vital to the success of the US economy.'

Vincente Fox, Mexican President 2000–2006

'Mexico is killing us on trade.'

Donald Trump, US Presidential hopeful, 2015

31.7 Impact on businesses of trading blocs

Each year the global market in passenger aircraft is worth about $120 billion. About half is received by Airbus Industrie and of that $60 billion, about 30 per cent comes to Britain. This income creates upwards of 100,000 jobs in Britain – and is the main source of high-value income and innovation among our engineering companies.

Back in 1970, three US airplane manufacturers had a near-100 per cent grip on the world market for 100+ seat passenger aircraft. In 1988, one of the three withdrew to focus on military aircraft and, in 1997, Boeing swallowed up its only remaining US rival.

In the meantime, after years of discussion, French, German and British aerospace companies (backed financially by their governments) combined to form Airbus Industrie and, in 1974, to launch their first plane. The Europeans had agreed two key strategies: all their planes would use 'fly-by-wire' technologies pioneered in military aircraft and all would use the same cockpit design/controls, etc. This cut design and production costs, and also cut pilot training and maintenance costs for the airlines. Airbus share of the world market crept up to 13.3 per cent by 1993 but then jumped to 44.7 per cent by 1997. In the period 2000–2015 Airbus and Boeing enjoyed a 50/50 split of the $120 billion market for large passenger planes.

Figure 31.4 Airbus A380

Advantages to business of trading blocs	Drawbacks to businesses of trading blocs
• Free movement of goods between members gives the potential to create a large 'single market'	• Competition increases due to freer trade, so those with monopoly power may find it competed away
• External tariff walls insulate the business from competition from another part of the world	• To create a single market, new rules and regulations may be agreed, including minimum wage rates
• As trade grows between neighbours, it becomes economic (and necessary) for governments to provide infrastructure support	• The availability of easily accessed neighbouring markets may reduce enterprise in relation to distant but dynamic ones such as China
• The advantages become much greater if there's free movement of labour as well as free movement of goods	• Within a geographically proximate bloc, there may be common factors that together become common problems, e.g. low commodity prices

Table 31.3 Advantages and drawbacks of trading blocs to businesses

Could this success have happened without the links formed by the trading bloc? Probably not. When Britain's Engineering Employers' Federation asked its members about withdrawal from the EU in early 2015, 93 per cent wanted Britain to remain. There is no doubting that manufacturers see the benefits of a trading bloc. But what about the service businesses that form 80 per cent of our economy? Does EU membership matter to Tesco, to Marks & Spencer or to Barclays Bank? Not as much, to be sure. The City of London has actually grown fabulously since Britain joined Europe, as it has become Europe's leading banking sector. But the benefits of belonging to a trading bloc are most obvious to manufacturing businesses – and they represent just 10 per cent of the British economy.

'The European Union is the world's most successful invention for advancing peace.'

John Bruton, former Prime Minister, Ireland

'I'm a great supporter of the European Union. I didn't support entry to the Euro, not because I'm against it in principle but because I didn't think it was economically right for Britain. But that doesn't make me any less pro-European.'

Gordon Brown, former Prime Minister

Five whys and a how

Questions	Answers
Why do countries get together to form trading blocs?	Because they believe the benefits outweigh the drawbacks, leading to improved economic growth.
Why not scrap all trading blocs and allow the WTO to ensure there's free trade globally?	Nice idea, but unrealistic. Especially during economic downturns, countries will act to protect their home industries – the WTO is too toothless to stop that.
Why is Switzerland able to do so well even though it's not part of a trading bloc?	It is unique for its very powerful positions in global watch-making, banking, chocolate production and the manufacture of top-end machinery (but also, don't forget it's strongly linked to the EU with free-trade agreements).
Why does Britain always seem to be questioning the benefits of trading bloc membership?	Perhaps because we were once the global superpower, and don't like sharing! It's notable that the US keeps questioning NAFTA.
Why is it so expensive to be part of a trading bloc such as the EU?	It isn't. The UK government spends over 25 per cent of UK GDP; the EU spends about 1 per cent of the EU's GDP.
How damaging might it be for a country to withdraw from a trading bloc?	It happens so rarely that no one can be sure. Judging by business lobbying, UK manufacturing would be hit hard but the service sector might be fine.

31.8 Trading blocs – evaluation

Although businesses can lobby in support of their viewpoint, it is politicians and voters who decide whether or not a country joins or remains in a trading bloc. In or out, businesses will simply get on and try to make the best of the situation. If a country joins the EU, its companies will probably switch to a strategy based on the opportunities across this huge single market. After all, it will know that sales in its home country are likely to be hit by greater competition from elsewhere in the EU. So it needs more sales abroad to make up for its home market losses.

But all that is said in the bland terms of economics. It fails to mention the difficulties and the short-term pain. New competition is difficult and new opportunities can be much harder to achieve than to talk about. So entering a trading bloc can mean huge short–medium-term upheaval; so can leaving one. Key decisions should be made on the basis of long-term benefits, but short-term problems can mean job losses, job relocations and even the need to cut costs by cutting wages. The short term can be nasty.

Key terms

Home market: the number of customers that can be reached without needing to jump administrative hurdles; the Empire once provided Britain with the world's biggest home market; today the European Union provides a smaller equivalent.

Single market: dismantling trade barriers within Europe so that all 28 countries can treat the whole region as their home market.

31.9 Workbook

Revision questions

(25 marks; 25 minutes)

1 Explain two possible disadvantages to a British shoe manufacturer of a decision by Britain to withdraw from the European Union. (6)

2 Explain why businesses are especially keen to have free movement of labour within a trading bloc such as the 26-member European Union. (4)

3 a) Use Table 31.1 to calculate the GDP per head of population (per capita) in the ASEAN compared with the EU trading blocs. (4)

b) Assess two ways in which a global company such as Unilever (Walls ice cream and many other global brands) could use that information. (8)

4 Figure 31.3 looks at median real income. Explain what that means. (3)

Revision activities

Data response

Toyota in Europe

It could almost be said that Toyota is the world's only truly global car company. In East Africa, in Pakistan and Afghanistan, you won't find many, if any, Audis or Chevrolets – but you will find Toyota Rav4s. Across the world the three great car makers are Toyota, Volkswagen and America's General Motors. The world's most profitable, by far, is Toyota.

Toyota is not especially strong in Europe (844,000 cars sold in 2014) but the European business does make a healthy profit. By contrast General Motors made a loss of $1.37 billion in 2014. Toyota's business success is to see how to make money in a trading bloc.

Toyota first began selling cars in Europe in 1963. Since then, the company has matured into the leading Japanese car manufacturer employing approximately 93,400 people, both directly and through retailer channels. Toyota's operation in Europe is supported by a network of 31 National Marketing and Sales Companies representing 56 countries, approximately 2,700 sales outlets and nine manufacturing plants in seven countries.

Toyota's basic strategy is localisation, adapting its vehicles to meet the specific needs of Europe's varied customers. This means the company's operations in Europe – be they manufacturing, research and development or marketing – are generally located within the continent to serve the local market.

The first Toyota vehicles to be made in Europe were produced under licence in Portugal in 1971. In 1992, Toyota began full production of cars and engines in the UK with the introduction of the Carina. A new Toyota facility in France began producing the Yaris in 2001. In April 2002, Toyota opened a new plant in Poland to build transmissions. Today, Toyota UK builds the Avensis and Auris models that are then exported throughout the EU.

Toyota's diesel engine plant in Jelcz-Laskowice, Poland, began operations in 2005, as did the new vehicle manufacturing plant in Kolin, Czech Republic, which is a joint venture between Toyota Motor Corporation and PSA Peugeot Citroën. Around two-thirds of Toyotas sold in Europe are made in Europe by Europeans.

Questions (40 marks: 45 minutes)

1 Assess the advantages Toyota may gain from making most of its cars for European sale in its own European Union factories. (10)

2 Toyota has important research and development centres in Belgium, France and Germany. Assess the importance of locally focused innovation to a business such as Toyota. (10)

3 Evaluate the importance to Toyota of Britain remaining within its trading bloc: the European Union. (20)

Extended writing

1 Mars UK launched the 'Merryteaser Reindeer' as a Christmas novelty chocolate in 2014. Now it plans to launch the product next Christmas throughout Europe. Evaluate the importance to Mars of operating within a 28-member trading bloc. (20)

2 From a business point of view, evaluate whether Britain should stay in the European Union or leave. (20)

Section 4.2 Global markets and business expansion

32 Conditions that prompt trade

Definition

The decision to build markets or develop supplies from abroad can be caused by market conditions in the UK (push factors) or opportunities overseas (pull factors).

Linked to: International trade and business growth, Ch 28; Trading blocs, Ch 31; Assessment of a country as a market, Ch 33; Assessment of a country as a production location, Ch 34; Global competitiveness, Ch 36

32.1 Introduction

The trade being referred to in this unit is between a business in one country and businesses or consumers in other countries. The reasons for the development of international trade such as this can be found in changing conditions of demand and in changes in the supply structure of markets. These reasons are many and can be subtle, but can be categorised into push and pull factors, namely, reasons why it makes sense to leave unfavourable domestic markets – **push factors** – and **pull factors** – attractive features of trading abroad.

Until recently it was agreed that goods are traded, but services are produced and consumed in the same place. You cannot export a haircut. But author Thomas Friedman suggests that 'we are coming close to exporting a haircut, the appointment part. What kind of haircut do you want? Which barber do you want? All those things can and will be done by a call center far away' (T. Friedman, *The World is Flat*).

32.2 Push factors

Trading internationally may well be caused by conditions in a firm's domestic market. Businesses looking to grow, or in some cases survive, may be unable to do this at home, thus pushing them into trading internationally, entering new, foreign markets in the search for new sales. These push factors tend to be about avoiding weaknesses or threats. Push factors include:

- saturated markets at home
- competition
- the need to extend the product life cycle.

Saturated markets

A key objective for most established businesses is growth. This is especially true for public limited companies, where stock market investors tend to expect growth in sales and profits every year. Therefore, once a business has managed to sell its products to just about everyone in a market, the only routes for growth are to sell a wider range of products or find new markets where their existing products can be sold. In markets for consumer durables, such as televisions, phones or toasters, a **saturated market** can mean falling sales. If every potential customer has already bought a durable such as an electric kettle, the only scope for further sales is replacements or upgrades. Often this forces a business into entering new geographical markets; Ansoff called this strategy 'market development' – and warned of the risks involved.

Figure 32.1 A saturated market in consumer durables can result in falling sales

Typically, a business looking to escape a saturated market through entering new countries will tend to look for markets where consumers share similar characteristics. This can lead to slightly surprising choices from a geographical perspective, with UK firms finding success in Australia rather than France, or Russia rather than nearby Belgium.

Real business

Chocs away to Oz

Choc on Choc was founded in 2004 in a small barn near Bath. Father–daughter team Kerr Dunlop and Flo Broughton make hand-made extremely expensive 'artisan' chocolates, supplying a market for 'posh chocs' that has grown substantially in the last decade. With so many players in the market, from Hotel Chocolat to Choccywoccydoodah, the market segment was becoming very crowded. This prompted Choc on Choc to explore opportunities for international expansion, since the 'posh chocs' segment was not so well developed in other countries. As a small business, the firm was keen to enter markets that would not require significant changes to its packaging and branding, but would still value its 'Made in Great Britain' promise. Although it now exports its products to nine different foreign markets, the top, by some distance, are Australia and the US. Both countries are English-speaking and are attracted by the British image. Expansion has allowed the firm to successfully achieve growth, even when its home market was becoming saturated.

(Source: Adapted from http://www.telegraph.co.uk/finance/newsbysector/retailandconsumer/11146330/Cheddar-Cheese-to-Gin-and-Tonic-the-British-flavours-they-love-abroad.html, 8 October 2014)

Competition

The arrival of new competitors may threaten a firm's market share. A powerful competitor may be able to bring significant financial resources to support its products or services. Therefore an existing business may decide to sidestep the new competitor by focusing on a foreign market, using the same product or service. This strategy may be the only real route to survival. If a global multinational decides to muscle in on your market, with all of the production and marketing resources it can bring, a small- to medium-sized UK business might flee. This flight could take place by moving into a foreign market.

This has often happened in the past. Ovaltine used to be an important brand in Britain (a sort of hot chocolate drink), but today is more important in Brazil and Nigeria. And a clothing fabric called Harris Tweed is now bigger in Japan, America and Germany than in Britain.

Extending the product life cycle by selling in multiple markets

Product life cycle theory implies that once a product hits its decline stage, it may be too late to save it. Those who want to extend the overall life cycle of their products may look to international sales as a successful way to boost sales. This helps to avoid the heavy investment and uncertainty involved in designing and launching a brand new product, as long as the international markets can be successfully accessed and served. In effect, launching into new territories serves as a series of extension strategies. This has been an important part of the growth of British retailers such as Ted Baker plc and SuperGroup plc.

Real business

Brompton Bicycle Ltd

Brompton Bicycle Ltd is a British-based manufacturer of folding bikes, selling mainly to affluent commuters. It has been trading for over 30 years with major UK growth happening in the late 1980s and early 1990s. As UK growth began to slow, Brompton looked overseas for other markets that would also value its products. This extension strategy proved hugely successful, allowing sales to more than double. Today the company sells to over 45 countries and in 2014 made and sold over 45,000 bikes, making it the UK's biggest bicycle manufacturer.

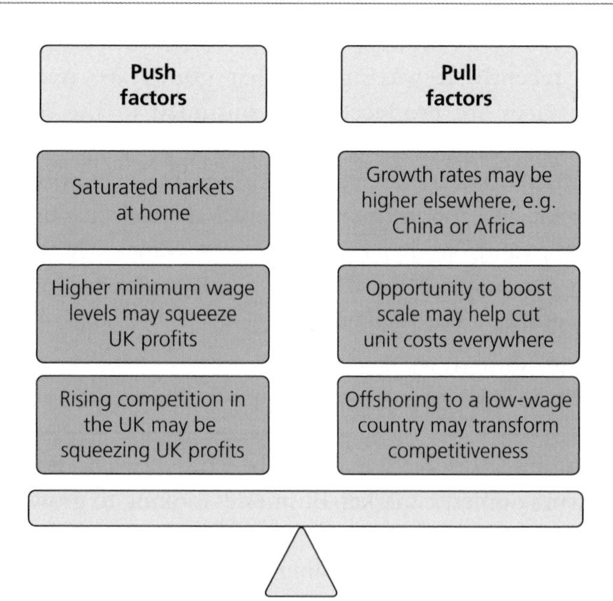

Figure 32.2 Logic balance: push and pull prompts to overseas trade

32.3 Pull factors

Sometimes the decision to trade or operate abroad is based on irresistible opportunities. Jaguar Land Rover chose to target its Evoque car on China because it saw the opportunity to price the car in China at £70,000 instead of £30,000 in the UK. And European aeroplane giant Airbus chose to set up factories in China because labour was cheaper (and to encourage Chinese airlines to buy from Airbus).

In a world of developing economies, it's fair to suggest that market opportunities are the main pull factor. But the lure of cost minimisation is also important. Key pull factors include:

- economies of scale
- possibilities for offshoring and outsourcing
- risk spreading.

Economies of scale

Often production facilities for a multinational become widespread but fragmented as the business grows into more markets. Moving production to a single site covering a whole continent, or even the global market, will allow the company to operate production on a huge scale – offering it the chance to enjoy economies of scale.

Even without centralising facilities, growing into new international markets will allow a firm to operate at a larger scale, thus gaining economies of scale. So Jaguar Land Rover's decision to build a new plant in China in addition to its existing plants in the UK provides purchasing economies of scale through bulk buying.

Possibility of offshoring and outsourcing

The terms offshoring and **outsourcing** are used quite interchangeably, but boil down to one idea: finding a lower-cost source of supply overseas than you're able to find at home. In effect that means losing jobs in the UK in favour of jobs overseas. This seems harsh, but can sometimes be a necessity: in other words, there's a possibility that a business will not survive

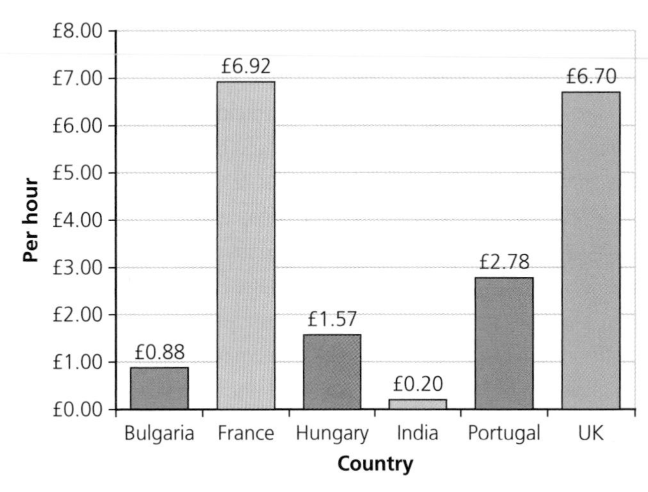

Figure 32.3 National minimum wages in selected countries (all EU except India) (sources: Eurostat and *Indian Economic Times*)

unless it switches to overseas supply. Figure 32.3 shows why British drinks multinational Diageo (Guinness, Baileys Irish Cream) decided to outsource much of its accounting and financial services work from London to Hungary back in 2002. Many others such as Aviva insurance have moved sections of their operations to India.

Offshoring usually means taking a section of your own business and relocating it to another country. This is what Aviva did when it set up a 2,500-strong unit in India in 2004 to handle insurance claims. The job losses were largely felt in and around the company's base in Norwich. Various other stages of offshoring have happened since.

> 'In the long run, outsourcing is another form of trade that benefits the US economy by giving us cheaper ways to do things.'
>
> *Janet Yellen, economist and chair of the US Federal Reserve (Central) Bank*

> 'For everything we don't want to do, there's someone out there who's really good, wants to do it and will enjoy it.'
>
> *Josh Kaufman, business author*

Real business

In May 2013, insurance group Aviva announced 600 jobs at offices in York, Sheffield and Norwich would be moved to India. The company revealed plans to cut 6 per cent of its global workforce, amounting to about 2,000 people losing their jobs. Aviva said 600 of those jobs would be 'offshored' and claimed the decision had not been taken lightly. The Unite trade union said it was an 'appalling way to treat' staff and called for the decision to be reversed. Aviva said the administrative roles would be moved to India by 2014. Aviva, which then employed about 31,000 people worldwide, was trying to reduce costs by more than £400 million.

Outsourcing usually means finding a new supplier for items that a company used to produce for itself. So instead of setting up its own factory or offices overseas, it stops doing the work itself and finds a new supplier. This happens within the UK as companies realise they're not very good at running their own cleaning or catering services. In these cases, the outsourcing is still within the UK so no jobs are lost (though wages often fall and job security may be lost). Big companies such as BT may outsource their call centre or administrative functions to specialist companies overseas, often based in India. The purpose is simple: cutting costs. See Table 32.1 for an overview of outsourcing.

Advantages over building own facilities	Disadvantages compared with building own facilities
Easier to change location quickly and cheaply	May be a lower priority for the contractor, causing delays
Far quicker to begin production – all facilities are already there	Local manufacturer's mark-up will add to costs
Easier to start production – local firms will have any local knowledge required	Control over quality can be harder to ensure
Pay and working conditions won't be compared directly with western levels – making it easier to cut costs	Customers and media will still hold you responsible for the behaviour of your subcontractors

Table 32.1 Outsourcing manufacturing abroad – from the viewpoint of a UK company

Risk spreading

A pull factor that is unrelated to costs and competitiveness is the spreading of risk. The strategy of moving into new international markets is one that allows the firm to spread the risk of demand collapsing in one particular market. A firm that sells solely to the UK may be at risk of failure if the UK's economy plunged into recession. However, if the same firm sold in a range of international markets, where economic conditions were more favourable, the risk of failure is reduced. Entering foreign markets allows a firm to avoid putting all its eggs in one basket – i.e. being totally reliant on one marketplace. This way of reducing risk is a common pull factor in prompting a business to decide to trade internationally. It is important to remember, though, that theorist Igor Ansoff has shown why market development is more challenging and therefore more risky than many businesses expect.

'Watch the *product life cycle*; but more important, watch the market life cycle.'

Phillip Kotler, business author

'India's great economic boom, the arrival of the Internet and outsourcing, have broken the wall between provincial India and the world.'

Aravind Adiga, Indian author of White Tiger

Five whys and a how

Questions	Answers
Why are some competitors best avoided?	A massive competitor can use all its financial clout to drive rivals out of business, from multi-million pound marketing campaigns to less obvious tricks such as lobbying politicians for changes in the law to favour bigger firms.
Why are so many firms desperate to sustain growth?	Shareholders in many UK plcs expect record dividends each year. This sustained growth in profits is only really achievable in the long run if revenues grow every year.
Why does trading with new foreign markets spread risk?	Over-reliance on a single market means that if there is a problem with demand in that market, the firm's total sales can collapse overnight. If a business trades in many markets, a problem in one means that the firm's overall performance will be less affected.
Why can outsourcing be a sensible route into foreign markets?	Getting local businesses to do your work for you may reduce your margins, but makes your business less likely to make the mistakes typically associated with operating in different cultures and business environments.
Why can offshoring be a mistake?	As several UK businesses have found, quality levels can slip, delivery times can be extended to impractical levels and the promised cost reductions can either fail to materialise or be eroded over time as wages rise, e.g. in China.
How can trade lead to economies of scale?	Selling to more markets means higher volumes of production are needed. It is these increases in total capacity that can prompt the reductions in cost per unit that are defined as economies of scale.

32.4 Conditions that prompt trade – evaluation

When making judgements on causes of increased foreign trade, it is usually interesting to explore the balance between push and pull factors. The decision to trade internationally is likely to be prompted by a combination of the conditions explained in this unit. In some cases, it may be hard to pinpoint exactly which of the conditions has led to the move to international trade. Generally, a healthy and successful business is likely to be prompted to 'go international' due to pull factors. Specifically, they are likely to be attracted by the opportunities offered by international trade. For firms that are struggling, the move overseas may be 'pushed' by the need to slash costs in order to survive an increasingly tough competitive environment.

All one would ask of the directors of the companies concerned is that their decision-making should bear in mind the main stakeholders, not simply the interests of the shareholders. And that the decision has been thought through in relation to the long-term consequences.

Key terms

Pull factors: positive factors overseas that entice a UK business to look outside the UK.

Push factors: negative factors within the UK that push a UK business to look overseas.

Outsourcing: contracting another business to perform a business function on your behalf. This could be anything from outsourcing catering at your school to Apple outsourcing iPhone assembly to Foxconn.

Saturated market: market where growth has ceased and there are no significant opportunities to boost sales other than stealing market share from existing rivals.

32.5 Workbook

Revision questions

(30 marks; 30 minutes)

1 From Figure 32.3 calculate the ratio of minimum wage pay in India to the level in the UK. (3)

2 Explain two possible risks to a UK firm of outsourcing its customer service call centre to a lower-wage country. (6)

3 Explain how starting to sell a product overseas can extend its life cycle. (4)

4 Explain three potential reasons why a UK business may decide to reverse a decision to offshore manufacturing. (9)

5 Assess how entering foreign markets might lead to two different types of economy of scale. (8)

Revision activities

Data response

Innocent International

Innocent Drinks, Britain's number one smoothie maker, is also Europe's number one. Its expansion into European markets was partially accidental, and partially strategic, but even then the strategy went a little wrong in several markets. Its first foreign market, when the company was only four years old, was Ireland, run from a shed in its Irish sales manager's garden. This came at a time when the company was riding the crest of a wave of sales success in the UK, with sales rocketing. The expansion to France took place in 2005, with the UK business stretched to its limits, when a distributor contacted Innocent, offering to start trying to get the products into Paris. Things went so well that the distributor could not cope with the workload and Innocent decided to employ its own sales and marketing team for France.

This model, of setting up a local team for sales, marketing and product development in each country, was one the management followed for the first few markets. However, co-founder Adam Balon said: 'the approach was only semi-successful. While invigorating local teams, it created a huge amount of navel gazing about small details that didn't matter. Certain elements of the brand's message may have played more strongly in some countries than others. But generally we found consumers were more alike than we'd expected.'

Entering Austria, and from there Germany, did bring cultural problems. Austrians tended not to be keen on the tried-and-tested distribution method of selling through independent health food stores to generate word of mouth and press coverage. Its locally employed Austrian sales manager spotted the problem and approached supermarkets directly – with significant success.

(Source: Adapted from http://realbusiness.co.uk/article/27010-innocent-drinks-co-founder-shares-his-lessons-for-international-growth, 24 June 2014)

Questions (40 marks; 45 minutes)

1 Explain the impact of Innocent's 'number one in Europe' market leadership on its unit costs. (4)

2 Assess the possible motives for Innocent's expansion to Ireland and France. (10)

3 Explain two reasons why Innocent's expansion to foreign markets experienced problems. (6)

4 All of Innocent's manufacturing is outsourced, even UK production. Evaluate the extent to which such outsourcing can cause problems for a firm with a reputation for high ethical standards. (20)

Extended writing

1 By 2020, it is expected that China will be exporting low-priced cars to Europe. This may cause BMW Mini (which produces in Oxford) to look overseas to help cut its production costs. Evaluate whether this is likely to prove a successful strategy for the business. (20)

2 'Successful international expansion is more likely to be driven by pull factors than push factors.' Evaluate this statement. (20)

33 Assessment of a country as a market

Definition

To assess a country as a market means weighing up the market strengths of one country against another.

Linked to: International trade and business growth, Ch 28; Trading blocs, Ch 31; Conditions that prompt trade, Ch 32; Assessment of a country as a production location, Ch 34; Global competitiveness, Ch 36

33.1 Introduction

British companies seeking to expand overseas have a series of decisions to make. The first is how seriously they are taking this expansion and therefore how much capital they wish to put behind it. They might decide to construct an e-commerce website that works globally, but means everything can be run from the British base (perhaps with language options covering Spanish, Mandarin, French and German as well as English). A really slick website might cost £50,000 to develop, but that's a tiny sum compared with setting up an office and hiring staff in just one overseas city. From the website you could take orders and export items globally; some clever celeb-based marketing plus effective use of global social media might ensure sales success without needing the huge cost and risk of setting up offices or subsidiaries around the world.

Effective though the above approach might be when selling fashion clothing or sportswear, there are many types of product that couldn't benefit from this approach. Could Innocent sell smoothies this way? Or McVities sell Jaffa Cakes? Not really. So if they want to expand overseas they will need to choose which countries to prioritise. Then a decision is needed on whether to build their own infrastructure locally (offices, warehouses, sales teams, delivery drivers, etc.) or whether to do a deal with a local joint venture partner or agent.

This chapter focuses on a key issue: which country or countries to prioritise – based on their **market attractiveness**.

33.2 Factors to consider in market attractiveness

You work for Innocent Drinks and your job is to decide which Eastern European country should be the first for Innocent to work in. Coca-Cola, your parent company, has provided a budget of £5 million but you must decide whether to go for Hungary, Poland or the Czech Republic. What would be the key criteria? In this case, all three are part of the European Union, so that's not a variable. But what about:

- levels and growth of disposable income
- ease of doing business
- quality of infrastructure
- political stability
- exchange rate?

Many other factors could be added in, but these five are hugely important and could form the basis for an effective decision. Ultimately you hope to produce a grid which might rank each of the three countries out of ten for each criterion – and then find the winner. It might look like Table 33.1.

1 is poor; 10 outstanding	Hungary	Poland	Czech Republic
Levels and growth of disposable income	5	7	8
Ease of doing business	6	8	8
Quality of infrastructure	7	6	8
Political stability	4	8	7
Exchange rate	5	7	6
Total	27	36	37

Table 33.1 Grid for assessing market attractiveness

So Hungary can be rejected, and because the figures for Poland and the Czech Republic are so close you might look at a few other factors including the market structure (is the fruit juice market dominated by very strong brands? If so, it might be harder to succeed) and current market prices (if juice is cheap it might be hard to find profitable niches). Despite these other factors, it is the five listed in Table 33.1 that will be our focus.

33.3 Levels and growth of disposable income

Disposable income is the amount a household has left after income taxes have been deducted. Generally it equates to GDP (national income) divided by the population size, i.e. GDP per capita. Figure 33.1 shows the differences between the Czech Republic, Hungary and Poland. Here, the implied level of disposable income is significantly higher in the Czech Republic than in the other two countries.

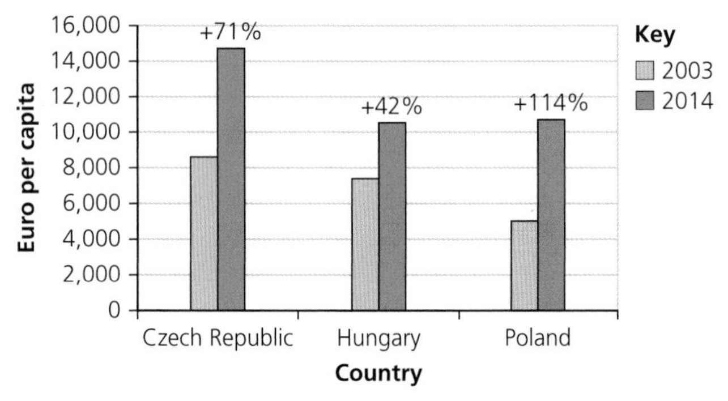

Figure 33.1 GDP per capita in three Eastern European countries in 2003 and 2014 (source: Eurostat September 2015)

The level of disposable income influences how the income is spent. In the UK, 9.6 per cent of household income is spent on restaurants and hotels. In the Czech Republic the figure is 8.4 per cent and in Poland it's just 3.1 per cent.

Figure 33.1 also gives a clear idea of the different growth rates within the three countries. For Poland to have leapfrogged Hungary since 2003 is impressive indeed; the graphic shows that it's due to Poland's terrific 114 per cent growth in per capita GDP. In the UK, the equivalent growth rate was 19.8 per cent between 2003 and 2014.

Nevertheless comparing 2014 with 2003 carries a problem: it doesn't help you analyse what happened when. The is why it's helpful to look at growth using a line graph as in Figure 33.2. This shows that Poland did hugely better than Hungary and the Czech Republic in the period 2007 to 2013 – especially in the 2009 recession. But possibly the data for 2013 and 2014 signal a recovery for Hungary and the Czech Republic. In other words, perhaps Poland's relative growth spurt is over.

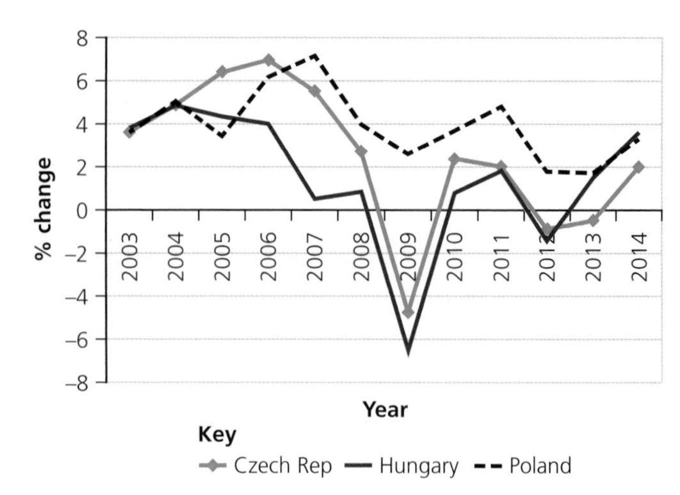

Figure 33.2 Economic growth rates in three Eastern European countries 2003–2014 (source: Eurostat 2015)

The reason the rate of growth is so important is that growth opens up opportunities. As people get wealthier, they don't just spend more, they spend differently. They switch from buying food to buying restaurant meals; and switch from buying cheap cartons of orange juice to buying freshly squeezed or smoothies. There is room for debate about whether it's better to target richer Czech Republic or faster-growing Poland; the economic data clearly rules out Hungary.

A further factor to consider is the sustainability of each country's growth rate. If a country is running large public and external deficits, it is living beyond its means and its level of GDP may not be sustainable in the long term. Table 33.2 shows that the Czech Republic is in a particularly secure position, with relatively low national debt and a positive balance of payments. The figures for the UK are there to help place the data into a wider context (they show that all three Eastern European countries have relatively stable economies).

	Current account balance (as % of GDP)	Government net debt (as a % of GDP)
Czech Republic	+1.6	43.5
Hungary	+4.8	78.2
Poland	–1.8	45.6
UK	–4.8	79.1

Table 33.2 How stable is the country's economic position? (source: Courtesy of the Central Intelligence Agency, *CIA World Factbook* 2015)

33.4 Ease of doing business

In the UK, it takes six days to set up a company and five days a year will be taken up in sorting company tax bills. In China, starting up a company takes 31 days and 11 days (solid) will be needed for the tax bills. On these criteria the UK scores much more highly than China. In fact out of 189 countries the UK comes eighth for 'ease of doing business' while China comes 90th.

What businesspeople want is to be able to do what they want, as quickly as possible and with the minimum of government involvement. In Nigeria, it takes 257 days to get electricity brought to new premises; that must be a huge disadvantage for an entrepreneur eager to get going. Also in Nigeria, it takes 34 days (and $1,960!) to get a container of items through the import regulations. Clearly there are many potential overlaps between infrastructure and 'ease of doing business'.

In a decision between Hungary, Poland and the Czech Republic, ease of doing business would be a factor. As shown in Table 33.3 there are remarkable differences between the countries. But it would be wrong to overstate the importance of some of these things; many may irritate but are unlikely to influence a decision. Does it really matter to Innocent if it takes five days to start its local company or 30? Of more importance would be the ongoing issues of days to import an item and the tax being paid on any profits. On those grounds Poland comes out on top.

	Hungary	Poland	Czech Republic
Days to start a business	5	30	19
Days for construction permit	91	212	143
Days to get electricity	252	161	129
Total tax rate (% of profit)	48%	38.7%	48.5%
Days to import an item	19	14	17
Days to enforce a contract	417	685	611

Table 33.3 Ease of doing business in three Eastern European countries (source: World Bank 2015)

33.5 Quality of infrastructure

The quality and quantity of infrastructure within a country are an important element in market attractiveness. Infrastructure is the provision of the underpinnings of modern life: roads, railways, running water, reliable electricity, Wifi and broadband connections. In some countries getting from A to B is a slow, unreliable and perhaps dangerous task.

The World Economic Forum (WEF) publishes an annual assessment of the key factors determining a country's international competitiveness. It always incorporates infrastructure. In its 2015 survey, WEF measured infrastructure on nine criteria, but the ones in Table 33.4 seem the most interesting. Note that the Czech Republic comes out quite a bit better than Poland.

Scale of 1–7 with 7 the best	Czech Republic	Hungary	Poland
Quality of roads	3.7	4.2	3.5
Quality of railways	4.5	3.8	2.9
Quality of ports/docks	4.0	3.8	4.0
Quality of electricity supply	6.4	5.9	5.5

Table 33.4 Quality of infrastructure in three Eastern European countries (source: Global Competitiveness Report 2015–16 WEF)

With a better infrastructure, goods can be transported faster and more reliably, making a just-in-time operation possible and keeping costs down and goods fresh. For a business like Innocent, this information would be very important.

> 'It is more important to do what is strategically right than what is immediately profitable.'
>
> *Philip Kotler, marketing guru*

33.6 Political stability

This is a topic that is taken for granted in a stable country such as Britain. In the Middle East and in parts of Africa, it's of vital importance. And even in Europe it matters, especially in Eastern Europe where there can still be huge policy movements between free market and communist governments. Table 33.5 shows that in 2015, businesspeople in Hungary saw policy instability as their most problematic factor in doing business. It is interesting to note that businesspeople working in Poland saw it as a minor matter compared with factors relating to bureaucracy and regulation. The table also provides an insight into the differential importance of corruption when operating in different countries. The Poles may grumble about over-regulation, but there seems to be a payoff in much lower levels of corruption.

	Average 1997–2006	2007	2008	2009	2010	2011	2012	2013	2014
Annual GDP % change	3.5	6.4	2.7	–0.8	5.0	–62.1	104.5	–13.6	–24.0

Table 33.6 Annual percentage change in Libyan real GDP (source: IMF 2015, used courtesy of The World Bank)

% saying it's a big problem	Czech Republic	Hungary	Poland
Policy instability	9.1%	15.1%	3.3%
Tax regulations	8.0%	11.0%	23.2%
Labour regulations	9.0%	1.0%	15.5%
Government bureaucracy	18.6%	10.3%	14.6%
Corruption	16.3%	13.0%	3.4%

Table 33.5 Problematic factors for doing business in three Eastern European countries (source: World Economic Forum 2015)

Making judgements about political stability is fraught with problems. No one foresaw that the attempt to achieve democracy in Egypt (eventually crushed by a military coup) would lead to the collapse of Libya. Libya had long been an important market for western businesses, especially those from Italy. Table 33.6 shows the International Monetary Fund (IMF) estimate of the changes in Libyan GDP over the period 1997–2014. The net effect was to cut Libyan living standards by more than 50 per cent between 2010 and 2014.

33.7 Exchange rates

In the long run, exchange rates move around so erratically and unpredictably that it would seem odd to hold back on an attractive market because of the exchange rate. Yes, Czech crowns might be low for a while, making it expensive to import products from the UK, but that could easily change within a year or two. Figure 33.3 shows the number of crowns a pound would buy in the two years up to September 2015. The variation from £1 = 29 crowns to £1 = 39 crowns is like the difference between paying £290 for a phone and paying £390.

So the exchange rate should not be the decider about which country to enter, but it might help decide *when* to enter. Consider the possibility that Innocent Drinks wants to buy a 39 million crown plot of land in Prague for a head office plus warehousing. In October 2013, with the pound at 29 crowns, the cost would be £1.34 million. In August 2015, with 39 crowns to the pound, it would cost £1 million. Quite a saving. So it's best to start up in a new country when the pound is strong against the local currency. It makes the start-up cheaper.

> 'When looking at market attractiveness, as well as profit, consider the probability of success, the costs involved and the timescales involved.'
>
> *www.changingminds.org*

> 'Markets change, tastes change, so the companies and the individuals who choose to compete in those markets must change.'
>
> *An Wang, Chinese computer pioneer*

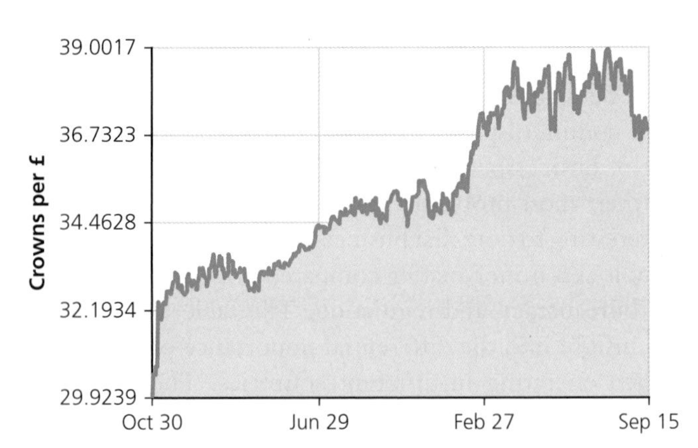

Figure 33.3 Pound sterling vs Czech crown 2013-2015 (source: www.exchangerates.org.uk)

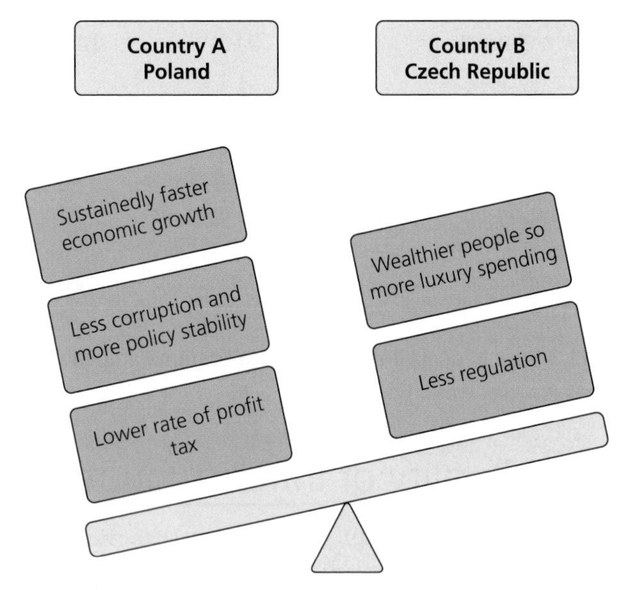

Figure 33.4 Logic balance: final decision: Poland vs Czech Republic

Five whys and a how

Questions	Answers
Why not just choose the country with the lowest input costs, e.g. wages?	Ultimately you're there for profit, so the market opportunities and potential are probably more important (or else everyone would locate in South Sudan).
Why might a business choose rich but slow-growth Germany in preference to poorer but high-growth Poland?	Some products or (especially) services only come into their own when income levels are high enough, e.g. dry-cleaning pick-up and delivery.
Why might political instability seem more important a concern than corruption?	Morally it isn't, but many businesses treat corrupt payments as a normal business expense, whereas instability – by definition – cannot easily be 'budgeted' for.
Why may a eurozone member prefer to start up in a market that's also in the euro currency area?	Because a common currency removes the uncertainties involved in exchange rate variability – business is tough enough without that.
Why might 'ease of doing business' get worse over time?	A government might decide to skew things in favour of locally owned businesses, perhaps by creating new barriers for foreign firms.
How does a firm make the final decision over Country A or Country B?	By weighing up all the numerical evidence, including investment appraisal data, and then making a judgement based on the views of the executives closest to the countries concerned.

33.8 Assessment of a country – evaluation

The idea of market attractiveness in the abstract is quite strange. It all depends on the company and its product range. Toyotas sell by the truckload in America, but far less in the UK; curiously VWs, which sell well in the UK, are a flop in the US. So whatever the overall judgement about the apparent market attractiveness of Poland over the Czech Republic (or whatever), it's vital to get some quantitative research done on the ground. The Poles may understand and like the proposition of a smoothie much more than the Czechs, in which case the final decision is an easy one. As with every question in business, it all depends on circumstances.

Key terms

Disposable income: household earnings minus direct taxes such as income tax and national insurance.

Market attractiveness: an analysis of the current and future sales and profit potential of a country or market.

33.9 Workbook

Revision questions

(30 marks; 30 minutes)

1. Explain why businesses prefer to do business in countries with relatively light government regulation. (5)
2. Look at Table 33.2 and explain the difference between the current account balance and government net debt. (4)
3. Assess two possible ways in which the quality of infrastructure would matter to a delivery business selling 'Fresh Dough Pizza'. (8)
4. Poland seems to be the most heavily regulated of the three Eastern European countries (see Table 33.5) yet has the fastest growth. Assess two possible reasons for this. (8)
5. Explain why the exchange rate is unlikely to be important in deciding on the best country to set up a business in the long term. (5)

Revision exercises

Data response

Naked in Nairobi

Naked Pizza was set up in 2006 in New Orleans, USA. 'Naked' refers to the fact that the pizzas are made from fresh natural ingredients and the mission of Naked Pizza was to provide healthy alternatives to other takeaway pizza outlets. They offer the opportunity to open franchises across America.

In 2011 Ritesh Doshi, an investment banker was visiting his parents in Nairobi, Kenya. When they had to wait 90 minutes for their takeaway pizza to be delivered he decided that wasn't good enough! He decided to move back to Nairobi and establish a franchise of Naked Pizza in the city. It was opened in 2012. This was followed in 2014 by another outlet in a prosperous neighbourhood of Nairobi.

Figure 33.5 Pizza made from fresh natural ingredients

Naked Pizza offers a variety of pizzas served on bases that contain 'pro-biotics' that promise to 'optimize nutrition and promote balance and digestive health'. A small pizza sells for 850 Kenyan shillings (about £5.80).

Doshi believes that love of pizza transcends international boundaries. He wants to capitalise on the increasing number of Kenyans who have lived abroad and are returning to the country – he believes that want the same level of convenience and quality of produce they will have experienced elsewhere.

There have been some challenges to setting up in Kenya though, he needs licenses to conduct lots of his business activities and it can be hard to source ingredients. However, he has aims to grow the business in the future.

Questions (45 marks; 50 minutes)

1. Explain why Naked Pizza may have looked for expansion overseas instead of in America. (5)
2. Assess why sourcing might be a problem when operating in less developed countries. (10)
3. Assess whether Doshi was right to use an American pizza franchise, or whether he might have been better off making it an entirely independent, local business. (10)
4. Evaluate the attractiveness to Doshi of Kenya as a market. (20)

Extended writing

1 When Tesco decided to enter the US grocery market it ended up wasting £2,000 million before having to give it away. Evaluate the main areas in which mistakes might be made when a business expands to a brand new country. (20)

2 Your 'Waffle Shop' business has mushroomed from one to 150 outlets in Britain and you think it's time to take your first step overseas. You've decided to try Italy or Sweden. Evaluate the difficulties you might have in making the right decision between the two. (20)

34 Assessment of a country as a production location

Definition

Businesses make location decisions on the basis of quantitative and qualitative factors. The quantitative factors are analysed using investment appraisal (see Chapter 12); this chapter focuses on the broader economic and business factors.

Linked to: Investment appraisal, Ch 12; International trade and business growth, Ch 28; Trading blocs, Ch 31; Conditions that prompt trade, Ch 32; Assessment of a country as a market, Ch 33; Global competitiveness, Ch 36; The impact of multinational corporations, Ch 40

34.1 Introduction

Many businesses will quite regularly weigh up the pros and cons of opening up a production location overseas. Some are looking to take advantage of offshoring, while others may already be **multinational** in their structure, or are growing at a pace that marks them out as future multinationals. A wide range of factors will need to be considered when selecting the right country as a production location. Not all of them are obviously linked to the cost of production, though that is where most firms start their assessment.

34.2 Costs of production

For most businesses considering setting up production operations in a new country, a major motive is to find a lower cost base for manufacturing. As a result companies want data on the costs of production relative to their existing locations. In 2014, a report by the Boston Consulting Group showed the overall cost of manufacturing in different countries compared with America – and measured the changes since 2004. They included labour, electricity, gas and other costs and the results were shown in index form, with the figures for America equalling 100. The labour cost data takes into account the productivity of the labour (as it should). Table 34.1 shows, for example, that China was 13.5 per cent more cost-competitive than America in 2004, but only 4.4 per cent in 2014. Indonesia and India, by contrast, have tended to maintain their cost advantages.

Country	Indexed manufacturing costs 2004 (USA = 100)	Indexed manufacturing costs 2014 (USA = 100)
China	86.5	95.6
Germany	117.4	121.1
Japan	107.2	111
UK	107.4	108.7
Indonesia	82.3	83.1
India	86.8	87.2
Mexico	92.1	91.5

Table 34.1 Boston Consulting Group data on manufacturing costs in selected countries relative to the cost of manufacturing in the USA (source: www.bcgperspectives.com)

'We are a much more flourishing company now because of what we did and it's doubtful if we could have survived in the long term if we had not done so.'

Sir James Dyson reflecting on his decision to shift manufacturing of Dyson cleaners from the UK to Malaysia

In fact, though, labour costs are not necessarily as important an element in total costs as you might expect. Figure 34.1 shows the composition of the total costs of Jaguar Land Rover in 2014. Given the low proportion of costs that are labour, is there really a strong reason to shift production to lower labour countries?

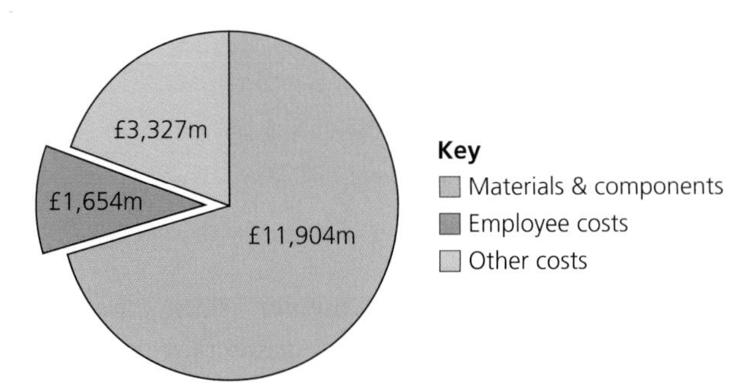

Figure 34.1 Jaguar Land Rover cost breakdown 2014 (source: JLR accounts; all figures in £ms; total costs: £16,885m)

34.3 Skills and availability of workforce

Most manufacturing requires a significant level of skill, even semi-skilled work operating sewing machines or assembling electronic goods such as mobile phones. In addition, manufacturing workers in a modern factory need strong enough literacy to read instructions and safety notices. So businesses cannot take it for granted that there will be sufficient staff with the right qualities to make a production location viable. Research carried out by the McKinsey Global Institute indicates that the global economy is likely to be facing a skills shortage over the coming decade. Key issues reported include:

- '38 million to 40 million fewer workers with tertiary education (university or postgraduate degrees) than employers will need, or 13 per cent of the demand for such workers'
- '45 million too few workers with secondary education in developing economies, or 15 per cent of the demand for such workers'
- '90 million to 95 million more low-skill workers (those without college training in advanced economies or without even secondary education in developing economies) than employers will need, or 11 per cent oversupply of such workers'.

(*Source:* Exhibit from 'The world at work: Jobs, pay, and skills for 3.5 billion people', June 2012, McKinsey Global Institute, (www.mckinsey.com) www.mckinsey.com. Copyright © 2012 McKinsey & Company. All rights reserved. Reprinted by permission)

These facts make it clear that global businesses looking for a production location will need to ensure that they identify countries where the pool of labour offers a sufficiently high level of education in order to ensure that the promised benefits of potentially lower cost manufacturing can occur.

34.4 Infrastructure

For companies considering choosing production locations in less economically developed countries, where costs may be lowest, the quality of local infrastructure must be carefully considered. For some major production facilities, the company building the factory will also build local infrastructure in their chosen location. For example, steelworks can be so huge that they have their own railway system to take hugely heavy materials and finished product to different parts of the factory complex. (N.B. Infrastructure was dealt with in more detail in Chapter 33.)

> 'Smart businesses do not look at labour costs alone anymore. They do look at market access, transportation, telecommunications infrastructure and the education and skill level of the workforce, the development of capital and the regulatory market.'
>
> *Janet Napolitano, American politician*

34.5 Location in a trading bloc

Trading blocs, such as the European Union, allow free trade to take place between members of the bloc. This is important to firms looking to establish a production location from which to sell to other major markets. So, for example, a Japanese firm looking to sell to any European Union market can do so without incurring tariffs – which is why Nissan, Honda and Toyota built manufacturing plants in the UK in the 1980s and 1990s – in order to access the whole EU market. The EU is not the world's only trading bloc. (See Chapter 31.)

Trading bloc	Member countries
ASEAN (Association of South East Asian Nations)	Brunei Darussalam, Cambodia, Indonesia, Laos, Malaysia, Myanmar, Philippines, Singapore, Thailand and Vietnam
EU (European Union)	Austria, Belgium, Bulgaria, Croatia, Cyprus, Czech Republic, Denmark, Estonia, Finland, France, Germany, Greece, Hungary, Ireland, Italy, Latvia, Lithuania, Luxembourg, Malta, Poland, Portugal, Romania, Slovakia, Slovenia, Spain, Sweden, the Netherlands, and the United Kingdom
MERCOSUR (Mercado Común del Sur – Southern Cone Common Market)	Argentina, Brazil, Paraguay, Uruguay and Venezuela.
NAFTA (North American Free Trade Agreement)	Canada, Mexico and USA

Table 34.2 The world's four major trading blocs, with member countries as at 2015 shown

'You guys have got to stay in the EU. You're the only sane ones there.'

An unnamed US Government official

34.6 Government incentives

Many national governments will be keen to attract foreign investment, in other words encourage foreign firms to choose their country as the place to build new manufacturing facilities. Incentives may include grants to help purchase land and machinery, tax breaks and investment in local infrastructure. Attracting foreign production facilities should bring jobs, tax revenues and other benefits to their country – thus explaining why governments may be keen to offer incentives to businesses to locate in their country.

Real business

In September 2015, Europe's hugely successful Airbus opened its first US factory in Mobile, Alabama. In the vast 210,000 sq. ft hangar the Airbus A320 will be assembled. Each retails at around $100 million and when maximum production is reached in 2017, four will roll off the production line per month. Airbus needs the extra capacity because it has global orders for over 5,000 of these planes. But why is Europe's Airbus opening a factory in America?

One chunky reason is $150 million in tax incentives, offered by Alabama. So Airbus won't be paying local and state taxes until the $150 million allowance is used up. The two other main factors are to do with staff and potential customers. Quite a number of US airlines buy Airbus planes, but others (such as the massive South West Airlines) only buy Boeing. It always makes a better story to say 'we buy American to protect American jobs'. Now airlines can buy Airbus and protect Alabama jobs. And then there's the staffing issue. Perhaps surprisingly, labour in Alabama is significantly cheaper than in Europe, and as another incentive, the Alabama State is paying the training bill for up to 1,000 locals.

34.7 Ease of doing business

In order to run a business, certain basic legal and other systems must be in place. The Doing Business Project, set up by the World Bank, considers the following factors when drawing up its index of the ease of doing business in different countries:

- ease of starting a business
- ease of receiving construction permits
- getting electricity
- registering property
- getting credit
- protecting minority investors
- enforcing contracts
- resolving insolvency
- ease of exporting.

Many of these issues will involve some level of **bureaucracy**. Efficient systems of bureaucracy will make a country an attractive location. The ease or speed with which these basics of doing business can be accomplished in a potential production location will affect its attractiveness. Table 34.3 shows the overall global ranking for selected countries in the 2015 Doing Business Rankings.

Global ranking	Country	Global ranking	Country
1	Singapore	14	Germany
2	New Zealand	39	Mexico
3	Hong Kong	90	China
4	Denmark	114	Indonesia
5	South Korea	142	India
7	USA	170	Nigeria
8	UK	173	Bangladesh

Table 34.3 Overall global ranking for selected countries in the 2015 Doing Business Rankings (source: www.doingbusiness.org/rankings)

Figure 34.2 Singapore is first in the Doing Business Rankings

34.8 Political stability

The role of governments in setting laws, tax levels and trade policies means that a stable system of government is a major consideration for companies looking to locate production abroad. In some countries, governments change a little too regularly to provide a stable legal and business environment, perhaps due to faulty democratic systems or the overthrow of regimes by the military. Although these problems may seem common in less economically developed nations, even seemingly well developed countries, such as the Ukraine, can undergo tremendous political instability. War in the

Eastern Ukraine has made the country virtually a no-go area for companies looking to move production facilities abroad. For further detail, see Chapter 33.

34.9 Natural resources

For businesses at early stages in the supply chain, local sources of natural resources are vital, especially given the tendency for these resources to be bulky and expensive to transport long distances. Therefore, locating close to an abundant supply of the natural resources required for the production process makes great sense. This is why processes that needed coal in the UK originally clustered around the coalfields of South Wales and Yorkshire. Figure 34.3 shows the huge bulk of raw materials needed to make 1 tonne of 'pig iron' (from which steel is made). Now, huge mining companies place processing facilities close to extraction facilities to reduce transportation costs of the bulkiest materials in the supply chain.

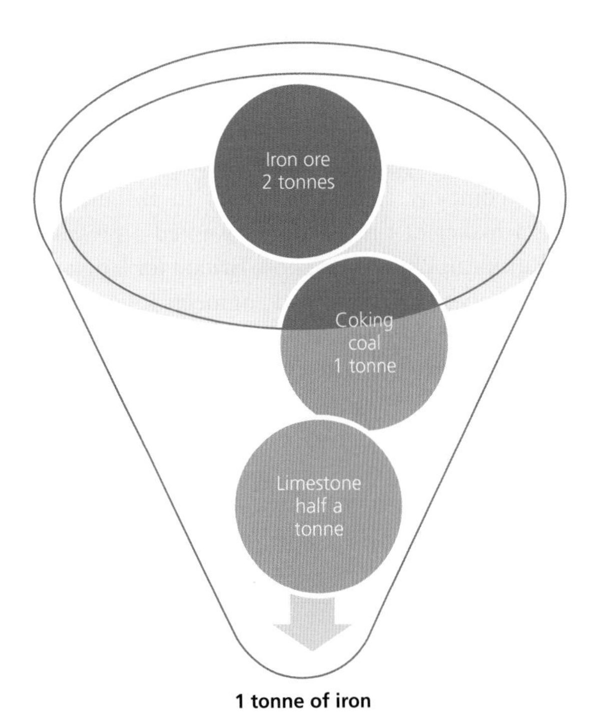

Figure 34.3 Logic chain: keeping steel production close to coal and iron ore mines

34.10 Likely return on investment

Ultimately, most business decisions are made according to the likely return on investment generated by each option being considered. When choosing a production location, lower costs are going to boost return on investment because profits will be larger each year that costs stay low. However, the equation may not simply be based on the costs of the location. A company that is able to access new foreign markets easily through choosing a production location in a trading bloc may be able to increase revenues significantly. This is because sales volumes should rise and there's also a real possibility of finding overseas markets where prices can be higher. Thus, although a cheap location may seem

Five whys and a how

Questions	Answers
Why might the cheapest location not be the best?	Although cost will be a strong feature in decision-making, other, qualitative issues such as the ease of doing business and political stability may mean the cheapest production location is not the best choice. In addition, cheaper locations may not generate the same revenues as more expensive locations in a country with stronger domestic demand for example.
Why is it easier to do business in some countries than others?	Laws covering what businesses can and cannot do vary between different nations. In addition, the extent to which those laws are actually enforced may differ. Businesses tend to favour nations where legal systems are embedded and protect their interests. Yet, ironically, they like consumers and employees to have very light legal protections.
Why do countries with low production costs often score less well on other location factors?	This is market forces at work. A country offering great infrastructure and a highly skilled workforce is likely to have higher standards of living – meaning that wage, material and land costs are also higher.
Why does EU membership make a country look attractive as a production location?	As part of the EU, any products manufactured within the EU can be exported to any other EU country without any trade restrictions or taxes.
Why have the costs of manufacturing in China risen over the past ten years?	As the standard of living in China has risen, and the pool of labour moving from the countryside to factories in cities has reduced, wage rates (and living standards) have risen dramatically.
How do firms make quantitative decisions on the best production location?	Investment appraisal techniques such as payback, ARR and NPV are likely to be the main quantitative techniques used, although other techniques such as break-even analysis or decision trees may also be used.

likely to give a higher return on investment, decisions on production locations should also consider the likely impact of the decision on revenues in the future.

There are also qualitative factors to consider. The first ever Japanese company to start a factory in Britain was Nittan UK, a maker of fire alarms. It wanted a presence within the European Union and chose Britain for language reasons. The Japanese managers and engineers knew some English, but no other European language. And why choose Woking, Surrey? Partly because it's near Heathrow airport and partly because there are lots of golf courses nearby. When explaining this, the Japanese managing director was quite embarrassed that the location reasons were so unbusinesslike. But it has served the company well; Nittan has been in the same premises for nearly 50 years.

34.11 Assessment of a country as a production location – evaluation

In many cases, the most important factor considered when choosing a production location will be costs of production. Sensible firms will produce sophisticated calculations of cost of production, bearing in mind infrastructure strengths and weaknesses as well as labour costs, energy costs and local tax regimes.

The purpose of gaining accurate cost information is to use it as part of the investment appraisal calculations. For these one also needs to know the revenue flows and the initial cost of setting up the factory or service centre. Then, having calculated the ARR and the NPV, qualitative factors can be considered.

One theme, however, that emerges from the data in Table 34.1 is that the relative attractiveness of production locations changes over time. The real skill to choosing the best location is to be able to forecast future production costs and revenues to be generated over the potential lifetime of the production facilities. The impossibility of getting this right with any consistency emphasises that location decisions are always high risk.

Key terms

Bureaucracy: from the French word for desk or office, a business or government that's bound up in rules – often strangling initiative and enterprise.

Multinational: a company based in one country but with operations in many.

34.12 Workbook

Revision questions

(35 marks; 35 minutes)

1 State three costs of production a firm may hope to lower by relocating production from the UK to a less economically developed nation. (3)

2 List three trading blocs. (3)

3 State three services that would be included as part of the term infrastructure. (3)

4 State three factors that affect the ease of doing business in a particular country. (3)

5 State three possible incentives governments may offer companies considering building a new factory. (3)

6 Use the data in Table 34.1 to identify two countries that became more attractive as manufacturing locations between 2004 and 2014. Briefly explain your answer. (4)

7 Explain why locating a factory inside a trading bloc may boost forecasted returns on investment for a business. (4)

8 From Figure 34.1, calculate the percentage that staff costs represent of all Jaguar Land Rover's costs. (4)

9 Assess why a decision by the UK to leave the EU might lead to some UK factory closures. (8)

Revision activities

Data response

British clothing manufacturer Superdry is considering building a brand new factory as part of a strategy to boost market share in the USA. This will be the company's first factory on the other side of the Atlantic and the choice has been narrowed down to two possible options.

Option A – Mexico

Following a path that many European firms have followed, Mexico will offer a relatively stable political environment and a large pool of suitably skilled labour. With transport costs to the US market relatively low, Superdry would also benefit from Mexico's membership of NAFTA. The availability of highly skilled workers means that factory defect rates should be no more than 1 per cent.

Option B – Venezuela

With a growing clothing manufacturing sector, the current Venezuelan government is keen to offer incentives to foreign manufacturers to locate there. Some Superdry staff have noted the ease with which this location would allow the firm to enter the huge Brazilian market in the future. However, the greater distance to the US market would add five days to delivery times. The availability of skilled workers means that factory defect rates should be no more than 4 per cent.

Financial data for the two options is shown in Table 34.4.

	Mexico	Venezuela
Variable costs per unit (£) (excludes transport)	3.30	2.45
Transport cost per unit to US (£)	0.20	0.35
Fixed costs per year (£m)	5.7	4
Average (ex factory) selling price per unit (£)	13	11
Tariff per unit for importing goods to the US (£)	0	0.2

Table 34.4 Financial data for Mexico and Venezuela

Questions (40 marks; 45 minutes)

1 Calculate the break-even point for both factories. (10)

2 Assess the main factors other than costs that should be considered when making the decision. (10)

3 Based on all the information available, evaluate which site the directors of Superdry should choose. (20)

Extended writing

1 'Although many factors may be considered when selecting a country in which to locate new production facilities, most major multinationals base their decisions on the lowest cost location.' Evaluate this statement. (20)

2 China is no longer the lowest cost choice for most multinationals looking to build factories in Asia. Evaluate why so many still choose China as a production location. (20)

35 Reasons for global mergers or joint ventures

Definition

A global merger is an agreement between two companies from different countries to join forces permanently; a joint venture is an agreement to work together on a specific project or region for a specified time (such as ten years).

Linked to: Mergers and takeovers, Chapter 9, International trade and business growth, Ch 28; Trading blocs, Ch 31; Conditions that prompt trade, Ch 32; Assessment of a country as a production location, Ch 34; Global competitiveness, Ch 36

35.1 Introduction

In September 2015, the Dutch giant Philips announced that it would sell off its lighting division to focus on 'digital health': collecting and analysing huge amounts of data about people's wellbeing. The company suggested that the global market for medical technology was already worth more than £100 billion a year, including consumer products such as Fitbit plus more complex diagnostic systems.

For Philips, the future will see more co-operation between traditional pharmaceutical companies and digital healthcare businesses. With that in mind it formed a **joint venture** with Teva, the giant Israeli drug maker. Together they will invest in digital healthcare start-ups. Just a month before, in August 2015, American Google announced a tie-up with French pharmaceutical heavyweight Sanofi. Their rationale was the same – linking digital expertise to pharmaceuticals. At the same time Panasonic Healthcare of Japan spent €1 billion buying the diabetes-monitoring division from Bayer of Germany. Each of these corporate tie-ups features companies from different countries – all pursuing the same global market opportunities.

When companies see value in joining forces with others (often their rivals) they have a straight choice between a permanent arrangement via takeover/merger, or a less permanent joint venture. Getting this decision right is the subject of this chapter.

> 'The time of big mergers is over, for the moment, but we can see more strategic alliances of the Renault and Nissan kind.'
>
> *Patrick Solaro, French commentator*

35.2 Spreading risk over different countries/regions

Years ago, Jaguar cars sold primarily in two markets: the UK and the US. They were manufactured in the UK and nearly half were shipped to America. Then, in 1980, UK interest rates as high as 15 per cent caused the pound to leap in value to $2.40, making Jaguars hopelessly expensive in the US. At the same time, the high interest rates caused a savage recession in the UK, causing home sales of Jaguars to collapse. Squeezed on both sides, the company collapsed too, causing huge numbers of job losses.

The bitter memory of 1980 led many companies to say never again. Many British engineering companies such as Rolls Royce, JCB and GKN started building factories overseas, to be less dependent on the pound. Oddly, Jaguar stayed British only until the 2008 takeover of the business by Indian-owned Tata Motors. Since then there has been investment in a Jaguar Land Rover factory in China and in Brazil. The logic is simple: if you have production bases in several countries, the ups and downs of the foreign exchange market will largely cancel themselves out. Whereas if you only produce in the UK but export half your output, a rising pound hits your competitiveness and your profit margins.

Spreading risk is also an important strategic move in terms of sales. In the first quarter of 2015, sales of Apple products slipped in one of the company's biggest markets: Japan. They fell from $4,047 million in 2014 to $3,457 million in 2015, causing profits in Japan to fall. Fortunately a sales boom in China smoothed over the disappointment in Japan. In just three months, Apple sales in China were $16,823 million, an amazing rise of $7,000 million compared with the same first three months of 2014. Operating in several markets can help you through the bad times in one region, e.g. the eurozone in 2012–2014.

35.3 Entering new markets/ trade blocs

When a UK business looks to expand internationally, it faces a dilemma. Should it set up its own operation in – let us say – China, or should it rely on local people with local expertise? A joint venture is often the solution. This is usually a 50/50 agreement to co-operate in a specific venture within a specific country for a limited period of time (five years, perhaps, or ten years). When Burberry first went to China, this is exactly how it operated. Later, when it realised that its China operation could become the heart of its future strategy, it bought out its Chinese joint venture partners. The net effect has been hugely beneficial to the company. A joint venture has the advantage of local expertise plus clear financial incentives for the local partner, without the UK company risking losing control of this branch of its operations. As a method of growth, it is tried, tested and very widely used.

In China, there is little alternative to operating a joint venture as the Chinese government will not allow foreigners to take over a large Chinese business. In Britain, by contrast, it's amazingly easy to buy up even a British business icon. In 2010, US Kraft bought Cadbury. In 2014, Turkey's Yildiz biscuit business bought United Biscuits plc including brands such as McVities Digestives, Hobnobs, Jaffa Cakes and many more. At one fell swoop (and £2 billion) Yildiz bought itself market leadership in the UK plus sales and distribution channels worldwide. Going the other way, in May 2015, UK company Just Eat plc paid £450 million for the Australian online fast food ordering business Menulog. Just Eat wanted to consolidate its position as the world's number one online delivery business by making a serious entry into the Australian fast food sector.

Businesses that are looking to access new markets face a choice between three options:

- do it organically (go in and build up slowly, learning from your mistakes along the way)
- look for a locally based joint venture partner (but will you ever learn enough about the local market?)
- look for a local business to buy up (but if you lack local knowledge, do you really know enough to buy the right company? In 2011, Thai steelmaker SSI bought the huge Redcar steelworks. In 2015, it closed it down and liquidated the business. It hadn't known how difficult it would be to run this plant profitably).

Real business

Joint ventures don't always work. After several years of court cases, in September 2015, Suzuki bought back the 120 million Suzuki shares bought in 2009 by Volkswagen as part of a joint venture arrangement. Suzuki was attractive to VW because it was (and is) the market leader in the fast-growing Indian car market. The VW/Suzuki partnership was supposed to cover technology, especially fuel efficiency, and India – but soon after the deal was made, disagreements broke out. Suzuki accused VW of failing to share information while VW objected to Suzuki's deal to buy diesel engines from Fiat. Court cases began in 2011 and finished when the joint venture was dissolved in 2015.

35.4 Acquiring national/ international brand names/ patents

When, long ago, Nestlé (of Switzerland) bought the British chocolate maker Rowntree, it wasn't particularly interested in the UK market or the factories in York. It wanted KitKat, After Eight and Quality Street – brands that it has transformed from a British to global presence. In Japan, KitKat is famous for having launched 200 flavour varieties since 2000 (I think I'll pass on 'European cheese', 'green tea' and 'red bean sandwich').

In recent years, there has continued to be a steady stream of overseas companies buying British brands. Many of these brands have a history that gives them credibility globally. What follows is a short list of who's bought what.

Nationality of purchaser	Company purchasing	British brands acquired	When acquired
India	Tata Motors	Jaguar Land Rover	2008 (for £1.15bn)
America	Kraft Foods	Cadbury, Bourneville, Creme Eggs, etc.	2010 (for £11.9bn)
China	Bright Foods	Weetabix	2012 (for £1bn)
Japan	Suntory	Ribena, Lucozade	2013 (for £1.35bn)
America	Coca-Cola	Innocent Drinks	2013 (undisclosed, but perhaps £300m)
Turkey	Yildiz	McVities, Jacobs, Jaffa Cakes	2014 (for £2bn)
America	Middleby or Whirlpool (both US)	Aga cookers	2015 (battle for Aga unresolved as at September 2015; approx. £150m)

Table 35.1 Who's been buying our brands?

Acquiring patents can be another important spur to global takeovers or mergers. The world's biggest pharmaceutical company is Teva of Israel. It was facing a probable collapse in its profits as one of its major drugs was coming out of patent in 2014. When drug patents lapse (as they will do after 20 years), manufacturers of **generic products** usually rush in with a chemically identical copy, resulting in a collapse in the price. Knowing this was inevitable, Teva looked around for young companies with newly patented drugs that it could buy up. In 2014, Teva paid $140 million for Nupathe, a lossmaking American pharmaceutical business with a patented system for treating migraines (called Zelrix). For Teva, this was a strategy of buying a potential rising star to make up for the cash cow that was about to become a dog.

Among the world's classic patents are:

- Cat's Eyes, the reflective road markings patented by Percy Shaw of Halifax, Yorkshire and used globally
- The intermittent windscreen wiper (the inventor patented it in 1964, then successfully sued Ford and Chrysler when they introduced the idea from 1969 onwards)
- 'Stay-tab' openings for aluminium cans, invented in 1975 in America and still used globally.

35.5 Securing resources and supplies

Such is the openness of the UK economy that few of our companies would feel they need to make a huge effort to secure supplies. Many of the world's commodities trade through the City of London and the UK has trading arrangements with every country in the world (perhaps excepting North Korea).

In the past, things were different; the whole economic set-up of the British Empire was to secure resources for UK firms and to prevent competitors from obtaining them (and to keep manufacturing in Britain and to force our colonies to only produce primary products such as raw materials). Today, China – and, to a lesser extent India – think in that same way. Between 2000 and 2015, China made significant investments into Africa and Brazil in order to secure resources – especially minerals such as copper and iron ore. But although there have been many articles on 'Chinese imperialism' the fact remains that the main investors in Africa are wealthy countries such as America, Britain, Japan and Belgium.

Where it becomes more important to secure your supplies is when the supplying organisations are operating with disregard for ethical standards. If your cocoa supplier in Ghana is using child labour – despite your regular inspections – it may be necessary to make a **backwards vertical takeover** (see Chapter 9) by buying up your supplier. Only then could you be sure that your suppliers meet the standards that you may wish to boast about on your pack or website.

35.6 Maintaining/increasing global competitiveness

Many businesses believe that scale is critical to long-term survival. They suspect that those with a small market share will suffer declining profitability due to the absence of economies of scale. In the UK in 2015, the most consistent strategy in retailing was to cut down on product lines. The success of Lidl and Aldi persuaded retailers from Tesco to B&Q to cut stockholding costs and to increase bulk-buying power by cutting out slow-selling product lines. Clearly this threatens the survival of niche brands; without distribution a brand is nothing.

With all this in view, and in a global marketplace, it seems to make sense to build scale by joining with overseas rivals: by merger/takeover or by joint ventures. In July 2015, the British engineering company GKN plc paid a bit over £500 million for Fokker Technologies – a German producer of aircraft parts. This was a clever purchase because it consolidated GKN's position in an area where it was already strong. It knew Fokker's business well, because it had been a competitor; now it would be an important part of GKN's status as one of the main suppliers to both the world's great aeroplane manufacturers: Boeing and Airbus.

GKN also uses joint ventures from time to time as a way to expand. In July 2015, it announced that its Powder Metallurgy Division had agreed a joint venture with a local company in China's Hebei Province. The new venture will be the first producer of international grade ferrous powders in China – which will make it an important supplier for GKN's own manufacturing plants in the Far East.

35.7 Real challenges from global growth via merger or venture

It's easy to think it's easy. Take two businesses that share an ambition; get them to work together. In fact it's amazingly difficult. With joint ventures the fundamental problem is that it's time-limited. Both sides know the venture will end in the future; so both are tempted to get more out of it than the other. Imagine United and City forming a single Manchester Youth Academy ('Merging two of the world's greatest clubs to create the world's greatest youth set-up'). Each side would work against each other as much as with each other. It wasn't really very different for Burberry when it had a joint venture with a Chinese retail business. Both sides wanted a 'fair share' of the overall profits but didn't agree on what was fair. Many joint ventures end with messy, premature divorces.

While takeovers and mergers are permanent and therefore haven't got the problems of the joint venture, they have their own difficulties. History shows that even within Britain, the biggest curse on mergers comes from clashing corporate cultures ('We are entrepreneurial and growth-orientated; you are cautious, bureaucratic and, well, dull.') Imagine how much harder it must be to overcome cultural problems between companies from different countries. It can be done successfully, as in the case of Renault and Nissan, but so often there's a problem. The business disaster that was the merger between German Mercedes and American Chrysler probably cost more than $100 billion. American Hewlett-Packard's $10 billion losses over its purchase of British Autonomy plc is on a smaller scale, but still a disaster. And then there's the RBS/NatWest $50 billion takeover of the Dutch bank ABN Amro, following which RBS had to be bailed out by the British government.

In the 'logic target' diagram you can see the stages involved in getting two organisations working as one.

Real business

In 2012, after a boom in its sales to China, Jaguar Land Rover (JLR) entered into a 50/50 joint venture with the Chinese car maker Chery Automobile. The purpose was to build a factory in China to manufacture JLR models, especially the hugely popular Evoque. Chery's understanding of local suppliers and local working practices would help get the factory up and running faster and more efficiently than if JLR did it on its own. By late 2014 the factory was ready to start test runs and in 2015 it started producing cars. A huge benefit of the factory was to avoid the 50–75 per cent tariffs China places on imported luxury cars. This would help JLR's competitiveness in China – the world's largest car market.

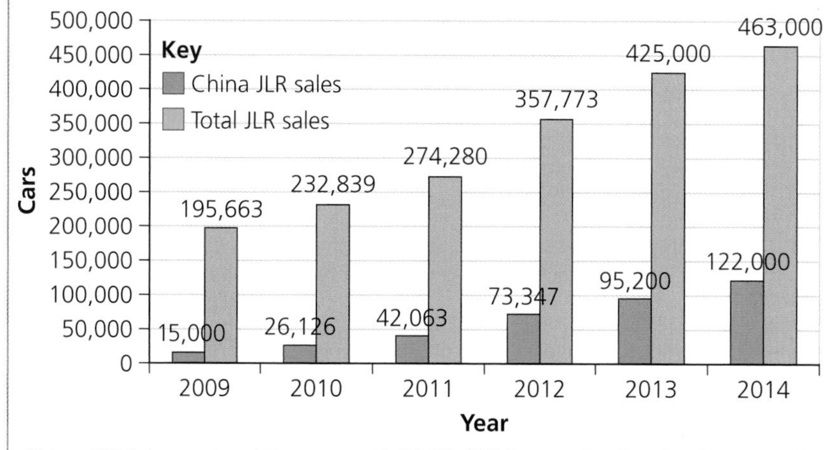

Figure 35.1 Jaguar Land Rover growth 2009–2014: annual unit sales (source: JLR press releases and financial statements)

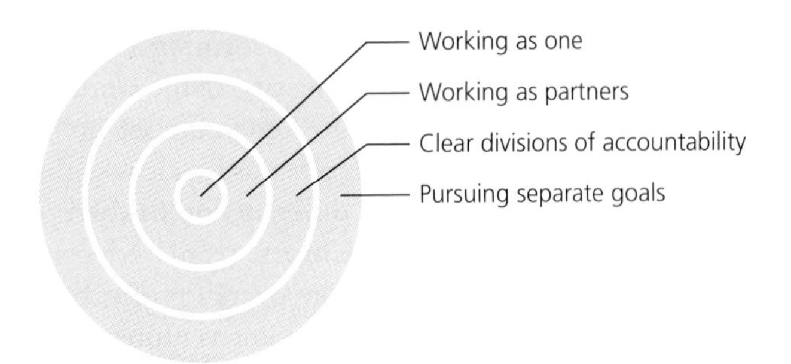

Figure 35.2 Logic target: challenges getting two organisations working together

'This joint venture represents an important expansion of GKN's long established working relationship with China.'

GKN press release

'Successful enterprises are built from the ground up. You can't assemble them with a bunch of acquisitions.'

Louis Gerstner, former CEO, IBM

'Every time you make a merger, somebody is losing his identity. And saying something different is just rubbish.'

Carlos Ghosn, CEO Nissan/Renault

35.8 Reasons for global mergers – evaluation

It would be nice to think that major business decisions, perhaps involving billions of pounds, are logical and far-sighted. Some are, of course, such as JCB's joint ventures in Japan and China. But a remarkable number bear no scrutiny at all. RBS bought an indebted Dutch bank for £50 billion without having undertaken 'due diligence' (a careful look at the books). HSBC bought Household – a US sub-prime lender – for £10 billion and ended up writing off the entire sum. Global mergers make sense only if a business has the right strategy; that's rarely about diversification – the most successful strategy is to use takeovers and mergers to strengthen your position within an existing market. Competition authorities, of course, may object – but it's the job of business to push for what suits it best; if government steps in, so be it.

Key terms

Backwards vertical takeover: buying a business in the same industry but at an earlier stage in the supply chain, e.g. bakery buys flour mill.

Generic products: generic products are undifferentiated; in the case of pharmaceuticals they'll be chemically identical.

Joint venture: a legal agreement between two businesses to work together on a specific project; in the context of this chapter it's a venture between companies from different countries.

Five whys and a how

Questions	Answers
Why do businesses feel the need to go from national to global?	In an ideal world, an international merger could bring new ideas and create new opportunities for both sides.
Why might an overseas joint venture (JV) be better than a takeover or merger?	JVs can be used as a test market; Burberry used a JV partner in China for five years, then bought it out (took it over) when it was sure that China had great potential.
Why might a merger be better than a JV?	A merger is for life, so even though there may be teething problems, eventually all staff should see they share a common purpose.
Why might organic growth be better for overseas expansion than either merger or JV?	Look at Fever-Tree's amazing organic international growth (75 per cent of sales are exports); as expressed in the quote from Lou Gerstner, you can't build a successful enterprise with acquisitions.
Why may the topic of mergers and joint ventures be supplanted by a new digital world?	Online businesses of the future may need fewer mergers, as businesses such as Amazon and Google are so dominant on their own.
How might a business maximise its chances of success by merger or JV?	By doing a huge amount of preparatory research and then holding several business and social meetings to make sure that the cultures don't conflict.

35.9 Workbook

Revision questions

(30 marks; 30 minutes)

1 a) Look at Figure 35.1 and calculate the percentage of Jaguar Land Rover's sales achieved in China in 2014 compared with 2009. (4)

b) Explain how this change may have influenced JLR's decision to form a joint venture with Chery Automotive. (4)

2 Explain how a business could use a merger to spread risk within its business operation. (4)

3 Explain two possible ways in which an overseas joint venture could be used to secure supplies for Bremont, one of Britain's leading manufacturers of expensive watches. (6)

4 Table 35.1 shows some of the British brands bought up in recent years by overseas companies. Explain the possible implications for the UK's international competitiveness. (4)

5 After many years of sales growth, sales of the UK-produced BMW Mini flattened in 2014 and 2015. Explain how a joint venture might be used to help boost the Mini's international competitiveness. (4)

6 Explain why the pursuit of global growth through takeover/merger can be hard, even for a business as large and experienced as McDonald's. (4)

Revision activities

Data response

Extract A

SuperGroup plc (trading as Superdry) press release, July 2015

'Following the appointment of Euan Sutherland as CEO in October 2014, we have developed and launched a new long-term strategic plan focusing on three key areas – to build a global lifestyle brand; to drive awareness of the breadth of the Superdry range; and to build a broad cross-channel relationship with customers. We are also focusing hard on our four key product attributes – design detail; quality obsession; innovation; and affordability.

In March 2015, SuperGroup announced the acquisition of our North American business from a former joint venture partner, which immediately gave us an estate of 15 stores and around 250 employees, with revenues of nearly $36 million. We have a structured plan in place to drive a substantial expansion plan across the US, Canada and Mexico by 2020. In July 2015 we announced the creation of a joint venture business in China, in partnership with the established Chinese retailer Trendy International, giving us a solid platform for a major entry into the Chinese market.'

Extract B

Punchline: Gloucestershire means business, July 2015

Figure 35.3 Superdry store

'Cheltenham-based fashion retailer SuperGroup plc has signed a ten-year 50:50 partnership contract with Chinese rival Trendy International Group. The deal has seen both companies invest a combined amount of £18 million with SuperGroup entering the Chinese market in a controlled and managed way "without imposing significant organisational demand".

The company, famous for its Superdry and Cult Clothing brands said: "The two key drivers of our growth are international expansion and improving efficiency. China is a very exciting market and forecast to overtake the US as the largest apparel and footwear market in the world. Customer tastes are evolving from luxury brands to brands influenced by 'pop' culture and we believe that the Superdry brand, with the right product, pricing model and infrastructure, is well positioned to be successful.

"The most appropriate model for us to enter this market is to join forces with an established Chinese company and as such we have agreed a ten-year minimum 50:50 joint venture with Trendy International Group."'

Questions (40 marks; 50 minutes)

1 Explain the likely reason for SuperGroup buying out its American partner. (4)

2 Given the goals outlined in the first paragraph of Extract A, assess whether SuperGroup would be wiser to develop its business in China through a merger rather than a joint venture. (12)

3 Explain the likely reason for SuperGroup wanting to develop its business in China 'without imposing significant organisational demand' (Extract B). (4)

4 Evaluate whether SuperGroup was right to go for a 50/50 joint venture in order to develop Superdry in China. (20)

Extended writing

1 Sainsbury's is considering whether to enter the Chinese grocery market through takeover/merger or a joint venture. Evaluate which option might be preferable. (20)

2 Jaguar Land Rover's Chinese joint venture built a factory on time – but just in time for the 2015 slump in demand for luxury cars in China. Evaluate whether JLR would be better off buying up its Chinese partner. (20)

36 Global competitiveness

Definition

Global competitiveness measures a business's ability to compete both at home and abroad against foreign firms. Internationally competitive firms are successful because they offer a better combination of price and quality than their rivals.

Linked to: Growing economies, Ch 25; China versus India, Ch 26; Business potential in Africa, Ch 27; International trade and business growth, Ch 28; Trading blocs, Ch 31; Conditions that prompt trade, Ch 32; Assessment of a country as a market, Ch 33

36.1 Introduction

Internationally competitive businesses succeed because they sell products that offer consumers better value for money than their foreign rivals. This could be because the firm has a cost advantage. Superior cost competitiveness matters because it can help firms to out-compete their rivals by offering consumers lower prices. Examples include Ryanair, Primark and Lidl.

Economists have a tendency to over-play the importance price plays in modern consumer decision-making. In many markets product quality and brand image are more important than price. There is far more to competitiveness than being the cheapest. Indeed, some very competitive firms sell their products at a price premium; they do not rely on low production costs and low retail prices to create their competitiveness. Companies like Mercedes, BMW and Toyota out-compete their rivals by producing highly differentiated products.

The benefits of being globally competitive are significant. Firms in this position are able to stop imports from penetrating their domestic market. German cars are popular with German car buyers. For example, in 2014, Volkswagen sold more cars than Honda, Mazda, Nissan, Mitsubishi, Renault and Peugeot combined. Unsurprisingly, products supplied by globally competitive firms like Volkswagen also sell well in export markets. In China, which is the biggest car market in the world, Volkswagen sold more cars than anyone else.

2013 rank	2014 rank	Brand and model	Sales 2014	Sales 2013
1	1	VW Golf	255,044	244,249
2	2	VW Passat	72,153	72,048
4	3	VW Polo	68,103	68,343
5	4	Audi A3	65,199	60,978
6	5	VW Tiguan	61,947	57,838
8	6	Mercedes C-Class	60,350	52,433
3	7	BMW 3 Series	55,681	69,486
10	8	Opel Corsa	55,151	49,595

Table 36.1 Best-selling car models in Germany in 2014 (full year, units)

'The German export successes are not the result of some sort of currency manipulation, but of the increased competitiveness of companies.'

Wolfgang Schauble, German politician (Christian Democratic Union)

36.2 The impact of movements in exchange rates on competitiveness

The exchange rate measures the quantity of foreign currency that can be bought with one unit of another currency, for example, £1 buys 2 dollars. Movements in the exchange rate can dramatically affect a firm's global competitiveness because the exchange rate affects both the price of imported and exported goods. Firms cannot influence the exchange rate. The pound's rate of exchange against the US dollar is determined by the supply and demand for the pound on international currency markets. An individual firm is too small to affect the exchange rate. It is a good example of an external factor that is beyond the control of any one manager.

Exchange rates affect firms in different ways.

The impacts of a high exchange rate

On firms with large export markets

UK firms, such as Jaguar, JCB and Bentley cars, that sell a high proportion of their output overseas, worry about the pound's value going up, i.e. the **appreciation** of the pound. Why is this so? The best way of explaining is via a numerical example.

America is an important export market for Bentley. The company's most popular model is called the Flying Spur and is priced at £150,000 in the UK.

To achieve the same profit margin in America, Bentley will have to charge a price in US dollars that will convert into £150,000. In July 2013 the exchange rate against the US dollar was £1: $1.45. To obtain £150,000 per export, Bentley charged its American customers:

£150,000 × $1.45 = $217,000

Two years later in July 2015, the exchange rate had gone up to £1: $1.55. To generate the same £150,000 of export revenue per car sold, Bentley now had to charge its American consumers:

£150,000 × $1.55 = $232,500

In other words, the rise in the pound sterling meant that Bentley needed to increase the US price of its cars by $15,500 dollars to maintain the current profit per car. If Bentley reacts to a rising pound by putting prices up in the US, price competitiveness will fall. Higher prices for Bentleys sold in America will almost certainly cause demand for its cars to drop (slightly). On the other hand, if Bentley decides against raising its prices in America, the company will have to accept a lower profit on each car sold. This means that there will be less retained profit available to finance research and development into producing the next generation of Bentley cars; either way Bentley loses out as a result of a higher pound.

Conclusion: exporters lose price competitiveness when their currency appreciates in value; they like it to fall, not rise. So the impact of a high exchange rate is to make it harder for UK manufacturers to trade profitably. This can threaten jobs in the UK. The loss of UK steelworkers' jobs in 2015 was blamed, in part, on the fact that the pound had appreciated against currencies, including the euro and the Japanese yen.

On firms that face competition from imports

The Scotch whisky industry contributed £5 billion to the UK economy in 2015, employing over 40,000 people in Britain. Much of what is produced is exported. However, the domestic market for whisky is still very significant. According to the Scotch Whisky Association, 87.5 million 70cl bottles of whisky were consumed by British households in 2014. Unsurprisingly, whisky producers in other countries target the British market. One of these companies is America's Jack Daniels. A high exchange rate reduces the price of imports. If the price of a case of twelve bottles of Jack Daniels is $70, the price paid by Tesco will be as follows:

If the exchange rate is £1: $1.40, the case will cost Tesco $70 / 1.40 = £50.00.

However, if the exchange rate appreciates to £1: $1.60, the same case of Jack Daniels will now cost Tesco £43.75 ($70 / 1.60 = £43.75). A high exchange rate will enable Tesco to cut the price of a bottle of Jack Daniels because the company can now buy imported goods more cheaply.

Some UK-based firms that import a high proportion of their raw materials from abroad will benefit from a stronger currency because it will reduce the sterling cost of buying these imports. Whisky is made from water, malt and other locally sourced ingredients. Therefore, a strong pound is unlikely to reduce the operating costs of a typical Scottish distillery. This means that Scotch whisky producers will lose some of their price competitiveness because unlike the producers of imported whisky, a stronger currency will not enable them to lower their prices.

The impacts of a low exchange rate

The impacts of a **depreciation** in the exchange rate are the reverse of those from a strong exchange rate. Firms like Bentley that were damaged by a strong currency find life easier when the exchange rate falls. A weak pound makes their exports seem cheaper to foreign consumers, so Bentley should be able to sell more of its cars in America.

On the other hand, retailers like Tesco will be damaged by a depreciated exchange rate because it will now cost Tesco more in pounds sterling to buy in its imported stock of Jack Daniels. If Tesco reacts to the falling exchange rate by raising the price of Jack Daniels, it will sell fewer bottles. If this happens, demand for whisky in the UK will probably be diverted away from imports towards domestically produced alternatives. This could encourage Tesco into giving more shelf-space to domestically produced Scotch whisky.

So a depreciation of the pound helps UK manufacturers who export – and those that face competition from overseas. But the upward push to import prices may hurt UK retailers – and, of course, UK households.

36.3 Competitive advantage through cost competitiveness

One way of being competitive is to charge customers low prices.

It is an old cliché that 'there's always room at the top and bottom of every market'. In other words, while wealthy people can always be persuaded to buy a new, super-luxury-top-of-the-range product, there's always a market for the lowest-priced item. But there is only one way to offer sustainedly low prices and that's to have resource advantages that keep costs lower than those of your rivals. This is easy to write but extremely hard to achieve. It may also require a combination of innovation and toughness to squeeze costs down to the minimum.

Real business

The Romanian car manufacturer Dacia is a good example of a business that competes successfully on price by targeting the budget segment of the market. In 2013, the company sold nearly 20,000 Sandero cars in the UK, which was a record for a UK new car launch. The launch price was £5,995, which also made it Britain's cheapest new car. To make a profit from rock-bottom prices firms must be efficient; they need to have low operating costs.

Figure 36.1 Low-cost Dacia from Romania

Dacia achieves the low unit costs it needs in several ways. First, wages paid by Dacia to its Romanian workforce are low by Western European standards. According to Eurostat, in 2014 the average monthly wage paid to a Romanian worker was under £300. In comparison, workers in Britain received over £1,600 per month. The second factor that has helped Dacia's cost competitiveness is investment. In 1999, Dacia was bought by Renault, which immediately modernised the company's only factory. The result was a dramatic increase in productivity. Before the modernisation programme the factory in Bucharest employed 30,000 workers who made a total of 110,000 cars a year. By 2014, the same factory produced 340,000 cars per year with a workforce of just 14,000.

Strategies to achieve cost leadership

Raising productivity

A cost leader is a business that operates with the lowest average cost in its industry. Cost leadership can be used as a source of competitive advantage. If a firm can produce its product for the lowest possible cost, it will be able to charge consumers the lowest possible prices. This is especially important in markets where there is very little product differentiation. In markets like this consumers tend to buy the cheapest brand that is for sale. One way to achieve low costs is to maximise labour productivity (output per worker). This is rarely about one group of workers working harder and faster than another; it's more about efficient planning and organisation of the workplace. In the most productive businesses, this organisation and planning is helped by discussion with and ideas from the workforce.

In the case of Ryanair (Europe's lowest-cost airline), the key to its cost minimisation strategy is to eliminate waste (classic lean production). It realised early on that the daftest waste was to have aircraft idle at airports. Ryanair was the first in Europe to make sure that passengers are ready for the plane's arrival, helping get plane turnaround times down to about 20 minutes. This ensures that the planes do more journeys per day, increasing the company's **capital productivity**.

Many media commentators suggest that high wages are the cause of poor cost competitiveness. This need not be true as long as labour productivity is high enough. Wage rates in Germany are comparatively high. According to Eurostat, the average monthly wage in Germany in 2014 was €2,154. Despite this, thanks to impressive levels of productivity, Germany's unit labour costs were still below their European rivals, as Figure 36.2 shows.

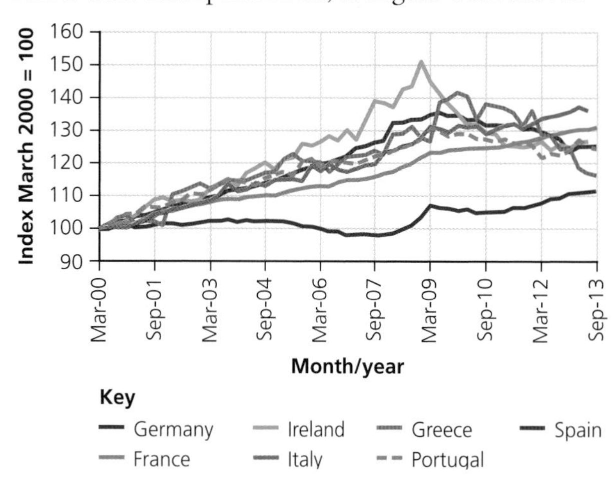

Figure 36.2 Unit labour costs in Western Europe (source: EconoMonitor. Index: March 2000 = 100)

'Over the long term, the only way we're going to improve international competitiveness is by investing in our people; especially their education.'

Robert Reich, US political economist

Germany achieves its cost competitiveness through high productivity, rather than via low wages. German workers produce more than British workers because German firms invest more heavily in training and in new machinery than their UK rivals. The German government also helps by supplying German firms with an educated workforce and modern transport infrastructure. Cutting wages to improve competitiveness lowers living standards. The fall in demand caused by lower wages will also make life harder for most firms by reducing the demand for goods and services. Therefore, it is better for a country to create its cost competitiveness in the German way by raising productivity.

Outsourcing

Firms outsource when they contract out to another firm activities that used to be done in-house. There are two motives for outsourcing. The first is to reduce costs. In the past, many firms used to employ their own teams of cleaners and catering staff. Today, these activities are likely to be undertaken by specialist cleaning and catering companies which provide these services at a lower cost. Some banks and airlines have outsourced telephone call centres to specialist companies operating in English-speaking countries, such as India. Wages in India are substantially lower than wages in the UK. Therefore, the strategy of outsourcing in this case can dramatically lower operating costs, creating a cost-based competitive advantage.

Offshoring

Offshoring is not the same as outsourcing. When a firm 'offshores', factories or offices are closed down and are moved to a new location overseas. However, unlike outsourcing, the newly opened factory or office overseas is still owned by the business. Offshoring can also be prompted by a desire to avoid environmental regulations and employment laws that add to a firm's costs. In some cases, firms offshore to take advantage of lower rates of corporation tax overseas.

36.4 Competitive advantage through product differentiation

Cost competitiveness on its own does not guarantee global competitiveness. This is because consumers consider other factors apart from price when making purchasing decisions. In a competitive market, firms that produce cheap but poor quality products may struggle to attract enough customers to break even; consumers will only purchase a product if they like it.

Businesses based in high wage economies know that they will find it hard to match the low prices charged by their competitors who operate from countries where wages and other overheads are lower. These firms therefore cannot compete on price. Instead they use product differentiation to create non-price competitiveness. Product differentiation is the extent to which consumers

	2003	2004	2005	2006	2007	2008	2010	2015
Management	3,500	15,000	34,000	42,000	48,000	64,000	106,000	259,000
Business	30,000	55,000	91,000	105,000	120,000	136,000	176,000	356,000
Computer	102,000	143,000	181,000	203,000	228,000	247,000	322,000	542,000
Architecture	14,000	27,000	46,000	54,000	61,000	70,000	93,000	191,000
Life sciences	300	2,000	4,000	5,500	6,500	9,000	16,000	39,000
Legal	6,000	12,000	20,000	23,000	26,000	29,000	39,000	79,000
Art, design	2,500	4,500	8,000	9,000	10,000	11,000	15,000	30,000
Sales	11,000	22,000	38,000	47,000	55,000	67,000	97,000	218,000
Office	146,000	256,000	410,000	475,000	541,000	616,000	815,000	1,600,000
Total	315,000	540,000	830,000	960,000	1,100,000	1,200,000	1,700,000	3,400,000

Table 36.2 Impact on America of offshoring: estimated number of US jobs moving offshore, 2003–2015 (source: www.umakemelaugh.newsvine.com)

believe that a brand is unique and in some way superior to other brands of the same product. It can be achieved through clever marketing and branding, or by genuinely creating a distinctively designed and engineered product. The huge success of the Land Rover Evoque is due to two main factors: good design and clever engineering that uses aluminium instead of steel. This makes the car lighter, ensuring that it's more fun to drive and is more fuel efficient and less noxious in its exhaust emissions.

Another example of great product differentiation is Swiss-made Lindor chocolate. Even though the Swiss franc is very strong on the exchange rates, sales of Lindor are growing at more than 10 per cent a year in Britain, boosting the market share of parent company Lindt. And price is certainly not the driving force. At the time of writing, a 100g bar of Lindor is £1.69 at Tesco, while Cadbury's Dairy Milk 120g is £1.40.

In a world in which hourly wage rates can be as low as 20p, it's hard to see many British companies succeeding on the basis of cost competitiveness. Far better to imitate the Americans, Germans and Swiss by focusing on added value products with clear product differentiation.

36.5 Skill shortages and their impact on international competitiveness

A skill shortage exists when firms are unable to recruit extra workers with the necessary skills. Such shortages can stop firms expanding – and therefore stop the economy from growing. An example might be a construction company that has to turn away work because it cannot find the additional structural engineers needed to complete these contracts.

Skill shortages are usually a consequence of poor decision-making and short-termist thinking by both the private sector and government. Firms can cause skill shortages if they fail to invest sufficiently in training schemes and apprenticeships. Governments can also contribute to skill shortages by supplying the wrong type of education. For example, over the last two decades the national curriculum has forced state schools to give pupils IT lessons in how to *operate* computer software that somebody else has already designed. This decision has meant that there is a shortage of young people in Britain who have the coding skills needed to *create* new computer software.

Firms can overcome skill shortages in several ways. Some try **poaching** the additional skilled labour they need from rivals by offering higher wages to persuade them to move. The problem with this solution is that the higher salaries paid will push up the firm's wage bill, which will undermine the business's cost competitiveness. In the construction sector firms look to import the talent that they need by hiring foreign engineers from elsewhere within the European Union. In extreme cases skill shortages can even prompt UK firms to outsource or offshore to other countries to get around a domestic skills shortage. (See Chapter 34 for more on workforce skills and availability.)

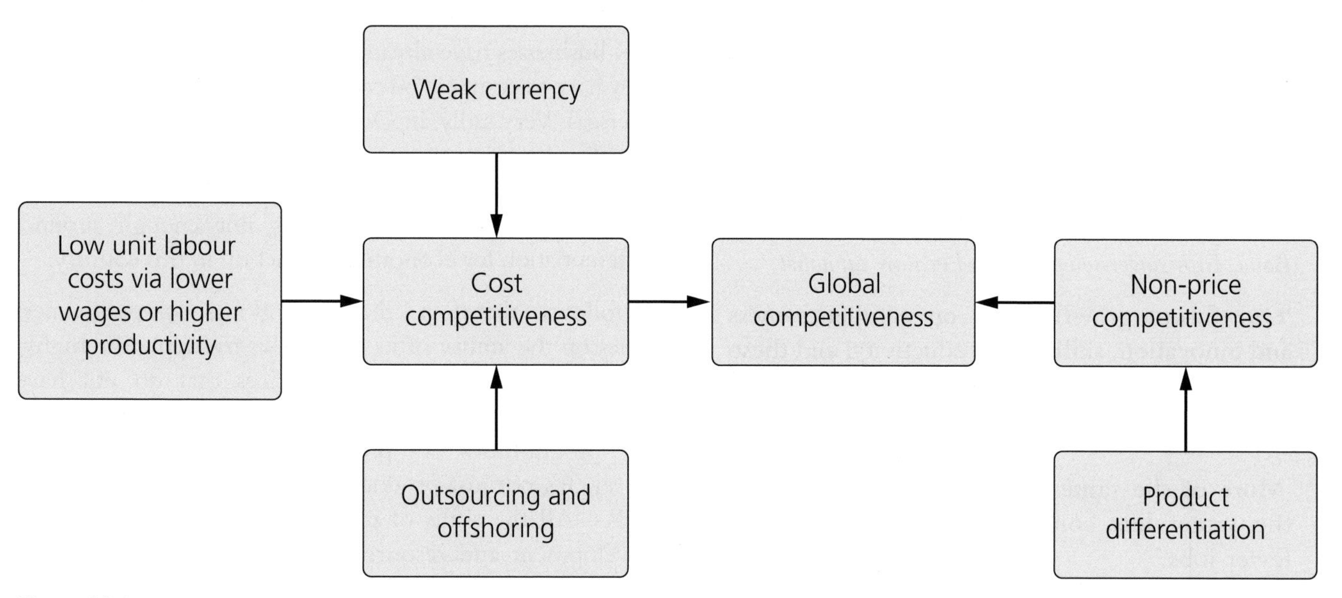

Figure 36.3 Logic chain: ways to achieve global competitiveness

Five whys and a how

Questions	Answers
Why do airlines try to achieve cost leadership?	Cost leaders are able to operate with the lowest average costs in their industry. This allows them to profitably charge customers the lowest possible prices.
Why might a firm choose to close down a factory to transfer production to a new facility abroad?	In highly competitive markets where there is little product differentiation, firms will need to charge low prices in order to survive. To achieve this goal firms might try to move production to another country where wages, taxes and other overheads are lower.
Why do some firms pursue growth as a way of becoming globally competitive?	Expansion should help a firm to achieve economies of scale, which cause a firm's average costs to fall in the long run. Lower costs help firms to become more competitive because it allows them to cut prices without losing profit margin.
Why might a clothes manufacturer prefer to use overseas outsourcing, rather than offshoring?	Companies are conscious about the bad publicity that they can attract if they 'exploit' low-cost labour abroad. Outsourcing is likely to attract less criticism because the firm that has used outsourcing can quite rightly point out that it is not paying low wages.
Why do firms try to increase productivity?	If productivity increases, the same workforce will now be able to produce more units of output. If output rises whilst the wage bill remains the same, unit labour costs will fall. This will help the business to become more cost competitive.
How might a skills shortage compromise a firm's global competitiveness?	To obtain the extra labour needed to expand, firms will have to poach labour from their rivals by paying higher wages. The resulting increase in costs might force the firm into raising its prices.

Key terms

Appreciating: when the value of a currency rises, i.e. it buys more of other currencies.

Capital productivity: the efficiency with which capital is used, e.g. output per £000 of capital investment.

Depreciation: when the value of a currency falls.

Poaching: poaching labour means hiring staff trained by others: they pay for the training but you benefit from it.

'At the heart of the Irish economy has always been the philosophy of tax competitiveness. On the cranky left, that is very annoying; I can see that.'

Bono, Irish singer-songwriter and venture capitalist

'Our future growth relies on competitiveness and innovation, skills and productivity, and these in turn rely on the education of our people.'

Julia Gillard, former Australian Prime Minister

'More of the same will just produce more of the same: less competitiveness, less growth, fewer jobs.'

David Cameron, UK Prime Minister

36.6 Global competitiveness – evaluation

In 2008/2009, at the time of the financial crisis, the value of the pound depreciated by more than 20 per cent against other currencies. Logically, this should have boosted our companies' competitiveness by 20 per cent, encouraging UK exports to rise and imports to fall. In fact, there was hardly a flicker in either. It is reasonable to conclude that UK businesses have already dropped out of markets where they have to compete on cost/price with products produced overseas. Very sadly, in October 2015, 1,700 jobs were lost due the closure of the steelworks at Redcar, Yorkshire. In August 2015, one hundred times more steel was produced in Asia than in Britain; there's not enough product differentiation for economic production in this country.

It follows, therefore, that UK global competitiveness relies on the ability of its companies to supply the highly differentiated products and services that do not have to sell on the basis of low prices. It's not just producing TV programmes, it's producing *Sherlock* and *Downton Abbey*. It's not just producing cars, but producing Jaguar XJRs. All the skills of marketing, design, research and development and resource management are needed for global competitiveness.

36.7 Workbook

Revision questions

(45 marks; 45 minutes)

1 What is meant by the term 'global competitiveness'? (2)

2 Explain why a decision by management to pay car workers a pay rise might not increase the cost of producing each car. (4)

3 In 2014, 3,036,773 cars were sold in Germany, compared with 2,952,421 the year before. Using the information in Table 36.1, calculate what happened to the VW Golf's market share between 2013 and 2014. (4)

4 Before modernisation, the Dacia factory employed 30,000 workers who made a total of 110,000 cars a year. By 2014, the same factory produced 340,000 cars per year from a workforce of just 14,000.

a) Calculate Dacia's labour productivity level then and in 2014. (4)

b) Explain how Dacia benefits from that change. (4)

5 Using Figure 36.2, compare the change in Greece and Germany's unit labour costs over the period shown. (5)

6 Explain two ways in which a firm might choose to lower its unit labour costs. (8)

7 Distinguish between outsourcing and offshoring. (4)

8 Product differentiation and cost competitiveness both affect a firm's profitability. Assess the view that product differentiation will always be more important than cost competitiveness for businesses like BMW and Lindt. (10)

Data response 1

A tale of two bicycle manufacturers

Thanks to the success of Bradley Wiggins, Chris Boardman and others, bicycle sales in Britain have been soaring. According to Mintel, 3.6 million bicycles were sold in Britain in 2014. The total amount spent on buying these bicycles was £745 million.

In the past, most of the bicycles bought in Britain were also manufactured in Britain by companies such as Raleigh. Raleigh was set up in 1887 by Frank Bowden. It was one of the first companies in the world to mass produce high-quality and affordable bicycles. Raleigh also used innovation to create product differentiation. It was the first company to sell bikes with gears in 1932; and their 1970s Chopper children's bike is still regarded as a design classic today. Raleigh used to produce its bicycles from a factory in Nottingham. At the company's peak in the mid-1970s Raleigh produced over 4 million bicycles per year in Britain, employing 12,000 people. They made seven in every ten bikes sold in the UK. Unfortunately, by the late 1990s Raleigh was in decline, unable to compete against cheap imported bicycles. The management responded by moving production from the UK to China and Taiwan. Raleigh's bikes are still designed in the UK, but by 2015 the company's UK workforce had been reduced to just over 100 people. Raleigh's UK market share in the same year was 20 per cent.

Some bicycles are still manufactured in Britain. Perhaps the best known example is Brompton which sells folding bikes that can be taken on trains by London commuters. Brompton is still relatively small. The business employed 240 workers in 2014. The company's only factory in Brentford produced 45,000 bikes in the same year, which generated a revenue of £25 million.

Questions (50 marks; 60 minutes)

1 a) Calculate the average price of every bicycle sold in the UK in 2014. How does this compare with the average price of a Brompton bike in the same year? (4)

b) Comment on your findings. (6)

2 Assess the relative importance of cost competitiveness to Brompton Bicycle Ltd. (10)

3 Assess the implications of Raleigh's decision to offshore production to the company's various stakeholder groups. (10)

4 Evaluate whether Brompton Bicycle Ltd should attempt to move out of its niche market in foldaway bicycles and diversify into producing conventional mass-market bikes. (20)

Data response 2

IKEA is a great example of a globally competitive company. The Swedish furniture retailer has 353 stores worldwide, operating in 46 different countries. In 2014, the company generated a global turnover of €28.7 billion – making IKEA the biggest furniture retailer in the world.

Product design has played a very important role in creating IKEA's global competitiveness. When he set up the business in 1943, Ingvar Kamprad's wanted his furniture to appeal to the mass market. To achieve high sales volumes, Kamprad knew that he would have to make his furniture affordable. This meant charging low prices. To make a profit from these low prices, costs have to be kept to a minimum. IKEA furniture was designed to be sold to customers in flat packs. This helped the company to cut costs in two ways. First, the flat packs reduced the cost of transporting and storing furniture. And second, labour costs were reduced, because the customer assembled the furniture, rather than a company employee.

IKEA also uses design to compete using product differentiation. The company's Scandinavian minimalistic designs are popular with consumers in most countries – even in conservative Britain, where homeowners have been successfully persuaded by IKEA's advertising to 'Chuck Out Your Chintz'.

Questions (50 marks; 60 minutes)

1. Explain how design can help a company like IKEA to establish competitive advantage through differentiation. (4)
2. Figure 36.4 shows that IKEA's revenues have more than doubled over the period shown. Explain whether IKEA should be pleased with this performance. (4)
3. Assess how an appreciation of the Swedish currency might affect the global competitiveness of IKEA. (12)
4. IKEA targets price-conscious consumers. In the light of this, assess whether cost competitiveness is more to IKEA than competitiveness achieved via product differentiation. (10)
5. Evaluate the possible future threats to IKEA's global competitiveness. (20)

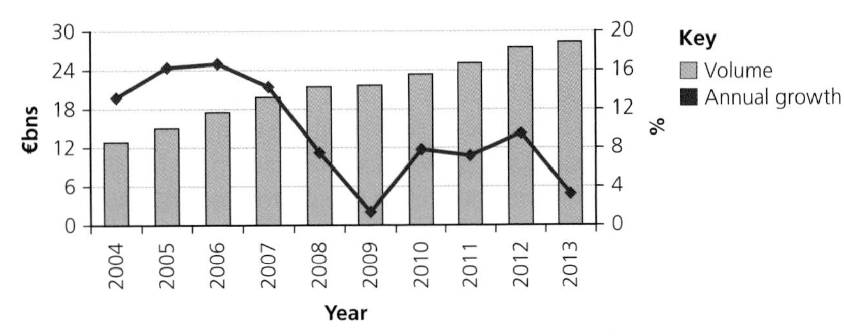

Figure 36.4 Ikea's fiscal year revenue (source: Quartz, qz.com. © Quartz. Reprinted with the permission of Quartz)

Extended writing

1. Some producers of luxury fashion clothing (such as Burberry) are considering returning production from the Far East to the UK. Evaluate whether this would be a wise move. (20)
2. JCB is one of the world's top three producers of construction site vehicles. It employs 6,500 staff at its site in the Midlands, but also has factories in India, Brazil and China. Evaluate the factors that will determine the global success of JCB over the coming years. (20)

Section 4.3 Global marketing

37 Global marketing

Definition

The choice of marketing strategy to find a fit between an individual company's objectives and its unique market position.

Linked to: International trade and business growth, Ch 28; Assessment of a country as a market, Ch 33; Global competitiveness, Ch 36; Global niche markets, Ch 38

37.1 Introduction

Manchester United and Real Madrid show what every business aspires to in global marketing: an image that is clear and unchanging in every part of the world: thrilling, starry, romantic, aspirational and successful. The image adds value to the brand and the brand's image is indivisible. For fifty years Coca-Cola followed the dictum: one drink, one bottle, one price, i.e. zero innovation in pursuit of an image for the brand as 'the real thing'. This was a huge help to its global success.

Today it's extremely hard to replicate Coca-Cola's approach or the strengths of a brand such as Real Madrid. BMW may come some way towards it, with its image as the 'driving machine' beloved of real, sporty-minded drivers. But needless to say, BMW cannot quite match the brand loyalty of the Real fan.

37.2 Global marketing strategy and global localisation (glocalisation)

The Coca-Cola marketing approach of the 1950s through to the 1990s was global. The same product with the same taste in the same can size and with the same advertising. Even though the TV commercials were in English, the simple messages came across, helped by the spread of American TV and Hollywood films. In 2015, German global giant Volkswagen was able to use 'Das Auto' as its global slogan, but this approach was becoming less common.

Figure 37.1 McDonald's restaurant in Moscow

When McDonald's opened its first restaurant in Russia in 1990, 30,000 people turned up to queue *because* it was an authentic American menu. Today McDonald's menus vary hugely around the world as they've been tailored to local tastes. McDonald's learned that they could boost sales by localising their menus. They kept the brand images constant and global, but localised the offer; this combination is known as glocalisation.

In today's markets it has proved increasingly difficult to use a one-size-fits-all global strategy in the lower and middle parts of the market. In other words, and quite curiously, mass markets in each country prove to be quite different. A good example is street food, which is remarkably different in different places. It's at the top end of markets where national differences tend to flatten out. The rich in London, Paris, Beijing and Mumbai tend to adore Hermes, Burberry, Bentley, Chanel and fine French wines.

So glocalisation is especially important for producers operating in mass markets. Mass market multinationals such as Unilever and Procter & Gamble spend a lot of time localising their global brands. Looking at the 'brands UK' and 'brands France' sections of Unilever's website shows that Lynx = Axe and Walls = Miko and in France there are brands such as Cajoline, Skip and Zendium. But Unilever is hugely proud of its 'power brands' with global sales of more than £1 billion. These include Magnum, Persil, Dove and Knorr. In other words Unilever is thrilled when it has truly global brands, but in many other cases has to localise in order to be successful.

Strengths of global brands	Strengths of localising your brands (glocalisation)
• Huge sales provide production opportunities to enjoy significant economies of scale	• Tailoring to local tastes and habits should boost market share, e.g. green tea Magnums in Japan
• Over 1.1 billion people travelled abroad in 2014; global brands can be bought for reassurance and familiarity, i.e. globalisation helps sales	• Local buyers can assume you're a local producer, which may help sales (e.g. many Brits believe Ford to be a British car maker, not American)
• Many promotional tools are global (e.g. sponsoring Formula 1 or buying the rights to Arsenal's shirt front) and can only be economic if the brands sell globally (e.g. Emirates airline)	• An innovative product designed for local tastes may end up being a global success, e.g. the Nissan Qashqai, designed in Sunderland, but now an important global brand
• Global scale provides strong negotiating power with retailers (helping those 'power brands' get better display and distribution)	• Localising brands probably means localised production, which cuts costs and may help establish a greener image for the business

Table 37.1 Global versus glocal branding

'There will be two kinds of chief executive in the next five years: those who think globally and those who are unemployed.'

Peter Drucker, business guru

'We are not a global business. We are a collection of local businesses with intense global co-ordination.'

Percy Barnevik, chief executive, ABB

37.3 Different marketing approaches

Domestic/ethnocentric

Linked to the issue of global versus glocal marketing strategy is whether the managers at a business have attitudes that are **ethnocentric**. In other words, managers whose national pride strays towards national arrogance in assuming that 'we French (or British) know best'. Perhaps this explains why a perennially underperforming British car producer (Jaguar Land Rover) has performed so much better since being bought by an Indian company who appointed a German as managing director. An ethnocentric management would be inclined towards a global strategy in which they simply take what works in Britain and market the product in the same way everywhere else.

Another aspect of ethnocentricity to consider is the approach of consumers. In some countries there is a fundamental preference for home-produced goods. The French are very reluctant to drink wine from outside France – so the local producers have a (possibly undeserved) competitive advantage. Global car makers only gain a 4 per cent market share in Japan. Some may complain about protectionist tricks by the Japanese, but no one doubts that Japanese car-buyers focus on home-produced cars. In China there's almost a reverse-ethnocentricity as Chinese customers trust western brands more than home-produced ones, especially in foods in general and baby food in particular.

International/polycentric

Managers with a **polycentric** approach believe that every market is different, and therefore that a high degree of delegation is called for. Local managers are empowered to develop new products and new brands to suit the local market – perhaps only drawing upon the global corporation for bulk buying advantages. Years ago, that's how Mars treated the UK. So local managers renamed the American 'Milky Way' as the Mars Bar; Snickers was called Marathon and Starburst was called Opal Fruits. Later the US head office changed its mind and rebranded Marathon and Opal Fruits (though the Mars Bar remains as it is).

Implicitly a polycentric management believes that local markets are unknowable by outsiders. Some have suggested that a polycentric approach to marketing still has a degree of nationalistic arrogance at its heart ('you Chinese are so different from us that we'll never understand you; we know we're better and we aren't going to waste our time getting to know you).

Mixed/geocentric

The geocentric approach has a clear world view, with an understanding that truly global brands are possible and desirable, but not in every circumstance. For managers to believe this, they implicitly believe that there are similarities between all people (we may be of different ethnicities, but we both love Cadbury's Dairy Milk). This makes it a significantly different approach from either ethnocentric or polycentric. By implication, then, this is the 'best' approach to global marketing.

In a business dominated by a geocentric view, there would be delegation to local regions but within a framework of understanding that, where possible, global is best. This quite flexible mixture of global and glocal allows situations such as that of Coca-Cola in India. Despite the global marketing of the brand, India has been accepted by head office as being an exception. In India, Coca-Cola is sold in smaller cans and bottles and priced significantly below the price charged elsewhere. And the company felt the need to bolster itself by acquiring local brands Thumbs Up and Limca.

37.4 Applying the marketing mix to global markets

Even for a business with a global marketing strategy it's hard, perhaps impossible, to adopt an unchanging global marketing mix. It may be possible to keep the branding the same (Ronald McDonald is iconic everywhere) but 'Place', in particular, may have to vary quite significantly. Britain is the home of delivery food, often ordered on a mobile device (which is great for Domino's Pizza). In other countries this approach is little developed. For McDonald's that's quite a problem in the UK market, where delivering burgers is not very realistic. A pizza can survive a 15-minute delivery time; a Big Mac can't.

Figure 37.2 shows how distribution channels can vary between countries. Although China's grocery distribution is quite similar to those of developed UK and USA, India's is completely different. Instead of supermarkets and hypermarkets together accounting for 60–65 per cent of grocery spending, in India the figure is below 2 per cent. India's grocery market is dominated by 10 million small grocers. To get a new product distributed successfully in India requires a huge sum spent on door-to-door selling. So Place in India requires a different mindset from elsewhere.

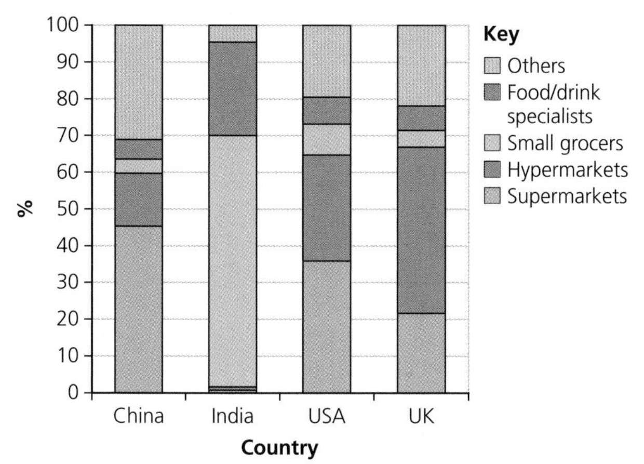

Figure 37.2 Grocery distribution (Place) in India compared with China, USA and UK (source: Euromonitor 2014)

Other factors in the marketing mix may be varied to good effect. Promotion in the UK or China, today, requires serious thought about social media as well as traditional channels such as TV. This is much less the case in countries such as New Zealand and Italy. And then there's Price. In the past, companies used **price discrimination** on a national basis, perhaps charging 40 per cent more in Germany than in Portugal for an identical product. Today a combination of the European single market and the advent of online shopping has made this much harder to achieve. Pricing these days is a bit more consistent, country by country.

37.5 Applying Ansoff's Matrix to global markets

Igor Ansoff was an important thinker and writer on business strategy. He encouraged businesses to think in a more long-term way about where to position themselves. He warned against sticking to the comfort zone represented by existing products in existing markets – yet also warned of the risks involved in straying away from what he called market penetration. (Ansoff was covered in more detail in Chapter 3.)

Real business

When on-a-roll Tesco announced in 2007 its five-year plan for breaking into the US grocery market, most commentators repeated the company's PR about the successes of chief executive Terry Leahy. In fact Tesco's attempt at international market development quickly turned sour. Because the company ended up with a different store concept in the US than existed in its UK product portfolio, you could even call Tesco's initiative a diversification (simultaneous product development and market development). Seen within the prism of Ansoff's theory, the risks involved in Tesco's initiative were clear. Ansoff's matrix is a valuable way to appraise a company's global marketing and corporate strategy.

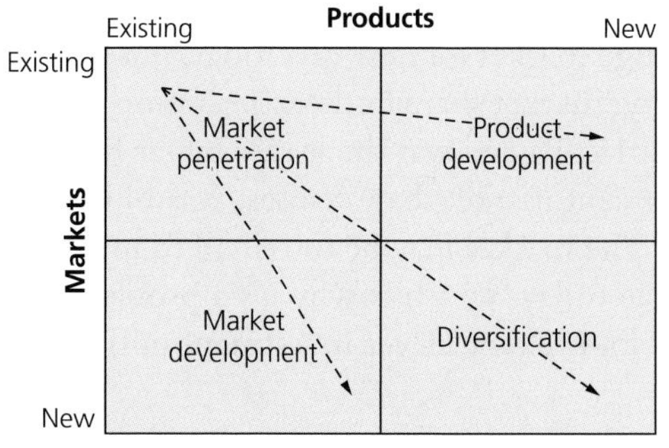

Figure 37.3 Ansoff's Matrix: the arrow shows the progressively greater risks involved in moving away from existing products in existing markets

37.6 Applying the Boston Matrix to global markets

The Boston Consulting Group's Product Portfolio Matrix is an important way to help businesses allocate their marketing budgets. As shown in Figure 37.4, it encourages firms to identify the brands that need greater marketing support (all the rising stars and some of the problem children). And shows where to get the resources from – by 'milking' the cash cows, i.e. using their positive cash flows to give a boost to brands thought to have a promising future. By transferring resources from the present to the future the business hopes to always have a portfolio of profitable brands (rather than feast, then famine).

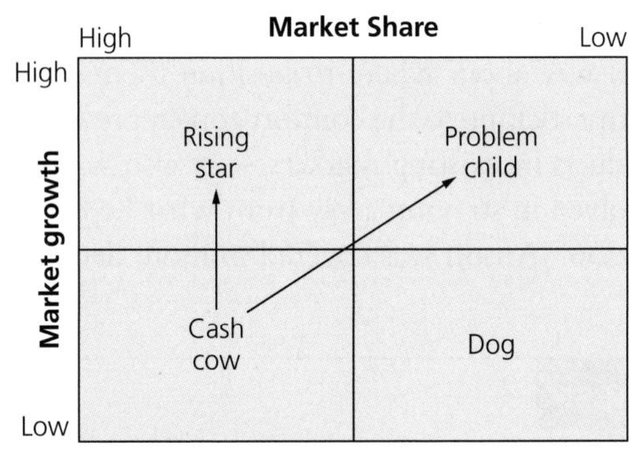

Figure 37.4 The Boston Matrix

It is interesting to consider how to take the Boston Matrix further and apply it to global business and marketing strategy. Figure 37.5 shows how the model can be adopted to make some interesting points about global marketing strategy. Even though the Chinese car market fell back slightly in 2015, both Jaguar Land Rover and Volkswagen continued with their long-term approach which is based on China as the future – and sales in Britain and Germany as a useful piggy bank to be raided at will to build sales in Asia. Note also that Ghana may have too low a level of household income to represent a huge market for new cars today, but it may be worth building market share in the expectation of future growth. In 2015, Toyota was the leader by far in Ghana, with a 33 per cent market share (closest was Nissan with 13 per cent). The market may be too small to make these sales profitable today, which is why it's a problem child. But this may look a very clever investment in five to ten years' time.

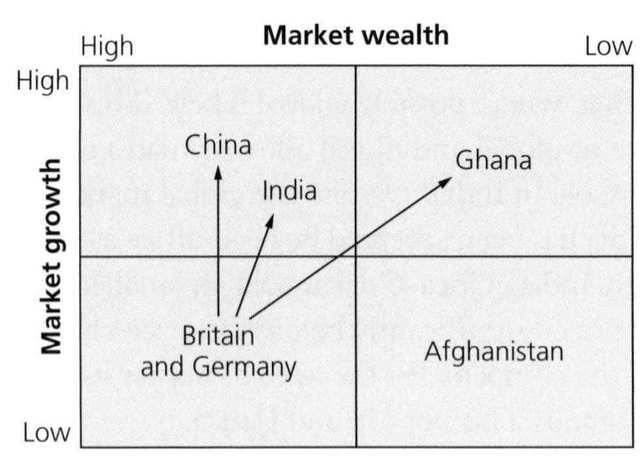

Figure 37.5 Boston Matrix adjusted and applied to global markets

'Think global. Act local.'

Sony company motto 1988

'There's no locality on the web - every market is a global market.'

Ethan Zuckerman, author

Five whys and a how

Questions	Answers
Why might a company such as Burberry be successful worldwide despite making few changes to localise its product range?	Luckily for Burberry, wealthy buyers worldwide seem to have similar tastes, perhaps generated by international travel.
Why might an ethnocentric population be helpful to an economy?	If they are proud nationalists in their purchasing habits, it means extra business for local firms and extra jobs for the population.
Why might Ansoff's theory be criticised for encouraging businesses to be too cautious in their strategic decisions?	The risk part of Ansoff's theory may have been over-emphasised compared with the opportunities that Ansoff also identified.
Why might a company such as L'Oréal use the same models for its TV commercials worldwide?	It may believe the model is a star globally – or may want to convey the same message in every country, i.e. act globally not glocally.
Why might it prove unwise to put too much cash behind a problem child?	With Tesco USA it was clear by 2008 that the business had problems, but it only withdrew from the US in 2013, after perhaps £2,000 million of losses.
How might a business such as Toyota decide which problem children to support and which to leave alone?	Clearly it would help if the brands are at or close to break-even and also Toyota could look for which markets have the most rapid economic growth.

37.7 Global marketing – evaluation

In the past global brands were largely a construct, needed to differentiate one product from another. The skill in making Coca-Cola seem different from Pepsi, or Ford different from Renault, was a lot to do with marketing and branding. Today the world's outstanding brands are largely backed by genuine differences, often based on technology. Apple, Google, Facebook and IBM have great brand names – but the heart of their businesses is great technology rather than simply great marketing.

Outside these huge names, posh brands such as Hermes, Chanel and Gucci are genuinely global, with little concession to local differences. But elsewhere there tends to be a great deal of localisation. This is good because it pays respect to different cultures; but less good in that it prevents goods from being mass produced and therefore great value for money.

Before each individual marketing director decides how best to develop sales internationally, a careful appraisal is needed, probably consisting of trial runs. A global, no-adaptation launch into a smallish market such as Austria will give a clear understanding of whether that approach can work. At the same time, a localised launch into Sweden or Denmark will give a valuable comparison. In the big corporate world, test marketing is always more persuasive than market research.

Key terms

Ethnocentric: centring on your own ethnicity, in other words sticking with the habits and attitudes that are common within your culture. It implies a refusal to change the product to suit local tastes (because your product is 'best').

Polycentric: welcoming of all cultures, and therefore willing to try to absorb new things such as foods and flavours from other countries. Polycentric marketing implies a clear ambition to spread a product internationally, localising as necessary.

Price discrimination: charging different people different prices for the same product or service.

37.8 Workbook

Revision questions

(30 marks; 30 minutes)

1. It costs an average of £21 per salesperson visit in India. Calculate the cost of getting a salesperson to visit every one of the 10 million Indian small grocers. (3)
2. Explain two possible risks to a UK firm of using a glocalisation marketing strategy worldwide. (6)
3. Explain two possible benefits to a business of a geocentric marketing strategy. (6)
4. Look at the 1988 quote from Sony. Explain what it means. (3)
5. Explain the changes that may be needed to turn the Boston Matrix into a tool for assessing global corporate strategy. (4)
6. Assume that Tesco used Ansoff's Matrix as part of its assessment of the US grocery market. Assess two possible reasons why Tesco's move into America failed anyway. (8)

Revision activities

Data response

Market developments in the global chocolate industry

In March 2015, Mars announced its first confectionery factory in India, producing Snickers and Galaxy. It will cost more than $160 million (about £100 million) and provide at least 200 jobs. The president of Mars Chocolate Asia Pacific remarked that 'India is a high priority for Mars ... India is one of the most rapidly emerging chocolate markets in the world and we hope to capitalise on that through this manufacturing plant.' In fact Mars is playing catch-up as Cadbury has a factory opening in India in 2015 – whereas the Mars factory is more likely to be ready in 2017.

Even more of a catch-up process for Mars is that it has just a 6 per cent share of the market for chocolate in India, behind Nestlé with 18 per cent and Cadbury with 62 per cent. The Indian chocolate market is currently worth about $850 million a year, but is expected to grow to $2 billion by 2019. Its pace of growth is 15–20 per cent a year – but from a very small base. In 2015, chocolate sales in India will be just under $1 billion compared with more than $5 billion in the UK. And the population of India is 20 times that of the UK. If, one day, the Indians eat as much as the Brits, sales of chocolate in India would be around $500 billion a year!

For the multinational chocolate makers, there is no doubt about the attractions of the markets in both India and China. Western consumers have been bombarded with health messages which have sucked the growth out of the market for confectionery. Facing static markets in the west, emerging markets become especially attractive. But of course there's a catch. Emerging markets tend to be in hot countries. And hot weather is no friend to chocolate. At 28°C chocolate melts; and if it melts and then re-cools, the mouthfeel of the chocolate stays ruined.

For the multinationals, the long-term solution is to develop chocolate that can withstand heat. US chocolate maker Hershey has a patented method for achieving this; Cadbury has a different, patented approach. And in April 2015, Nestlé filed a patent for a method that is heat resistant up to temperatures as high as 40°C. The Nestlé method adds fibre from sources such as wheat or citrus fruits and it claims that the mouthfeel of the product is unaffected by the new production method. Better still, all the ingredients are natural and pass the required tests of what is allowed, by law, to go into a bar of chocolate.

In the past the main battles between the major chocolate producers have been fought in the marketing departments. The future battle for India and – later – Africa may be fought in the laboratory. A very big prize is up for grabs.

	China market share 2014	India market share 2014
Cadbury (Mondelez International)	Negligible	62%
Nestlé	12.5%	18%
Mars	39%	6%
Ferrero	12%	12%
Hershey	12%	Negligible

Table 37.2 Market shares held by leading manufacturers (sources: various)

	Population (ms) 2014	Population (ms) 2018
India	1,236	1,298
China	1,356	1,380
UK	64	65

Table 37.3 Size of population 2014 and projected for 2018 (source: Courtesy of the Central Intelligence Agency, *CIA World Factbook*)

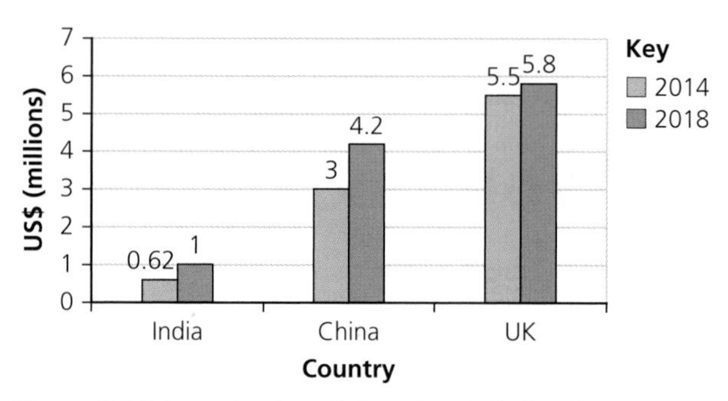

Figure 37.6 Annual sales of chocolate in India, China and the UK, 2014 and forecast for 2018 (sources: various trade publications)

Questions (40 marks; 45 minutes)

1 Explain how Mars is using Ansoff's concept of market development. (4)

2 a) Use Figure 37.6 to calculate the percentage growth rates in chocolate sales between 2014 and 2018 in India, China and the UK respectively. (4)

b) If you were the boss of Cadbury, assess which of the three countries you would see as the most attractive for future investment. (12)

3 Evaluate the factors that are most likely to determine whether Nestlé succeeds with its newly patented heat-resistant chocolate. (20)

Extended writing

1 Fat Face (retailers of clothes targeting 15–25-year-olds) decides to develop a retail presence overseas, starting in continental Europe. Evaluate whether the business would be better off using either the Boston or Ansoff's Matrix. (20)

2 Managers may have ethnocentric, polycentric or geocentric attitudes. Evaluate which might be the most successful for a newly appointed global marketing director of Jaguar Land Rover. (20)

38 Global niche markets

Definition

Some businesses want globalised marketing while others are happy in niches. This might be the same niche worldwide, e.g. Porsche sports cars for wealthy men; or a business finds different niches in different markets.

Linked to: International trade and business growth, Ch 28; Assessment of a country as a market, Ch 33; Global competitiveness, Ch 36; Global marketing, Ch 37; Cultural and social factors in global marketing, Ch 39; The market, AS Ch 2

38.1 Introduction

A niche market offers products that match closely the requirements of a distinct minority within a sector. An example might be non-alcoholic lager. Consumers within a niche market might be regular and loyal (teetotalers, perhaps) but others will be occasional (buying non-alcoholic lager as the nominated driver). Although the customer usage and attitudes may be quite different, a well-positioned niche product should appeal to a wide range of consumers at the specific time they want it.

38.2 Cultural diversity

According to the World Health Organization, only 30 per cent of adults in India drink alcohol. Interestingly, then, a non-alcoholic lager that would clearly be a niche product in Britain might be the mass market one in India. It is clear that groups of people across the globe have different interests and values. Therefore it's an interesting business challenge to try to meet those needs.

In 2015, Cadbury launched Dairy Milk Silk Bubbly into India, using Bollywood stars in their TV commercial. But it is hard to see how aerated chocolate fits in with the heat of India; furthermore Cadbury has priced the bar stiffly, with two sizes at 70p and £1.60. This launch smacks of 'it worked (reasonably well) in the UK so we'll sell it to India' – rather than an attempt to offer something that matches the different needs of Indians. The success or otherwise of this launch will depend on Cadbury's remarkable market dominance (it has a 62 per cent market share) and whether others such as Mars leap to launch something more appropriate for a hot and relatively poor country.

Even across Europe **cultural diversity** is a hugely significant force. Among the factors influencing that diversity are:

- economic factors, especially levels of real disposable income
- weather factors, especially the temperature; Mediterranean countries have a lifestyle with afternoon siestas and late-evening cafe socialising; northern Europeans are more likely to stay in from the cold
- history and tradition: an important influence on diet, on attitudes to religion, to gender, to racial diversity and lifestyle.

Although there's a danger of stereotyping, certain cultural characteristics hold good:

- Germans combine deep respect for science and engineering with huge concern for the environment; as long ago as 2005, when England recycled 17 per cent of its household waste, Germany recycled 65 per cent; in 2015, Germany is still Europe's recycling champion.
- The French and Belgians may not be as good at recycling, but they take cycling extraordinarily seriously. Apparently 48 per cent of Belgians cycle at least once a week; the equivalent UK figure is 7 per cent. The Belgians combine this love of cycling with an equivalent love of food, especially chips and chocolate; Belgians eat 8.3kg of chocolate a year; in neighbouring Holland the figure is 5.4kg.

The point is a simple one: cultural diversity makes a huge difference to markets and therefore businesses. It affects

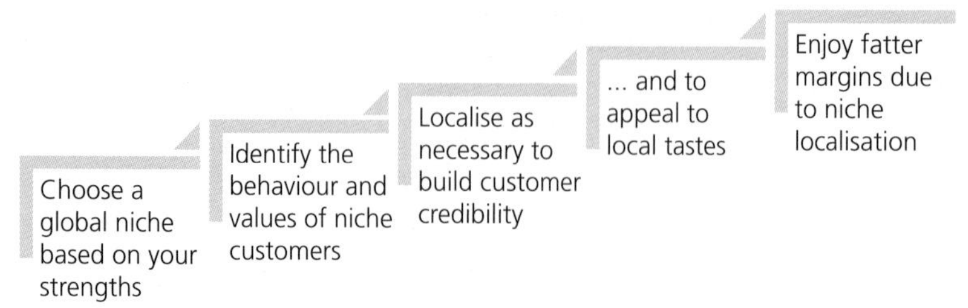

Figure 38.1 Logic chain: building a global niche

the market for products such as chocolate or bicycles – but also services such as restaurants and cafes. It's one of the factors at the heart of Igor Ansoff's warnings about the risks involved in attempting radical market development. Businesspeople often underestimate the differences in tastes and habits between different cultures. Yet the appeal is clear, as shown in the logic chain: successful niche localisation can boost profit margins.

Different interests

As suggested above, people in different parts of the world have different interests. Football's World Cup is the only single sport that brings all countries together (as long as the US team has got through). The Americans have their World Series in baseball – but only North American teams compete. It is true to say that television has globalised many sports and games, such as snooker – now a big thing in China. But still there remain huge national differences.

Away from sport, Figure 38.2 shows some interesting data in relation to different interests. India is a poor country. In 2014, its per capita GDP (at purchasing power parity) was a seventh of the UK's. Yet Indians go to see more films per year than the British. The graph shows that Germany and Russia are particularly poor cinema-goers in relation to their income levels. That, of course, is their choice.

Different values

The term 'values' is a complex one. It suggests the moral code we live by, i.e. the standards of behaviour, including issues such as susceptibility to bribes and the willingness to cut corners in the pursuit of a goal such as profit or career advancement.

In business an important issue is corruption. Each year the World Economic Forum carries out its Global Competitiveness Report. It asks businesspeople in every country of the world: what are the biggest problems you find in doing business in this country? Corruption is one of the options that respondents can choose. When you look at all the figures, it's clear that corruption broadly correlates inversely with GDP per capita: the higher the level of affluence the lower the problem of corruption. Beyond that, however, there are national, cultural issues at play. For a super-wealthy country, Germany has an issue with corruption, whereas Japan has none. For a middling country Russia has a serious corruption problem whereas China and Swaziland come out relatively well. The United Kingdom is bang on the line of best fit, between Germany and Japan. At the other end of the line is Uganda, with 22.5 per cent of businesspeople considering corruption a major problem (see Figure 38.3).

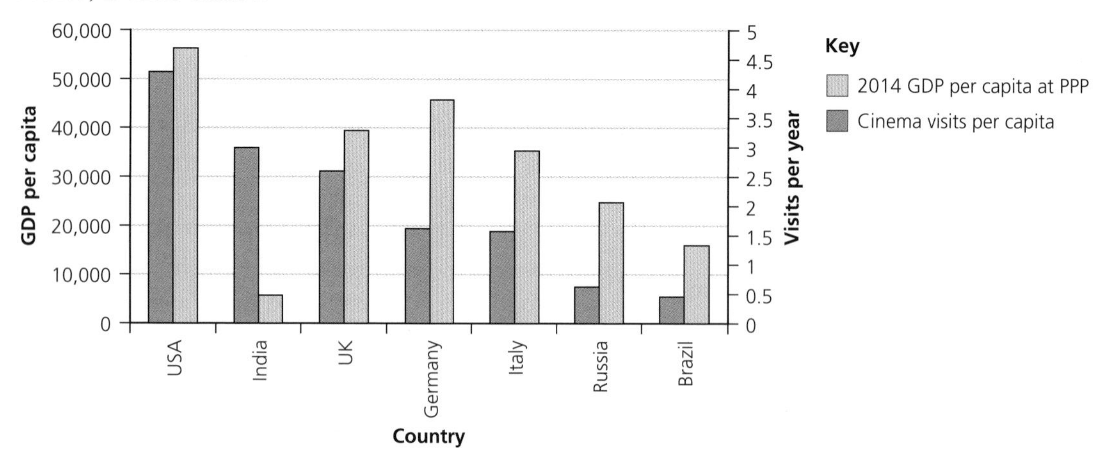

Figure 38.2 Cinema attendance related to income per head of population (source: *CIA World Factbook* and BFI statistics)

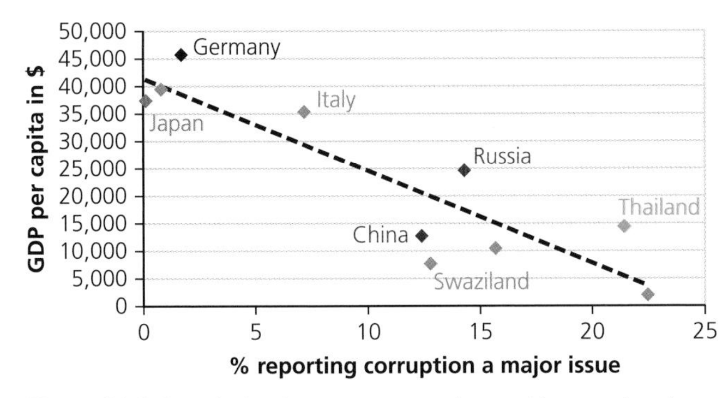

Figure 38.3 Correlation between corruption and income level (source: Global Competitiveness Report 2014/2015 and *CIA World Factbook* 2014)

In autumn 2015, Germany's Volkswagen was caught up in an extraordinary scandal about deliberately cheating on diesel car emissions tests. There is clearly an issue of values within the company.

> 'If people believe they share values with a company, they will stay loyal to the brand.'
>
> *Howard Schulz, chief executive, Starbucks*

38.3 Features of global niche markets

Especially at the luxury end of the market, global niches abound. In the market for perfumes and fragrances in Italy, brands include Askett, Memo, Tuscan Soul and Neroli. No sign of Katie Price. But at the top end of the Italian market there are a series of global brands including Bulgari, Armani as well as French Chanel No 5.

In the UK in recent years, Domino's Pizza has been hugely successful in the fast food business. But Domino's accounts reveal the huge losses the business has made in its expansions to Switzerland and, especially, Germany. In 2014, Domino's operation in Germany made operating losses of £8.3 million on a sales turnover of £5.7 million. That means total costs were £14 million compared with revenues of £5.7 million. The point is simple: niches can be quite different in the middle and lower ends of the market – because of cultural differences. It's only at the top end that niches become more standardised globally, because wealthy people travel a lot and therefore pick up tastes and habits in a more global way.

38.4 Adapting the marketing mix to fit global niche markets

At the top end of markets, where niches are based on luxury and exclusivity, the marketing mix needs little adaptation. This is the world of glossy magazines aimed at business travellers, such as *Monocle*, *Vogue* or *Condé Nast Traveller*. It's about distribution in airports, in posh shopping malls and in all the right streets: Bond Street, London; the Kurfürstendamm, Berlin and so on. And it's about pricing with boldness and imagination. All that's needed is a product with a long heritage or a newcomer with a brilliant story. Would Sir like a watch from a brilliant British company started by two brothers in 2002? That'll be £8,450 please, for the Bremont 'Jaguar' MKI.

Figure 38.4 The Bremont 'Jaguar' watch. Used with kind permission

Outside the luxury sector things can get harder. Targeting young consumers, perhaps those in the market for a new smartphone, can be much harder. Cultural differences mean that although Facebook may be quite global, many other marketing options are closed. Instagram is huge in America, big in Britain but little used in many other countries. Social media can be complex, with sites such as KWICK and Yappy (Germany) and VKontakte and Moi Mir (Russia).

To achieve success in non-luxury niches, huge local knowledge is essential: knowledge of the distribution system, of promotional methods, especially social media and local attitudes to price. It is said that Russians and Chinese like the combination of **aspirational pricing** and western imagery. This might work brilliantly for SuperGroup, due to open its first Superdry store in China in 2016.

> 'What marketers need to do is realise that the shopper needs to feel that she is making smart choices. It does not help the brand if she feels that she is being taken for a ride.'
>
> *Bindu Sethi, chief strategy officer, Grey Asia Pacific*

> 'This may seem simple, but you need to give customers what they want, not what you think they want. And, if you do this, people will keep coming back.'
>
> *John Ilhan, entrepreneur*

Five whys and a how

Questions	Answers
Why is global niche marketing any different from ordinary niche marketing?	It isn't. Both require a deep understanding of the current and potential customers within the niche.
Why use the term 'values' when it means the same as 'ethics'?	It doesn't quite. Values include behavioural traits as well, such as being hard-working.
Why might marketing to different niches in different countries be unsustainable?	It might simply be too expensive. If the West African car market requires an extra row of seats because of bigger family sizes, that may be impossible to justify economically.
Why don't more new entrants flood into the global niche market for luxury goods?	They try all the time; it's clear that there are huge profits to be made, but hard for newcomers to break through the shield provided by the powerful images of existing brands from Gucci to Givenchy.
Why might cultural diversity be seen as a problem by a UK business thinking of exporting?	Every business would love to sell the same thing to more people. Cultural diversity implies needing to develop new products to suit different cultures; each being costly to develop, and each with the risk of marketplace failure.
How might a newcomer break in to the global niche market for luxury goods?	By a combination of product innovation and clever branding based on something authentic (e.g. shirts hand-made and stitched in London).

38.5 Global niche markets – evaluation

Five years ago commentators thought that the future of business rested with the internet: online ordering from anywhere across the globe, making it easy to find a profitable niche. Since then it's become clearer that that approach might work for established niches such as '60s hippy music, but is much harder for newer niche markets. Customers like to see and touch – and need to, if the market is so new that they are still trying to understand it. The dramatic rise of street food in Manchester is a great case in point. No online delivery system here; it's about direct smells and experience.

So it's probably true to say that global niche marketing non-luxury markets will continue to require on-the-ground experience and a flexible, localising approach by companies. This links back to polycentrism, as explained in Chapter 37. Only in luxury sectors can ethnocentric or geocentric approaches be undertaken, in either case perhaps deciding on a standardised, globalised method for tackling the niche.

Key terms

Aspirational pricing: this means ignoring costs and competitors in pitching a price so high as to tempt those who wish to show off their wealth. (A London restaurant boasts the world's priciest burger: $2,000.)

Cultural diversity: the different interests and values of people from different national backgrounds.

38.6 Workbook

Revision questions

(25 marks; 25 minutes)

1 Explain why average price levels may be higher in niche than in mass markets. (4)

2 Give three reasons why a large firm may wish to enter a non-luxury, global niche market. (3)

3 Explain the value to a business of understanding the different interests of consumers in different countries. (4)

4 Look carefully at Figure 38.2. Use the data to explain whether America is a relatively enthusiastic cinema-going country. (4)

5 Explain two reasons why values may differ in different countries. (6)

6 Look carefully at Figure 38.3. Explain why it's possible to conclude that Thailand's record on corruption is relatively worse than that of China. (4)

Revision activities

Data response

Just Eat

On 2 April 2014, Just Eat floated on the London stock market at a valuation of £1.47 billion; even though it owned no restaurants, no consumer recognition and no patents, it was overnight worth more than long-established Pizza Express. It did have one important and valuable claim, though: Just Eat is the world's largest online takeaway ordering service, operating in 13 countries.

Just Eat started up in Denmark in 2001. Founded by Jesper Buch, the idea was simple: take the hassle of website development away from restaurant owners. Instead of devising an independent, but probably clunky, web presence, sign up with Just Eat and advertise on its super-slick e-commerce site. With every order, Just Eat takes 10–11 per cent of revenue as its commission. Needless to say, if volumes are high enough, this can become a vastly profitable business.

Between 2001 and 2006 the Danish Just Eat grew relatively slowly. Then Jesper Buch read that half Europe's takeaway food business is generated by Brits. In 2006, Just Eat came to Britain. By 2009 the British operation generated 1 million orders, which mushroomed to 10 million by 2011. Seeing the writing on the wall, Buch moved the whole operation to London in 2008. This is where the business is now headquartered. The 2014 flotation confirmed that, although born in Denmark, the business is now British. Its British chief executive is David Buttress.

Just Eat Mission:

> 'Empower consumers to love their takeaway experience'
>
> *(Source: Just Eat plc 2014 annual report)*

Just Eat is an interesting business for two reasons: its extraordinary rate of growth, especially in profitability; and its very clear sense of strategy. It wants to grow, but in a thoughtful way: building on strengths rather than risking taking on too much competition. In America, for example, Grubhub was there before Just Eat.

Just Eat is a great example of a modern, online business that can develop amazingly quickly from a good idea to a stunningly profitable enterprise. Once sales revenue is high enough to move above the break-even point, extra business is highly profitable. In the first half of 2015 Just Eat boasted 45 per cent growth in the number of takeaway restaurants signed up, but generated 54 per cent more revenue and 62 per cent more profit.

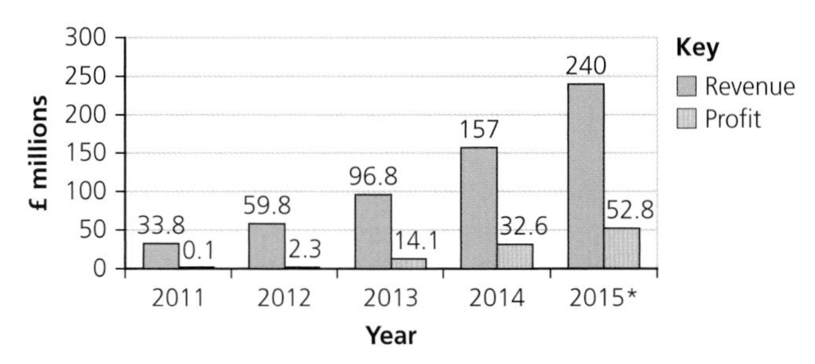

Figure 38.5 Rising profitability at Just Eat plc (source: all data from Just Eat accounts. *The 2015 figure is an estimate based on Jan–June 2015 figures)

For boss David Buttress, the main objective is to manage the company's spectacular growth to keep it as worldwide number one. Astonishingly, although the business is the number one provider in 10 of the 13 markets in which it operates, all the profit in 2014 came from the UK and Denmark. The 'other countries' division made operating losses. This is because the takeaway delivery market remains quite small in countries such as France, Italy, Mexico and Brazil (and in much of the rest of the world). Just Eat believes that the growth will show through in future, bringing in serious profits. In 2014, the 'other countries' revenue stream grew by 83 per cent compared with 66 per cent in Britain (and just 10 per cent in Denmark), so the plan looks on track.

The other major concern for David Buttress is to keep up with technological change. In 2014, for example, 60 per cent of orders were placed from a mobile device; in 2011 virtually none were placed this way. The position of Just Eat relies hugely on being at the forefront of convenient customer ordering.

Figure 38.6 Just Eat advertising logo. Used with kind permission

David Buttress also has firm ideas about branding. Perhaps surprisingly this modern business believes in traditional TV advertising for brand-building. Social media are seen as hugely important, but as a way to engage existing customers rather than a means to build the brand. To create brand awareness among potential rather than actual users, TV is the chosen medium. Surprisingly, though, for a business that wants to be the go-to brand in its field, Just Eat has surprisingly little visual presence. The 'fist-pump' logo is a recent attempt to tackle this weakness.

What's not in doubt is that things are working out well for boss David Buttress. In 2013, his 'remuneration' (total earnings) amounted to £367,000; a year later they were £3,824,500. Just Eat is a fantastic business success, but when the financial rewards become this great, company directors sometimes lose focus. As in everything, sometimes less is more.

Questions (40 marks; 40 minutes)

1 Whereas Denmark and the UK are profitable, the eleven 'other countries' generate losses. Assess whether that loss-making can be attributes to cultural diversity. (10)

2 **a)** Calculate Just Eat's 2015 profit as a percentage of revenue and compare it with the percentage for 2012. (6)

b) Outline two conclusions you can draw from that. (4)

3 Assume you've been given £2,000 to be used for saving or investing. Evaluate whether it would be wise to invest it buying shares in Just Eat plc. (20)

Extended writing

1 Brompton manufactures collapsible bikes for commuters, priced at around £1,000–£2,000. Evaluate its likelihood of succeeding if it makes a push into new markets globally. (20)

2 The Jaguar F-Pace 'practical sports car' was launched in 2016 into a luxury niche at the top end of the market for sports utility vehicles (SUVs). Evaluate the factors that may determine its success in this global niche market. (20)

39 Cultural and social factors in global marketing

Definition

Different traditions, religions and social conventions lead to significant variations in culture across the globe. Even a true global brand like Coca-Cola has to make adjustments to its marketing to appeal to differing local tastes and attitudes.

Linked to: International trade and business growth, Ch 28; Assessment of a country as a market, Ch 33; Global competitiveness, Ch 36; Global marketing, Ch 37; Global niche markets, Ch 38

39.1 Introduction

Entering foreign markets is a hazardous activity for most business, with so much scope for plans to be delayed operationally, or for technical problems to be discovered. However, many of the problems of entering foreign markets are a little more subtle, stemming from social and cultural differences between countries. A failure to understand different societies and cultures can lead to major marketing mistakes – in branding and advertising, and in the personal relationships on which successful selling relies.

39.2 Cultural differences

Normal everyday activities can be carried out in very different ways in different cultures – get them wrong and you can end up causing grave offence. Often, simple personal interactions can be fraught with difficulties in different cultures. This can be shown by considering the following potential mistakes that can be made when meeting people with whom you need to do business in China:

- Failing to exchange business cards *before* a meeting: in China (and Japan) it is expected that business cards be exchanged at the beginning of a meeting, and some time is taken to study one another's cards, admiring the design – failing to do so is like refusing to shake hands in the West.
- Dignity is critical: this can translate to politeness dictating that one should never directly say no – to do so would cause a dreadful loss of face to whomever is making the offer. This can have the knock-on effect of meaning that a yes in China is not quite as positive a response as it is in the west (yes may mean 'yes, maybe').
- Bad table manners at a meal: table manners will often be a key part of consolidating a business relationship, and bad manners will bring shame. Table manners themselves can be somewhat complex in China.

(Source: Bloomberg Business, 7 October 2014)

Often cultural norms can be influenced by religion. A past Coca-Cola summer advertisement featured bikini-clad beach volley-ballers; it did not go down well in India or the Middle East. And global advertisers have been caught out by different attitudes to dogs – cuddly pets in the west, but street-pests in many developing countries. It is easy to cause offence without meaning to. Upsetting for an individual, but potentially a major issue in a business context, where a marketing mistake can undermine a brand or a business relationship between two firms.

This issue relates back to globalisation versus glocalisation – covered in Chapter 37. Few companies today produce a TV advertisement in New York and tell its national subsidiaries to run it. They realise that local differences in taste and **culture** make this too risky an undertaking.

Real business

B&Q – CIY in China

B&Q, the British do-it-yourself retailer, was one of the earliest western retail firms to try to enter the Chinese market. Once there, bosses realised they faced a massive cultural problem – the absence of any DIY culture in China. When most Chinese homes or flats are bought, they are bought new, unfitted. Those buying these properties rarely possess any DIY skills. As manual labour is cheap, property-owners hire workers to fit out their flats for them. So it didn't work to build big DIY stores. B&Q needed to adapt its offering to suit the Chinese approach of Create It Yourself (then get someone in to do it for you). This early cultural lesson brought B&Q a certain degree of success. Yet the going was still so difficult that B&Q's owner Kingfisher plc sold its Chinese outlets to a local business in 2015.

39.3 Different tastes

The most popular flavours of crisps in the UK are ready salted and cheese and onion. Across most of mainland Europe, it is paprika. In the UK, Cadbury's Dairy Milk is *the* taste of chocolate; in America Hershey's is considered the real thing. In India Cadbury is number one with a market share of more than 65 per cent; in China Mars Dove (Galaxy) is the number one with a 40 per cent share. When it comes to taste in any consumer goods being sold, getting it right is crucial – failing to meet the needs of local customers is a sure-fire way to fail in the marketplace.

Market research can help here, but although large-scale quantitative research can be useful, a business with limited experience in a new foreign market may fail to ask the right questions of the right people. This is where research that relies heavily on local experts can be more useful and cost-effective. Many fashion brands will employ local fashion journalists as advisors when trying to break into a new market. These locals can offer a more indepth perception of which of the firm's items will appeal to local tastes.

Language

Language	Speakers (million people)
Chinese	1,197
Spanish	399
English	335
Hindi	260
Arabic	242

Table 39.1 The five most widely spoken languages in the world 2015 (source: www.themindunleashed.org)

The most widely spoken language in the world is, of course, Chinese (including several different languages such as Mandarin and Cantonese). Businesses looking to enter the country need to ensure that their staff can communicate effectively with Chinese speakers with whom they must deal. This can include locally hired staff, government officials and local suppliers and customers. And the business must ensure that marketing materials are checked by Chinese locals to avoid problems of translation.

Spanish is widely spoken throughout Central and South America – regions where economic development is occurring rapidly and potential markets for products sold by many firms from developed countries. Yet even a firm as large as General Motors made the mistake of launching the Nova in Mexico – where 'no va' translates to 'no go' – not a great name for a car.

Language	Learners (million people)
English	1,500
French	82
Chinese	30
Spanish	14.5
German	14.5

Table 39.2 The five most popular languages being learned around the world – 2015 (source: www.themindunleashed.org)

Table 39.2 gives a clear indication as to which language dominates international communication – English. With roots in the old British Empire, and further encouragement by the export of American culture, English is a commonly spoken second language for many, and thus becomes the common language that many people use where they do not speak one another's language.

What is clear from most businesses that have successfully managed to enter foreign markets is that:

- speaking even a little of the home language is always appreciated as a sign that the firm is treating its new market with respect
- access to fluent speakers of the new language is vital if the business is to avoid the problems that follow and get its marketing right.

Regrettably, the study of modern languages in the UK is declining from an already low base. Canny business students study Business and Chinese or Business and Japanese at University.

> 'If I'm selling to you, I speak your language. But if I'm buying, dann müssen Sie Deutsch sprechen.'
>
> *Willy Brandt, former German Chancellor*

39.4 Unintended meanings

With Google's translate service, we perhaps all feel that we can translate any foreign language accurately enough. However, the nature of language is such that a literal, word-for-word translation often leads to a different meaning to that which was originally intended. The examples below all show evidence of literal, rather than meaningful, translation and help to illustrate the problems faced by a business starting to operate in a language with which staff are not familiar:

Where?	What did it say?
In a hotel lift in Belgrade	To move the cabin, push the button for the wishing floor. If the cabin should enter more persons, each one should press a number of wishing floor. Driving is then going alphabetically by national order
In a dry-cleaner in Bangkok	Drop your trousers here for best results
A diversion sign, in Japan	Stop – drive sideways
In a Serbian hotel	The flattening of underwear with pleasure is the job of the chambermaid

Table 39.3 Unintended meanings (sources: various)

As silly as these sound, they illustrate the need for careful translation by a native speaker, rather than reliance on a literal word-for-word translation. Failure to get it right can lead to consequences that create irreparable damage to a brand, since much of the marketing material being translated may be seen by millions of potential new consumers. It is important to remember that foreign products entering new markets will face competition from others. And local rivals will not be making errors with language.

> 'Like many Easterners, Indians don't like to say "no" outright. Sometimes the lack of an answer is tantamount to a "no". In other instances, a "yes" without a follow-up is a "no".'
>
> *Manoj Joshi, author of* **Passport India**

39.5 Inappropriate or inaccurate translations

Translation problems tend to fall into one of three categories:

- Wrong words being used: using the wrong words in a translation tends to obscure the actual meaning intended and confuses potential consumers.
- Sounds like something else: taking a brand name and attempting to sell it in a foreign market can lead to problems if the brand name sounds like something else in the local language. Although the Nestlé ice cream range in Europe features the 'Bum bum' ice cream, launching the same product in the UK would need a change of product name.
- Slang: a brand name can seem to be perfectly acceptable in one language once the formal translators have checked that the name of the brand does not translate to anything inappropriate.

> 'No two languages are ever sufficiently similar to be considered as representing the same social reality. The worlds in which different societies live are distinct, not merely the same world with different labels attached.'
>
> *Edward Sapir, academic*

39.6 Inappropriate branding and promotion

Developing products or services that simply do not meet the needs of, or, even worse, offend local consumers will lead to failure in any market. It is thus vital to ensure that any branding, whether that be wording or imagery, will be appropriate for the local market. From social or cultural norms to religious imagery, the potential to come up with inappropriate branding is great. A soft drink featuring a number of six-pointed stars on its label caused offence in a number of Arab countries, where the stars were interpreted as being pro-Israeli. Unsurprisingly the German soft drink Pschitt has never made it in the UK.

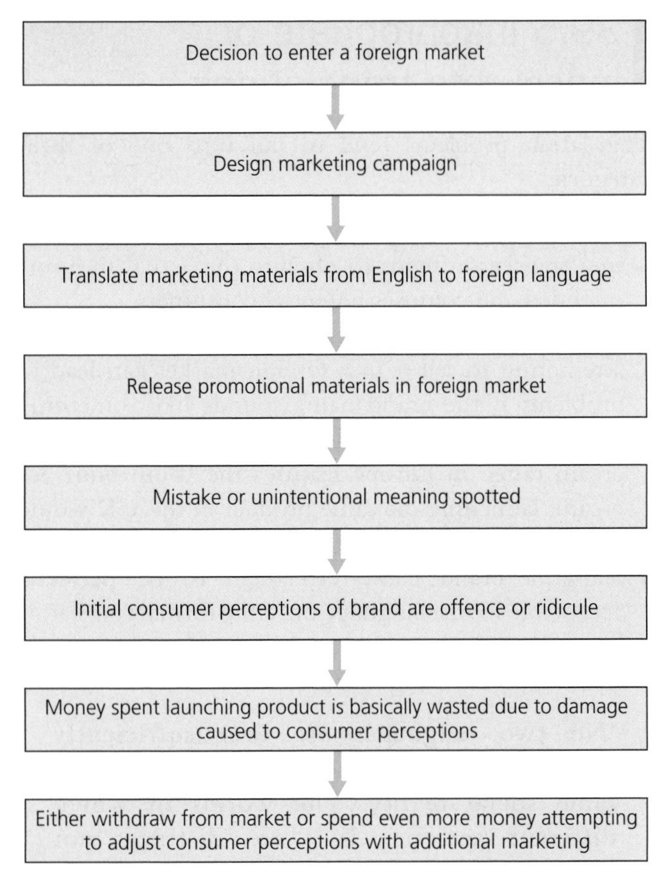

Figure 39.1 Logic chain showing effects of a translation problem

'In English culture a certain amount of eye contact is required ... in South Asian and many other cultures it's aggressive and rude.'

www.1000ventures.com

39.7 Cultural and social factors in global marketing – evaluation

Cultural and linguistic problems can completely undermine entry to a foreign market. Even if the operational side of the business is fully geared up to provide products and services to a new market, a marketing mistake can destroy the good work carried out by the rest of the business. Without correctly translated materials, marketing can be embarrassing, causing a loss of potential customers. Without a proper understanding of the social and cultural norms within the target country, a company may well find itself selling a product that does not suit customers' needs to a market that has been offended by the product or marketing materials. Businesses can underestimate the impact of national differences between markets, but they do so at their peril. Concentrating on getting translation and local market understanding right is critical to companies operating in a globalised economy selling to diverse markets.

Key terms

Culture: the commonly accepted values, beliefs and behaviours within a country.

Five whys and a how

Questions	Answers
Why is it vital to avoid offending local cultural norms?	It's hard enough to win when launching a new product without scoring a lot of own goals.
Why is it hard to succeed even though British firms are using the world's most common learned (second) language?	As the quote from Willy Brandt illustrated, anyone buying a product expects to be treated with respect – for many this means being addressed in their native language.
Why is Google Translate not the answer?	Machine translations tend to be over-literal in their translations, often producing odd meanings.
Why can UK firms especially be prone to linguistic problems?	A shortage of UK trained linguists linked to an attitude that others should speak English are both particular UK problems.
Why is it so vital to get marketing right for local tastes?	Marketing creates an image for a business or product. Once an initial image has been created, it tends to be far harder to change that image – so initial mistakes can be very costly to correct.
How can inappropriate marketing materials be avoided?	Check, check and check again using staff from the country in which you are planning to launch.

39.8 Workbook

Revision questions

(35 marks; 35 minutes)

1 List five types of promotion where translation errors could occur. (5)

2 Explain two examples of how different cultural norms in a foreign market could make a product you buy in the UK unacceptable. (6)

3 Briefly explain three reasons why poor translation of marketing materials can occur. (6)

4 Explain three consequences of launching a product in a foreign market with an inappropriate brand name. (9)

5 Analyse the benefits of setting up a local marketing office staffed at least partly by locals before entering a new foreign market. (9)

Revision activities

Data response

Oreos in China

Oreos are America's number one biscuit brand and have grown increasingly popular in the UK. In 1996, Oreos' owner, Kraft Foods, launched the brand in China. It had assumed that what made the product popular in the US would work in China just as well, amongst a growing middle class hungry for western brands. After nearly a decade, during which time Oreos never became the hit that Kraft had hoped for in China, the company was considering pulling out of the Chinese market altogether. Before taking this drastic step, Kraft carried out market research in China, aimed at finding out why the product had not been successful. The key findings were as follows:

- Biscuits as a whole are not as popular in China as elsewhere in the world.
- Chinese consumers found the biscuit element a little too bitter and the cream inside a little too sweet for their tastes.
- Prices had been set too high for value-conscious Chinese consumers.

By 2006, Kraft had made significant changes to cater for the Chinese market. Smaller packs had been introduced at far lower prices. The biscuit itself had been radically redesigned, now to be made of four layers of crispy wafer filled with vanilla and chocolate cream, coated in chocolate. In addition, recipes had been adjusted to reduce the sweetness of the vanilla cream and the bitterness of the chocolate.

Lessons have been learned and Oreos sales have increased dramatically, prompting Kraft to continue to tinker with the product to better suit local tastes, with Oreo green-tea ice cream now being sold in China. Kraft's willingness to adapt to local tastes helped Oreo become the first biscuit brand ever to have sales of more than $3 billion (2014) with more than $1 billion coming from developing countries, including China.

Figure 39.2 Oreo ice cream flavoured biscuits from Indonesia

(Source: Business Today, 1 March 2013)

Questions (50 marks; 60 minutes)

1 Use the example of Oreos to assess the importance of local market research being conducted before launching into a foreign market. (10)

2 Assess two possible reasons why Kraft management failed to carry out effective research before launching its brand in China. (8)

3 Assess the issues Kraft may have considered before deciding whether to pull out of China in 2004. (12)

4 Evaluate the extent to which adapting a product like Oreos to local tastes may be the most important part of a successful product launch in a new foreign market. (20)

Extended writing

1 Mastering national cultural differences requires time, sensitivity and people on the ground – all of which costs money. Evaluate whether this is possible for UK plcs focused on the next set of profit figures to be published. (20)

2 British firms are unlikely to achieve significant global success while British schools see a decline in the popularity of students taking modern foreign languages at GCSE level and beyond. Discuss. (20)

40 The impact of multinational corporations

Definition

A multinational corporation is a firm that has its headquarters in one country and branches, manufacturing or assembly plants in others. In other words, it is not just an exporter. It has business operations in many countries.

Linked to: Growth, Ch 7; China versus India, Ch 26; Business potential in Africa, Ch 27; International trade and business growth, Ch 28; Factors contributing to increased globalisation, Ch 29; Protectionism, Ch 30

40.1 Introduction

Some multinationals are giants. Table 40.1 compares the turnover of several large multinationals with the total output of various entire countries.

Country/company	2014 GDP/sales ($ billion)
UK	2,490
Poland	514
1. Walmart	478
2. Shell	451
3. Sinopec-China	445
4. Exxon	394
5. BP	379
South Africa	354
Pakistan	237
Kenya	45

Table 40.1 Comparative size of top five multinational corporations and selected national economies (source: *Forbes* magazine 2014 and *CIA World Factbook* March 2015)

Traditionally, multinationals had their headquarters in Europe, the USA or Japan. Over coming years, an increasing number of multinationals will be based in India or China. Examples may include the Indian companies Tata (owners of Jaguar Land Rover) and Mittal, plus the Chinese giants Lenovo (owners of IBM computers) and Alibaba.

40.2 Impact of multinational corporations (MNCs) on the local economy

Local labour, wages, working conditions and job creation

By the end of 2015 Yum Food (owners of KFC, Pizza Hut and Taco Bell) had 5,000 outlets across 100 cities in China. It was also developing rapidly in Russia and India (811 stores in India by October 2015). In total, Yum had 42,500 restaurants across 130 countries from America to Zambia.

The whole focus of managing a brand such as KFC globally is to look for consistency. Staff in frantic Lagos (Nigeria) must serve customers as professionally as in slow-moving Seattle. So the arrival of multinational company (MNC) service operations has a huge impact on local labour. Staff undergo training and are expected to work to rules that are quite different from traditional, quite casual practices. Timekeeping, cleanliness, politeness and efficiency are qualities that local labour learns to adopt and respect. And, for the most part, MNCs in service industries pay staff above local average pay rates. These pay rates may be far below western levels, but as long as they are above local averages they represent good jobs without raising any moral issues.

On the other hand, some MNC sourcing of products can be overly profit-driven. The awful Rana Plaza building collapse that killed 1,134 Bangladeshi garment workers highlighted their powerlessness in the face of bullying local management, driven by the cost pressures imposed by western companies such as Primark, H&M, Benetton and Gap. Part of the problem is the attitude of employers towards trade unions. Individuals have no negotiating power in a country such as Bangladesh, where no job means no food. At the time of the Rana Plaza collapse just 3 per cent of the workers belonged to trade unions. Better representation would create a better, fairer balance between employees and employers. This would allow pressure to be put on employers to provide better, safer and healthier working conditions. Western MNCs could stop using suppliers that refuse to recognise trade unions. They don't.

	Positive impact of MNCs	Negative impact of MNCs
Local labour	• Western training methods may make the local workforce more productive/ employable	• Western employers may attract over-qualified people – possibly stripping local businesses and public services of skilled staff
Wages	• MNCs usually pay higher wage rates than local firms, improving standards of living	• Some locals may feel bitter that they are paid less than westerners for doing exactly the same job
Working conditions	• MNCs have international reputations to maintain, so they will tend to provide above-average conditions • Yum Foods has a 'Human and Labour Rights Policy' and claims to employ it in all 125 countries	• Conditions may be above-average, yet still quite shocking to westerners • Some MNCs may have impressive policies in place yet the workplace reality may be worse than the paper theory
Job creation	• Yum Foods employs 1.5 million people worldwide; in Africa it provides more than 20,000 jobs	• The success of MNCs may sometimes be at the expense of local independent firms; the key measure is *net* job creation

Table 40.2 Positive and negative impact of multinational corporations

Impact of MNCs on local businesses

In 2014, Honda started production at its 450-acre car factory in Tapukara, India. This, the first-ever car factory in Rajasthan, employs 3,200 people. Just consider the impact on local businesses. There will be small businesses that open up to supply the factory directly. All the way from providing security guards and delivering catering services through to supplying car parts or raw materials. Then there's the huge secondary impact caused by 3,200 relatively well-paid jobs. Cafes will spring up locally, grocers will build extensions and local private schools will be affordable by more people. The impact on local businesses will be huge and almost entirely beneficial.

Honda's arrival in Rajasthan is entirely positive because it's the first car company in the region – and the overall growth of the Indian car market means the 3,200 jobs in Tapukara are not at the cost of jobs elsewhere. But what about when a multinational comes to compete with an established business? BP and Shell have a long history of breaking into local markets for energy, especially oil exploration and extraction. Their financial muscle and distribution potential makes it hard for local oil businesses to compete. They would be inclined to sell their business to the multinational rather than risk being out-competed.

Overall, though, if you asked Chinese and Indian businesspeople whether they have benefited from multinational firms, they would say yes. They would point to the business opportunities created plus the amount they learned from the MNC's ways of recruiting, training and managing staff.

Impact of MNCs on the local community and environment

It is important to remember that many local businesses in developing countries have no real concept of environmental standards. Despite the air pollution that can be unpleasant in London, it's nothing like as bad as in the main cities of India. It is naïve to think that happy, honest locals are environmentally good and MNCs are environmentally bad. Either or both can be good or bad depending on different influences. For a multinational such as Coca-Cola, ignoring local green issues can backfire not only in the host country but also globally. Coca-Cola has long had an image problem in India; its supposed environmental mistakes in India have upset green campaigners throughout the west. This means that Coca-Cola has a clear incentive to be environmentally sound in all its future operations.

Nevertheless, incentive is one thing, reality is another. There are plenty of examples of poor behaviour by multinationals. The car manufacturer Volkswagen has had to face the consequences of cheating on its diesel emission tests. Both BP and Shell have had a series of environmental scandals in Nigeria and America. But then so too have non-MNCs. In 2008, the industrial chemical melamine was found in baby milk in China. Over 300,000 babies fell ill and at least three died directly from the poisoning. Executives from the Chinese Sanlu Group were arrested and punished severely. The point is simple. Seriously unethical practices can be traced to some MNCs and to some local businesses.

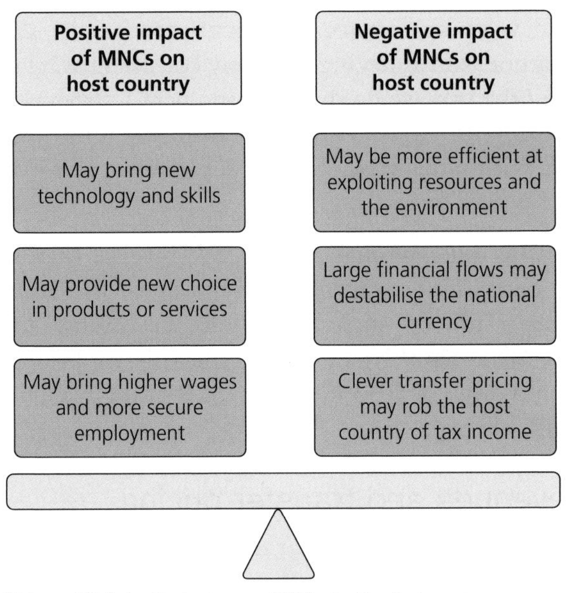

Figure 40.1 Logic balance: MNCs in the balance

40.3 Impact of multinational corporations (MNCs) on the national economy

FDI flows

Foreign direct investment (FDI) comes from many sources, one of which is multinational corporations. In 2012, the Staffordshire-based JCB opened a £100 million factory in Brazil. The £100 million came from profits saved by JCB plus some borrowings – and therefore was £100 million taken from UK banks and sent to Brazil. There it was invested in land, buildings and construction plus used for buying equipment and recruiting and training staff. All these uses of the money represent injections into the Brazilian economy – creating jobs in the short and medium term.

Although there is no doubting the benefits to be gained from FDI, some worry that the FDI flow may be positive in the short term but negative in the long term. If JCB's investment is successful its Brazilian **subsidiary** will make good profits. If those are sent back to the UK year after year, it may be that Brazil loses out financially in the long term. Others would say that this is a curious way to look at it. If JCB Brazil is successful, JCB will be keen for it to expand and won't, therefore, simply treat Brazil as a cash cow.

Figure 40.2 shows how FDI inflows were rising sharply in India before the global recession, but haven't quite recovered since.

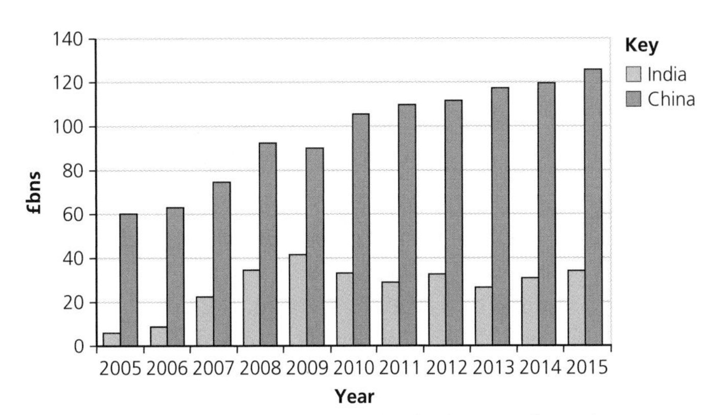

Figure 40.2 FDI inflows in China and India (source: Central Statistics Office of China and Central Statistics Office of India; 2015 is estimated)

Balance of payments

If a country has higher imports than exports, it runs a current account deficit. That is likely to push the value of a currency down, creating a risk of inflation. FDI inflows would counter that. If a country imports £200 million more than it exports, but an outside multinational promises to invest £200 million in a new shopping centre, the FDI inflows will cancel out the current account outflows.

But what if, at a time a country was suffering a £200 million current account deficit, a multinational decided to withdraw £200 million of capital from the country? It's going to sell to a local, then withdraw its cash. This means the balance of payments now has a £400 million deficit. This might be very tough for the value of the currency.

For a huge economy such as Britain's, the power of any one multinational is relatively unimportant. For a country such as Kenya, however, with GDP a tenth of the size of the biggest multinationals (see Table 40.1), the withdrawal of a large amount of capital could push the value of the currency down sharply.

Technology and skills transfer

It's important to bear in mind that much of human progress is based on theft of ideas. It was Toyota and Nissan's success in using Japanese lean production techniques in their American and British factories that persuaded western companies to 'borrow' those ideas. So the arrival of a multinational company is bound to bring technology and skills from the developed west, a process known as technology or **skills transfer**. In the period up to 2005, western advisors going to China to talk about environmental improvement would find little interest in the subject, but huge interest in laptops, memory sticks and software. Today China is a leading producer of all those things.

In the long run technology makes a difference, but nothing like as much as skills and attitudes. Ford once had the exact same factory layout at Halewood, Liverpool and Saarlouis, Germany. The technology was the same and the car model was the same. The Germans were more than 20 per cent more efficient. Their higher technical skill meant they looked after the machinery better and therefore there were fewer breakdowns. If a new MNC makes locals think more seriously about education and skills training, the benefits could be massive. As Figure 40.3 shows, multinationals can be a progressive force for economic development.

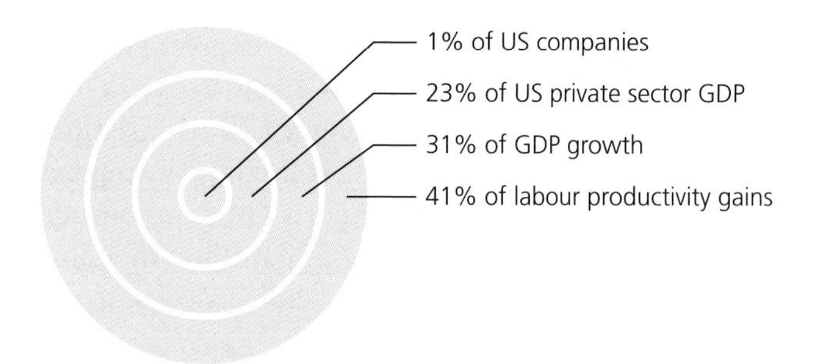

Figure 40.3 Logic target: multinationals in America (source: McKinsey Global Institute)

Consumers

Although most people take pride in their own customs and traditions, consumers are easily seduced by choice. I love Cadbury's Dairy Milk, but like the occasional Swiss indulgence: Lindor. Therefore it's a rare consumer who rejects the advantages of new suppliers with new ideas and new forms of service.

The only downside would be if a wave of Starbucks put a series of local, high-quality cafes out of business. But this is the heart of capitalism: for the strong to succeed the weakest must go to the wall. If people talk nostalgically about independent cafes while they're sitting in Starbucks, presumably there was a flaw in the local, independent offering. Chain stores such as Starbucks may be irritatingly same-y, but they are clean, efficient and consistent.

Business culture

The ethos of a multinational company is usually very driven, profit-focused, efficient and governed by clear objectives. It may or may not have a culture that is entrepreneurial or one based on clear ethical standards. What a developing country may benefit from is the idea of the corporation as having relatively consistent ways of working ('the way we do things round here'). Producers of raw materials will find professionalism and long-term thinking within the MNC buying department; this may rub off.

It would be quite wrong, though, to imagine that all western companies are bringing high ethical standards. Volkswagen proved that with diesel emissions, and Britain's GlaxoSmithKlein proved that in its bribery scandal in China in 2013 (for which it eventually paid a $500 million fine).

Tax revenues and transfer pricing

Multinationals have a particular temptation to minimise their tax payments by utilising the spread of their business over a series of different tax authorities. As Figure 40.4 shows, tax rates vary a lot between developed countries. Furthermore there are **tax havens** such as the British Virgin Islands where the rate of corporation tax is zero.

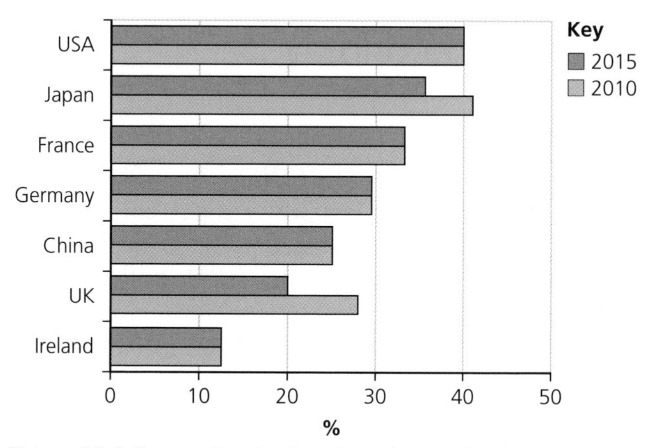

Figure 40.4 Corporation tax in selected countries (source: KPMG 2015)

The existence of different tax rates in different countries allows multinationals to practise **transfer pricing**. This is a way to boost profits by taking advantage of different tax levels in their countries of operation. It involves declaring high profits in countries where tax rates are low and minimal profits in countries where tax rates are high. For example, if Tesco UK sold goods cheaply to Tesco Ireland, its profits would rise in Ireland (where profit tax is low), and would fall in Britain. This would reduce Tesco's overall tax bill. The legality of transfer pricing tends to vary from country to country. As a result, it is difficult to clamp down on this practice, which many feel to be unfair.

An even more significant problem, in recent years, has been the increasing use of tax havens such as Bermuda or the Virgin Islands. Multinationals can register their businesses on these islands, where corporation tax may be 0 per cent. By channelling profits to these islands the multinational company can minimise its tax bill.

In 2014, the UK-based drinks multinational Diageo (Smirnoff, Baileys, Guinness) paid a corporation tax rate of 16.5 per cent. Local, probably smaller, British breweries would have had to pay the full 22 per cent tax. The scope for **tax avoidance** unfairly favours multinational corporations.

Real business

In October 2015 the European Commission ordered that Starbucks should pay $34 million in back taxes to the Dutch government. In 2001, Starbucks had made Amsterdam its European headquarters after reaching a deal with the Dutch tax authorities. This allowed for a double tax-reduction mechanism: the company would buy all its beans through low-tax Switzerland, at a 20 per cent mark-up (transferring profit to Switzerland). In addition Starbucks Holland would syphon profits from the other European branches by means of an 'Intellectual Property' (IP) levy of 5 per cent.

The European Commission managed to discover that the IP involved was nothing more than the temperature at which coffee should be roasted. As it noted, acidly, this was more like instructions than intellectual property. No other Starbucks companies or other roasters paid royalties for this information. In 2014, Starbucks Holland paid just €2.6 million of profit tax on €407 million of profit – a rate of less than 1 per cent. Perhaps the European Union's new-found firmness on this issue will see a significant reduction in transfer pricing by multinationals.

Five whys and a how

Questions	Answers
Why might it be significant that Shell's sales revenue is ten times that of Kenya's GDP (Table 40.1)?	It might imply that Shell has the financial muscle to get its own way when dealing with the Kenyan government.
Why are workers at Jaguar Land Rover thrilled with their Indian multinational owner?	JLR was a poorly run business before Tata of India. Under British ownership and under American (Ford) ownership the workers' future looked very uncertain.
Why do people get more angry with multinationals than badly behaved national companies?	People believe that the sheer size of many multinationals gives those businesses a sense of entitlement – they can get away with whatever they want.
Why do firms use transfer pricing?	To transfer their profits from high tax to low tax countries.
Why might the data in Figure 40.4 tempt a French firm to move to the UK?	Corporation tax in France is about 33 per cent whereas here it's now 20 per cent (and moving down to 18 per cent). Surely that must be tempting!
How might a multinational minimise its tax bill?	By locating a head office in a low tax country, then 'charging' its subsidiaries a fee for the right to use the logos and intellectual property of the business. This captures the profit where profit tax rates are low.

'The multinational corporation and international production reflect a world in which capital and technology have become increasingly mobile, while labour has remained relatively immobile.'

Robert Gilpin, academic

'Can you believe it? Fifty miles from McDonald's. I didn't think there was anywhere in the world that was fifty miles from McDonald's.'

Neil Gaiman, humourist

'Leaders (of multinationals) will have their most positive influence if they have a willingness to recognise the limitations of their own cultural norms and accept and adapt to the culture of the host country.'

A.J. Fernandez, academic

'My guiding principle is that prosperity can be shared. We can create wealth together. The global economy is not a zero-sum game.'

Julia Gillard, former Prime Minister, Australia

40.4 The impact of multinational corporations – evaluation

Multinationals get a bad press. It is assumed that their lack of a solid connection to a single country weakens their sense of moral and social responsibility. It's not difficult to see why that would be true. Many are so large that, as shown at the start of the chapter, they can rival nations in their size and wealth. So they can be expected to develop their own culture and their own sense of right and wrong. What's not in doubt is that a failing by McDonald's or Shell anywhere in the world can bite them all over the world. So in some ways multinationals may have to work harder at being 'good' than other companies. They have more to lose from bad publicity.

The use of extreme tax avoidance by several prominent multinationals such as Apple and Google is a reminder, though, that companies can allow themselves to lose sight of their moral responsibilities. They succeed thanks to the education and health of the people who work for them, so they should be *proud* to contribute to the tax base of the countries in which they operate. Sadly, their failure to do so affects many other companies as well. Richard Branson's Virgin Group gets much of its income from UK government sources (rail income and operating outsourced health and social care businesses) – but it keeps its tax base in offshore havens such as the Virgin Islands.

Figure 40.5 The Virgin Islands are a tax haven

Key terms

Skills transfer: the way that technologies and management practices used by multinationals can generate spin-off benefits locally, e.g. an IT manager for Wal-mart quits to start up her own e-commerce business in Cambodia.

Subsidiary: a company set up to be subordinate to another, e.g. Cadbury starting a sweet shop subsidiary business.

Tax avoidance: legal, but perhaps not moral, ways of artificially minimising the taxes companies owe to society.

Tax havens: countries or districts where taxes on company profits are at or close to zero. Multinationals and many other businesses artificially register their company headquarters in these – often tiny – 'homes'.

Transfer pricing: a way multinationals can minimise their worldwide tax liabilities by transferring their profits from high-tax to low-tax countries.

40.5 Workbook

Revision questions

(35 marks; 35 minutes)

1 a) State four advantages to businesses of operating in several countries. (4)

b) Which of the four would be the most important for each of the following businesses? Explain your reasoning:

i) Rolls Royce Motors, if its management decided to open a factory overseas. (6)

ii) Cadbury's, if it wanted to open a factory in India. (6)

iii) King Interactive, owners of the Candy Crush saga, if it moved half of its key software development team from London to Beijing. (6)

2 Explain one potential problem for a British business opening up operations in several overseas markets. (4)

3 Explain the meaning of the term 'transfer pricing'. (3)

4 Explain two advantages of producing in the country in which you are selling. (6)

Revision activities

Data response

Fever-Tree plc: the enterprising UK manufacturer

Britain's biggest manufacturing sector is food and drink. Although the UK has a huge current account deficit in food and drink, we still sell plenty of food exports, often at very good profit margins. The sector is characterised by old established firms such as Cadbury and Schweppes, plus lively newcomers such as Fever-Tree. Founded in 2005 by two experienced food marketing executives, the company was launched onto Britain's junior stock market (AIM) in early November 2014. Sixty per cent of the shares were floated raising £93 million. Almost all this cash was to reward the shareholders; only £4 million was to help finance growth.

But growth potential there certainly is. Fever-Tree's brand proposition is 'all-natural', from the quinine that goes in the tonic water to the ginger in the ginger ale. And no artificial sweeteners. This has helped it get 75 per cent penetration in the world's top restaurants, yet it has a market share of less than 0.5 per cent in US retail market. Curiously, its highest market penetration is in Spain, with 5 per cent. Clearly there's plenty of scope for growth.

Although the Fever-Tree founders worked hard to source and test the recipes in their products, they saw no need to produce them themselves. They outsource production to a soft drinks factory in Shepton Mallet, Somerset. This provides English provenance, which lends credibility to the brand, especially as a mixer to as classically English a spirit as gin. Such has been the success of the brand that around 75 per cent of all sales come from abroad. 2014 saw a big push into India – Fever-Tree's fiftieth country in which it operates.

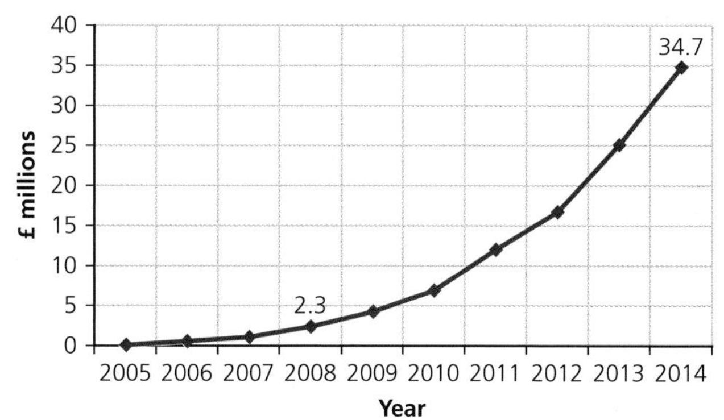

Figure 40.6 Fever-Tree: annual sales turnover (£ms) (source: various, including Sunday Times Fasttrack)

As the graph shows, sales have grown consistently and dramatically at an average growth rate of over 50 per cent a year. Profits have clearly been exceptional as well, judging by the company's ability to finance its own growth. In 2014, the company's stated operating profit was £8.1 million.

Questions (40 marks; 45 minutes)

1. Assess why Fever-Tree may have chosen to target overseas markets. (10)
2. Assess whether Fever-Tree should continue to be based in England or should build a more multinational structure. (10)
3. If financial constraints forced Fever-Tree to choose whether to focus on China or India, evaluate which market they should choose. (20)

Extended writing

1. 'To succeed in the long term, every car manufacturer has to develop a strong multinational presence.' Evaluate this statement. (20)
2. A Chinese electrical goods manufacturer is considering building a new plant in Britain to serve the European market. Evaluate whether this inward investment should be welcomed or rejected. (20)

41 Ethics in global business

Definition

Ethics are the moral principles that should underpin decision-making. Although the principles are no different for global as for local business, in practice there are different issues that must be considered.

Linked to: Corporate objectives, Ch 1; Corporate culture, Ch 16; Shareholders versus stakeholders, Ch 17, Business ethics, Ch 18; The impact of multinational corporations, Ch 40; Controlling multinational corporations, Ch 42

41.1 What are business ethics?

As explained in Chapter 18, ethics can be defined as a code of behaviour considered morally correct. Business ethics provide moral guidelines for the conduct of business affairs. There is a natural tension between these guidelines and the single-minded pursuit of business objectives – especially profit. This tension is especially acute when businesses from developed economies operate in less developed ones. This has been highlighted recently in relation to whole industries (such as alcohol and fast food) and to businesses that use child labour in less developed countries.

Among the important ethical considerations in global business are the following:

- Do businesses implement everywhere the best practice they operate in certain (probably developed) countries, e.g. if a global fast-food business prints calories on US menus, does it do the same in Thailand or Nigeria?
- Do western companies check back throughout the entire supply chain when buying supplies from less developed countries? Apple received bad publicity when there was a spate of staff suicides at its Taiwanese-owned but China-located supplier Foxconn.
- Do companies make sure that there are neither slave nor child labourers working for a subcontractor, a supplier or a provider of outsourcing services?
- Are companies paying their way? Are they paying standard rates of profit tax or are they organising their business activities in a contrived way to avoid paying corporation tax?

41.2 Stakeholder conflicts

A useful starting point may be to consider business objectives in relation to ethical behaviour. Many businesses operate within the corporate objective: 'make the maximum profit possible in order to satisfy the owners of the business'.

Some notable academics support this view. Milton Friedman, a famous American economist, held the view that all businesses should use the resources available to them as efficiently as possible. Friedman argued that making the highest possible profit creates the maximum possible wealth, to the benefit of the whole society.

Friedman's view, however, ignores the fact that the interests of the stakeholders may differ. Most people would consider it unethical to make staff redundant if the motive was purely to add to the bonuses earned by directors and dividends paid to shareholders.

Conflicting stakeholders	Example	Ethical solution
Retailers and their suppliers	In 2015, Arcadia plc (Topshop) cut 2% from all payments to suppliers from 1 September. Young designers squealed at the threat to their finances	Price negotiations should be tough, but once a price is agreed, it's unethical to bully a small supplier into receiving less
Directors and staff	In May 2015, Tesco told staff it would in future contribute 5% of pay towards their pensions; before it was 11%; new boss Dave Lewis gets 25% of his salary paid 'in lieu of pension'!	Staff understand that bosses receive higher remuneration, but unfairness such as this is quite simply unethical
Management and shareholders	Bafflingly, owners of bank shares have allowed senior bank staff to pay themselves bonuses that strip the banks of their profitability (Lloyds Bank shares: 976p in 1999; 575p in 2007; 75p in 2015)	Ethics should apply in all cases; using negotiating power is fine; but many bonuses were for things that cost the bank in the long term e.g. mis-selling Payment Protection Insurance (PPI)

Table 41.1 Conflicting stakeholders – ethical solutions

41.3 Pay and working conditions

Broadly, the pay people receive is in line with the supply and demand for their skill level within a specified country. Bus drivers in England earn a little more than £9 an hour – slightly more than shop workers at Lidl. Are the bus drivers paid fairly? Well, no, if the bus companies are making fat profits. But yes, if there's no problem recruiting more bus drivers.

But in this section on ethics the focal point is pay internationally. A bus driver in New Delhi, India, earns about 60p an hour. Is that fair? All we know is that there's not much point in comparing the wages in Delhi with those in Britain. Many people find it distasteful that they are wearing garments made by poorly paid staff, probably working in poor working conditions. But look at Figure 41.1. It shows economic growth rates in Cambodia. In 1995, it was starting to recover from one of the most vicious civil wars of all time. It chose to adopt clothing production as its way to grow. This has given the country 15 years of solid growth, transforming average incomes from $300 a year in 2000 to $3,300 in 2014. Today more than 70 per cent of Cambodia's manufactured goods' exports are textiles; the poorly paid garment workers are leading the country's growth.

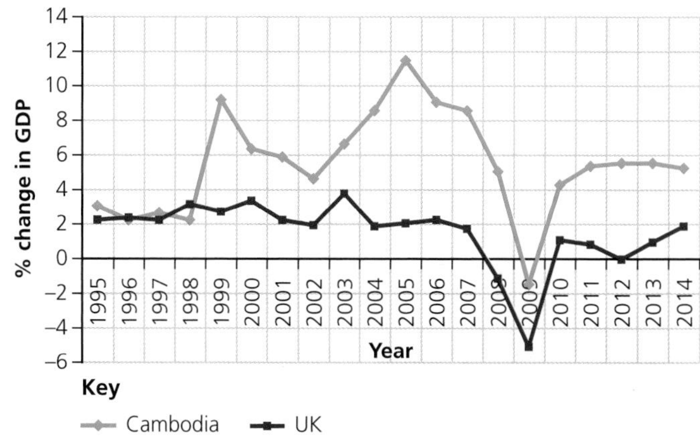

Figure 41.1 Cambodia growth miracle: percentage change in annual per capita GDP at constant prices (source: World Bank 2015)

Yes, underpaying staff is wrong; but paying the right rate for local circumstances can be justified. But there remains the issue of working conditions.

Working conditions that could be seen to be ethically acceptable	Working conditions that are unconditionally unacceptable
• Cramped and hot, where profit margins are too low to allow more space and air conditioning	• Dangerous conditions with machinery and fire risk – and perhaps chemical air pollution
• Long working hours, perhaps up to 12 hours a day	• Forcing people to work long hours, perhaps by threats of dismissal
• Agricultural workers planting rice – bending over for perhaps 12 hours a day	• Long, back-breaking hours in agriculture with little pay – while farmers and dealers get rich

Table 41.2 Working conditions and ethics

41.4 Environmental considerations

Emissions

In Autumn 2014, the US Environmental Protection Agency fined Hyundai $100 million for mis-stating its carbon emissions. This should have been a warning to Volkswagen which, a year later, was caught in a similar (but much more scandalous) way. For businesses, meeting government regulations on emissions is necessary; but in the case of cars there's a double factor. Customers are influenced by the environmental claims made for a car, so low emissions add value to the proposition. The Toyota Prius (an eco-friendly hybrid car) sold its 5 millionth car in August 2015 – a notable achievement.

Figure 41.2

It seems that the temptation to overstate emissions performance is too much for car companies. In America, the state makes sure that regulatory testing is independent of the car company; in Europe companies pay for their own testing from the 'independent' testers they appoint.

Ethically, the key thing is honesty – not just in the promises made but also behind the scenes. If a company finds out something bad that no one else knows, it's up to it to publicise the fact. The reality is often the opposite. In her book *Confessions of an Rx Drug Pusher*, former pharmaceuticals saleswoman Gwen Olsen explains that she was trained to keep quiet about the dangerous side-effects of the drugs she was selling to doctors. This is completely unethical on the part of the company and the individual.

Waste disposal

In December 2013, the United Nations published a report about the developed world dumping its electronic waste (e-waste) on Africa. Britain was responsible for disposing of 21kg of e-waste per person, including old-style computer screens that can contain up to 3kg of lead (a serious poison). At the time, Interpol reported that one-third of containers leaving the EU contained illegal e-waste. Dumped in weakly regulated African countries, the e-waste contains many toxic chemicals that can affect groundwater or pollute the air. In 2015, the story was updated in West Africa, when it emerged that stricter rules in East and South Africa were channelling the waste towards Ghana, Liberia and the Ivory Coast.

Companies lobby hard to persuade government that minimal regulation is best for all concerned, but the evidence makes this a tough argument. Food waste from UK supermarkets is the highest in Europe – cementing the UK's position as the biggest waster of food by far in the EU. France has passed legislation making it illegal for French supermarkets to throw away unsold food. Now they have to pass the food on to charities. In the past, the House of Lords has blamed UK supermarkets for using Buy One Get One Free (BOGOF) promotions that encourage over-buying and therefore waste. But no government has yet regulated on the subject.

A problem in exams can come from the fact that many companies are very clever at creating a green image for themselves, even when it may not be warranted. Always be alert to the difference between a company that's serious about its environmental footprint and one that's simply clever at **greenwash**.

> 'I often wince when companies talk too enthusiastically about their social or environmental responsibility. It often sounds like window dressing.'
>
> *Gillian Tett, award-winning Financial Times columnist*

41.5 Supply chain considerations

The specification uses the term 'exploitation of labour'. Surely no labour is exploited if the supply is willing; in other words, if the employees are free to work or not work. But exploitation certainly exists. Until 2005 it was legal in the UK to act as a 'gangmaster' – bringing in workers who were 'bonded' to their boss by 'debt bondage' and forced to work. The Gangmasters Licensing Authority now accepts or rejects applications based on the known behaviour of those who want to use 'gangs' of seasonal labour to pick strawberries or other agricultural produce.

The Gangmasters (Licensing) Act was passed in 2004 after 23 Chinese workers drowned in Morecambe Bay (they had been forced to pick cockles on a notoriously tidal beach – but couldn't swim). The use of gangmasters had been allowed after the Deregulation and Contracting Out Act 1994 – a deregulatory piece of legislation pushed through by John Redwood MP, then a government minister. According to the Borgen Project charity, there are more than 20 million slaves in the world today. Without question, no UK company should be dealing with any supplier suspected of using slave labour.

Another factor to consider is child labour. According to the International Labour Organization (ILO), there are 168 million children employed worldwide. Most work for their parents – usually in agriculture – and more than 40 per cent do what the ILO considers 'hazardous work'. There are positives, such as that the total number of child workers has fallen by a third since 2000 (girls by 40 per cent). But there remain many incidences of children working in brick kilns, mines or construction – dangerous places for anyone, especially children. Nestlé has had problems with child labour at supplier cocoa plantations in the Ivory Coast. To its credit, it now publishes the work of its auditors, even though the December 2014 one found evidence of 27 workers under 15 at the Nestlé farms. The issue of child labour is not a simple one. If a twelve-year-old is working on the farm because it's the only way to feed the family, who are we to condemn? But of course no ethical business would want to see children in mines or on construction sites.

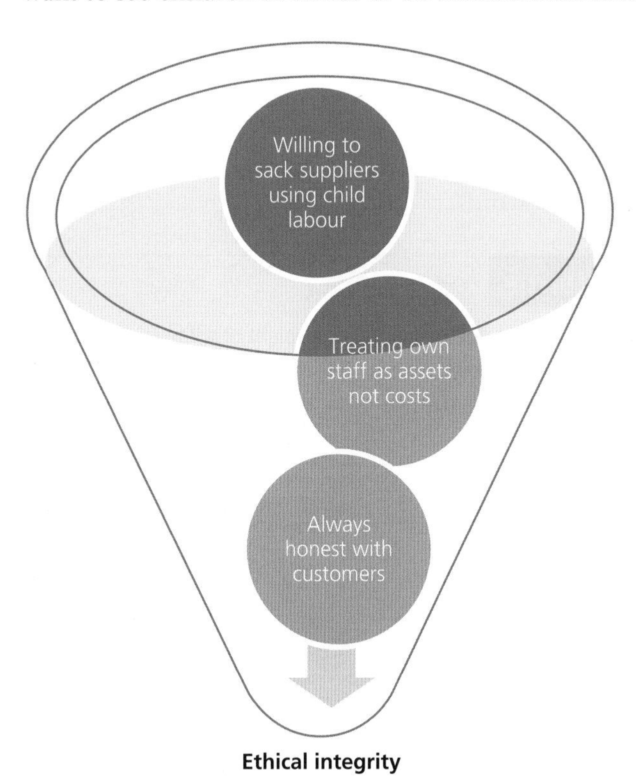

Figure 41.3 Logic funnel: ethical integrity

41.6 Marketing considerations

Misleading product labelling

The UK consumer is protected by the Trades Descriptions Act 1968, which makes it a criminal offence to make false statements about goods or services offered. So, almost always, actual claims made on a pack or on an advertisement will be true. The devil is in the detail: lots may be implied but not claimed. So consumers may buy something they think is made in a natural way, but is actually factory-made and subject to lots of processing. The French food business managed to push global sales of Activia yogurt up to $4.2 billion a year on the basis of claims about its benefits to digestion and vitality. In 2013, the EU banned the company from making any more health claims for the brand, but sales were still growing in parts of the world outside Europe – where Activia could still overstate its case.

Inappropriate promotional activities

As mentioned earlier, the BOGOF promotion can be criticised for encouraging over-buying and therefore food wastage. Perhaps more important is that promotional devices such as this (or 'the round £1') tend to focus on the things we like, but know we shouldn't have. Ben & Jerry's at £2, nice fat slabs of chocolate for £1 and so on. Tesco proudly pursues a strategy of de-listing added-sugar soft drinks for kids – but doesn't hold back on many other ways to keep us eating and drinking too much of the wrong stuff. Ever remember a BOGOF on apples?

Real business

Capri-Sun is consumed in 200ml pouches. Each contains 20mg of sugar, which is 5 teaspoons (4gm = 1 teaspoon). It is now banned from Tesco stores.

Buying 2-for-1 Coca-Cola 1.75 litre bottles means consuming the following number of teaspoons of sugar:

- Coca-Cola contains 27gm of sugar per 250ml (source: Tesco website).
- That is 189gm per 1.75 litre bottle ...
- ... which is 189 × 2 = 378gm in total
- A teaspoon contains 4gm of sugar so there are 378/4 = 94.5 teaspoons of sugar in Tesco's BOGOF deal.

Yes, 94.5 teaspoons of sugar. Thanks, Tesco.

'The time is always right to do what is right.'

Martin Luther King, Nobel Prize winner

'Apart from values and ethics which I have tried to live by, the legacy I would like to leave behind is a very simple one – that I have always stood up for what I consider to be the right thing, and I have tried to be as fair and equitable as I could be.'

Ratan Tata, Indian business leader

'Live one day at a time emphasising ethics rather than rules.'

Wayne Dyer, business author

'Consumers have not been told effectively enough that they have huge power and that purchasing and shopping involve a moral choice.'

Anita Roddick (founder of the Body Shop), human rights activist and environmental campaigner

Five whys and a how

Questions	Answers
Why might ethics be stronger in businesses with long-term corporate objectives?	Those with long-term planning horizons can factor in the reputational benefits from establishing a strong ethical culture.
Is it unethical to buy from suppliers who pay staff 50p an hour?	Not necessarily. If average pay levels locally are lower than that, 50p an hour may be a good wage; surely it's better than having no job because pressure groups have made it impossible to use 'cheap' labour.
Why might achieving a strong ethical culture be harder for businesses that operate on a global scale?	If staff are dispersed widely, it is very hard to achieve a consistent and strong culture in every part of an organisation that might have 200,000 staff spread over 60 countries.
Why is Marks & Spencer so proud of its 'Plan A'?	Because it is its own initiative for improving the company's environmental performance – and its employees and shareholders seem to value it.
Why might a shareholder criticise 'over-focus' by a company on its wider stakeholders?	Because some shareholders buy purely with the intention of selling at a higher price; they want a focus on profits today rather than image-building for tomorrow.
How might a company such as GSK rebuild its corporate culture on the basis of ethical values?	Slowly and quietly. It needs a clear lead from the top; and make sure that promotions (and sackings) reflect the new ethical climate.

41.7 Business ethics – evaluation

Evaluation involves making some sort of informed judgement. Businesses are required to make a judgement about the benefits of ethical behaviour. *Their* key question may well be whether ethics are profitable or not. Yours should not. It shouldn't have taken the $42 billion loss made by BP as a result of the Gulf of Mexico spillage, or the – perhaps – $50 billion cost to Volkswagen of its diesel emissions fiasco to persuade you or anyone else that the right reason to do the right thing is that it's right. The problem then is that it's easy to judge outcomes but hard to know about motives. In 2015, Lidl shocked the grocery world by announcing a big pay rise to staff (to take their pay up to the 'living wage'). Was that for operational and PR reasons or because of a sudden conversion to an ethical approach to staff pay?

Overall, though, it is fine to make a judgement about a business's motives, but beware of accepting that a company is ethical because it says it is. Actions speak louder than words.

Key terms

Greenwash: the environmental equivalent of whitewash, i.e. painted on to cover the reality beneath – a business that dresses itself up to pretend to be environmentally conscious.

41.8 Workbook

Revision questions

(30 marks; 30 minutes)

1 What is meant by the term 'business ethics'? (2)

2 Outline two factors that may shape the moral behaviour of a business. (4)

3 Explain one circumstance in which a company may face an ethical dilemma. (4)

4 Explain the difference between a business behaving legally and a business behaving ethically. (4)

5 Explain why decisions made upon the basis of ethics may conflict with profit. (4)

6 Why could a policy of delegation make it more difficult for a business to behave ethically? (4)

7 Assess two positive effects the adoption of a more ethical culture may have on a business's workforce. (8)

Revision activities

Data response

The VW disaster: objectives, strategy and an ethical void

How is possible for a business like Volkswagen to make an illegal decision to install 'defeat' software that misleads regulators about its dirty exhaust emissions? With consequences that might cost it €50 billion over the next few years.

The events themselves are quite easily explained. Diesel engines are naturally dirty. Although they are fuel-efficient, they create far more nitrous oxide and particulate matter (fragments that cause smog) than petrol cars. With large diesel trucks and cars, this isn't too much of a problem, because filtration devices can be effective. But no one has found how to filter smaller (say 1,600cc) engines without causing a marked loss in engine power and performance.

So VW cheated. They commissioned a piece of software that could detect when the emissions were being tested, and temporarily add the fix that would hurt the car's performance. Hey presto – the car passes America's tough emissions rules, but the drivers still have powerful cars.

But now VW faces fines of up to £12 billion in America, the cost of recalling 11 million cars, lawsuits from car owners and a massive downturn in sales. Why, oh why?

The issues involve a mix of two of the most potent exam topics: business objectives and business ethics. In a sense, the ethical issue is straightforward: it's wrong to cheat; it's wrong to deceive your customers and it's wrong to cause excessive pollution. Happily, in this case, VW is certainly paying for ignoring morality. Less obvious is what the VW crisis says about objectives. For 75 years from 1931 and 2007 the world's biggest car maker was General Motors. The desire to become number one caused problems at Toyota and now at VW.

Figure 41.4 puts things into context. In 2007, General Motors (GM) was about to lose its crown to Toyota. Volkswagen wasn't really in the picture. But the sharp fall in sales for GM and Toyota in 2009 made VW executives think differently. Helped by its number one position in China, VW started to see itself as the new General Motors. The global sales figures for 2014 show how extraordinarily close the race had become. VW had its eyes on the prize: global number one.

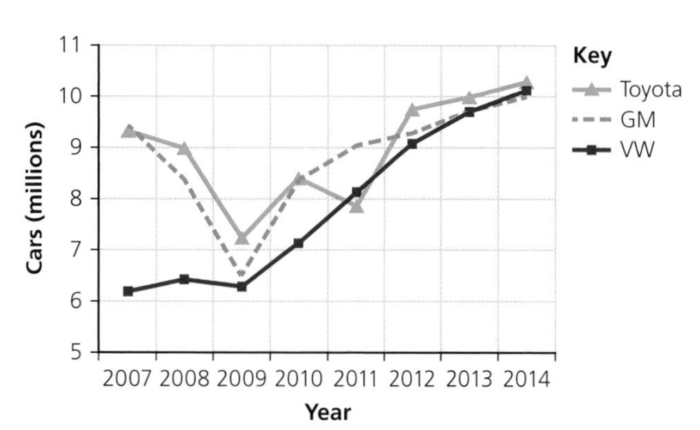

Figure 41.4 Battle to be global number one car maker (sources: OICA and press reports)

In 2009, Toyota was hit by a wave of quality issues in America, which it handled poorly. After several weeks of fumbling in the face of severe media pressure, Akio Toyoda, grandson of the founder, took over as president of the company. After some weeks of investigation he announced that Toyota had been pursuing the goal of becoming the world's number one car maker – and had taken shortcuts in attempting to achieve it. He announced that he would be working on a new culture based on the company's founding principles: customer satisfaction and quality come first. In the period since then he surprised other car makers by refusing to open new car factories (in China, for example) until he was sure the company had learned the lessons from the quality crisis.

Then VW allowed itself to be dazzled by the thought of the number one prize. To achieve it, VW had to overcome its sales weakness in America (see Figure 41.5). It set out to differentiate itself by focusing on diesels. But whereas diesels have a 50 per cent market share in Europe, in America it's 3 per cent. So VW decided to persuade Americans by marketing their brands under the slogan 'Clean Diesel'.

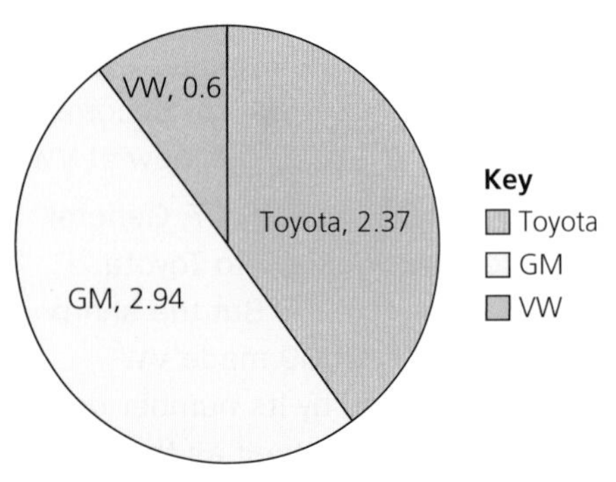

Figure 41.5 USA car sales 2014 (in millions)

The scene was set. VW had an ambitious objective to be met by a strategy based on selling diesels to Americans. America's exhaust emissions regulations are among the world's toughest. Solution? Cheat.

High though the short- to medium-term cost is going to be, the long-term implications may be greater. The diesel strategy followed by many German, French and Italian car makers may come unstuck.

In December 2014, in response to smogs in Paris, the mayor announced that diesels would be banned from the streets of the capital by 2020. In January 2015, the French government announced that it would progressively ban diesels from the country. Given that diesels represent two-thirds of Renault and Peugeot production, this is quite something. Further moves against diesels are being discussed in London, especially after a July 2015 report estimated that 9,500 people die in London each year from air pollution. European car manufacturers are suddenly facing a serious threat to their competitiveness. Eighty-one per cent of BMWs are diesel; 71 per cent of Mercedes are the same – and Volvo's diesel percentage is 90 per cent! In Asia and America, hybrid petrol/electric and pure electric cars are seen as the future; perhaps Europe will have to follow that lead.

Corporate objectives are a powerful force, but some textbooks make them sound only a force for good. The VW case shows they must be handled with great care.

Questions (50 marks; 60 minutes)

1. Explain the reason why businesses set objectives. (3)
2. Explain the possible effect of VW's trouble on two of its stakeholders. (6)
3. Use the text to analyse why business objectives 'must be handled with great care'. (9)
4. To what extent do you think that the environmental factors in this case will affect costs and demand for Volkswagen? (12)
5. Volkswagen has always been exceptionally strong at Corporate Social Responsibility, publishing annual 'Sustainability Reports'. Evaluate whether it's possible that CSR may get in the way of business ethics. (20)

Extended writing

1. 'A modern, democratically led company with an empowered workforce would be the type of organisation that would be expected to operate an ethical policy.' To what extent do you agree with this statement? (20)
2. Discuss the view that few businesses take truly moral decisions and that most implement ethical policies to gain a competitive advantage. (20)

42 Controlling multinational corporations

Definition

A multinational operates in many countries and may be so large that it feels able to persuade governments to act in the company's best interests. This makes the control of multinationals a difficult challenge for the international community.

Linked to: Growth, Ch 7; Business potential in Africa, Ch 27; International trade and business growth, Ch 28; Factors contributing to increased globalisation, Ch 29; Protectionism, Ch 30; The impact of multinational corporations, Ch 40

42.1 Introduction: influence or control?

There are many forces that influence multinational corporations: they are largely the same as their list of stakeholders. Governments, customers and pressure groups are among that list. Control is quite a different issue. Customers and pressure groups influence but rarely have control. Governments can have control, due to their powers to legislate and to tax. Shareholders also have theoretical control as they own the business (theoretical because small shareholders often show little interest in the detail of how 'their' directors run the business).

When analysing the issue of control, a strong argument would come from the subtle borderline between control and influence. The most important grouping at that borderline may be the customers. Clearly they are a huge influence on business decision-making; perhaps that influence can also stray towards an element of control. In late 2013 Ryanair amazed the business world by announcing a new customer-friendly policy. Boss Michael O'Leary was not going soft in his old age – falling market share and profits forced Ryanair to rethink its competitive struggle with easyJet. Customer demand exercised a degree of control over the company. Figure 42.1 shows the zone of uncertainty between influence and control – and also points out that the influence of pressure groups is sometimes over governments as well as companies.

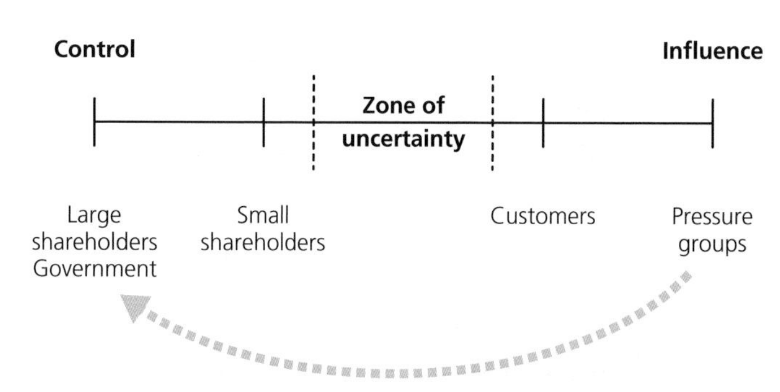

Figure 42.1 The subtle boundary between influence and control

42.2 Why may there be a need for control over the activities of multinationals?

Safety concerns

Some multinationals with production facilities in less economically developed countries are accused of operating sub-standard, outdated safety precautions. Often, safety regulations in these countries are not as tough as those in developed countries. As a result, multinationals can use older equipment and machinery, which is perhaps not as safe as that used in other parts of the world. The result may be higher numbers of accidents and injuries.

The world's worst-ever industrial accident, at Bhopal, India, killed 20,000 and injured almost 600,000 people. Poor safety precautions at (US) Union Carbide's chemical plant were to blame when toxic gas escaped from the factory, sending a cloud of poisonous gas onto the nearby town. Despite short-term damage to the firm's reputation and share price, no long-term ill effects were felt by the multinational. It closed the factory and left. Decades later, local residents are still suffering the physical and psychological after-effects.

Short-term mineral extraction may leave a host country poorer

Many multinationals set up production or mining facilities in less developed countries to extract valuable raw materials. Although the resources mined are irreplaceable, there is strong evidence that some companies have conspired with local politicians to allow short-term mineral extraction to be to the benefit of individuals, not the country. Many a Swiss bank account has been boosted by mineral exploitation. This can leave the multinational and the individuals richer, but the country poorer. Minerals can only be mined once.

Figure 42.2 Mineral extraction can have negative impacts for the country

Traditional, local cultures are weakened

It is said that, after 'OK', the world's best known piece of English is 'Coca-Cola'. This underpins the concern that traditional, local cultures are being weakened by the spread of multinational products. Some suggest that traditions should be preserved, untainted by imported cultures. This whole issue is a difficult one. The Coca-Cola Corporation is not forcing anyone to drink Coke. Multinationals argue that everyone has the freedom to choose.

Lack of commitment to the host country

Multinational firms may lack a real commitment to their host country. Therefore, if something happens such as a recession, an overseas plant may be closed down without any serious concern for the local workforce or society. Firms may also prove **footloose**; that is, open a factory one year, but close it and move on to another country where labour costs are even lower.

'The global system was not made to serve the good of all, but to serve multinational corporations.'

Ahmed Ben Bella, former President of Algeria

42.3 Multinationals and political influence

In 2012, at a parliamentary hearing, Rupert Murdoch (boss of the Sky TV/News Corporation multinational) admitted having met with Prime Minister David Cameron seven times since the 2010 general election. Cameron was also meeting with and exchanging regular texts with Murdoch's trusted advisor and editor Rebecca Brooks. This remarkable level of contact between a multinational boss and the prime minister implies a strong attempt to achieve political influence.

But was Britain's prime minister cosying up to Murdoch because he was the boss of a multinational? Or was it because News Corp controlled 34 per cent of British newspaper circulation (owning the *Sun* and *The Times*) plus Sky TV? In other words, wasn't he focused on the company's monopolistic position and therefore power within British media rather than Sky/News Corp as a multinational business? This matters, because although it's true to say that multinationals have power and influence, it may simply be because they are big, wealthy businesses. Perhaps all big wealthy businesses have political influence and power (just as, arguably, do wealthy individuals).

Note also the implication of the above. Some commentators write as if the political influence of multinationals is limited to developing countries. Not a bit of it. When the Volkswagen diesel emission crisis hit in 2015, it quickly emerged that European regulators had known for years that the industry was fudging its figures. But the governments of Europe effectively allowed car manufacturers to push diesel cars on the public, pretending they were clean and green. Large, powerful, wealthy businesses are amazingly clever at achieving political influence.

Despite the above, it is important to acknowledge that multinational corporations may have an even greater influence in developing countries than in developed ones. Since 1996, the Democratic Republic of Congo (DRC) has suffered a series of wars in which more than 4 million have died. DRC is home to fabulous mineral wealth (copper, gold, diamonds) and a series of civil wars have been battles for who controls the mines and therefore the wealth. Quite clearly, minerals can only be turned into

Real business

The Ford Motor Company is one of the original multinationals. Having become America's dominant producer by 1920, Ford began a steady transition to a multinational with the opening of Ford Dagenham in 1923 and then a series of other factories. Today it takes some time to list all the countries in which Ford has factories. Some produce engines; some produce other car parts, but all are vital in contributing towards final car assembly. In 2015, this is where Ford had factories:

• Argentina	• Malaysia	• Taiwan
• Australia	• Mexico	• Thailand
• Canada	• Romania	• Turkey
• China	• Russia	• United Kingdom
• France	• South Africa	• United States
• Germany	• Spain	• Venezuela
• India		

Table 42.1 Locations of Ford factories, 2015

This scale and breadth gives Ford powerful leverage against any individual government. If the government of Malaysia, Turkey or the UK proposes policies the company dislikes, it will have a credible threat to switch operations to a different, more 'friendly' country.

money if there are buyers. Those buyers have often been multinational mining companies with close relations to the militia leaders with control of the mines. It is hard to find words for such a contemptible way to run a business.

42.4 Legal control

In many ways multinationals operate under the exact same legal controls as any other company. In the UK, every company has to operate under the Trades Descriptions Act or the Health & Safety at Work Act. The only differences come at the margin – at the point where it's hard for individual governments to exert full authority.

In the case of multinationals, there are two obvious areas where governments can struggle: takeovers and taxes. If a UK-based business wants to buy another UK business, the rules are simple: if the combined market share is 25 per cent or more, the government's Competition and Markets Authority may investigate to see whether the acquisition is in the public interest. But what if it's a Swiss multinational buying up a British multinational? Such as Nestlé buying Rowntree (producers of KitKat, After Eights and Quality Street). There may be a reduction in competition spread over many markets in many countries, but none may create a larger than 25 per cent market share in the UK. So the British competition authorities will not look at it. But perhaps the European Commission should.

The other key issue in legal control relates to tax revenue. Apple in Ireland and Amazon in Luxembourg have come to tax arrangements that mean they pay virtually nothing to local tax authorities such as Britain. This topic was covered in more detail in Chapter 40.

In developing countries there are other aspects to consider within the phrase 'legal control'. In 2009, the magazine *African Business* estimated the Democratic Republic of Congo's mineral wealth at $24 trillion. That was more than the combined GDP of America and Europe. Yet the wealth of the annual mineral output (which is so widely stolen than no one can value it) has done nothing for the people of the DRC. In 2014, figures from the *CIA World Factbook* suggest that annual GDP per capita at purchasing power parity is only $700 – one of the world's lowest figures. Infant mortality is among the world's highest. In the DRC, legal control means the rule of law – which still looks some way off.

42.5 Pressure groups

In 2015, the government of India froze the assets of the Indian branch of the pressure group Greenpeace. That meant staff couldn't be paid. A long-running dispute between the government of Narendra Modi and Greenpeace is about new coal mines to be opened in the woods of Mahan, central India. Greenpeace has protested internationally about the environmental damage to the area and the probable displacement of thousands of inhabitants. The Indian government has accused Greenpeace of being a western agency determined to hinder the economic rise of India.

In the middle of this is the mining company, Essar Energy. This is an Indian power and fossil fuel giant that operates electricity-generating plants. Its interests here are simple – it wants to mine coal to provide more fuel for making electricity – and of course it's aiming to make a profit. From the government's point of view, the important thing is to generate electricity (about 70 per cent of Indian electricity is from coal).

Interestingly, in this case it's Greenpeace that is the multinational. It is applying western environmental standards to India. It may or may not be right in its judgement about coalmining in Mahan, but there can be no doubt that it would have hugely greater leverage if Essar Energy were a well-known MNC. If it were BP or Shell, pressure could be applied in Britain and America that would have made it hard for the company and the Indian government. As the company involved is Indian, few in the west are interested.

From this one can draw a clear conclusion: western pressure groups are more likely to have success with global multinationals than local businesses. The only clear counter-argument is to say that perhaps multinational pressure groups are a bad thing. Modi's government can easily get away with dismissing Greenpeace as a western group pursuing western interests. This would have been a harder issue for Modi if the complainant had been a powerful Indian pressure group.

Real business

In September 2015, multinational Shell announced that it was ending its exploration for oil and gas off the coast of Alaska. Its $7 billion investment had been criticised from the start by environmental pressure groups – worried that the extremely harsh Arctic operating conditions made spillages likely. Shell said that its decision to withdraw was based purely on economic factors. Its first test drilling yielded disappointing quantities of oil and gas and the 2014 collapse in the global price of oil made it impossible to see how profits could be made. Environmentalists pointed out that their pressure had persuaded US Presidential candidate Hillary Clinton to speak out against Shell's operations – and that perhaps Shell was seizing an excuse to withdraw.

Aspect of business activity	Important pressure group	Example of action
Actions against tax avoidance	UK Uncut	Blockading shops owned by Vodafone UK, because of tax avoidance in the UK and India
Threats to the environment	Friends of the Earth	The UK's Friends of the Earth is one of 70 national FoEs. In the UK it has recently campaigned to protect our bees
Fairer conditions and pay for developing world textile workers	Clean Clothes Campaign	Organised a global day of action on the 2015 anniversary of the Rana Plaza disaster as a reminder that not all clothing retailers have paid the worker compensation they promised
Actions against the spread of genetically modified (GM) foods	Greenpeace	Campaigns and demonstrations against GM foods plus direct action to disrupt field trials of GM crops

Table 42.2 Pressure group influence on multinationals

42.6 Social media

Reasons why social media may impact on company behaviour

It is fair to say that company bosses globally go in fear of a social media firestorm. If poor service, a cat's eye in the soup or a caught-on-camera pollution fiasco hits a company, it could quickly be seen by multi-millions of potential customers. This might mean that companies would be far more careful than in the past. Social media might be an effective way to police corporate activity.

This would be especially important in relation to multinational enterprises. As shown in Figure 42.3, the huge number of global users of Facebook, Twitter and other social media sites and apps makes it clear to see why businesses should be very wary of misdemeanours in an online world.

When Shell started its Arctic oil exploration (see the 'Real business' feature above), environmental commentators such as George Monbiot launched daily attacks on the business. Monbiot has 138,000 Twitter followers who in turn are likely to have discussed his points with others. Multinational businesses monitor social media constantly to find out possible impacts on their corporate image. Figure 42.3 shows the global scale of social media usage.

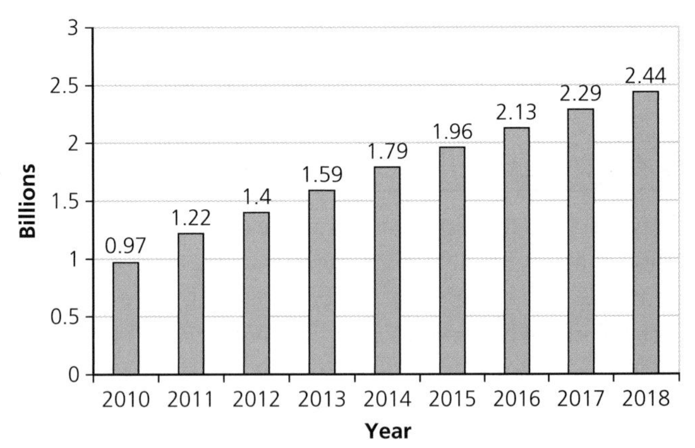

Figure 42.3 The global rise of social media usage (forecast from 2015) (source: www.statista.com)

Reasons why social media may have little impact on company behaviour

The philosophy behind the free market suggests that governments do not need to control businesses, because the market ensures that companies behave. Those that misbehave are shunned by consumers and therefore go out of business. The rise of social media could accentuate that view. After all, if a local factory sneakily tips pollution into a river, killing fish, a few tweets can create a global Twitter-storm.

That's probably true for highly visible companies, especially multinationals. But many, many companies hide in plain sight. By tomorrow, today's scandal loses impact because people can't remember the name of the (little-known) business. On 25 March 2015, company director Peter Mackereth of Pyranha Mouldings was sentenced to nine months in prison and the business fined £200,000 for corporate manslaughter. The details of the death of an employee are too awful to repeat. But accidents through negligence keep happening because people don't remember who's to blame. Social media will do little to change that.

Five whys and a how

Questions	Answers
Why is it assumed by some that multinationals are especially in need of control?	Size matters, but perhaps there's an over-estimation of the importance of size compared with market share; local but dominant businesses also have huge power.
Why might a multinational close a factory in one country and re-open it in another?	Partly, perhaps, to show it can. This warns other governments about the danger that footloose companies can up and leave if they're not given what they want.
Why are multinationals so reluctant to pay their taxes?	It's perhaps because it's easier for them to avoid tax than it is for national businesses; and, because 'everyone does it', they feel it's essential for their competitiveness.
Why might it be a mistake to leave the control of MNCs to pressure groups?	Because pressure only works if people care; they care about sick animals and babies, but less about accidents or illnesses among thousands of adults.
Why might the EU be better at controlling multinationals than individual governments?	Power counts for a lot, so multinationals will take more notice of EU rules than UK ones.
How might an ethically sound MNC behave?	It would reject proposals for 'legal tax avoidance' and simply pay profit taxes when due.

'Multinational corporations do control. They control the politicians. They control the media. They control the pattern of consumption, entertainment, thinking. They're destroying the planet and laying the foundation for violent outbursts and racial division.'

Jerry Brown, former Governor of California

42.7 Controlling multinational corporations – evaluation

There are good reasons to be wary of multinationals. Coca-Cola once invested in a device to supply Coke on tap at home. Where would obesity be today if that had taken off? The problem for MNCs such as Coca-Cola, Nestlé, BP, Shell and Volkswagen is that they get so big that it becomes progressively harder to ensure an ethical culture. In its place come targets – passed down from on high. In pursuit of growth, VW ended up with the diesel emissions scandal.

But it can be argued that much the same is true of other companies; the only difference is that MNCs are usually bigger. A rare exception is the NHS which employs more than most multinationals. It has suffered some ghastly scandals, such as the treatment of patients by the mid-Staffordshire Hospital Trust. This was caused by cost-cutting targets that were managed inhumanely.

Whether the problem is being a multinational or just being too big for your own good, there is no doubt that there's a huge suspicion of multinationals globally. Their case is not helped by eager seizing of the opportunities to avoid national taxes.

Key terms

Footloose: a company that has no commitment to the countries it's operating in, making it comfortable closing down factories and moving elsewhere, despite the unemployment left behind.

42.8 Workbook

Revision questions

(30 marks; 30 minutes)

1 Explain why local businesses might be concerned about the political influence of large multinational corporations. (4)

2 a) From Figure 42.3, calculate the percentage change in global social media usage between 2010 and 2015. (4)

b) Explain the importance of this growth to a multinational company such as BP. (4)

c) The world population in 2015 reached 7.3 billion. Calculate the percentage of the globe's population who used social media in 2015. (4)

3 When the Volkswagen emissions scandal hit in September 2015, satirists and cartoonists unleashed a Twitter backlash against the company. Explain the effect that could have on the company. (4)

4 Re-read Section 42.3. Assess whether Rupert Murdoch or any other business leader should be allowed exceptional access to the prime minister. (10)

Revision activities

Data response

Evidence A. From GlaxoSmithKlein (GSK) third quarter 2013 results announcement*

'Operations in China were clearly disrupted in the third quarter with sales down 61 per cent but we remain fully committed to supplying our products to patients in the country. At this stage, it is still too early for us to quantify the longer-term impact of the investigation to our performance in China. The investigation is ongoing and is complex and detailed. We continue to co-operate fully with the authorities and to respect the process of the investigation. As such, there is very little further I can say until it has reached its conclusion.

However, I do want to reiterate that the activities described by the authorities are very serious and totally unacceptable. They are contrary to our values and to everything I believe in. We very clearly recognise there is a profound need to earn the trust of the Chinese people again, and we shall take every action to do so.'

*GSK is Britain's biggest pharmaceuticals multinational company operating in more than 150 countries and with an annual turnover of more than £20 billion.

Evidence B. UK drug maker handed largest ever corporate fine in China

GlaxoSmithKlein plc said a Chinese court found the drug maker's local subsidiary guilty of bribery and fined the company nearly $500 million, capping a scandal that has shaken China's pharmaceutical industry. Five of the company's managers, including Mark Reilly, its former top China executive, were convicted of bribery-related charges and received suspended prison sentences, a Glaxo spokesman said on Friday.

Chinese authorities began investigating the company in June 2013, laying bare a tale of intrigue involving a mysterious sex tape, whistleblowers, private investigators and a culture of bribery and graft in China's vast medical industry.

'The illegal activities of GSKCI [GSK China Investment Co.] are a clear breach of GSK's governance and compliance procedures; and are wholly contrary to the values and standards expected from GSK employees,' Glaxo said on Friday.

The company added that it has co-operated fully with the authorities and has taken steps to rectify the issues identified at the operations of the unit. Glaxo issued a separate apology to the people of China in English and Chinese on Friday, saying, 'GSK plc sincerely apologises to the Chinese patients, doctors and hospitals and to the Chinese government and the Chinese people.'

(Source: Wall Street Journal, 19 September 2014)

Questions (40 marks; 45 minutes)

1 Assess whether a multinational such as GSK needed to be controlled more effectively by the Chinese government. (10)

2 Assess whether the power of social media is sufficient to prevent a multinational business such as GSK from acting unethically. (10)

3 The British government has done nothing to penalise GSK plc for bribing Chinese doctors. Evaluate whether our government should use legal controls to ensure that British multinationals act lawfully in every country in which they operate. (20)

Extended writing

1 Re-read Section 42.5. The Indian government does not want western pressure groups interfering in national decisions about economic development. Evaluate whether Greenpeace is right to get involved in Indian decisions about coal mining. (20)

2 Evaluate whether multinational corporations operating in Britain should face stronger government controls than UK-only businesses. (20)

43 Quantitative skills for Business A level

Definition

Quantitative skills are needed to calculate, interpret and analyse business data, whether numerical or graphical.

Linked to: every chapter in the book

Introduction

Unlike the other chapters of the book, this one purely provides questions and (in a few pages) answers. It is to help you test your knowledge and understanding of an important aspect of the subject. Page 51 of the Edexcel Specification sets out the exact skill requirement for A level exams. The questions below provide good practice for the quantitative skills required for the A level. Candidates should be aware, though, that they might be expected to use quantitative skills within higher mark questions, including the 20-mark question. The questions that follow go no higher than an 8-mark tariff.

43.1 Calculate, use and understand ratios, averages and fractions

All figures in £000s	53 weeks ending 31 January 2015	52 weeks ending 25 January 2014
Sales revenue	£387,564	£321,921
Gross profit	£235,205	£198,470
Operating profit	£49,759	£39,588
Profit for the year	£35,850	£28,852

Table 43.1 Extract from Statement of Comprehensive Income for Ted Baker plc

1 a) Calculate Ted Baker's operating profit margin for 2014 and 2015. Show your workings. (4)

b) Explain one possible reason why the profit for the year is lower than the operating profit. (4)

2 a) Calculate Ted Baker's average weekly sales in 2014 and 2015. Show your workings. (4)

b) Calculate the percentage increase in weekly sales in 2015 compared with 2014. (4)

c) Explain one possible reason why sales changed in that way. (4)

3 In one of its London stores, Ted Baker has weekly sales of £60,000, of which £36,000 is of women's clothes and £24,000 men's. The store has an inventory value amounting to £720,000.

a) What fraction of the week's sales are accounted for by menswear?

b) By what percentage would menswear sales need to rise to match womenswear?

4 Ted Baker is contemplating launching a new aftershave. There are two options, Product A and Product B.

a) On purely numerical grounds, use the decision tree to calculate (and recommend) what Ted Baker should do. (6)

b) Explain **one** other factor Ted Baker should consider before a final decision. (4)

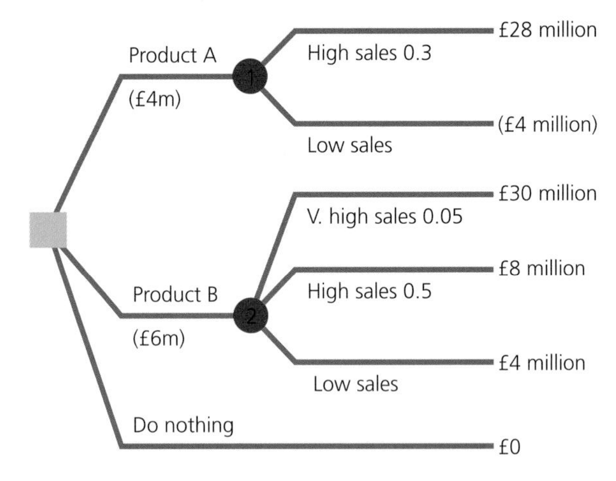

Figure 43.1 Decision tree

43.2 Calculate, use and understand percentages and percentage changes

	Value		Volume	
	£ms	Y-o-Y* %	Litres (m)	Y-o-Y* %
Heinz Tomato Ketchup	128.2	–0.1	42.3	0.3
Hellman's Mayo	101.8	0.4	27.1	2.2
Heinz Salad Cream	41.8	–4.0	10.7	–0.9
HP Sauce	36.9	–1.8	10.3	–5.3
Blue Dragon	13.2	–14.7	2.4	–16.2

Table 43.2 Sales figures for top-selling sauces in the UK, 52 weeks ending 18 July 2015 (*Y-o-Y means comparison with previous year)

5 a) Calculate the price per litre achieved by Blue Dragon compared with Hellman's. (4)

b) Calculate Blue Dragon's sales by value in the previous year. (4)

c) The sales volume for HP Sauce has fallen by a higher percentage than the sales value. How might you explain that? (4)

d) Calculate Heinz Ketchup's volume share of the sauces listed. (4)

43.3 Construct and interpret a range of standard graphical forms

A bar chart is effective at showing how two sets of data compare with each other. Figure 43.2 shows Morrisons (supermarkets) sales and profits 2010–2015. Look at the chart, then answer questions 6a–c.

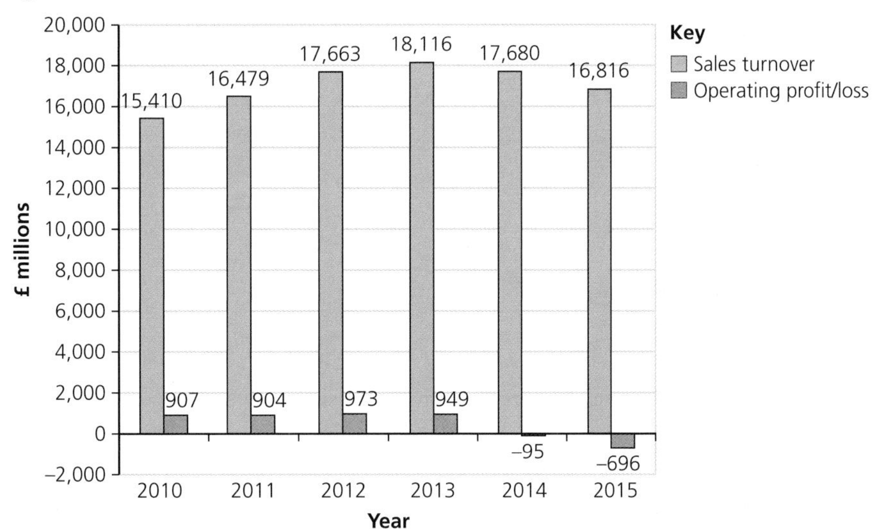

Figure 43.2 Morrisons' annual sales and profits 2010-2015 (source: Morrisons annual accounts)

6 a) Explain two important features of the data shown on the graph. (6)

b) i) Calculate what was happening to the company's profit margin in the growth years 2010–2013. (4)

ii) Explain the implications of this profit margin data. (4)

c) In 2015, Morrisons' sales were higher than in 2011, but the profit position was dramatically worse. What might explain this? (4)

7 These questions on correlation use the graph below (Figure 43.3).

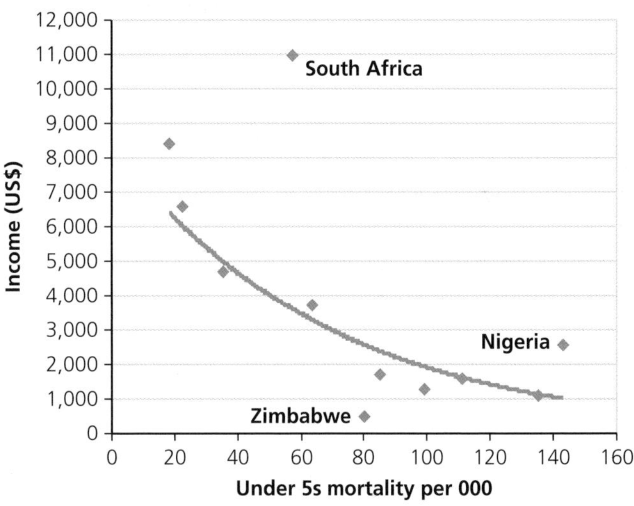

Figure 43.3 Correlation: income (GDP per capita at PPP) and infant mortality in developing countries (sources: Unicef and *CIA World Factbook*)

a) Describe your overall conclusions from the correlation data. (5)

b) i) Explain the implications of being above the line of best fit. (4)

ii) Briefly consider the position of South Africa compared with Zimbabwe. (6)

c) Explain why scatter graphs such as this can be useful. (4)

43.4 Interpret index numbers

In business, data series are often converted into index numbers. It makes the data easier to interpret and far easier to compare with data that might be correlated.

Look at the graphs showing pre-tax profits at Ted Baker versus Next (Figures 43.4 and 43.5) then answer question 8.

8 a) i) Explain what is meant by 'Index 2006 = 100'. (4)

ii) Explain two benefits from presenting this data in index form. (6)

b) Explain why the Next profit line appears faster-growing in the first graph than in the second. (4)

43.5 Calculate cost, revenue, profit and break-even

9 An independent pizza delivery shop has an average revenue per customer of £20, with variable costs of £8. Weekly fixed costs are £1,800 and there are 250 orders per average week.

a) Calculate the weekly profit. (2)

b) Calculate the margin of safety. (6)

c) Just Eat says that using its online promotion will add 50 per cent to the shop's sales, though at a cost of 15 per cent of the revenue. Use calculations to help decide whether the business should accept. Briefly explain your decision. (8)

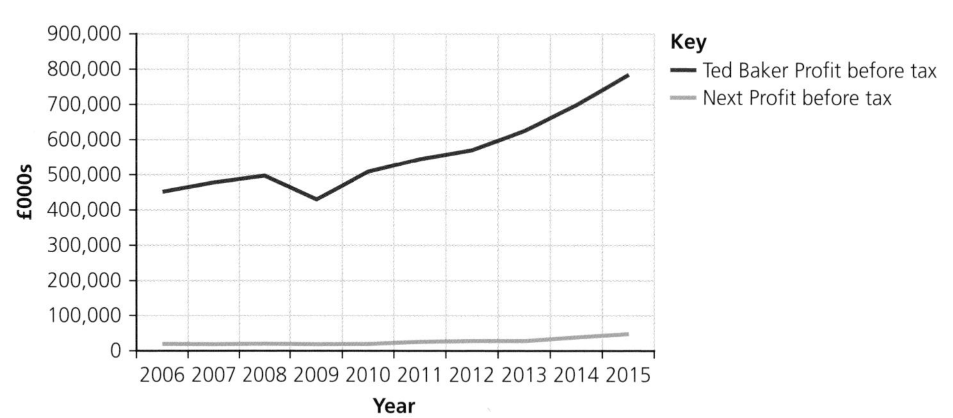

Figure 43.4 Ted Baker vs Next pre-tax profits stated in absolute terms (source: annual accounts)

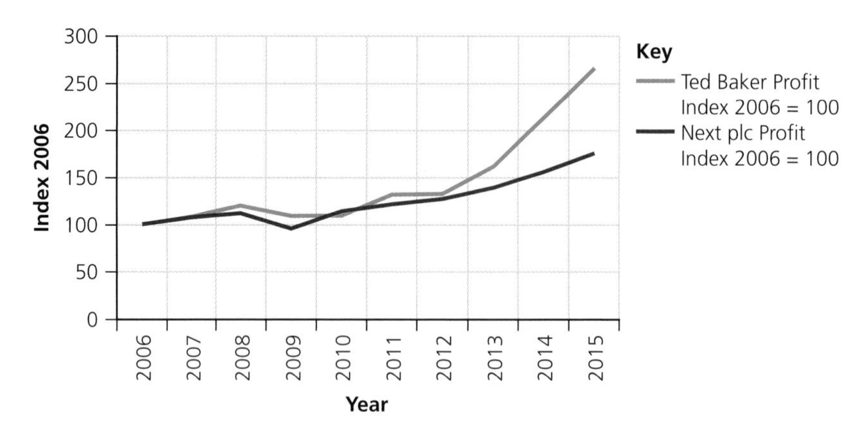

Figure 43.5 Ted Baker vs Next pre-tax profits stated in relative terms using indexing to 2006 (source: annual accounts)

43.6 Calculate investment appraisal outcomes and interpret results

Nestlé is considering launching a new upmarket chocolate brand to the UK market called Cailler of Switzerland. It's aware that this will be a slow process, because the British are very set in their ways when it comes to chocolate. The marketing and distribution launch cost will be about £12 million. Nestlé operates strict criteria that demand a minimum average rate of return of 10 per cent and a maximum payback period of 3.5 years. Use the data below to help decide whether or not the brand should be launched.

	Cash in	Cash out
NOW		(£12m)
End of Year 1	£10m	£9m
End of Year 2	£8m	£8m
End of Year 3	£12m	£9m
End of Year 4	£16m	£11m
End of Year 5	£20m	£11m

Table 43.3 Cash flows on Nestlé's investment

10 a) Calculate and set out the data columns for Cailler's net cash flow and cumulative cash positions. (6)

b) i) Calculate the average rate of return for Cailler. (6)

ii) On the basis of this result, would you suggest there are grounds for going ahead with the launch? (4)

c) i) Calculate the payback period. (3)

ii) With both sets of data, would you now recommend proceeding? (6)

43.7 Interpret values of price and income elasticity of demand

11 In the year to July 2015, Mars put the price of Galaxy down by 3 per cent. The result was an increase in total sales volume from 22.39 to 24.41 million kg.

a) Calculate Galaxy's price elasticity of demand. (4)

b) If the original price per kilogramme was £9.50, what was the revenue after the price cut? (4)

c) Cadbury had a poor year with its Dairy Milk brand. Explain one possible reason why. (4)

12 Next year the economy is forecast to grow by 2.5 per cent, bringing up household disposable incomes by the same amount. This is likely to have a notable effect on sales of white gold jewellery, which have an estimated income elasticity of +5.

a) Calculate the percentage increase in sales of white gold that can be expected next year. (4)

b) While white gold has an income elasticity of +5, pure gold has an income elasticity of +8. Explain what this means about each product. (5)

43.8 Use and interpret quantitative and non-quantitative information in order to make decisions

Read this short case study, then tackle the questions below.

In 2015, sales of Cadbury's Dairy Milk fell by 5.6 per cent to £466.7 million. This was despite a series of new product launches (included in the above figure), the biggest of which was the launch of Cadbury Puddles, with sales of £7.2 million. Part of the explanation may have been Cadbury's cunning ways of improving profits. In August 2014 a 'Sharing Bag' of Giant Buttons contained 155gm. Cadbury withdrew all the bags from stores and launched the New Sharing Bag containing 119gm.

(Source: The Grocer, 3 October 2015)

13 a) i) Calculate Cadbury's Dairy Milk sales in 2014. (4)

ii) Explain two possible reasons for the fall in overall sales of Cadbury's Dairy Milk in 2015. (8)

b) Cadbury would argue that cutting the size of its Sharing Bags was part of its fight against obesity. Assess two other ways of viewing this action. (8)

Figure 43.6

43.9 Interpret, apply and analyse information in written, graphical and numerical forms

The final set of questions on quantitative skills relate to Table 43.4 and Figure 43.7. The data is based on the best estimates available in November 2014 of the sales performance of the Sony PS4 console compared with its rival Microsoft Xbox One.

All figures in millions	PS4	Xbox One	PS3*
Oct–Dec 2013 (launch November)	4.5	3	1.7
Jan–Mar 2014	3	2	1.9
Apr–Jun 2014	2.7	0.8	0.7
Jul–Sep 2014	3.3	1.7	1.3
Oct–Dec 2014	6.4	3.5	4.9
Jan–Mar 2015	2.4	1.2	2.3
Apr–Jun 2015	3	1.4	1.6

Table 43.4 Global sales for PS4 vs XBox One vs PS3 (*launch: corresponding months, but 2006/2008)

14 a) From the data in Table 43.4, what conclusions can Microsoft draw so far about its Xbox One? (4)

b) On the basis of Table 43.4, what sales forecast might Sony make for PS4 in Oct–Dec 2016? Give an estimate and explain your reasoning. (6)

c) Figure 43.7 shows the cumulative sales figures for each console. Assess whether this information is more or less useful than the ordinary quarterly sales figures shown in Table 43.4. (6)

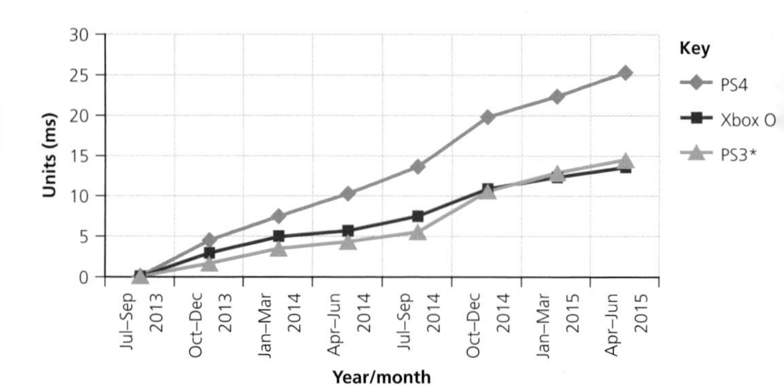

Figure 43.7 Cumulative sales since launch: PS4 v Xbox One vs PS3 (source: VGChartz plus company accounts)

All the answers to these questions are on page 313, at the end of Chapter 45.

44 Understanding assessment objectives

In order to maximise the chances of launching a great new product, a business will use market research to discover just what the target market wants. In the same way, your answers are produced, by you, with a target market in mind – your examiner. This chapterexplains the four key skills that you are expected to demonstrate when answering A level Business questions. They have equal weightings; in other words, each one is worth 25 per cent of the exam mark total.

44.1 Knowledge and Understanding (AO1)

Every question you are asked will test your knowledge of terms, concepts, theories, models and methods. In addition, the 'points' you make when answering a question are considered as knowledge. Your business knowledge must be seen as the foundation of every answer you write. It is an opportunity to show what you have learned. Good answers are rooted in the knowledge gained during your A level Business course. It is this that will discriminate between the type of answer that a top business student would produce and well-written waffle. Use appropriate terminology whenever possible in your answers – just don't force it in where it does not belong.

The tougher challenge presented by A levels is the expectation that you have not simply learned definitions and formulae like a parrot. Excellent A level Business students *understand* the concepts and formulae that they have learned. Understanding a term helps you to remember it. Knowing that gearing is about company borrowings helps you to remember the formula.

Understanding is born of good study skills throughout your course. Never unquestioningly copy things a website or a teacher tells you. Think about the meaning of what is being explained – that will help to develop a proper understanding of the subject.

44.2 Application (AO2)

You need to apply your knowledge to the specific context provided by the text, numbers, graphs and bar charts within each question. To master this requires you to read and think about the material with care, writing your thoughts alongside the text and data. This skill is important because it forms the basis for good application and evaluation.

The way that you will show application will vary from question to question depending on which paper you are tackling. Some short-answer questions expect you to show application by using numbers provided by the question to complete a calculation.

Data response questions require you to use information about the context provided within the data to develop your explanations and arguments. When there's a large amount of numerical or graphical material, make sure that you:

- understand what the graph/table is showing
- use the appropriate units when quoting figures
- check the dates of the data you are using – note that sometimes accountants record the most recent year to the left of previous years' data.

On other data response questions, much more of the data provided will be text, about a company or perhaps industry. Read and annotate that carefully, looking to draw out the key issues raised by the data provided. Often you will need to infer (read between the lines) rather than expect to be explicitly told everything. Making notes in the margin next to the text helps you remember the key parts of the business story. Sometimes there will be a mix of numerate and written information about the business. Combine the good habits described above to get the most out of the data provided.

Twenty-mark questions (usually the final part of each A level question) allow you to develop your answer a bit more widely. This is why you have been reading around the subject for the whole of your A level course. Knowing real business examples adds depth of application to your answers – but the examples must be relevant. If the exam material is on Jaguar Land Rover, your knowledge of BMW Mini is relevant; your knowledge of Fever-Tree Tonic Water is less so.

The final, perhaps most important, hint provided for application may be in the question. Even without a case study or data to respond to, better students pick up on aspects of the question to show their ability to apply knowledge to different contexts, e.g. 'a business operating in a highly competitive market' or 'a small bakery'. Check the following to see if you can spot the context to which you need to apply to each:

1 Explain two methods of promotion that could be used by a firm trying to break into a highly competitive consumer goods market.
2 Analyse the benefits to a rapidly growing firm of using financial methods of motivation.
3 To what extent is greater use of digital technology an appropriate strategy for an established luxury goods manufacturer whose unique selling point is its 200-year history of unsurpassed customer service?

Good students will have picked up on the following features of each question to show their ability to apply knowledge to context:

Question 1	• Trying to break into a new market • The market is for consumer goods • The market is highly competitive
Question 2	The firm is rapidly growing
Question 3	• The USP is customer service • The firm is traditional • Luxury goods are being sold

Table 44.1 Key features of exam questions 1-3

Where possible, look to draw together several aspects of the information provided in order to help to build your arguments. This should help to ensure that your answer is fully rooted in the context provided.

44.3 Analysis (AO3)

Analysis involves breaking down information into component parts. That generally means starting to show an awareness of cause and effect. The construction of a logical argument is also a vital component of strong analysis. So a key ability is building chains of logic that answer the question.

When building a chain of logic, the basic rules to consider are as follows:

- Start your chain from the question.
- Do not miss out links in the chain.
- Ensure every link is logical.
- Finish your chain back at the question.

A question such as 'analyse the financial benefits of increased capacity utilisation' can be used to illustrate these four rules:

Start your chain at the question – in this case increased capacity utilisation is the starting point for your journey. From here you should begin to work through the consequences of increased capacity utilisation:

Increased capacity utilisation – more output without extra fixed costs – meaning fixed costs are spread over more units – so fixed costs per unit are lower – allowing a higher profit per unit.

Note that in the chain above there are no obvious steps forward within the chain that are illogical. In addition, there are no missing links in the chain. Finally notice the illustration of the fourth rule of analysis – the chain finishes back at the question – in this case, by showing the financial benefit that the question asked for.

44.4 Evaluation (AO4)

Evaluation means making judgements, but they must stem from arguments (your analysis) that have been built on evidence from the scenario being considered.

The skill of evaluation can be thought of as making judgements. Of course, without evidence to back up those judgements and arguments explaining why, you will not score highly. It is vital that when you make a judgement, it flows logically from the arguments you have put forward. There are only two trigger terms towards evaluation: assess and evaluate. Each requires a subtly different form of judgement:

- Assess: weigh up the evidence, comparing points for and against to come to a conclusion that is in keeping with the arguments put forward.
- Evaluate: consider several issues on both sides of the argument before deciding on the most important. Make a judgement that answers the question directly, make recommendations when relevant and draw conclusions that reflect upon the importance of the issues under discussion.

What these have in common is the need to do something extra, beyond the knowledge, application and analysis you show within your answer. As your judgement should flow from your answer, it is sensible to offer it at the end of your response to the question, i.e. in your conclusion. Within the conclusion, you should maximise your evaluation marks by ensuring that you:

- make a clear judgement specific to the question asked
- explain why the judgement you have made is more appropriate than other judgements you could have made
- use the context of the question to show why your judgement is most appropriate.

The best judgements should show an element of weighing up alternatives before settling on a final decision.

Five whys and a how

Questions	Answers
Why must I learn key terms?	You will be asked to show knowledge of definitions of key terms, not only within multiple-choice questions but also short-answer sections.
Why must I make sure I understand the theories I have learned?	Students with hazy understanding of key terms struggle to understand what the question is trying to ask. That can lead to a serious loss of marks.
Why is it helpful to stay abreast of current business news stories?	Not only will this deepen your understanding of business concepts, it will also help you enrich the quality and depth of the answers you give.
Why is it so important to read the question carefully?	Top marks are only awarded to answers that fully address the question. Make sure you have not missed a subtle clause within the question.
Why is evaluation more than a summary?	Evaluation implies a judgement – some kind of weighing up of alternative arguments you have presented. That needs you to go beyond simply re-stating your arguments.
How can I get a clearer idea of the assessment objectives?	Using the past papers* and mark schemes published on the internet will allow you to see plenty of examples of what examiners expect to see to award good analysis, application and evaluation.

*In the early years of this specification, there will be a shortage of usable papers. If you feel the need for more, email the lead author of this book (Ian Marcousé at marcouse@btopenworld.com). His company A–Z Business Training Ltd has produced a pack of exam-style questions with mark schemes – written by Ian Marcousé but not reviewed by the senior examining team. As a dedicated reader of this book, he'll be happy to let you have an extra paper or two.

44.5 Understanding assessment objectives – evaluation

The single most important way to meet *all* the assessment objectives is to answer the question. Take the time to think what *exactly* the question is asking you to do. Just because a question includes a piece of terminology such as training does not mean that the answer should be 'all about training'. If the question wants to know whether increased training is the best way to improve productivity, the question is really about how to increase productivity – a concept that must be at the heart of your answer.

Ultimately, exam technique can be summed up in one phrase: 'ANSWER THE QUESTION!'

Key terms

A01/Knowledge: Demonstrate knowledge of terms, concepts, theories, methods and models to show an understanding of how individuals and organisations are affected by and respond to business issues.

A02 /Application: Apply knowledge and understanding to the business context set out by the examiner, to show how individuals and organisations are affected by and respond to issues.

A03/Analysis: Analyse issues within business, using chains of logic to build arguments about the causes and effects of problems or opportunities.

A04/Evaluation: Evaluate quantitative and qualitative information to make informed judgements and propose evidence-based solutions to business issues.

45 Tackling data response questions

45.1 Introduction

A data response question requires you to do three things simultaneously:

1 understand and use the data (perhaps an article)

2 keep in mind the relevant classroom/textbook theory

3 answer the precise terms of the question.

It would not be crazy to suggest that most human beings can do only one thing at a time; two at a push. But three? That is why data response papers are harder than they look.

For students who revise at the last minute, the problem is especially acute. Cramming blocks out the other two factors, making the answers one-dimensional. The examiner can see the knowledge, and may admire it, but the marks for application, analysis and evaluation are few and far between.

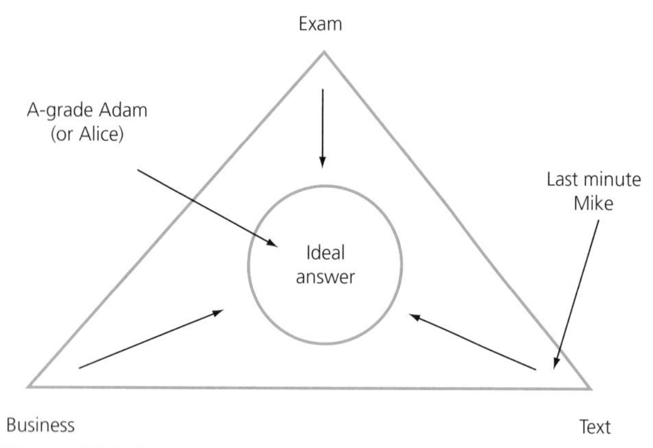

Figure 45.1 The three-way answer

45.2 Using the data

The key is to find a way to get the guts out of the short passage of text; that is, to find the real business bits that matter. Many students use a highlighter pen, but seem to mark up too much, turning the page from white to pink. That achieves little. It's better to jot down the key points as you go. These amount to:

- key points about the business context: competitors, consumer fashions, and so on
- key points about the business: its products, its image, its efficiency its sales trends and its culture
- key points about the people running it: their experience, their enthusiasm and their judgement.

Below is a short piece of text on PD Ltd. Identify at least three key points that you could use to enrich the application within exam answers. Give yourself a few minutes, then look at the suggestions given at the end of the unit.

Real business

PD Ltd

Den and girlfriend Pam started PD Ltd with £15,000 borrowed from a friend and £15,000 from HSBC. Both keen surfers, their plan was to open the first surfing school in north-east England, on the coast above Newcastle. They were confident that they could persuade the Geordies to take up surfing, despite the cold weather.

Figure 45.2

This exercise shows the enormous importance of reading the text with great care.

When in the exam room, you can make use of every subtlety built into the text, but some of the more common issues worth looking out for are listed in Table 45.1.

Topic or issue	From one extreme ...	... to the other
Seasonal sales	70% of the whole year's sales occur in the three-week run-up to Christmas (e.g. toys, posh perfume)	Sales vary little month by month (e.g. toilet paper)
Degree of competition	Fiercely competitive market in which customers care greatly about price	Few competitors, and they focus on giving high service levels to their own customers
Product life cycle	Very short product life cycles; a brand's sales can be ended by a technological breakthrough by another	Long life cycles protected by the conservatism of consumers (e.g. Heinz Tomato Ketchup – people won't try another)
Risk	A sole trader has started a new restaurant using borrowings secured against the family home	Tim started a limited company to run a small education business offering maths tutoring

Table 45.1 Some common issues to look out for

45.3 Using numerical data

Quite often, data response questions include numerical data such as budget statements or cash flow forecasts. These are very helpful. They offer a quick and easy method for getting high marks.

The valuable thing about numbers is that they:

- give you a starting point for investigating the business situation and answering the question set in an analytic manner, while ...
- ... pressing the examiner to give you extra marks for application (because if you use the specific data to build an argument, your answer is automatically applied to the context).

So an answer that uses the numbers effectively is automatically getting double marks. It can also be argued that numbers provide a good student with the opportunity to show both their knowledge of the course and provide a basis for making judgements. In other words, it can generate every one of the assessment objectives.

With numerical data (such as sales figures), it will always be valid to ask yourself certain questions (see Table 45.2).

Valid questions about data	Example of good data	Example of bad data
Is the data actual or forecast?	Actual data on weekly sales over the last 18 months	A forecast of next year's sales made by a businessman wanting a loan
Is it based on a valid sample?	Based on a sample of 600 people within your target market, carried out by Gallup, an independent research company	Based on research carried out by a sales department
Is there a valid way to make comparisons?	The figures show sales of all our brands compared with the same period last year and the year before	The figures show the huge success of Brand P, which has seen a 70% sales increase in the past two months

Table 45.2 Questions to ask yourself about numerical data

45.4 Bringing it all together

The amount of data provided in a data response exam question may be quite substantial. It cannot, therefore, all be used to answer every question. Don't worry: the important thing is *not* to 'know it all'; the key is to have picked out enough key features to show that you're really trying to think for yourself while in the exam room. Examiners are giving you the opportunity to break away from your teacher and show that you're far from just being a puppet, with your teacher pulling the strings.

Having read the text and thought about the numbers, make sure to jot down the key points. If you don't, there's a risk that you'll forget the details by the time you tackle your third question. Every answer requires the context (that is, an effective analysis of the case being looked at).

Real business

Application points: PD Ltd

Things to look out for include the following.

- *The 'first' surfing school in north-east England.* This may mean that there is a fortune to be made, but it also suggests high risk (whereas being the 15th surfing school in Newquay, Cornwall, would probably not be a total disaster).
- *'They were confident that ...'* The key here is what it does *not* say. It does *not* say: 'They'd done some market research, which gave them confidence that ...'. Their confidence may mean nothing. Anyone who watches *The Apprentice* has seen no end of people with confidence but startlingly little ability. The key requirement in this case is evidence not confidence.
- *'£15,000 borrowed from a friend and £15,000 from HSBC'.* No bank would lend unless it has seen the owners invest at least half the start-up capital, so Den and Pam have probably not told the bank that they have borrowed it all. Having such high debts (relatively) must increase the riskiness of the investment.

Other possibilities include: the importance of the Ltd status (protection from unlimited liability); the importance of seasonality (especially in the north-east); the possible significance of the boyfriend/girlfriend relationship – how long have they been together?

Answers to the questions in Chapter 43

1 a) Calculate Ted Baker's operating profit margin for 2014 and 2015. Show your workings. (4)

$$\text{Operating margin} = \frac{\text{operating profit}}{\text{Revenue}} \times 100$$

$$2014 = \frac{£39,588,000}{£321,921,000} \times 100 = 12.3\%$$

$$2015 = \frac{£49,759,000}{387,564,000} \times 100 = 12.8\%$$

b) Explain **one** possible reason why the profit for the year is lower than the operating profit. (4)

One answer from:

- The net financing cost is taken after operating profit, so that could be eating away at the figure (if the cost of finance outweighs any finance income).
- The other item is corporation tax; as Ted Baker plc pays its corporation tax that figure must be deducted. In that financial year it would have been 21 per cent of the pre-tax profit.

2 a) Calculate Ted Baker's average weekly sales in 2014 and 2015. Show your workings. (4)

$$\text{Average weekly sales} = \frac{\text{Annual sales}}{\text{no of weeks}}$$

$$2014 = \frac{£321,921,000}{52} = £6.19 \text{ million a week}$$

$$2015 = \frac{£387,564,000}{53} = £7.31 \text{ million a week}$$

b) Calculate the percentage increase in weekly sales in 2015 compared with 2014. (4)

$$\% \text{ change} = \frac{\text{change}}{\text{original}} \times 100$$

$$\frac{£1,12\text{m}}{£6.19\text{m}} \times 100 = \text{an } 18.1\% \text{ increase}$$

c) Explain **one** possible reason why sales changed in that way. (4)

It may have been that Ted Baker launched its clothing range in a new country (China?) creating a sales increase through market development (as Ansoff describes it).

3 a) What fraction of the week's sales are accounted for by menswear?

A fraction is one part of a whole, so it's $\frac{£24,000}{£60,000} = \frac{4}{10}$ $(= \frac{2}{5})$.

b) By what percentage would menswear sales need to rise to match womenswear?

Menswear sales would need to rise by £12,000, so $\frac{£12,000}{£24,000} \times 100 = +50\%$.

4 a) On purely numerical grounds, use the decision tree to calculate (and recommend) what Ted Baker should do. (6)

At point 1, expected value: (£28m × 0.3 = £8.4m) + (–£4m × 0.7 = – £2.8m) = £5.6m.
So the Net Expected Value for Product A is £5.6m – £4m = £1.6m.
At point 2, expected value: (£30m × 0.05 = £1.5m) + (£8m × 0.5 = £4m) + (£4m × 0.45 = £1.8m) = £7.3m.
So the Net Expected Value for Product B is £7.3m – £6m = £1.3m.
Therefore Product A should be chosen.

b) Explain **one** other factor Ted Baker should consider before a final decision. (4)

Although it comes out better using the weighted average method known as expected value, Product A actually gives a 0.7, i.e. 70 per cent chance that £4m will be spent with the result that a further £4m is lost, i.e. a net loss of £8m. Perhaps that makes it too risky and Product B might therefore be chosen.

5 a) Calculate the price per litre achieved by Blue Dragon compared with Hellman's. (4)

Formula: $\frac{\text{Value}}{\text{Volume}}$ = price

Blue Dragon = $\frac{£13.2m}{2.4m}$ = £5.50 per litre

Hellman's = $\frac{£101.8m}{27.1m}$ = £3.76 per litre

b) Calculate Blue Dragon's sales by value in the previous year. (4)

$\frac{£13.2m}{0.853}$ = £15.47m (to check, note that £15.47m – 14.7% = £13.2m).

c) The sales volume for HP Sauce has fallen by a higher percentage than the sales value. How might you explain that? (4)

If volume has fallen more than value, there must have been a price increase of perhaps 2 or 3 per cent (and HP must be fairly price elastic).

d) Calculate Heinz Ketchup's volume share of the sauces listed. (4)

Add up the volume total for the 5 brands (= 92.8m litres).

Then take 42.3 as a percentage of 92.8 = 45.6% share.

6 a) Explain two important features of the data shown on the graph. (6)

- The sales turnover data looks like maturity, then the start of decline on a product life cycle. Is this the Morrisons' company life cycle?
- The impact on profitability of the relatively slight decline in sales is breathtaking. In 2014, profits fell from £949m to minus £95m, i.e. a turnround of minus £1,044m – and then 2015 saw further huge declines.

b) i) Calculate what was happening to the company's profit margin in the growth years 2010–2013. (4)

2010: 5.9%

2011: 5.5%

2012: 5.5%

2013: 5.2%

ii) Explain the implications of this profit margin data. (4)

- Profitability was declining quite sharply. A fall from 5.9 to 5.2 per cent means a loss of 0.7 per cent on £18bn of sales, i.e. £126m. This should have alerted Morrisons' bosses to the need for change – much earlier than 2014/2015.

c) In 2015, Morrisons' sales were higher than in 2011, but the profit position was dramatically worse. What might explain this? (4)

- The simple answer is that the more than £1.5bn turnround in profit must mean that total costs in 2015 were more than £1.5bn higher than in 2011.
- One possible explanation is that the business was slow to realise it needed to be in cost-cutting mode; perhaps in the period after 2011 it was still trying to expand the business.

7 a) Describe your overall conclusions from the correlation data. (5)

- There's clear inverse correlation between GDP and infant mortality, i.e. the higher a country's income, the lower the infant mortality; nevertheless there are outliers such as South Africa and Zimbabwe.

b) i) Explain the implications of being above the line of best fit. (4)

- Being above the line of best fit is shameful; it means an excess of infant deaths bearing in mind the affluence of the country. Given its wealth, Nigeria should have an infant mortality rate of about 75 per 1000 instead of 145.

ii) Briefly consider the position of South Africa compared with Zimbabwe. (6)

- South Africa's infant mortality is really shocking, given its affluence; its figure should be well under 20, instead of 50–60; by contrast Zimbabwe is doing superbly (given its abjectly poor income level); in the UK, Zimbabwe is always presented as a shambles; perhaps the press should be more critical of South Africa.

c) Explain why scatter graphs such as this can be useful. (4)

- They illuminate; they show correlations which might help provide insight into causation; in this case there's only one plausible causal link, i.e. that infant mortality is affected by income levels; in other cases it may be more difficult, with no clear indication of the direction of the causal link.

8 a) i) Explain what is meant by 'Index 2006 = 100'. (4)

- Within a time series, one year has been chosen to represent the base period to which all the rest of the data will be related. So the 2006 figure is converted to 100, and all other numbers are given their proportionate connection to 100.

ii) Explain two benefits from presenting this data in index form. (6)

- It makes it easier to see at a glance the relative changes going on with the data.
- It makes it hugely easier to compare changes in two sets of data on a different scale (as shown by the two graphs in Figures 43.4 and 43.5).

b) Explain why the Next profit line appears faster-growing in the first graph than in the second. (4)

- In Figure 43.4 the figures are in absolute terms, so Next's bigger scale of operation means its profit rises by more £000s than Ted Baker's – so it rises more steeply.
- The second shows the two in relative terms, showing that in fact Ted Baker's profit growth rate is higher than Next's.

9 a) Calculate the weekly profit. (2)

- £1,200

b) Calculate the margin of safety. (6)

First, the break-even point:

$$\frac{£1,800}{£20-£8} = 150 \text{ orders per week.}$$

Then safety margin:

250 – 150 = 100 orders.

c) Just Eat says that using its online promotion will add 50 per cent to the shop's sales, though at a cost of 15 per cent of the revenue. Use calculations to help decide whether the business should accept. Briefly explain your decision. (8)

- 15 per cent of £20 = £3, so that's lost to Just Eat.
- So the contribution per order is now £17 – £8 = £9.
- Sales will rise to 375 orders at £9 cpu (= £3,375).
- So the new profit is £3,375 – £1,800 = £1,574.

My decision would be to check carefully with other pizza independents that have used the service; will sales really rise by 50 per cent? If they only rise by 20 per cent, the result would be (300 × £9) – £1,800 = £900 profit (£300 down on the current level); only if you're reasonably sure of the +50 per cent promise should you proceed.

10 a) Calculate and set out the data columns for Cailler's net cash flow and cumulative cash positions. (6)

	Cash in	Cash out	Net cash	Cumul. cash
NOW		(£12m)	(£12m)	(£12m)
Year 1	£10m	£9m	£1m	(£11m)
Year 2	£8m	£8m	£0m	(£11m)
Year 3	£12m	£9m	£3m	(£8m)
Year 4	£16m	£11m	£5m	(£3m)
Year 5	£20m	£11m	£9m	£6m

b) i) Calculate the average rate of return for Cailler.

$$\text{ARR} = \frac{\text{Average annual profit}}{\text{Sum invested}} \times 100$$

$$\text{Average annual} = \frac{£6\text{m}}{5 \text{ yrs}} = £1.2\text{m a year}$$

$$\text{ARR} = \frac{£1.2\text{m}}{£12\text{m}} \times 100 = 10\%$$ (6)

ii) On the basis of this result, would you suggest there are grounds for going ahead with the launch? (4)

- On the face of it it's marginal because 10 per cent is the minimum return the company's looking for, but the growth in annual cash flows suggested that the brand could be making good profits in years 6, 7 and beyond – which would push the ARR above 10 per cent; the 5-year cut-off point is arbitrary and shouldn't hold the company back.

c) i) Calculate the payback period. (3)

- Pay-back occurs after the end of year 4 but before the end of year 5.
- Within year 5 monthly contribution is $\frac{£9\text{m}}{12 \text{ months}}$ = £750,000 a month.
- $\frac{£3 \text{ million}}{£750{,}000} = 4$
- So the payback period is 4 years and 4 months.

ii) With both sets of data would you now recommend proceeding? (6)

- I'd fight hard to overcome the company's short-sighted approach to investment. Why the need for a 3.5-year payback when successful chocolate brands have decades or even centuries of profitable life? But on the face of it the senior managers will turn the proposition down.

11 a) Calculate Galaxy's price elasticity of demand. (4)

The increase in sales volume was $\frac{(24.41 - 22.39)}{22.39} \times 100 = +9\%$.

So the PED is $\frac{+9\%}{-3\%} = -3$.

b) If the original price per kilogramme was £9.50, what was the revenue after the price cut? (4)

New revenue = New price (£9.215 per kg) × New volume (24.41m kg) = £224.94 million.

c) Cadbury had a poor year with its Dairy Milk brand. Explain one possible reason why. (4)

You'd expect Galaxy and Cadbury's Dairy Milk to be directly competitive, so any sales gains by Galaxy could well be at the expense of Cadbury; perhaps Cadbury failed to match the price discounting used by Galaxy.

12 a) Calculate the percentage increase in sales of white gold that can be expected next year. (4)

- Next year, white gold sales should increase by 2.5% × 5 = 12.5%.

b) While white gold has an income elasticity of +5, pure gold has an income elasticity of +8. Explain what this means about each product. (5)

- It implies that although white gold is a luxury, because it has high, positive income elasticity, pure gold is even more of a luxury.

13 a) i) Calculate Cadbury's Dairy Milk sales in 2014. (4)

- In 2014, Cadbury's Dairy Milk's sales must have been $\frac{£466.7\text{m}}{94.4} \times 100 = £494.4\text{m}$.

(You need to work out the figure that, with 5.6 per cent taken away, equals £466.7m; the only way to do it is to divide £466.7m by 100% – 5.6% = 94.4%.)

ii) Explain two possible reasons for the fall in overall sales of Cadbury's Dairy Milk in 2015. (8)

- There may have been a social force pushing consumers from chocolate to supposedly healthy muesli and 'natural' snacks; if the whole chocolate market suffered, CDM would as well.
- The other reason (which we know to be true) is that price cuts on Galaxy could have inflicted sales damage on CDM.

b) Cadbury would argue that cutting the size of its Sharing Bags was part of its fight against obesity. Assess two other ways of viewing this action. (8)

- Cutting the weight of a sharing bag by nearly a quarter to 119gm would allow Cadbury to cut the price per bag by, say, 15 per cent, yet still be better off in terms of income per gm. Or, more probably, it would give the company a better overall profit margin to help it run more price cut promotions in supermarkets (Sharing Bag for £1!).
- This could be regarded as a gross deception on the public; if you're cutting nearly 25 per cent from the pack size it seems only right to rename it ('A decent bag size for a normal person', perhaps?).

14 a) From the data in Table 43.4, what conclusions can Microsoft draw so far about its Xbox One? (4)

- Clearly Xbox One's sales have slipped into a pattern that's around half the sales achieved by Sony's PS4; as sales in the first six months were proportionately better for Microsoft, there must be concern that the brand is on the slide, i.e. that future sales will see Xbox One achieve less than half the sale gained by PS4.

b) On the basis of Table 43.4, what sales forecast might Sony make for PS4 in Oct–Dec 2016? Give an estimate and explain your reasoning. (6)

- A sales forecast such as this requires a calculation of the sales trend onto which one can add a seasonal adjustment to allow for the Christmas sales peak.
- In this case, I'm going to take the growth figure from the latest quarter (sales up by approx. 11 per cent and assume that the 2015 Christmas period will see sales of 6.4m + 11% = 7.1m; and that the figure for 2016 will be 7.1 + 11% = 7.9m).

c) Figure 43.7 shows the cumulative sales figures for each console. Assess whether this information is more or less useful than the ordinary quarterly sales figures shown in Table 43.4. (6)

- It certainly helps illustrate how sales of PS4 are accelerating away from the Xbox One; if I ran Microsoft I would want actions taken asap to try to avoid this situation becoming permanent.
- But cumulative figures must always keep rising, so they can create an illusion. PS4's sales in 1st Q 2015 were 20 per cent lower than in the corresponding period in 2014; you can't get that from the cumulative sales chart, so in some ways raw data is more useful.

Acknowledgements

The Publishers would like to thank the following for permission to reproduce copyright material. Every effort has been made to trace all copyright holders, but if any have been inadvertently overlooked, the Publishers will be pleased to make the necessary arrangements at the first opportunity.

p.2: © Oliver Knight / Alamy Stock Photo; p.6: © John Crowe / Alamy Stock Photo; p.14: © REUTERS / Mansi Thapliyal; p.15: © Prykhodov / Thinkstock; p.26: © aviationimages / Alamy Stock Photo; p.33: © REUTERS / Luke MacGregor; p.38: tupungato © 123RF.COM; p.44: Michael Spring © 123RF.COM; p.48: HONGQI ZHANG © 123RF.COM; p.53: nyul © 123RF.COM; p.62: fotointeractiva © 123RF.COM; p.67: pitrs © 123RF.COM; p.77: © Smileus / Thinkstock; p.88: Francis Dean © 123RF.COM; p.93: Jojobob © 123RF.COM; p.105: basphoto © 123RF.COM; p.113: © Kristoffer Tripplaar / Alamy Stock Photo; p.118: © peplow / Thinkstock; p.125: basphoto © 123RF.COM; p.131: jwsc101 © 123RF.COM; p.147: Georgios Kollidas © 123RF.COM; p.151: © Pradipkotecha / Thinkstock; p.161: © Anna Clopet / CORBIS; p.166: Thammanoon Praphakamol © 123RF.COM; p.172: mtaira © 123RF.COM; p.180: Maurizio Migliorato © 123RF.COM; p.186: © ronniechua / Thinkstock; p.194: © BirgitKorber / Thinkstock; p.204: © MagicBones / Thinkstock; p.211: Evgeny Atamanenko © 123RF.COM; p.216: © Jim West / Alamy Stock Photo; p.226: Olga Besnard © 123RF.COM; p.229: Maksym Yemelyanov © 123RF.COM; p.240 Jakub Gojda © 123RF.COM; p.244: Dmitry Rukhlenko © 123RF.COM; p.253: © Kevin Britland / Alamy Stock Photo; p.257: © Marin Tomas / Alamy Stock Photo; p.263: © Mike Nicholson / Alamy Stock Photo; p.271: © Bremont Watch Company; p.274: © Just Eat; p.279: © Martyn Evans / Alamy Stock Photo; p.286: Robert Ranson © 123RF.COM; p.290: Joseph Belanger © 123RF.COM; p.296: Dennis Van De Water © 123RF.COM; p.305: Antonio Munoz Palomares © 123RF.COM; p.310: Graham Oliver © 123RF.COM

Index